TWENTY-SEVEN
MAJOR AMERICAN SYMPHONY ORCHESTRAS

A HISTORY AND ANALYSIS OF THEIR REPERTOIRES

SEASONS 1842-43 THROUGH 1969-70

Kate Hevner Mueller

INDIANA UNIVERSITY STUDIES/BLOOMINGTON

For John Henry Mueller

1895–1965

Distributed by Indiana University Press

Copyright © 1973 by Kate Hevner Mueller

Library of Congress Catalog Card Number: 72-96549

ISBN: 0-253-36110-9

Manufactured in the United States of America

ACKNOWLEDGEMENTS

It is a pleasure to acknowledge my great indebtedness to the Rockefeller Foundation and to Dr. Norman Lloyd, Director for Arts and Humanities, for the original grant of $12,000, later supplemented by $4,000, which in 1967 enabled me to carry forward this study of orchestra repertoire history. Mr. Lloyd's original confidence and his continued interest was appreciated through four years of slow progress until the 568 pages of data were finally completed.

During these years Indiana University generously provided space, materials, services and encouragement, and in 1972 the Indiana University Foundation has provided an ample subsidy for publication.

My husband, John Henry Mueller, and I had begun these studies in 1940, and he continued them in 1950 with his own history and analysis in The American Symphony Orchestra: A Social History of Musical Taste. His purpose was to explore the relationship of the performing arts to the society which surrounds it and the culture in which it is embedded. But without some "hard data" in this borderline area between social science and music, neither the armchair sociologist nor the musician, be he theorist, listener, performer or critic, can make much headway. Surely, after The American Symphony Orchestra in 1951, there can be no question of the influence of economics, politics, and business on at least one of the musical arts. The sole purpose of the present study is to provide the basic data and to indicate via a few charts and summaries the trends and relationships which may be inferred from such data.

It is always a pleasure to thank the resourceful and energetic graduate students in the School of Music who worked with me in the first two years: Mrs. Elizabeth Kirkpatrick Vrenios supervised the undergraduate workers; Miss Ann Louise Davidson served as typist-linguist-chartmaker-researcher; and both Mr. and Mrs. Robert Griffith devoted many tedious hours to timings.

iii

Conferences with Mr. Philip Hart while writing his own history of the orchestras, Dr. Thomas Willis, Music Critic for the <u>Chicago Tribune</u>, and Professor of Music at Northwestern University, Dr. Jack Watson, Dean of the Conservatory, University of Cincinnati, Mrs. Helen Thompson, Executive Vice President of the American Symphony Orchestra League, and Miss Harriett Johnson, Music Critic and Editor of the <u>New York Post</u> were especially useful in the early days. Mr. Martin Bookspan of the American Society of Composers, Authors and Performers and Mr. Oliver Daniel of Broadcast Music Inc., gave me access to some of their files and showed many other courtesies.

At Indiana University Mr. Walter Albee of the Press provided invaluable technical advice and the Office of Publications assisted generously in setting up the copy and in proof reading.

More than we can ever say, both my husband and I have long been indebted to President (later Chancellor) of Indiana University, Herman B Wells, for that contagious enthusiasm and dynamic support for which he is so justly famous.

Eventually these data must be transferred to the computer, so that future scholars may be spared the tedious tabulations and calculations which constitute the major drawback for socio-musical research. In the meantime the inevitable errors and omissions will be discovered, and the one thing for which I would be most grateful would be correspondence with readers who will call them to my attention.

CONTENTS

PART I: ANALYSIS AND SUMMARY

PART I: ANALYSIS AND SUMMARY

INTRODUCTION: THE HISTORY,

SOURCES AND METHODS OF REPERTOIRE STUDIES

This study of orchestra repertoires is one more contribution to the
history of American music. In his 1951 analysis of eleven major American
orchestras, John H. Mueller was able to trace the origins and movements of
their conductors, the development of concert halls and audiences, and the
successive patrons who paid their bills. He also reported some of the
social and historical facts which stamped each of them with its own individual characteristics.[1] In the 1970's, with 27 major orchestras, this task
becomes too formidable for one person working alone. Therefore the present
study can do no more than provide the basic data for every composition
through the 130 years, 1840-1970 with its performance time in minutes and
the dates of all performances, together with the name of its composer, his
life span and national origin. A few charts are also offered to indicate
the general trends, and from these data other scholars will be able to
uncover more significant facts and theories about this most important insti-
tution in our American musical culture.

To a sociologist searching for keys to unlock the mysteries of musical
taste, the raw materials must be found in some phase of musical history
which runs continuously through many decades and thus parallels other events,
social, political, economic, commercial, and cultural. In 1940[2] and again
in 1950 Mueller searched for such data in the concert series of various
cities and music halls, in the sales of recordings, in the radio programs,
in critics' reviews in newspapers and magazines, even in copyrights and
publishers' catalogues but was everywhere frustrated by the paucity,
omissions, irregularity, and inaccessibility of records. Finally in the
orchestras he found that the year-by-year series of program booklets pre-
served in the city libraries and in the headquarters of orchestra management

offered a large and important segment of music history that gave him the complete and uninterrupted data which he sought.

In the earlier publications only the method and some of the resulting charts were presented to the musical world, since in both publications lengthy lists of composers and years would have made them too unwieldy and costly. In the present work however, the actual data, every composer, every composition, every year, is presented, a procedure which will reveal all the errors and omissions which are inevitably involved in such a large undertaking.

Another important value of these enumerative details is the opportunity given to any musicologist to make his own analysis and his own interpretation of the relation of music to the society which surrounds it and to the culture in which it is embedded. These data represent music as it is played and heard not in any previous century which must be reconstructed from an uncertain past, but music of the twentieth century, music of the everyday world of our own time. This world is known and has been experienced by the musicians now living and working in it, and therefore they can relate it to the immediacy of their own times.

In 1970 almost every orchestra is facing not only serious financial problems but also dilemmas 1) in meeting the widely varying tastes, indeed demands, of the more sedate and devoted audiences they wish to hold, and at the same time 2) in attracting the newer, younger, more adventurous listeners they must also satisfy. These crises in orchestra management and programs make it all the more important to continue the repertoire studies of America's 27 major symphony orchestras, and to round out their history through the recent decades of their unchallenged popularity and their greatest successes.

These orchestras are peculiarly American institutions, quite different in their history and function from orchestras in other parts of the world,

either eastern or western. In addition to these 27 "Major" groups whose
expenditures exceed $500,000, listed in 1972 by the American Symphony
League, 74 "Metropolitan" orchestras are also listed with expenditures between
$100,000 and $500,000 and 23 "Urban" orchestras with annual budgets
of $50,000 to $100,000. They include organizations from Sacramento, California to Portland, Maine and from Flint, Michigan to El Paso, Texas. There
are also many special chamber orchestras, summer orchestras and festival
orchestras, plus college, university and conservatory orchestras whose
repertoires would be available and important for understanding the American
musical heritage.[3]

To achieve continuity in a society as complex, rich and varied in its
musical culture as twentieth century America, means establishing regrettable
limits. Since the 1951 history of the eleven older and most noteworthy
orchestras it has been necessary to go back into the century for histories
of the sixteen who have more recently met the criteria of "Major". Unfortunately in the present sampling, only the regular subscription concerts of
the 27 orchestras have been tabulated, a sad limitation imposed by the almost
unmanageable dimensions and varying definitions of the non-subscription
concerts. Nevertheless the many Popular, Youth, Pension Fund, and other
Special concerts are a growing and lively part of any orchestra's history,
a "sideline" in the earlier years which may eventually become the main
attraction in the orchestra's future development.

THE TIMING OF EACH COMPOSITION

To interpret the trends and analyze the differences among the orchestras as well as the changes made by successive conductors within the same
orchestra, it was necessary to devise some measure of the volume of any one
individual composer, that is to tabulate the actual amount of time given to
his work year after year, relative to the work of every other composer, and

relative also to the orchestra's repertoire as a whole. This volume is the <u>time</u> given to his output divided by the <u>total time</u> the orchestra gives its audience in each successive year.

In the 1942 study[4] a very loose and arbitrary measure or weight was given by way of the titles of the compositions: a symphony would be weighted as four, a concerto as three, an overture or tone poem two, and other items one, with greater weights given to certain compositions known to be longer, such as symphonies of Mahler or Bruckner, tone poems of Strauss, and requiems, masses, ballets, oratorios and opera excerpts.

In 1951 however, a more laborious but more accurate approximation of time allotted to each composer or national group seemed imperative, and therefore the actual playing time of each composition was found and recorded, and thus the total playing time for each orchestra in every successive year. These timings were found for the most part through the catalogues of Fleischer; the American Society of Composers,Authors,and Publishers (ASCAP); Broadcast Music, Inc. (BMI); Aranowsky; the Gramaphone Shop; the card files of radio broadcast studios; and publishers' lists. The playing time of more obscure works could be approximated by noting their position on the program in relation to the other program items whose timings were readily available.[5]

With the playing time ascertained for each composition, an individual tabulation of these timings was made for a number of the more prolific composers, and for all the others in eight categories according to their national origins. These individual and group records could then be totalled for each successive year and finally accumulated in five year periods to be charted for the study of apparent trends.

It is immediately obvious that such a gigantic project involving dozens of typists, tabulators, friends, students and professionals, and the copying, transferring, adding and dividing cannot be done without error. By checking,

crosschecking and proofreading, errors can be minimized but never wholly
eliminated.   Errors of omission are the most serious and they may occur through
moments of inattention or carelessness, or when pages in bound volumes are
missed, as well as by misreading or by failure to record dates.

Several orchestras who could not send bound volumes were generous
enough to send copies of the title pages of all their programs for as many
as twenty years.   However these title pages rarely include the composer's
first name or the exact identification of the composition since these facts
would have been given in the program notes unavailable to the author.   Thus
a Prelude in C minor or a Concerto for Oboe or even a Symphony in A flat
could remain obscure because encyclopedias and catalogues may not list both
opus number and key.   Opus numbers and dates are more often than not omitted
on title pages, but in only a few instances has a composition been included
in these data which is not listed in some encyclopedia or catalogue or published list.

Many of the 27 orchestras were very helpful in providing the sources
for this record.   Current program booklets were provided week by week but for
earlier years it was usually impossible to lend the bound volumes, because
often the only copies available were those in the orchestra's own archives.
For distant cities, friends, students and professionals were pressed into
service to work in city libraries, e.g.,Seattle, New Orleans, Houston, and
Rochester, copying the programs page by page and year by year.[6]   City libraries,
e.g.,St. Louis, Indianapolis, the Lincoln Center Library in New York, as well
as Indiana University, were well stocked with bound volumes of programs, but
these were invariably irregular and at the most covered relatively short
periods of time.   Only Chicago and Cincinnati publish an annual cumulative
repertoire and Cincinnati with its complete record of full name, birth and
death dates and places is an invaluable source for historians.   St. Louis

has an accumulated repertoire covering a substantial period of time, and
Buffalo made such an accumulation at the request of the author, but even
these lists do not give the national origin, dates or first names of composers.

For each composer whose work appeared on any program from 1842 to 1970,
one or more cards were made on which to list the items played in each
orchestra in each successive year, so that the total performances throughout
these seasons could then be read from the procession of the composer's file
cards. Some 8,000 three by five inch cards were made, and another 1,000
larger cards to accommodate the more prolific composers, Bach, Beethoven,
Brahms et al. Machine made copies of all cards were eventually made for
safety.[7]

THE NATIONAL ORIGINS OF COMPOSERS

In the data presented for these 27 orchestras, the national origin for
each composer and his birth-death dates are included in so far as they could
be found. In these origins and dates however, there is no wish to imply a
national idiom, a national school or form or spirit, but only to indicate the
sources, chiefly European, of the music which was offered to listeners in the
United States during these thirteen decades. The histories of the individual
orchestras as they are plotted in five year periods will in many cases illus-
trate how the choices of each conductor are related to his background and
training.

The composite picture for all 27 orchestras taken together also reveals
the relative importance of one musical culture rather than another in our own
American heritage. It will be clear that the Central European tradition which
gave these orchestras many, indeed most, of their early conductors would in
itself account for the dominance of the Austro-German music in the early
repertoires; it always comprised more than half of the music presented. This
dominance continues however through the later decades when conductors from

many other cultures were on the podiums, and when audiences were very much
aware of the richness and variety of musical resources from many other
European and Far Eastern countries.

For most composers the place of birth gives immediate national identification, except in those cases where political boundaries have shifted in two
world wars, notably in the Balkan areas. There are always those special cases
however, of composers who change their citizenship either by choice or
necessity. "Unless there are strong reasons to the contrary a composer is
allocated for present purposes to the country in which he has produced his
major works and in whose culture he has shared and participated. . . Handel
is counted as British, Chopin as French. . . Theodore Thomas and Walter
Damrosch as American. . .Stravinsky, Schoenberg and others who migrated with
mature reputations to the United States are assigned to their respective
European origins."[8]

As in earlier studies of these repertoires, Austria and Germany have
been treated as one because they represent a cultural unity even though a
geographical shift may be noted from the early Vienna with Haydn, Beethoven,
Brahms, Schubert et al, to the more northern cities, Munich, Berlin, and
Leipsig with Wagner, Mendelssohn, Schumann, Liszt, and R. Strauss along with
Mahler, and Bruckner. Although the charts show these Austro-Germans plotted
as one, the repertoire listings separate the German from the Austrian origins
so that scholars in the future may separate the two groups to meet their own
research objectives.

After the Austro-Germans, the Russian repertoire is next in importance,
followed by the French. As the earlier generation of Rubinstein, Tchaikowsky,
Rimsky-Korsakoff, Scriabin, Glazounov declined in prestige there seemed
always newer names to claim the time evacuated: Stravinsky, Prokofieff,
Rachmaninoff, Miaskowsky, Shostakovich and Khatchaturian. Naturally the

Russians, together with our better known allies, the French and British, received some impetus from the two world wars, but relatively less than the Americans themselves received.

Native American composers maintain a low but stable position in the major orchestras, a minority position which is more clearly evident when their record is compared with those of such dominant individual figures as Beethoven, Brahms, Mozart, Strauss, Wagner, and Tchaikowsky.

That more time is not given to the American composers in these subscription concerts represents a complex problem, although some superficial comments come to mind as the records of native composers are studied. For one thing, the average length of the compositions is short; one Mahler symphony would swallow up a half dozen of these typically shorter American contributions. Rehearsal time for new works is costly, while most of the seasoned players are already familiar with the "standard" repertoire, and with the "fifty pieces" which occur and reoccur in our repertoires. This means that very often the new composer will rightly complain that the subtleties and excellencies of his work are not brought out in its first hearing, which unfortunately may also be its last. The appetite for new and newer and commissioned works from contemporary composers seems insatiable.

The record of the Americans would be better if items rather than timings were used as measures, a fact that has been demonstrated in the annual record published by Broadcast Music Incorporated.[9] Since these annual BMI studies also include every appearance, not only in subscription concerts but also those in the popular and youth concerts and those which are carried by the orchestras when they travel to other cities and other countries, the records are considerably enhanced in comparison with both the older and the newer foreign generations. Another and better test of the American composers to compete in the repertoire would be to match such

established artists as Barber, Copland, Bloch, Ives, Bernstein, Schuman,
Shuller, Gershwin, Harris, Menotti, Mennon, Sessions, et al and in fact all
those born within the modern era, with all foreigners of similar age span.
When this was done in 1950, the discrepancy was not so pronounced as it had
at first seemed.[10] Comparisons can also be made according to the geographical
distribution of American composers and studies are also in order to compare
the local groups, especially in Boston, New York, and Philadelphia, with
composers scattered throughout other areas of the United States. With the
data now available, such studies might be very revealing.

THE TWENTY-SEVEN MAJOR ORCHESTRAS:

THEIR FOUNDING AND EARLY HISTORY

A major symphony orchestra in any of our great cities does not spring
fully grown as Athena from the head of Zeus. Such a majestic organization is
built up gradually over a period of years, sometimes over a full century of
musical activity: arranging its housing, accumulating its financial resources,
recruiting its players and conductors and even more important, building its
audiences. Such pioneer cities as Boston, Chicago, New York and Philadelphia
each had a century or more of local chamber music groups, of travelling solo
artists and opera, in America's colonial history. Housing was always a
problem as well as finding generous patrons with both money and musical taste.
In St. Louis and Cincinnati the orchestras were associated with choral groups
in the German tradition and with annual musical festivals. In the early
years following the founding dates, the purely orchestral concerts were few;
overtures and symphonies were interspersed with singers using piano accompani-
ments, and with trumpet, bassoon, violin, and other solos by members or by
guest artists. Their programs are unavailable except perhaps via newspapers
or journals, for rarely does an orchestra publish a fifty-year summary or a
centenary commemorative volume covering its full history as did the German,

British, and Scandinavian cities, or as Philadelphia and Boston in the United
States.[11]

At the turn of the century six of these 27 orchestras had been firmly
established and were offering concerts which continued without interruption
through the seven decades to 1970, the date which marks the end of the
present study: the New York Philharmonic from 1841, the New York Symphony
Society from 1878, which merged with the Philharmonic in 1928, Boston from
1881, Chicago from 1891, Cincinnati from 1895, and Philadelphia from 1900.
Two other cities had also established symphony orchestras, St. Louis in
1881 and Pittsburgh in 1895, but their concerts were few and the earlier
programs not available for these studies. Pittsburgh's orchestra began with
conductors Archer in 1895 and Victor Herbert in 1898, but had a long period
of silence from 1909 to 1925. It was reestablished in the 1930's with
Klemperer when the records became available in bound volumes of program notes.

The continuous records for Dallas, although it began offering some concerts from 1900, became available only from 1925 and it was silent during the
war years 1942-44. Houston was silent for an even longer period, 1918 to
1929, although it too had been organized much earlier in 1913.

Minneapolis, like St. Louis and Cincinnati, was another early orchestra
operating with a choral society but was firmly established as an orchestra
in 1903 with Oberhoffer. However programs were not available for this
orchestra until the early 1920's with the Belgian Verbrugghen. Seattle also
entered at this time, although the city had been enjoying concerts irregularly
from a much earlier date.

The continuous programs of San Francisco, Cleveland and Los Angeles
entered before 1920, with Dallas and Rochester immediately after them in
the early twenties.

In the decade of 1930-1940 five more orchestras were fully operating
after their earlier beginnings: Indianapolis, the National in Washington,

Kansas City, New Orleans, and Buffalo. Another two, Utah and Atlanta, came
in with the decade of the '40's and finally Milwaukee in 1959. Yet all of
these could point to a substantial background of artists and performances and
audiences extending over a period of years and with various degrees of success
and patronage.

THE CONDUCTORS AND THEIR TENURES

The histories of the American orchestras have always been closely inter-
woven with the conductors, composers and performers of Europe and with the
Western music traditions. The orchestras' sponsors, financial problems,
travels, labor relations, recordings and their promotional activities with
their publics are inevitably reflected in their programs.[12] Their conductors
especially, as they moved from one city to another and sometimes from one
country to another, have had a widespread and lasting influence on the development of American music. It is therefore essential to incorporate into any
study of the orchestra repertoires an account of the tenures of the conductors and their movements from one to another of these major orchestras.
The present list, covering the years 1842 to 1969, was obtained from the
orchestras themselves by constructing a trial chart of all the orchestras.
This chart was submitted to the managers and returned by them with corrections
of dates, spelling and sequences.[13]

The list also gives the abbreviations employed in recording their
repertoires, and since the ultimate transferring of all the data to computer
cards and tape was anticipated, the use of either I or 0 was avoided because
of possible confusion with the numerals one and zero. Thus Indianapolis is
not IN but NA and New Orleans is not NO but NR. All dates refer to seasons,
i.e., 1945 indicates the season which began in the fall of 1945 and continues
through the spring of 1946; 1969 is the season which ends in the spring of
1970. The tenure of one conductor continues through all the intervening years

to the next name and date listed. Recently the man primarily responsible for the repertoire has been given the title musical director, or in some cases principle or chief conductor.

ORCHESTRA CONDUCTORS WITH DATES OF TENURE
FIRST SEASON THROUGH 69-70*

Atlanta, AT,Sopkin, 1945; Guests, 1966; Shaw, 1967.

Baltimore, BA, Strube, 1916; Siemonn, 1930; Schelling, 1935; Janssen, 1937; Barlow, 1940; Stewart, 1942; Freccia, 1952; Adler, 1959; Priestman, 1968; Comissiona, 1969.

Boston, BN, Henschel, 1881; Gericke, 1884; Nikisch, 1889; Paur, 1893; Gericke, 1898; Muck, 1906; Max Fielder, 1908; Muck, 1912; Rabaud, 1918; Monteux, 1919; Koussevitzky, 1924; Munch, 1949; Leinsdorf, 1962; Steinberg, 1969.

Buffalo, BU, Autori, 1936; Steinberg, 1945; Krips, 1954; Foss, 1963.

Chicago, CH, Thomas, 1891; Stock, 1905; Guests, 1942; Defauw 1943; Rodzinski, 1947; Guests, 1948; Kubelik, 1950; Reiner, 1953; Martinon, 1963; Hoffman, Acting 1968; Solti, 1969.

Cincinnati, CT, Van der Stucken, 1895; (Suspended) 1907; Stokowski, 1909; Kunwald, 1912; Ysaye, 1918; Reiner, 1922; Goossens, 1931; Johnson, 1947; Rudolf, 1958.

Cleveland, CL, Sokoloff, 1918; Rodzinski, 1933; Leinsdorf, 1943; Szell, 1946.

Dallas, DA, Kreissig, 1900; Fried, 1907; Venth, 1912; Fried, 1914; Van Katwijk, 1925; Singers, 1937; (Suspended) 1942; Dorati, 1945; Hendl, 1949; Kletzki, 1958; Solti, 1961; Johanos, 1962.

Denver, DE, Tureman, 1912; Disbanded 1917, Reorganized 1934 with Tureman; Caston, 1945; Golschmann, 1964.

Detroit, DT, Gales, 1914; Gabrilowitsch, 1918; Guests, 1936; (Suspended) 1942; Kreuger 1943; (Suspended) 1949; Paray, 1952; Ehrling, 1963.

Houston, HN, Blitz, 1913; Berge, 1916; (Suspended) 1918; Nespoli, 1931;

St. Leger, 1932; Guests, 1935; Hoffman, 1936; Guests, 1947; Kurtz, 1948;

Fricsay, Beecham, 1954; Stokowski, 1955; Stokowski, Sargent, 1960;

Barbirolli, 1961; Previn, 1967.

Indianapolis, NA, Schaefer, 1930; Sevitzky, 1937; Solomon, 1956.

Kansas City, KC, Kreuger, 1933; Kurtz, 1943; Schwieger, 1948.

Los Angeles, LA, Rothwell, 1919; Schneevoigt, 1927; Rodzinski, 1929; Klemperer,

1933; Guests, 1939; Wallenstein, 1943; Walter, Beinum, 1956; Beinum, 1957;

Guests, 1959; Mehti, 1961.

Milwaukee, ML, Brown, 1959; Schermerhorn, 1968.

Minneapolis, MN, Oberhoffer, 1903; Guests, 1922; Verbrugghen, 1923; Ormandy,

1931; Guests, 1936; Mitropoulos, 1937; Dorati, 1949; Skrowaczewski, 1960.

New Orleans, NR, Zach, 1936; Windingstad, 1939; Freccia, 1944; Hilsberg, 1952;

Yestadt, 1961; Guests, 1962; Torkanowsky, 1963.

New York Philharmonic, NP, Hill, Timm, Loder, Eisfeld, L. Damrosch, 1842;

Thomas, 1879; Seidl, 1891; Paur, 1898; W. Damrosch, 1902; Safanoff, 1906;

Mahler, 1909; Stransky, 1911; Mengelberg, Furtwängler and Guests, 1922;

Toscanini, 1930; Barbirolli, 1936; Rodzinski, 1941; Guests, 1947;

Mitropoulos, 1950; Mitropoulos, Bernstein, 1957; Bernstein, 1958.

New York Symphony, NS, L. Damrosch, 1878; W. Damrosch, 1885; Merged with

New York Philharmonic, 1927.

Philadelphia, PH, Scheel, 1900; Pohlig, 1907; Stokowski, 1912; Ormandy, 1936.

Pittsburgh, PT, Archer, 1895; V. Herbert, 1898; Paur, 1904; (Suspended) 1909;

Breeskin, 1926; Modarelli, 1930; Klemperer, 1937; Reiner, 1938; Guests,

1948; Steinberg, 1952.

Rochester, RC, Coates, 1923; Goossens, Coates, 1925; Goossens, 1925; Guests,

1931; Iturbi, 1934; Guests, 1944; Leinsdorf, 1946; Guests, 1956;

Bloomfield, 1959; Guests, 1963; Somogyi, 1964.

St. Louis, SL, Otten, 1881; Ernst, 1894; Zach, 1907; Ganz, 1921; Guests, 1927;

   Golschmann, 1931; Remoortel, 1958; De Carvalho, 1963; Susskind, 1968.

San Francisco, SF, Hadley, 1911; Hertz, 1915; Cameron, Dobrowen, 1930;

   (Suspended) 1934; Monteux, 1935; Guests, 1952; Jorda, 1954; Krips, 1963.

Seattle, SE, West, 1903; Kegrize, 1907; Hadley, 1909; Spargur, 1911; Davenport,

   Engbert, 1921; Kreuger, 1926; Cameron, 1932; Sokoloff, 1938; Beecham, 1941;

   Bricken, 1944; Rosenthal, Linden, 1948; Rosenthal, 1950; Guests, 1951;

   Katims, 1954.

Utah, UT, Heniot, 1940; Guests, 1942; Heniot, 1944; Sample, 1945; Janssen,

   1946; Abravanel, 1947.

Washington, National, WA, Kindler, 1931; Mitchell, 1949.

*Three orchestras also classified as major were not included in these studies
because of short histories and difficulty in securing records: The American
Symphony founded 1962, Honolulu, Hawaii, and San Antonio, Texas, founded 1939.

INDIVIDUAL COMPOSERS AND THEIR LIFE CYCLES

There are many ways to group composers together for the purpose of
summarizing their characteristic qualities: esthetic, theoretical or historical.
Thus we speak of classicists, romanticists, serialists, or of program music or
abstract music, of those who use the twelve tone scale, or electronic techniques;
other groups are described more simply as eighteenth century, or baroque,
or modernists. For the present analysis composers are grouped according to
their volume in the repertoire, i.e., by the proportion of time allotted to
their compositions in 27 major American orchestras, in the regular subscription
concerts over the time span of one hundred thirty years. By this measuring
device, volume through time, composers who display similar patterns form
describable groups. Any one five-year period, in fact any moment of time,

would find some composers whose volume was rising, others maintaining a

fairly stable position, either high or low, and still others whose proportion

of the programs was diminishing in quantity.

As this volume through time is followed for a composition or a composer

the term life span or life cycle seems appropriate, and just as with a human

person, this life span of a musical career is determined by the vitality of

the individual as well as by the environment in which he lives. In the

orchestra repertoires, the vitality might be translated as musical quality or

esthetic worth; some might speak of the inspiration of the artist, or the

greatness of his concept, or his mastery of musical form. A favorable

environment would also be varied in musical language: enthusiastic audiences,

available teachers and schools, ample financial resources, or sympathetic

conductors. Composers themselves affect their own environments; they may be

burdened or stimulated by earlier traditions and may or may not influence the

music of the future.

Whatever the theories or the language, the life cycles of individual

composers fall into patterns which repeat themselves decade after decade.

They are continually rising and falling, and undoubtedly if composers could

be grouped together in schools or theories, such designated groups would

exhibit a similar waxing and waning through successive centuries.

As in the two earlier studies, the composers whose individual records

are here studied can be differentiated for purposes of description and summary

into six groups:

I.   A small group with a long time span, diminished volume and little

fluctuation,designated as low but stable: Handel, Mendelssohn, Schubert and

Weber.

II.   Composers in the ascending phase, either A) with higher volume and

longer range, perhaps nearing their maximum successes, or B) with a shorter

and more recent time span, showing promise of still greater success: A) Bach,
Bruckner, Haydn, Mahler, and Mozart; B) Barber, Bartok, Britten, Copland, Ives,
Prokofieff, Shostakovich, and Stravinsky.

III. Composers whose greatest success came in the very early years but
more recently are clearly descending, perhaps phasing out or destined for a
low but stable status: Liszt, Saint Saens, Schumann, Tchaikovsky and Wagner.

IV. Composers whose full life cycle can be followed within our twentieth
century. These are also separated into two groups: A) Composers with earlier
time spans and greater volume, and B) those entering the repertoire somewhat
later and with smaller volumes: A) Debussy, Franck, Rachmaninov, Rimsky-
Korsakov, and Sibelius; B) Bloch, Hindesmith, Milhaud, Rispighi, and Vaughn
Williams.

V. Composers whose cycles are labelled indeterminate in the 1960-69
decade and who might by the end of the century join one or another of the
groups described above: Berlioz, Dvorak, Ravel and Strauss.

VI. The twentieth century's most played composers, eminent in history
and importance, including several whose names have already appeared on the
above charts: Bach, Beethoven, Brahms, Mozart, Tchaikovsky, and Wagner.

In order to separate the records of these individuals for better inspec-
tion, it has been necessary to use different percentage scales as noted on the
margins for each chart, and the movement of the composer through the decades
will look a little different when the scale is changed, e.g., Strauss in
Charts V and VI; Mozart and Bach in Charts II and VI. The rises and falls
seem exaggerated when the percentage scale is finer.

GROUP I, Chart I, Low but Stable Composers:
HANDEL, MENDELSSOHN, SCHUBERT AND WEBER

For adequate profiles of the four composers today characterized as low
but stable, their careers in the nineteenth century should also be presented,

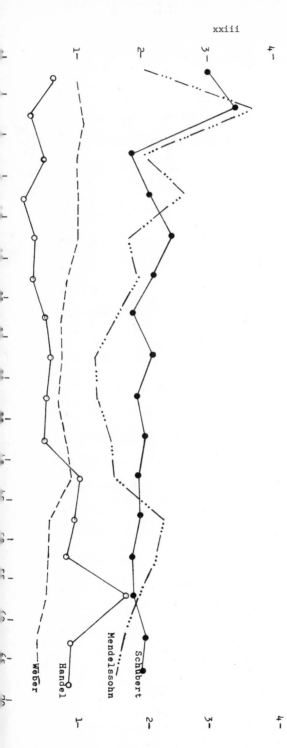

INDIANA UNIVERSITY-ROCKEFELLER FOUNDATION ORCHESTRA REPERTOIRE RESEARCH PROJECT Kate Hevner Mueller

TWENTY-SEVEN MAJOR AMERICAN SYMPHONY ORCHESTRAS 1890- 1970

PROPORTIONATE REPRESENTATION OF SPECIFIED COMPOSERS

Low But Stable

CHART I

xxiii

for all of them had held much more important places from 1850 to 1900 than they occupy on today's charts.[14] Schubert lay claim to as much as six percent of the repertoire, Mendelssohn fifteen percent; Handel whose fame rested mainly on his choral and religious work was more irregular, and Weber represented only by shorter works, mainly the overtures, had nevertheless held as much as six to nine percent in the 1850's.

Weber's Invitation to the Dance has not been heard in the 1960's in any of the excellent arrangements made for it and the Konzertstück for Piano and Orchestra only six times in that decade, but two of the three overtures, Euranthe and Freischütz were heard more than twenty times, and Oberon more than forty. These totals have been keeping Weber at half a percentage point, but the curve is obviously gently falling.

It does not take many performances of Handel's oratorios to lift his curve into a peak, as in the five year period from 1955 to 1960. In that time there were ten full length performances of the Messiah, plus four at full length of Judas Maccabeus and one each of Samson and Israel in Egypt. Six of the suites, in Beecham's arrangement, had many performances, and there was also the usual quota for the Water Music, plus an occasional concerto.

Mendelssohn, with his mid-nineteenth century standing of fifteen percent, was at that time heard as much as Beethoven today in the twentieth. By the year 1900 however, he had inevitably dwindled to three percent, and more recently to just under two. From 1945 to 1955 he made some gains in part because of five performances of the Oratorio Elijah. The Violin Concerto in E minor still remains as popular as ever in the 60's. Of the symphonies, Number Four (Italian) has long been the most frequently played with the Third (Scotch) next in popularity, and the Fifth (Reformation) a poor third.

Schubert was a contemporary of Beethoven but died at the early age of 31 in 1828, and the C Major Symphony, the Great was lost and not recovered until

ten years later when Mendelssohn then introduced it in Germany. In 1851 the
New York Philharmonic presented it and data show that this Symphony, Number
Seven, now also listed as Number Nine, together with Number Eight, the Unfinished,
are still played regularly by practically all orchestras. Liszt carried Schubert
throughout Europe with some fifty transcriptions of his songs, and today
many of them are a standard choice of singers but for lieder concerts only,
and not with the orchestras. Schubert's two Masses, the Overture to Rosamunde,
and occasionally each of the other symphonies have appeared on these programs
in the decade of the 60's.

GROUP II A, CHART II A ASCENDING RECORDS, LONG RANGE
COMPOSERS: BACH, BRUCKNER, HAYDN, MAHLER, MOZART

Bach was categorized in 1950 as Low and Stable, yet he has shown more
irregularity among the orchestras than others in this category such as Weber
and Haydn, and taking a long view, from 1890 to 1970, there seems to be a
general upward trend. After Stokowski, who was succeeded by Ormandy in 1936,
and after Stock, whose 37-year career in Chicago ended with his death in 1942,
the curve for Bach declined rather sharply, but took an upward climb to three
percent of the repertoire from 1950 to 1955. This rise was at least partly
due to seven performances of the extremely long St. Matthew Passion and two
performances each of the St. John Passion and the B minor Mass. These large
choral works, the Passions and masses have been offered in one or another of
the orchestras almost every year, as well as one or two concertos and suites.
Except for these and the Brandenburg Concertos, Bach is usually heard in
transcription or arrangement, with a host of the most gifted composers from
whom to choose.

Perhaps Bach will stabilize again at a proportion higher by a few points
than his record in the first five decades of the century, but the complexities

which have contributed to his rise make any predictions uncertain. Bach is
probably less often heard in these orchestras than in other concerts, in
piano and organ recitals, choral societies, and chamber music programs. Of
the 101 cantatas, chorales, and choral preludes formerly catalogued in these
orchestras, more than half have not been performed in the 1960's in any
orchestra. The Brandenburg Concertos however, are even more popular than in
the earlier years, especially Numbers One, Three and Four, and in this decade
the Passions also keep recurring in the programs, St. Matthew ten times and
St. John seven times and the B minor Mass nine times.

Bruckner's volume of compositions for orchestra is small, with only a
mass or two and the Te Deum beside the nine symphonies. These are all very
long, although as with Mahler, they are much admired by most critics and
conductors, and in America he has never lacked for conductors to present his
work: Walter Damrosch in New York, Theodore Thomas, and Gericke before World
War I and later continuing with Bruno Walter, Koussevitzky, Steinberg,
Bernstein and Schweiger. The most often played symphonies are the Fourth,
Seventh and Ninth. Boston, New York and Chicago, and more recently Kansas
City, have presented more than the average but most of the younger orchestras
tend to neglect him.

Mozart himself might have been surprised at his rise in popularity
in the recent decades, for he wrote not for the future but only to please
his immediate public. Perhaps the very richness offered by the German
romantics and the variety to be found in the more adventurous Russians
enhances Mozart's delicate and unpretentious beauties. Now when so many
others throughout the seventy years are continuing a slow or sometimes
precipitous decline, Mozart slowly but surely rises in favor. Perhaps
he is more enjoyed because of the greater competency of the 20th century
players and more attention to the subtleties and excellencies of his symphonies. Occasionally a concert aria may still find its way into the programs,

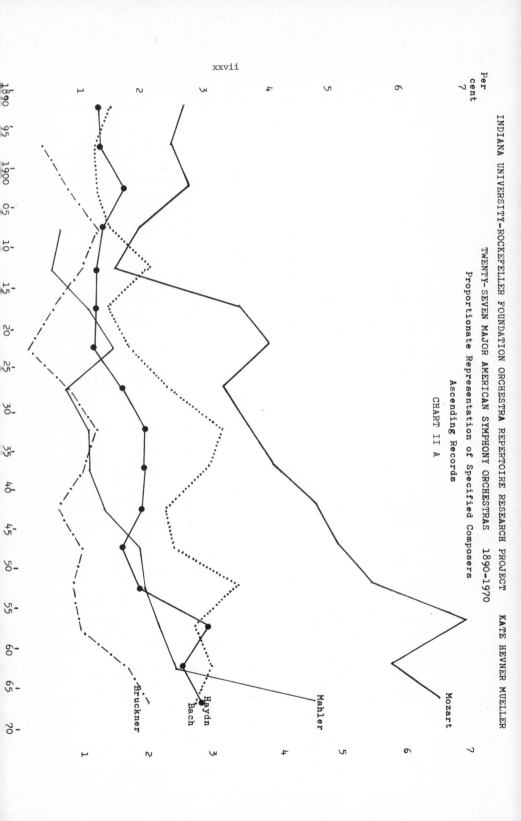

INDIANA UNIVERSITY-ROCKEFELLER FOUNDATION ORCHESTRA REPERTOIRE RESEARCH PROJECT   KATE HEVNER MUELLER

TWENTY-SEVEN MAJOR AMERICAN SYMPHONY ORCHESTRAS   1890-1970

Proportionate Representation of Specified Composers

Ascending Records

CHART II A

Per
cent

Mozart

Mahler

Haydn
Bach

Bruckner

occasionally a piano concerto, K 466 in D minor, K 491 in C or K 595 in B^b, or a violin concerto, K 218 in D or K 219 in A, but the substantial elements of his rise are the symphonies, especially four of them: K 385 Haffner, K 504 Prague, K 550, and K 551 Jupiter. Three overtures, Magic Flute, Figaro and Don Giovanni are also very much favored works, and periodically one or another of his not so well known compositions is likely to make a one-time-only appearance, introduced either by a solo artist or an admiring conductor.

There is little also to explain the steadily increasing record of Haydn except to note more symphonies introduced and many symphonies more often played. The recent publication of authentic scores has aroused new interest. In the 60's a round dozen of them appeared which had never before been heard: 12 in E, 21 in A, 39 in G minor, 44 in E minor, 52 in C minor, 60 in C, 67 in F, 75 in D, 77 in B^b, 79 in F, 84 in E^b and 91 in E^b, while the old favorites--the Oxford, Surprise, Clock, Drum Roll, and Military--continued as before. Occasionally Haydn's oratorios, The Creation and The Seasons, were presented complete and his three masses, together with a number of concertos for cello, for violin, for trumpet, for flute, for harpsichord or combinations of these instruments, were resurrected. All orchestras have participated in his rise, more especially Boston, Buffalo, and Chicago.

Mahler's overlong symphonies seem to be favorites of the critics who attend them devoutly and write about them eloquently, when they are well per-formed. Both his Lied von der Erde and the Kindertotenlieder were introduced by Stokowski in 1916 and the Lied has appeared in every orchestra but one since 1950 as many as four or five times, and the Songs of a Wayfarer no less often. Of the symphonies, Numbers One, Two, Four, Five and Seven are heard almost everywhere since 1965. Steinberg, Bernstein, Szell, Ormandy, and Abravenel have especially favored Mahler.

GROUP II B, CHART II B, ASCENDING RECORDS, NEWCOMERS

The patronage of Barber is quite evenly distributed among all his compositions. The four exceptions which do receive more attention and seem to
have persisted best through the 1960's are the short Adagio for Strings, Opus
11, first presented in 1939 and heard 22 times in the 1960's, Medea's Meditation and Dance of Vengeance, Opus 232 (23 times), the Overture to the School
for Scandal, Opus 5, (15 times) and Symphony No 1 (20 times).

Barber and Copland have led all other Americans in volume since 1955,
exchanging first and second places by small margins. Copland entered the
repertoire a decade earlier than Barber and his patronage is more evenly distributed among all 27 orchestras. Copland's compositions are on the average
shorter than Barber's. His Appalachian Spring, the Quiet City, El Salon
Mexico, and his longest work, the Third Symphony are most widely played.
Boston, Cleveland, New York and Washington have been especially generous.

Of all the newcomers to the American orchestras whose records are
examined here, Bartok is most favored with more than two percent of the
repertoire in our final decade. Reiner in Cincinnati in the 1920's and in
Chicago in the 1950's, Koussevitzky, Ormandy, and Szell have perhaps shown
the greatest enthusiasm, but his leadership in general seems firm and he
matches the present record of such old masters as Bruckner, Handel, Mendelssohn,
Schubert, Rachmaninov, Sibelius, Debussy, Franck, and Ravel, and even the more
modern Shostakovich. The Concerto for Orchestra, one piano concerto (the Third)
and one violin concerto (the Second), the Miraculous Mandarin Suite, and
especially the Music for Strings, Percussion and Celesta are most popular
today.

Charles Ives, unknown in the repertoire until his death in 1954, has been
rising at a good pace in these last fifteen years. The very titles of his

INDIANA UNIVERSITY- ROCKEFELLER FOUNDATION ORCHESTRA REPERTOIRE RESEARCH PROJECT   KATE HEVNER MUELLER

TWENTY-SEVEN MAJOR AMERICAN SYMPHONY ORCHESTRAS   1890-1970

PROPORTIONATE REPRESENTATION OF SPECIFIED COMPOSERS

Ascending Records

CHART II B

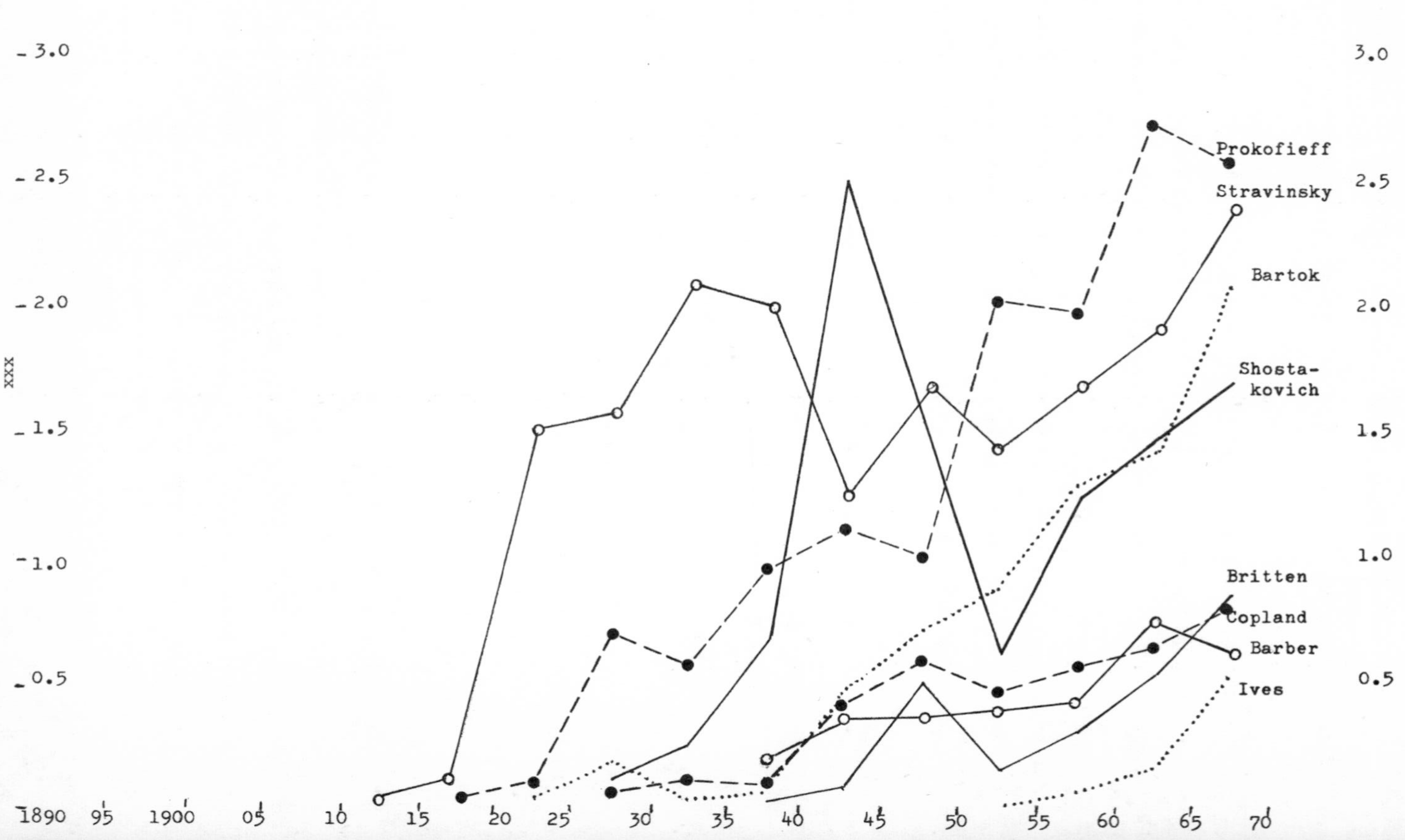

Per cent

1890 95 1900 05 10 15 20 25 30 35 40 45 50 55 60 65 70

3.0
2.5
2.0
1.5
xxx
1.0
0.5

Prokofieff
Stravinsky
Bartok
Shosta-kovich
Britten
Copland
Barber
Ives

compositions seem to stamp him as indigenous to America: <u>Central Park in</u> <u>in the Dark</u>, <u>Three Places in New England</u>, <u>The Housatonic at Stockbridge</u>, and his use of well-known American tunes makes him seem even more so. From the <u>Holidays Symphony, No 2</u>, the separate movements, <u>Thanksgiving</u>, <u>Fourth of July</u>, etc., are often presented as separate items, which makes them more timely and useful in the programs.

In the 1940's Britten's reputation was established by the <u>First Piano</u> <u>Concerto</u> and especially by the <u>Sea Interludes</u> from his opera <u>Peter Grimes</u>. More recently his <u>Young Person's Guide to the Orchestra</u>, the <u>War Requiem</u> and the <u>Sinfonia da Requiem</u> have replaced them in public favor. Occasional hearings are also given to eighteen of his other numbers, so that his growth continues firmly and steadily among the newcomers.

Prokofieff appeared first in Chicago in 1918 and has continued in favor with that city which also first put on his opera, <u>The Love of Three Oranges</u>. Otherwise enthusiasm for him waxed and waned irregularly, now in one, now in another of the cities, but especially with conductors Koussevitzky (who also introduced him in Paris), Reiner, Mitropoulos, Rudolph, Leinsdorf, and Münch. Prokofieff settled in the United States for a short time in 1918, but, after 1927 and his return to Russia, travel has been rare. Practically all orchestras play the <u>Piano Concerto Number Three in C</u> and the <u>Violin Concerto in D, Opus 19</u>, and two of his Symphonies, <u>Number One in D</u>, the <u>Classical</u>, and <u>Number Five</u>, <u>Opus 100</u> at least two or three times each decade, which probably earns them right to be labelled "standard".

Stravinsky has a wealth and variety of compositions but nothing in this large repertoire touches the popularity of the ballets, the <u>Firebird</u> and <u>Petrouchka</u>, or the <u>Rite of Spring</u>. Following his first visit to the United States in 1925, a period in which he was very active as guest conductor, his curve accelerated, and this upward swing was repeated in the decade of the 60's.

The Symphony of Psalms (1930) and the Symphony in Three Movements have been welcomed cordially as well as the Pulcinella Suite. Probably a few of Stravinsky's works suffer to some extent because of the additional players who must be hired, and the additional rehearsal time, which is always expensive. In Chicago both Reiner and Martinon played him generously; in New York Mitropoulos played more and Bernstein less.

Plucked out of relative obscurity in 1942, with his picture in fireman's helmet on the front cover of Time, the 36 year old Shostakovich was presented to the American conductors and orchestras via an overwhelming publicity campaign. Perhaps audiences were moved by patriotism, perhaps by the sheer enjoyment of the novelty, perhaps by a kind of mass mesmerism, but whatever the motives they quickly wore off, and within the decade Shostakovich returned to his obscurity. The notorious 1942 Seventh Symphony, the Leningrad, has been played only once since 1943. Of the fifteen symphonies only the Fifth, heard 58 times in the 1960's, has persisted in the repertoire. Since 1955 Shostakovich has been slowly climbing and with fifteen symphonies to choose from, most of them explored at least once or twice by various orchestras for a total of 70 hearings, he may achieve for himself a secure place in the repertoire.

GROUP III, CHART III, DESCENDING RECORDS: LISZT,
SCHUMANN, TCHAIKOVSKY, SAINT-SAENS, WAGNER

Tchaikowsky's peak in 1940-45 was probably helped both by the centenary of his birth and by the War, with a few orchestras who almost doubled his average: Baltimore, Buffalo, Detroit, Kansas City, and Utah, and another few who were well below it: Boston, Chicago, Minneapolis, and San Francisco. Most orchestras overplayed him in their early years but as they grew older, with longer seasons and more concerts, tended to underplay him, especially

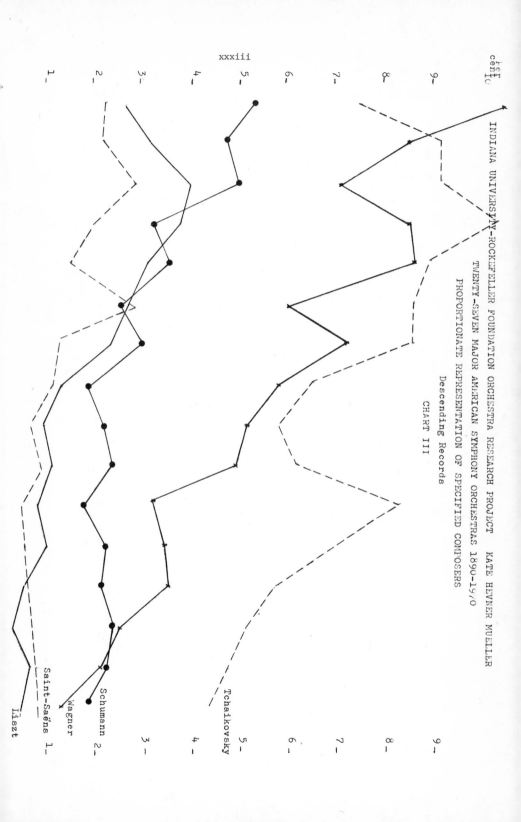

INDIANA UNIVERSITY—ROCKEFELLER FOUNDATION ORCHESTRA RESEARCH PROJECT   KATE HEVNER MUELLER
TWENTY—SEVEN MAJOR AMERICAN SYMPHONY ORCHESTRAS 1890–1970
PROPORTIONATE REPRESENTATION OF SPECIFIED COMPOSERS

Descending Records

CHART III

Tchaikovsky

Schumann

Wagner

Saint-Saëns

Liszt

after 1940. The <u>Fourth</u>, <u>Fifth</u> and <u>Sixth</u> symphonies, with the two fantasy overtures, <u>Francesca da Rimini</u> and <u>Romeo and Juliet</u>, and the two concertos, the <u>Piano Number One, Opus 23</u>, and the <u>Violin in D, Opus 35</u>, continue as the most frequent presentations.

Wagner's repertoire suffered during the first World War partly from patriotism, but partly also because the intellectual curiosity and controversy which he had aroused were fading. He recovered from that period but the decline continued steadily. Wagner lost again in World War II recovered as before, and lost again slowly and steadily as before. In the decades of the 40's, 50's and 60's his repertoire no longer boasted of the arias for which opera artists had been brought in as guests. No longer were the singing stars imported for whole acts of <u>Tristan and Parsifal</u>; rather the most frequently played items were the <u>Siegfried Idyll</u>, <u>Forest Murmurs</u>, <u>Liebestod</u>, <u>Good Friday Spell</u>, the <u>Meistersinger Prelude</u> and <u>Siegfried's Death Music</u> from <u>Gotterdamerung</u>. Some orchestras, Boston, the New York Philharmonic, and Chicago after Thomas, already offered less than half the national average.

Schumann had been very popular in the early years in both the New York Philharmonic and with Thomas in Chicago where his record was second only to that of Beethoven, but decline after the first quarter of the twentieth century has been fairly regular with little variation among the orchestras. All the symphonies had been equally popular in the early decades of these concerts but today the <u>Second in C minor, Opus 61</u> and the <u>Fourth in D minor, Opus 120</u> are now heard more than twice as often as the <u>First (Spring)</u> and the <u>Third (Rhenish)</u>. The songs and choruses of which he wrote hundreds are rarely heard today, but his one piano concerto is still frequently the choice for today's artists.

After 1905 the decline of Liszt was slow but steady. Of his twelve symphonic poems only <u>Les Preludes</u> is heard today, and the once so popular

Hungarian rhapsodies have been heard not more than once or twice since 1950,
nor have the symphonies. The two piano concertos, the First in E^b and the
Second in A are still chosen by some pianists in all the orchestras.

Saint-Saëns too is most often heard today in concertos: the Cello
Concerto in C, Opus 33, and the Piano Concerto Number Two in G minor, Opus 22,
and Number Four in C minor, Opus 44. Of the symphonies only the Third, with
piano and organ has survived. Except for the peak in 1915-20 his record
seems to have stabilized and continued strongly at a low level in the last
two decades. Since his visit to the United States in 1906 and again in 1915,
which improved his record in the orchestras of cities he visited, there is
singularly little fluctuation of his record in the 27 orchestras.

GROUP IV A, CHART IV A, FULL LIFE CYCLES, 1900-1970:

DEBUSSY, FRANCK, RACHMANINOFF, RIMSKY-KORSAKOV, SIBELIUS

In the year 1950 it was possible to discern six composers, portrayed
over a period of 75 years, whose life cycles in these concerts had run a full
course, rising from their early beginnings and reaching a central peak which
was followed by a downward slope that did not necessarily presage imminent
oblivion but did indicate that their appearances were at that moment ominously
thinning out. These six were Dvorak, Grieg, K. Goldmark, MacDowell, Saint-
Saëns, and Smetana, and among them only Dvorak has experienced some slight
rejuvenation.

Now in 1970, in an 80-year span, from 1890 to 1970, there are in these
series of subscription concerts five of the curves of earlier composers with
similar contours: Debussy, Franck, Rachmaninoff, Rimsky-Korsakoff, and Sibelius.
They show in this period of years not only the decline which is inevitable for
any of the earlier composers as they meet the competition of the younger

generation, but also their first entrance, followed by their rise to a volume of two to four percent before the decline sets in. There may be others, today classified as rising, who have already achieved or soon will reach the high point of their careers; likewise, perhaps one or another of the six designated now as cycles near completion, will return in the next decade or two with improved records.

Of the present six, Sibelius and Rachmaninoff have the strongest showing. Both entered the American repertoire in the first decade of the century and both finish in the final decade, 1960-69, not only with the highest records, but also each with a slight upturn which may mean a reawakening of interest in their works. Rachmaninoff's peak came in the decade of his death, and Sibelius' between 1935 and 1940. Boston continued as the most enthusiastic patron of Sibelius until the era of Münch in 1949, and Cleveland also has been generous until the era of Leinsdorf. Both Stokowski and Ormandy also favored Sibelius in Philadelphia as well as Iturbi in Rochester. In the 1960's all but one of the orchestras have played the Violin Concerto, and all but one the Second Symphony, which has always been the most popular, with the First and Fifth also often heard. Sibelius' other compositions however, the once popular Finlandia, the Swan of Tuonela and the other five symphonies are rarely presented today.

The hospitality which the American orchestras extended to Rachmaninoff as he travelled in these decades playing and conducting his own compositions was indeed enthusiastic and generous. It would be surprising therefore to find that his peak volume of two and a half percent in 1940-1945 could remain at that high level after his death in 1943 which denied the audiences his personal presence. The Third Piano Concerto is now a little more widely played than the Second, favored in earlier years, and the Second Symphony far outstrips any of the others. None of the songs have been heard since the 1950's,

INDIANA UNIVERSITY-ROCKEFELLER FOUNDATION ORCHESTRA REPERTOIRE RESEARCH PROJECT   KATE HEVNER MUELLER

TWENTY-SEVEN MAJOR AMERICAN SYMPHONY ORCHESTRAS 1890-1970

PROPORTIONATE REPRESENTATION OF SPECIFIED COMPOSERS

Life Cycles

CHART IV A

Nearing Completion

Per cent

-3.5 -3.0 -2.5 -2.0 -1.5 -1.0 -0.5

05 10 15 20 25 30 35 40 45 50 55 60 65 70

Sibelius 2.0
Rachmaninov
Debussy 1.0
Franck 0.5
Rimsky-Korsakov

3.5 3.0 2.5 2.0 1.5 1.0 0.5

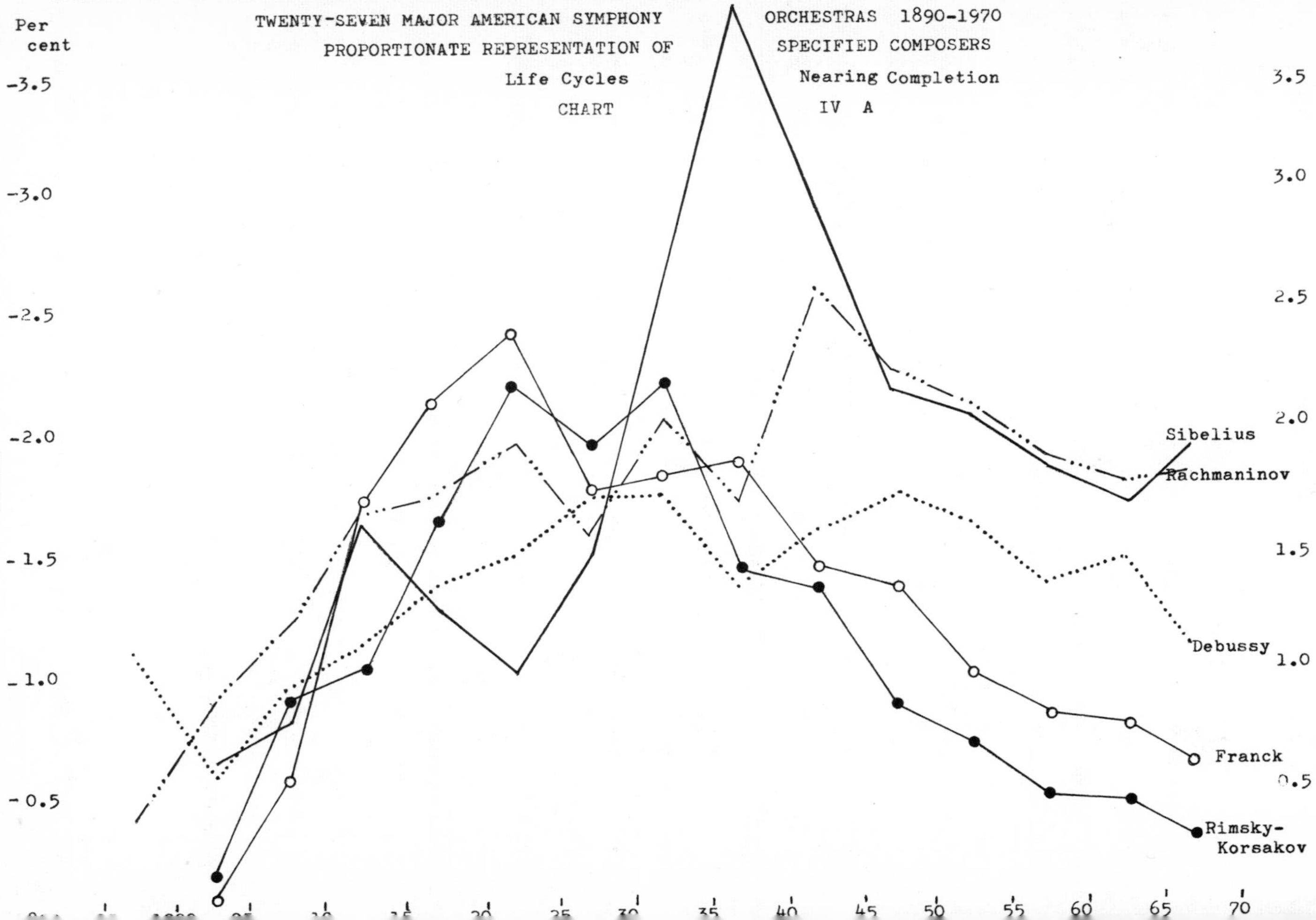

and the Rhapsody on a Theme of Paganini is also very much on the wane.

Debussy's La Mer has been heard in the decade 1960-69 in every orchestra and in most of them not once but four or five times. Other compositions still popular are The Afternoon of a Faun, Iberia (Number Two of the Images), Nuages and Fetes from the Nocturnes. These few compositions account for most of Debussy's present day repertoire which has been cut in half from the peak years. Various excerpts from Le Martyre de St. Sebastian appear more often today than in earlier years.

The rise of Franck, an earlier compatriot of Debussy, was more sharp, his peak a little earlier and his decline more steady. It seems to be the disappearance of the many shorter pieces and the diminishing record of the Symphonic Variations for Piano and Orchestra which account for most of the decline since 1950. Franck's one symphony appeared in all orchestras in the 1960's for a total count of 42, a better record than any of the symphonies of Mahler, Bruckner, or Prokofieff, and not too far behind the less popular of Beethoven's.

With so many lively, varied and richly orchestrated compositions, how could Rimsky-Korsakoff fail to hold his audiences? He did so, very firmly, from 1895 to 1945, but in the following 25 years up to 1970 his decline has been rapid except in the popular concert series. There are many newer and younger composers to claim the Russian repertoire: Khatchaturian, Prokofieff, Shostakovich and Stravinsky. There has been little variation among the orchestras in these last declining decades, except that some have dropped his name from their programs for five or even ten years. The Scheherazade Suite, the Russian Easter, and the Spanish Caprice, in that order, are the most frequently played, with some of the younger orchestras, Atlanta, Denver, Indianapolis, Kansas City, Milwaukee and Washington showing the most cordiality.

INDIANA UNIVERSITY-ROCKEFELLER FOUNDATION ORCHESTRA REPERTOIRE RESEARCH PROJECT   KATE HEVNER MUELLER

TWENTY-SEVEN MAJOR AMERICAN SYMPHONY ORCHESTRAS   1890-1970

PROPORTIONATE REPRESENTATION OF SPECIFIED COMPOSERS

Life Cycles Nearing Completion

CHART IV B

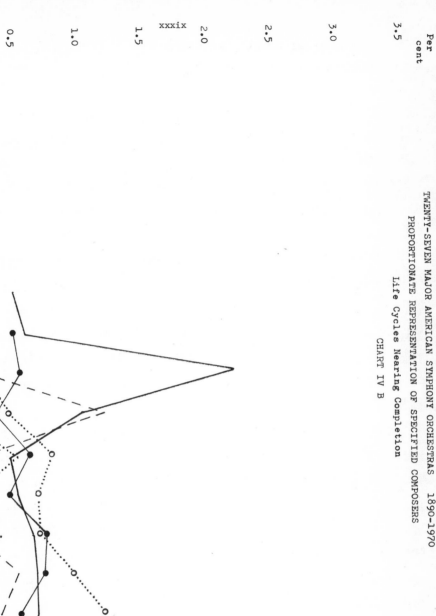

Per cent

Hindemith
Respighi
Vaughn Williams
Bloch
Milhaud

GROUP IV B, FULL LIFE CYCLES OF RECENT COMPOSERS, CHART IV B:

BLOCH, HINDEMITH, RESPIGHI, VAUGHN WILLIAMS

Nothing of Bloch's has equalled the record of <u>Schelomo</u>, his <u>Rhapsody for Cello and Orchestra</u>, although the <u>Israel Symphony</u> and the <u>Three Jewish Poems</u> have come rather close. Only <u>Schelomo</u> continues in the last decade, and his volume even at its highest point never reached that of Ives' present position.

Vaughn Williams grew rather unevenly from his beginnings in 1920-1924 with now one, now another, of the orchestras doubling his usual small quotas. It is likely that his repertoire rose slightly because of interest in our British Allies during the Second World War period, 1940-1945. <u>Symphony No 2, London</u>, his longest, has been played more than any of his other nine, and his short <u>Fantasia on a Theme of Thomas Tallis</u> is by far the most popular of his works. He has written many song cycles and choruses, but the American orchestras do not very often make use of compositions for group singing in the subscription series.

Respighi in his heyday, which coincided with his visit to the United States, achieved in 1925-1929 more than two percent of the American repertoire. In that period it was rather the older and larger orchestras which contributed most: Boston, Cincinnati, Cleveland, the New York Philharmonic, Rochester, and San Francisco. In the World War II period, 1940-1945, he fell to his lowest point, as did the total Italian repertoire, but he has since recovered substantially, due almost entirely to the continuing interest in his symphonic poem, <u>The Pines of Rome</u>.

Milhaud's record is unique to the American repertoire in that so very few of his long list of more than sixty orchestral compositions have been heard more than once or twice. Some of them have been written on commission for special occasions. His college teaching and residency in this country(California) make him more readily available for producing music to order. The <u>Suite</u>

Française and especially the Suite Provençale, which first established him in the United States, and more recently La Création du Monde have had a wider reception, but of his twelve symphonies, no one has been heard more than once.

Hindemith's symphony from his opera Mathis der Maler has been unequaled by any other of his compositions and its popularity through the decade of the 1960's is unabated, with forty performances. The Symphonic Metamorphosis on a Theme of Weber is also widely played, thirty five times in the last decade, and his six concertos are frequently chosen by individual artists. Unlike the many short compositions of Copland, those of Hindemith are, with few exceptions, of substantial length.

GROUP V, CHART V, INDETERMINATE RECORDS:

BERLIOZ, DVORAK, RAVEL, STRAUSS

The amazing fact about the Berlioz repertoire for these orchestras today is that there is hardly any one of his works not given a place in the programs. The exceptions are the Rackoczy March from The Damnation of Faust, the Funeral March from the final scene of Hamlet, a reverie entitled The Captive, the Rob Roy Overture, and his long opera, The Trojans. In the fifty years since 1920, Berlioz has doubled his standing in these orchestras, and his hold on listeners today seems to be quite firmly established. All orchestras participate in his gains and there is little variation from one to another of them.

In contrast to Berlioz, Dvorak displays great irregularity in the orchestras, often moving from very low to very high records in successive years. His pattern does not follow the tenure of any one conductor and in certain cities with large Czech populations, e.g., Chicago and Cleveland, there is no overflow of his work. Neither is he favored in New York where he once held a three year tenure as Director of its Conservatory.

Yet the revival in the decade of the 1960's is unmistakable. In this period both the _Fourth_ and the _Fifth (New World)_ Symphonies have been played in every orchestra, in all, more than fifty times for each, and the _Fourth_ in six orchestras where it has never been heard before. The _First_ and _Second_ were also played some forty times and on occasion after a gap of fifteen, twenty or even fifty years. Every orchestra except one also played the _Cello Concerto_ and all but three the _Violin Concerto_. On the other hand, except for _Carnival_, almost none of the other compositions have been heard since the 1940's or 1950's.

The career of Richard Strauss in the American orchestras has been irregular and it seems impossible to escape the conclusion that his extreme losses during the periods of World Wars I and II were due to political situations. Thwarted in mid-career by the prejudices of audiences against listening to contemporary German composers in 1915-1920, Strauss made a spectacular recovery up to the 1925-1930 period. Perhaps after this high point the usual life cycle decline had begun to set in, but the decline was accelerated by the Second World War. Again in the immediate post-war period Strauss recovered his temporary political loss although in the long range view from 1925 to 1970, the general trend seems gently downward. The slight upward turn following Strauss' death in 1949 may be the usual attention given to a famous composer in the decade after his death.

The great vogue for his symphonic poems has kept them in the repertoire of all but a few orchestras in the 1960's: _Til Eulenspiegel_, 71 performances; _Don Juan_, 59; _Death and Transfiguration_, 48; _Thus Spake Zarathustra_, 28; and _Ein Heldenleben_, 25. Occasionally one of the shorter operas is given in its entirety, e.g., _Electra_, or in special concert form, e.g., _Salome_. Many arias, dances and especially prepared excerpts from the operas are also given, e.g., the _Suite_ made by Strauss from _Der Rosenkavalier_, or his _Potpourri_ from _Die_

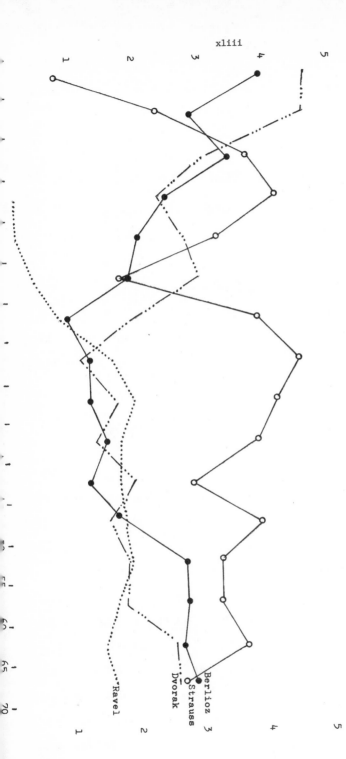

INDIANA UNIVERSITY-ROCKEFELLER FOUNDATION ORCHESTRA REPERTOIRE RESEARCH PROJECT   KATE HEVNER MUELLER

TWENTY-SEVEN MAJOR AMERICAN SYMPHONY ORCHESTRAS   1890- 1970

PROPORTIONATE REPRESENTATION OF SPECIFIED COMPOSERS

Indeterminate records

CHART V

Per
cent

xliii

Schweigsame Frau. Except for the _Four Last Songs_, Strauss' songs are rarely heard today. His stage works seem to be appearing frequently in both American and European opera houses, but there is no systematic survey by which to estimate their relative popularity at this time.

Perhaps the Second World War helped bolster Ravel's record just at the time when it might have been expected to begin a decline. Perhaps however he will become one of those "low but stable" composers, maintaining his four decade level of one and a half percent for several more decades. His most popular items are the _Second Daphnis and Chloé Suite_ and _La Valse_, each of which has been heard more than 60 times in the decade of the 1960's, with about half as many for _Bolero_, the _Rhapsodie Espagnole_, and the _Piano Concerto in G_. His records vary little from one orchestra to another, and few of his compositions have lacked some hearing in this decade.

GROUP VI, CHART VI, THE MOST PLAYED COMPOSERS, THE EMINENT GROUP:

BACH, BEETHOVEN, BRAHMS, TCHAIKOVSKY, WAGNER

A search for the most played composers would reveal different candidates from one decade to another. To set quite arbitrarily a volume of 3.5 percent in minutes devoted to one composer gives fourteen men who have met this standard in some five-year period between 1890 and 1970. They are, in order of magnitude, with their records and years, as follows:

Composer	Volume in Percent	Years
Beethoven	14.55	1895-99
Wagner	10.47	1890-94
Brahms	10.30	1945-49
Tchaikovsky	10.03	1905-09
Mozart	6.49	1965-69
Schumann	5.36	1890-94

Composer	Volume in Percent	Years
Dvorak	4.61	1895-99
Mahler	4.57	1965-69
Strauss	4.39	1925-29
Liszt	3.94	1900-04
Berlioz	3.93	1890-94
Bach	3.67	1930-34
Mendelssohn	3.64	1895-99
Sibelius	3.63	1935-39

From this high criterion there seems to be a natural break to a second group approximately one percentage point below the records above. Eleven names appear on this second list;

Haydn	2.88	1955-59
Saint-Saens	2.84	1900-04
Prokofieff	2.73	1960-64
Schubert	2.52	1910-14
Shostakovich	2.50	1940-44
Rachmaninoff	2.50	1965-69
Stravinsky	2.43	1965-69
Franck	2.38	1920-24
Respighi	2.20	1925-29
Rimsky-Korsakoff	2.17	1930-34
Bruckner	2.00	1965-69

Below the criterion of two percent, four composers will find their places, as follows:

Debussy	1.93	1935-39
Handel	1.87	1955-59
Ravel	1.86	1945-49
Weber	1.30	1895-99

A host of other names will come to mind who as it happens were not
singled out for individual study in this series: Elgar, Falla, Glazounov,
D'Indy, Krenek, Rubinstein, Schoenberg, Smetana, and Webern, together with
many distinguished Americans who are not considered here and will deserve
further attention and analysis. And also to be considered in the longer
sweep of the history of the American orchestras are such forgotten names as
Spohr, who had ten percent of the New York Philharmonic's programs in 1850 to
1855, Joachim Raff, Peter Lindpaintner, John Kalliwoda, J. H. Hummel, Niels
Gade and many others.[15]

The histories of many of these most played composers have already been
pictured in charts and described in some detail. Wagner, Tchaikovsky, Schumann,
Liszt, and Saint-Saens are now losing ground in the face of their competition.
Berlioz, Ravel, Dvorak, and Strauss seem to be in 1970 at an indeterminate stage,
while Debussy, Franck, Rachmaninoff, Respighi, Rimsky-Korsakoff, and Sibelius
have apparently brought their life cycles to near completion. In contrast,
Bruckner, Haydn, Mahler, Mozart, Prokofieff, Shostakovich, and Stravinsky,
along with many other newcomers who have experienced the high points of their
careers in the 1960-69 decade, are in ascending phases of their performance
history.

It is Beethoven and Brahms who have held the highest places in these
orchestra repertoires, not only in these eighty years but also in many of the
earlier decades. Little can be said of either which would add any special
luster to their already massive influence and importance in these years and
these orchestras, although much remains to be discovered which would afford
new insights as these data are more carefully searched and analysed. Some
superficial observations are always possible and the most obvious is the challenge of Brahms, who actually by a small fraction exceeded the titan Beethoven
in the 1940-1945 period. So small is this challenge, however, that minor

INDIANA UNIVERSITY-ROCKEFELLER FOUNDATION ORCHESTRA REPERTOIRE RESEARCH PROJECT   KATE HEVNER MUELLER

TWENTY-SEVEN MAJOR AMERICAN SYMPHONY ORCHESTRAS   1890-1970

PROPORTIONATE REPRESENTATION OF SPECIFIED COMPOSERS

The Most Played Composers

CHART VI

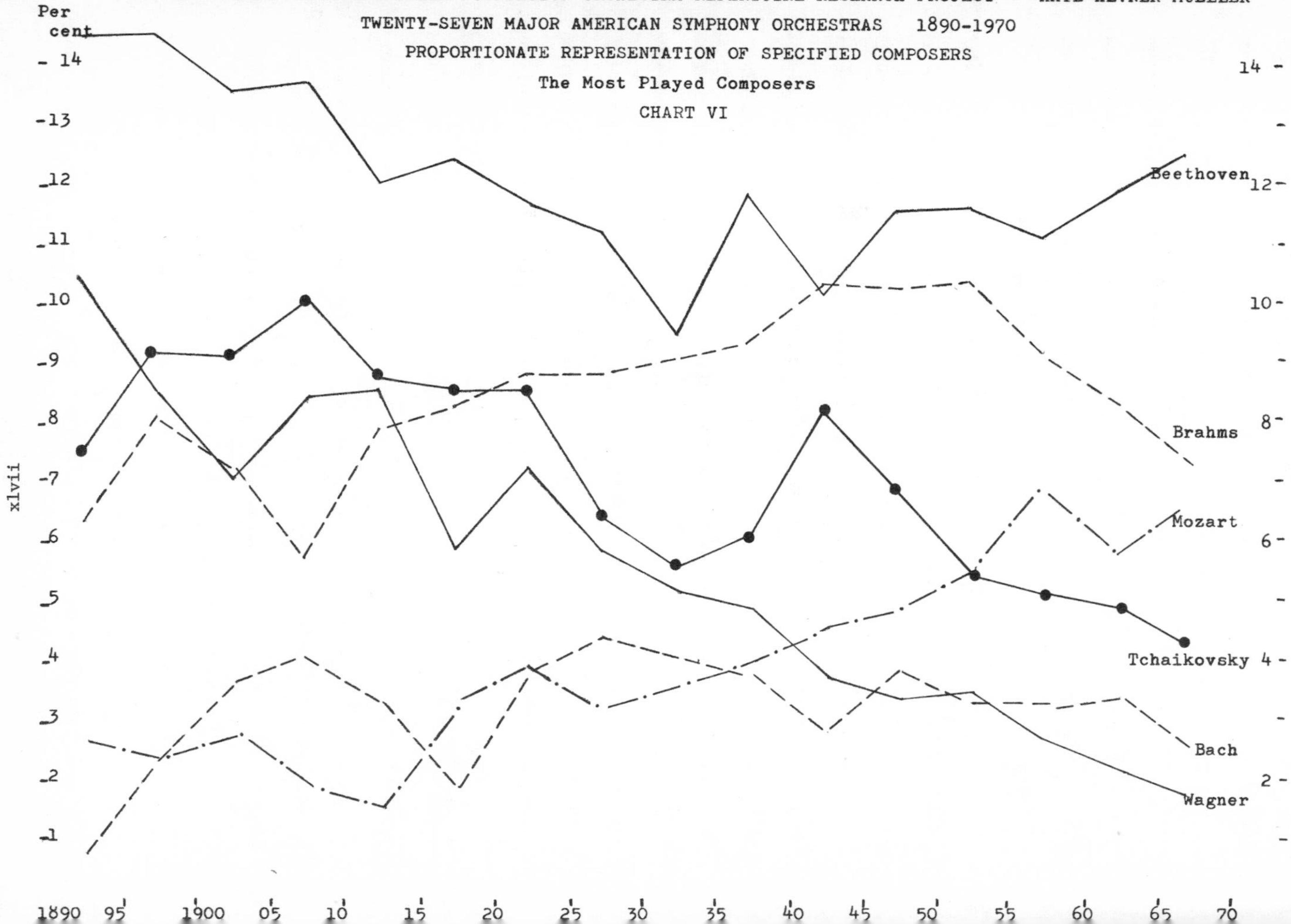

Per cent

- 14
- 13
- 12
- 11
- 10
- 9
- 8
- 7
- 6
- 5
- 4
- 3
- 2
- 1

1890 95 1900 05 10 15 20 25 30 35 40 45 50 55 60 65 70

Beethoven 12 -   14 -
Brahms 8 -   10 -
Mozart 6 -
Tchaikovsky 4 -
Bach 2 -
Wagner 1 -

revisions in the timings of the symphonies, or a different arrangement of the
time periods might whisk it away. This challenge in 1940-1945 was occasioned
by unusually high records in Buffalo, Pittsburgh, Seattle and Washington as
well as by the orchestras who have continuously favored Brahms: Baltimore,
Philadelphia under Ormandy, St. Louis, and especially Los Angeles. Beethoven's
two low points in 1930-1935 and 1940-1945 are difficult to explain. Rochester
in 1930-1935 neglected Beethoven giving him only three percent and Brahms
eleven percent. Was there a Brahms festival or some other specific celebra-
tion? Why did Indianapolis at the opening of its history with the German-born
Maestro Ferdinand Schafer give Beethoven so little attention? Or why did
Washington, another beginning orchestra, offer only a third of its usual
Beethoven volume in the later periods?

In 1940-1945 Seattle dropped even below its usually rather low quotas to
5.62 and the New York Philharmonic dived from 15.15 to 10.12 and back to 16.17
in 1945-49. Perhaps even Beethoven suffered from the general boycott of all
things German in the War years, 1940-1945, but if so, why not also the even
younger Brahms? Beethoven's record has been consistently higher than average
in Buffalo and Utah, in Cleveland under Szell and in St. Louis and Seattle
since 1950. The attention given him because of the bicentenary of his birth
(1770) showed itself in some orchestras in the 1969-70 season while others
will choose to celebrate this occasion in 1970-71, which is not recorded in
the present history. Brahms may have been the man to lose most in these
Beethoven celebrations; in Minnesota he dropped to less than four percent with
Beethoven's rise to thirteen percent, but in Boston, Brahms dropped to four
percent and with no compensating rise in Beethoven's record.

Both Beethoven and Brahms offer a rich variety for their listeners in the
compositions surviving through the 1960-69 decade, mainly overtures, concertos,
and symphonies. No songs of Beethoven and only one of Brahms survive. With

only four symphonies to Beethoven's nine it is surprising to find Brahms com-
peting so well in this special field. Only the Brahms Third, given 65 performances, falls short of a hundred hearings, while with Beethoven, only the
Third and Seventh can claim so large a share of symphonic time. In all, Brahms'
four have been heard a total of some 370 times, and Beethoven's nine offer a
total just short of 600 hearings. Beethoven's five piano concertos accumulate
a total of 252 and Brahms' two, a total of 145. Brahms' two violin concertos
add up to a 124 and Beethoven's one, to 86.

But keeping score in this way reveals little of the significant history
of these two giants. It does not touch on the wealth of personal preferences
of conductors and artists, nor of the rivalries of classicists, romanticists
and modernists of every variety who must be given their own needed representation in the programs. Does not the development of esthetic taste in the performing arts demand the education of older listeners to new experiences as
well as a parallel tolerance for the classics on the part of new listeners?
The tedious counting from which the successive life cycles, of all these most
prolific composers have been projected,as well as similar life patterns for
the hundreds of smaller contributors within their own special groups, should
provide some of the answers to these cultural riddles and to the future of the
American orchestras.

CHART VII

AMERICAN COMPOSERS: 1900-1970

Boston has been the most consistently generous orchestra to the Americans,
keeping well above the average through all decades and all conductors. Chicago
was also generous until the end of Stock's long tenure. Philadelphia and
Minneapolis are usually low and Kansas City unusually low. Cincinnati has
taken a lead after 1930 with Goossens, Johnson, and Rudolph, and Washington,
with a shorter history, has also maintained very high rates of performance.

In recent decades Indianapolis and New York, and of the Western orchestras, Utah, play generous amounts of American music. Other orchestras have some very good years, but are for the most part irregular.

Very early in the orchestras' history native composers raised their voices against the neglect of their work.[16] On the other hand they protest any token patronage, for example,when they are recognized only on those concerts labelled All-American. Perhaps it is quite to be expected that local composers will find places in their city's repertoire denied to Americans from far away centers. Up to midcentury, in the period from 1925 to 1950, the proportion of composers heard in only one orchestra was 49 percent of the total list of Americans, while six percent of all composers (18 men) accounted for 45 percent of all American music played. These 18 were represented by more compositions and given repeated performances.

Fron 1950 to 1965, 343 American names appeared but 82 percent of them appeared in fewer than five orchestras, and a glance through the pages of the repertoire lists will reveal many a composer who is accorded that once-only performance as year after year he produces his new composition. In the early years, 1925 to 1950, the American music performed by the Chicago Orchestra was contributed largely by composers of the local metropolitan area, and in Boston, 30 percent of its American music was Boston-American, although these same Bostonians achieved only nine percent in all other orchestras. One is led to the conclusion therefore that when the orchestras seem apathetic toward Americans, it is at least partly because of the lesser prominence of their cities as musical centers, which deprives them of the opportunity to fatten their American averages via local composers.

Not so much to be expected, perhaps, is the reluctance of conductors to play American works commissioned by other orchestras, with the general result that few compositions by Americans are played more than once in these sub-

INDIANA UNIVERSITY-ROCKEFELLER FOUNDATION ORCHESTRA REPERTOIRE RESEARCH PROJECT   KATE HEVNER MUELLER

TWENTY-SEVEN MAJOR AMERICAN SYMPHONY ORCHESTRAS   1840-1970

RELATIVE STANDING OF LEADING AMERICAN COMPOSERS

WITHIN THE TOTAL AMERICAN REPERTOIRE

At Intervals of Twenty years: 1905-09; 1925-29; 1945-49; 1965-69

CHART VII

Per Cent of Total U.S. Time	1905-1909	1925-1929	1945-1949	1965-1969
.14	MacDowell			
-12	Loeffler		Copland	Copland
-10	Stock Strube			
-8	Chadwick	Scheling	Gershwin Copland Thomson	Barber Ives
-6	Converse	Loeffler	Barber	Bernstein
	Hadley	Carpenter		
-4	Scheling	Hanson Bloch Taylor	Bloch	Schuller Schumann
-2	VanderStucken	Wetzler Sowerby Stock	Gould Schuman Piston Hanson Creston Thomson	Bloch Menotti
-2 (lowest cluster)		GoossensMason MacDowellChadwick Kelley WhithorneGruenbergEicheim DeLaMarterHillConverse GoldmarkGershwinBorowski MooreTochSessionsPowell PistonStrubeCoplandHarris	DiamondHarrisAntheil CarpenterBernstein MacDonaldDellaJoio MenninFossMenotti CowellSessionsStill BorowskiChadwickToch	Mennin SessionsVarese DiamondHansonHarris PistonCarterFoss CrestonDellaJoio Hovhaness TochThomson R.R.Bennett GouldStillCowellThompson

scription concerts. When foundations or other subsidies commission American works they are often presented at nonsubscription concerts such as gala occasions or festivals for All-American programs. The Orchestra League-Broadcast Music reports, for example, which include samplings of all kinds of concerts, show much longer lists of American composers and compositions than the present studies limited to subscription concerts.

In the 1965 season the 28 most frequently played composers (See Chart No.VII) those who appeared in all or at least half of the major orchestras, accounted for 50 percent of the American repertoire, indeed in each of the five-year periods since 1950, the proportion of these 28 men has fallen little if any below 50 percent. In most recent decades the general picture in all the arts is changing for many reasons, but undoubtedly the gradual shifting of support from the philanthropists to the listening public is of great importance. One could speculate that the mass media might homogenize programs from all parts of the country, giving to the local composers broader coverage and wider acceptance. But these 28 leading composers have with few exceptions (Harris from the Midwest, Foss, German born) been born in New York, have lived or studied either there or in the Boston vicinity, held teaching or training posts in the New York or Boston areas, used fellowships or other subsidies for studies abroad, but leave this Eastern Seaboard Megalopolis only for brief periods or toward the end of their careers (Creston in Ellensburg, Washington).

Another reason that the percentage of American music as compared with German or Russian or French remains low is that on the average their compositions tend to be of shorter length. This may be true also of modern compositions from foreign cultures, but its effect is felt more in American music because there is no heritage of Old Masters from the 18th and 19th centuries to undergird American programs, no Beethoven, Berlioz, Mozart, Tchaikowsky, Dvorak, not even some half-century-Old Masters, such as Debussy, Franck,

Stravinsky, Strauss, no outstanding figures whose birth dates could command occasional festivals. Yet the original American rhythms and harmonies are not totally lost; they have profoundly affected all Western music as in the case of jazz, and other new forms, perhaps electronic music may also produce some long felt changes in future repertoires.

NOTES

1. Mueller, John H., <u>The American Symphony Orchestra: A Social History of Musical Taste</u>, Bloomington, Indiana, Indiana University Press, 1951, 437 pp.

2. Mueller, John H. and Hevner, Kate, <u>Trends in Musical Taste</u>, Bloomington, Indiana, Indiana University Publications, Humanities Series No. 8, 1942, 111 pp.

   This monograph recorded the history and analysis of the repertoires of eight major American symphony orchestras, the Royal Philharmonic of London, and two American opera companies. The purpose of this "prosaic and quantitative treatment" was to note the fluctuation of public taste or consumer preferences and thus "to supplement and illuminate the more conventional histories."

3. American Symphony Orchestra League, <u>Newsletter</u> for April 1971, Vol. 22, Nos. 1-2, Vienna, Virginia, 22180.

4. Mueller and Hevner, op. cit., p. 17.

5. Mr. Robert Griffiths, graduate student at Indiana University, and presently Conductor, Memphis State University, Tennessee, made a tentative timing catalog by tabulating, analysing and finally resolving or averaging the differences reported by the various standard sources. Sources found useful in timing were:

   Catalogues of the Edwin Fleischer Private Collection of Orchestral Music, Philadelphia, The Free Library.

   Reis, Claire, <u>Composers in America</u>, New York, Macmillan Co., 1947, 399 ;

   York, T.C., <u>How Long Do They Play</u>? London, Oxford University Press, 192*

   American Society of Composers, Authors and Publishers, <u>Symphonic Catalogue</u>, New York, 2nd Edition, 1963, with supplement, 1966.

   Broadcast Music, Inc., <u>Symphonic Catalogue</u>, New York, 1965.

The Gramophone Shop Encyclopedia of Recorded Music, Simon and Schuster, New York, 1942, p. 558 and Crown Publishers Third Edition 1948, p. 639.

Aronowsky, Solomon, *Performing Times of Orchestral Works*. This was a very good source for times of standard (roughly pre-1920) works. His figures compared favorably with radio broadcasters card files in 70 percent of the cases.

Card files of Indiana University Radio Broadcasting Station, WFIU. All such files from radio card files are limited by the particular orchestra recording used for any composition.

More than fifty publishers catalogues were also consulted.

6. I am greatly indebted to the many managers of orchestras for the time and attention they gave to my requests for information, for the loans of bound volumes, and the copies made for me of announced programs as well as for the historical sketches and brochures.

In Houston, Mr. Robert Jobe, at that time Assistant Professor of Music at the University of Houston and program annotator for the Orchestra, typed the repertoire from 1950 to 1965.

Friends and former students generously copied repertoires at inconvenient times and for very low wages, in Seattle, Baltimore, New Orleans and Utah. Former colleagues now located in distant cities helped to find careful workers to supply special needs.

7. These cards and other documents are now available for private study at Indiana University on solicitation from the author.

8. Mueller, op. cit., pp. 256-58.

9. *The Orchestral Program Survey of Broadcast Music Inc.*, 589 Fifth Avenue, New York, N.Y. 10017, published annually in cooperation with the American Symphony League. The tenth report, 1968-69 season, included 582 American orchestras, with more than 5,877 concerts performed. It includes lists of the most performed composers, both Standard and 20th century, and

separates the subscription and tour concerts from all others. The
interested reader should by all means study these annual reports.

10. Mueller, op. cit., p. 280 ff.

11. Erskine, John, The Philharmonic-Symphony Society of New York: Its First
Hundred Years, New York, Macmillan Co., 1943.

   Howe, M. A. DeWolfe, The Boston Symphony Orchestra, 1881-1931,
Boston, Houghton Mifflin Co., 1931.

   Otis, Philo A., The Chicago Symphony Orchestra; Its Organization,
Growth and Development, Chicago, Clayton F. Summy, 1924.

   The Philadelphia Orchestra, Fiftieth Season, 1900-1950, Philadelphia,
1950.

12. Mueller, op. cit., Chapter III, "Profiles of Major American Orchestras,"
pp. 36-179, and reference notes, pp. 408-413.

13. The creation of the original charts sent to the orchestra managers was
entrusted to Mr. Robert Griffiths, a Master's candidate in the Indiana
University School of Music, and presently Conductor, Memphis State
University, Tennessee. He has listed the following as his chief sources:

   Stoddard, Hope, Symphony Conductors of the U.S.A., New York,
Crowell, 1957, 405 pp.

   Schonberg, Harold C., The Great Conductors, New York, Simon and
Schuster, 1967, 384 pp.

   Mueller, op. cit., pp. 48-49.

   Musical America, various volumes since 1915, and especially the
special edition of December 15, 1967.

14. Mueller, op. cit., p. 235 and p. 212 for Mendelssohn and Schubert;
Handel p. 212; Weber, p. 214.

15. Mueller, op. cit., p. 250 and charts p. 206.

16. Mueller, op. cit., pp. 266-70.

1900   AMERICAN COMPOSERS   1970

LISTED ACCORDING TO THE NUMBER OF ORCHESTRAS IN WHICH THEY HAVE BEEN PLAYED

Copland, 27	Riegger, 15	Shepherd, 9	Finney, 6
Gershwin, 27	Rorem, 15	Smith, 9	Grofé, 6
Barber, 26	Still, 15	Strube, 9	Helm, 6
Creston, 25	Dubensky, 14	VanVactor, 9	Johnson, 6
Hanson, 25	Varese, 14	Wagenaar, 9	Labunski, 6
Ives, 25	Hadley, 14	Antheil, 8	Kay, 6
Della Joio, 24	Schelling, 14	Beach, 8	Kennan, 6
Schuman, 24	Sessions, 14	Blackwood, 8	Kirchner, 6
Gould, 23	Carter, 13	Elwell, 8	Mohaupt, 6
Harris, 23	Powell, 13	Erb, 8	Morris, 6
Piston, 23	Bennett, 12	Etler, 8	Nordoff, 6
Schuller, 23	Foote, 12	Giannini, 8	Saminsky, 6
Thomson, 23	Kelley, 12	Kurka, 8	Robertson, 6
Bernstein, 22	Loeffler, 12	Nabokov, 8	Siegmeister, 6
Griffes, 22	Rogers, 12	Rodgers, 8	Stock, 6
Minnin, 22	Thompson, 12	Ruggles, 8	Stoessel, 6
Menotti, 22	Borowski, 11	Swanson, 8	Stojowski, 6
Weinberger, 22	Mason, 11	Yardumien, 8	Stringham, 6
Bloch, 21	Read, 11	Zemachson, 8	Ballantine, 5
Havhaness, 21	Converse, 10	Eppert, 8	Cadman, 5
Chadwick, 20	De La Marter, 10	Chasins, 7	Chou, 5
Cowell, 20	Eicheim, 10	Hageman, 7	Clapp, 5
Macdowell, 20	Moore, 10	Hoffman, 7	Dukelsky, 5
Toch, 20	Rochberg, 10	Koutzen, 7	Fine, 5
Foss, 19	Skilton, 10	Lamontaine, 7	Fried, 5
Korngold, 19	Ward, 10	Parker, 7	Gardner, 5
Carpenter, 18	Wetzler, 10	Persichetti, 7	Gutche, 5
Diamond, 18	Whithorne, 10	Phillips, 7	Heiden, 5
McDonald, 17	Zador, 10	Salzedo, 7	Josten, 5
Sowerby, 17	Ganz, 9	Sanders, 7	Kilpatrick, 5
Grainger, 16	Gilbert, 9	Shulman, 7	Luening, 5
Kern, 16	Gillis, 9	Sousa, 7	McKinley, 5
Krenek, 15	Goldmark, 9	Vincent, 7	Meyerovitz, 5
Taylor, 16	Haieff, 9	Amfitheatrof, 6	Noble, 5
Herbert, 15	Hill, 9	Babin, 6	Paine, 5
Lees, 15	James, 9	Colgrass, 6	Smit, 5
Lopatnikoff, 15	Ruggles, 9	Damrosch, 6	Weill, 5
			Zimbalist, 5

LISTED ALPHABETICALLY WITH THE NUMBER OF ORCHESTRAS IN WHICH THEY HAVE BEEN PLAYED

Amfitheatroff, 6	Gruenberg, 9	Piston, 23
Antheil, 8	Gutche 5	Powell, 13
Babin, 6	Hadley, 14	Read, 11
Ballantine, 5	Hageman, 7	Riegger, 15
Barber, 26	Haiefe, 9	Robertson, 6
Beach, 8	Hanson, 25	Rochberg, 10
Bennett, 12	Harris, 23	Rodgers, 8
Bernstein, 22	Heiden, 5	Rogers, 12
Blackoood, 8	Helm, 6	Rorem, 15
Bloch, 21	Herbert, 15	Ruggles, 8
Borowski, 11	Hill, 9	Salzedo, 7
Cadman, 5	Hoffman, 7	Saminsky, 6
Carpenter, 18	Hovhaness, 21	Sanders, 7
Carter, 13	Ives, 25	Schelling, 14
Chadwick, 20	James, 9	Schuller, 23
Chasins, 7	Johnson, 6	Schuman, 24
Chou, 5	Josten, 5	Sessions, 14
Clapp, 5	Kay, 6	Shepherd, 9
Colgrass, 6	Kelley, 12	Shulman, 7
Converse, 10	Kennan, 6	Siegmeister, 6
Copland, 27	Kern, 16	Smit, 5
Cowell, 20	Kilpatrick, 5	Skilton, 10
Creston, 25	Kirchner, 6	Smith, 9
Damrosch, 6	Korngold, 19	Sousa, 7
DeLaMarter, 10	Koutzen, 7	Sowerby, 17
DellaJoio, 24	Kurka, 8	Still, 15
Diamond, 18	Krenek, 15	Stock, 6
Dubensky, 14	Labunski, 6	Stoessel, 6
Dukelsky, 5	Lamontaine, 7	Stojowski, 6
Eicheim, 10	Lees, 15	Stringham, 6
Elwell, 8	Loeffler, 12	Strube, 9
Eppert, 7	Lopatnikoff, 15	Swanson, 8
Erb, 8	Luening, 5	Taylor, 16
Etler, 8	MacDowell, 20	Thompson, 12
Fine, 5	Mason, 11	Thomson, 23
Finney, 6	McDonald, 17	Toch, 20
Foote, 12	McKinley, 5	VanVactor, 9
Foss, 19	Mennin, 22	Varese, 14
Fried, 5	Menotti, 22	Vincent, 7
Ganz, 9	Meyerovitz, 5	Wagenaar, 9
Gardner, 5	Mohaupt, 6	Ward, 10
Gershwin, 27	Morris, 6	Weill, 5
Giannini, 8	Moore, 10	Weinberger, 22
Gilbert, 9	Nabokov, 8	Wetzler, 10
Gillis, 9	Noble, 5	Whithorne, 10
Goldmark, 9	Nordoff, 6	Yardumian, 8
Gould, 23	Paine, 5	Zador, 10
Grainger, 16	Parker, 7	Zemachson, 8
Griffes, 22	Persichetti, 7	Zimbalist, 5
Grofe, 6	Phillips, 7	

PART II: THE CATALOGUE

ABBREVIATIONS USED

NATIONALITY DESIGNATIONS

Argentina	Arg	Scotland	Scot
Australia	Austr	Spain	Sp
Austria	Aust	Sweden	Swed
Belgium	Belg	Switzerland	Swiss
Britain	Brit	United States	
Canada	Can	of America	US
Czechoslovakia	Czech		
Denmark	Dan		
England	Eng		
Finland	Fin		
France	Fr		
Germany	Ger		
Hungary	Hung		
Ireland	Ir		
Israel	Is		
Italy	It		
Mexico	Mex		
Netherlands	Neth		
Norway	Nor		
Poland	Pol		
Roumania	Roum		
Russia	Russ		

KEY SIGNATURES

A	A major
a	A minor
A^b	A flat major
a^b	A flat minor
A#	A sharp major
a#	A sharp minor

NOT ABBREVIATED

Bass

Bassoon

Harp

Horn

Suite

COMPOSITIONS AND INSTRUMENTS

C	Cello
Conc	Concerto
Chor	Chorus
Clar	Clarinet
Contr	Contralto
Fl	Flute
Harpsi	Harpsichord
Mvt	Movement
Ob	Oboe
O	Orchestra
Org	Organ
Quart	Quartet
Rhaps	Rhapsody
Sopr	Soprano
Str	Strings
Symphon	Symphonic
Symph	Symphony
Ten	Tenor
Trom	Trombone
Trump	Trumpet
Vla	Viola
V	Violin

Any date before 1900 is written in full -- 1862, never '62, except when several years in the 1800's appear in sequence, e.g., 1862, 68, 72, etc. Dates within the 20th century are written without the 1900, e.g., '00, '18, '24, '69. Punctuation is omitted except as needed to make the meaning clear.

Time in
Minutes

ABACO
  see Dall'Abaco

ABSIL, Jean 1893- Belg	12	Rhaps No 2 Op 56 CH 45	
ABT, Franz 1819-1885 Ger	4 4 4	Cradle Song NP 1852 Die Stille Wasserrose NP 1864 Ich Denke NP 1859	
ACHRON, Isidor 1892- US	30 9	P Conc in e^b NP 37 Suite Grotesque SL 41	
ADAM, Adolph 1803-1856 Fr	48 4 9 10	Giselle, Ballet DA 66; MN 42 O Holy Night NS 16 Overt If I Were King HN 38, 44 Var on Mozart Theme CT 39; HN 39	
ADASKIN, Murray 1906- Can	12	Saskatchewan Legend DT 60	
ADDINSELL, Richard 1904- Eng	7	P Conc, Warsaw WA 66	
ADLER, Samuel 1907- US	8 6 5 27 29 15	Elegy for Harp and Str DA 62 Jubilee Fanfare for O DA 59 Overt, Summer Stock DA 62 Symph No 1 DA 52 Symph No 2 DA 57 Vision of Isaiah DA 65	
ADOMIAN, Lan (Adohmyan) 1905- Russ/US	17	Suite for O SL 50	
AHN, Eaktay 1920- Korea	30	Symphon Fantasy DA 57	
AKIMENTO, Feodor 1876-1945 Russ	12	Lyric Poem Op 20 BN 03	
AKUTAGAWA, Yasushi 1925- Japan	11	Music for O AT 58; CT 55, 57	
ALARD, Delphin 1815-1888 Fr	15	Souvenir de Mozart Op 21 NP 1864	

ALBENIZ, Isaac
1860-1909   Sp
	7
	6
	7
	
	6
		Aragon arr Figueras RC 42
		Brisas de Marbella DE 58
		Catalonia, Rhaps for O Suite No 2 BN 19; CH 20,
		   26; CT 25, 35; LA 26; MN 43; NS 26;
		   RC 25, 37; SL 19; SF 43; UT 48
		Cordoba Op 232 No 4, Dance DE 58; RC 37, 39, 43	

ALBENIZ (cont.)

7	Danza de Mallorca CT 43
30	Iberia arr Arbos BN 28, 43, 48, 61; BU 48, 57; CH 69; CT 33, 59; CL 48, 51, 60; KC 40; MN 51; PT 56, 60; SE (three parts) 61
5	-EL Puerta, The Harbor CH 55; CT 43, 45, 52; SL 29, 52, 58
4	-Evocation CH 42; CL 30; DE 60; SL 30, 31, 39, 52, 53, 58, 60; SF 36, 55, 58
7	-Fête-Dieu à Séville AT 58, 61; BA 42, 45, 50; CH 42, 47, 57; CT 43, 45, 52; (dance only) 42; CL 29, 33, 36, 41; DE 60; DT 34, 45; KC 37; LA 32 (2), 43, 49, 66; MN 36; NP 28, 45, 46, 56; NS 27; PH 24, 25 (2), 26, 28, 35, 36, 37, 51, 56 (5 dances); RC 39, 57; SL 29, 31, 39, 53, 58
5	-L'Albaicin SL 29
5	-Malaga MN 66
5	-Triana BA 43, 50; CH 40, 42, 44, 53, 55, 57, 62; CT 31, 42, 43, 44; CL 29, 34, 38, 41; DA 32; DE 59; DT 28, 52, 61; KC 37, 65; LA 43, 66; MN 36, 37, 43; NP 28, 36; NS 27; PT 39, 54; RC 29 (arr Grignon), 37, 41, 43, 57; SL 28 (2), 29, 30, 31, 39, 52, 53, 58, 60; SF 36, 43, 55, 58; WA 40,
5	Jota Aragonesa arr Figueras RC 43; WA 36
6	Leyenda for Guitar MN 66; PT 60
6	Navarra arr Arbos CH 57; CL 30, 34; MN 34, 37, 43; NS 27; PH 34, 43; PT 38; SL 39
	Pepita Jimenez Opera 1869
8	-Dance DE 58
6	Seguidillas Arr Figueras DE 41
12	Spanish Rhaps for P and O Op 70 BN 22; CH 22; CT (arr Iturbi) 56; CL 22; RC 44
10	Suite Espanola, Excerpts arr Fruhbeck LA 68
2	Tango KC 33; PH 17
4	Torre Bermeja for Guitar DE 54; NR 67; SL 54
10	Two Pieces arr Arbos BN 30
10	La Vega arr for Guitar Marshall BU 69

d'ALBERT, Eugene	24	C Conc in C Op 20 BN 00; CH 01, 15, 17, 37; CL 01,
1864-1932 Ger		29; DT 20; NP 00, 04, 13; NS 10; PH 08, 16; PT 3 SL 17; SF 21
	20	P Conc No 2 in E Op 12 BN 04
		Overtures
	7	Esther BN 1893
	5	Der Improvisatore 1902 BN 03, 07; CH 02, 03, 06, 07, 08, 09, 12, 20, 36; CT 03; DA 35; NS 04; RC 33; SL 22, 24
	9	Kain 1900 CH 02
	4	Der Rubin, The Ruby 1893 BN 1895, 02; CH 1895, 13
	4	Song, Medieval Hymn to Venus LA 20
	49	Symph No 1 in F Op 4 BN 1892; NS 1887

ALBINONI, Tommaso	10	Adagio in g arr Giazotto LA 59
1671-1750 It		

ALESSANDRESCO, Alfred   20   Actaeon, Symphon Poem BN 37;   NP 37
1893-   Roum

d'ALESSANDRO, Raffaelo 12   Conc Grosso for Str   PH 55
1911-   Swiss

ALEXANDER, Carlos   8   Penthesilea, Lament   UT 54
              US

ALEXANDER, Josef   15   Andante and Allegro for Str SL 52
1910-   US   23   Epitaph for O NP 50
                        12   New England Overt SL 42
                        12   Quiet Music for Str DE 65

ALFANO, Franco   4   Resurrection Opera 1904: Aria, Dieu de Grace MN 31
1876-1960   It

ALFVÉN, Hugo   10   Festival Overt Op 52 HN 45
1872-1960   Swed   4   Land, Der Valsignade SF 39
                        13   Midsommarvarka, Midsummer Wake, Swedish Rhaps 1904
                               CH 13, 14, 15, 16, 17, 19, 21, 24, 25, 26;   CT
                               47, 48, 49;   CL 33;   DE 25;   LA 22;   ML 65;   MN 29;
                               NS 22;   PH 26;   SL 14;   SF 26;   WA 40, 46
                        40   Symph No 2 in D Op 11 NP 20
                        34   Symph No 3 in E BN 17; CH 15 (2), 16, 17, 18, 20,
                               23, 27, 33; LA 27; SL 19

ALGAZI, Leon   7   Col Nidre, Largo SL 48
1890-   Roum/Fr

ALIFERIS, James   6   Minnesota 1849, A Fantasy for O MN 49
1913-   US   18   Symph No 1 MN 47

ALLANBROOK, Douglas   20   Symph in Three Movts WA 60
1921-   US

ALLEGRI, Gregorio   4   Chorus, Misèrere   CH 38
1582-1652   It

ALMOND, Claude   5   John Gilbert, A Steamboat Overt CT 49
1915-   US

ALVAREZ, Fermin Maria   5   Chanson Espagnole NS 22
     -1898   Sp

AMANI, Nicholas   10   Orientale for V PH 17
1875-1904   Russ

d'AMBROSIO, Alfred   25   V Conc in b Op 29 BN 07; CH 22, 34; SL 15, 17, 20
1871-1914   It

AMFITHEATROF, Daniele   14   American Panorama BN 37; MN 37; RC 39
1901-   Russ/US 15   Christmas Rhap for Org and O CH 28
                         9   Prelude to a Requiem Mass LA 45; PT 43
                        10   The Miracle of the Rose SL 27

AMRAM, David	8	Autobiography for Str WA 66
1930- US	20	Conc for Horn and O PT 69
	14	King Lear Var NP 66; WA 66
	22	Shakespearean Conc AT 68;
AMIROV, Fikret	9	Two Azerbaijan Mugams: I Kyurd Ovshari BN 59
1922- Russ	9	-II Shour HN 58; NP 59
ANDERS, Erich	12	Symphonietta for O SF 64
1883- Ger		
ANDERSEN, Arthur Olaf	5	Fantasia for FL on Dutch Nat'l Anthem CH 1892
1880- US		
ANDERSON, Leroy	4	Fiddle Faddle CT 54
1908- US	20	Irish Suite AT 63
	8	Saraband SE 51
	6	Squares AT 68
	5	Var on Negro Spiritual, Lord, Lord, Lord CL 46
ANDERSON, T. J.	15	Chamber Symph AT 69
ANDRE, Jose	8	Impressiones Fortenas DT 36; RC 36
Sp		
ANDREAE, Volkmar	14-15	Concertino for Ob and O Op 42 RC 52
1879-1962 Swiss	16	Little Suite Op 27 DT 23; NS 23; SL 22
	20	Symphon Fantasy for tenor chor org and O Op 7 CT 05
ANDRIEU, Mihail	8	Dance in C Op 3 No 2 NP 37
1894- Roum		
ANDRIESSEN, Hendrik	9	Ricercare PH 53
1892- Neth	11	Symphonische Etude CL 55; LA 55; RC 55
ANERIO, Felice	6	Christus Factus MN 43
1560-1614 Ital		
ANGYAL, Laszlo	12	Valse Macabre PH 58
1902- Hung		
ANROOY, Peter G.	10-15	Piet Hein Dutch Rhaps DA 27, 30; MN 24, 29, 41
1879-1954 Neth		
ANTHEIL, George	30	Capital of the World, Ballet Suite SL 55; SE 56
1900-1959 US	5	-Excerpt NA 55
	10	Capriccio 1930 SL 32
	27	V Conc No 1 in D 1946 DA 46
	4	Decatur in Algiers, Nocturne 1943 CL 45; SL 44; WA
	8	McKonkey's Ferry, Concert Overt CT 51; LA 48; WA 48
	8	Over the Plains UT 49

ANTHEIL (Cont.)   16   Spectre of the Rose Suite, Film Music
    6   -Excerpts: Waltzes   SL 48
   27   Symph No 4 1942   CL 42;   SL 46;   SF 45;   WA 45
   21   Symph No 5 1946   PH 48
   24   Symph No 6   SF 48
    7   Tom Sawyer, or Mark Twain Overt   SL 49

ANTILL, John H.   20   Corroborree, Concert Suite from the Ballet CT 46;
1902-   Austr   NR 68

APOSTEL, Hans Erich   20   Var on a Haydn Theme Op 17   PH 64
1901-   Ger/Aust

APPOLONI, Guiseppe   4   Fu Dio Che Disse Aria from Opera, L'Ebreo, 1855
       It   CT 28

ARAMBARRI, Jesus   6   Prelude to a Fairy Story   SL 31
1902-   Sp

ARBOS, Enrique   5   Andalusian Dance   RC 40
1863-1939   Sp   10   Guajiras for V and O   PH 13
    5   Tango for V   BN 03

ARCADELT, Jacob   4   Ave Marie arr MacDonald   BU 45;   PH 39
1505-1567   Neth

ARENSKY, Anton   8   Carillon of Kharkov for Chor and O arr Goossens   CT 41
1861-1906   Russ   6   Dance Capricieuse for C and P   MN 47
    6   A Dream on the Volga Overt from Opera 1890   CT 1899
    8   Nal and Damayanti Overt from Opera 1899   BN 02
   30   P Conc in F Op 2   BN 1899;   CH 19
    4   Song, The Eagle   NS 17
    4   Song, Little Fish's Song   DT 20
    4   Song, Lullaby   RC 24
   15   Var on Tchaikovsky Theme for Str Op 35a   BN 30;
           CH 42;   CT arr Glazounov 31;   NP 39, 42;   PH 12,
           16, 17;   PT 43;   SF 21, 23;   SE 33;   WA 37, 39, 44
    5   Waltz arr Koshetz   DA 32

ARLENS, Harold   27   Blues Opera Suite for O arr S. Mattowsky   NR 57
1905-   US

ARMANDO, Gualterio   15-20   Night in the Escurial   NA 52
1897-   Ger

ARNE, Thomas   3   Air: Where the Bee Sucks, from the Tempest   NP 17
1710-1778   Brit   10   Overt to the Masque of Comus   ML 66
    4   Song: The Lass with the Delicate Air   MN 27

ARNELL, Richard   6   Ceremonial and Flourish for Brass Instruments   HN 56
1917-   Brit   8   A Song of Gambia: Var   DA 69

ARNOLD, Malcolm   8   Beckus the Dandipratt, Comedy Overt   CH 54, 56
1921-   Brit   7   Tam O'Shanter Overt Op 52   AT 59;   CT 61;
           DT 58, 65;   HN 61, 66;   SE 59
   30   Symph No 2 Op 40   AT 58;   BA 56;   DE 57;   WA 58
    4   -Vivace   DE 57

ARRIAGA

- 6 -

AULIN

ARRIAGA Y BALZOLA,	32	Sinfonia A Gran Orquesta KC 55
Juan C.	25	Sinfonia A Grave-Dulce LA 56
1806-1826 Sp	29	Symph in D CL 63; SF 56

ARRIGO, Girolamo   14   Thumos for Wind Instruments and Percussion   SL 66
1930   It

ARTCIBOUCHIEFF,Nikolay 3   Var on a Russian Folk Song   NS 03, 05 with Lliadov,
1858-1937   Russ   Rimsky-Korsakov, Sokolov, Glazounov, et al

ARTOT, Alex   10   Concert Var for Sopr with V Obligato   NP 1864
1815-1845   Belg

ASCHAFFENBURG, Walter 16   Ozymandias, Symphon Reflections   CL 53
1927-   US   8   Three Dances for O   AT 68

ASIOLI, Bonifacio   20   Vla Conc in A   BN 27
1769-1832   It

d'ASTORGA, Emanuele   5   Recitative and Aria for Sopr arr Molinari   CL 31
1680-1750   Sp

ATTERBERG, Kurt   9   Ballad and Passacaglia on Theme in Swedish Folk
1887-   Swed   Style Op 38   CH 38
                   9   Eine Varmlands Rhaps Op 36   PH 37
                  45   Symph No 1 in b Op 3   CH 29
                  40   Symph No 2 in F Op 6   PH 24
                  37   Symph No 3 in D Op 10 Ocean Symph   MN 26
                  25   Symph No 4 in G Sinfonia Piccola   PH 26
                  32   Symph No 6 in C Music as Song Op 31   NA 49; MN 28; NP 28
                  13   Symphon mvt on Indian Themes Op 51   NA 50

AUBER, Daniel Francois 4   Aria: from Fra Diavolo Opera 1830   CT 53;   KC 54;
1782-1871   Fr   PT 43, 53
                        Overtures
                  10   Carlo Broschi   BN 1894, 97
                   7   Domino Noir, Black Domino Opera 1837   BN 1898
                   8   Fra Diavola Opera 1830   BN 65;   CT 58;   CL 57;
                            KC 60;   RC 26, 55
                  10   Lac des Fées, Opera 1839   BN 1882
                  10   L'Enfant Prodique, Prodigal Son, Opera 1850 BN 1894
                  10   La Part du Diable, Opera 1843 BN 1881, 1882
                   8   Masaniello or La Muette de Portici, Opera 1828
                            BN 1882, 53;   CH 02;   CT 1898;   HN 41

AUBERT, Louis   5   Air for Fl   NS 15
1877-   Fr   3   Chanson Espagnole for Voice and O   PH 19
                   6   Cinema: Tableaux Symphoniques: Excerpts   DT 58
                  10   The Dryad, A Musical Picture   NS 24
                  17   Fantasie in b for P and O Op 8   MN 37;   NP 53
                  12   Feuille d'Images   SL 47
                  12   Habenera, Symphon Poem 1919   BN 23, 26;   NS 19;
                          PT 38;   SL 32
                  20   La Nuit Ensorciler, after Chopin   NS 26

AULIN, Tor   31   V Conc No 3 in C Op 14   CH 10;   CT 09;   SL 09
1866-1916   Swed

AURIC, Georges	10	Ecossaise CT 57
1899- Fr	5	Nocturne PH 22
	8	Overt 1938 PH 52; PT 50
	20	Symphon Suite from ballet Phèdre 1950 MN 65; SL 56
AUSTIN, Larry	12	Improvisations for O and Jazz Soloists NP 63
1930- US		
ASUTORI, Franco	8	Four Italian Folksongs BU 42
1845-1924 It		
AVERY, Stanley	9	Taming of Shrew, Overt Op 49 CH 18
1879- US		
AVISON, Charles	10	Conc for Str O No 1 in g arr Warlock CL 49
1710-1770 Brit		
AVSHALOMOFF, Aaron	34	Symph No 2 in e Chinese Symph CT 49
1894-1965 Russ	12	Tone Poem, Peiping Hutings, Streets of Peiping LA 50; SF 48
AVSHALOMOV, Jacob	8	The Taking of Tung Kuan DT 52
1919- China/US		
BABBITT, Milton	7	Composition for 12 Instruments SL 64
1916 Russ/US	15	Relata I PH 65
	20	Relata II NP 68
BABIN, Victor	13	Capriccio for O CL 63; NP 50
1908- Russ/US	23	Conc No 2 for 2 P and O CH 39; CL 56; NA 57; NP 40; PT 59
BACEWICZ, Grazyna	10	Conc Grosso for Str WA 52
1913- Pol		
BACH, Carl Phillip Emanuel	5	Andante molto Lento from Conc for O in D SL 39, 47, 50, 54
1714-1788 Ger	5	Andante from Conc in E NA 66
	13	C Conc in A PH 26
	14	Conc for O in D arr Steinberg BN 24, 26, 28, 31, 34, 37, 43, 54; CH 44; CT 47, 49, 52, 53, 2nd mvt only 56; CL 38, 42, 50; DT 29; HN 51; NA 38, 56, 67; LA 43, 48; MN 44; NP 44, suite 41, 44; NS 22; PH 22, 29, 44, 52, 56, 61; SL 33, 43, 44, 64
	15	Conc for 2 P and O in F AT 64; DT 55; KC 41; NP 64; SL 47; UT 1st mvt 41
	15	Conc for 2 P and Str O in E^b CH 23, 24; DT 24; WA 37
	18	Conc for 2 P and O BN 24
	14	Conc for Vla UT 57
	15	Magnificat: Excerpts PH 39
	14	Serenade for Str and O No 2 in B^b PH 61
	15	Symph No 1 in D BN 1881, 94; CH 1898, 01; CT 32; DE 53
	15	Symph No 2 for Str O in B^b BN 07, 12; CT 61; NA 50
	12	Symph No 3 for Cembalo and Str BU 41, 42; CH 36; NP 33; PH 46; WA 35, 38, 45, arr Kindler 47
	12	Symph No 5 in b PH 60

BACH, Johann   14   Conc Bassoon and O in B^b UT 64
  Christian   13   C Conc   SE 60
  1735-1782   Ger   10   Fantasia and Fugue in g for Org   DT 24
                       6   Overt Orione   PH 61
       6   Recitative and Rondo   MN 39;   SL 39
      14   Sinfonia for Double O in D Op 18 No 3   SF 29
      12   -Allegro Assai, Andante, Presto   SF 35
      20   Symph B^b Op 3 No 4   CT 55;   DT 57;   LA 44, arr Fritz Stein 63;
             NS 24;   RC 65, 68;   WA 37, 39, 44, 47
      13   Symph E^b Op 18 No 1   BN 69;   CH 58, 65, 66;   CT 49, 50;   NP 31
            Symph in B^b Lucia Silla Op 18 No 2   AT 67;   CL 35, 40, 61;   DA 62;
             HN 53;   MN 65;   NP 26;   PH 69;   PT 37, 61;   RC 65, 68;   SF 61, 67
      14   Symph D Op 18 No 3   BA 48;   CH 38;   NP 30;   PH 40, 42, 56, 59, 60;
             SF 67
      12   Symph Op 18 No 4   CH 38, 43;   CT 67;   KC 62;   NP 69;   PH 68; SE 69
      13   Symph in g Op 6 No 6   NP 62;   SE 63
      12   Symph in B^b BA 62;   PH 27, 35, 39,   arr Stein 41
       9   Cantata for Soli and Chor, Childhood of Christ   CT 54

BACH, Johan   5   Adagio for Str arr Hellmesberger   NS 1896
  Sebastian   9   Adagio and Fugue in g for V   NP 1873
  1685-1850   Ger   6   Air for Str arr Wilhelm   DA 27; arr L. Damrosch
                           NS 03, 24, 27;   SL 49
       6   Andante and Prelude arr Stock   SE 35
       4   Aria, Strike, O Strike   NS 17
       4   Aria, unidentified   SL 49;   SF 47
      30   Arias from Cantatas Nos 8, 10, 68, 97, 114, 146, 159, 202   NR 60
      30   10 Arias, unidentified   DE 60;   SF 61
      20   Arias from Cantatas No 8, 32, 92, 97, 151, 159   WA 68
       6   Arias from Cantata No 10   WA 63
       4   Ariosa arr Almeida   MN 66
       4   Arioso   NS 16
       4   Arioso in g   AT arr Franko 58;   DT 33, 34
       4   Ave Maria   AT 46;   HN 42
       3   Bourrée from Partita in b   MN 66
       4   Bourrée in g arr Reger   DT 33
       4   Bourrée, unidentified   SL 54
  CANTATAS
       5   Cantata for Domenica Quasi Modogoniti arr S. Franks   NS 16
       6   No 1 Wie Schon Leuchtet der Morgenstern Erfuellet   SF 42
      24   No 2 Freut Euch, Ach Gott, von Himmel sich darein: Eight Short mvts AT 54
      16   No 4 Christ lag in Todes banden   BN 59;   CT 65;   CL 58;   DA 53;
             DE 45;   PH 32, 39, 54;   PT 49, 59;   SL 63, 65
       4   -Choral Prelude   NP 46;   WA 35, 40
       4   No 5 Wo Soll Ich Fliehan Hin? Aria, Ergiesse dich reichlich   CH 15
       5   No 8 Dach weichet ihr tollen, vergeblichen sorgen   DA 68
      20   No 10 Meine Seele Erhabit den Herrn   WA 49
       4   -Aria for Sopr   WA 63
      30   No 11 Lobet Gott in seinen Reichen, Ascension Oratorio   CT 61
      15   No 12 Weinen, Klagen, Sorgen, Zagen   CL 34
       4   -Sinfonia   BA 47;   NR 69
       4   No 14 War Gott nicht mit unsdiese Zeit: Recitative, Ja, Ja, die
             Stunden Sind   CH 1899
       8   No 18 Gleich wie der Regen und Schnee: Sinfonia and Chorale   BN 62
       4   -Sinfonia only   CL 45
       4   No 21 Ich hatte viel Bekummernis, I had much grief: Sinfonia RC 48, 49
       4   No 26 Ach wie fluchting, ach wie nichtig: El wie Schmeckt der Kalfe
             Suisse   CT 61

BACH, J.S. (Cont.) Cantatas, No 26 (Cont.)
4   -Overture   SL 38
4   No 29 Wir Danken die Gott, Ratswahl Cantata: Sinfonia   BN 29, 50;
           CL 31, 33, 45;   PH 40;   SF 62;   WA arr Kindler 39, 42, 44, 47, 49
4   -Introduction   CL 31, 33;   NS 17
4   -Aria   WA 39
4   No 31 Der Himmel lacht, die Erde Jubiliret, The Heaven Laughs, The
           Earth Rejoices: Sinfonia   CL 60;   RC 48, 49
4   -Sonata   NP 35;   NR 69
10   No 35 Geist und Seele ver wirret for Contral, Chor, Org obligato BN 67
5   No 38 Aus tiefer Not Schrei, Her Zu dir   HN 60
5   No 41 Jesu nun sei gepreiset: Choral Fantasy   DA 48;   MN 49
6   No 42 Am Abend aber dessel biggen Sabbats: Sinfonia No 1 CH 36; CL 60
6   No 50 Nun ist das Heil und die Kraft   CH 29;   PH 57
4   No 51 Jauchzet Gott in allen landen, Sopr and O   CH 25, 35;   CT 61;
           CL 63;   DA 68;   KC 56;   NR 68;   NP 58;   PH 58
6   No 53 Schlage doch, gewunsschte Stunde   CT 51;   MN 49
20   No 56 Ich will den Kreutzstab gerne tragen   CT 54;   CH 45; CL 57
4   -Bass Solo   NP 25
4   -Choral prelude   PT 66
6   No 68 Also hat Gott die Welt Geliebt: Aria No 2, My Heart ever Faithful,
           Mein glaubiges Herz   BA 45;   CH 09, 45;   NS 15;   PH 14, 52
4   No 75 Die Elenden sollen Essen, The Meek Shall Eat: Sinfonia RC 48, 49
20   No 78 Jesu der du Meine Seele, Jesus, thou my wearied spirits LA 49
30   No 80 Ein feste Berg is unser Gott, A Mighty Fortress, Reformation
           Cantata   NP arr Stock 39;   PH 33, 34, 35
4   No 1 Chorale Ein feste Berg   BA 63, 68; BN 1883; CH arr Stokowski 62
8   -Chorale and Chor   BA 68;   CH 1897
4   -Choral Prelude   AT 69; CH 38, 42, 44, 46;   DA 54;   DE 45, 52;
           DT 67;   HN 56;   PT 51;   RC 63;   SL 54;   WA 38, 40, 48, 52
4   -Aria   NP 54
26   No 82 Ich habe genug: Recitative, Ich habe genug AT 62;   CH 22
3   -Aria, Schlummert ein ihr matten Augen   CH 22
4   No 85 Ich bin ein guter Hirt: Aria No 5 Seht! was die Liebe thut
           CH 15;   DA 68
4   No 88 Siehe ich will viel Fischer aussenden Aria   MN 39
16   No 93 Wer nur den Lieben Gott lasst walten, Only be Still SF 38; SE 60
30   No 106 Gottes Zeit ist die allerbeste ziet, God's Time is the Best SL 37
6   -Sinfonia   CL 60
4   No 131 Aus der Tiefe rufe ich: Chorale   PH 23, 26
4   No 133 Ich freue mich in dir: Choral Prelude arr MacMillan WA 38
16   No 140 Wachet auf, ruft uns die Stimme, Sleepers Awake   BN 69;
           PH 4 parts 50;   WA 32
5   -Choral Prelude   BA 28, 54; BU 48; CL 52; DE 45, 53, 54; NA 56;
           63, 64;   LA 43;   NP 47;   PH 23, 24, 25, 28, 31, 33, 34, 35, 39, 44,
           46;   PT 64;   RC 45;   SL arr Filippi 52;   SE 56;   WA 46, 48
4   -Chorale   DA 49;   PH 14, 25, 26, 29, 34, 42, Respighi 50, Ormandy
           51, 63, Stokowski, 69
4   -Recitative, When on that Great Day   PH 19
10   -Variations   PT 54, 59;   SL 29
4   -No 7 Gloria sei dir gesungen, Now let every tongue adore Thee DT 48
30   No 142 Uns ist ein Kind geboren, Unto us a Child is Born   CL 43
5   No 144 Nimm was dein ist und gehe hin, Murmur not, O My Soul; Recita-
           tive and aria for tenor DA 68;   MN 47;   NS 24;   PH arr Respighi 30
5   No 146 Wir Mussen durch viel Trubsal: Sinfonia for Org and Str DT 57;
           PH arr Stokowski 37

Time in BACH, J.S. (Cont.)
Minutes   CANTATAS (Cont.)

 6 No 147 Herz und Mund und Tat und Leben: Chorale, Jesu Joy of Man's
     Desiring: AT 46; DE 47, 50, 53, 57, 64; NA 49; NR 60; SL 62; WA 32
 6 -arr Calliet for Org and O MN 36, 42; PH 36, 56
    No 156 Ich steh mit einem Fuss im grabe: Sinfonia Ariosa CH 36, 44; NP 4
 4 -Ariosa: arr Frank NS 16; PH 54
 4 No 159 Schet, Wir geb'n hinauf gen Jerusalem: Aria: Es ist
     vellbracht, das Lied is alle DA 68
 5 No 174 Ich liebe den Hochsten von ganzum Gemute: Sinfonia: BN 64;
     CL 45; NP 49
 4 -Prelude NP 24
 25 No 191 Gloria in Excelsis Deo, for Christmas Day CL 66; MN 65
 20 No 202 Wedding Cantata: Weichet nur Betruebte Schatten, for Sopr
     and O BN 56; CL 53, 62; DA 68; DT 57
 4 No 205 Secular Cantata Der Zufrieden gestellte Aeolus: No 3 Aria,
     Wie will ich lustig lachen; CH 1899
     -No 14 Recitative, Ja, Ja, die Stunden Sind; CH 1899
 5 No 208 Secular Cantata, or Birthday Cantata, Was mir behagt, ist
     nurdie: No 9 Sheep May Safely Graze, Schafe konnen sicher
     weiden HN 56, 60; SL 54
     -arr Barbirolli DT 60; NP 40; RC 41; SE 42
     -arr Cailliet ML 62
     -arr Grainger under title "Blithe Bells" SE 32; WA 32
 22 No 209 Secular Cantata, Non sa che sia dolore NP 33
 4 No 210 Wedding Cantata: No 1 Recitative, O Holder Tag and Aria
     Spielet ihr beseelten Lieder CH 56
 4 -No 9 Recitative, Hochtheurer Mann, and Aria Seid begluckt CH 56
    No 211 Schweigt stille, plaudert nicht: El Wei Schmeckt der Kaffe
     susse CT 61

CHACONNES
 15 Chaconne from VI Partita No 1 LA 64
 13-18 Chaconne CL arr Casella 31, 36; DA arr Gesensway 59; DT arr Str O
     31, 33, 37, 41; LA arr Steinberg 31; MN 32, 34; NS 1878, 80, 23;
     SF arr Steinberg 24, 29
 13 Chaconne in d: Partia No 2 AT arr Sopkin 51, 53, 57; BN arr Raff
     1888, 89, 35(2); CH for Vla 23; HN arr Stokowski 55; NP 1874(2);
     PH 30, 31, 32(2), 33, 53, 54; RC 34, 57; SF 31; SE 60

CHORALES and CHORAL PRELUDES, unidentified
 5 2 Chorales arr Gui: DT 29; NP 28
 7 3 Chorales for Org arr Weiner KC 38
 12 3 Chorales or Choral Preludes arr Respighi CL 38; HN 51, 38;
     NR (2 chorales) 50; NP 30, 43; PT 38; CH arr Castro 41;
     MN arr Kodaly for C and P 47
 16 4 Chorales LA 49

CHORALE and CHORAL PRELUDES by name in English
 4 Before Thy Throne I Stand arr Leinsdorf RC 49
 6 Choral Var on Christmas Song, From Heaven Alone to Earth I Come,
     Chor and O CH 59
 4 Christians be Joyful NA 59

BACH, J.S. (Cont.)

CHORALES and CHORAL PRELUDES by name in English (Cont.)

4   Fervent is my Longing arr Cailliet BA 43; NA 46; MN 34, 35
4   I Call on Thee arr Stewart BA 42, 49, 51
4   My Soul is Athirst HN 58; PH 36
4   When Thou Art Near or If Thou be Near CH 45; WA 38
5   Watch ye, Pray ye: Rec and Aria PH 19
4   Zion hears the Watchmen Calling arr Sevitzky NA 50

CHORALE and CHORAL PRELUDES by name in German
4   Chorale Ach Gott von Himmel Sich derain, O God from Heaven Look
          Below CH arr McDonald 49; HN 49; PH 39, 48, 49, 51, 63, 65
8   Chorale Prelude No 16 from Orgelbüchlein, Das alte Jahr
          vergangenist, The Old Year is Gone BN arr Munch 51, 53, 54, 56,
          57, 58, 60, 61; RC 36, 49; SL 54
4   Bist du bei mir, Geistliche Gesange, Aria for Contralto CT 37;
          LA 36, 37; WA 49
4   Christe du Lamm Gottes, arr Leinsdorf RC 49
4   Durch Adam ist ganz Verderbt, Through Adam came our fall,
          Orgelbüchlein No 39 SL 39
4   Es ist Volbrach arr Stokowski NP 49
5   Gott, der du Selber bist das Licht arr   McDonald for Woodwinds,
          Brass and Timpani PH 46
4   Herzlid Thut, Kyrie, Gott Heilich Geist NP 35
4   Hier, in meines Vater's Statte   MN 24
4   Ich Ruf' zu dir, Orgelbüchlein No 42 DT 23, 46; HN 50; LA 28;
          NP 30; PH 26, 28, 33, 39; WA 35
4   In dir ist Freude, Orgelbüchlein No 17 CT 28, 37; RC 36
4   Jesus bleibet meine freude, Orgelbüchlein No 12 WA 45
12   Komm Gott, Schöpfer, Heiliger Geist, and Schmücke dich O liebe
          Seele, Two Preludes arr Schoenberg BN 27, 31; CH 43, 48;
          CT 28; DT 68; LA 34, 36; MN 32; NP 22, 51, 57; PH 42, 48, 61;
          UT 61
7   Komm Susser Tod, Come Sweet Death, from Cantata No 161, Chorale,
          AT arr O'Neill 46; BA 43, 44, 46; CH arr Stock 57; DA 38;
          DE 45, 46, 52(2), 54, 56, 57; DT 34; HN 57; NA arr Sevitzky
          46, 49, 52, 53, 54; KC 48, 61; LA 29; MN 53; NP 46, 50;
          PH 33, 34, 35, 41, 50, 53, 60, 67; PT 40, 50; SL 41, 45, 50, 54,
          56, 58; WA 39, 41, 42, 46, 49
          -arr for Str and Harp by Heerman CT 48
4   Liebster Jesu wir sind hier, Dearest Jesus SE 34, 36
4   Mein Jesu was fur Seelenweh befallt dich in getsemane CH 57;
          HN 57; PH 36, 37; SL 54
4   Mein glaubiges Herz froloche SL 58
4   Mein Gott ich haffe auf dich arr MacMillan WA 38
4   Nun Freut euch, lieben Christen, Miscellaneous Prelude No 22 PH 36
5   Nun Komm' der Heiden Heiland, Now comes the gentle Savior, Cantata
          No 61: Prelude No 9 CH 57; CL 43, 51; HN 57; LA 36, 38; PH 30,
          31, 33, 36, 39, 41, 42, 43, 44, 45, 49; RC arr Leinsdorf 49;
          SL arr Tansman 39, 41, 42, 43, 44, 45, 49; WA arr Kindler 43,
          47, 48

BACH, J.S. (Cont.)

CHORALE and CHORAL PRELUDES by name in German (Cont.)
5   O mensch bewein dein Sünde gross, O Man, Thy Grievous Sins Bemoan,
     Orgelbüchlein No 24 arr Stock CH 17, 25, 29, 32, 35, 37, 38, 40, 41,
     42, 52;   CT 28, 37;   MN 39, 44;   NP 20(2), 49;   PH 39, 44(2), 54,
     60, 69;   WA 37, 40
4   Schafe Konnen Siener Weiden PT 64
4   Schleicht Sprelente Wellen, May Providence Surround and Protect You
     Final Chorus from Secular Cantata, dated 1734 NA 50
6   Schmücke dich, O liebe Seele arr Leinsdorf RC 49
4   Vater Unser in Himmelreich, Catechism Prelude No 10 arr Ormandy PH 37
12   Von Himmel Hoch var arr Stravinsky HN 57;   LA 65;   NP 56
     -arr Ormandy PH 42
5   Wen wir in höchsten Nothen Sind, In our hour of deepest need NP 41
3   Wir glauben all, the Crede, We All Believe in One God BA 61;   CH arr
     Stokowski 57;   CL 41, 51;   DE 54;   DT 28;   HN 55;   NA 46, 49, 51,
     53;   KC 52;   LA 28, 42;   MN 42, 35(2), 39, 50;   NP 30, 41, 51, 53;
     PH 23, 24, 25, 28, 29, 31, 33, 34, 35, 48;   PT 50, 54, 59, 64;
     RC 43, 45;   SL 29, 52;   SE 56;   WA 32, 46, 48, 49

100   Christmas Oratorio AT 67;   CT 64;   CL 58;   DA 53, 63;   LA 53, 64; SF 56
4   -Aria NR 60
4   -Bereite dich Zion SL 58
12   -Three Chorales from Oratorio NP 38
15   -Excerpts NR 54
4   -Jauchzet fro lachet NP 59
40   -Part I BN 84, 50
60   -Part I and IV CL 64
5   -Pastorale Sinfonia BN 1884, 87, 89, 97, 98, 05, 09, 11, 14, 52,
      57, 60;   CH 1891, 96, 98, 02, 06, 07, 09, 10, 11, 12, 14, 15, 16,
      17, 19, 22, 25, 26, 27, 30, 31, 35, 36, 37, 38, 39, 40, 41, 43;
      CT 62;   CL 27, 52, 60;   DE 47;   MN 57;   NP 1889, 27, 52;   PH 14,
      19, 22, 41, 48, 51, 54, 59;   PT 49, 63;   SL 15, 56;   SF 45, 48
10   -Pastorale and Chorale BN 55;   CH 54
4   -Prepare Thyself DT 54, 56
4   -Slumber Song, Schummerleid DT 56;   NP 30

CONCERTOS
15   Conc for O after Vivaldi NA 49, 58;   WA 32, 33 Adagio only
18   Brandenburg No 1 in F BA 67;   BN 47, 65;   BU 65;   CH 07, 43, 45,
     49, 51, 63;   CT 28, 34;   CL 48, 64;   DA 46;   DE 58;   DT 58, 67;
     LA 34;   MN 14, 47, 61;   NR 63, 69;   NP 17, 20(2), 35, 51;   NS 1888,
     10, 12, 14, 20, 25;   PH 26, 62;   SL 27, 61;   SF 40
12   Brandenburg No 2 in F BN 01, 18, 25, 27, 36, 45, 50;   Ch 12, 14,
     19, 23, 27, 33, 34, 37, 42, 62;   CT 04, 34, 40, 59;   CL 42, 68;
     DE 50, 60;   DT 55, 66;   HN 49;   LA 38, 55;   ML 63;   MN 28, 56, 61;
     NR 57;   NP 35, 46;   NS 26;   PH 03, 07, 08, 09, 11, 20, 21, 26, 28,
     30, 33, 35, 42, 44, 58, 60, 62;   RC 67;   SL 26;   SF 31;   UT 60; WA 37
     -Andante only CH 14
12   Brandenburg No 3 in G AT 49, 54, 60;   BA 42, 47, 50;   BN 06, 10, 13,
     24, 26, 29, 33, 35, 41, 42, 49, 53;   CH 1891, 10, 13, 14, 15, 16, 18,
     19, 21, 22, 23, 24, 25, 27, 29, 30, 32, 35, 37, 38, 39, 40, 41, 44,
     45, 47, 51, 53, 62;   CT 12, 16, 22, 31, 38, 47, 49;   CL 25, 28, 32,
     36, 38, 50, 58;   DA 29, 54, 58;   DE 53, 56, 59;   DT 23, 33, 56, 64;
     HN 46, 48, 54;   NA 40, 45, 50;   KC 45, 56;   LA 32, 35, 44, 52, 57, 65;

BACH, J.S. (Cont.)

CONCERTOS (Cont.) Brandenburg No 3 (Cont.)
MN 24, 28, 31, 33, 43, 58, 61; NR 65; NP 1880, 83, 87, 95, 02, 04, 11, 13, 23, 26, 37, 38, 48, 59, 64, 68; NS 27; PH 13, 16, 20 1st part, 26, 27, 38, 53; PT 38, 42, 43, 58, 65, 69; RC 25, 56; SL 28, 31, 33, 38, 39, 40, 46, 53, 67; SF 44, 48; SE 34, 47, 58; UT 62, 65; WA 38, 40, 41, 42, 46, 53, 55

20   Brandenburg No 4 in G AT 50; BN 26, 28, 45, 63; CH 29, 30, 41, 49, 51, 56, 61; CT 05, 65; CL 37, 57, 68; DT 32, 65; HN 33; NA 63; LA 26, 47, 64; ML 64; MN 24, 61, 64; NR 58, 68; NP 29, 59; PH 26, 54, 69; PT 63; RC 49; SL 37; SF 52; SE 46; WA 44, 68, 69

22   Brandenburg No 5 in D AT 67; BA 61; BN 21, 34; BU 59, 62, 64; CH 23, 31, 50, 51, 54; CT 31, 46, 52; CL 56, 59; DE 56; DT 28, 46, 60; HN 52; LA 31, 46; MN 24, 37, 44, 61; NR 53; NP 59, 64, 68; NS 21, 23; PH 22, 26, 30, 32, 33, 35, 37, 41, 49, 54; PT 40, 45, 59; RC 45; SL 21, 45, 52; SF 30, 32, 38, 56, 66; SE 28; UT 59; WA 69

18   Brandenburg No 6 in B^b BN 37, 50, 54, 59; BU 68; CH 1899, 10, 22, 25, 26, 28, 30, 34, 38, 47, 48, 51; CT 30, 39; MN 53; NP 32, 36, 59, 62, 68; PH 26, 29, 43, 55, 69

12   Piano or Harpsichord No 4 in A CL 60; WA 69
15   Piano in C WA 53
20   Piano in D BN 21; NS 13, 17, 24 allegro only, 27; WA 69
18   Piano No 1 in d AT 67; BN 51; BU 40, 60, 63, 67; CH 25, 32, 51, 59; CT 31, 32, 35, 56, 68 for Harpsichord; CL 27, 58, 61; DE 48, 59, 65; DT 21, 60; HN 60; LA 62; PH 11, 16, 21, 25, 50, 57; SL 13, 28, 50; SF 45, 55, 62, 66; SE 57; WA 36, 40, 41, 49, 59, 69
15   Piano in E PH 51
12   Piano No 6 in F AT 69
12   Piano No 5 in f BN 12; BU 66; CT 26, 53; CL 29, 62; DE 58; DT 58,66 NA 48; MN 26, 46; PH 24, 54; PT 54; SL 25, 57; SF 28, 56; SE 48 for Harpsichord; RC 59
12   Piano No 5 in g NP 58, 62; PH 29, 57; SF 66; WA 59, 69
12   Two Pianos No 1 in c BN 40; CH 21, 32 allegro only, 33, 39; CT 39, 51; CL 28; DA 54; NA 53; NS 21; PT 58, 64; WA 47
12   Two Pianos No 2 in C BN 40; CH 45; CT 39, 55, 68; DE 52, 58; HN 68; NA 54; LA 52; MN 52,with Harpsichord 27 and 66; NP 11; PT 51; RC 52; SL 51; SE 68; UT 68; WA 32, 36, 53
12   Three Pianos, unspecified AT 65; BU 54; DE 68; NA 51; MN 23, 67; NS 22
12   Three Pianos No 1 in d BA 36, 53; CH 51; CT 50; NP 15, 50, 57, 58; PH 35, 41, 62; PT 50; SL 50
12   Three Pianos No 2 in C CH 23, 24, 34, arr Gunn 47; CT 01, 59; CL 25; DE 58; DT 19; HN 42; NR 65; NP 59; PH 17; PT 66; SE 68; WA 32
12   Four Pianos in a BU 40, 53; CT 54; DT 56; HN 50; NA 53; KC 67; PH 33; RC 40
12   Harpsichord in F, Italian PH 23
12   Organ and Str in d after Vivaldi Conc Grosso Op 3, No 11 BN 22; DA 58; PH 54
12   Organ and O No 1 in D NP 54
 5   Organ, C and O Grave and Allegro only, arr Kindler WA 32, 36, 39, 42, 43

BACH, J.S. (Cont.)

Concertos (Cont.)
12   Violin No 1 in a from Clavier Conc No 7 in g AT 49, 68; BA 63, 67;
      BN 02, 27, 49, 59, 60, 66; BU 50; CH 27, 41, 46, 51; CT 12, 47,
      65; CL 27, 66; DE 51; DT 48, 53; HN 57; NA 34, 65; LA 50, 51;
      MN 63; NR 62; NP 31, 38, 50, 53, 54, 64; NS 26; PH 26, 45;
      PT 49, 54, 63, 68; SL 48, 54, 66; SF 31, 37, 51, 57; SE 36
      Andante only, 37; WA 49, 53, 62, 65, 69
18   Violin No 2 in E from Clavier Conc No 3 in D BA 45, 50, 68; BN 04,
      45; BU 68; CH 37, 40, 52; CT 05, 15, 28, 31, 66; CL 24, 30, 32,
      38, 52, 63, 69; DA 57; DT 25, 41, 61; HN 55, 64; MN 22, 51;
      NP 01, 60, 64, 65, 67; NS 14; PH 04, 06, 13, 54; PT 44, 58, 63;
      RC 28; SL 33, 46, 53; SE 45; UT 49; WA 60, 68, 69
18   Violin in g DA 53, 61; DT 54; NP 49, 54; PH 22; SF 54
15   Violin in f from Piano Concerto No 5 in f CL 49
4   -arioso arr Stokowski PH 40
18   Violin in d from Clavier Conc No 1 in d PH 45
17   Two Violins in d from 2 P Conc No 3 in c AT arr Sopkin 48, 61;
      BA 50; BN 90, 14, 64; BU 52, 64; CH 1892, 00, 15, 21, 31, 34;
      CT 07, 17, 60; DA 50; DT 57, 64; KC 55; LA 22; MN 37, 54, 57,
      64; NR 67; NP 1881, 28, 33, 40, 58, 69; NS 24; PH 03, 29, 35,
      40, 52, 59; RC 49; SL 66; SF 19, 20, 60; SE 30, 34, 52
      -arr for Str O AT 57
15   Flute, V and P in A WA 52
15   Piano and Two Flutes in F PH 51
12   Oboe, V and O in c from 2 Clavier Conc No 1 in c NR 65; NP 65
16   Oboe or Flute, V and Str in D BU 66; CL 26; HN 66; LA 52;
      PH 14, 50, 54, 55; PT 55, 61
15   Triple Concerto in a for V, Clavier and Fl PT 54

12   Divertimento, Suite from several works arr Seidl CT 1895; NP 1893

65   Easter Oratorio CL 67; PH 62; SE 55
5   -Chorale CL 52
4   -Kommt, Eilet und Laufet CH 50
4   -Overt WA 53
6   -Sinfonia and Adagio CT 59

5   Etude, for ballet MN 43

FANTASIAS and FUGUES
10   Chromatic Fantasy and Fugue in d CT arr Mraczek 28; DT 48;
      NP arr Bristow 1879
5   Fantasia Contrapuntistica arr Busoni-Stock CH 11
4   Fantasia in G BN 32; CH 41; LA arr Volkel 49; ML arr Rusch 63,
      arr Stoessel 67; SL arr Volkel 41, arr Stoessel 42, 49
12   Fantasia and Fugue in g, "Great" BA 42, 43, 45, 47; BN 35; CH 34(2),
      40; CL 38, 44; NA 52; MN 36, 38, 41, 46; NR 58; NP 40, 48, 52,
      57; PH arr Stokowski 26, 28, 33, 36, arr Smith 55, 62; PT arr
      Goedicke 40; RC 24, arr Elgar 25, arr Mitropoulos 49
17   Fantasia and Fugue No 6 AT arr Villa Lobos 56
10   Fantasia and Fugue in c arr Elgar BA 51; BN 24; CH 37, 53; CT 34;
      CL 39; DT 48; NP 1876, 54; NS 21, 25; PH 53; PT 44, 45
90   Art of the Fugue BN 49; CL 3 Fugues 49; MN 2 Fugues 40; RC 7
      Fugues arr Munch 49
10   -Four Contrapunti, Nos I, II, III and IX arr Tureck WA 68, 69

BACH, J.S. (Cont.)

FANTASIAS and FUGUES (Cont.)
3   Fugue a la gigue arr Holst BA 42; DT 33, 34
4   Fugue in a arr Hellmesberger CH 1891, 93, 97, 08; NP 1894, 99, 47;
     NS 1889
4   Fugue in C arr Weiner KC 37; NP 18
4   Fugue in c from WTC Book I PH 32, 33, 36
5   Fugue in D from WTC Book II WA 32
4   Little Fugue in g BA 42, 43, 45, 47, 50; CH 40, 46, 57, with
     canzone 37, 39; CL 44; DE arr Caston 49, 50, 52, 55, 57, 60;
     DT 41; HN 42, 44, 45, 56, 57; NA arr Cailliet 55; LA arr
     Stokowski 39; ML 60; NP 40, 48, 52, 57; PH 30, 31, 33, 34,
     35, 39, 50, 54; PT arr Cailliet 43, 49; RC arr Cailliet 57

GAVOTTE
4   Gavotte NS 03
4   Gavotte arr for Guitar AT 58; DE 54; NR 57
4   Gavotte arr for Harpsichord DT 23
3   Gavotte in D NS 25, 27
4   Gavotte in E NS 08, 24

15   Goldberg Var arr for O Nabokov CL 38; MN 38; PH 57

14   Magnificat CH 29; CT 49; CL 60; DT 60; LA 59; MN 50; NP 15,
     58, 59; PH 58, 67; PT 63, 67; SL 53; SF 50
4   -Exultate WA 63

120 Mass in b AT 69; BA 66; BN 54; CH 34, 41, 62; CL 57, 66;
     DE 49; HN 58; LA 58; MN 61; NP 64; PH 34, 61; PT 54; SF 58;
     WA 63, 65
5   -Benedictus LA 33; MN 39
4   -Crucifixus RC 40
5   -Et incarnatus RC 40
4   -Et Resurrexit RC 40
4   -Et in Spiritum Sanctum MN 24
4   -Kyrie Eleison NP 33
3   -Sanctus RC 40

20   Mass in F PH 61 excerpts

MOTETS
4   The Spirit also helpeth us CH 32; MN 48; RC 40
4   Sing to the Lord CH 31; HN 45; LA 28; MN 44
4   I Wrestle and Pray CH 09
4   Be not afraid KC 34

60   Musical Offering, Ricercare, Six part fugue SF 52; WA 69
     -arr Heerman for Str and Harp CT 48
     -arr Ferguson NP 39, 40, 53
     -arr Markevich for solo octet and Str O BN 56
     -arr Webern CH 57; HN 69; LA 68; MN 61; PT 58, 63; RC 66;
     SL 64, 67

4   Overt in D WA 32

BACH, J.S. (Cont.)

12   Partita in e SL arr Levy 48

15   Passacaglia and Fugue in c DT 28, 39, 41, 43; SE 45, 52
            -arr Boessenroth CT 40; NA 41; MN 34, 35, 45, 49
            -arr Esser NP 1871(2), 94, 98, 01, 03, 15
            -arr Ormandy CH 48, 57; DT 50; HN 50; NA 48; MN 47; PH 46,
            48, 50, 60, 62
            -arr Respighi BU 45, 49; CH 55, 61; CT 30, 38, 45, 55; NP 29,
            32, 46, 56; PT 49, 54; RC 30, 39, 40; UT 46, 50
            -arr Stock CH 29(2), 30, 31, 32, 36, 38, 41, 42
            -arr Stoessel CT 47
            -arr Stokowski CH 65; DT 47, 55, 56, 67; HN 47, 55, 56, 67;
            MN 51, 53; PH 21(2), 22, 23, 24, 25(2), 26, 28, 29, 31, 33, 34,
            35, 37, 39, 41, 44; PT 50; WA 51
12   Passacaglia   BA 43, 44, 45, 46, 50, 51, 60, 64, 69 NR 54, 56;
            SE 29;   WA 44
                -arr Goedicke CL 30, 31; PT 38
                -arr Respighi CL 34; DA 37; DE 64; LA 30, 44, 46; SL 30, 32,
                34, 37, 51, 54, 55; SF 35, 48, 60; UT 46, 50
                -arr Sevitsky NA 54
                -arr Stokowski DE 52, 53, 62; LA 39, 68; NR 54, 56, 66

13   Passacaglia and Fugue in d arr Stokowski DE 50

8   Passacaglia in E   PT 39

134   The Passion according to St. John AT 68; BN 34, 49, 51, 55, 57, 66;
            BU 63; CH 65; CL 61; LA 36; NP 65; PH 67
4   -Aria DA 58; NR 60
4   -Alto Aria WA 58
4   -All is Fulfilled DT 53
4   -Aria, Dissolve Oh My Heart CH 51
4   -Aria, I Follow Thee Also, My Savior CH 51
4   -It is Finished NS 15; PH 14, 34, 35, 36

220   The Passion according to St. Matthew BN 10, 17(2), 50, 52, 58;
            BU 47, 58; CH 34, 35; CT 56; CL 59(90min., Gabrilovich version);
            DA 57, 60; DE 51; DT 58; LA 60, 67; MN 54; NP 39, 42, 60;
            PH 16, 30, 54; PT 52, 60; RC 49; SF 52, 60, 65; SE 62; UT 63, 69
4   -Ah, Jesus Dear WA 43
4   -Alto Aria WA 58
4   -Aria NR 60
4   -Chorale No 63 BN 57
10   -Three Chorales CH 44; DT 43, 44
4   -Ergarme Dich DA 68; MN 39
30   -Excerpts PH 40; SL 35
6   -Final Chorus CT 63; NP 33, 43, 44, 45
4   -Gladly Will I All Resigning Aria CT 40
4   -Herzliebsten Jesu, Chorale PH 39, 40, 43
4   -Herzlich tut mich Verlaugen, Chorale DT 46; NA 36, 40, 42; LA 51;
            PH 34; WA 36, 41
4   -In Love My Savior, Aria CH 51
4   -Oh Pardon Me, Aria CH 14; NS 13; PH 13; SL 30
100   -Part II BN 56

BACH, J.S. (Cont.)

4   Pastorale in F arr Damrosch   NP 1882;   WA 37

5   Polonaise and Badinerie for Flute   NS 25

PRELUDES and FUGUES
   14   Prelude, Adagio and Gavotte arr Bachrich   BN 1884(2), 86, 90, 92, 98,
           04, 05, 17;   NP 38(with Rondo also);   NS 1883, 11
    8   Prelude and Fugue in a for Org   CL 31;   NP 21 for piano;   SF arr
           Cailliet 41(2), 49
    8   Prelude and Fugue in b   BN 36;   CH 39;   MN for cello 37, 42;   NP arr
           Mitropoulas 42;   PH arr Cailliet 37, 38;   RC arr Read 39;   SE 26
    5   Prelude and Fugue in C No 17 arr Koussevitzky   BN 40
    5   Prelude and Fugue in C# arr Verbrugghen   MN 28, 29
    5   Prelude and Fugue in c from Cello Suite No 5   PH arr Ormandy 50, 53;
           RC 42;   WA 33, 38, 42;   NP 1883
   15   Prelude and Fugue in D WTC Vol I No 5   CT arr Mitchell 41, arr
           Respighi 29, 30, 51;   CL 37;   DT 34;   LA 32;   MN 36, 37, 47;
           NP 34, 48, 52, 55;   PH 31;   RC 32;   SL 54
   10   Prelude and Fugue in D, Book II WTC   PT 39;   WA 32
    9   Prelude and Fugue No 6 arr for O Villa Lobos   HN 57;   SE 54
    8   Prelude and Fugue in E from V Sonata in E arr Bloomfield   SF 45, 49
    8   Prelude and Fugue in e No 18 of WTC   LA arr Cailliet 45;   MN 32;
           PH arr Stokowski 37
   12   Prelude and Fugue in Eb, St. Anne   AT 66;   BA 36;   CH arr Stock 30,
           32, 34, 36, 39, 40, 41, 57;   LA 30, 34, 65;   MN 27, 29, 33;   WA 39,
           51, 56
   12   -arr Schoenberg   BN 29, 30, 33, 36, 43;   BU 67;   CH 33;   CT 39, 43;
           DT 68;   LA 54;   NR 69;   NP 32, 34;   PH 31, 33, 54;   PT 69;   SF 31;
           SE 69;   UT 61
   10   Prelude and Fugue in f   NA 49;   LA 49;   MN 36;   PH arr Cailliet 36,
           40, arr Zador 48
   10   Prelude and Fugue in g   PT 67
   12   Prelude, Chorale and Fugue WTC Book I No 4 arr Abert   AT 48;   CH 92,
           95, 96, 04, 06, 08, 16, 26, 27;   CT 97, 98, 00, 05;   CL 26;   DE 46,
           62;   DT 14, 23;   NA 38;   LA 26;   NP 97, 01, 07, 13, 17, 18, 19,
           20(2), 21;   SF 17;   WA 41
    8   -Chorale and Fugue   CH 17, 20, 24, 36;   NA 34;   SL 28
    4   -Chorale   CH 05, 43
    3   -Prelude   AT 59

PRELUDES
    4   Prelude in b   DT 46(2);   PH 26, 29
    4   Prelude in D from Organ Fugue   RC 31
    4   Prelude in E from 3rd Partita   RC 31
    5   Prelude in E from V Partita No 6 in E   BA 43, 49;   HN 60;   NR 52;
           PH 31, arr Cailliet 36;   PT 39;   RC 31;   SF 41;   WA 35
    5   Prelude in e   BA 45(2);   LA 45
    4   Prelude in E^b PT 41
    4   Prelude in e^b DE arr Cailliet 57;   NP 47
    4   Prelude in G   WA 40
    4   Prelude in g   DT 33

BACH, J.S. (Cont.)

PRELUDES (Cont.)
Preludes from Well Tempered Clavichord
3   -Book I No 8 DT 38
3   -Book I No 6 in c HN 57 with Fugue
3   -Prelude in B♭ BA 43, 45
3   -Prelude in c♯ CH 37
3   -Prelude in e♭ Book I arr Stokowski PH 26, 28, 30, 31, 33(2),
      35; NP 47
10   -Three Preludes MN 27
4   Prelude unidentified arr Sopkin AT 63
9   Two Preludes from Fugue in d and V Sonata No 6 arr Pick-Mangiagall
      for Str O BN 30, 32, 35, 42, 47; DA 32; DT 38; NA 46; NR 50

6   Saraband and Gavotte WA 34

5   Siciliano or Arioso from Sonata in c for V and Cembalo arr
      Stokowski PH 33

5   Sinfonia Concertante AT 66

20   Sinfonia Concertante in C NR 64

5   Sinfonia in B♭ HN 47; LA 50; UT 48, 52

9   Three Sonata Mvts BN 1884, 86, 94, 98

12   Sonata in E♭ from Pedal Clair arr Ormandy PH 56
      -First Mvt arr Stokowski PH 39

10   Sonata in E♭ for Organ arr Wetzler CT 07; NP 06

SONATAS for V
6   No 1 in g: Adagio and Fugue PT 50
6   No 2 in a: Andante and Allegro arr Stock CH 03(2)
      -Allegro assa DT 32: Andante Sostenuto arr Stokowski 41;
      SE arr Stokowski 44, 46
20   No 3 in C arr Thomas CH 1896; NP 1896
4   -Andante arr Weiner KC 37, 39; SE 44, 46
      No 5 in d Fugue in C NP 1899
5   -arr Thomas for V and P CH 1892, 94, 95, 05, 07; NP 1896
6   -Chaconne CT 24, 31, 32, 44
8   -Largo and Vivace CH 02
5   No 6 in E: Prelude NR 59

BACH, J.S. (Cont.)

SUITES

34	Suite No 1 in C for Woodwinds, Str and Continuo BA 69; BN 68; CH 50; CL 49; HN 54; LA 48; MN Overt 30; NP 35; NS arr Weingartner 16, 18, 19, arr Damrosch 26; SL 30; SF 67; WA 49, 62
25	Suite No 2 in b for Flutes, Str and Continuo At 46, 62; BA 42, 43, 53; BN 1893, 06, 11, 14, 18, 31, 52, 56, 61; CH 1893, 96, 98, 00, 02, 03, 05, 06, 08, 10, 11, 12, 13, 15, 19, 20, 21, 24, 28, 32, 33, 38, 39, 40, 43, 50; CT 20, 23; CL 54; DE 49; DT Overt 47, 53, 59, 65; HN 50, 55, 68; NA 41, 48, 49; KC 36; MN 35, 50, 56, 58; NP 1885, 96, 21, 25, 28, 35, 39; NS 06, 12; PH 01, 03, 10, 12, 15, 17, 22, 23, 24, 27, 28, 33, 37, 44, 53, 60; PT 49; RC 54; SL 44, 47, 48, 49, 50, 55, 57, 59, 62; SF 35, 52; SE 27, 54, 67; WA 32, 35, 38, 45, 47, 61
10	-Chaconne for Solo Voices NP 49, 50
15	-Excerpts SL 30
5	-Overt MN 24
20	Suite No 3 in D for Oboes, Bassoons, Trumpets, Timpani, Str and Continuo BA 42, 50, 68; BN 1887, 88, 92, 95, 05, 07, 12, 18, 22, 25, 45, 46, 51, 54, 59, 60, 66, 50; BU 43, 51, 59; CH 1891, 94, 97, 01(2), 03, 05, 07, 08, 09, 12, 13, 14, 15, 17, 20, 22, 24, 25, 33, 34, 40, 43, 46, 64; CT 1898, 06(2), 09, 19, 25, 48, 60, 67; CL 46, 49, 54, 66; DA 55, 58, 61; DE 54, 68; DT 16, 28, 30, 52, 58, 68; HN 31, 35, 44, 46; NA 31, 32, 34; LA 35, 51, 63; MN 26, 43, 59, 61; NR 55, 60, 64; NS 27; PH 06, 09, 11, 23, 34, 38, 39, 41, 49, 58, 61, 64, 66; PT 52, 54; RC 39, 49; SL 09, 52, 56; SF 36, 42, 46, 55, 63; SE 33, 34, 44, 49, 65 arr Woodhouse; UT 47, 64; WA 50, 52, 58
4	-Air AT 56; BA 42; BU 53; CH 1895(2), 03, 04, 06, 42, 46, 48, 53; CT 13, 63; CL 68; DE 57; HN 40; NA 33, 49, 59; KC 56; LA 37; ML 62; MN 22, 37, 48, NP 33, 51, 56; NS 1893; PH 35, 36, 39, 40, 55; RC 23, 26, 32; SL 28, 51; SF 37; SE 40; UT 57, 63
4	-Gavotte I CT 13, I and II 33; NR for guitar 67
4	-Gigue CT 33
4	-Overt CT 13, 33; NA 49; KC 52; MN 41, 43; NS 1893 Excerpts; SL 32, 34
15	-Overt, Air, and Gavotte NP 1868, 87, 98, 03, 14, 15, 16, 18, 20, 26, 29, 38, 51, 53, 55, 56, 63, 66(2); NS 1890, 93
20	Suite No 4 in D for Oboe, Bassoons, Trumpets, Timpani, Str and Continuo BN 21, 54, 58, 60, 68; CH 14, 16, 18, 21, 24, 26, 27, 33, 35, 36, 40, 50; CT 65; CL 60, 69; ML 64; MN 50; NP 57, 61; PH 54, 67, 69; RC 40, 60; SL 58; SF 54, 61; WA 51
	-Bouree I and II, Gavotte and Rejouissance Ch 01
16	Suite from Ballet, The Wise Virgins arr Walton, from 12 Cantatas BA 47, 48; DE 55; NA 46; NR 60; PH 49, 51, 54, 61; RC 45; SE 53, 61; WA 52, 53, 65
4	-Praise be to God CT 53
4	-See What His Love Can Do CT 53
4	-Sheep may safely graze CT 53
4	-What God Hath Done CT 53
20	Orchestral Suite from Cantatas MN 54
20	Suite in E arr Bachrich NS 1886
10	-Adagio and Gavotte only NS 1891, 93

Time in   BACH, J.S. (Cont.)
Minutes   SUITES (Cont.)
  17   Suite No 6 for C and Str O arr Wood for full O BA 51;   CT 36, 44;
               CL 44;   KC 35 Finale;   LA 28;   SF 25, 44 Selections;   SE 29
  25   French Suite No 5 in G CT arr Goossens 32, 38, 45;   MN 32;   SL 28
  12   Suite arr Honegger from French Suites NP 53;   PH 54, 58, 60
   4   English Suite No 2: Bouree PH 35
   4   -Gavotte CH 33
   4   English Suite No 3 Sarabande PH 35, 36;   SE 27
              -Gavotte, as Harpsichord solo CH 23
  20   Suite arr Mahler from French Suite II and III CL 34, 40;   DT 23;
               LA 29;   NP 09, 10;   RC 32;   SF 21

           Toccata and Fugue in a arr Leonardi PT 37
  16   , Toccata, Adagio and Fugue No 1 in C Peters Vol III No 6 BA 44(3),
               45, 46, 48, 50, 53;   DE arr Weiner 55, 61;   LA arr Weiner 51, 53;
               NP 35;   PH arr Weiner 27, 34, 35, 37, 43, arr Ormandy 47, 49, 50,
               60;   RC arr Weiner 31, 32, arr Bloomfield 61;   SE arr Weiner 66
   4   -Adagio only HN 58;   KC arr Stokowski 48;   NA arr Stokowski 55;
               NP 24;   MN 41;   PH arr Stokowski 33, 35, 39;   SL arr Siloti 25;   WA 36
   8   -Adagio and Fugue only NA arr Guerrini 47;   PH arr Ormandy 50;   PT 61
   8   -Adagio and Toccata only BN arr Siloti 24
              -Fugue only KC arr Weiner 37
   4   -Toccata only arr Weiner BN 36, 44;   CT 27(2), 28, 30(2), 32, 42,
               46, 50;   DE for organ 48, 51;   MN 40, 43, 46;   NR for organ 60;
               SL 41;   WA 49
   8   -Toccata and Fugue arr Weiner CH 37, 53;   CL 35;   DA 32, 48;
               DT 38;   HN 38;   LA 36, 60;   MN 49, 52, 55;   NP 33, 36, 52;   PT 37,
               41, 44, 47, 53, 56;   SF 51, 52
              -arr Bloomfield NP 46;   SF 45, 49
   8   Toccata and Fugue in c DT 39;   WA 49
   9   Toccata and Fugue in d, also called Dorian or Dorian Cantata AT 55,
               58;   BA 56;   BN arr Tansman 38;   BU arr Autori 41, 52;   CH Tansman
               47(2), Wertheim 61;   CT arr Wood 35, 40, 45;   CL 32, 35, 36, 37,
               42, 44, toccato only 51, 61;   DA 49, 66, 67;   DT 35, 36, 52, 59;
               HN 45, 54, 55, 60;   NA 50, 51, 53;   KC 50;   LA 29(2), 31, 32, 52;
               ML 64;   MN arr Ormandy 33, 34, 52, 66, 68;   NR 51, 55, 62;   NP 30,
               arr Wood 35, 41, 46;   PH 25(2), 26(3), 28, 29, 30, 31, 32, arr
               Stokowski 33, 34, arr Ormandy 36, 37, 38, 40, 41, 47, 49, 51, 52,
               53, 54, 57, 58, 59, 61, 67;   PT arr Leonardi 37, 46, 48, 50, 62;
               RC arr Wood 37, 38, arr Stokowski 58;   SL arr Leonardi 35, arr
               Tansman 36, 38, 40(2), 41, 43, 48, 50, 51, 54, 57;   SF arr Leonardi
               40, arr Tansman 45, arr Leonardi 53;   SE arr Stokowski 52, 59;   UT 68
   5   -Toccata only DE arr Tansman 65
   8   Toccata and Fugue in F arr Esser NP 1883, 95, 00, 08;   SE 30
              -Toccata only BN 1881, 84, 90;   CH 23;   KC 34;   NP 18, 47;   NS 1879,
               86;   SE 30
   9   Toccata and Fugue in g DT 39;   WA 49
   8   Toccata and Fugue arr Villa Lobos WA 49

BACH, Wilhelm F.   15   Conc for P or Harpsichord and Str in f DA 34
  1710-1784   Ger   18   Symph for 2 Fl and Str No 31 PH 56;   PT 57;   SF 57, 61

BACHELET, Alfred G.   4   Song, Chére Nuit CT 46;   HN 56;   MN 29, 40;   SL 46
  1864-1943   Fr

BACON, Ernest	15	From These States 1943 DA 46
1898- US	20	Great River, The Rio Grande DA 56
	20	Suite, Ford's Theatre 1943 DT 48
	35	Symph No 1 in d 1932 SF 23

BADINGS, Henk   9   Ballade, Symph Var on They Were Two Royal Children
1907-   Neth   PH 59
                20   Conc 2 V   PH 61
                16   Symph Var on a South African Theme   SF 59

BAIRD, Tadeusz   12   Four Essays for O   NP 63, 65;   PT 64
1928-   Pol

BAIRSTOW, Sir Edward   12   I sat down under His shadow, for Chor and O   CH 31
1874-1946   Brit

BAKALEINIKOFF,   16   Symphon Miniature   PT 51
   Vladimir   12   Three Oriental Dances   PT 42
1885-1953   Russ

BAKER, Robert   6   Var on each other   SL 65
1933-   US

BALADA, Leonardo   11   Guernica   NR 67
1923-   Sp   18   Sinfonia en Negro, NR 69

BALAKIROV, Mily   13   In Bohemia Symphon Poem 1906   RC 36;   SL 17
1837-1910   Russ   12   Islamey, Oriental Fantasy 1869 arr Casella   BN 20;
                         CH 09, 30;   CT 27;   CL 24, 33;   DT 26, 28, 30;
                         LA 30;   NP 43, 51;   NS 14;   PH 25, 28, 30, 42, 60;
                         PT 55;   RC 28, 38;   SL 28;   SF 27;   WA 39
                8   Overt on Three Russian Themes 1858   CH 11;   CT 43;
                         LA 43;   PT 46
                11   Overt on Theme of a Spanish March 1857   BN 11;
                         CH 12, 39
                40   Symph in C No 1   BN 07;   CH 06;   PH 07, 08, 09, 11;
                         RC 45
                20   Symphon Poem Thamar, or Tamara 1867   BN 16, 17, 19;
                         CH 1896, 04;   CT 31;   DT 27;   MN 34;   NP 31, 36,
                         37;   PH 27;   SF 42

BALENDONCK   8   Metropolis, Impressions of Life in a Modern City
1893-   Belg/US   DE 49

BALES, Richard H.   8   Music for Str   SE 42;   WA 42
1915-   US

BALLANTINE, Edward   6   Prel to The Delectable Forest   CH 16;   SL 17
1886-   US   12   From the Garden of Hellas, Suite for O   BN 22;
                         CT 25
                20   Symphon Poem, The Eve of St. Agnes   BN 16;   CH 17;
                         SL 18

BALOGH, Erno   14   Divertimento   BA 48
1897-   Hung/US

BANTOCK,
  Sir Granville
	20	Curse of Kehama, Procession and Jaga-Naut 1894
		  SL 13

1868-1946 Brit	12	The Frogs, Comedy Overt 1935 BA 38
	18	Dante and Beatrice, Tone Poem No 2 1910 BN 11
	30	Fifine at the Fair, Drama for O 1901 CH 15
	10	Omar Khayyam Pt I for Soli, Chor and O 1906 BN 10
	14	Overt to a Greek Tragedy 1911 CH 13

	11	Pierrot of the Minute, Comedy Overt 1908 BN 09;
		  Ch 10, 19, 23; CT 32; DT 26; MN 27; NS 14,
		  17, 21; SL 11, 18; SF 14

	8	Sapphic Ode, Poem for C 1906 NS 13

BARATI, George
1913-   US

    13   The Dragon and the Phoenix SE 63

BARBER, Samuel
1910-   US

8	Adagio for Str O OP 11 AT 52, 56, 60, 62, 66; BA 47, 58, 62; BN 52, 58; BU 40, 43; CT 48, 53; DA 60; DE 49, 51, 52, 56, 61, 62, 63(2), 67; DT 44, 46, 55, 61; HN 47, 49, 60; NA 55, 64, 69; KC 43, 57, 61, 64; LA 59; ML 64; MN 40, 44; NR 58, 64, 68; NP 39, 54(2), 60; PH 43, 48; PT 40, 51, 54; SF 65; SL 39, 49, 53, 55, 56, 61; SE 44; UT 42, 47, 59, 66; WA 49
12	Andromache's Farewell for Sopr and O Op 59 CL 64; DA 62; NA 64
5	Anthony and Cleopatra: Cleopatra's Death SE 69
8	Commando March 1943 BN 43; WA 44
14	Capricorn, Conc for Fl, Ob, Trump and Str Op 21 BU 64; DE 57; NR 52; NP 46
20	C Conc Op 22 BN 45; BU 49; CH 48, 52; NP 47, 58; SL 47, 65
26	P Conc Op 38 AT 63; BN 62; CH 65; CT 64; CL 63, 64; DA 63; DE 65; DT 67; NA 63; LA 64; ML 67; MN 62; NP 63; PH 65; PT 63, 67; SF 63; SL 66; SE 65; UT 66; WA 62
22	V Conc Op 14 AT 67; BN 41, 48, 61; CL 41, 53, 61; DA 49, 55; DT 64; NA 68; MN 47, 49, 60; NP 60, 63; PH 40, 57; SF 42; WA 41
16	Die Natalie, Choral Preludes for Christmas Op 37 BN 60, 62, 69; CH 64, 68; CT 62; DE 61; PH 62; PT 62
8	Essay for O No 1 Op 12 AT 54, 61; BN 40; CT 53, 61; CL 46; DA 46; DE 53; DT 54; NA 41, 46, 48; KC 48, 60; LA 43; ML 63; NP 50; PH 40; RC 61, 65; SF 53; SL 44, 46; SE 42, 54, 66; WA 49, 51, 59, 66
10	Essay for O No 2 Op 17 BA 65; BU 60; CT 51, 69; NA 65; KC 64; LA 68; MN 46; NR 66; NP 41, 44, 59, 67; PH 42, 45, 52; PT 65; RC 46, 51, 65; SF 66
16	Knoxville Summer of 1915 for Sopr and O Op 24 BA 50, 60; BN 47; CT 50; CL 60; DT 54; HN 68; MN 48; NP 59; RC 53; SL 50
22	Media, The Cave of the Heart, Ballet Op 23 PH 47; WA 59

BARBER, S (Cont.)

13   Medea's Meditation and Dance of Vengeance Op 23a
AT 69; BA 57; BN 56, 59, 65; CH 56; CT 49;
CL 57, 62; DA 55, 60, 68; DE 60; DT 57, 62;
HN 65; NA 56; LA 56, 64; ML 69; MN 55, 56,
61, 65; NR 60, 65, 68; NP 55, 57, 61, 64;
PH 58, 65; PT 57, 67; RC 60; SF 61; SL 56,
61; SE 57; UT 69; WA 56, 60, 66

8   Music for a Scene from Shelley Op 7 BA 37;
BN 65; CH 45; CT 41; CL 43, 56; DT 57, 66;
NR 63; PH 36; SF 40; WA 53, 57

8   Night Flight Op 19b CL 64

8   Overt to Sheridan's School for Scandal Op 5
AT 68; BA 61, 66; BN 40, 42, 49, 51; BU 50,
67; CH 39(2), 44, 50; CT 47, 52, 58; CL 40,
47, 50, 59; DA 57, 64, 68; De 51, 55; DT 43,
51, 57, 62; HN 53, 55; KC 53, 66; LA 49, 53,
54, 60; ML 61, 65; MN 41, 66; NR 50, 59;
NP 37, 51, 55, 64; PH 56, 64; PT 46; SL 44,
52, 61; SE 49; UT 46, 56; WA 33, 53, 57, 59, 68

18   Prayers of Kierkegaard for Mix Chor and Sopr Op 30
BN 54; CH 54; CT 68; CL 60; MN 65; NR 65;
WA 55

19   Souvenirs, Ballet Suite in six mvts Op 28 CH 53;
CT 54; DA 53; DE 53; HN 53; SL 53; UT 54

19   Symph No 1 in one mvt in E Op 9 BN 63; BU 41;
CH 37, 64; CT 63; CL 36, 48; DA 57, 61, 66;
DE 64; DT 40, 54; HN 49, 54, 63; NA 55;
LA 52, 69; MN 63; NR 64; NP 36, 43; PH 38,
43, 55, 63; PT 61, 65; RC 63; SL 69; SF 62,
68; SE 46, 52, 68; WA 45, 50, 61, 63

27   Symph No 2 Op 19 BN 50; PH 48; SF 56

14   Toccata Festiva for Org and O Op 36 DA 62, 66;
DT 63; PH 60, 62

6   Vanessa, an Opera: Intermezzo CL 58; DE 58;
HN 57; NA 67; ML 64; NR 57, 63; NP 62; UT 58

BARBIROLLI,
Sir John
1899-1970   Brit

11   Conc on a theme of Corelli KC 47

20   Conc for Str and Oboe on Pergolesi Themes NP 36

10   Elizabethan Suite arr fr Fitzwilliam Virginal Book
AT 59; BN 58; CH 59; CT 41, 48; HN 65;
KC 59; LA 41, 58; MN 59; NR 59; NP 41, 58;
SF 58; WA 58

BARGIEL, Woldemar
1828-1897   Ger

5   Adagio for C Op 38 BN 1881, 82, 96; NP 1872,
74, 11

9   Overt for O, Medea BN 1884, 86, 03; CH 00;
NP 1864, 70, 82, 89

8   Overt for O, Prometheus Op 16 BN 1883, 87;
NP 1865, 71, 78, 87

BARKLEY, Robert O.
1898-   US

7   Sunday Evening in Bloomfield, fr Iowa Suite WA 41

BARLOW, Sammuel 1892- US	13 6 21	Alba, Symphon Poem 1927 CT 29 Overt, Mon Ami Pierrot, Opera 1934 WA 37 P Conc RC 30
BARLOW, Wayne 1912- US	4 8	Rhaps, The Winter's Passed 1938 BU 40; CT 29; CL 53 Vistas NA 62
BARRAINE, Elsa 1910- Fr	16	Symph No 2 SL 49

BARRAUD, Henry
1900-   Fr
	54
	
	12
	
	25
	14
	13
	15
	
	27
	
	25
	20
		Le mystère des Saints Innocents, Oratorio for
		   Soli, Cho and O, 1947 BN 50
		Offrande à une Ombre 1941 CL 54; DT 56; SL 46;
		   SE 41, 59
		P Conc 1939 NP 46
		Rhaps Cartessiene CL 61
		Rhaps Dionysienne MN 63
		Symphon Suite, La Kermesse, The Fair, Ballet
		   CT Overt only 59; DT 57; SL 55
		La Symphonie de Numance, Overt and Interludes
		   from Opera CL 57; SL 49, 57; WA 55
		Symph No 3 BN 57; MN 60; SL 63
		Te Deum for Chor and O BN 56

BARRERA y CALLEJA, Gomez 1874-1938 Sp	4	Song Granadinas SL 46
BARROZO, Netto Ary 1881-1941 Brazil	6	Aquarelle Brasileira RC 40
BARRYMORE, Lionel 1878- US	12 6 13 20 13 5 4	Fugue Fantasia NA 45, 49 Intro and Scherzo NA 48 Partita NA 43 Piranesi Suite NA 46 Prelude and Fugue NA 44(2) Symphon Poem In Memoriam CL 44 Valse Fantasia PT 44
BARSANTI, Francesco 1690-c.1776 It	15	Conc Grosso Op 10 SL 58
BARTH, Hans 1896-1956 US	8-10	Conc for 1/4 tone P and Str 1929 CT 30; PH 29

BARTOK, Bela
1881-1945   Hung
	55
	
	17
	
	38
		Bluebeard's Castle Op 11 CH 51, 66;
		   CL 60; DA 48; LA 68; MN 52; NP 66; PH 60;
		   PT 65, 69; RC 66; SL 68
		Cantata Profana for Tenor, Baritone, Chor and O
		   1930 CT 65; CL 57
		Conc for O 1943 AT 66, 69; BN 44(2), 49, 51, 54,
		   58, 60, 62, 65, 67; CH 48, 51, 55, 56, 63, 68;
		   CT 50, 53, 56, 62, 64; CL 45, 49, 52, 61, 64,
		   65; DA 58, 61; DE 67; DT 53, 55, 61, 64, 66;

BARTOK, Bela (Cont.) Conc for O 1943 (Cont.)
HN 57, 59, 69; NA 58, 69; KC 68; LA 46, 48,
50, 52, 55, 59, 60, 62, 65; ML 66, 68;
MN 49, 53, 54, 56, 62, 64; NR 64, 68; NP 45,
52, 59(2), 60, 68; PH 47, 52, 56, 61, 65, 66,
67; PT 45, 50, 59, 61; RC 59, 61, 67; SL 48,
52, 54, 60, 62, 64, 67, 69; SF 46, 49, 55, 59,
63, 67, 69; UT 52, 62, 68, 69; WA 58, 67

6   -Elegy PT 63; WA 68
23   P Conc No 1 1904 BN 27; CH 59, 65, 68; CT 27;
CL 61, 69; LA 66, 68; MN 66; NP 59, 68;
PH 65; SF 68
25   P Conc No 2 1930 BN 62; CH 38, 41, 56, 64; CT 67;
CL 40, 55; DA 62, 66; DE 50, 69; DT 67; NA 66;
LA 62, 67; NR 68; NP 50, 63, 68; PH 59, 67, 69;
PT 40, 69; RC 63; SL 62; SF 45, 56, 63, 66;
SE 64; UT 59; WA 61, 65
23   P Conc No 3 1945 AT 58, 68, 69; BA 57; BN 64;
CH 57, 60, 68; CT 55, 65, 68; CL 56, 59, 63,
66; DA 46, 67; DE 66; DT 63, 67; HN 62, 69;
NA 49; LA 48, 56, 59, 61; MN 68; NR 59, 64,
67; NP 57, 66; PH 45; PT 55, 66; RC 65;
SL 53, 55, 60, 65, 67; SF 55, 62, 65; SE 69;
UT 55; WA 60, 63
24   Conc for 2 P and Percussion 1937 BN 66; HN 65;
LA 65; NP 42, 65; SL 59
20   Conc for Vla and O Op Post BN 51, 60; BU 67;
CH 58; DA 59; LA 51; MN 49; PH 67; SL 49;
SF 64; SE 57
21   V Conc No 1 Op Posth BA 63; CH 64; DA 54, 68;
DT 68; NA 67; LA 48, 52, 56; RC 68; SL 69;
SF 47, 50, 57, 65; WA 61, 68
32   V Conc No 2 1928 AT 64; BA 46, 63; BN 45, 53, 63;
CH 44, 57, 60, 69; CT 49, 57, 63; CL 42, 50,
62, 66, 69; DT 55; LA 63, 66; MN 43, 57, 69;
NP 43, 54, 57, 64, 66; PH 45, 59, 60, 67;
PT 44, 53, 57, 62; SL 48, 66; SE 65; UT 57;
WA 44, 59
16   Dance Suite 1923 AT 67; BN 26, 53; CH 25, 65;
CT 24, 25, 61, 65, 68; CL 66, 67; DA 59, 65;
HN 54, 60; NA 62; LA 55, 62; MN 47, 67;
NR 65; NP 47, 54, 64; PH 51, 66, 69; PT 51,
57; RC 50, 58, 69; SL 55, 57, 60; SF 51, 53;
SE 49, 68; UT 63; WA 66;
8   Daemonic ballet piece AT 65
20   Deux Images for V and O Op 10 BN 52; CH 62;
CT 27; CL 67; DA 49; PH 39, 61, 62, 65
-Andante NP 54
22   Divertimento for Str O 1939 CH 56, 68; CT 60;
CL 50, 51, 64; DA 64; DE 69; DT 60; HN 53;
LA 58, 69; MN 49; NR 67; NP 51; PH 40, 64,
67; PT 41, 56; SL 40, 43(2), 54; SF 53, 66
25   Four Orchestral Pieces Op 12 PH 69
11   Five Hungarian Folk Songs for Mezzo Sopr Op 15
BN 61; PH 65

BARTOK, Bela (Cont.)

	11	Hungarian Sketches 1931 CH 54, 58; MN 55, 56; PH 35; PT 46; RC 57
	20	Miraculous Mandarin Suite Op 19 AT 68; BN 60; CH 43, 53, 59, 64; CT two scenes only 26, 65; CL 65; DA 50, 61; DT 65; NA 48; LA 56, 60, 69(2); MN 53, 56, 65; NR 53, 63; NP 59, 61, 66; PH 48, 58, 62, 67, 68; PT 46, 52; RC 65; SL 62; SE 60, 67
	16-17	Mikrokosmos Suite 1926 arr Serley NP 55; SL 43
	25	Music for Str, Percussion and Celesta 1936 AT 68; BN 50, 53, 55, 57; CT 59, 67; CL 53, 61; DA 62; DE 68; DT 56, 68; LA 57, 63; MN 50, 63(2); NR 66; NP 37, 49, 53, 60, 67, 68; PH 48, 61, 63; PT 63, 67; RC 62; SL 51, 65; SF 49, 64, 66
	17	Rhaps for P and O Op 1 DT 66; NP 27; PH 27; SL 40, 64; SF 48
	11	Rhaps for V and O No 1 1928 CH 61; CT 33, 60; LA 65; MN 53; NP 57, 61; SF 59, 67
	12	Rhaps for V and O No 2 1928 NP 55; SL 53; SF 54
	29	Scherzo for P and O Op 2 NP 64(2)
	18	Suite for O No 1 Op 3 CH 24, 58; CT 22, 26
	25	Suite for O No 2 Op 4 CT 64; MN 55; PT 65
	15	Suite for O Op 14 arr for small O Dorati MN 68
	12	Seven Roumanian Folk Dances for Str O Op 8 DE 46; HN 63; KC 45; LA 44; MN 55, 56, 57; SF 57; SE 44; WA 3 dances 35, 47, 48
	9	Two Roumanian Dances arr Weiner CH 53, 58; NA 61; PT 40, 46, 47
	10	Three Village Scenes for Women's Chor CT 62
	11	Two Portraits Op 5 WA 46, 54, 63
	5	-No 1 only CH 53; CL 55; KC 63; PT 46; WA 69
	30	The Wooden Prince, Suite from Ballet Op 13 PH 68

BASART, Robert
1926-   US
| | 8 | Kansas City Dump SF 67 |

BASSANI, Giovanni
1657-1716   It
	6	Cantata, L'amorosa Lontananza for voice arr Malipiero PH 27
	5	Song, Dormi Bella NS 04
	4	Song, Per Lontananza di Donna Crudele LA 30; SF 30

BASSETT, Leslie
1923-   US
| | 23 | Var for O DT 66; PH 65 |

BATE, Stanley
1913-   Eng
| | 28 | Symph No 3 Op 29 RC 57 |

BAUER, Marion
1887-1955   US
| | 4 | Orientale, Song for O 1932 WA 32 |

BAUMANN, H.
1825-
| | 10 | Horn Duo fr Araby's Daughter NP 1853 |

BAUMGARTNER, H.   6   Adagio from a Symph   BN 1885
           Ger

BAX, Sir Arnold   17   Garden of Fand, Tone Poem 1916   BN 24, 34;   CH 20(2),
1883-1953   Eng   30;   CT 22;   RC 39
                      15   In the Fairy Hills 1909   BN 20;   CH 30, 32
                      15   November Woods, Symphon Poem 1917   BN 22;   CH 22,
                                32, 36, 39;   CT 32;   RC 28
                      10   Overt to a Picaresque Comedy 1930   BA 51;   BN 40;
                                CT 35;   DT 55;   NP 33, 35, 51;   RC 34
                      16   Phantasy, Vla and O 1920   CT 27;   KC 37
                       9   Summer Music 1920   NP 33
                      30   Symph No 1 E^b mi and mj 1930   BN 27;   CH 23, 27;
                                CL 24, 25
                      35   Symph No 2 in e and c 1924   BN 29, 32
                      30   Symph No 3 in C 1928   MN 45;   NP 35, 37
                      35   Symph No 4, E^b 1930   NP 38
                      43   Symph No 5 in C# 1931   CT 33
                      18   The Tale the Pine Trees Knew, Symphon Poem 1931
                                NP 36
                      12   Tintagel, Tone Poem 1917   BN 45;   BU 40;   HN 62;
                                NS 25;   RC 29;   SF 31;   SE 33, 36
                      30   Winter Legends, Symph Concertante for P and O 1930
                                BN 32(2)

BAZELON, Irwin   18   Dramatic Mvt for O   SE 65
1922-   US   25   Excursion for O   KC 65
                      12   Symph No 5   NA 68
                      14   Testimonial to a Big City, A short Symph   WA 62

BEACH, Mrs. H.H.   35   P Conc in c# Op 45   BN 1899, 16;   CH 15;   SL 16
1867-1944   US   40   Symph in e Gaelic Op 32   BN 1896, 97;   CH 1897;
                                DT 18;   PH 14, 18
                       4   Songs
                                My Sweetheart and I   CT 03
                       5   June   NP 19
                       6   from Mary Stuart   NS 1892

BEACH, John   20   The Asolani, after Bembo, Three pieces for Str Quart,
1877-   US   Wind Quart and Harp   MN 26
                      12   New Orleans Street Cries at Dawn   PH 26

BEALE, John   22   Symph No 2 Cressay   Op 26   SE 61
1924-   US

BEALL   10   Essay for O   DA 65
1942   US

BEETHOVEN,   13   Ah Perfido, Scene and Aria for sopr and O Op 65
  Ludwig van   AT 55;   BA 51;   BN 68;   CH 97, 01, 06, 07, 20,
1770-1827   Ger   49;   CT 09, 25, 33, 47, 61, 68;   CL 25;   DE 68;
                                DT 23, 29, 61;   KC 66;   LA 50, 60, 65;   MN 22,
                                26, 38, 42, 46;   NP 1869, 73, 74, 75, 78, 85,
                                95, 06, 09, 37, 48, 50, 64;   NS 1888, 07, 08,
                                25, 27;   PH 49, 65;   PT 37, 56;   SL 69;   UT 45;
                                WA 40, 56, 62

BEETHOVEN, L.v. (Cont.)
4   Aria, Undesignated HN 50, 51, 52; NS 1895, 23
        Calm Sea and Prosperous Voyage, for P, Chor and O Op 112 NP 65
5   Canon for Three Voices, Down the Scale in E-flat NS 23
5   Canon for Six Voices, Helpful be, O man arr Damrosch NS 23
15   Cantata on the Death of Emperor Joseph II Op 196 NP 64
19   Choral Phantasy for P, Chor and O Op 80   CT 58, 65; MN 66;   RC 40;
        WA 36, 49, 64
38   P Conc No 1 in C Op 15 AT 68; BA 52, 60; BN 48, 66; BU 61;
        CH 14, 34, 38, 42, 43, 50, 59, 62, 67(2), 69; CT 36, 37, 46, 53,
        62, 65; CL 48, 53, 60, 63, 67; DA 46, 55, 59; DT 24, 33, 69;
        HN 45, 50; NA 46, 38; KC 41, 46(2); LA 53, 54, 55; ML 64;
        MN 39, 45, 61; NR 58, 66; NP 26, 38, 39, 41, 45, 56, 60, 62;
        NS 18, 20, 21; PH 18, 33, 38, 39, 48, 53, 57, 68; PT 45, 49,
        53, 61, 66; RC 36, 46, 58, 62, 67; SL 22, 26, 38, 39, 46, 47,
        59, 60, 66, 69; SF 38, 44, 50, 55, 64, 66; UT 58; WA 38, 41,
        50, 51, 55, 59, 64
28   P Conc No 2 in B^b Op 19 AT 62, 68; BA 65; CH 25, 53; CT 49, 58,
        65; CL 53, 56, 62, 69; DA 63; DE 48, 53, 61, 67; DT 56, 60,
        67; HN 51; NA 64; KC 52; LA 66; ML 63; MN 56, 60, 68; NR 57,
        66; NP 49, 53, 56, 61; PH 53; PT 58, 64, 65; RC 57, 67; SL 48,
        53, 60, 61, 66; SF 50, 53, 60, 61, 66; SE 63; UT 51; WA 51,
        57, 64, 66
39   P Conc No 3 in c Op 37   AT 50, 63, 67, 68;
        BA 45, 49, 51, 54, 60, 64, 67;
        BN 1887, 10, 19, 20, 33, 38, 54, 56, 58;
        BU 53, 55, 67;
        CH 10, 18, 26, 37, 47, 48, 49, 51, 52, 53, 56, 58, 65, 66;
        CT 12, 18, 20, 26, 29, 32, 37, 38, 46, 48, 54, 55, 57, 60, 63,
        65, 68;
        CL 22, 31, 38, 47, 49, 57, 59, 60, 62, 66;
        DA 50, 55, 64, 67;
        DE 60, 62, 65, 66;
        DT 21, 25, 33, 44, 47, 53, 55, 62, 64, 67;
        HN 42, 47, 50, 51, 54, 63, 65, 67, 69;
        NA 47, 52, 65, 68;
        KC 36, 40, 48, 51, 63, 65;
        LA 25, 28, 30, 46, 51, 54, 56, 58, 65, 67, 69;
        ML 69;
        MN 23, 33, 35, 42, 50, 61, 62, 67;
        NR 56, 59, 63;
        NP 1861, 64, 70, 77, 26, 36, 38, 42, 44(2), 45, 46, 50, 51, 52, 54,
        56, 57, 58, 62, 63, 66;
        PH 14, 20, 35, 36, 48, 49, 56, 57, 61, 65, 67, 68;
        PT 46, 52, 56, 59, 65, 66, 67, 68;
        RC 50, 55, 60, 66, 67;
        SL 15, 18, 23, 29, 31, 33, 39, 40, 47, 51, 54, 56, 59, 60, 62, 65,
        66, 69;
        SF 20, 35, 43, 44, 47, 49, 50, 51, 54, 56, 58, 60, 62, 65, 66, 69(2)
        SE 46, 58, 64
        UT 47, 58;
        WA 36, 38, 43, 45, 48, 50, 51, 55, 61, 64;

BEETHOVEN, L.v. (Cont.)
34   P Conc No 4 in G Op 58   AT 50, 54, 56, 59, 67, 68;
            BA 26, 42, 47, 50, 52, 59, 61, 65, 67;
            BN 1881, 82, 84, 85, 86, 91, 93, 99, 06, 10, 12, 14, 16, 20, 22,
            23, 29, 34, 39, 42, 46, 51, 55, 61, 65, 68;
            BU 40, 46, 53, 56, 59, 65;
            CH 1892, 97, 00, 06, 13, 14, 16, 22, 26, 29, 33, 34, 36, 38, 39,
            42, 46, 47, 48, 49, 50, 51, 57, 58, 60, 61, 62, 65, 68;
            CT 05, 11, 12, 23, 27, 30, 31, 33, 36, 38, 40, 43, 44, 47, 49, 51,
            55, 57, 59, 62, 63, 65, 67;
            CL 23, 27, 28, 34, 39, 43, 46, 49, 51, 54, 55, 56, 57, 58, 59, 60,
            62, 63, 66, 69;
            DA 46, 57, 61, 65;
            DE 47, 53, 58, 61, 64, 66, 68;
            DT 17, 20, 25, 28, 30, 34, 36, 37, 40, 43, 52, 53, 55, 59, 61,
            64, 68, 69;
            HN 32, 40, 49, 52, 56, 59, 62, 65, 66, 68, 69;
            NA 50, 51, 57, 59, 61, 65, 69;
            KC 35, 42, 44, 50, 54, 62, 67;
            LA 23, 33, 37, 38, 44, 46, 48, 52, 54, 55, 56, 60, 63, 68, 69;
            ML 63, 66;
            MN 23, 26, 29, 37, 42, 44, 46, 49, 53, 55, 56, 58, 61, 62, 69;
            NR 50, 52, 54, 55, 57, 61(2), 63, 66, 68;
            NP 1862, 66, 68, 79, 81, 85, 92, 04, 17, 20, 22, 24, 26, 33, 35,
            37, 38, 41, 45, 50, 51, 52, 53, 54, 55, 56, 57, 59, 60, 62, 63,
            64, 68, 69;
            NS 1889, 91, 16, 17;
            PH 04, 06, 07, 12, 14, 17, 22, 23, 29, 30, 39, 42, 46, 47, 49, 53,
            54, 56, 57, 59, 61, 63;
            PT 38, 42, 47, 49, 54, 57, 58, 60, 62, 65, 66, 68;
            RC 23, 30, 51, 54, 56, 67;
            SL 11, 12, 24, 30, 32, 37, 38, 40, 42, 46, 48, 49, 50, 51, 52, 54,
            55, 56, 60, 61, 62, 64, 66, 68;
            SF 26, 37, 46, 50, 53, 55, 57, 58, 62, 65, 66, 69;
            SE 45, 52, 61, 68;
            UT 49, 56, 60, 63, 64, 69;
            WA 36, 37, 43, 46, 49, 54, 58, 61, 63, 64, 65
9   -One mvt NP 1869; SL 66
9   -Andante BU 63
36   P Conc No 5 in E^b Emperor Op 73 AT 52, 56, 62, 64, 68;
            BA 48, 49, 50, 51, 55, 58, 61, 66;
            BN 1881, 84, 86, 87, 89, 91, 94, 98, 99, 05, 09, 11, 13, 14, 18,
            21, 26, 28, 30, 35, 37, 41, 43, 45, 47, 50, 52, 54, 57, 61, 67;
            BU 42(2), 48, 53, 57, 60, 64;
            CH 1899, 00, 02, 03, 04, 06, 07, 11, 12, 14, 16, 18, 19, 21, 23,
            26, 28, 29, 31, 32, 36, 37, 40, 43, 46, 48, 49, 54, 57, 60, 61,
            63, 64, 65, 66, 67;
            CT 1897, 01, 06, 10, 14, 18, 28, 31, 33, 35, 38, 39, 45, 50, 52,
            54, 56, 57, 59, 61, 63, 65, 68;
            CL 21, 23, 29, 34, 36, 38, 42, 45, 47, 49, 52, 55, 57, 58, 59, 61,
            63, 64, 66;
            DA 49, 52, 56, 58, 63, 65;
            DE 46, 49, 51, 54, 57, 59, 61;
            DT 16, 19, 29, 30, 39, 45, 51, 53, 56, 59, 61, 62, 65;
            HN 39, 43, 48, 52, 53, 57, 58, 67;

BEETHOVEN, L.v. (Cont.) P Conc No 5 in E^b (Cont.)
        NA 35, 38, 42, 44, 48, 51, 60, 65;   KC 53, 56, 61;
        LA 22, 24, 26, 32, 37, 45, 47, 49, 51, 52, 58, 64, 67;
        ML 60, 65, 67; MN 22, 23, 27, 32, 37, 40, 43, 47, 48, 49, 51, 54,
        58, 61, 63, 66; NR 51, 55, 58, 60;
        NP 1854, 66, 68, 69, 70, 71, 75, 83, 87, 90, 95, 00, 03, 05, 10,
        15, 20, 23, 34, 36, 39, 43, 44, 47, 48, 49, 50, 51, 53, 54, 55,
        56, 58, 61, 62, 64, 65, 66;
        NS 1878, 84, 89, 96, 11, 12, 14, 17, 21, 22;
        PH 05, 07, 13, 15, 18, 21, 23, 25, 33, 34, 36, 41, 43, 45, 46, 47,
        48, 49, 50, 51, 60, 61, 62, 63, 64, 67;
        PT 38, 45, 47, 49, 55, 57, 58, 61, 63, 64, 66;
        RC 25, 35, 37, 49, 54, 62;   SL 13, 16, 24, 28, 30, 33, 34, 36, 46,
        47, 48, 49, 50, 53, 55, 57, 58, 60, 61, 62, 63, 66;
        SF 13, 45, 47, 49, 50, 51, 55, 59, 64, 66;   SE 47, 54;
        UT 40, 45, 50, 57, 63, 66, 68;
        WA 33, 39, 41, 47, 49, 51, 53, 54, 56, 59, 61, 62, 63, 64, 65, 67;
        -2nd and 3rd mvts NP 1859

41   V Conc in D Op 61 AT 48, 51, 57, 63, 66;
        BA 42, 43, 44, 50, 57, 59, 63, 65;
        BN 1885, 87, 93, 95, 96, 98, 00, 02, 03, 05, 10, 12, 14, 15(2), 17,
        18, 19, 22, 23, 25, 30, 38, 41, 44, 51, 53, 55, 56, 60, 61, 64, 67;
        BU 41, 49, 53, 56, 58, 61, 62, 66, 69
        CH 1893, 97, 98, 00, 02, 03, 05, 09, 12, 14, 16, 17, 19, 20, 22, 23,
        26, 28, 30, 31, 33, 34, 36, 37, 38, 39, 40, 41, 42, 44, 47, 48, 49,
        50, 51, 52, 53, 55, 58, 60, 61, 64, 65, 66, 69;
        CT 1895, 97, 05, 09, 13, 14, 16, 22, 23, 26, 27, 29, 34, 41, 45, 47,
        52, 54, 60, 62, 64, 69;   CL 50, 51, 54, 57, 59, 60, 61, 64, 66, 68;
        DA 38, 48, 49, 50, 57, 60, 63; DE 50, 53, 54, 55, 57, 58, 61, 63,
        64, 68;   DT 17, 23, 30, 36, 39, 40, 43, 44, 45, 51, 54, 56, 59, 65, 66;
        HN 31, 43, 48, 49, 51, 53, 57, 60, 62, 69;
        NA 39, 45, 48, 50, 52, 55, 59, 62, 65;   KC 33, 40, 45, 52, 64;
        LA 19, 20, 22, 24, 26, 35, 37, 38, 39, 44, 49, 52, 53, 56, 60, 63,
        67, 69;   ML 61, 63, 66;   MN 22, 25, 31, 32, 33, 36, 37, 40, 45,
        47, 48, 49, 51, 52, 56, 57, 59, 61, 63, 65, 66, 69;
        NR 50, 51, 54, 56, 57, 59, 66;
        NP 1861, 70, 76, 92, 94, 96, 00, 05, 06, 11, 14, 18, 19, 20, 22,
        23, 24, 27, 31, 33, 34, 37, 38, 39, 40, 42, 43, 44, 45, 46, 47, 48,
        50, 51, 53, 54(2), 56, 57, 58, 59, 60, 66;
        NS 1878, 87, 97, 10, 11, 16, 17, 19, 20, 23(2), 26, 27;
        PH 01, 02, 04, 05, 12, 13, 15, 16, 17, 20, 21, 22, 23, 25, 26, 32,
        33, 36, 38, 39, 42, 44, 46, 48, 49, 50, 52, 53, 54, 55, 57, 58, 60,
        61, 69;   PT 37, 38, 40, 41, 42, 43, 46, 47, 48, 49, 52, 53, 54, 55,
        57, 58, 60, 61, 62, 64, 65, 68;   RC 27, 38, 48, 49, 57, 65, 67;
        SL 12, 14, 19, 22, 25, 26, 28, 30, 32, 33, 34, 40, 42, 44, 46, 47,
        48, 49, 50, 51, 52, 53, 54, 56, 57, 58, 59, 60, 62, 63, 66, 67, 69;
        SF 13, 14, 15, 20, 23, 26, 28, 31, 34, 35, 36, 37, 40, 43, 50, 53,
        57, 61, 64, 65, 66;   SE 31, 45, 53, 59, 66, 69;
        UT 47, 48, 51, 53, 61, 65, 69;
        WA 35, 37, 40, 43, 44, 48, 50, 51, 56, 62, 65, 67, 69

8   -One mvt NP 1863, 67, 68, 72

BEETHOVEN, L.v. (Cont.)
37   Conc in C for P, V, C, and O Triple Concerto Op 56
         BA 61;   BN 1881, 88, 65;   BU 51, 64;   CH 1899, 13, 26, 30, 51, 53, 55;
         CT 26, 56;   CL 27, 50, 65;   DA 63, 68;   DT 52;   HN 51, 56;   NA 57;
         KC 53, 64;   MN 65;   NP 14, 22, 48, 53, 59;   NR 68;   NS 16;   PH 25, 40;
         PT 43, 56, 62, 67;   RC 54, 61, 67;   SL 39, 54, 55, 60;
         SF 50, 58, 64, 66;   SE 65;   UT 61,   WA 51

11   Consecration of the House Overt Op 124   AT 69;   BN 1881, 82, 83,
         88, 91, 95, 97, 01, 09, 20, 30, 55, 65, 69;   BU 50, 68;   CT 14,
         26, 41, 69;   CH 1897, 02, 07, 54, 66;   CL 55;   DA 53;   DT 56;
         NA 31, 66;   KC 59;   LA 66, 69;   ML 63;   MN 39, 57, 66;
         NR 64;   NP 1872, 79, 81, 09, 14, 37, 62;   NS 1882;   PH 53, 62;
         PT 53, 62, 68;   RC 46;   SL 68;   UT 58

15   Contradances, Twelve Dances,Op 141   BA 48;   BN 60;   MN 56;
         NP 4 dances 31;   SF 6 dances 56

 7   Coriolanus Overt Op 62   AT 48, 60, 63;   BA 53, 58, 60, 67;
         BN 1881, 84, 85, 88, 89, 90, 92, 93, 96, 00, 03, 07, 08, 10,
         12, 13, 15, 18, 22, 24, 31, 36, 45, 48, 53, 55, 58, 60;
         BU 46, 55, 63;   CH 1891, 93, 96, 97, 98, 00, 02, 03, 04, 05,
         06, 07, 08, 09, 11, 12, 13, 14, 20, 21, 23, 26, 28, 33, 37, 38,
         41, 43, 44, 46, 47, 49, 55, 56, 57, 58;   CT 1895, 97, 07, 10, 12,
         14, 18, 20, 21, 26, 27, 29, 31, 40, 43, 46, 51, 61, 65, 69;
         CL 21, 28, 30, 37, 38, 48, 54, 58;   DA 46, 49, 59;   DE 55, 56;
         DT 15, 18, 29, 32, 37, 40, 43, 45, 53, 61;   HN 51, 56;
         NA 39, 56, 63, 68;   KC 35, 45, 55, 60, 64;   LA 34, 37, 41, 43,
         46, 53, 58, 60, 61, 64;   ML 65, 68;   MN 22, 24, 29, 39, 41, 43,
         47, 52, 55, 60;   NR 51, 63, 65;   NP 1857, 63, 69, 71, 75, 80,
         84, 88, 92, 99, 02, 04, 09, 10, 14, 15, 16, 17, 19, 20, 21, 23,
         25, 28, 29, 33, 35, 36, 37, 38, 39, 44, 46, 47, 48, 50, 53, 55,
         61;   NS 1881, 82, 86, 90, 07, 08(2);   PH 02, 05, 07, 09, 10,
         11, 12, 13, 15, 16, 17, 18, 19, 21, 22, 23, 24, 27, 29, 35, 36,
         41, 43, 48, 51, 53, 61, 65, 69;   PT 37, 38, 43, 48, 49, 54, 58,
         64, 68;   RC 30, 34, 36, 39, 58, 63;   SL 10, 14, 17, 21, 29, 30,
         31, 33, 34, 35, 37, 39, 54, 57, 58, 60, 64;   SF 11, 17, 22, 26,
         29, 30, 32, 35, 37, 39, 41, 43, 50, 52, 59, 63, 66;   SE 28, 34,
         39, 44, 62, 65, 66;   UT 50, 65, 69;   WA 31, 34, 36, 40, 49, 60, 66

      The Creatures of Prometheus,Die Geschöpfe des Promethus, Ballet, Op 43
         BN 1888, 33, 45, 51, 59;   CT 25, 41, 61, 65;   SF 37;   CL 66;
 8   -Adagio, Andante quasi Allegretto   BN 67;   CH 91, 99, 03;
         CL 29;   DT 59;   PH 69
         -Excerpts   BN 1881, 83, 96, 08, 19;   CH 6 excerpts 61;   NP 12
         excerpts 53, 59;   PH 27, 45;   SE 69
 5   -Finale, Allegretto   BN 67;   CH 1899, 03, 61;   NS 23;   PT 59
 4   -Introd to Act I   BN 67;
 5   -Overt   AT 52;   BA 53, 60;   BN 67;   BU 48, 51;   CH 1899, 01,
         03, 15, 24, 26, 29, 36, 37, 39, 42, 55, 56, 60, 61(2), 62, 63, 67;
         CT 31, 48, 52, 54;   CL 29, 38, 46, 49, 51, 53, 57, 62, 64, 65;
         DA 65;   DE 56, 58;   DT 21, 30, 33, 46, 55, 57, 58;   HN 50, 51,
         65, 66;   NA 58, 65;   KC 44, 61;   LA 43, 50, 62, 69(2);   ML 67;
         MN 25, 40, 45, 47, 50, 58, 59, 69;   NR 50, 54, 56, 58, 59;
         NP 12, 33, 69;   PH 13, 15, 16, 18, 19, 36, 48, 55, 59;

BEETHOVEN, L.v. (Cont.)   The Creatures of Prometheus Op 43,   Overt (Cont.)
        PT 37, 38, 43, 52, 57, 59, 65, 67;   RC 59, 68;   SL 45, 46, 48,
        51, 53, 60;   SE 68, 69;   UT 52, 63, 69;   WA 33, 37, 41, 46, 47,
        48, 51, 65;

40   Egmont, Incidental Music for Goethe's Tragedy Op 84   BA 60, 63;
        BN 1885, 33;   CH 1892, 01;   NA 49;   NP 1870, 73, 77, 85;
        PH 49;   SF 54
4   -Clarchen's Songs, Aria and Death   BN 1894, 56;   HN 47;   NS 07,
        08, 12, 14, 21, 23;   PH 27;   SF 40, 42;   WA 44
4   -Die Trommel gerühret, Drums Loudly Beating   CT 12, 26;   DE 47;
        DT 44;   MN 22, 48;   PH 43;   RC 38, 44;   SF 47;   UT 53;   WA 42
6   -Excerpts   LA 44;   NP 31
4   -Freudvoll und leidvoll   CT 02, 12, 26;   DT 44;   MN 22, 48;
        PH 43;   RC 38, 44;   SF 16;   UT 53;   WA 42
8   -Overt   AT 51, 60, 64, 68;
        BA 26, 41, 42, 47, 49, 52, 54, 56, 58, 66;
        BN 1881, 83, 84, 87, 89, 90, 91, 93, 94, 95, 97, 98, 01, 05, 06,
        08, 10, 11, 12, 14, 16, 18, 21, 23, 24, 26, 27, 29, 30, 35, 44,
        46, 51, 56, 58, 68, 69;   BU 40, 42, 44, 46, 56, 57, 58, 66;
        CH 1899, 04, 06, 08, 09, 11, 13, 15, 19, 21, 24, 26, 37, 38, 46,
        49, 51, 53, 56, 60, 63, 67, 69;   CT 1896, 06, 11, 17, 18, 22,
        24, 26, 30, 31, 34, 46, 52, 56, 60, 66;
        CL 20, 23, 26, 29, 30, 32, 33, 36, 40, 41, 42, 43, 45, 46, 53,
        58, 59, 63, 67;   DA 37, 49, 57, 58, 61, 66, 68;
        DE 45, 46, 48, 51, 53, 54, 60, 62, 63, 64;
        DT 16, 24, 27, 29, 31, 34, 38, 47, 48, 53, 54, 56, 59, 68;
        HN 38, 49, 51, 54, 55, 62, 66, 68;   NA 31, 45, 48, 49, 54, 56, 62, 65;
        KC 35, 37, 48, 69;   LA 22, 23, 24, 30, 38, 45, 52, 53, 56, 61, 62,
        65, 69(2);   ML 60, 67;   MN 22, 23, 27, 30, 31, 33, 34, 35, 36,
        40, 43, 46, 48(2), 51, 53, 56, 57, 58, 67(2);
        NR 51, 53, 54, 56, 57, 61, 63, 69;
        NP 1847, 53, 56, 60, 64, 84, 95, 00, 05, 15, 23, 24, 25, 31, 33,
        35, 36, 37, 39, 40, 41(2), 42, 45, 46, 48, 52, 53, 54, 55, 59,
        62, 64, 66;   NS 1880, 85, 94, 10, 20, 21, 23, 24, 26, 27;
        PH 01, 07, 08, 11, 12, 13, 16, 18, 21, 24, 26, 27(2), 30, 33, 34,
        36, 39, 43, 44, 46, 50, 52, 57, 60, 61, 62, 64, 65, 66, 67, 69;
        PT 37, 38, 40, 44, 50, 51, 52, 55, 58, 59, 65, 68;
        RC 29, 32, 38, 40, 44, 45, 46, 55, 57, 60;
        SL 10, 12, 13, 15, 17, 19, 20, 22, 24, 26, 27, 28, 29, 30, 31,
        32, 36, 38, 39, 45, 46, 47, 48, 50, 51, 53, 54, 55, 56, 57, 59,
        60, 61, 63, 66, 69;   SF 15, 20, 32, 33, 35, 37, 40, 42, 47, 52,
        53, 59, 61, 66, 68, 69(2);   SE 27, 30, 38, 42, 56, 67;
        UT 43, 45, 46, 48, 49, 53, 59, 69;
        WA 31, 35, 36, 40, 42, 48, 51, 54, 55, 68
8   -Songs   NA 2 songs 43;   KC 62;   SL 3 songs 45;

10   3 Equale for Four Trombones Grove No 195   CT 33;   HN 56; MN 26;   NP 38
        PH 17, 26;   SF 37;   WA 41

19   Fantasy for P, Chor and O in c Op 80   CH 1896, 31;   CL 57;
        DA 52;   KC 58;   LA 26;   NP 1876, 09, 61;   PH 06(2), 19, 50, 58;
        PT 56, 66;   RC 67

BEETHOVEN, L.v. (Cont.)
120   Fidelio, Opera Op 72 Complete   MN 67;   NS 25;
  4   -Abscheulicher, wo eilst du hin? Scene and aria, Act I   BA 45;
         CH 04, 07, 30, 37, 55;   CT 16, 26;   CL 43;   DT 26;   KC 40, 60;
         NA 40, 50;   LA 27, 35, 47;   MN 36, 40, 46;   NP 1842, 68, 70, 76,
         78, 87, 92, 05, 07, 36;   PH 03, 06, 41, 49, 58;   PT 44;   RC 38;
         SL 15, 38;   UT 65;   WA 49
  4   -Ah Welch ein Augenblick   MN 23
 30   -Act I   BN 1890
 30   -Act II   BN 1887
 60   -Two Acts   KC 66
         -Concert Version   BA 61;   CT 67;   NP 69;   PT 58, 69
  4   -Gott! Welch Dunkel hier, aria Act II   CT 01;   LA 47;   PH 03
  6   -Introduction and Scene   DA 55, 66
  4   -In des Lebens Frühlingstagen, aria Act II for Tenor   AT 64;
         KC 64;   MN 23, 38;   SL 33
  4   -Komm, O Hoffnung, aria Act I   CH 04, 07, 30, 37, 55
  7   -Overt   AT 55;   BA 51, 67;   BN 1882, 84, 86, 94, 96, 98, 00,
         03, 11, 19, 50, 53, 55, 67;   BU 67;   CH 1894, 98, 06, 08, 10,
         13, 15, 19, 23, 33, 37, 44, 52, 55, 58, 66;   CT 20, 25, 29, 36,
         40, 47;   CL 27, 35, 40, 51, 55, 66;   DA 49;   DE 48, 55, 61;
         DT 19, 29, 52, 54, 59, 61;   HN 40;   NA 55, 65;   KC 52, 54, 67;
         LA 44, 47, 50, 54;   ML 66;   MN 23, 26, 35, 39, 45, 55;
         NR 55, 65;   NP 1859, 61, 69, 01, 13, 20, 36, 37, 38, 41, 42, 51,
         52, 55, 66;   NS 07, 08;   PH 03, 14, 18, 19, 36, 55, 68;
         PT 39, 42, 49, 55;   RC 28, 32, 46, 49, 55, 57;   SL 23, 31, 33,
         35, 55, 66;   SF 13, 32, 47, 49, 55;   SE 29, 58;   UT 55, 69;
         WA 43, 46, 50, 54, 62, 67
  4   -O war ich schon mit der vereint, aria, Act I   KC 65
  8   -Prison Scene and Chorus   MN 64;   NP 1858
  6   -Quartet, Mir ist's so wunderbar   CH 39, NP 1844;   NS 07;
         PH 06
  4   -Recitative and Aria   SF 28

 16   Grand Fugue in Bb for Str Op 133   BN 16, 57;   BU 64;   CH 04, 26;
         CT 25, 62;   KC 69;   LA 38;   MN 38, 67;   NP 26, 41, 59, 65, 67;
         PH 39, 53, 61;   PT 50, 58, 66,   SL 65;   SF 37, 42, 46, 69

  8   Hymnus, Orchestration of Andante fr Trio in Eb by Franz Liszt
         PH 08, 10

  7   King Stephen Overt Op 117   AT 56;   BA 60;   BN 1883, 85, 93, 95,
         00, 11, 19, 62;   CH 1896, 04, 08, 12, 20, 50;   CT 1898, 02, 19;
         CL 50, 63, 66, 69;   DT 25, 32;   NA 41;   MN 26;   NP 10, 66;
         PH 27, 52;   PT 62, 65, 67;   WA 69

 10   Lenore Overture No 1, Op 138   BN 1881, 86, 99, 07, 13, 15;   CH 02;
         CL 64, 66;   CT 15, 32, 55, 63, 68;   DA 66;   DT 20;   HN 52;
         LA 56;   ML 69;   MN 23, 45;   NR 61;   NP 19, 24, 28, 33, 52;
         NS 07, 08;   PH 53, 58, 60, 67;   PT 66, 68;   SL 63, 66, 69;
         SF 56, 64;   WA 38, 56

 13   Lenore Overture No 2, Op 72a   BA 61;   BN 1881, 87, 90, 91, 97,
         99, 02, 03, 25, 34, 35, 54, 55, 64, 66;   BU 46;   CH 1892, 97,
         00, 08, 10, 11, 14, 15, 16, 25, 34, 35, 39, 47, 49, 53, 57, 60,
         68;   CT 16, 23, 29, 55, 62, 69;   CL 38, 42, 44, 48, 54, 66;

BEETHOVEN, L.v. (Cont.)   Lenore Overture No 2 (Cont.)
          DA 52;   DT 23, 31, 60;   HN 53;   NA 36, 41, 43, 47, 63;
          KC 39, 57;   LA 57, 62, 67;   MN 36, 41, 43, 63;   NR 58, 61;
          NP 1869, 73, 77, 83, 87, 01, 26, 40, 42, 45, 48, 50, 54, 69;
          NS 07, 08, 09, 22, 23;   PH 68, 69;   PT 38, 42, 47, 52, 66;
          RC 53, 59, 61;   SL 30;   SF 50, 60;   WA 40, 49

14   Lenore Overture No 3, Op 72b   AT 49, 53, 56, 61, 64;
      BA 26, 52, 54, 58, 59, 62, 66;
      BN 1881, 84, 85, 87, 89, 92, 93, 94, 95, 96, 97, 01, 10, 11, 12,
      14, 15, 17, 18, 20, 22, 23, 26(2), 28, 29, 33, 37, 39, 40, 43,
      45, 51, 59, 62;   BU 40, 43, 48, 53, 55, 57, 65;
      CH 1891, 93(2), 94, 95(2), 97, 99, 00, 01, 03, 04(2), 05, 06, 07,
      08, 10, 11, 12, 13, 14, 15, 16, 17, 18, 19, 20, 21, 22, 23, 24,
      25, 26, 27, 29, 31, 36, 39, 40, 42, 44, 45, 48(2), 49(2), 51, 54,
      56, 58, 60, 61, 62, 67;
      CT 1895, 97, 99, 03, 04, 09, 12, 14, 15, 17, 18, 19, 20(2), 21,
      22, 24, 26, 29, 33, 34, 37, 38, 39, 41, 47, 51, 53, 55, 62, 64;
      CL 18, 20, 23, 25, 29, 31, 33, 35, 36, 37, 38, 40, 43, 46, 47,
      49, 53, 56, 58, 62;
      DA 27, 28, 46, 48, 49, 50, 54, 55, 57, 61, 63, 68;
      DE 45, 46, 50, 51, 55, 57, 59, 60, 65, 67;
      DT 17, 26, 28, 29, 35, 36, 39, 40, 41, 43, 44, 45, 46, 54, 56,
      58, 60, 62, 63, 66, 69;   HN 34, 36, 39, 40, 42, 44, 49, 51, 54,
      56, 61;   NA 38, 55;   KC 33, 35, 38, 40, 44, 50, 56, 63, 64;
      LA 24, 25, 26, 28, 29(2), 33, 34, 39, 41, 45, 46, 48, 49, 50, 55, 58
      ML 62;   MN 22, 23, 25, 27, 29, 31, 32, 34, 38, 44, 45, 47, 48, 50,
      52, 55, 57, 60, 64;   NR 52, 54, 55, 56, 59, 61;
      NP 1852, 57, 58, 62, 65, 68, 71, 74, 76, 78, 81, 86, 93, 96, 99, 03
      05, 06, 09, 10, 11, 14, 15, 16, 18, 23, 25(2), 26, 28, 29, 32, 37,
      43, 44, 45, 46, 47, 48, 51, 54, 55, 56, 57, 58, 63, 65, 67;
      NS 1879, 80, 81, 84, 88, 04, 07, 08, 11, 12, 16, 21, 23(2), 25, 26;
      PH 00, 01, 04, 05, 06, 07, 08, 09(2), 10, 11, 12, 13(2), 15, 17,
      18(2), 19(2), 20(2), 21(2), 23, 24, 25, 26(2), 28, 29, 30, 31, 32,
      33(2), 35(2), 36, 37, 38, 40, 41, 44, 46, 47, 50, 52, 56, 57, 60,
      61, 62, 63, 64;   PT 34, 38, 43, 45(2), 48, 51, 57, 61, 67, 69;
      RC 23, 25, 27, 29, 31, 34, 36, 38, 42, 54, 61, 65;
      SL 10, 12, 13, 15, 17, 19, 20, 22, 24, 26, 27, 28, 29, 30, 31, 32,
      36, 38, 39, 45, 46, 50, 52, 53, 55, 56, 57, 60, 61, 68;
      SF 12, 15, 16, 18, 25, 29, 32, 43, 57, 58, 59, 63, 64, 66, 67;
      SE 26, 29, 33, 40, 43, 45, 52, 55, 67;
      UT 42, 53, 59, 63, 64, 66;
      WA 31, 34, 36, 37, 38, 39, 40, 43, 45, 47, 48, 49, 51, 54, 56, 58, 6

37   Mass in C Op 86   PH 65;   WA 54

7   Military Marches for Winds arr Foss   BU 64;   CL 64;   MN 67;
      NP 65(2)

5   Minuet in G arr Stock   CH 12

5   Minuetto   BA 26

BEETHOVEN, L.v. (Cont.)
74   Missa Solemnis in D Op 123   AT 67;   BA 65;   BN 38;   BU 66;
        CH 60, 67;   CT 60;   CL 56, 63, 66;   DA 61, 67;   DT 59, 66;
        KC 62;   ML 69;   LA 51, 61, 69;   MN 51, 60, 68;   NP 33, 34,
        47, 53, 59, 66, 68;   PH 65;   PT 53;   RC 69;   SL 64;   SF 55,
        62, 66;   SE 65;   UT 68
5   -Gloria   LA 26
5   -Benediction   CH 00;   CL 30;   MN 26;   NS 07, 18

5   The Mount of Olives, Christus am Olberge, Oratorio Op 85   PH 62
        -Hallelujah Chorus   CH 95
4   -Aria O, my heart is sore within me   CH 17, 20

15   Music to a Knightly Ballet, Musik zu einem Ritterballett, Grove
        No 149   CT 26;   DT 23

9   Namensfier Overt in C Op 115   BN 1882, 03;   CH 1896;   CT 16;
        MN 51;   WA 41, 69

4   Primo amore piacer del ciel, for Sopr, Flute, 2 Oboes, 2 Bassoons,
        2 Horns and Strs   SF 37

30   Quart in C for Str No 3 Grove No 152   BN 1884, 91

40   Quart No 5 in A for Str Op 18 No 5   BN 58
8   -Theme and Var   CH 1891, 94
8   -Andante   CT 18;   NS 21

8   Quart No 6 in B^b for Str Op 18 No 6: Allegro   AT 51

40   Quart No 9 in C for Str Op 59 No 3   BN 1884, 91;   NP 1881, 88, 95,
        00, 07
8   -Minuet and Finale   CH 1899, 04, 06, 08, 10, 26;   ML 59
5   -Fugue   PT 50

20   Quart in f for Str Op 95   MN 35

5   Quart No 13 in B^b for Str Op 130: Alla danza tedesca   CH 03
5   -Cavatina   CH 03;   PH 62

        Quart in c# for Str Op 131 arr for O   BN 36, 51;   MN 37;   NP 40;
        NS 1883
8   -Lento assai   BN 56
8   -Cavatina   PH 62

8   Quart in F for Str Op 135: Lento assai   NS 07
8   -Lento Vivace   NP 33
6   -Lento   UT 61

8   Romance No 1 in G for solo instrum and Str Op 40   CT 60;   LA 45;
        MN 62;   NS 04, 08;   PT 46;   RC 24;   SL 60;   SF 66

9   Romance No 2 in F for solo instrum and Str Op 50   BN 1897;
        BU 60;   CH 04, 59, 65;   CT 60;   CL 64;   MN 62;   NS 04, 07;
        SF 66;   UT 55;   WA 43

BEETHOVEN, L.v. (Cont.)
8   Romance for P, Fl, Bassoon, and O   BN 54

8   Rondino in E^b for 8 Wind Instr, Grove No 146   BN 33;   CH 02, 03;
     CT 34, 39;   NS 23;   SF 38

9   Rondino for Str Op 48   MN 23;   PH 01

6   The Ruins of Athens, Incidental Music Op 113: Chorus   CH 1896;
     NP 1876;   PH 27
5   -Duet   NP 1876
5   -Marsia Solemne   NP 1876
6   -Overt   BN 1883, 87;   CH 44;   DT 64;   NA 58, 65;   NP 35, 64
4   -Turkish March   CH 1896, 08;   CL 43, 53;   DA 28;   HN 39, 42
     NP 1876;   NS 07, 08;   PH 27;   SL 53;   SF 58;   WA 32
8   -Version arr by Rubinstein   NS 1891

5   Scherzo, Unidentified, Orchestration Chauncey V. Kelley   CT 45

25   Septet in E^b for Clar, V, Vla, C, Bassoon, Horn and double Bass Op 20
     CH 1891, 92, 97;   LA 49;   NR 58
6   -Var, Scherzo, Finale   NP 1842, 86, 89
6   -Adagio Cantabile, Theme and Var   NS 1892

5   Serenade for V, Vla, and C Op 8: Polonaise   CH 1892, 26;   MN 22;
     NS 23

5   Serenade for Fl, V, Vla, Op 23: Adagio and Finale   NS 23

20   Sonata in F Op 10 No 2, arr Black for Str O   HN 14

8   Sonata for V and P in A, Kreutzer Op 47: Andante con variazioni
     arr Thomas   CH 00(2), 04, 06, 08, 16

6   Sonata No 12 in A^b for P Op 26: Marcia Funèbre arr Thomas   CH 1899

26   Sonata No 29 in B^b for P Op 106 Hammerklavier, Orchestrated by
     Weingartner   CT 31;   CL 35;   MN 38;   RC 52

SONGS
4   Adelaide Op 46   CH 1891, 20;   CT 13, 26, 37;   DT 46;   NA 54;
     MN 23, 39, 47;   NP 1862, 64, 14;   NS 1881, 12;   PH 15(2);
     WA 38
4   An die Hoffnung Op 32   CH 02;   NS 09, 10;   PH 11
4   Chant Elegiaque for Voice and Str Op 118   CH 44;   MN 26
4   Cottage Maid, fr Welsh Songs Op 226 No 3   CT 12
     Gellert Lieder Op 48   Cycle of 6 songs
4   No 1 Bitten   NS 07, 08
4   No 2 Vom Tode   NS 07, 08
4   No 4 Die Ehre Gottes in der Nature, or Die Himmel ruhmen, or
4   Creation's Hymn   BU 53;   CH 20;   CT 29, 43;   CL 28;   DA 35;
     DE 52;   DT 21, 44(2);   HN 47, 51;   MN 22, 30, 42, 48;   NP 16;
     NS 1892, 07, 08, 14, 22, 23;   PH 33;   RC 44;   SL 30;   WA 37
4   No 5 Gottes Macht und Vorschung   WA 42
4   Ich liebe dich: Groves No 235   NS 22;   WA 42
4   In questa tomba oscura, arietta Grove No 299   CH 07;   CT 49;
     DE 47, 55;   DT 47, 54;   MN 47;   NP 39;   NS 07;   SF 47

BEETHOVEN, L.v. (Cont.) Songs (Cont.)
        Der Küss, arietta Op 128   CT 29;   NS 07, 23
        Neue liebe, Neues Leben, Op 75 No 2   NS 22, 23
  4   Scottish Folk Songs Op 108 with O: one song unidentified   NS 07,
        08, 23
  4   -No 20, Faithful Johnnie   CT 12
 10   Song Cycle undesignated   NS 08
 16   4 Songs   PH 16
  4   Song of the Flea   NS 07, 23
  4   Two airs from Goethe:
  4   No 1 Prufung des Küssens   CT 29
        No 2 Mit Madeln sich vertragen   CH 07;   CT 29
  4   Wachtelschlag Grove No 237   NS 1881, 07
  4   Wonne der Wehmut Trocknet nicht Op 83 No 1   MN 22;   NS 14

 28   Symphony No 1 in C Op 21
        AT 46, 58, 64;   BA 43, 50, 54;
        BN 81, 82, 83, 84, 86, 90, 93, 95, 96, 00, 02, 07, 09, 13, 15,
          17, 20, 25, 26, 30, 35, 37, 39, 41, 45, 48, 50, 60, 68;
        BU 41, 43, 50, 59, 63;
        CH 1893, 95, 02, 03, 09, 13, 19, 20, 23, 25, 26, 30, 32, 43,
          44, 47(2), 49, 54, 60, 62, 64;
        CT 14, 20, 23, 25, 26, 35, 38, 44, 49, 52, 61, 67;
        CL 28, 38, 40, 41, 42, 49, 51, 54, 61, 64;   DA 62, 67;
        DE 45, 49, 52, 53, 56, 59, 62;
        DT 14, 17, 19, 24, 32, 34, 41, 45, 51, 52, 58, 61, 63, 65, 68;
        HN 16, 35, 47, 51, 52, 53, 55, 56, 58;   NA 35, 66;
        KC 44, 47, 55, 59, 65;   LA 19, 22, 38, 46, 49, 53, 60, 63, 64;
        ML 64;   MN 23, 30, 37, 40, 43, 44, 46, 55, 66;
        NR 50, 53, 57, 60, 65;
        NP 1853, 68, 91, 01, 12, 21, 25, 28, 29, 30, 32, 33, 35, 38(2),
          40, 41, 43, 44, 46, 48, 50, 53, 58, 63, 69;
        NS 1887, 88, 07, 08(2), 10, 20, 21, 23, 24;
        PH 01, 03, 04, 06, 12, 18, 19, 24, 28, 30, 32, 34, 36, 37, 38,
          39, 41, 42, 44, 45, 49, 51, 53, 60, 61, 62, 65, 69;
        PT 38, 41, 44, 45, 48, 51, 54, 58, 63, 69;
        RC 34, 37, 51, 59, 63, 67, 69;
        SL 26, 27, 31, 43, 54, 57, 59, 63, 67;
        SF 17, 21, 27, 30, 39, 43, 46, 47, 54, 55, 60, 64, 66, 67, 69;
        SE 35, 53, 62;   UT 42, 49, 54, 58, 68;
        WA 32, 42, 47, 56, 62, 66, 69

        -Minuet and Finale   MN 43

 36   Symphony No 2 in D Op 36
        AT 48, 59;   BA 37, 53, 61, 67, 69;
        BN 1881, 82, 83, 84, 85, 87, 89, 92, 94, 97, 99, 01, 05, 07, 10,
          12, 15, 17, 19, 26, 36, 38, 39, 42, 43, 51, 53, 59, 63, 66;
        BU 51;   CH 1893, 96, 01, 04, 07, 16, 19, 24, 26, 30, 32, 36,
          37, 40, 44, 46, 48, 49, 53, 55, 59, 61, 64, 66;
        CT 1895, 98, 10, 13, 15, 20, 25, 26, 27, 30, 33, 37, 38, 42, 50,
          58, 62, 65, 67;
        CL 22, 31, 38, 42, 45, 47, 49, 52, 53, 56, 58, 63, 64, 67;
        DA 52, 60, 67;   DE 49, 55;

BEETHOVEN, L.v. (Cont.)   Symphony No 2 (Cont.)
        DT 20, 25, 31, 36, 38, 46, 48, 54, 58, 64, 69;
        HN 50, 51, 52, 53, 56, 59, 69;   NA 30, 50, 52, 65, 68;
        KC 39, 45, 52, 64, 69;
        LA 22, 47, 50, 54, 56, 59, 60, 64;   ML 66;
        MN 23, 24, 29, 35, 38, 41, 46, 51, 56, 58, 68;   NR 58, 67;
        NP 1842, 50, 53, 59, 66, 90, 97, 04, 18, 24, 27, 28, 29, 31, 33,
           34, 36, 37, 39, 42, 44, 46, 48, 49, 50, 53, 55, 56, 60, 62,
           63, 67;
        NS 1882, 86, 94, 05, 07, 08, 15, 17, 23;
        PH 04, 11, 13, 16, 17, 23, 26, 28, 35, 36, 39, 51, 53, 54, 57,
           58, 61, 65;
        PT 38, 44, 46, 55, 59, 63, 68;
        RC 27, 38, 41, 44, 47, 56, 66, 67;
        SL 15, 30, 36, 53, 56, 57, 68;
        SF 15, 23, 28, 30, 41, 45, 50, 53, 57, 60, 62, 64, 66, 69;
        SE 36, 54, 65;   UT 50, 56, 67;   WA 44, 51, 56, 61

  9   -2nd movement   MN 47
 18   -3rd and 4th movements   MN 47
  9   -Larghetto   CH 01, 02, 04, 11

 50   Symphony No 3 in E^b, Eroica Op 55
        AT 49, 68;   BA 45, 52, 54, 56, 57, 60, 63, 68;
        BN 1881, 82, 83, 84, 85, 86, 87, 88, 90, 91, 92, 93, 94, 97, 98, 00,
           02, 04, 05, 06, 08, 11, 12, 14, 16, 17, 18, 21, 24, 26(2), 28,
           31, 33, 34, 37, 39, 41, 42, 43, 44, 45, 46, 50, 52, 56, 57, 59,
           61, 62, 63, 65, 68;
        BU 45, 49, 51, 53, 54, 56, 58, 63, 69;
        CH 1891, 94, 95, 97, 98, 00, 01, 03, 05, 06, 07, 08, 09, 10, 11,
           12, 13, 14, 15, 17, 18, 19, 20, 21, 22, 23, 25, 26, 28, 32, 34,
           35, 39, 40, 41, 42, 44, 45, 46, 47, 49(2), 50, 51, 52, 54, 56,
           58, 59, 60, 61, 64, 66, 68;
        CT 1896, 00, 01, 05, 09, 11, 12, 14, 16, 20, 21, 24, 26, 29, 30,
           32, 34, 37, 40, 45, 47, 56, 57, 61, 63, 65, 67, 68;
        CL 20, 23, 25, 26, 30, 32, 34, 38, 41, 42, 43, 44, 46, 47, 49, 51,
           53, 55, 56, 60, 62, 64, 66, 69;
        DA 46, 48, 49, 53, 56, 59, 61, 64, 66, 67;
        DE 47, 49, 50, 52, 55, 58, 63, 64, 68;
        DT 18, 23, 25, 32, 35, 36, 39, 41, 43, 44, 45, 46, 48, 51, 52, 56,
           59, 62, 64, 69;
        HN 40, 43, 47, 49, 51, 53, 55, 56, 60, 62, 65, 68;
        NA 32, 40, 46, 51, 54, 55, 56, 60, 62, 66, 69;
        KC 35, 47, 50, 56, 62, 67;
        LA 21, 26, 27, 30, 37, 38, 40, 44, 46, 48, 50, 52, 56, 58, 60, 62,
           64, 67;   ML 62;
        MN 22, 23, 25, 28, 33, 37, 40, 42, 44, 48, 50, 52, 54, 56, 58, 60,
           64, 69;
        NR 51, 53, 63, 66, 69;
        NP 1842, 44, 46, 48, 51, 54, 56, 61, 68, 71, 78, 80, 82, 85, 87,
           90, 93, 97, 00, 05, 06, 08, 11, 13, 14, 15, 16, 18(2), 19(2),
           20(2), 22, 24, 25(2), 26, 28, 29, 31(2), 33(2), 35, 38, 39, 44,
           45, 46, 48, 51, 52, 54, 60, 62, 63, 64, 66, 68;

BEETHOVEN, L.v. (Cont.) Symphony No 3 (Cont.)
  NS 1879, 81, 82, 84, 88, 90, 92, 95, 97, 04, 06, 07, 08, 10, 11,
    14, 16, 17(2), 18, 19, 21, 22, 23(2), 24, 25;
  PH 02, 04, 05, 06, 07, 08, 09, 13, 14, 16, 20, 24, 26, 27, 28, 29,
    30, 33(2), 50, 53, 55, 56, 58, 59, 60, 61, 62, 63, 64, 65, 67,
    68, 69;
  PT 37, 38, 41, 43, 46, 50, 52, 55, 57, 63, 65, 67, 68;
  RC 31, 35, 36, 39, 43, 45, 47, 52, 56, 58, 60, 61, 65, 67, 69;
  SL 12, 14, 16, 21, 26, 29, 31, 34, 36, 38, 39, 41, 42, 43, 46, 48,
    50, 51, 55, 57, 58, 63, 67, 69;
  SF 11, 15, 18, 20, 23, 24, 26, 29, 31, 45, 47, 49, 50, 51, 53, 57,
    59, 61, 62, 63, 64, 66, 67, 69;
  SE 27, 30, 39, 49, 58, 64;
  UT 41, 47, 52, 55, 58, 62, 63, 65, 68
  WA 35, 39, 44, 48, 49, 50, 52, 55, 56, 58, 59, 62, 64, 65, 66, 67, 69

12 -2nd movement   PT 40
10 -Scherzo, 3rd movement   MN 44, 48
12 -Allegro con bric   CH 16
12 -Marche funebre   BA 26, 43;   BN 63;   CH 16, 27, 29;   CT 25, 29,
    44;   CL 64;   DA 56;   LA 38;   NP 1864, 56;   PH 13, 18;
    UT 68

34 Symphony No 4 in B^b Op 60
  AT 51, 54, 63;   BA 38, 57;
  BN 1881, 82, 83, 84, 86, 88, 89, 91, 92, 93, 96, 98, 00, 02, 03, 04,
    07, 09, 11, 12, 14, 16, 17, 19, 25, 26, 29, 31, 36, 37, 39, 42,
    47, 48, 50, 52, 56, 60, 63;
  BU 40, 42, 48, 53;
  CH 1892, 96, 98, 00, 02, 04, 05, 06, 08, 09, 10, 12, 13, 16, 17, 20,
    23, 25, 26, 28, 31, 35, 36, 37, 38, 40, 41, 43, 44, 45, 48, 49,
    52, 56, 57, 58, 62, 63, 66, 67;
  CT 1898, 02, 08, 13, 15, 19, 24, 26, 28, 31, 35, 41, 48, 53, 57, 60;
  CL 24, 27, 38, 46, 50, 54, 57, 60, 62, 67;
  DA 48, 50, 53, 55, 58, 59, 65, 67;   DE 49, 54;
  DT 20, 24, 27, 29, 30, 34, 46, 53, 60, 63, 68;
  HN 49, 51, 52, 56;
  NA 36, 61, 65;
  KC 38, 43, 54, 67;
  LA 27, 45, 51, 56, 62, 64;
  MN 23, 34, 38, 40, 44, 47, 50, 55, 64, 67;
  NR 55, 63, 68;
  NP 1849, 55, 58, 62, 66, 70, 73, 75, 78, 81, 83, 86, 88, 93, 99, 06,
    16, 23, 26, 27, 29, 30, 33, 35, 38, 39, 40, 47, 48, 50(2), 51,
    56, 61, 64, 67(2);
  NS 1880, 89, 07, 08, 11, 16, 20, 23, 27;
  PH 00, 06, 14, 16, 20, 22, 24, 26, 30, 35, 36, 41, 43, 44, 45, 46,
    53, 57, 60, 64, 68, 69;
  PT 38, 40, 42, 47, 49, 55, 58, 61, 64, 65, 68;
  RC 26, 47, 55, 57, 62, 67;
  SL 24, 28, 35, 36, 39, 40, 44, 47, 50, 51, 55, 57, 58, 60, 61, 69;
  SF 15, 22, 27, 37, 42, 44, 49, 53, 60, 63, 64, 66, 67, 69;
  SE 36, 43, 47, 68;
  UT 57, 65, 69;
  WA 41, 49, 50, 51, 53, 56, 62, 67

BEETHOVEN, L.v. (Cont.)
   29   Symphony No 5 in c Op 67
         AT 49, 60, 64, 69;
         BA 28, 40, 42, 44(2), 47, 49, 51, 57, 58, 61;
         BN 1881, 82, 83, 84, 87(2), 89, 90, 91, 93, 95, 97, 98, 00, 02, 04,
            05, 06, 07, 08, 10, 11, 12, 13, 14, 17, 18, 19, 22, 23, 24,
            26(2), 27, 29, 33, 34, 36, 38, 40, 42, 43, 45, 47, 51, 54, 57,
            59, 62, 67;
         BU 40, 42, 45, 49, 52, 55, 60, 63, 64;
         CH 1891, 93, 94, 95, 96, 97, 98, 99(2), 00, 01, 02, 03, 05, 06, 07,
            08, 09, 10, 11, 12, 14, 15, 16, 18, 20, 21, 23, 24, 25, 26, 28,
            29, 31, 32, 34, 35, 36, 37, 38, 39, 40, 41, 42, 43, 44, 47, 48,
            50, 52, 53, 55, 58, 63, 66, 67, 68;
         CT 1895, 97, 99, 01, 03, 05, 07, 09, 10, 11, 12, 13, 15, 17, 18,
            20, 21, 22, 23, 24, 25, 26, 29(2), 30, 31, 34, 36, 38, 40, 41,
            42, 43, 46, 52, 53, 56, 58, 66, 67;
         CL 18, 19, 21, 24, 25, 26, 28, 29, 31, 32, 34, 36, 38(2), 39, 40,
            41, 42, 44, 45, 46, 48, 50, 52, 54, 55, 56, 57, 59, 61, 63, 66;
         DA 26, 37, 46, 49, 52, 55, 58, 61, 63;
         DE 45, 46, 48, 49, 50, 52, 54, 56, 60, 64, 68;
         DT 15, 17, 18, 19, 22, 25, 26, 28, 29, 31, 32, 36, 37, 39, 47, 53,
            57, 59, 61, 64, 66;
         HN 31(2), 35, 37, 39, 42, 46, 48, 51, 53, 54, 55, 56, 58, 61, 67;
         NA 33, 39, 41, 43, 47, 48(2), 53, 56, 59, 61, 64, 66, 69;
         KC 34, 38, 41, 42, 44, 45, 48, 55, 58, 63, 64, 67;
         LA 19, 20, 21, 22, 23, 25, 26, 27, 28, 29, 33, 34, 39, 42, 43, 48,
            53, 55, 57, 59, 61, 63, 64, 66, 68;   ML 69;
         MN 23, 26, 28, 31, 34, 35, 37, 40, 42, 45, 49, 50, 52, 54, 57, 58,
            59, 61, 65, 67;
         NR 50, 53, 56, 58, 61, 62, 64;
         NP 1842, 43, 45, 47, 50, 52, 56, 61, 69, 72, 74, 76, 79, 81, 83, 84,
            87, 94, 98, 01, 03, 05, 07, 09, 10, 11, 12, 13, 14, 15, 17, 18,
            19, 20(2), 21(2), 26, 27, 28, 30, 31, 32, 33, 34, 35, 36, 38, 39,
            41, 44, 45, 47, 48, 51, 52, 53, 56, 59, 62, 63, 65, 69;
         NS 1878, 82, 87, 96, 03, 05, 07, 08, 09, 10, 11, 15, 17(2), 18(2),
            19, 20, 21, 22, 23, 24, 25, 26, 27;
         PH 00, 01, 05, 07, 08, 09, 10(2), 11, 12(2), 14, 15, 17, 18, 19,
            20, 21, 22, 23, 24, 25, 26(2), 27, 28(2), 29, 30, 31(2), 32, 33,
            34, 36, 37, 38, 39, 40, 41, 42, 43, 44, 45, 46, 47, 48, 49, 50,
            51, 53, 59, 61, 62, 64, 65, 67(2), 69;
         PT 37, 38, 39, 41, 45, 47, 48, 50, 51, 52, 53, 56, 58, 60, 64, 68;
         RC 23, 25, 32, 36, 42, 45, 47, 53, 59, 63, 65, 67;
         SL 11, 13, 15, 17, 19, 21, 24, 27, 28, 29, 31, 33, 34, 35, 37, 38,
            40, 42, 44, 49, 52, 57, 58, 59, 60, 61, 63, 65;
         SF 12, 14, 16, 17, 19, 21, 22, 26, 29, 31, 33, 35, 42, 43, 52, 53,
            56, 58, 60, 63, 64, 66, 69;
         SE 26, 28, 32, 38, 44, 47, 52, 63;
         UT 40, 42, 44, 46, 48, 53, 56, 60, 64, 69;
         WA 31, 39, 40, 41, 44, 46, 49, 53, 54, 56, 58, 62

    7   -First movement   CT 45;   MN 45

   36   Symphony No 6 in F Op 68 Pastoral
         AT 50, 57   BA 41, 58, 63, 65
         BN 1881, 82, 83, 84, 85, 86, 88, 89, 91, 93, 95, 97, 99, 01, 05, 07,
            09, 13, 15, 17, 18, 20, 23, 24, 26, 28, 29, 35, 39, 40, 41, 43,

BEETHOVEN, L.v. (Cont.) Symphony No 6, BN (Cont.)
        45, 54, 56, 58, 60, 62, 64, 68;
    BU 46, 53, 60, 67, 69;
    CH 1893, 94, 95, 96, 97, 00, 01, 02, 04, 06, 08, 10, 12, 14, 15, 17,
       25, 26, 29, 33, 37, 41, 42, 44, 47, 48, 50, 54, 55, 56, 58, 60,
       61, 64, 67;
    CT 1896, 00, 02, 04, 12, 14, 16, 18(2), 24, 26, 30, 33, 35, 39, 40,
       43, 51, 55, 58, 63, 67, 69;
    CL 22, 31, 37, 38, 43, 44, 47, 48, 50, 52, 54, 56, 58, 61, 64, 67,69;
    DA 49, 50, 53, 58, 63;
    DE 49, 67, 69;
    DT 19, 23, 26, 30, 37, 44, 45, 46, 51, 54, 58, 62, 64;
    HN 31, 38, 41, 47, 50, 51, 59, 62, 68;
    NA 42, 47, 52, 58, 63, 66;
    KC 38, 41, 48, 61, 66;
    LA 21, 28, 35, 45, 47, 51, 54, 57, 61, 64;
    MN 23, 24, 35, 38, 39, 43, 46, 49, 53, 56, 57, 62, 65;
    NR 52, 61, 65, 69;
    NP 1845, 46, 51, 55, 60, 63, 67, 71, 74, 77, 80, 84, 87, 91, 96,
       00, 07, 10, 12, 13, 16, 20, 26, 27, 30, 32, 33, 37, 38, 43, 46,
       47, 48, 49, 50, 51, 52, 54, 55, 56, 61, 62, 64;
    NS 1879, 85, 92, 06, 07, 08, 11, 13, 16, 19, 21, 23, 25;
    PH 01, 03, 05, 08, 10, 15, 19, 20, 25, 31, 34, 36, 38, 42, 45, 46,
       50, 51, 52, 53, 55, 57, 59, 61, 62, 63, 68, 69;
    PT 38, 43, 47, 48, 51, 56, 58, 62, 64, 66, 68;
    RC 30, 37, 40, 47, 51, 54, 60, 63, 67;
    SL 10, 14, 18, 25, 32, 35, 45, 51, 57, 60, 63, 65, 67;
    SF 17, 32, 38,   47, 52, 54, 58, 61, 63, 64, 66, 69;
    SE 31, 46, 50, 60;
    UT 48, 54, 59, 63, 69;
    WA 37, 62, 68;

27   -3rd, 4th, 5th movements   MN 46

40   Symphony No 7 in A Op 92
    AT 47, 52, 67;
    BA 42, 43, 50, 53, 55, 57, 61, 65, 68;
    BN 1881, 82, 83, 84, 85, 87, 88, 89, 90, 92, 94, 95, 97, 99, 01,
       03, 06, 08, 10, 11, 13, 15, 18, 21, 23, 24, 26, 27, 30, 32,
       35, 37, 38, 39, 40, 41, 43, 44, 46, 48, 49, 52, 54, 57, 60, 63,
       66, 67;
    BU 41, 44, 45, 47, 52, 53, 55, 57, 59, 61, 63, 65;
    CH 1892, 94, 95, 97, 98, 99, 00, 01, 02, 03, 04, 05, 07, 08, 09,
       10, 11, 13, 15, 16, 17, 18, 19, 20, 21, 22, 23, 24, 26, 29, 31,
       33, 37, 42, 44, 45, 46, 47, 48, 50, 52, 53, 55, 56, 57, 61, 62,
       63, 67, 68;
    CT 1899, 06, 10, 12, 14, 16, 17, 19, 23, 26, 28, 30, 32, 43, 46,
       50, 51, 55, 57, 59, 64, 67;
    CL 21, 22, 23, 25, 27, 30, 33, 35, 38, 39, 40, 42, 43, 44, 45, 46,
       47, 49, 51, 53, 54, 56, 57, 59, 61, 63, 65, 67, 69;
    DA 38, 46, 48, 50, 51, 54, 56, 59, 62(2), 66, 67;
    DE 45, 46, 47, 49, 50, 51, 52, 53, 55, 57, 59, 61, 63, 65, 67;
    DT 17, 18, 22, 24, 27, 28, 33, 38, 39, 40, 47, 48, 52, 54, 57, 61,
       62, 63, 65, 67, 69;
    HN 34, 39, 46, 49, 50, 52, 53, 54, 55, 58, 60, 61, 63, 66, 69;

BEETHOVEN, L.v. (Cont.)   Symphony No 7 (Cont.)
        NA 38, 40, 43, 45, 48, 55, 57, 61, 65;
        KC 33, 36, 43, 46, 49, 53, 57, 60, 61, 63;
        LA 20, 23, 24, 26, 28, 29, 34, 39, 41, 42, 44, 46, 55, 56, 58, 59,
           60, 61, 64, 69;
        ML 61, 64, 67;
        MN 23, 27, 30, 31, 34, 37, 38, 41, 45, 49, 52, 53, 54, 57, 59, 63,
           66, 68;
        NR 51, 52, 54, 55, 58, 62, 63, 68;
        NP 1843, 44, 46, 49, 54, 58, 60, 62, 65, 70, 72, 76, 78, 79, 82,
           84, 86, 89, 92, 95, 98, 02, 03, 08, 10, 11, 14, 17, 21, 22, 23,
           25, 28, 29, 31, 33(2), 34, 35(2), 37, 38, 39, 40, 42, 43, 44,
           45, 46, 47, 48, 50, 52, 54, 57, 58, 62, 63(2), 66, 67, 69;
        NS 1879, 80, 83, 87, 89, 91, 94, 07, 08(2), 12, 15, 18, 20(2), 21,
           23, 24, 25, 26;
        PH 07, 08, 09, 12, 13, 15, 18, 19, 21, 22, 23, 25, 26, 27, 28, 29,
           31, 32, 33, 35, 36, 37, 38, 39, 40, 41, 43, 44, 45, 47, 48, 50,
           52, 53, 54, 56, 58, 59, 60, 61, 62, 63, 65, 66, 67, 68;
        PT 38, 39, 42, 45, 46, 48, 49, 51, 52, 54, 57, 60, 64, 65, 67;
        RC 23, 25, 29, 32, 35, 38, 42, 44, 46, 47, 50, 54, 57, 61, 62;
        SL 11, 13, 16, 18, 20, 22, 25, 27, 29, 30, 32, 33, 35, 38, 41, 44,
           50, 52, 54, 56, 57, 60, 61, 62, 64, 65, 67, 68;
        SF 13, 16, 18, 20, 25, 28, 30, 31, 35, 42, 45, 52, 53, 55, 58, 59,
           61, 63, 64, 65, 66, 69(2);
        SE 29, 30, 33, 37, 42, 44, 48, 51, 55, 59, 66, 68;
        UT 43, 48, 51, 52, 53, 58, 64, 66, 69;
        WA 35, 37, 41, 43, 45, 47, 49, 51, 53, 54, 56, 62, 63, 64;

10   -Allegro   CL 67;   SE 26
10   -Second movement   NR 53;   PH 18
10   -Allegretto   CL 27, 67;   HN 38;   LA 24;   PT 58;
10   -Fourth movement   MN 49

25   Symphony No 8 in F Op 93
        AT 48, 55, 61, 62;
        BA 41, 51, 58, 60, 64, 67;
        BN 1881, 82, 83, 84, 86, 88, 89, 90, 91, 92, 93, 96, 97, 99, 02,
           03(2), 04, 06, 09, 12, 14, 16, 18, 20, 22, 25, 26, 31, 33, 35,
           39, 46, 47, 51, 55, 61, 64, 67, 68, 69;
        BU 48, 52, 53, 58, 60;
        CH 1891, 94, 96, 98, 00, 01, 02, 03, 05, 08, 12, 13, 15, 18, 20, 22,
           24, 26, 28, 33, 36, 44, 45, 48, 53, 54, 57, 59, 61, 64, 65
        CT 96, 01, 03, 10, 13, 15, 17, 19, 22, 25, 26, 29, 31, 36, 39, 42,
           44, 46, 54, 60, 62, 67;
        CL 21, 28, 35, 37, 38, 40, 46, 50, 53, 55, 57, 58, 60, 62, 65;
        DA 46, 48, 51, 56, 60, 62, 67;
        DE 46, 49, 52, 54, 56, 61;
        DT 19, 21, 25, 28, 29, 43, 47, 51, 52, 55, 59, 62, 66, 68;
        HN 32, 45, 51, 54, 56, 62, 64;
        NA 37, 42, 49, 58, 62, 66;
        KC 37, 45, 51, 60, 63;
        LA 19, 23, 31, 37, 43, 46, 48, 52, 54, 55, 57, 62, 64;
        ML 63;
        MN 22, 23, 27, 33, 39, 42, 44, 47, 51, 54, 57, 60, 64, 67;
        NR 56, 62, 67, 69;

BEETHOVEN, L.v. (Cont.) Symphony No 8 (Cont.)
<pre>
        NP 1844, 52, 57, 65, 70, 77, 82, 86, 89, 94, 98, 02, 05, 07, 11,
            13, 15, 19, 21, 26, 29, 30, 32, 33, 34, 35, 38, 45, 46, 47, 48,
            49, 50, 51, 54, 56, 63, 66, 67;
        NS 1881, 84, 91, 97, 05, 07, 08, 12, 13, 22, 23, 27;
        PH 02, 10, 12, 14, 16, 17, 18, 19, 26, 28, 29, 36, 40, 44, 45, 46,
            48, 53, 57, 67;
        PT 37, 38, 40, 44, 50, 53, 58, 62, 64, 65, 67;
        RC 24, 31, 36, 41, 44, 47, 50, 56, 61, 67;
        SL 12, 17, 19, 20, 23, 28, 34, 38, 44, 45, 49, 56, 57, 61, 62, 65, 68;
        SF 18, 19, 24, 25, 29, 38, 40, 43, 46, 51, 52, 53, 55, 59, 64, 66, 69;
        SE 29, 34, 51, 61;
        UT 43, 49, 55, 59;
        WA 33, 37, 39, 47, 48, 50, 54, 56, 60, 62;

        -Allegretto   PH 42
        -Second and Fourth movements   DA 48
        -Second movement   NR 53;   PH 67
</pre>

70   Symphony No 9 in d Op 125
<pre>
        AT 67   BA 36, 48, 49, 56, 60, 63, 66;
        BN 1881, 82, 83, 85, 87, 92, 99, 03, 08, 09, 17, 23, 25, 28, 32, 35,
            44, 45, 46, 48, 53, 55, 56, 58, 61, 65, 68;
        BU 41, 42, 43, 50, 53, 59, 61, 63;
        CH 1892, 93, 95, 97, 00, 02, 03, 09, 11, 13, 26, 28, 39, 44, 49, 51,
            54, 58, 60, 63;
        CT 44, 50, 52, 59, 64, 66, 67;
        CL 23, 30, 34, 36, 38, 50, 51, 53, 55, 57, 60, 62, 64;
        DA 57, 59, 65, 67;
        DT 23, 52, 53, 61, 65;
        HN 41, 45, 48, 56, 64;
        NA 37, 44, 48, 66;
        KC 38, 48, 55, 60, 65;
        LA 25, 33, 34, 38, 48, 55, 57, 60, 64, 69;
        MN 23, 24, 26, 33, 39, 47, 50, 52, 55, 59, 63, 67;   NR 56, 64;
        NP 1845, 59, 67, 76, 80, 85, 89, 95, 01, 04, 09, 12, 15, 17, 27, 29,
            33, 35, 43, 45, 48, 58, 61, 63, 66, 67, 69;
        NS 1878, 79, 85, 88, 93, 08, 09, 18, 23, 24, 26;
        PH 01, 03, 06, 13, 19, 20, 28, 33, 36, 40, 42, 50, 53, 57, 62, 68;
        PT 38, 45, 50, 54, 56, 59, 60, 61, 63, 65, 67;
        RC 34, 38, 47, 52, 59, 67;
        SL 28, 34, 37, 54, 57, 59, 61, 63, 65, 67;
        SF 36, 50, 51, 56, 59, 63, 64, 66, 69;
        SE 37, 57, 67;
        UT 47, 54, 60, 67;
        WA 37, 43, 50, 53, 56, 60, 68;
</pre>

55   -Without Chorus BN 1885, 96, 97, 22;   CH 1899, 05, 24, 33;
            NP 1897, 23;   NS 07, 14;   SF 22, 46, 47, 49
6   -The Ode from Symph No 9 arr Stock   CH 43
12   -Second movement   MN 47

16   Terzetto, Tremante, empi tremate, for Winds, Drums and Str
            Op 116   CH 95

BEETHOVEN, L.v. (Cont.)
  6   Trio No 7 in B^b Archduke Trio Op 97: Andante Cantabile, arr Liszt
          CH 1891;   NP 30, 33

 15   Trio for Harpsichord, Flute, Bassoon in G   NS 07, 08, 23
  6   -Theme Andante   NS 10

 28   Trio for Oboe, Clarinet and Horn   NS 18

 25   Trio for two Oboes and English Horn in C Op 87   MN 26;   NS 07, 15
  6   -Allegro and Vivace   NS 10

 14   Wellington Siege Wellington's Victory or Battle Symphony Op 91
          BU 63;   KC 59, 69;   NS 04, 23

BECERRA, Gustavo   15   Symph No 1   PH 65;   WA 67
1925-   Chile

BECK, Conrad   20   Serenade for Fl, Clar and Str 1935: Largo   DE 54
1901-   Swiss 25   Symph No 3 for Str 1927   BN 27

BECKER, John J.   18   Symph Brevis   NP 58
1886-   US

BEDFORD, Herbert   16   Tone Poem: Hamadryad   SE 35
1867-1945   Eng

BEHNKE, Emil   4   My Heart Was Like a Swallow, Song   CT 03
1836-1892   Belg

BELLINI, Vincenzo   OPERAS
1801-1835   It   4   Beatrice di Tenda 1833: Aria Ma la Sola   NP 32
                     4   The Capulets and Montagues 1830: Aria Oh Quante
                              Volti   CH 18, 46
                     4   Norma 1831: Cavatina, Casta Diva   CH 1898;   CT 37;
                              DT 66;   MN 29, 46, 59;   NP 13
                     4   -Aria: Oh Remembrance   AT 61
                     4   -Aria unidentified   NS 1882, 16, 17;   PH 02
                     4   -Aria: Ah Per Sempre   NP 20;   SL 40
                     4   The Puritan, I puritani di Scozia 1835: Aria Qui la
                              voce soave   CT 58, 65;   DT 26, 62;   MN 30;
                              NP 10, 16;   PT 58;   SL 16
                     4   -Vien Diletto   DT 26, 62;   NP 01
                          The Sonambulist, La Sonnambula 1831
                     3   -Ah mon credea, Rondo   CT 39, 43, 48, 54, 64;
                              DE 57;   ML 64;   NP 02
                     4   -Ah mon grunge   CT 54, 64
                     4   -Aria   DA 30;   NP 05, 20;   NS 16
                     6   -Ballet   WA 55, 60
                     4   -Come per me sereno   MN 28
                          Arias, unidentified:
                     4   Liana, Nanna, a Liana   SF 38
                    20   The Romantic Age, Ballet   MN 42
                     8   Symph in d   NA 51

BEMBERG, Herman	5	Le Morte de Jeanne d'Arc, Cantata for Sopr, Chor,
1859-1931 Fr		and O 1886: Arioso CL 27
		Songs
	4	Aime-moi NS 90
	4	Nymphs and Fauns CH 1894
BENDER, Natasha	6	Soliloquy for Ob and O HN 56
1919- US		
BENDIX, Victor E.	25	Symph in d No 4 BN 06
1851-1926 Dan		
BENEDICT, Sir Julius	20	Concertino for 2 P and O Op 29 NP 09
1804-1885 Eng	4	The Wren KC 34
BEN-HAIM, Paul	20	V Conc NA 65; LA 68; SF 64
1897- Is	15	From Israel, Suite for O DE 57(2), 59
	4	-Fanfare only SL 57
	12	Pastorale Varies for Clar, Harp and Str BA 62
	26	The Sweet Psalmist of Israel NP 58
	30	Symph No 1 NA 58
	15	To the Chief Musician NA 60
BENJAMIN, Arthur	11	Cotillion, Suite, English Dance Tunes 1938
1893-1960 Austr		BA 42; CL 43; NA 56
	2	Jamaican Rumba 1938 BA 46; SL 45; WA 46
	11	North American Square Dance CT 55; NA 52;
		PT 54; SE 55
	6	Overt to an Italian Comedy 1937 AT 46, 47;
		BU 45; CH 41; CT 54; KC 48; ML 62;
		NA 45; NR 52; SF 41; WA 46
	11	Prelude to Holiday 1940 NA 40; SE 42
	23	Romantic Fantasy NA 57
BENNETT, Robert R.	8	Adagio Eroico, To the Memory of a Soldier 1933
1894- US		RC 36
	12	Classic Serenade for Str 1940 DT 48
	18	Eight Etudes for Symph O 1938 NP 42; PH 40
	8	Maria Malibran, Opera: Three Orch Fragments LA 34
	13	Nocturne and Appassionata, P and O 1941 PH 41
	7	Overt to an Imaginary Drama 1946 RC 47
	9	Overt, Mississippi NA 49
	28	Sights and Sounds 1929 BN 4 parts only 42
	17	Six Etudes for O 1936 CH 58; PT 42
	16	Symphon Story of Jerome Kern 1946 ML 60
	30	Symph Abraham Lincoln 1929 LA 32; PH 31
	18	Symph Four Freedoms 1943 CL 43; LA 43; PH 43
	22	Symph Stephen Foster PT 60
	20	Symph No 1 DE 67; PH 66
	20	Symph CH 62; LA 66
BENNETT, Richard R.	22	Symph No 1 DE 67; LA 66
1936 Brit	25	Symph No 2 NP 67

BENNETT, Sir	25	P Conc Op 19 No 4 BN 1883
William Sterndale	6	-Barcarole NP 29
1816-1875 Eng	10	Overt for Moore's Paradise and the Peri Op 42 NP 33
	10	Overt The Naiads Op 15 BN 1882, 89; NP 03, 10
	10	Overt Woodnymphs Op 20 NP 07, 10, 14
BEN-YOHANSEN,	8	Festive Overt NA 60
Asher		
1929-		
BENIOT, Piere	7	Charlotte Corday, Lyric Drama 1876 Overt CH 1892,
1834-1901 Belg		CT 1897
	5	-Entr'acte Valse CH 1892
	6	-Scene de bal CT 1896
	15	Symphon Poem for Fl and O 1866 BN 1894;
		CT 1899
BENTZON, Niels V.	12	Variazioni Brevi Op 75 NP 56
1919- Dan		
BEREZOWSKY, Nikolai	8	Christmas Festival Overt 1943 DE 46; KC 50;
1900-1953 Russ/US		NP 43
	23	Conc Lirico for C and O Op 19 BN 34
	22	Conc for Harp and O Op 31 PH 44
	24	Vla Conc Op 28 BN 41; CH 41
	20	V Conc Op 14 BN 31
	11	Hebrew Suite for O Op 3 NP 28
	9	Introd and Waltz for Str O Op 25 NP 40
	4	Soldier on the Town 1942 NP 43
	12	Sinfonietta Op 17 CH 32; CT 32; NP 33;
		PH 36; SL 37
	20	Symph No 1 Op 12 MN 36; PH 43; RC 38
	35	Symph No 2 Op 18 BN 33
	25	Symph No 3 Op 21 BN 36, 40, 45; RC 36; SL 44
	35	Symph No 4 Op 27 BN 43
	23	Toccata, Var and Finale for Str Quart and O Op 23
		BN 38; CT 55; CL 38; DE 59; PH 38;
		SF 39
	8	Ukranian Noel RC 44
BERG, Alban	26	V Conc 1935 AT 67; BA 69; BN 36, 59, 63;
1885-1935 Aust		BU 68; CH 38, 52, 64, 67, 68; CT 59; CL 40,
		66, 68; DT 65; HN 66; LA 45, 61, 66, 68;
		MN 44, 60, 67; NA 68; NP 49, 59, 62, 68;
		PH 37, 68; PT 52, 58, 66; SL 59, 63; SF 60;
		SE 61; UT 62;
	35	Lulu,Opera 1937: Symphon Suite BA 50; BN 34, 66;
		CH 35, 65; DA 61; HN 69; LA 59, 66; MN 53;
		NP 35, 64, 69; PH 62, 66; PT 64; SL 69
	3	-Song of Lulu CL 64
	6	-Adagio BA 65; BU 65; CL 64; KC 67;
		MN 63; NP 65
		-Ostinato BU 63; CL 64; MN 63; NP 65
	35	Lyric Suite for Str O 1925 BN 55; SL 54
		-3 mvts DT 67; MN 39, 68; NP 31

BERG, Alban (Cont.)

	18	Sieben Fruehe Lieder 1905 CH 66; SL 64
		-3 songs BU 63; NP 65
	10	Five Orchestral Songs, Altenberg text Op 4 SL 65
	18	Three Pieces for O Op 6 BN 68; CH 61, 68;
		CL 67; LA 68; ML 69; MN 67; NP 52, 60, 67;
		PH 64, 69; SL 64
	15	Der Wein: Concert Aria for Sopr and O 3 Poems of
		Baudelaire 1920 BN 51, 64; PT 56
	120	Wozzeck, Opera 1925 NP 51
		-Two Excerpts HN 58
	20	-Three Excerpts for Sopr and O BN 57, 63, 69;
		BU 63; CH 30, 56, 58, 66; CT 50; CL 69;
		DA 56; LA 53, 69; MN 47; NR 65; NP 30,
		65, 67; PH 30, 47; PT 44, 67; RC 65;
		SL 48, 66, 67; WA 49
		-Act III MN 64

BERGER, Arthur
1912-   US

	12	Ideas of Order BN 53
	15	Polyphony BN 64
	10	3 Pieces for Str 1944 PT 50

BERGER, Jean
1901   Ger/US

	20	Carribean Conc for Harmonica and O CT 46

BERGER, Theodore
1905-   Aust

	10	Legende von Prinzen Eugen 1942 BA 56
		Rondino giocoso Op 4 KC 66
	12	Rondo Ostenuto on a Spanish Theme for Winds and
		Percussion 1947 BA 60, 64; PT 59

BERLIOZ, Hector
1803-1869   Fr

	7	Béatrice et Bénédict Opera, 1860: Overt BN 49, 58;
		CH 34, 38, 48, 53, 54, 56, 57, 60, 62; CL 48, 62;
		DE 64; MN 48; NR 54, 60; NP 51, 56, 64, 68;
		NS 03; PH 35, 57; PT 47, 56, 63; RC 33;
		SF 52, 58, 61, 66, 69; SE 67; WA 61, 63
	80	-Concert Version LA 69(2)
	5	-Duet, Act II NS 1881, 03
	11	Benvenuto Cellini, Opera Op 23: Overt BA 66;
		BN 1887, 88, 90, 92, 94, 96, 98, 00, 07, 09, 11,
		12, 16, 17, 20, 22, 25, 27, 39, 58, 64, 67;
		BU 51, 68; CH 1893, 98, 02, 04, 05, 07, 09,
		12, 16, 17, 18, 21, 22, 23, 26, 36, 40, 46, 53,
		57, 58, 59, 64; CT 06, 13, 22, 25, 30, 35, 46,
		54, 56, 60; CL 31, 37, 52, 55, 58, 63, 67;
		DA 53, 60; DE 57, 64, 68; DT 18, 28, 36, 41,
		54, 63, 67; HN 35, 39, 41, 60, 63; NA 30, 39,
		54, 58, 62, 69; KC 54, 67; LA 21, 36, 38, 60;
		ML 63; MN 32, 36, 39, 45, 49, 58, 60; NR 59,
		62; NP 1884, 91, 98, 02, 03, 12, 15, 24, 32, 33,
		36, 37, 38, 39, 46, 52, 55, 60, 66(2), 69; NS 1890,
		92, 03, 04, 06, 09, 11, 18; PH 07, 08, 09, 10,
		11, 12, 13, 15, 27, 32, 36, 49, 54, 66; PT 38,
		42, 45, 46, 55, 58; RC 24, 31, 32, 51, 63;
		SL 12, 17, 24, 31, 53, 56, 62, 66, 68; SF 18,
		23, 30, 42, 46, 58; SE 29, 48, 60; UT 60;
		WA 50, 57, 64

BERLIOZ, H. (Cont.)   Benvenuto Cellini (Cont.)
   4   -Air from Act III   NS 03
   5   -Cavatina from Act I   NS 03

  10   La Captive, Reverie Op 12 for Voice and O   CH 1891;   NP 02, 07,
            13, 41;   NS 1878, 94, 22;   PH 18, 26

   7   Le Corsaire, Overt Op 21   AT 69;   BA 57, 67;   BN 1894, 16, 49,
            58, 63, 67;   BU 66;   CH 1896, 33, 37, 48, 56, 58, 61, 65;
            CT 15, 21, 29, 32, 38, 63, 69;   CL 55, 62, 69;   DE 63, 64, 66;
            DT 46, 57, 66;   HN 53, 54, 56, 68;   NA 55, 64, 68;   KC 38;
            LA 51, 53, 55;   ML 63, 65, 69;   MN 38, 65;   NR 57, 67, 69;
            NP 11, 25, 37, 56;   NS 1887, 27;   PH 15, 59, 65;   PT 40, 59,
            64;   RC 28, 69;   SL 62, 67;   SF 47, 50, 51, 65, 68;   SE 54;
            UT 66;   WA 49, 51, 62, 69

 120   La Damnation de Faust   Cantata, Solo Voices, Chor and O Op 24
            Complete   BA 53;   BN 1882, 97, 01, 06, 11, 12, 25, 27, 34, 53,
            54;   CH 46;   CL 39;   DA 65;   DT 54;   NA 62;   LA 55, 68;
            NP 67;   NS 1879, 80, 82, 85;   PH concert form 58;   PT 50;
            RC 2 cuts 48;   SL 36;   SF 51, 54, 60;   SE 55

   3   -Ballet of Sylphs   AT 65;   BA 46, 49;   BN 1886, 92, 93, 94,
            98, 19, 23, 33, 39, 43, 49, 63;   CH 1891, 95, 96, 97, 99, 00,
            02, 03, 04, 07, 09, 11, 12, 14, 18, 19, 22, 23, 24, 39, 41, 53,
            59;   CT 1895, 96, 99, 11, 17, 31, 36, 46, 51, 58;   CL 25, 36,
            48, 50, 53, 57, 58, 61, 65;   DA 32;   DE 46, 51, 59;   DT 22,
            29, 45, 51, 53, 57, 64;   HN 33, 38, 49;   NA 35;   KC 57, 64;
            MN 31, 34, 43, 47, 52, 66;   NP 04, 14, 22, 23, 26, 28, 39, 42,
            50, 51, 53, 60, 64;   NS 03, 23, 24;   PH 06; 12, 13, 17, 18, 19,
            21, 24, 25, 27, 29, 51;   PT 44, 47, 49;   RC 23, 24, 35, 40;
            SL 10, 54, 55;   SF 17, 27, 48;   SE 26, 52;   UT 49;   WA 32,
            42, 57

   4   -Chanson Gothique   NS 22
   6   -Chorus of Soldiers and Students   CT 61
  20   -Excerpts   DA 27, 46, 52, 55;   DE 64, 68;   DT 48, 69;   KC 53,
            62;   LA 19, 39, 45;   MN 53, 57, 63;   NR 53, 57, 63;   NS 09,
            18;   SL 15, 21, 29, 31, vocal excerpts 48, 49

   5   -Mephistopheles Serenade   AT 68;   BA 46, 49;   CH 1897;   CT 55;
            CL 68;   DA 69;   DT 17;   NA 48;   KC 64;   MN 46;   NS 24;
            PH 12, 13, 15, 17, 18, 19, 24, 25, 27, 29, 51

   8   -Minuet, Will'o'the Wisp   BA 46, 49;   BN 1886, 92, 93, 94, 98,
            19, 23, 33, 39, 43, 49, 63;   CH 1891, 95, 96, 97, 99, 00, 02,
            03, 04, 07, 09, 11, 12, 14, 18, 19, 22, 23, 24, 39, 41, 53, 59;
            CT 1896, 99, 03, 11, 31, 36, 39, 46, 51, 58;   CL 25, 36, 48, 50,
            53, 57, 58, 61, 65;   DE 46, 51, 59;   DT 51, 53, 57, 64;   HN 33,
            38, 49;   NA 35;   KC 57, 64;   MN 31, 34, 43, 47, 52, 66;
            NP 04, 14, 22, 23, 26, 28, 39, 42, 50, 51, 53, 60, 64;   NS 03,
            23, 24;   PH 12, 13, 17, 18, 19, 21, 24, 25, 27, 29, 51;   PT 44,
            47, 49;   RC 23, 40;   SL 10, 54, 55;   SF 17, 27, 48;   SE 52;
            WA 57

BERLIOZ, H. (Cont.)   La Damnation de Faust (Cont.)
  4   -Rackoczy March   BA 42, 46, 49;   BN 1886, 92, 93, 94, 98, 19,
           23, 33, 39, 43, 49, 63;   BU 49;   CH 1891, 92, 94, 95, 96(3),
           27, 99(2), 00, 01, 02, 03, 04, 06, 07, 09, 11, 12, 14, 18, 19,
           22, 23, 24, 33, 39, 41, 49, 53, 59;   CT 1896, 97, 99, 03, 07,
           11, 17, 18, 20, 27, 29, 31, 35, 36, 37, 40, 45, 46, 51, 58;
           CL 22, 25, 26, 27, 29, 30, 36, 48, 50, 53, 57, 58, 61, 65;
           DE 45, 46, 51, 59;   DT 17, 22, 29, 37, 51, 53, 57, 64;   HN 16,
           33, 38, 47, 49;   NA 30;   KC 35, 37, 57, 64;   MN 22, 23, 26,
           31, 34, 43, 47, 52, 56, 59, 66;   NP 04, 11, 14, 17, 18, 19, 22,
           23, 24, 26, 28, 30, 39, 42, 50, 51, 53, 54, 56, 60, 64;   NS 03,
           23, 24;   PH 12, 13, 17, 18, 19, 21, 22, 24, 25, 27, 29, 51;
           PT 41, 44, 47, 48, 49, 63;   RC 23, 24, 26, 29, 35, 40;   SL 10,
           28, 54, 55, 60, 61;   SF 17, 21, 48, 62;   SE 52;   UT 49;
           WA 32, 34, 36, 43, 57
           -Rose's Aria   BA 46, 49;   NR 68;   PH 51
           -Song of the Flea   BA 46, 49;   PH 51
           -Suite   SF 54

 93   L'Enfance du Christ, Cantata Op 25   Complete AT 60;   BA 59;
           BN 53, 56;   CL 59;   DE 56;   DT 57;   HN 56;   NA 59;   KC 66;
           MN 58;   PH 61;   SL 59;   SF 54, 60, 68;   UT 67;   WA 59
  5   -Epilogue   CT 50
  8   -Farewell of the Shepherds   SF 38, 47;   WA 46
 16   -The Flight into Egypt   CH 36, 45;   MN 43;   NP 07;   SF 38, 47
 10   -Herod's Dream   CT 50
  4   -Joseph, Mary, Hear our Voices   CT 50
  5   -Now Take thy Rest   CT 50
  4   -0, My Son   CT 50
  4   -0, My Soul, Bow Down   CT 50
  4   -Overt   DT 54;   SF 38, 47
  8   -Prologue   CT 50;   DT 54;   MN 43,   SF 38, 47
  4   -The Repose of the Holy Family   CT 50;   MN 32;   NS 1883;
           PH 37;   SF 38;   WA 37
  7   -Serenade, for 2 Fl and Harp   NS 1883
  4   -Thou Must Leave Thy Lowly Dwelling, De vant la Maison   CT 50;
           KC 60, 64;   NR 68
  8   -Trio of the Ishmalites, Op 25   DT 54, 60;   BN 66

 52   Symphonie Fantastique in C Op 14   AT 57, 68;   BA 52(2), 54, 57(2),
           60, 63, 69;   BN 1885, 87, 90, 93, 94, 97, 00, 04, 08, 17, 19, 22,
           25, 29, 32, 36, 38, 40, 43, 45, 47, 50, 51, 54, 59, 61, 63, 68;
           BU 45, 53, 55, 66;   CH 1892, 01, 03, 07, 33, 39, 41, 43, 45, 46,
           47, 49, 51, 53, 56, 59, 64, 67, 69;   CT 1897, 02, 04, 05, 12, 19,
           36, 45, 46, 55, 59, 62, 64, 66;   CL 23, 32, 40, 47, 48, 51, 53,
           55, 59, 64, 66;   DA 50, 54, 56, 60, 63, 65, 68, 69;   DE 60, 63,
           65, 67, 69;   DT 19, 31, 36, 40, 51, 53, 56, 59, 63, 68;   HN 50, 51,
           52, 55, 58, 60, 63, 65, 67, 69;   NA 45, 58, 63;   KC 45, 56, 59,
           63, 66, 68;   LA 30, 33, 36, 46, 49, 52, 54, 56, 59, 63, 66(2);
           MN 22, 32, 37, 40, 46, 50, 52, 55, 60, 64, 68;   NR 51, 52, 55, 57,
           61, 66;   NP 1865, 68, 84, 98, 1903, 09, 13, 18, 28, 30, 33, 37,
           39, 41, 42, 43, 47, 49, 52, 54, 56, 58, 60, 62, 67, 68;   NS 1878,
           81, 90, 05, 07, 09, 12, 14, 24;   PH 02, 07, 09, 10, 11, 13, 26,
           32, 35, 38, 50, 51, 53, 54, 57, 58, 59, 62, 64, 65, 67, 68;
           PT 46, 48, 49, 53, 57, 60, 62, 63, 64, 66;   3 mvts 27, 41;

BERLIOZ, H. (Cont.) Symphonie Fantastique (Cont.)
           RC 34, 42, 47, 53, 55, 58, 68;   SL 10, 18, 28, 38, 46, 47, 48, 50,
           52, 55, 56, 61, 63, 67;   SF 19, 36, 38, 43, 47, 49, 54, 56, 60,
           61, 64, 68;   SE 49, 57, 64, 69;   UT 52, 59, 65;   WA 36, 50, 53,
           55, 59, 64, 68
    5   -March to the Scaffold   CT 32;   NA 52;   NR 69;   RC 24, 27; WA 41
    5   -Scene in the Fields   CT 32;   RC 27
    5   -The Ball   WA 41
    5   -Waltz   NR 69
    5   -Witches Sabbath   CT 32, 34, 40;   NA 52;   RC 27

   10   Les Francs-Juges, Overt Op 3   BA 69;   BN 02, 17;   CH 94;   CT 44,
           66;   CL 68;   DA 63;   MN 68;   NP 1845, 55, 60, 65, 74, 79, 68;
           PH 68;   PT 64

    8   Funeral March for the Final Scene of Hamlet, 1848   CH 34;   DT 47;
           LA 36;   RC 34;   SF 57, 62

   47   Harold en Italie, Symph No 3 with solo Vla Op 16   AT 56;   BA 54, 66;
           BN 1883, 85, 88, 91, 95, 98, 03, 06, 10, 14, 19, 41, 42, 43, 44, 46,
           51, 53, 57, 61;   BU 65;   CH 1891, 00, 19, 43, 45, 48, 54, 61;
           CT 1898, 06, 19, 44, 51, 63;   CL 50, 54, 68;   DA 68;   DE 52;
           DT 45, 59;   HN 62, 69;   NA 64;   LA 25, 35, 46, 61, 65;   ML 63;
           MN 25, 38, 41, 44, 51;   NR 50;   NP 1880, 04, 07, 11, 29, 34, 53,
           61, 65;   NS 1887, 93, 03, 09, 17, 18, 20, 24;   PH 18, 42, 57, 64;
           PT 44, 54, 61, 67;   RC 66;   SL 16, 51, 66;   SF 44, 50, 65;
           SE 59;   UT 58;   WA 48
   13   -Pilgrim's March   CH 1896;   MN with Prayer 30;   NS 1888

   12   Le Roi Lear Overt in c Op 4   AT 62;   BN 1883, 86, 93, 99, 04, 17,
           18, 66;   CH 1892, 97, 01, 06, 11, 14, 15, 21, 22, 27, 40, 58, 64;
           CT 1897, 16, 19;   CL 52;   HN 58;   MN 42, 45;   NP 1846, 53, 64,
           69, 79, 83, 85, 94, 13, 42, 68;   NS 1878, 87;   PH 03, 58;
           PT 62;   RC 30, 59;   SL 09

   25   Lélio, ou Le Retour à la vie, Sequal to the Symphonie Fantastique,
           Monodrama for actors, solo Voices and O Op 14^b   PT 62

    6   La Mort de Cléopâtre, for Voice and O   Overt 1829   NP 61
    4   -Scene lyrique   AT 63;   NP 61, 68

   32   Nuits d'été for Sopr and O Op 7   BN 54;   CL 67;   DE 59;   DT 60;
           HN 69;   SF 67
    5   No 1 Absence   CH 62;   CT 1896;   DE 46;   NP 1876
    5   No 2 Villanelle   CH 62;   DE 46
    5   No 3 Le Spectre de la rose   CH 62;   CT 18;   NP 41;   NS 13
    5   No 4 Sur les lagunes, On the Lagoons   CH 03, 62;   NS 1890, 03
    5   No 5 Au cimetière, In the Cemetery   CH 62
    5   No 6 L'Ile inconnue, The Unknown Isle   CH 62;   NP 1886

   92   Requiem messe des morts for Tenor, Chor and O Op 5   AT 69;   BN 50,
           58;   BU 59;   CL 58;   MN 57;   NP 68;   PH 63;   SL 64;   SF 49,
           57, 62, 66;   UT 68
    5   -Sanctus   NS 03

BERLIOZ, H. (Cont.)

11   Reverie et Caprice for V and O Op 8   NP 58

12   Rob Roy, Overt   BN 09, 13, 15;   CH 00;   MN 47;   NP 50;   PT 52

8   Le Carnaval romain, Overt Op 9   AT 52, 60, 64, 66, 67;   BA 26, 52,
    55, 63;   BN 1882, 85(2), 86, 92, 94, 97, 00, 02, 05, 06, 08, 10,
    11, 12, 15, 18, 21, 24, 26, 28, 38, 55, 64;   BU 55, 57, 59, 61,
    63, 68, 69;   CH 1893, 95, 99, 01, 02, 03, 05, 08, 09, 12, 16, 17,
    18, 20, 21, 22, 24, 25, 26, 27, 30, 33, 40, 45, 55, 57, 58, 61, 62;
    CT 1896, 13, 15, 16, 17, 18, 26, 28, 29, 31, 32, 41, 45, 46, 48,
    57, 59, 61, 64, 68;   CL 19, 23, 26, 35, 40, 45, 46, 49, 51, 56,
    57, 59, 61, 63, 64, 69;   DA 26, 29, 35, 38, 49, 51, 54, 55, 57,
    58, 66;   DE 45, 48, 49, 53, 54, 55, 57, 63, 65, 67;   DT 15, 18,
    27, 28, 31, 33, 35, 37, 40, 44, 51, 54, 56, 61, 65;   HN 45, 49,
    51, 52, 55, 57, 61, 64, 67;   NA 36, 38, 42, 44, 48, 56, 64, 65, 68;
    KC 41, 48, 52, 56, 58, 62, 69;   LA 23, 32, 36, 37, 41, 45, 61;
    ML 61, 64, 67;   MN 22, 24, 27, 29, 31, 33, 35, 41, 44, 46, 48(2),
    50, 51, 55, 57, 59, 61, 66, 68;   NR 52, 53, 55, 57, 60, 64;
    NP 1861, 64, 66, 70, 74, 78, 00, 09, 13, 14, 15, 17, 20, 21, 22,
    26, 34, 36, 37, 38, 42, 45, 50, 51, 53, 54, 52(2), 58, 69;
    NS 1880, 84, 89, 96, 03, 14, 16, 22, 23;   PH 02, 04, 05, 06, 07,
    08, 09, 10, 11, 13, 15, 16, 17, 18, 20(2), 24, 27, 28, 29, 30, 31,
    33(2), 35, 39, 43, 47, 49, 50, 52, 53, 56;   PT 39, 41, 48, 49, 50,
    51, 54, 58, 61;   RC 23, 25, 27, 31, 32, 33, 37, 43, 46, 56, 60, 63;
    SL 14, 18, 23, 25, 27, 28, 31, 33, 35, 39, 40, 45, 49, 52, 55, 65,
    68;   SF 15, 17, 29, 35, 38, 49, 51, 52, 60, 66, 68;   SE 33, 41,
    47, 49, 51, 62;   UT 41, 49, 56, 63;   WA 33, 36, 39, 43, 44, 48,
    49, 52, 54, 55, 59

95   Roméo et Juliette, Symph No 4 Soli, Chor and O Op 17;   Complete
    BN 52, 53, 60, 67;   BU 50, 64;   CH 59, 69,   CL 61;   LA 51;
    MN 54;   NR 61;   NP 25;   NS 1881, 86, 91;   PH 08, 14;   PT 52,
    59;   SF 48;   WA 61
6   -The Combat   CH 27;   RC 52
6   -Concert and Ball   CH 1891, 92, 95, 98, 00, 03, 06, 17, 27, 35;
    CT 1897, 99, 05, 14, 40, 46;   NP 1866;   NS 23, 26;   RC 35, 52
20   -Excerpts   BN 1887, 88, 93, 95, 99, 02, 15, 17, 18, 20, 21, 23,
    42;   DA 50, 62;   LA 66;   NP 15, 27, 31, 41, 52, 55, 68;
    NS 1894, 08, 09, 15, 19;   PH 49, 55;   RC 67;   SL 13, 15, 19, 35;
    SF 61;   SE 50, 62;   WA 67
8   -Fête au Capulets   BA 58, 60;   CH 63;   CT 1897, 99, 05, 14, 40,
    46;   DT 55, 59;   NP 10, 42, 59, 60, 66;   NS 1896, 23, 26;
    RC 35, 52, 58;   WA 51, 60
20   -Love Scene   CH 1894, 99, 03, 27, 63;   CT 14, 18;   CL 50;
    DA 62;   DE 64;   HN 63;   MN 43;   NP 1872, 77, 80, 02, 10;
    NS 23, 26;   PH 02, 14, 56;   RC 52, 56;   SL 56;   SF 37, 40;
    WA 51, 60
8   -Overt   BA 58;   CH 63;   NS 1881, 86;   RC 58
6   -Romeo in Solitude   CH 35, 63;   CT 1897, 99, 05, 14, 40, 46;
    CL 50;   RC 35, 52;   SF 37, 40;   WA 51, 60
8   -Scherzo, Queen Mab   BA 38, 58;   CH 1892, 94, 99, 05, 14, 22,
    27, 35, 49, 63;   CT 19, 23, 29, 61;   CL 50;   DA 50, 62;
    DE 59;   LA 23, 33, 37;   MN 24, 34, 35, 43;   NP 10, 29, 32, 37;

BERLIOZ, H. (Cont.) Roméo et Juliette, Scherzo (Cont.)
          NS 23, 26;   PH 02, 04, 23, 34, 39, 41, 49;   PT 40;   RC 35, 52,
          58;   SF 37, 40

   8   Song: Le Cinq Mais for Chor and O Op 6   NS 1880

  35   Symphonie funèbre et triumphale for Chor, Str and Military Band
          Op 15   NP 64;   SE 65

  49   Te Deum Op 22   PH 64

   4   Les Troyens, Opera 1856: The Greeks have disappeared   CH 01, 03,
   4   -Aria   PH 01
   4   -Aria, Unhappy King   CH 01, 03
   5   -Dido's Lament   KC 39
   6   -March   BA 56;   CH 53, 56;   CT 53;   DT 58;   HN 49;   NR 56;
          PH 55;   RC 45;   WA 49
   6   -Overt   SF 44
  10   -Quintet, Septet and Chor   NP 1876
  10   -Royal Hunt and Storm   AT 67;   BA 68;   BN 18, 27, 52, 58, 62;
          BU 67;   CH 69;   CT 53;   CL 32;   DA 55;   DT 61;   NP 27, 31,
          PH 55;   RC 34;   SF 54;   SE 41;   WA 52

BERNARD, Emile   15   V Conc in g   BN 1885
1843-1902   Fr

BERNAT, Robert   8   In Memoriam   JFK Passacaglia   PT 66
                US

BERNAT, Saul   12   Symph No 1: Scherzo   NA 35
1907-   US

BERNERS, Lord Gerald   7   Fantasie Espagnol 1919   CT 27;   NS 21;   PH 26
1883-1950   Brit   25   The Triumph of Neptune, Ballet 1926: Suite   LA 51;
                            NR 56;   NP 35;   PH 28, 51;   SF 51;   WA 51

BERNSTEIN, Leonard   30   Age of Anxiety Symph No 2 1949   BN 48, 67;   BU 63;
1918-   US   DT 57;   HN 62;   NA 62;   MN 67;   NP 49;
                            PT 49;   UT 68;   WA 54, 69
                    4   Candide, Operetta, Overt   AT 58, 68;   BA 68;
                            BU 63;   CT 61;   CL 64;   DT 59;   HN 62;   NA 62;
                            KC 61, 63, 69;   NR 61, 65;   NP 56;   RC 69;
                            SE 57, 61;   UT 58, 65, 66, 69;   WA 58, 64
                    6   -Glitter and Be Gay   CT 64
                   10   Chichester Psalms   BU 69;   CL 65;   NP 66;   UT 67
                   21   Facsimile Suite 1946   RC 46
                20-25   Fancy Free Suite,Ballet 1944   DE 51
                   23   Jeremiah Symph No 1 1942   AT 63, 69;   BN 43;
                            NR 66;   NP 43, 68;   PH 64;   PT 43, 69;
                            RC 45;   SL 44;   SF 48
                   43   Kaddish Symph No 3   BA 64;   BN 63;   BU 65;
                            NP 63;   SL 64;   SF 64;   SE 65
                    8   The Lark: French Choruses   BU 63
                    5   -Latin Choruses   BU 63
                   10   On the Town, Three Dance Episodes 1944   RC 45

BERNSTEIN, L. (Cont.)
	23	On the Waterfront, Symphon Suite NP 59; SF 65 WA 65
	4	Serenade for V and O after Plato's Symposium BN 54; CL 66; MN 65; NP 65, 67; PT 55
	22	West Side Story, Symphon Dances BU 63; NP 62
	4	-Fete AT 63

BERWALD, Franz
1796-1868   Swed
	10	Dramatic Overt CH 19
	28	Symphon in C Singuliere No 5 CH 52; CT 58, 64; MN 64, 68; RC 57; SE 64
	30	Symph No 6 in E^b CT 68

BETTINELLI, Bruno
1913-   It
	6	Carovane Notturne HN 31

BEVERSDORF, Thomas
1924-   US
	10	Conc Grosso PT 49
	9	Mexican Portrait NA 51
	9	New Frontiers HN 52

BEZANSON, Philip
1916-   US
	22	P Conc NP 53

BIBER, Heinrich Von
1644-1704   Ger
	7	Sonata No 6 arr Marquardt RC 42

BILOTTI, Anton
1906-   US
	30	P Conc CT 39

BINDER, Abraham Wolfe
1895-   US
	15	Concertante for Str O 1938 DT 48
	20	Holy Land Impressions, Symphon Suite No 1 1927 DT 32

BINGHAM, Seth
1882-   US
	13	Passacaglia for O 1918 BN 20

BINKERD, Gordon
1916-   US
	23	Symph No 1 SL 58
	20	Symph No 4 SL 63

BIRD, Arthur
1856-1923   US
	30	Symph No 1 in A NS 1886
	15	2 Episodes for O BN 1889

BISCHOFF, Hermann
1868-1936   Ger
	60	Symph No 1 Op 16 in E BN 07(2), 12; CH 09

BISHOP, Sir Henry
1786-1855   Eng
	4	Lo, Hear the Gentle Lark DE 57; NA 52; SE 36
	4	Love Has Eyes SE 60
	4	Pretty Mocking Bird, Song arr La Forge CT 43

BIZET, Georges
1838-1875   Fr
	14	L'arlésienne, Incidental Music 1872 Suite No 1 BA 40; BN 1892, 94, 97, 02, 09, 13, 15; CH 1894, 99, 03; CT 09, 17; CL 18, 27, 43, 52; DA 34, 56; DT 14, 17; HN 45; NA 31, 32; KC 35; NR 57; NP 10, 12, 13, 14, 21, 24, 55; NS 19; PH 06, 12, 16, 19, 24, 28; RC 52; SF 11, 60, 62; SE 42, 49; UT 42, 43; WA 31

BIZET, G. (Cont.) L'arlésienne, Suite No 1 (Cont.)
    8   -Minuet and Adagio   CT 1896;   WA 37, 39, 47
    6   -Selections   MN 44, 67, 68;   NR 60;   SE 42, 49
   17   Suite No 2   CH 12;   DA 34, 56;   HN 31, 35, 40;   NA 36;   NR 57;
            PH 22, 24, 25;   RC 52;   SF 62;   UT 42, 43, 61;   WA 34
    4   -Carillon   WA 37, 39, 41
    3   -Fandango   WA 37, 39, 47
    4   -Farandole   BA 28;   CT 96;   WA 37, 39, 47
    3   -Minuet   BA 28;   CT 96;   WA 37, 39, 47
    6   -Pastorale   CT 96
    8   -Selections fr Suites No 1 and 2   MN 44, 67;   NR 60;   SE 42, 49

   30   Carmen, Opera 1874: Concert Version   BU 50, 60;   DT 59;   NA Act IV
            50, 55
    4   -Arias, unidentified DE three 58, 61;   KC 44, 61;   PT 64
    5   -Card Song Act II   KC 35, 41;   SL 61;   WA 35
    8   -Duet Act IV   AT 64
             -Excerpts   SF 43
    4   -Flower Song, La fleur que tu m'avais jete   AT 64;   CL 27;
            DT 46;   HN 46;   SL 14, 15, 24;   WA 33
    4   -Gypsy Dance, Dance Boheme Act II BA 42;   CT 55;   NS 14;   RC 42;
            SL 61;   UT 56;   WA 35, 64
    5   -Habenara   AT 64;   BA 42, 59;   DA 28, 30;   DE 63;   HN 41;
            NA 41;   KC 41;   SL 61;   WA 35, 36, 64
    8   -Guard Mount Act I   BA 42
    3   -Intermezzo Act IV   CT 55;   RC 42, 43, 44
    4   -Micaela's Aria, Je dis que rien Act III   CH 12;   CT 13, 28;
            CL 19;   DA 25;   DT 17;   HN 42;   MN 41;   RC 25;   SL 14, 45
    4   -Prelude Act I   DE 58;   HN 39, 42;   KC 41;   RC 44;   NA 37;
            WA 35, 37, 39, 47, 64
    2   -Prelude Act II   HN 39, 42;   RC 44;   WA 35, 64
    3   -Prelude Act III   HN 39;   WA 35
    2   -Prelude Act IV   HN 39;   WA 35
    4   -Seguidilla   BA 42, 43;   CT 49;   CL 21;   DA 29;   KC 35;
            NS 1888, 21;   UT 56;   WA 35, 46, 64
    5   -Smuggler's Chorus, Écoute, Compagnon, Act III   DA 27
             -Torreadors' Chorus Act II   AT 42;   DA 26, 27;   HN 13, 36;
            MN 66;   PT 51;   UT 56

    9   Children's Games, Jeux d'enfants, Suite Op 22   BN 1896, 00;
            CH 1898;   MN 47;   NP 55;   PT 62;   RC 28

   20   P Conc No 2   MN 65

   11   Djamileh, One Act Opera 1871: Egyptian Dance   CH 1895
    7   -Overt   BU 56

    4   Jolie Fille de Perth, Opera 1866: Aria, Quand la flamme d'amour
            CT 26;   PH 11
   16   -Suite SF 40

   12   Patrie, Overt Op 19   BN 1895, 07, 18;   CH 1896, 99, 03, 17, 19, 26,
            45;   CT 21;   CL 22;   DT 57;   LA 29;   NP 03;   PT 44   RC 28;
            SL 21, 24;   SE 39, 43

BIZET, G. (Cont.)
    4   Pearl Fishers: Opera, Les Pêcheurs de Perles 1863: Aria of Leila
             CL 20;   DA 35;   PH 11;   PT 37
    4   -Cavatina, me Voile Seule   CH 20, 23;   CT 20;   DT 20
    4   -Je crois entendre   PT 37;   SL 41
    4   -Quand La flamme   SL 20
    4   -Serenade   NS 22

    30   Roma: Symphon Suite also called Symphony, or Suite No 3 1868
             BN 1883;   CT 1895, 06;   CL 54;   NP 10
             -Allegretta Vivace   CH 01
    6   -Scherzo   PH 24

         Songs
    4   Agnus Dei   BN 42;   CT 43;   DE 47, 48;   NA 48;   NS 21
    4   Ouevre ton Coeur, Spanish Serenade   CT 45;   HN 43;   WA 38, 45
    4   Tarantelle 1872   NS 1882
    4   Vieille Chanson 1865   NS 05

    28   Symph in C No 1 1855   AT 48, 50, 60;   BA 58;   BN 49, 63, 66, 68;
             BU 66;   CH 42, 45, 47, 52, 58, 65;   CT 35, 61;   CL 44, 51, 55,
             65, 68;   DA 64;   DE 51, 56, 61, 65;   DT 44, 63, 68;   HN 49, 58;
             NA 48, 56, 59;   KC 52, 57, 66;   LA 40, 58;   ML 66;   MN 42, 52,
             65;   NR 51, 53, 56, 67;   NP 40, 44, 48, 50, 53, 55, 57, 62, 64;
             PH 55(2), 58, 60, 66;   PT 51;   RC 35, 58, 62;   SL 50, 51, 53,
             55;   SF 69;   SE 50, 55, 65;   UT 54;   WA 38, 59, 67

BLACHER, Boris   10   Capriccio for O Op 4   DT 37
1903-   Ger   11   Concertante Musik Op 10   CH 67;   DA 62;   DE 57;
                                LA 59;   NR 67;   PH 68
                      20   Orchestral Fantasy Op 51   HN 60;   PT 57
                      10   Music for Cleveland Op 53   CL 53, 57, 62
                      14   Orchestral Ornament Op 44   NP 53
                      16   Var on a Theme of Paganini Op 26   AT 62;   BN 62;
                                CH 53, 63;   CT 58;   CL 53;   DA 53;   DE 56;
                                DT 58;   KC 62, 63;   LA 61;   MN 54, 64;
                                NP 54;   PH 55;   SL 58;   SF 55, 62;   SE 56,
                                67;   UT 56, 67;   WA 53, 57, 62
                      25   Symph Op 12   PH 68

BLACKWOOD, Easley   15   Clar Conc Op 13   CT 64
1933-   US   10   Symphon Fantasy Op 17   CT 65;   CL 66;   NA 65
                      30   Symph No 1 Op 3   BN 57, 58, 59;   CT 61;   CL 59;
                                LA 59
                      24   Symph No 2   CL 60;   NA 63

BLISS, Sir Arthur   20   Checkmate, Dances from Ballet 1937   NP 39
1891-   Eng   20   Color Symph 1922   BN 23;   CT 24;   SF 40
                      30   P Conc 1938   CH 42;   LA 46;   NP 59
                      12   Conc 2 P and O 1920   BN 24;   CH 24;   CT 39;
                                NP 39;   PH 24
                      10   Hymn to Apollo 1926   CT 26
                      12   Introd and Allegro 1926   BN 34;   PH 28
                      14   Mélée Fantastique 1921   CH 25;   CL 26, 28;
                                LA 24;   PH 24;   SL 23
                      10   Pyanepsion   CH 36

BLITZSTEIN, Marc	12	Lear: a Study NP 57
1905- US	52	The Airborne Symph 1943 NP 66
	12	Symphon Poem, Freedom Morning 1943 PH 43

BLOCH, André	8	Au Benguinage BU 55
1873-1960 Fr	18	Kaa, Symphon Poem after Kipling's Jungle Book DT 57

BLOCH, Ernst
1880-1959   Swiss/US

47   America, Epic Rhaps 1926   BN 28(2), 38;   CH 28(2);
    CT 28;   CL 28;   NA 37, 54;   LA 28;   MN 28, 29,
    45;   NP 28;   PH 28;   RC 45

55   Avodath Hakodesh, Sacred Service for Baritone,
    Chor and O 1933   AT 57, 61, 69;   CL 65;   DT 68;
    KC 65;   NP 59

13   Baal Shem for V and O, Three Poems of Chassidic
    life 1923   AT 54;   BN 50;   CT 52
    -No 2 Nigen   LA 53

39   Conc Symphonique for P and O 1948   BN 52;   SF 51

35   V Conc 1938   BN 39;   CH 40;   CL 38;   NA 60;
    NP 57;   RC 60;   SF 44, 51, 61

22   Conc Grosso No 1 for Str with P obbligato 1925
    AT 60;   BN 25;   CH 25, 29, 36, 50;   CT 25;
    CL 33, 63;   DT 29;   NA 43;   KC 52;   LA 25, 26,
    29;   NR 54, 64;   NP 32, 47;   PH 25, 29;
    SF 25;   UT 59, 67;   WA 67

18   Conc Grosso No 2 for Str O and Str Quart 1952
    BN 53;   CT 59;   CL 55;   DE 53;   DT 54, 67;
    MN 53;   PH 54(2), RC 54;   SL 29, 53

14   Four Episodes for Chamber O 1926   BN 27;   DT 38

17   Evocations, Symphon Suite 1937   CH 39;   NP 40; SF 37

23   Helvetia, Symphon Fresco 1929   CH 31;   CT 34

30   Israel, Symph for soli and O 1916   BA 51;   CH 25,
    30;   CL 26, 27, 32, 51;   HN 60;   NA 63;   LA 31;
    NP 26, 28, 44;   PH 17;   UT 53, 54, 66;   WA 53, 54

25   Three Jewish Poems 1913   BN 16, 25, 27, 35, 38;
    CH 27;   CL 21, 50;   DE 51;   DT 24;   LA 23, 25;
    NP 43;   NS 17;   PH 17, 23;   RC 48;   SL 18; SF 24
    -Cortège Funèbre   CH 59

4   Jubilee Var on a Goossens Theme 1944   CT 44, 45

11   Macbeth Opera 1909: Two Symphon Interludes   BN 38;
    CH 55;   CT 58;   CL 54;   DE 54;   NA 63;
    NP 49;   PH 53;   PT 39;   RC 52;   SF 39

18   Poems of Autumn 1906: Two Songs   NP 18

6   Proclamation for Trump and O   NR 56

7   Psalm 22 for low voice and O 1914   CT 22;   CL 22

6   Psalm 114 for high voice and O 1914   BN 19; PH 17;
    PT 60

6   Psalm 137 for high voice and O 1914   BN 19;
    PH 17;   PT 60;   WA 48

20   Schelomo, Jewish Rhaps for C and O 1916   AT 54;
    BA 50, 55, 69;   BN 22, 29, 33, 38, 58;   BU 43, 66;
    CH 23, 31, 33, 37, 43, 53, 62, 67;   CT 37, 55, 68;
    CL 27, 30, 33, 52, 55, 63, 69;   DA 50, 55, 60;
    DE 47, 52, 62;   DT 36, 45, 68;   HN 54;   NA 59, 69;
    KC 47, 55, 61;   LA 28, 33, 54, 60, 66;   ML 60, 64;
    MN 40, 47, 67;   NR 56;   NP 30, 45, 50, 53, 55,

BLOCH, E (Cont.) Schelomo, NP (Cont.)
61, 67;   PH 17, 22, 30, 42, 54;   PT 57, 64;
RC 29, 58;   SL 31(2), 47, 55, 62, 68   SF 18,
20, 23, 26, 29, 51, 55, 62;   SE 31, 35, 51, 58,
69;   UT 41, 48, 50, 54, 60, 63, 66;   WA 41,
50, 54, 63

18   Sinfonia Breve 1952   CT 57;   CL 55;   DE 55;
NP 53;   RC 55, 60

25   Suite for Vla and O 1919   BN 25, 44;   CH 27,
42, 50;   CT 29;   CL 29, 36;   PH 21, 68;
SL 29;   SF 48, 51, 61;   SE 56;   UT 55

12   Suite Hebraic for Vla, V and O 1951   CH 52

20   Suite Symphonique 1914   CT 49;   KC 59;   PH 45;
SF 45;

24   Symph in E   CT 56

47   Symph in C   CL 20;   NP 17, 27;   PH 18;   SF 26, 27

17   Symph with Trombone Solo   SE 64;   UT 61

13   Two Last Poems for Fl and O   NR 69

16   Two Poems, Winter and Spring   BN 20;   CH 19, 29,
36, 43;   CL 42;   DT 19, Winter only 46;
LA 21, 33, 49;   NP 33;   PH 43;   RC 24;
SL 21, 31;   SE 40

25   Voice in the Wilderness, Symphon Poem with C
Obbligato 1936   LA 36;   SF 48

BLOCKX, Jan   15   Carnaval from Princess d'auberge, Opera, 1892
1851-1912   Belg   LA 19;   SL 20

4   Flemish Dance No 4 Op 26   CT 04

5   Kermesse Flamande from the Ballet, Milenka, 1886
CT 00

16   Triplyque Symphonique   CH 06, 07;   CT 06

4   -Noël from Symphonique   CH 11

BLOMDAHL, Karl-Birger 11   Forma Ferritonans   NP 66
1916-1968   Swed   23   Symph No 3 Facets 1948   CH 63;   CT 64;   CL 63;
DT 61

BLUMENFELD, Harold   6   A Festival Overt   SL 61
1923   US   8   Miniature Overt   SL 59
20   Symph, Amphitryon   SL 65

BOCCHERINI, Luigi   22   Concertos:
1743-1805   It   22   No 1 Op 34 in B^b for C   AT 61;   BA 44, 64, 68;
BN 23, 48;   CH 25, 27, 31, 37, 43, 45;   CT 37;
CL 25, 35, 42;   DA 61;   DE 46;   DT 25, 44;
NA 38;   KC 45;   LA 23, 47;   MN 49;   NP 29,
35, 51, 53;   NS 23, 26;   PH 42;   PT 43, 57;
RC 39, 59;   SL 31, 35, 48;   SE 58;   WA 60

18   No 2 in D for C   BU 42;   NR 53;   SL 50

6   Flute Op 45   AT 59;   WA 64

17   Guitar in E   AT 61;   BA 61, 68;   BU 66;
CT 62;   DT 66;   MN 62;   NR 61, 67;   PT 60;
SF 62

10   Violin in D   CH 25;   NS 23

2   Minuet from Str Quart in E Op 13 No 5   BA 46;
BN 1881, 84;   CH 02;   DT 36;   NA 36

BOCCHERINI, L. (Cont.)
	6	Overt in D Op 43 MN 43; NP 31
	12	Pastorale for Str NS 1893
	20	Suite for Str in C BN 37; MN 37
	19	Symph in A BA 68; CT 37; NA 42; ML 68; MN 40; NP 38, 45, 52
	8	Serenade RC 67
	24	Symph in C No 3 Op 16 BN 24; PH 27; SL 22; WA 36
	18	Symph in c CH 57
	12	Symph in D No 16 PT 55
	17	Symph in G LA 39
	15-18	Symphonie Concertante Op 41 SL 65

BOCHSA, Robert   12   Dialogo Brillante for Fl and Cl   NP 1843, 44, 52
1789-1856   Fr

BODA, John   25   Sinfonia 1960   RC 60;   WA 60
1922-   US

BOEHE, Ernst   22   Taormina: Tone Poem Op 9   BN 07;   CH 08
1880-1938   Ger   18   Ulysses' Departure and Shipwreck Op 6 No 1, BN 05;   CH 06;   PH 04

BOELLMANN, Léon   11   Fantaisie dialoguée for Org and O   LA 28
1862-1897   Fr   13   Var Symphonique Op 23 for C and O   BN 11;   CH 02, 12, 15, 23, 34;   CL 20;   HN 32;   LA 34;   NS 08, 15;   PH 05, 06, 13;   RC 24, 37;   SF 17;   SE 40

BOGOROFF   4   Prayer   HN 41
               Russ

BOHLMANN, T. H.   15   Lyric Tone Poem for O   CT 10;   SL 15
1865-1931   US

BOHM, Yohanen   10   Scottish Fantasia for Fl Op 25   CH 04
1844-1920   Ger

BOIELDIEU, Francois   Operas
1775-1834   Fr   7   Le Calife de Bagdad 1800: Overt   BN 1883
                        8   La Dame Blanche 1825: Overt The White Lady CH 46;   MN 23, 29
                        4   Jean de Paris 1812: Aria   NP 30
                        8   Les Voitures Versées 1808: Duet for Soli and O CT 1896

BOLCOM, Wm. Elden   12   Fives   SE 68
1938-   US

BOITO, Arrigo   36   Mephistopheles, Mefistofele Opera 1868: Excerpts
1842-1918   It   KC 55
                              Prologue, Bass, Chor and O   AT 68;   BA 49; CT 55;   CL 68;   DA 49, 69;   DT 52;   KC 64; NR 68;   NP 59
                              -Arias
                        4   -L'altra notte in fundo CT 20;   ML 65;   SL 48;   SE 58
                        4   -L'aggio tra guinche   SE 35

BOITO, Arrigo (Cont.) Mephistopheles, Arias (Cont.)
                    4   -Ecco li mondo   NA 66;   KC 60, 64
                    4   -Son lo spirito che nega   AT 53;   DT 52
                    4   -Unnamed   DE 59

BOLLINGER, Samuel   8   The Sphinx Op 18   SL 16
1871   US 5   -The Sphinx's Slumber   SL 13

BOLOGNESI   4   Apres la valse   HN 13
            It

BOLZONI, Giovanni   5   Minuetto for Str O   HN 45;   SL 24
1841-1919   It

BONDEVILLE, Emmanuel de 10 Ophélie, Illuminations No 2 1932   WA 53
1898-   Fr   22   Symph Poem Gaulitier-Garguille   DT 58

BONNER, Eugene   25   3 Poems: Whispers of Heavenly Death for Voice and
1889-   US   O after W. Whitman, 1922   BA 29
                    4   Prelude to Scene 2 of La Femme Muette, Opera 1923
                              BA 26
                    15   Prelude for O, White Nights 1925   PH 41

BONNET, Joseph   10   Ariel, Org Solo   CH 18
1884-1944   Fr   15   Rhaps Catalane, Org Solo   CH 18

BONONCINI, Giovanni 4   No oh Dio from Calfurnia, Opera 1724   BA 67
1670-1755   It

BONPORTI, Francesco 10   Conc Grosso No 8 in D Op 11   CH 69;   NP 54
1672-1749   It   15   Concerto a Quattro Op 11 No 2   NP 68

BOONE, Charles   5   Song of Suchness   SF 67
1939-   US

BORCHARD, Adolphe   12   L'Élan for O   BN 24
1892-   Fr

BORDESE, Luigi   4   Aria from Jeanne d'Arc à Rouen   NP 1852
1713-1796   It

BORGHI, Luigi   15   Conc for Harpsichord and Wind O in D   BN 27;   NS 26
18th cent.   It

BORISHANSKY, Eliot 15   Music for O   NP 57
1930-   US

BORNSCHEIN, Franz   15   The Earth Sings 1944   BA 43
1879-   US   12   The Mission Road, Symphon Poem 1937   BA 38
                    8   Moon over Taos 1943   WA 45
                    12   Ode to the Brave 1945   WA 44
                 12-14   Southern Nights, Symphon Poem 1936   WA 36

Time in
Minutes

BORODIN, Alexander	9	Nocturne fr Str Quart arr Sargent DA 35; PH 56
1833-1887 Russ	7	On the Steppes of Central Asia, Musical Picture for O 1880 BN 1891, 95, 02, 16, 19; CH 02, 04, 09, 18, 24, 30, 37, 38, 47, 52; CT 1899, 02, 11, 16, 21, 26, 51; CL 27, 28, 39; DT 38, 52, 58; MN 25, 36, 40; NP 21, 44; PH 28, 35, 58; PT 50; RC 23, 26, 39, 68; SL 10, 19, 21, 26, 27, 32; SF 20, 55; SE 26; UT 64; WA 31, 39
	14	Petit Suite HN 33; PH 02
	6	-Scherzo DT 29
		Prince Igor, Opera, completed by Rimsky-Korsakof 1890: Arias, Undesignated CL 28; DE 53, 60
	4	
	4	-Joroslavna's aria DT 29; LA 32
	4	-Khan Konchak's aria DA 46; MN 34
	4	-No Sleep No Rest KC 60
	4	-Prince Galsky's aria NA 61; RC 29
	4	-Vladimir's Cavatina CL 32; RC 23, 27
	4	-Yara Shavna's aria NS 27
	30	-Ballet MN 37, 43; SF 30
	11	-Excerpts BA 40, 42; PH 17
	3	-March of the Polovetsi CH 58; DA 28
	10	-Overt CH 12, 18; CT 28, 35, 50, 69; CL 31, 39; DE 53; HN 55; NA 34, 35, 41; KC 69; MN 43; NP 31; PH 41; PT 42; RC 31, 60; SF 54; UT 57
	14	-Polovetsian Dances AT 47, 49; BN 19, 23, 33, 53; BU 53; CH 24, 25, 26, 30, 36, 50, 53; CT 23, 32, 48; CL 24, 25, 26, 27, 28, 29, 30, 32, 33, 41, 53, 57, 69; DA 28; DE 45, 46, 57; DT 24(2), 25, 30, 33, 35, 52, 54, 58; HN 38, 42, 49, 56; NA 40; KC 38, 39, 53, 54, 57; LA 29; ML 60; MN 30, 36, 37, 38, 39, 45, 67; NP 29, 32; NS 21, 24, 27; NR 56, 63; PH 17, 21, 22, 23, 24, 25, 27, 28(2), 30, 32, 36, 37, 42, 46; PT 40, 43; RC 24(2), 27, 36, 42; SL 24, 25, 31, 35, 52; SE 28, 34, 35, 37, 38; UT 42, 43, 55, 57, 63, 67; WA 32, 34, 36, 42, 44, 46
	10	-With Chorus BN 24(2), 25, 28, 42; CT 35, 61, 63; SF 37, 58
	4	Song: Dissonance MN 41
	33	Symph No 1 in E^b 1867 BN 1889, 99; CH 12; DT 25; LA 22
	32	Symph No 2 in b Heroic Op 5 AT 48, 51; BA 37; BN 12, 14, 18, 26, 29, 34, 66; BU 45; CH 08, 10, 14, 24, 33, 35, 39, 45, 46, 52; CT 1899, 01, 23, 30, 36; CL 27, 37; DA 53; DE 57; DT 23; HN 23; KC 55, 69; LA 26, 50; MN 36, 41, 43, 48, 51; NP 1896, 20, 27, 44, 53; NS 18, 21; NR 67; PH 16, 32; PT 40, 52, 62, 68; RC 28, 34, 35, 62; SL 11, 22, 32, 41, 44; SF 16, 47, 54; SE 55; UT 46; WA 49, 65
	17	Symph No 3 in a unfinished, completed by Glazounov CL 26; DT 24, 55; NP 57; PT 51

BOROWSKI, Felix	10	Allegro de Concert for Org and O 1915 CH 15
1872-1956 Brit/US	12	Ecce Homo Tone Poem 1923 CH 39, 42, 45; CT 53; NA 57; KC 43; PH 57; SF 43
	8	Élégie Symphonique 1916 CH 16; DT 18; NS 18
	5	Fanfare for the American Soldier CT 42
	9	The Mirror CH 55; SE 58
	5	Overt to a Pantomine for Chamber O 1925 NA 42
	25	Paintings, three mvts for O 1917 CH 17; CT 18; DT 20; SL 18
	10	The Passionate Springtime, Tone Poem 1920 CH 20; SL 21
	8	Requiem for a Child 1944 CH 44
	12	Semiramis Tone Poem 1923 CL 27; DT 32; SL 31; CH 25
	10	Suite from Ballet Pantomine Boudoir 1918 CH 18
	20	Symph No 1 in d 1932 CH 32
	26	Symph No 2 in e 1933 CH 36, 40, 43, 51; CT 37; KC 52(2); PH 50; SF 49
	28	Symph No 3 in G 1937 CH 38
	12	Youth Fantasie Overt 1922 CH 23; DT 25; MN 29; NP 23; SL 23
BORTKIEWIEZ, Sergei	24	P Conc in B Op 16 CH 26; WA 42
1877- Russ		
BOSMANS, Henrietta	18	Concertstück for V and O BN 40; CT 40
1895-1952 Neth		
BOSSI, Marco E.	25	Conc for Org in a Op 100a CH 1898

1861-1925 It	20	Intermezzi Goldoniani Op 127 BN 07, 11, 14;
		    CH 07, 29; CT 29; CL 32; DT 15, 23, 26,
		    34; NP 10, 32; PH 06, 08; SL 16

	22	Three Pieces, Interludes, Suite Op 126 CH 08
	13	Theme and Var Op 131 BN 22; CT 30
BOTTESINI, Giovanni	10	Fantasy on Bellini's La Sonnambula, Double Bass and O BA 68
1821-1889 It	14	Tarantelle, Double Bass and O CH 09
LEBOUCHER, Maurice	12	Trois Morceaux Symphoniques DT 56
1882- Fr		
BOULANGER, Lili	30	Faust et Hélène, Cantata 1913 NS 18
1893-1918 Fr	8	Pour Les Funerailles d'un Soldat Baritone and Mixed Chor BN 24; NS 24; PH 49; WA 39
	10	Psalm 24 BN 61; NP 61
	12	Psalm 129 BN 61; NP 61
	10	Psalm 130 BN 61; NP 61
BOULEZ, Pierre	10	Livre pour Cordes CH 68
1926- Fr	30	Figures, Double Prisms CL 64
	6	Improvisation sur Mallarmé I BU 63, 64; NP 59
	11	Improvisation sur Mallarmé II NP 60
	12	Sonatine for Fl and P SF 65

BOURGAULT-DUCOUDRAY,   6   Burial of Ophelia, L'Enterrement d' Ophélie, for O
  Louis   BN 1896
  1840-1910   Fr

BOURGUIGNON,   20   Jazz Triumphant, Symph Poem Op 33   MN 30
  Francis de
  1890-   Belg

BOURK   15   The Fall of Nokomis from Hiawatha   NS 18
                 US

BOWEN, Edwin Y.   25   Vla Conc in c   BN 23;   CH 23
  1884-   Eng

BOYCE, William   4   The Cambridge Ode in d 1749 arr Lambert NA 54;
  1710-1779   Eng   RC 18
                        8   Conc Grosso in d   NP 38
                        8   Symph No 1 arr Lambert   BA 42, 45;   BU 41, 42;
                                DT 41;   KC 56;   NP 50, 56;   WA 42, 47
                       18   Symph No 5   DA Minuet and Allegro arr Lambert 65
                                HN 69;   RC 18;   SF 55, 62
                        8   Symph No 8 arr Lambert   WA 51

BOYD, Jeanne   12   Song Against Ease, Symphon Poem   AT 49
  1890- Austr/US

BOYLE, George   23   C Conc in a   CH 24;   SF 25
  1886- Austr/US   25   P Conc in d   CH 14
                       15   Symphon Fantasy for O 1916   CT 20;   NS 17;   SL 16

BRAEIN, Edward   6   Concert Overt Op 2   WA 56
  1924-   Nor

BRAGA, Ernani   12   Var on a Popular Brazilian Theme   CH 47
  1898-   Brazil

BRAHMS, Johannes   9   Academic Festival Overt Op 80   AT 49, 51, 58, 66;
  1833-1897   Ger   BA 44(2), 45(2), 46, 50;   BN 1882, 87, 88, 89,
                                93, 94, 96, 97, 98, 00, 01, 03, 06, 10, 11, 12,
                                14, 16, 22, 25, 27, 32, 36, 43, 45, 46, 57, 64,
                                67;   BU 40, 43, 54, 58, 60, 61;   CH 1892, 94,
                                95, 01, 04, 05, 06, 08, 09, 10, 11, 12, 13, 14,
                                15, 21, 23, 24, 28, 33, 37, 39, 42, 43, 45, 52,
                                53, 54, 59, 61, 62, 64;   CT 11, 13, 19, 21, 25,
                                30, 31, 32, 33, 34, 35, 36, 38, 43, 46, 47, 48,
                                50, 53, 54, 56, 61, 66;   CL 24, 25, 26, 30, 32,
                                33, 40, 49, 51, 53, 56, 59, 60, 66, 67;   DA 29,
                                46, 50, 51, 55, 57, 62, 66;   DE 45, 47, 48, 49,
                                51, 52, 54, 57, 59, 61, 62;   DT 20, 25, 31, 34,
                                51, 63, 69;   HN 53, 59, 67;   NA 33, 56, 61, 64,
                                67;   KC 35, 42, 49, 61, 64, 65;   LA 24, 27, 31(2),
                                34, 38, 40, 44, 47, 52, 57;   ML 66;   MN 23, 29,
                                33, 36, 37, 41, 43, 47, 48, 50, 54;   NR 55, 57,
                                61, 62;   NP 00, 16, 21, 23, 25, 31, 34, 36, 40,
                                48, 50, 53, 54, 56, 61;   NS 1881, 07, 11, 14, 20,
                                22(2), 25, 26, 27;   PH 02, 05, 07, 11, 12, 13,

BRAHMS, J. (Cont.) Academic Festival Overt (Cont.)
          27, 30, 33, 38, 40, 41, 45(2), 46, 50, 52(2), 56, 62, 68;   PT 38,
          47, 49, 51, 54, 56;   RC 26, 28, 32, 37, 44, 49, 50, 53;   SL 10,
          13, 21, 22, 26, 44, 60, 61, 62, 64, 66;   SF 17, 24, 37, 38, 41,
          43, 49, 54, 59, 63, 67;   SE 28, 33, 34, 50, 51, 62;   UT 41, 48,
          53, 62, 64, 66;   WA 32, 35, 39, 41, 42, 46, 52, 54

26	Choral Preludes (11) Op 122 arr V. Thomson SF 57
20	-Eight Preludes CH 59
10	-Prelude and Fugue for Strings arr Mason PH 60
10	-Two Preludes CL 45; PT arr Leinsdorf 48, 60; RC 47, 53
6	No 7 arr Leinsdorf NP 52; RC 53; SL 53
15	Nos 3, 4, 5, 8, 10, 11 arr V. Thomson PH 57; SL 4 only 60
4	1 only 62
12	-Six Chorale Preludes for Org arr V. Thomson CT 63
10	-Choral Prelude for Org and O arr V. Thomson NR 56, 64
4	No 11 arr Voice and O, O Welt ich muss dich lassen, World I must leave thee DE 55

44	P Conc No 1 in d Op 15 AT 52, 57, 61, 65; BA 49, 54, 59, 62, 65; BN 00, 13, 20, 25, 31, 32, 38, 41, 44, 46, 48, 50, 53, 55, 57, 63; BU 41, 50, 55, 57, 61; CH 1899, 06, 08, 13, 16, 22, 28, 32, 33(2), 36, 37, 40, 41, 44, 48, 50, 52, 53, 55, 58, 61, 62, 63, 66, 68; CT 24, 27, 28, 30, 32, 36, 42, 46, 51, 54, 55, 56, 61, 64; CT 67, 69; CL 26, 27, 32, 37, 41, 45, 46, 48, 50, 52, 53, 56, 57, 58, 61, 64, 67, 69; DA 46, 49, 50, 52, 56, 58, 61, 63, 65; DE 45, 52, 54, 62, 67; DT 21, 26, 31, 34, 44, 46, 53, 56, 63, 65, 69; HN 34, 53, 54, 59, 63, 67; NA 45, 49, 53, 58, 64, 69; KC 41, 52, 55, 65; LA 24, 27, 31, 43, 47, 49, 52, 57, 61, 65, 66, 67, 68; ML 67, 68; MN 29, 38, 42, 43, 45, 50, 53, 54, 55, 56, 57, 66; NR 53, 64, 67; NP 1875, 11, 12, 17, 19, 34, 36, 40, 42, 45, 48, 50, 51, 53, 54, 55, 56, 59, 60, 61, 63, 65, 66, 69; NS 05, 14, 18, 23, 27; PH 13, 16, 22, 23, 25, 30, 40, 45, 46, 47, 49, 52, 54, 61; PT 39, 41, 45, 47, 52, 55, 59, 63, 66; RC 28, 32, 52, 57, 59, 69; SL 13, 30, 34, 36, 41, 45, 49, 50, 58, 60, 63, 65, 66; SF 27, 43, 48, 50, 51, 52, 57, 63, 65; SE 50, 59, 65, 69; UT 48, 54, 58, 62, 65, 67; WA 35, 42, 44, 45, 49, 53, 59, 62, 64, 67
43	P Conc No 2 in B^b Op 83 AT 53, 55, 60, 62, 66, 69; BA 44, 46, 48, 53, 55, 60, 67, 69; BN 1883, 85, 88, 95, 98, 04, 06, 15, 16, 17, 18, 23, 26, 32, 35, 36, 38, 40, 50, 52, 58, 60, 64, 68; BU 42, 48, 51, 54, 58, 60, 66; CH 1894, 12, 15, 17, 21, 24, 27, 29, 31, 34, 36, 39, 40, 42, 43, 45, 46, 48, 51, 52, 54, 56, 59, 63, 65, 67; CT 1896, 14, 15, 19, 25, 27, 31, 35, 41, 43, 47, 50, 51, 55, 56, 59, 62, 65, 67; CL 30, 31, 33, 35, 36, 37, 41, 43, 46, 49, 52, 55, 57, 59, 60, 62, 65, 66, 68; DA 46, 54, 58, 60, 62, 68; DE 51, 55, 57, 58, 69; DT 19, 21(2), 26, 33, 46, 51, 54, 57, 60, 62, 64; HN 41, 46, 47, 49, 51, 52, 54, 65, 68; NA 41, 46, 52, 56, 61, 67, 68; KC 35, 45, 47, 50, 62; LA 26, 32, 34, 35, 42, 44, 47, 50, 51, 52, 54, 56, 58, 60, 62, 64, 66, 69(2); ML 66; MN 25, 33, 40, 41, 45, 49, 51, 52, 55, 59, 62; NR 50, 55, 57, 62, 65, 67, 69; NP 1882, 86, 98, 22, 24, 26, 28, 31, 33, 35, 36, 37, 38, 41(2), 43, 45(2), 47, 48, 50, 51, 52, 53, 54, 56, 57, 58, 61, 62, 67; NS 1895, 11, 13, 15, 16, 18, 22; PH 15, 16, 18, 28, 29, 36, 38, 41, 44, 45, 48, 49, 50, 52, 55, 57, 58, 59, 62;

BRAHMS, J. (Cont.) P Concerto No 2 (Cont.)
PT 40, 46, 48, 51, 54, 56, 58, 62, 64, 68, 69;   RC 30, 47, 53,
60, 68;   SL 15, 19, 23, 25, 29, 33, 37, 41, 46, 47, 51, 52, 54,
57, 58, 59, 62, 64, 65, 67, 69;   SF 28, 37, 41, 48, 50, 51, 52,
53, 54, 58, 62, 65, 67, 68;   SE 44, 57, 62;   UT 48, 52, 57, 58,
59, 61, 64, 69;   WA 33, 34, 36, 42, 49, 51, 54, 58, 60, 62, 64,
65, 66

39   V Concerto in D Op 77   AT 51, 55, 62, 67;   BA 42, 46, 48, 50, 52,
54, 56, 58, 61, 64, 66, 69;   BN 1899, 91, 92, 96, 00, 02, 03, 04,
05, 07, 10, 11, 13, 16, 20, 22, 25, 27, 28, 30, 31, 37, 43, 45, 46,
47, 52, 54, 55, 57, 58, 60, 65, 66;   BU 40, 44, 46, 51, 54, 56,
58, 60, 62, 64, 67;   CH 1893, 95, 96, 99, 02, 04, 07, 10, 12, 13,
14, 16, 17(2), 20, 21, 25, 28, 29, 30, 34, 37, 38, 39, 41, 43, 44,
45, 47, 48, 50, 52, 53, 55, 57, 59, 60, 61, 62, 63, 64, 66, 68, 69;
CT 1898, 06, 09, 13, 14, 21, 23, 25, 27, 29, 34, 41, 45, 48, 50,
53, 55, 57, 58, 61, 66;   CL 20, 23, 26, 27, 29, 30, 34, 36, 37,
40, 41, 43, 44, 46, 49, 52, 54, 57, 58, 61, 64, 65, 66, 67;
DA 46, 49, 53, 60, 62, 67;   DE 46, 49, 51, 53, 56, 59, 60, 61,
66, 68;   DT 21, 23, 31, 34, 37, 39, 41, 45, 46, 52, 56, 60, 62,
64, 66, 67;   HN 42, 44, 47, 49, 50, 53, 56, 59, 62, 64, 69;
NA 39, 41, 43, 46, 52, 56, 58, 66, 69;   KC 35, 39, 41, 44, 47,
51, 56, 58, 63, 65, 67, 68;   LA 28, 33, 36, 38, 39, 40, 43, 47,
49, 54, 57, 59, 61, 64, 68, 69;   ML 64, 65;   MN 24, 26, 34, 35,
38, 40, 43, 45, 47, 48, 50, 52, 53, 54, 55, 58, 59, 66;
NR 53, 55, 57, 59, 61, 64, 66;   NP 1893, 98, 99, 02, 05, 09, 12,
15, 16, 17, 18, 19, 20, 21, 22, 24, 29, 34, 37, 41, 42, 43, 44,
45, 46, 47, 48, 49(2), 50, 51, 53, 54, 55, 56, 58, 60, 61, 64;
NS 1891, 07, 10, 11(2), 13, 14, 16, 18, 20(2), 21, 22, 25, 27(2);
PH 07, 08, 11, 13, 14, 15, 16, 17, 18(2), 19, 22, 23, 25, 26, 27,
29, 32, 33, 34, 35, 37, 38, 40, 41, 43, 44, 46, 49, 50, 51, 52, 53,
54, 55(2), 59, 60, 62, 63, 65, 69;   PT 46, 47, 48, 49, 50, 51, 52,
53, 56, 58, 59, 60, 62, 65, 67;   RC 29, 41, 45, 46, 47, 52, 53,
55, 60, 63;   SL 12, 13, 16, 17, 19, 20, 24, 27, 28, 30, 31, 34,
35, 36, 37, 38, 39, 41, 42, 43, 44, 45, 47, 48, 50, 51, 52, 53, 54,
55, 56, 59, 60, 62, 63, 68;   SF 14, 16, 24, 27, 30, 31, 33, 36,
37, 45, 48, 49, 50, 51, 52, 55, 58, 60, 62, 63, 64, 65, 66;
SE 39, 41, 44, 46, 49, 52, 57, 62, 63, 68;   UT 47, 49, 54, 58;
WA 33, 37, 39, 43, 46, 49, 51, 53, 55, 58, 60, 63, 66, 67

33   Conc for V and C in a Op 102   AT 50, 53, 58, 62, 68;   BA 36, 46, 59;
BN 1893, 96, 01, 09, 16, 23, 55, 64;   BU 44, 51, 54, 61, 65;
CH 1894, 06, 16, 19, 23, 24, 34, 44, 48, 51, 54, 56, 59, 64, 69;
CT 23, 34, 40, 51, 59, 64;   CL 21, 30, 35, 46, 52, 62, 65, 68;
DA 46, 48, 54, 56, 59, 63;   DE 47, 52, 57, 59, 62, 69;
DT 20, 22, 29, 32, 46, 48, 54, 67;   HN 61, 68;   NA 54, 65;
KC 49, 59;   LA 44, 53, 62, 64;   ML 62, 63, 68;
MN 37, 41, 48, 50, 54, 58, 60, 61(2);   NR 51, 57, 63;
NP 12, 19, 29, 34, 38, 50, 54, 59, 62;   NS 22, 23, 24;
PH 38, 52, 59, 65;   PT 39, 52, 54, 60, 63;   RC 30, 37, 43, 50,
59, 66;   SL 21, 24, 29, 37, 46, 54, 57, 65;   SF 26, 35, 47, 57, 64;
SE 59;   UT 55, 66;   WA 41, 52, 54, 56, 61, 66, 69

BRAHMS, J. (Cont.)

60   Ein Deutsche Requiem, German Requiem for Sopr, Baritone, Chor and O
      Op 45   AT 59, 66;   BA 65;   BN 62;   BU 66;   CH 1897, 29, 45, 49,
      56, 59, 64;   CT 54, 68;   CL 25, 54, 60, 68;   DA 46, 58, 68; DE 54;
      DT 58, 67;   HN 59;   KC 51, 63;   LA 35, 47, 53;   MN 40, 62;
      NR 61;   NP 26, 34, 51, 54,   NS 11;   PH 20, 52, 63;   PT 46, 68;
      RC 53, 65;   SL 60, 62;   SF 53;   SE 68;   UT 60, 69;   WA 52

13   Gesang der Pargen, Song of the Fates, Fragment from Goethe, for
      Contral and O Op 89   DE 49;   PH 32

      Hungarian Dances originally for P
3   No 1   BA 46;   CT 16;   DA 29;   HN 43;   KC 36;   NR 56;   PT 42,
      45;   WA 34, 35, 36
3   No 2   BA 46;   DA 29;   WA 34, 44
3   No 3   BA 46;   HN 43
3   No 4 in g   CT 16;   DA 29;   HN 59
3   No 5 in F#   CT 01;   DE 45;   HN 43;   PH 01, 22, arr Dvorak 28,
      40;   PT 42;   RC 38;   UT 41;   WA 37, 44, 48
28   First Set   CH 1891, 93, 95, 00
8   Nos 17-21 arr Dvorak   CH 1892, 97, 08, 11, 12, 13, 15, 16, 17,
      19, 22, 23, 29, 31, 33, 35, 40, 41
3   No 6 in D   CT 01;   DA 29;   DE 45;   PH 01, 22, 28, arr Dvorak 40;
      PT 42;   RC 38;   UT 41;   WA 32, 48
3   No 7   HN 14,   PT 12, 13, 19, 42, 45
3   No 17 arr Dvorak   LA 53
4   No 18 arr Dvorak   KC 40
10   No 19, 20, 21 arr Dvorak   MN 34
3   No 21 arr Dvorak   LA 53;   PT 42
10   Three dances   DA 56;   NA 33;   NP 25, 28, 34, 42, 50
7   Two dances   KC 54;
10   Selections   BN 1881, 82, 84, 86, 95, 99, 02, 30, 31;   BU 65;
      DT 15, 45
4   Vagabond Dance   NS 18
28   Hungarian Dances for V arr Joachim   CH 1896

16   Liebslieder Waltzes Op 52a   AT 60;   DA 46;   LA 47, 52;   NP 34;
      NS 1889;   PH 43

4   Motet for mixed Chor and O, O Heiland, reiss die Himmel auf,
      Savior Throw the Heavens Wide Op 74   MN 44

15   Nänie for Chor and O Op 82   CL 39,   HN 51;   NA 50;   NS 11;   SF 51

15   Part songs for Female Voices with 2 Horns and Harp Op 17
      DA 46;   NA 33;   PH 40;   SF 31
4   No 2 Lied from Shakespeare's Twelfth Night   NP 34
4   No 3 Der Gärtner, The Gardener   NP 34
5   No 4 Gesang aus Fingal, Ossian, The Death of Trenar   NP 34

5   Psalm 113 for Female Voices and Org Op 27   DA 46

32   Quart for P and Str in g Op 25 arr Schoenberg   BN 41(2), 50, 62;
      CH 38, 61;   CT 42;   CL 38, 42;   LA 38;   NP 42;   RC 53;
      SL 65;   SF 36;   SE 66

BRAHMS, J. (Cont.)
40   Quint in F Op 88 arr Leinsdorf   CL 45;   RC 49
        -Andante arr Reisman   RC 40

13   Rhaps for Alto solo, Male Chor and O Op 53   AT 65;   BN 1881, 46,
        64;   BU 69;   CH 38, 45, 53, 67;   CT 26, 69;   CL 34;   DA 46, 58;
        DE 47;   DT 59, 64;   HN 49, 59;   NA 50;   KC 48;   LA 57, 63;
        MN 23, 55;   NR 54, 66;   NP 1882, 28, 32, 55;   NS 07;   PH 38,
        41, 69;   RC 49;   SL 58;   SF 61

15   Schicksalslied Song of Destiny for Chor and O Op 54   BN 16, 29,
        42;   CT 41;   CL 27;   DA 48, 54, 66;   HN 51;   MN 46;   NP 17;
        PH 32, 52, 63;   PT 59;   WA 40, 51, 58, 69

35   Serenade No 1 in D Op 11   BA 46;   BN 1882, 97, 01, 58;   CH 1895,
        01, 02,13, 25, 66;   CT 16, 47;   CL 69;   DE 59;   DT 27;
        HN 59;   NA 31;   LA 47, 52;   NP 16, 34, 69;   NS 11, 13, 22;
        PH 03, 52;   RC 52;   SF 22
6   -Allegro Molto   CH 45;   HN 53

32   Serenade No 2 in A Op 16   AT 53;   BA 46;   BN 1886, 94, 46;
        CH 1896, 03;   CT 24, 49;   NA 52;   LA 47;   NP 20, 34, 35;
        NS 15;   PH 31, 38, 52;   PT 58;   SF 57, 66
5   -Allegro non troppo SL 61
12   -Minuet, Rondo, Scherzo,   CT 34

10   Sextet No 1 in B^b Theme and Var Op 18   CH 1892;   DA arr Dorati 48;
        NP 1888;   NS 1895

32   Sextet No 2 in G for Str Op 36 arr Goossens   CT 45, 46

15   Song of Triumph, Triumphleid Op 55, for Chor and O   NS 11

SONGS Individual, in German
4   Auf dem Kirchhofe Op 105 No 4   CH 45;   CT 07
4   Ave Maria, for female Voices and O Op 12   NS 11
4   Botschaft Op 47 No 1   CT 16;   NP 14;   NS 13
4   Dein blaues Auge Op 59 No 8   CT 51;   LA 38;   MN 47;   PH 38
20   4 Ernste Gesänge, Four serious Songs Op 121   CT 50;   NA 51;
        MN 45;   LA 45, 52;   NR 55;   PH 25, 53;   PT 46;   RC 41, 51;
        SL 41;   SF 43
4   Feldeinsamkeit Op 86 No 2   CT 16, 25;   NP 14
4   Der Frühling, Op 6 No 2   NP 1899
4   Immer leiser wird mein Schlummer, Ever Lighter Grows my Slumber
        Op 105 No 2   CH 45;   CT 19, 51;   DT 31, 39;   MN 47;   NS 1889;
        PH 19, 38
4   In Waldeseinsam Keit, Op 85 No 6   CT 02
4   Lied aus dem Gedicht, Ivan Op 3 No 4   MN 28
4   Liebestreu Op 3 No 1   CH 95;   DA 32;   LA 38
4   Das Mädchen spricht, Op 107 No 3   CT 16
4   Die Mainacht Op 43 No 2   CT 1895;   NP 1898
4   Meine Liebe ist grün Op 63 No 5   CH 1891, 95;   CT 1895;
        NP 1898;   NS 1889
4   An die Nachtigall Op 46 No 4   NS 13

BRAHMS, J. (Cont.) SONGS Individual, in German (Cont.)
4   Sapphische Ode Op 94 No 4   CH 06;   DT 23, 26, 31;   NP 12;   PH 08
4   Der Schmied Op 19 No 4   CH 45;   CT 51;   DT 31;   LA 38;   MN 47;
        PH 13, 38
4   Sehnsucht Op 49 No 3   MN 41
4   Schwalbe sag mir an   NP 14
12   Songs, three unspecified   NR 62
4   Song, unspecified   LA 42
4   Spanisches Lied, Op 6 No 1   CT 27;   DT 26
4   Ständchen Op 106 No 1 Serenade   CH 1895;   LA 31;   SL 31
4   Sind es schmerzen sind es Frieden Op 33 No 3 Set II   MN 41
4   Von Ewiger Liebe Op 43 No 1   CH 26;   CT 27, 32, 51;   DT 26, 39;
        MN 47;   NP 1883;   NS 25;   PH 38
4   Vor dem Fenster Op 14 No 1   CT 16;   NP 14
4   Vorschneller Schurer Op 95 No 5   SL 10
        Weg Zuruck Op 63 No 8   NS 04
4   Wie bist du meine Königen Op 32 No 9   DT 23;   MN 49;   NS 1889
4   Wiegenlied, Cradlesong Op 49 No 4   BA 42;   DE 47;   NS 1882;
        PH 13;   KC 40
4   Willst du dass ich geh? Op 71 No 4   CH 26;   DT 26;   CT 27
4   Wir Wandelten Op 96 No 2;   NS 13
40   Zigeunerlieder Cycle of 11 songs for Vocal Quart and 0 Op 103   SF 30
4   No 1 He Zigeuner   CT 14, 30
4   No 2 Hochgetürmte Rimafluth   CT 14, 30
4   No 3 Wisst ihr, wer mein Kinder   CT 30
4   No 4 Lieber Gott, du weist   CT 14, 30
4   No 5 Brauner Bursche, fuhrt zum Tanze   CT 14
4   No 6 Roslein dreie in der Reihe   CT 14, 30
4   No 7 Kommt dir manchmal in den Sinn   CT 14, 30
4   No 11 Rote Abendwolken   CT 30

6   SONGS, Gypsy, unspecified   LA 28, 30

        SONGS, Individual, in English
4   Lady of the Lake   NP 34

48   Symphony No 1 in c Op 68
        AT 48, 51, 55, 59, 62, 65, 67
        BA 38, 40, 42(2), 43, 44(2), 45, 46, 49, 51, 52, 55, 57, 60, 61, 66, 68
        BN 1881, 82, 83, 85, 87, 89, 90, 91, 93, 95, 97, 99, 00, 02, 04, 06,
        08, 10, 11, 12, 14, 16, 19, 21, 25, 26, 27, 30, 31, 32, 33, 35,
        36, 37, 38, 40, 41, 43, 44, 45, 46, 47, 49, 50, 52, 53, 56, 59, 60,
        61, 63, 67
        BU 41, 42, 48, 52, 54, 56, 58, 60, 62, 63
        CH 1893, 98, 99, 02, 04, 05, 07, 08, 10, 12, 14, 16, 18, 19, 20, 21,
        22, 23, 24, 26, 27, 29, 30, 31, 32, 33, 34, 35, 37, 38, 39, 40, 41,
        42, 43, 44, 45, 46, 47, 48, 49, 50, 51, 52, 53, 55, 56, 57, 59, 61,
        62, 64, 66, 67, 69
        CT 1898, 01, 02, 04, 10, 11, 12, 14, 17, 22, 25, 28, 30(2), 31, 32,
        34, 36, 38, 39, 41, 42, 44, 45, 46, 48, 49, 51, 53, 57, 58, 60, 62,
        65, 69
        CL 20, 22, 24, 26, 28, 30, 32, 33, 35, 37, 39, 40, 41, 42, 43, 44,
        45, 46, 47, 49, 50, 52, 53, 54, 55, 56, 57, 59, 61, 63, 66, 67
        DA 46, 48, 54, 56, 57, 58, 61, 64, 66
        DE 46, 48, 50(2), 52, 53, 56, 58, 62, 63, 65, 68
        DT 14, 18, 20, 22, 25, 27, 28, 32, 33, 35, 36, 38, 40, 41, 43, 45,
        46, 47, 51, 52, 53, 55, 58, 60, 62, 64, 68

BRAHMS, J. (Cont.)   Symphony No 1 (Cont.)
    HN 39, 44(2), 46, 48, 50, 51, 52, 53, 54, 55, 57, 59, 61, 62, 64,
      66, 67, 68
    NA 33, 37, 43, 46, 48, 49, 50, 52, 53, 55, 57, 61, 64, 66, 69
    KC 34, 35, 37, 40, 42, 47, 49, 50, 53, 56, 60, 62, 67
    LA 21, 22, 23, 24, 25, 26, 27(2), 28, 29, 32, 33, 34, 35, 36, 38, 39
      40, 42, 45, 46, 47, 49, 52, 55, 56, 58, 59, 60, 61, 62, 64, 67, 68
    ML 63, 69;   MN 22, 23, 25, 27, 29, 32, 33, 34, 36, 38, 40, 42, 44,
      45, 47, 48, 49, 51, 52, 53, 55, 57, 58, 59, 61, 68
    NR 50, 51, 53, 57, 59, 62, 64, 69
    NP 1877, 88, 98, 01, 03, 10, 11, 17, 21(2), 23, 24, 25, 27, 28(2),
      29, 30, 32(2), 33, 41, 43(2), 44, 45, 46, 47, 48, 49, 50, 51,
      53(2), 54, 55, 56, 57, 58, 61, 64, 65, 66, 68
    NS 1880, 90, 93, 97, 04, 06, 08, 09, 11, 13, 18(2), 19, 20, 21, 22,
      24, 25, 26, 27(2)
    PH 02, 07, 12, 13, 15, 16, 17, 19, 20, 21, 22, 23, 24, 25, 26, 27,
      28, 29, 30(2), 31, 32(2), 33(2), 34, 35(2), 36, 37, 38, 40(2),
      41, 42, 43(3), 45, 46(2), 47, 48, 49, 50, 51, 52, 53, 54, 55,
      56, 57, 58, 59, 60, 62, 63, 64, 65, 66, 67, 69
    PT 38, 41, 43, 45, 46, 48, 50, 51, 53, 55, 57, 61, 63, 65, 67
    RC 23, 25, 28, 32, 35, 37, 39, 43, 46, 51, 53, 56, 57, 60, 63, 68
    SL 09, 12, 17, 20, 23, 25, 27, 29, 32(2), 33, 35, 36, 38, 39, 40,
      41, 42, 43, 44, 45, 46, 47, 48, 49, 50, 51, 53, 54, 55, 56, 57,
      59, 60, 61, 62, 65, 66, 68
    SF 11, 13, 16, 18, 20, 22, 23, 25, 26, 28, 35(2), 37, 41, 45, 49,
      51, 52, 53, 56, 59, 62, 63, 64, 66, 68
    SE 28, 29, 31, 33, 36, 39, 42, 45, 47, 52, 56, 64, 67
    UT 46, 49, 51, 54, 57, 60, 63, 67
    WA 35, 36, 38, 40, 41, 42, 44, 45, 47, 48, 49, 52, 54, 59, 65

12   -Second mvt   MN 48

43   Symphony No 2 in D Op 73
    AT 49, 52, 56, 60, 63, 66, 68
    BA 38, 43, 46, 48, 49, 51, 53, 58, 62, 63(2), 68
    BN 1881, 82, 84, 86, 88, 90(2), 93, 95, 98, 99, 01, 03, 05, 07, 09,
      11, 12, 14, 16, 18, 20, 22, 25, 26, 28, 30, 32, 33, 34, 35, 36,
      37, 39, 40, 41, 42, 43, 45, 46, 47, 49, 50, 53, 55, 56, 57, 58,
      59, 60, 61, 64, 67, 69
    BU 44, 45, 47, 52, 54, 58, 61, 67
    CH 1894, 97, 01(2), 03, 05, 06, 08, 09, 10, 11, 13, 15, 16, 17, 19,
      20, 21, 22, 24, 25, 26, 29, 30, 31, 32, 34, 36(2), 38, 40, 41,
      43, 45, 47, 48, 49, 50, 51, 52, 53, 54, 56, 57, 58, 60, 62, 63,
      67, 68
    CT 1896, 99, 03, 06, 11, 13, 16, 17, 19, 24, 26, 29, 31, 32, 35,
      40, 41, 44, 45, 46, 48, 52, 54, 57, 59, 61, 65
    CL 19, 21, 23, 24, 27, 29, 31, 32, 34, 36, 37, 39, 40, 42, 43, 44,
      45, 46, 47, 49, 51, 53, 55, 57, 59, 61, 63, 65, 66, 68
    DA 46, 48, 49, 50(2), 55, 57, 60, 61, 65, 69
    DE 45, 46, 49, 50, 51, 53, 54, 55, 57, 61, 62, 64, 66, 69
    DT 19, 24, 28, 31, 32, 34, 39, 40, 44, 46, 48, 53, 56, 59, 61, 62,
      64, 66
    HN 36, 40, 42, 47, 49, 50, 51, 53, 54, 55, 56, 59, 61, 64, 65, 68
    NA 35, 37, 39, 45, 47, 50, 54, 56, 59, 62, 64, 67
    KC 34, 36, 39, 41, 46, 48, 52(2), 57, 59, 63, 66, 69
    LA 20, 22, 24(2), 26, 31, 32, 33, 36, 39, 41, 44, 45, 46, 47, 50,
      51, 53, 55, 57, 58, 60, 61, 63, 65, 69(2)   ML 66

BRAHMS, J. (Cont.)   Symphony No 2 (Cont.)
    MN 22, 25, 28, 30, 32, 34, 35, 36, 37, 39, 43, 45, 47, 48, 50, 51,
        53, 56, 57, 58, 61, 63, 65
    NR 51, 53, 58, 60, 63, 68
    NP 1878, 80, 87, 97, 02, 05, 13, 15, 16, 18, 19, 22, 26, 27, 29,
        31, 41, 42, 43, 44, 46, 47, 48, 49, 50, 51, 52, 53, 54, 55, 56,
        58, 59, 61, 62, 63, 64, 66, 68
    NS 1888, 92, 05, 09, 10, 11, 12, 14, 15, 16, 17, 20(2), 22, 23, 25,
        26(2), 27
    PH 00, 02, 03, 05, 08, 09, 10, 11, 13, 14, 15, 17, 18, 19, 21, 23,
        27, 28, 29, 30, 31, 32, 33, 34, 35, 36, 37, 38, 39, 40, 41, 42,
        43, 44, 45, 46, 48, 49, 50, 51, 52, 53, 54, 56, 57, 58, 59, 60,
        61, 62, 64, 65, 66, 67, 68, 69
    PT 38, 40, 42, 44, 46, 48, 49, 50, 51, 55, 57, 60, 62, 64, 67, 69
    RC 01, 05, 07, 11, 15, 17, 20, 23, 26, 27, 29, 33, 37, 39, 42, 45,
        48, 51, 53, 55, 58, 61, 63, 66, 67
    SL 11, 13, 16, 18, 22, 24, 26, 28, 30, 31, 33, 34, 35, 37, 38, 39,
        40, 41, 43, 44, 45, 46, 47, 49, 51, 53(2), 55, 56, 57, 58, 60,
        61, 62, 64
    SF 15, 17, 19, 21, 24, 25, 27, 30, 31, 32, 35, 38, 40, 46, 48, 50,
        52, 53, 55, 58, 62, 64, 65, 68
    SE 27, 30, 32, 35, 42, 43, 44, 50, 55, 61, 63, 68, 69
    UT 47, 52, 56, 62, 65, 68
    WA 34, 36, 38, 43, 48, 50, 51, 52, 53, 54, 59, 63, 67, 69

12   -Third mvt   CT 63
24   -Two mvts   DA 28, 38, 46, 49
24   -Third and Fourth mvts   MN 43, 45

36   Symphony No 3 in F Op 90
    AT 50, 53, 57, 60, 64, 69
    BA 42, 43, 44, 45, 46, 50, 53, 56, 57, 62, 68
    BN 1884, 85, 87, 88, 92, 94, 96, 97, 98, 00, 02, 04, 08, 10, 12,
        15, 17, 21, 23, 27, 32, 33, 36, 37, 39, 42, 43, 47, 48, 51, 54,
        58, 62, 65
    BU 46, 51, 55, 64
    CH 1891, 96, 00(2), 04, 06, 07, 09, 12, 14, 16, 17, 19, 20, 21, 22,
        24, 25, 27, 28, 29, 30, 31, 33, 34, 35, 37, 38, 39, 40, 41, 42,
        43, 44, 45, 46, 48, 52, 54, 55, 56, 57, 58, 60, 61, 62, 64, 65, 69
    CT 1897, 07, 09, 14, 16, 18, 21, 24, 27, 29, 31, 33, 35, 40, 43, 45,
        46, 52, 56, 61, 67
    CL 22, 25, 28, 29, 32, 34, 37, 40, 44, 45, 46, 48, 50, 52, 54, 57,
        58, 60, 62, 64, 67, 69
    DA 52, 60, 63, 68
    DE 48, 50, 53, 54, 58, 65
    DT 15, 20, 22, 29, 30, 34, 37, 40, 44, 46, 51, 54, 58, 63, 65, 69
    HN 45, 50, 52, 53, 54, 56, 58, 63, 67
    NA 36, 41, 44, 53, 57, 62, 66
    KC 40, 47, 50, 55, 61, 65, 68
    LA 19, 21, 25, 28, 30, 32, 33, 34, 44, 47, 50, 52, 54, 58, 59, 63
    MN 26, 33, 35, 37, 40, 41, 43, 46, 49, 54, 60, 62, 67   NR 51, 57
    NP 1884, 00, 06, 09, 12, 17, 18, 20, 23, 26, 29, 30, 32, 33, 34,
        37, 38, 42, 43, 44, 45, 46, 48, 51, 53, 54, 55, 56, 57, 60, 61,
        62, 63, 64(2)
    NS 1887, 89, 03, 05, 07, 11, 15, 16, 18, 20, 21, 23, 24, 26

Time in   BRAHMS, J. (Cont.)
Minutes   Symphony No 3 (Cont.)
           PH 01, 11, 12, 13, 14(2), 15(2), 16(2), 18, 20, 21, 23, 24, 25, 28,
              30, 31, 32, 33, 34(2), 36, 37, 38, 39, 41, 42, 44, 45, 46, 47,
              48, 49, 50, 51, 52, 53, 58, 60, 61, 62, 64, 65, 66
           PT 39, 42, 45, 47, 49, 50, 53, 56, 59, 61, 64, 66, 68
           RC 34, 36, 41, 43, 44, 47, 50, 52, 53, 57, 59
           SL 10, 15, 21, 28, 31, 36, 39, 43, 47, 50, 51, 53, 56, 57, 58, 59,
              61, 69
           SF 12, 14, 15, 17, 21, 22, 24, 28, 30(2), 32, 36, 38, 39, 42, 46,
              49, 52, 54, 55, 59, 66, 69
           SE 35, 41, 43, 46, 49, 58, 65
           UT 48, 55, 61, 66, 68
           WA 40, 41, 47, 48, 49, 50, 52, 60, 61, 69

   9   -Third mvt   MN 49;   WA 32
  18   -Two mvts   DA 28, 38, 46, 49

  43   Symphony No 4 in e Op 98
           AT 51, 54, 58, 61, 65, 67
           BA 42, 52, 54, 56, 60, 66, 68
           BN 1885, 88, 91, 92, 93, 95, 96, 97, 99, 01, 03, 05, 07, 09, 11,
              13, 15, 17, 20, 22, 24, 25, 26, 27, 31, 33, 35, 36, 38, 39, 40,
              41, 42, 43, 44, 46, 47, 48, 49, 51, 53, 55, 56, 57, 60, 65, 69
           BU 40, 43, 44, 45, 48, 50, 52, 54, 57, 59, 66, 69
           CH 1892, 95, 98, 01, 03, 04, 06, 08, 11, 13, 15, 18, 19, 20, 21,
              22, 23, 24, 25, 27, 29, 30, 33, 34, 36, 37, 38, 41, 42, 43, 45,
              46, 47, 48, 49, 50, 52, 53, 55, 56, 57, 58, 59, 60, 61, 62, 63, 66
           CT 00, 05, 13, 15, 20, 22, 24, 25, 28, 29, 32, 34, 35, 38, 39, 41,
              44, 46, 47, 49, 54, 58, 60, 62, 64, 65, 68, 69
           CL 24, 25, 26, 27, 31, 33, 35, 37, 38, 39, 40, 41, 44, 45, 46, 47,
              48, 50, 51, 53, 56, 57, 58, 60, 62, 64, 65, 68
           DA 46, 48, 49, 50, 51, 55, 57, 61, 62, 66, 67(2)
           DE 45, 47, 49, 50, 51, 55, 57, 59, 63, 64, 67, 69
           DT 21, 25, 29, 30, 33, 35, 39, 41, 43, 45, 46, 47, 52, 54, 55, 57,
              60, 61, 63, 65, 66, 68
           HN 38, 41, 46, 48, 50, 52, 53, 54, 58, 59, 61, 63, 65, 68
           NA 34, 39, 42, 45, 48, 49, 51, 55, 56, 58, 60, 63, 65, 67
           KC 37, 42, 45, 51, 54, 58, 60, 64
           LA 23(2), 25, 26, 27, 30, 31, 34, 43, 45, 47, 49, 51, 52, 54, 56,
              57, 59, 60, 61, 62, 65, 67, 69(2);   ML 65
           MN 24, 27, 28, 30, 32, 34, 36, 38, 41, 44, 47, 48, 56, 57, 59, 61, 63
           NR 50, 52, 55, 56, 57, 59, 62, 66
           NP 1886, 94, 99, 04, 14, 16, 17, 19(2), 21, 22, 23, 24, 25, 29, 30,
              31, 32, 34, 36, 41, 42, 43, 44, 46, 47, 48, 49, 50, 51, 53, 54,
              57, 60, 61, 62, 63, 64, 67(2), 69
           NS 1886, 10, 11, 12, 14, 16, 19, 21(2), 22, 25(2), 27
           PH 01, 03, 04, 06, 13, 14, 17, 19, 20, 21, 22, 24, 27, 28, 29, 30,
              31, 32, 33(2), 34, 35, 36, 37, 38, 39, 40, 41, 42, 43, 44, 45,
              46, 47, 48, 49, 50, 51, 52, 53(2), 55, 56, 57, 58, 60, 62, 63,
              64, 65, 66, 67, 69
           PT 37, 40, 43, 46, 48, 50, 51, 54, 57, 58, 60, 62, 64, 66, 69
           RC 24, 30, 31, 34, 38, 40, 42, 44, 46, 50, 53, 56, 58, 62, 63, 68
           SL 12, 14, 20, 24, 26, 27, 29, 30, 32, 34, 37, 38, 39, 40, 41, 42,
              43, 44, 45, 47, 48, 49, 50, 51, 54, 55, 56, 57, 61, 62, 64, 65, 66

BRAHMS, J. (Cont.) Symphony No 4 (Cont.)
          SF 16, 19, 23, 26, 29, 39, 48, 50, 51, 52, 53, 55, 59, 60, 63,
             65, 68, 69
          SE 31, 40, 43, 51, 54, 60, 69
          UT 46, 50, 53, 55, 59, 64, 66, 69
          WA 32, 40, 44, 47, 49, 51, 52, 55, 57, 67

  10   -Second mvt   MN 47

  14   Tragic Overt Op 81   AT 62;   BA 46, 54;   BN 1881, 82, 83, 85, 89,
          91, 93, 95, 96, 99, 03, 04, 09, 13, 15, 17, 21, 23, 26, 32, 48,
          52, 53, 55, 58, 65;   BU 49, 55, 69;   CH 1893, 97, 07, 10, 13, 21,
          28, 35, 36, 40, 42, 45, 46, 53, 57, 65, 68;   CT 12, 29, 32, 49, 60;
          CL 20, 23, 27, 36, 43, 51, 57, 66;   DA 52, 63;   DE 49, 63;
          DT 23, 28, 46, 64;   HN 50, 56, 62, 67;   NA 42, 58;   KC 45, 57,
          63;   LA 25(2), 35, 36, 46, 52, 55, 57, 59, 63;   ML 62;   MN 23,
          38, 53, 64;   NR 59, 63, 68;   NP 1881, 85, 14, 15, 17, 18, 20,
          22, 24, 34, 40, 43, 47, 48, 50, 51, 52, 53, 54, 62, 63;   NS 16;
          PH 07, 13, 15, 28, 29, 34, 38, 45, 51, 56, 57, 58, 59, 63, 65;
          PT 40, 51, 58, 61, 68;   RC 36, 45, 53, 60, 62, 68;   SL 11, 14,
          19, 20, 23, 28, 32, 62, 67;   SF 19, 35, 42, 48, 53, 61, 68;
          SE 60, 63;   UT 46, 58;   WA 33, 36, 39

  15   Var on a Theme by Haydn in B^{b} Op 56a   AT 55, 68;   BA 40, 46, 48,
          51, 57, 64;   BN 1884, 86, 89, 93, 96, 98, 00, 04, 06, 08, 12, 14,
          16, 21, 23, 24, 27, 34, 38, 42, 44, 45, 46, 48, 49, 53, 58, 61, 62,
          64;   BU 68, 69;   CH 1892, 95, 97, 98, 02, 03, 04, 05, 06, 07, 09,
          14, 16, 19, 24, 25, 26, 27, 28, 29, 33, 39, 40, 48, 49, 52, 55, 60,
          62, 64, 67;   CT 15, 23, 25, 27, 33, 39, 43, 46, 48, 58, 63, 68;
          CL 22, 25, 31, 37, 40, 41, 44, 47, 50, 52, 55, 61, 63, 64, 68;
          DA 46, 48, 50, 55, 58;   DE 46, 48, 51, 53, 54, 56, 59, 61, 64, 66,
          69;   DT 69;   HN 42, 47, 50, 53, 55, 59, 61, 68;   NA 38, 43, 47,
          49, 54, 55, 58, 62, 66;   KC 39, 42, 46, 51, 60, 67;   LA 23, 25,
          35, 37, 45, 47, 52, 54, 56;   ML 62, 64;   MN 25, 28, 33, 41, 44,
          49, 52, 53, 55, 59, 63, 66, 68;   NR 50, 55, 57, 60, 68;   NP 1877,
          83, 90, 99, 11, 13, 18, 28, 29, 32, 34, 36, 43, 44, 50, 53, 54,
          56, 64;   NS 22;   PH 07, 09, 10, 11, 13, 15, 16, 17, 18, 20, 21,
          24, 25, 27, 29, 32, 37, 38, 39, 40, 41, 43, 45, 46, 47, 50, 52, 53,
          57, 59, 62, 65, 67, 68;   PT 38, 44, 52, 56, 58, 64;   RC 30, 37,
          39, 41, 43, 45, 50, 53, 56, 58;   SL 21, 30, 32, 34, 38, 40, 42,
          43, 46, 50, 52, 55, 56, 60, 61;   SF 14, 27, 30, 35, 39, 40, 42,
          45, 47, 50, 54, 62, 65, 66;   SE 44, 58, 65;   UT 53, 61;
          WA 35, 38, 46, 49, 52, 63

  27   Var and Fugue on a Theme by Handel Op 24   CT 39;   DT 16, 18, 24,
          29, 37, 39, 44, 48, 55, 59, 61;   PH 24, 44, 60;   SE 46;   SF 40

  17   Var on St. Anthony Chorale   LA 62;   UT 61;   WA 48

  25   Waltzes Op 39 arr Garrick   BN 1888, 97, 04
          -Two Waltzes   WA 39, 41

BRAINE, Robert   4   Habanera from Lazy Ciganetti   MN 41
  1896-   US   5   Prelude to Act III of Virginia   CH 30;   WA 37
                      3   S. O. S.   CH 30;   WA 37

BRAND, Max   11   The Wonderful One Hoss Shay   PH 49, 52;   SL 51
1896-   Aust/US

BRANT, Henry   12   Antiphony One   MN 60;   NP 59;   SL 60
1913-   US   10   Dedication 1945   PT 45

BRAUN, Edith   8   Carol Overt   NR 60
               US

BRAUNFELS, Walter   12   Carnival Overt from Opera, Princess Brambilla Op 22
1882-   Ger   BN 15;   CH 13
                              30   Don Juan, Var on Mozart Theme, from Don Giovanni
                                          Op 34   NP 26
                              46   Fantastic Var on Berlioz Theme   MN 26;   NS 24;
                                          PH 21
                              10   Die Vogel, The Birds, Opera Op 30: Prologue   CH 26
                              12   -Wedding of the Doves   MN 24;   SE 26

BRENTA, Gaston   8   Arioso et Moto Perpetuo   DT 57
1902-   Belg   20   Symph   SL 64

BRETON, Tomas   6   El Cortejo   MN 66
1850-1923   Sp   8   En Vieja Madrid, arr Chueca   CT 44
                               5   Mazurka from La Verbena de la Paloma, Operetta 1894
                                          CT 42, 43;   RC 40, 41, 43;   SF 43

BRICCETTI, Thomas B.   23   Symph No 1   DE 61
1936-   US

BRICKEN, Carl   5   Pastorale from Symph No 2 in F 1936   SE 45
1898-   US   17   Suite in E^b 1931   SE 46

BRIDGE, Frank   5   Dance: Sir Roger de Coverly 1922   DT 23
1879-1941   Eng   Songs
                               4   Love Went a-Riding 1914   CT 39
                               4   O That It Were So 1913   HN 44
                               4   Sally in Our Alley   RC 27
                              20   Suite The Sea 1910   BA 40;   BN 23;   CL 23
                              12   Summer, Tone Poem 1914   DT 23
                              10   Two Poems for O: The Open Air and the Story of my
                                          Heart 1915   NS 23

BRISTOW, George   10   Columbus Overt in D   NP 1866
1825-1898   US   10   Concert Overt Op 3   NP 1846
                              30   Jullien, Symph No 2 in d   NP 1855
                              30   Symph in e Arcadian   NP 1873
                              30   Symph Op 26 in f#   NP 1858

BRITAIN, Radie   6   Prelude to a Drama   AT 52;   CH 37;   LA 49
1903-   US   7   Three Nocturnes for Small O 1934   AT 47

BRITTEN, Benjamin   15   Ballad of Heroes Chor and O Op 14   BU 63
1913-   Eng   8   The Building of the House Overt   HN 69
                              20   Cantata Academica, Carmen Basiliense Op 62   CL 61
                              19   Cantata Misericordium Op 69   PH 64

BRITTEN, B. (Cont.)

31-33	P Conc No 1 Op 13	CL 48; HN 53; LA 48; NP 49; SF 48; UT 48; WA 49
21	V Conc No 1 Op 15	NP 39; WA 51
26	Gloriana, Symphon Suite from Opera Op 52 NR 55	
25	Diversions for P Left Hand Op 21 BA 67; PH 41; RC 65	
7	5 French Folk Songs, Baritone and O 1946 CH 48	
21	Les Illuminations Soli and O Op 18 CH 67; NA 61, 65; LA 51; PH 58; SL 61	
25	Nocturne for Tenor and Str Op 60 SL 60	
8	Peter Grimes Opera Op 33: two excerpts HN 58	
7	-Passacaglia Op 33b BN 45; CH 61; DA 49; HN 60; PT 46, 62; SE 46; WA 46	
15	-Four Sea Interludes Op 33a BU 46; CH 61, 66; CT 46, 58; CL 67; DA 46; DE 67; HN 69; NA 59, 69; KC 53; MN 63; PH 48; PT 48, 62; SL 47; SE 46, 69; UT 68; WA 46, 49, 52, 54	
12	-Three Sea Interludes BA 49, 50, 63; CH 46; CL 45; DE 48, 65; DT 55; MN 49; RC 46, 58	
13	Scottish Ballad for 2 P and O Op 26 AT 57; BA 56, 62; CT 41, 55, 58; DE 49; DT 52; NA 58; KC 57; LA 52; MN 47; NR 50; PT 59; WA 47	
24	Serenade for Tenor, Horn and Str Op 31 DT 44, 58; LA 49; SE 49	
16	Simple Symph Op 4 BU 41; SF 66	
20	Sinfonia da Requiem Op 20 BN 41; CH 46; CT 68; DT 69; HN 67; KC 64, 66; MN 45, 60; NP 55, 64; PH 64; RC 66; SL 62, 65; SF 64, 68	
45	Spring Symph for Soli, Chor and O Op 44 CL 66; DA 67; NP 62	
31	Symph for C and O BN 65; BU 65; MN 66; PT 66; SF 65	
11	Soirées Musicales, Suite fr Rossini Op 9 BU 43	
17-19	Var and Fugue on a Theme of Purcell: Young Person's Guide to O Op 34 AT 67; BN 54; BU 48; CT 69; DA 50; DT 69; HN 56, 65; LA 49 MN 48, 49, 66; PH 54, 61, 66; PT 58, 64; SL 57, 68; SE 50; UT 51(2), 54, 66; WA 59, 61	
25	Var on Theme of Frank Bridge, Op 10 BA 58, 68; BN 40, 49, 56; CH 55; CT 58; DT 62, 68; NA 66; LA 47; NP 62; SL 57	
85	A War Requiem Op 66 AT 68; BN 63; CL 64; DA 64; DT 64; NA 65; KC 65; MN 64; NR 65; NP 66; SE 64	

BROADWOOD, John   5   Song: Twankydillo   NS 1894
  c 1810-1890   Eng

BROCKWAY, Howard   8   Ballad: Hey Nonino, double chor a capella   CH 08
  1870-1951   US   Sylvan Suite Op 19   BN 00
                                  Symph in C Op 12   BN 06

BROEKMAN, David 1902-1958 US	35	Symph No 2 CT 46
BROMAN, Sten 1902- Swed	23	Symph No 4 DT 66
BRONSART, Hans von 1830-1913 Ger	30 15	P Conc in f# NP 1876 Frühlings-Fantasie for Grand O NS 1880
BROOKS, Ernest 1903- US	8 10	Chicabana, Op 157 RC 40 Three Units PH 32
BROTT, Alexander 1915- Can	15 9	Fancy and Folly SL 47 Symphon Poem: The Oracle SE 43
BROWN, Earle 1926- US	15-20 15	Available Forms II for O Four Hands, 98 Musicians and 2 Conductors NP 63 From Here CH 69
BRUBECK, Howard 1916- US	23 20	Dialogues for Jazz Combo and O NP 59 Elementals NR 65

BRUCH, Max   4   Achilles,Soli Chor and O Op 50: Aria, Andromache's
1838-1920   Ger   Lament   CH 21, 26;   CL 23;   DT 23, 28, 30
                            LA 23, 28;   MN 23;   NP 12;   NS 1891, 14, 16;
                            PH 14, 30;   SL 11, 13
                  25   V Conc No 1 in g Op 26   AT 52, 58, 61;   BA 26, 42,
                            45, 47, 55, 60, 63;   BN 1882, 86, 91, 92, 94, 04,
                            11, 17, 20;   BU 52, 67;   CH 1894, 00, 03, 14,
                            16, 20, 24, 26, 27, 35, 40, 42, 46, 60, 63, 69;
                            CT 1897, 01, 06, 11, 12, 14, 41, 47, 65;   CL 22,
                            31, 51;   DA 25, 29, 48, 54, 58;   DE 48, 55, 63;
                            DT 16, 17, 22, 25, 30, 34, 45, 51, 69;   HN 14,
                            33, 45, 61;   NA 35, 37, 47, 54, 60;   KC 36, 46,
                            64, 67;   LA 34, 44, 55, 58, 62, 65;   ML 63;
                            MN 22, 27, 38, 50, 63;   NR 60, 63;   NP 1871,
                            82, 85, 92, 00, 04, 12, 19, 20(2), 21, 50, 51,
                            54, 55, 67;   NS 1880, 03, 05, 14, 18;   PH 01,
                            02, 05, 08, 09, 12, 14, 23, 27, 30, 65;   PT 39,
                            42, 48, 55, 64, 67;   RC 54;   SL 13, 14, 16, 23,
                            36, 45, 58, 69;   SF 12, 29, 30, 39, 68;   SE 30,
                            39, 51, 58;   UT 63;   WA 33, 36, 45, 50, 52, 59, 66
                  30   V Conc No 2 in d Op 44   BN 1888, 04, 12;   CH 1897,
                            06, 12, 15, 24;   CT 03, 37;   HN 14;   LA 23;
                            MN 25, 27;   NP 1895, 97, 13;   NS 1889, 94, 13;
                            17;   PH 10;   SL 13, 26
                  6   -Recitative and Finale   CH 13
                  45   V Conc No 3 in d Op 58   BN 1891, 95, 08;   CH 1898,
                            35;   CT 1896;   NP 50;   NS 1891;   UT 57
                  30   2 P Conc Fantasy Op 88   NP 17;   PH 16
                  4   Cross of Fire, Das Feurer Kreuz,Soli, Chor and O Op 52
                            aria Ave Maria   HN 33;   MN 31;   NS 13
                  8   Kol Nidrei for C Op 47   BN 1888, 93, 11;   CH 14;
                            CT 00, 21;   KC 58;   NS 1882, 94, 22
                            -arr for Double Bass and O   BA 68

BRUCH, M. (Cont.)

4   Lorelei Opera Op 16: Prelude   BN 1882, 83;   CH 20; MN 23, NP 32;   SL 11

4   Odysseus for Soli, Chor and O Op 41: aria Hellstrah-lander Tag   CH 10, 12;   NS 15;   PH 01, 16

3   -Penelope Weaving   CH 15

9   Romance in F for V Op 85   BN 1893;   CH 1896

   Römische Leichenfeier Chor and O Op 34   NP 26

39   Scottish Fantasy for V and O Op 46   AT 65;   BN 1888, 95, 98, 03, 11, 21, 68;   CH 1893, 94, 01, 11, 12, 20, 23, 37, 41;   CT 1895, 16, 25;   CL 27; DA 64, 68;   DT 26, 31, 66;   KC 60;   LA 50; NP 1894, 07, 19;   NS 05, 11, 20, 24;   PH 19; PT 51, 62, 67;   SL 19, 31;   SF 19;   SE 66

8   Serenade for V and O Op 75   BN 04

14   Swedish Dances for V Op 63   CH 1893

36   Symph No 3 in E Op 51   BN 1882;   NS 1882

BRUCKEN Fock, Gerard von 1859-1935   Neth

15   Impressions on Midi   NP 27

BRUCKNER, Anton 1824-1890   Aust

12   Andante from Symph in f, Student work, 1863   NP 31

8   Adagio from Str Quin in F 1878   NP 33

25   Mass in e for Chor and Wind O 1866   DA 53

90   Mass in f No 3 Grosse Messe for Soli, Chor and O 1867 NP 64

12   Overt in g 1862   PH 61

9   Psalm 150 for Sopr, O, Chor and Org 1892   NP 62

SYMPHONIES

10   "O" in d 1863: Scherzo only   CL 41

44   No 1 in d 1863   CH 39

50   No 2 in c 1871   BN 50;   CH 02, 10;   CT 38; HN 48;   KC 47;   NP 25;   PH 02;   SL 65

60   No 3 in d Wagner Symph 1873   BN 60;   CH 00, 10, 32, 37, 40, 52, 58, 63;   CT 13, 46, 68;   CL 49, 63, 65;   HN 64;   KC 69;   NA 38;   LA 66; NP 64;   PH 67;   SF 64;   RC 2nd mvt only 37

60   No 4 in E^b Romantic 1874   BA 64;   BN 1898, 32, 65; BU 49, 55, 62;   CH 1896, 15, 34, 41, 48, 51, 52, 64, 67;   CT 06, 15, 28, 45, 64;   CL 44, 50; DA 64;   DT 26, 58, 63;   HN 42, 43;   KC 49, 65; LA 26, 33, 46, 51, 65;   MN 29, 42, 36, 66; NR 58;   NP 25, 32, 42, 48, 63, 66, 68, 69; PH 06, 14, 64, 67, 69;   PT 41, 49, 55, 59, 63; RC 33, 49, 62, 66;   SL 12, 41, 42, 62;   SF 50, 57, 66;   SE 61;   UT 60;   WA 42

65   No 5 in B^b 1875   BN 01, 59;   CH 13, 46;   CT 32, 62;   DT 65;   KC 67;   LA 58;   MN 68;   NP 11, 17, 32, 64;   PH 07, 34, 39, 65, 67;   PT 61; SF 68

50   No 6 in A 1879   BA 69;   BN 68, 69;   CH 50, 61; CT 34;   DE 55;   NP 12, 64;   PT 58;   WA 51, 61

BRUCKNER, A. (Cont.)   SYMPHONIES (Cont.)
                  70   No 7 in E 1884   BN 1886, 06, 09, 11, 12, 15, 34,
                          35, 39, 48, 51, 63, 67;   BU 48, 56, 59;   CH 05,
                          16, 28, 30, 49, 52, 55, 62, 63, 65, 67;   CT 16,
                          26, 59;   CL 31, 45, 48, 52, 62, 66;   DA 59;
                          DT 34, 59, 66;   HN scherzo only 43, 61, 69;
                          KC 61, 68;   LA 35, 54, 57, 66, 69(2);   ML 68;
                          MN 33, 35, 62;   NP 1886, 30, 34, 39, 41, 44,
                          54, 59, 62, 63, 65;   PH 24, 48, 52;   PT 53, 60,
                          67, 68;   RC 58, 69;   SL 39, 50, 69;   SF 46,
                          54, 60, 67;   SE 69
                  80   No 8 in c 1884   BN 08, 09, 28, 31, 36, 38, 46, 47,
                          61, 64, 69;   BU 54, 61;   CH 48, 49, 51, 60, 66;
                          CT 29, 52;   CL 38, 41, 57, 69;   KC 64;   LA 60;
                          MN 58;   NP 19, 33, 35, 40, 47, 50, 52, 61, 64;
                          PT 56, 59;   SF 65
                  60   No 9 in d 1887-96   BN 03, 07, 14, 36, 62, 66;
                          BU 66;   CH 03, 12, 23, 24, 26, 27, 30, 33, 35,
                          38, 49, 66, 68;   CT 22, 65;   CL 51, 57;   DT 68;
                          HN 65;   KC 66;   LA 59, 62, 64;   MN 52, 64;
                          NP 27, 33, 34, 45, 49, 53, 61, 64;   PH 47, 58,
                          65;   PT 66;   SF 54, 66
                  22   Te Deum in C for Sopr, Chor, Org and O 1881-83
                          BN 60;   CH 55;   CT 63;   CL 67;   NA 39;   KC 48;
                          NP 43;   PH 65;   PT 51, 66, 68;   RC 47;   SF 53;
                          UT 69

BRULL, Ignaz   30   P Conc Op 10   NP 1879
1846-1907   Austr   8   Overt to Macbeth Op 43   BN 00

BRUNE, Adolph G.   8   Ein Dammerungsbild, Twilight Picture, Capriccio Op 64
1870-1935   Ger/US   CH 17, CT 16
                     6   A Fairy Tale   CH 19
                     8   Overt to a Drama Op 61   CH 15, 28
                     8   Overt to a Tragedy, Op 62   CH 30
                     23   Symph No 2 Op 29   CH 26
                             -Scherzo and Adagio   CH 23
                     15   Symphon Poem: Das Lied des Singschwans   CH 12
                     20   Tone Poem, At Bernina Falls Op 83   CH 34

BRUNEAU, Alfred   7   L'Attaque du Moulin, Opera 1893: Air of Jacqueline
1857-1934   Fr   PH 12
                     15   -Suite   NS 15
                     12   La Belle au Bois Dormant,Sleeping Beauty Symphon
                             Poem Op 13   CH 03, 07, 08, 15;   NS 03
                     5   L'heureux Vagabond, Song from Leids de France Op 21
                             NP 1899
                     7   Messidor Opera 1897: Symphon Entr'acte   BN 03, 18;
                             CH 03;   CT 07;   DA 34

Brunswick, Mark   18   Symph in B^b 1945   MN 46
1902-   US

BRUNZ   20   Conc for Bassoon and O   DT 48
             Russ

BRUSSELMANS, Michel   17   Suite after caprices by Paganini   CH 39;   CT 39;
1886-   Belg   CL 39;   DT 40;   MN 41

BRYAN, Charles   8   The White Spiritual Symph 1946: Andante, Second mvt
1911-1955   US   CT 41

BUCHARDO, Carlos   15   Escenas Argentinas: Tone Poem for O   CT 37
1890-   Brazil
(or Lopez-Buchardo)

BUCHAROFF, Simon   8   Reflections in the Water, scene de Ballet from
1881-   US   opera Sakahra   NP 28

BUCK, Dudley   10   Prelude and March from Longfellow's Golden Legend,
1839-1909   US   for mixed Chorus   CH 39

BULL, John   5   The King's Hunt arr Bantock   CT 11;   NS 09
1562-1628   Eng

BULL, Ole   30   V Conc in A   NP 1868
1810-1880   Nor   15   Fantasia, after Bellini, Capulets and Montagues
                                NP 1869
                       15   Pollacca Guerriera V and O   NP 1868
                        5   The Shepherd's Sunday   DA 25

BÜLOW, Hans von   6   Funerale No 4   BN 1893
1830-1894   Ger   10   Julius Caesar, Overt from Incidental Music Op 10
                                NP 1877
                       15   Minstrel's Curse, Des Sängers Fluch, Ballad for O
                                Op 16   NS 1886, 89

BURGMÜLLER, Norbert   25   P Conc Op 1   NP 1865
1810-1836   Ger

BURLEIGH, Henry   4   Song: Deep River   HN 42
1866-1949   US

BURMEISTER, Richard   25   P Concerto Op 1 in d   BN 1889;   CH 00;   CT 00;
1860-1944   Ger   NS 1890;   PH 08
                       12   The Sisters: Poem for O   CT 02;   NP 01

BURT, Francis   13   Expressione Orchestrale Op 10   SL 68
1926-   Brit

BUSCH, Adolf   18   Psalm No 6 for Chor and O   PH 57
1891-1952 Ger/Swiss   18   Var and Fugue on a Mozart Theme Op 19a   NP 29

BUSCH, Carl   10   Elegie   KC 43
1862-1943   US   15   Indian Rhaps   CH 23
                        9   Minnehaha's Vision   KC 31, 41
                       10   A Song of Chibiabos, Symphon Poem   KC 33;   SL 26

BUSCH, Fritz   30   Symph in e   NS 27
1890-1951   Ger

BUSONI, Ferruccio   60   Arlecchino: Opera in one act 1917   NP Rondo only 51
1866-1924   It/Ger   10   Berceuse Élégiaque Op 42   BN 52;   CH 11, 24;
                              NP 10, 28, 32, 34, 53;   PT 50;   SL 21
                      17   P Conc Op 39 with final chorus for male Voices
                              CH 39;   CT 29, 55;   CL 65;   MN 69;   SL 69;
                              WA 43
                      25   V Conc in D Op 35a   CH 32;   MN 41;   WA 42
                      14   Dance-Waltz Op 53   NP 53, 65;   PT 62
                      30   Indian Fantasy P and O Op 44   CH 39;   DT 66;
                              PH 14;   WA 36, 48
                      27   Geharnischte Suite No 2 Op 34   BN 05
                       8   Lustpiel Overt Op 38   BN 05;   CH 06, 09, 29,
                              32, 49;   SL 10, 21
                      12   Rondo arlecchinesco, Harliquin, Tenor and O Op 46
                              BN 05, 64;   CH 28;   CT 65;   CL 65;   MN 66;
                              NP 27, 32
                      20   Sarabande and Cortège Op 51   SL 66
                      45   Turandot Suite Op 41   BA 58;   BN 10, 16;   CT 29;
                              CL 55;   MN 55;   NP 09;   PT 55;   SL 56
                      20   -Excerpts   CH 58;   NP 57;   RC 55, 57
                      40   Symphon Suite Op 25   BN 1891;   SF 19
                      20   Symphon Tone Poem Op 32a   BN 1892

BUTTERWORTH, George   11   A Shropshire Lad, Rhaps 1913   HN 66;   UT 45
1885-1916   Eng

BUXTEHUDE, Dietrich   8   Chaconne in e arr Chavez   BN 58;   BU 64;   CH 41;
1637-1707   Ger   CL 37, 65;   NA 64;   NR 57;   PH 63;   PT 37;
                              RC 65;   SL 38;   SE 55;   WA 40
                      12   Passacaglio, arr Cailliet   PH 36, 38, 40, 43, 62
                       6   Prelude and Fugue in e arr Leonardi   BA 38
                      12   Sarabande and Courant   PH 30

BUZZI-PECCIA, Arturo   8   Gloria a Te   SL 12
1853-1943   US

BYRD, William   The Seven Hills, from Cincinnati Profiles,
1926-   US   13   Suite for O, 1st mvt   CT 52

BYRD, William   4   Ave Verum Corps from Bk I, Part II Gradualia, 1605
1543-1623   Brit   CT 25
                       4   Motet for 3 Voices, Miserere Mei   CH 32
                       2   Pavane and Gigue arr Stokowski   PH 36, 37
                       5   Sellinger's Round   CT 11
                   12-13   Suite from Fitzwilliam Virginal Book arr Gordon
                              Jacob   CT 40;   CL 44;   NP 39;   PH 41;   PT 39;
                              WA 42

BYRON, Arthur   7   Pragmatism No 1   PT 64
1910-   Brit

CAAMANO, Roberto   18   Suite for Str Op 9   NP 54
1923-   Arg

CADMAN, Charles   10   American Suite for Str 1937   CH 38;   NA 44;
1881-1946   US   PT 38
               10   Dark Dances of the Mardi Gras 1933   DT 33
               9   Oriental Rhaps, Omar Khayyam 1917   LA 21
               23   Symph No 1 in e, Pennsylvania 1939   CH 41;   LA 39

CAETANI, Roffredo   32   Symphon Prelude in a Op 11 No 5   BN 04
1871-   It   14   Symphon Prelude in E^b NP 02

CAGE, John   10-25   Atlas Eclipticalis with Winter Music,Electronic
1912-   US   Version   CL 69;   DE 69;   NP 63
               19   Conc for Prepared P and O   BU 64, 67

CAILLIET, Lucien   7   Var on Pop Goes the Weasel   UT 53
1897-   US

CAIN, Llewellyn B.   5   Wake Up Sweet Melody, part song   CH 32
1896-   US

CALKER, Darrell   15   Penguin Island   WA 44
             US

CAMPBELL   4   Spirit Flower   SE 48
             US

CAMPO, Conrado del   8   Symphon Interlude, El infierno, The Divine Comedy,
1876-1953   Sp   SL 30

CAMPRA, André   4   Aria, Charmante Papillon fr Fêtes Venitiennes,
1660-1744   Fr   Opera 1699   PT 51

CANNING, Thomas   10   Fantasy on a Hymn by Justin Morgan   DT 59;
1911-   US   HN 59;   KC 61

CANTELOUBE, Joseph   18   Chants d'Auvergne for Mezzo and O 1924   BA 4 songs
1879-1957   Fr   44;   CT 47;   NA 48;   KC 39, 50;   MN 5 songs
                   39;   SL 49

CAPLET, André   20   Épiphanie, Musical Fresco for C and O 1923
1878-1925   Fr   BN 24;   CH 27;   MN 45;   PH 26
               5   -Dance of the Little Moors   MN 45

CARISSIMI, Giacomo   4   Song, Vittoria, Mio Core   CH 32
1605-1674   It

CARMICHAEL, Hoagy   8   Star Dust arr Morton Gould   CT 44;   MN 44
1899-   US   5   Brown County Autumn   NA 49

CARPENTER, John A.   24   Adventures in a Perambulator, Suite 1915   BN 15(2),
1876-1951   US   23, 27;   BU 47;   CH 14, 15, 22, 31, 35, 41;
                   CT 16, 26;   DT 32, 46;   LA 24;   MN 24;   NS 15,
                   Selections 21;   SL 12, 15, 18, 41

CARPENTER, J.A. (Cont.)	Time in Minutes	
	10	The Anxious Bugler 1943 NP 43
	30	Birthday of the Infanta, Ballet 1919 BN 20; CH 20, 29; NA 42
	26	Concertina for P and O 1917 BN 19; CH 15, 21, 25, 27, 35; CT 26, 40; NS 20; WA 47
	23	V Conc 1937 BN 38; CH 37; CL 37; LA 37
	15	Dance Suite 1942 BN 35; CH 35; LA 36; SL 50
	24	Gitanjali, Song Cycle for mezzo Sopr and Chamber O 1932 CT 38; NA 42; KC 35
	10	Hurdy-Gurdy SL 41
	10	Krazy Kat Ballet 1922 Excerpts CH 21; CT 22; NA 40; SL 22
	10	Lake SL 41
	4	On a Screen, Voice and O PH 18
	2	Odalisque, Voice and O PH 18
	18	Patterns for P and O BN 32; CH 32
	10	Pilgrim Vision CH 22, 23; DT 26; PH 20, 21
	15	Sea Drift, Symphon Poem 1933 BA 37; CH 33, 45; CL 35; NA 51, NP 34, 44; RC 34; SL 39
	19	The Seven Ages, Suite 1945 CH 45; NP 45; PH 46; SF 46
	15	Skyscrapers, Ballet 1926 BN 27, 28, 32; CH 26, 34, 39, 44, 47, 50; CT 27; CL 33; DT 27; LA 27; NP 28; PH 27; SF 28
	12	Song of Faith, Chor and O 1931 CH 31(2); HN 32; NA 44; LA 31
	18	Symph No 1 1940 BN 17; CH 17, 18, 40; NA 41; LA 40; PT 40
	21	Symph No 2 1942 CH 43; NP 42
	20	Symph Sermons in Stones NS 19
	7	War Lullaby SE 42
	4	When I Bring You Colored Toys, Song NA 50; PH 40; SL 42
CARRILLO, Julian 1875-1965 Mex	20 20	Concertino for C, Horn, Guitar and O 1926 PH 26 Horizontes for V, C and Harp and O 1947 MN 51; PT 51; WA 51
CARTER, Elliott, Jr. 1908- US	23 23 10	Conc for O NP 69 P Conc BN 66; BU 68; CL 69 Holiday Overt 1944 BA 47; CH 63, 69; DE 68; MN 60; NP 56, 60; PH 67; SF 65; WA 66
	25 24	The Minotaur, Ballet Suite 1946 NA 58 Var for O BN 64; MN 65; PH 62; SL 66; SF 62
CARVALHO, Eleazar de 1915- Brazil	8	Var on 2 Roros for Fl and Str SL 68
CARY US	4	Pastoral song WA 32
CASADESUS, Robert 1889-1972 Fr	22	Ballet Suite No 3 after Rameau Op 54 CL 60; NP 59; RC 42

CASADEUS, R. (Cont.)

15	C Conc Op 43 MN 48	
28	P Conc in E Op 37 CL 54; DE 50; MN 46; NP 47, 55; PH 49; RC 66; PT 50; SL 47, 67	
25	Conc for 2 P and O Op 17 CT 41, 63; CL 63; NP 50; RC 41; SL 64	
14	Conc for 3 P and O Op 65 CT 67; CL 65; NA 69; MN 67; NR 65; PT 66	
20	Suite No 2 in B^b Op 26 Mn 59; NP 51, 69; SL 43 Symph No 2 Op 33 CT 39	

CASALS, Pablo
1876-   Sp

90	El Pesselire, Oratorio, The Manger NR 63; SF 61

CASCARINO, Romeo
1922-   US

12	Divertimento for Woodwinds, Harp, Horns, Str, Celesta, and Percussion NR 59

CASELLA, Alfredo
1883-1947   It

10	Balakireff's Islamay, transcription for O BA 65
30	Conc Romano for Org and O Op 43 CH 28
16	Conc for P, Str, and Percussion Op 69 CH 63; DA 58; PH 67
25	Conc for P, V, C and O Op 56 BN 35; CH 35
30	V Conc in a Op 48 CH 28; CT 28
18	Conc for Clar, Bassoon, V, Trump and O CT 30
20	Convent on the Water, Symphon Suite for Ballet Op 18 BN excerpts 21(2); CT 33; CL 22; MN excerpts 30; NS 20(2), 25
10	LaDonna Serpente, Suite No 2 from the Opera Op 50 NA 37; MN 40; RC 33
12	Élégie Heroique, to The Unknown Soldier Op 29 PH 24
40	La Giarra, Ballet Suite Op 41 BN 26; BU 69; CH 26, 58, 69; CT 25; DE excerpts 61; DT 26; LA 52, 60; MN 55; NP 25, 26, 29, 68 PH 51; PT 50, 56; RC 56; SL 26
18	Italia Rhaps Op 11 BN 22; CH 13, 14, 17, 18, 21, 22, 24, 25, 26, 27, 34, 35; CT 21, 26(2), 29, 52, 61; CL 22; DE 52; DT 21, 31, 32, 59; KC 55; LA 25, 29, 50; MN 25, 64; NP 24, 25; PH 20, 27; RC 35, 49; SL 15, 22, 24; SF 20; SE 28
19	Paganiniana, Divertimento Op 65 CH 49; CL 50, 61; DA 48; LA 49; NA 69; MN 51; NR 68 NP 50, 58; PH 58, 59, 67; PT 47; RC 50, 60, 65; DT 66
22	Partita for P and O Op 42 BN 26; CT 25; DT 26; NP 25; NS 26
8	Puppazetti, Marionette Pieces, for nine instruments Op 27 BN 22; CH 22; CT 23; CL 22
22	Scarlatianina, Divertimento, P and O Op 44 NS 26; PT 59; SL 29; SF 62
13	Serenata for Small O Op 46 NP 30; PH 30
40	Symph No 3 Op 63 CH 40
13	Suite in C Op 13 CL 22; SL 17
15	War Pictures, Pagina di guerra Op 25 NS 19; PH 21

CASINIÈRE, Yves   10   Hercule et les Centaures   PH 28
1918-   Russ/Fr

CASSADO, Joaquin   12   Catalonian Rhaps   NP 28
1867-1926   Sp   15   Hispania, Fantasia Symphonique for P and O   DT 18

CASTAGNONE, Riccardo   5   Preludio Giocoso   BN 36;   MN 39
1906-   It

CASTALDI, Alfonso   14   Symphon Poem Marayas   CH 25
1874-   It/Roum

CASTELLINI, J. E.   15   Misty Dawn, Fantasy   CT 41
1905-   US

CASTELNUOVO-TEDESCO,   25   Birthday of the Infanta, Ballet Suite, 1944   NR 46
   Mario   5   Cipressi, Cypresses   BN 40
1895-   It/US 15   Conc for Guitar in D Op 99   AT 58;   BA 66;   BU 58;
                                  CH 54;   CT 55, 64;   DE 54;   DT 64;   HN 53;
                                  NA 55;   KC 58;   LA 49;   MN 57;   NR 59, 67;
                                  PT 54;   RC 65;   SL 54;   SF 54, 59
                       28   P Conc in F No 2   NP 39
                       33   V Conc in g Italian 1924   CL 30;   LA 30;   MN 28
                       35   V Conc No 2 The Prophet 1939   CL 35;   NP 32
                        8   Harvest Time, Liede   BA 49
                       10   Noah's Ark, Narrator, Chor and O   UT 46
                               Overtures
                       13   Merchant of Venice 1935   NP 40
                        9   Taming of the Shrew 1931   BA 54;   LA 45;
                                  NP 31, 32;   PH 43;   RC 43
                        9   Twelfth Night   NP 39;   SF 45
                       19   Suite, Indian Songs, Dances   LA 42
                       21   Symphon Var for V 1930   NP 29

CASTIGLIONI, Niccolo   6   Conc for O   BU 66
1932-   It   7   Consonante   SF 65

CASTRO, Jose Maria   8   Chorale, Aria, and Finale from Conc Grosso   RC 40
1892-   Sp

CASTRO, Juan José   20   Coralea Criollos   NP 57
1895-   Sp

CATALANI, Alfredo   4   Opera, La Wally 1892: Aria, Ebben ne andro lontana
1854-1893   It   DT 65
                        4   -Dance of Undine   DT 38
                        3   -Prelude Act III, AT Dusk   PT 48;   SL 27

CATEL, Charles   10   Overt to Semiramis Opera 1802   NP 1869
1773-1830   Fr

CATTOZZO, Nino   78   Misteri Dolorosi for Soli, women's Chor and O   DT 37
1887-   It

CATURLA, Alessandro   10   Two Cuban Dances   PH 31
1906-1940   Cuba

CAUFFMAN, Frank   6   Legende   PH 08
1850-   US   15   Symphon Poem, Salammbo   PH 03

CECE, Antonio   13   Passacaglia   MN 39
                  It

CELLA, Theodore   10   Through the Pyrenees 1931   NP 31
1897-   US

CESANA, Otto   20   Swing Septet 3 mvts   NA 41
1899-   It/US

CESTI, Pietro Antonio   4   Aria: E Dove d'agiri from Il Pomo d'Oro, Opera 1667
1623-1669   It   BA 47;   CT 36;   MN 33;   WA 33
(Marc' Antonio)

CHABRIER, Alexis   5   Bourrée Fantasque   arr Mottl   BN 1898, 99, 13, 40,
1841-1894   Fr   45, 52;   CH 1899, 18, 20, 23, 24, 28, 30, 38,
                                 44;   CT 04;   CL 20, 50, 57;   DT 31, 56;   MN 47;
                                 NP 58;   NS 14;   PH 27;   PT 51;   RC 36;   SL 28;
                                 SF 38;   WA 34
                         9   Gwendoline, Opera in two acts 1886: Overt   BA 28;
                                 BN 1896, 03, 07, 14, 20, 23;   BU 56;   CH 14, 24,
                                 32, 41, 45;   CT 18;   CL 22, 24, 25, 28, 35;
                                 DT 64;   PH 08, 10, 18(2), 23, 66;   PT 42, 50;
                                 SL 13, 17, 25;   SE 50;   WA 31, 37
                         5   -Entr'Acts   BN 1894, 97, 18, 21, 30
                         5   -Prelude Act II   CH 1893, 06;   CL 26;   NP 26
                         3   Habenera, trans from P Solo for O   CT 43
                         4   Marche Joyeuse   BN 51;   CH 02, 14, 17, 20, 21, 22,
                                 23, 29, 37, 39, 58;   CT 20, 21, 35, 44;   CL 22,
                                 26, 29;   DT 23;   HN 67;   MN 25, 47;   NP 49;
                                 NS 10;   RC 26;   SL 24;   WA 50, 69
                        10   Ode to Music for Soli, women's Chor and O   NP 10;
                                 SF 48
                         4   LeRoi Malgre Lui, Opera 1887: Fete Polonaise
                                 NR 67;   NP 49, 53, 54, 55;   UT 67;   RC 27;
                                 SL 11;   SF 36;   SE 49
                        12   3 Romantic Waltzes for O arr Mottl   SF 46
                        14   Spanish Rhapsodies   AT 50, 52, 56, 61;   BA 26, 42;
                                 BN 1897, 06, 07, 12, 14, 16, 18;   BU 61;   CH 1894,
                                 95, 05, 08, 09, 17, 18, 20, 29;   CT 1897, 07, 17,
                                 18, 20, 44;   CL 19, 21, 26, 31;   DA 29;   DE 45,
                                 57;   DT 15, 17, 18, 22, 28, 52, 54, 60;   HN 37,
                                 40, 42, 54;   NA 50;   KC 35, 54, 57, 62;   LA 19,
                                 21;   MN 29;   NP 10, 14, 16, 17, 18, 19, 23, 24,
                                 55, 56;   NS 07, 14;   PH 08, 09, 10, 11, 14, 17,
                                 18, 22, 26, 62;   PT 49, 64;   RC 24, 25, 28, 30,
                                 44, 50;   SL 09, 11, 12, 14, 18, 21, 25;   SF 17,
                                 57;   SE 26, 35(2), 38, 41, 46, 52;   UT 47, 68;
                                 WA 32, 34, 46, 50, 60
                        16   Suite Pastorale, five parts   CH 98, 04
                         6   -2 Excerpts, Village Dance and Woodland Scene,
                                 CT 41

CHADWICK, George W.   10   Adonais Overt after Shelley 1898   BN 1899;   SL 19
1854-1931   US   15   Angel of Death Symphon Poem 1917   BN 19;   CH 19,
                             32, 44;   NS 18;   SL 21
                      10   Anniversary Overt 1922   BN 22;   CH 22;   SL 23
                      15   Aphrodite Symphon Poem 1912   BN 12;   CH 12;
                             NS 16, 19
                      15   Cleopatra Symphon Poem 1891   BN 06;   CH 07;
                             CT 07
                       5   Euterpe Overt 1906   BN 03;   CH 04;   LA 19;
                             NP 13;   PH 07(2)
                      10   Lochinvar Ballad, Voice and O 1896   KC 39;   NS 23;
                             PH 16;   SL 17
                       4   Land of Our Hearts, Chor and O 1918   BN 18
                      12   Melpomene Overt 1891   BN 1887, 88, 95, 98, 01, 20,
                             41;   CH 91, 98, 13, 14, 30;   CT 1895;   CL 46;
                             DT 20;   NP 95, 10, 18, 58;   SL 14
                      10   Pastoral Prelude 1891   CH 1894;   BN 1891
                      15   Scherzo in F   BN 1883
                      40   Sinfonietta in D 1906   BN 09, 29;   NS 09, 20
                      15   Symphon Sketches, Suite in A 1896: Jubilee   BA 40;
                             BN 07, 14, 17;   CH 32;   CT 37, 51;   NA 54;
                             KC 40;   NP 42;   PT 41;   SL 28;   SE 54;
                             UT 45, 57, 60
                       5   -Overt   BN 07, 14, 17;   DT 41
                       7   -Noel   BA 40;   BN 07, 14, 17;   CH 11, 32;
                             CT 50, 52;   DT 41;   ML 61;   MN 35;   PH 36,
                             58;   UT 45;   WA 41, 45, 47
                      30   Suite Symphonique in E$^\flat$ 1911   BN 10;   CH 11;
                             NS 11;   SL 12
                      30   Symph No 2 in Bb 1888   BN 1886, 90
                      35   Symph No 3 in F 1896   BN 1894, 13;   CH 1896, 18
                       8   Stabat Mater Chor and O   NP 13
                      18   Tam O Shanter, Symphon Ballad 1917   BN 15, 26;
                             CH 15, 17, 19, 21, 27, 39;   CT 19;   CL 25;
                             NP 17;   PH 18;   SL 17
                      10   Thalia Overt 1883   BN 82
                      10   Theme, Var and Fugue for Org and O 1923   BN 08,
                             16, 21

CHAJES, Julius   26   P Conc in E   DT 53
1910-   Pol   7   Fugue No 1 in a   DT 57

CHAMINADE, Cecile   15   Concertino in D for Fl and O   MN 45
1857-1944   Fr   12   Concertstück Op 40 P and O   CH 1894;   PH 08
                      10   Four Songs   CT 1895
                       5   -Chanson Slave   NS 1890

CHARPENTIER, Gustave 34   Impressions of Italy, Suite   BN 00, 02, 12, 17, 19;
1860-1956   Fr   CH 1893, 00, 04, 05, 09, 13, 20, 25, 28, 31, 32,
                             37;   CT 02;   CL 26;   DT 15, 18, 30, 36;   LA 20;
                             MN 26, 39, 48;   NP 1898, 04, 13, without 2nd mvt
                             28;   NR 53;   NS 19, 24;   PH 08, 09, 10, 11, 17,
                             22, 26, 29;   SL 12, 18, 20;   SF 23;   SE 27
                       5   -Naples   MN 48;   RC 27, 38
                       5   -Serenade   RC 38

CHARPENTIER, G. (Cont.)

5   Louise, Opera, Aria: Depuis le Jour   AT 65;   BU 51;
      CH 12, 14, 18(2);   CT 11, 15, 21, 31, 32, 36, 45;
      CL 18, 25, 26, 29, 43;   DA 28;   DE 48, 59;
      DT 16, 17, 18, 24, 38, 40, 65;   HN 51, 56;
      NA 66;   KC 37, 56;   LA 19, 20, 25, 26, 29;
      MN 25, 31, 36, 40, 48, 56;   NR 66;   NP 14, 19;
      NS 17(2);   PH 02, 10, 12, 23, 39, 49;   RC 26,
      32, 37, 42;   SL 12, 14, 16, 18, 20;   SF 40, 42;
      SE 51

4   -Aria Paris, Paris   NP 28

8   Medea, Opera 1693: Passacaglia Act II   HN 55

30   Metropolis   NP 48

7   3 Songs   NS 14

CHASINS, Abraham   28   P Conc No 1 1929   PH 28
1903-   US   29   P Conc No 2 1932   NP 37;   PH 32
                      3   Flirtation in a Chinese Garden, from Three Chinese
                           Pieces 1929   NP 30
                      7   Parade 1930   LA 42;   NP 30
                      15   Period Suite   CL 50;   DE 50;   MN 50;   NP 49;
                           SL 50

CHAUSSON, Ernest   32   Conc for V, P and Str Op 21   BN 25;   CH 26;   CT 54;
1855-1899   Fr   CL 26;   DT 29;   LA 29;   NS 13
                     30   Conc for Str Quart Op 30 Trans for O   BN 25
                     10   Jardin Aux Lilas, Ballet   AT 54
                     22   Poéme de l'amour et de la Mer Voice and O Op 19
                           CH 58, 67;   CT 19;   CL 63;   DA 64;   DE 50;
                           DT 62;   LA 57;   ML 62;   PH 18;   WA 52
                     17   Poéme, V and O   Op 25   AT 49;   BA 61;   BN 17,
                           32;   BU 60, 69;   CH 18, 22, 31, 34, 36, 44;
                           CT 31, 35, 44, 47, 55;   CL 20, 24, 30, 38, 39,
                           44, 48, 57;   DA 55;   DE 47, 48, 56, 57, 63, 67;
                           DT 18, 28, 48, 57, 68;   HN 49;   NA 68;   KC 61;
                           LA 32, 43, 46;   MN 29, 33, 39, 51;   NR 51, 56,
                           67;   NP 48, 63;   NS 04, 10, 15, 23;   PH 17,
                           18, 25, 56;   PT 44, 63;   RC 28, 61;   SL 28,
                           33, 41, 51, 58, 66;   SF 38, 44;   UT 52, 62;
                           WA 34, 37, 40, 49, 57
                     6   Soir de Fête Op 32   BN 22
                     31   Symph in Bb Op 20   AT 51, 55;   BN 05, 16, 19, 22,
                           31, 37, 40, 52, 61;   BU 50;   CH 08, 09, 14, 15,
                           17, 18, 19, 21, 22, 23, 24, 25, 27, 32, 33, 35,
                           37, 44, 46, 50, 55;   CT 18, 31, 44, 50, 62;
                           CL 19, 20, 22, 26, 31, 37, 49;   DE 48, 54, 60;
                           DT 28, 39, 43, 44, 45, 46, 47, 54, 61;   HN 51,
                           59;   NA 47, 57, 68;   KC 54;   LA 30, 45, 49;
                           MN 35, 39, 45, 47;   NP 24, 40, 45, 55, 63;
                           NS 10, 15, 20;   NR 52, 67;   PH 18, 20, 22, 24,
                           32, 37, 51;   SF 20, 21, 39, 44, 45, 48, 49;
                           SE 40;   WA 33, 38, 42, 46
                     11   Vivianne, Symphon Poem Op 5   BN 01, 07;   CH 98;
                           CL 27;   DT 24, 26;   PH 30;   SF 16

CHAUSSON, E. (Cont.)
		Songs
	4	Le Temps de Lilas CH 19; DT 19; PH 19, 35
	4	Chanson Perpetuelle Voice and O Op 17 CT 21; CL 21, 27; PH 20
	4	Marine CT 36

CHAVARRI, Eduardo L. 6   Acuarelas Valencianas   RC 36
1875-   Sp   6   Andante for Str O   RC 40
                      6   Festival   RC 41

CHAVEZ, Carlos   23   Ballet Suite, Horse Power   1927   CL 37;   HN 46, 68;   LA 44;   NP 36;   PH 35;   PT 37
1899-   Mex   7   Chaconne, arr from Buxtehude   HN 63
                     33   P Conc 1940   NP 41;   PT 60;   SE 53
                     23   Conc 4 Horns and O 1938   CH 41;   PT 46;   SF 44
                     36   V Conc 1950   LA 51;   NP 65
                     23   Daughter of Golchis, Suite, La Hija de Colquide, Ballet 1944   HN 47
                      8   Elatio   HN 68
                     18   Resonances, La Paloma Azul   CL 66;   SE 66
                     10   Saraband for Str O   HN 46;   LA 44;   NR 61; SF 44
                     11   Symph Antigona 1933   BN 35;   CH 36;   NP 36; PH 35;   RC 40;   SF 39
                     11   Symph No 2 India 1936   BN 35, 58;   BU 67;   CH 41; CL 56(2), 65:   DT 68;   DA 59;   HN 46;   NA 59; KC 61;   LA 51;   MN 66;   NR 63;   NP 36, 60; PH 36, 65;   PT 46, 64;   SL 38, 45, 67, 69; SF 39, 42;   UT 65
                     26   Symph No 3 1951   NP 55;   RC 69;   SE 55
                     22   Symph No 4 Romantic 1952   BN 58;   DA 62;   NP 59; PT 60;   RC 69
                     18   Symph No 5   BN 54;   RC 68
                     30   Symph No 6   KC 67;   ML 67;   NP 63
                      8   Toccata for Percussion 1942   CT 49;   HN 56;   UT 66

CHENOWETH, Wilbur   10   Var on Lobe Den Herrn   LA 51
1899-   US

CHERUBINI, L.   4   Aria: Ave Maria   NP 04
1760-1842   Fr   18   Conc Grosso No 8   DT 46
                            OPERAS
                      7   Les Abencérages 1813 Overt   BN 1887, 06, 08, 16, 17;   CH 07;   CT 33;   MN 42;   PH 17;   SF 18; WA 34
                      8   Ali Baba 1833 Overt   BN 1881, 27;   CT 16, 38; CL 35, 52, 57;   DA 48;   MN 51, 57;   PT 56, 62; SL 29
                      9   Anacréon 1833 Overt   AT 53, 62;   BN 1884, 86, 89, 90, 94, 96, 98, 03, 13, 15, 17, 21, 52, 56; CH 1898, 99, 08, 09, 14, 16, 18, 23, 25, 37, 40, 45, 49, 60;   CT 1895, 16, 20, 32, 36, 46, 59; CL 32, 34, 36, 49;   DA 29, 34, 53;   DT 30, 51, 68;   HN 32, 35, 52;   NA 42;   KC 54;

CHERUBINI, L. (Cont.)   Anacréon Overt (Cont.)
                         LA 31, 34, 37, 44, 52, 56;   MN 46;   NR 61;
                         NP 1845, 55, 70, 79, 06, 10, 25, 27, 28, 32, 35,
                         44, 49, 56;   NS 1878, 83;   PH 01, 13, 15, 16,
                         30, 33, 34, 61;   PT 46, 60, 61;   RC 54;   SL 13,
                         29, 41, 64;   SF 15, 17, 29, 33, 34, 44, 49, 60,
                         68;   SE 27, 53;   WA 49

8	Faniska 1806 Overt BN 1881; NP 34
4	L'Hôtellerie Portugaise 1798 Overt BN 1882
11	Lodoiska 1791 Overt BN 11; CH 02
8	Medée 1797 Overt BN 1885, 90, 01; NP 15, 59, 61;
	PT 60; SL 61
4	-Entr'acte NP 1897
9	-Prelude Act III CH 1893, 03; NP 39
6	The Water Carrier, Les Deux Journées, 1801 Overt
	BN 1883, 84, 89, 94, 02; CH 1894, 13; CT 31,
	40; HN 34; MN 27; NP 09, 25, 27, 36, 50;
	PH 06; SL 19

10	Overt in G NS 92
50	Requiem in c CH 66
10	Scherzo from Quart No 12 in E^b for Str O NS 1893
30	Symph in D BN 57; CL 66; MN 56; NP 35, 53,
	57

CHESLOCK, Louis
1899-   Brit/US

17	Rhaps in Red and White BA 49
	Suite from Cantata, David BA 38, 43
15	Symphon Prelude BA 63

CHIAFFARELLI, Albert 8
1884-1945   It/US
                        Prelude to a Merry Play   NP 19

CHOPIN, Frederick
1810-1849   Fr
                        Compositions played as Piano solos, especially in
                         early years, or possibly arranged for Orchestra
                         -NS Piano Solos in 1879, 80, 86, 87, 88, 89(2),
                         90, 91, 93, 95, 16
                         SL Three Piano Solos in 1910

5	-Etude Op 25 No 7 CH 1897
4	-Nocturne Op 48 No 1 CH 1892
4	-Nocturne Op 37 No 1 CH 1892
4	-Two Chants Polonaise CH 1897
15	-Ten Piano Selections DA 29
10	-Three Piano Solos DA 30
14	-Mazurka, Waltz, Polonaise HN 59
4	-Waltz in e Posth CH 1893; MN 45
4	-Waltz Op 34 No 1 CH 1892
3	-Waltz Op 34 No 2 CH 1891

120	Complete Program of Chopin for Ballet Russe de
	Monte Carlo, Items unspecified UT 43

15	Andante Spianta and Grand Polonaise in e^b Op 22
	BN 1882; CH 07; CT 49; CL 60; DA 53;
	DT 26; NA 49; KC 65; MN 22; NS 82, 19;
	PT 43; SL 12, 59; SF 17;

CHOPIN, F. (Cont.)
    27   Chopiniana Suite arr Boutnikoff   BA 45

    35   P Conc No 1 in e Op 11   BA 58, 64, 67;
             BN 1882, 86, 87, 88, 01, 06, 15, 18, 23, 59;   BU 50, 64;
             CH 1898, 02, 06, 09, 18, 22, 23, 25, 30, 38, 42, 44, 47, 48, 64;
             CT 37, 45, 46, 53, 61, 69;
             CL 23, 30, 34, 38, 41, 42, 48, 69;
             DA 52, 58, 61, 62;   DE 48, 54;
             DT 18, 26, 30, 34, 37, 44, 52, 66;
             HN 31, 48, 65;   NA 40, 45, 64, 69;   KC 39, 46, 49, 68;
             LA 24, 47, 49, 52, 53, 59, 62, 65;
             MN 28, 30, 41, 43, 48, 55, 62, 68;
             NR 33, 51, 54, 56, 60, 69;
             NP 1898, 05, 12, 17, 18, 32, 34, 41, 43, 46, 47, 51, 53, 54, 67, 68;
             NS 1886, 88, 14, 16, 17, 20, 25;
             PH 02, 03, 06, 11, 12, 15, 26, 30, 39, 44, 52, 60, 64;
             PT 50, 52, 61, 64, 66;   RC 28, 38, 69;
             SL 11, 23, 27, 41, 46, 48, 49, 50, 51, 54, 55, 57, 59;
             SF 11, 24, 47;   SE 49, 54;   UT 56, 68;   WA 35, 48, 53, 56, 60, 64;
             -Romance and Finale only   DA 26

    24   P Conc No 2 in f Op 21   AT 69;   BA 36, 45, 49, 53, 56, 64, 67;
             BN 1882, 83, 84, 86, 90, 91, 94, 96, 04(2), 10, 11, 17, 35, 44,
             54, 61, 69;   BU 45, 52, 59, 67;   CH 1891, 01, 04(2), 10, 14,
             32, 35, 36, 37(2), 43, 47, 48, 51, 53, 66, 69;
             CT 1898, 00, 05, 32, 49, 54, 58, 63;
             CL 32, 33, 43, 52, 58, 60, 64, 66;
             DA 59, 60, 64, 66;   DE 47, 53, 56, 62, 65;
             DT 20, 44, 47, 53, 58, 63, 68, 69;
             HN 51, 52, 55, 56, 58;   NA 44, 48, 54, 67;
             KC 59, 64, 66;
             LA 19, 36, 46, 51, 55, 58, 63, 67, 69(2);   ML 67;
             MN 24, 27, 36, 40, 44, 46, 59, 63, 65, 69;
             NR 50, 58, 62, 67;
             NP 1899, 07, 11, 12, 20, 25, 28, 29, 31, 38(2), 43, 49, 50(2),
             51(2), 53, 54, 55, 56, 57, 58, 61, 64, 68;
             NS 1882, 90, 15, 17, 26;
             PH 01, 05, 36, 39, 41, 48, 51, 54, 62;
             PT 46, 51, 60, 65, 67;   RC 26, 45, 62;
             SL 11, 17, 20, 22, 38, 46, 53, 56, 58, 59, 64, 67;
             SF 31, 44, 54, 60, 62, 67, 69;   SE 52;   UT 44, 60;
             WA 34, 44, 47, 48, 55, 58, 68

    10   Krakowiak, Conc Rondo, Op 14   BU 40;   CT 49

    20   Les Sylphides, Ballet drawn from Chopin works and Orchestrated by
             Britten, Rieti, Glazounov and others   DE 69;   DT 36;   MN 37,
             38, 43;   PT 36;
             -Waltz   DE 59;
             -Pas de Deux   NR 60

     9   March Funèbres in B^b fron Sonata, Op 35   CH arr Thomas 1891(2), 92,
             93, 94, 95, 96, 98, 99, 00, 03;   LA 32;   NP arr Wood 41, arr
             Thomas 46;   PH arr Stokowski 25

CHOPIN, F. (Cont.)
14	Var on a Mozart Theme Op 2 CT 49; DA 53
6	Arrangements for O from P Compositions:Fantasia in f arr Rudorff NP 32
3	-Mazurka Op 68 No 4 arr Thomas CH 1891
5	-Mazurka arr Stokowski PH 36(2)
5	-Nocturne in E^b and Mazurka Op 7 in B^b NP 37
4	-Nocturne Op 31 No 1 arr Wilhelmj NP 37
8	-Polonaise Op 53 arr Thomas CH 1894(2), 95(3), 96, 97, 99, 04, 05, 07, 11, 16; WA arr Kindler 45
5	-Prelude arr Stokowski PH 36

CHOU, Wen-Chung
1923-   China/US
10	And the Fallen Petals, Triolet for O CT 60; MN 60; NP 60; SF 59
7	Landscapes CH 59; SF 53

CHRISTIANSEN, F.
  Melius
1871-   Nor/US
4	Father Most Holy MN 44
6	Fiftieth Psalm MN 48
4	Rock and Refuge, Swedish Melody MN 43

CHRISTIANSEN, Olaf
              US
4	O King of Glory MN 44
4	The Trumpets of Zion MN 43

CHRISTIANSEN, Paul
              US
6	Symphon mvt The Vials of Wrath MN 41

CHUECA, Federico
1846-1908   Sp
8	Scenes from Old Madrid arr J. Fiqueras and F. Reinisch RC 40, 43

CILEA, Franceso
1866-1950   It
4	Opera L'Arlesiana 1897: Aria DA 35
4	-Lament DE 55, 59; NA 55, 68; ML 68; MN 64; PT 59;
4	Opera, Adriana Lecouvreur 1902: Aria for Soprano KC 46;
4	-E La Solita Storia BA 67;
4	-Io Son L'Umile NA 66; ML 64

CIMARA, Pietro
1887-   It
4	Canto di Primavera, Song DA 58; DE 50; NA 33; WA 49
4	Stornello, Song arr Warren DA 58; DE 50; WA 49

CIMAROSA, Domenico
1749-1801   It
10	Conc for Oboe and Str DE 49; DT 45; MN 62; SL 47; SE 45, 50; UT 62
10	Conc for Oboe and Str arr for Harmonica by Benjamin DE 61
	OPERAS
4	Le astuzie femminili 1794 Aria, Le Ragazze Che Son Di Vent BU 45
8	II fanatico per gli antichi 1777 Overt BU 45; NP 54
6	Giannina e Bernardene 1781 Overt MN 55
6	Gli Orazi e Curiazi 1796 Overt LA 57; NR 57; PH 57

Time in
Minutes

CIMAROSA, D. (Cont.) Operas (Cont.)

9 The Secret Marriage or La Bella Greca 1784 Overt
   BN 52; BU 65; CH 47, 65; CT 25, 32, 35,
   63; CL 31; DT 32, 38, 48; HN 54; NA 57,
   61; KC 52(2); LA 48; MN 49; NP 53;
   PT 49; SF 51, 57; SE 57, 63; WA 52

5 -Aria, Tutti Udite BU 45

4 -Aria, Pardonate DT 38

4 -Aria Pria Che Spunti SF 38

6 -Scena BU 65

6 I Traci amanti, Three Brothers 1793, Overt RC 56

CLAPISSON, Antoine L. 4 My Soul to God, My Heart to Thee, Song NP 1862
1808-1866 Fr

CLAPP, Philip G. 10 Norge, Tone Poem CH 22; SL 19
1888- US 10 Overt to a Comedy MN 48; NP 49; SL 43
5 Summer, Prelude for O CH 27; SL 13
30 Symph in e BN 13
27 Symph in E^b BN 16
20 Symph in C No 8 NP 51

CLARKE, Jeremiah 5 Trump Voluntary arr Wood formerly attributed to
1673-1707 Brit Purcell AT 54; DE 52

CLEMENTI, Muzio 22 Symph in C DA 48
1752-1832 It 25 Symph No 2 in D BA 47; BN 36(2); DE 55;
LA 59; NP 44

CLIFF, Charles J. 6 Overt Pentatonic WA 53
1912- US

CLOKEY, Joseph 4 Two Kings, Xmas Carol AT 54
1890-1961 US

CLOUGH-LEIGHTER, H. 4 Possession Song PH 18
1874- US

COATES, Eric 10 Descriptive Fantasy, Three Bears SE 37
1886- Eng 16 Suite Ancienne RC 23; SE 43

COERNE, Louis 8 Overt to Zenobia, Opera Op 66 SL 14
1870-1922 US

COFFEY, 6 Virginia Reel DT 43
US

COGAN, Robert 11 Fantasia for O CL 54
1935- US

COHN, James 21 Symph No 3 in G DT 59
1928- US 11 Var on the Wayfaring Stranger DT 62

COHON, Baruch 30 Let There be Light, Cantata for Solo Mixed Chor and
1926- US O CT 53

COLE, Rossetter	13	Pioneer Overt Op 35 CH 18
1866- US	15	Suite No 1 from The Maypole Lovers 1934 CH 35
	8	Symphon Prelude CH 15, 17
COLE, Ulric	16	Divertimento for 2 P and Str O 1938 CT 38; WA 43
1905- US	22	P Conc No 2 1942 CT 45
COLERIDGE-TAYLOR,	12	Ballade in a Op 33 CH 02
Samuel	9	Bamboula, Rhapsodic Dance Op 75 CH 14; CT 17;
1875-1912 Brit		DT 39; NP 12; PT 51, SF 12; SL 12
	5	Christmas Oratorio, Overt SL 53
	8	Hiawatha's Song for Soli Chor and O Op 30: Onaway,
		Awake BU 45; CH 99; CT 42; MN 28, 30
	4	-Hiawatha's Vision and Departure HN 33
	14	Petite Suite, Op 77 AT 48
	4	Song Life and Death CT 43
	4	Beautiful is the Sun O Stranger HN 33
COLGRASS, Arthur	10-20	As Quiet As BN 66; CH 66; CL 68; DT 68;
1930- US		ML 68; SE 68
COLLINS,	15	Concert Piece for P and O CH 31
	30	P Conc in E^b CH 24
	10	Mardi-Gras CH 23
	5	Tragic Overt 1914 CH 26, 41; MN 28; SL 26
CONSTANT, Marius	10	Chaconne and Marche Military CH 68; DT 68;
1925- Fr		HN 69; PH 67
	14	24 Preludes for O BN 65; CH 64
CONUS, Jules	25	V Conc in e CH 18; CL 32; LA 27; RC 08;
1869- Russ		SF 27
CONVERSE, Frederick	13	Ave Atque Vale, Tone Poem 1916 BN 16; SL 16
1871-1940 US	8	Cahokia, Prelude to Masque of St. Louis, Chor and
		O 1914 SL 15
	15	California, Tone Poem, Festival Scenes 1927
		BN 27; NA 39
	18	Elegiac Poem 1928 CL 26
	6	Euphrosyne Overt 1903 NA 43, 54
	15	Endymion's Narrative Tone poem Op 10 BN 02, 09; CH 04
	18	Festival of Pan, Romance Op 9 BN 00; CH 05, 12;
		CT 05; NS 06
	12	Flivver Ten Million, A joyous Epic 1927 BN 26;
		DT 27; NA 41
	8	Jeanne d'arc, Incidental Music 1923 BN 07
		La Belle Dame Sans Merci, Ballad for Baritone and O
		BN 05; PH 18
	20	Mystic Trumpeter Orchestral Fantasy 1905 Op 19 BA 39;
		BN 06, 18; CH 06; CT 06, 17; CL 20; NA 38,
		46; NP 53; PH 04; SL 10, 18, 26;
	10	Night and Day for P and O Two Poems 1905 BN 04
	15	Ormazd, Symphon Poem 1912 Op 30 BN 11, 14;
		CH 14; SL 11
	10-15	Prophecy, Sopr and O 1932 BN 32

CONVERSE, F. (Cont.)
```
                  10   Song of the Sea Tone Poem 1924    BN 23
                  25   Symph No 1 in d 1898    BN 98
                  18   Symph No 2 in c 1920    BN 19, 21;    SL 19
                  30   Symph No 6    NA 40
                  30   Symphon Suite, American Sketches 1934    BN 34;
                          CL 38;    NA 37
```

COOLEY, Carleton
1898-   US
```
                  17   Caponsacchi, Epic Poem for O    CL 33;    PH 42
                  20   Song and Dance for Vla    CL 25
```

COPLAND, Aaron
1900-   US
```
                  20   Appalachian Spring, Ballet 1944
                          AT 55, 60;    BA 63;    BN 45, 52, 58;    BU 45, 55;
                          CH 47, 59, 69;    CT 45, 48, 60, 64;    CL 45, 54,
                          58, 64;    DA 50;    DE 50;    DT 58, 61;    NA 45,
                          62, 67;    LA 45, 52, 55;    MN 46, 55;    NR 64;
                          NP 45, 53, 61;    PH 68;    PT 45, 65;    RC 45, 58;
                          SL 52, 59;    SF 45;    SE 42, 49;    UT 47, 65;
                          WA 48, 51, 53, 55, 60, 63
                  22   Billy the Kid Suite from Ballet 1938    AT 55;
                          BN 41;    BU 66;    CL 42;    DA 59;    DE 68
                          LA 43;    MN 43, 69;    NR 60;    PH 43, 55;
                          PT 43;    RC 42;    SL 43, 60;    SF 42;    WA 54
                          -Waltz    DA 46, 49
                  16   Canticle of Freedom    AT 67;    WA 55
                  17   Conc for Clar, Harp and Str 1948    BA 62;    BU 52,
                          64;    CT 63;    CL 56;    DE 56;    HN 68;    LA 51;
                          NR 64;    NP 69    PH 50;    SE 60
                  16   P Conc 1926    BN 26, 53;    NP 63;    WA 68
                  19   Connotations    BA 65;    BU 67;    MN 66;    NP 62;
                          SF 65;    WA 66
                   8   Cortege Macabre from the Ballet Grogh 1932    PH 46
                  18   Dances from Opera Rodeo 1942    AT 50, 54, 57;
                          CT 61;    DA 46, 49;    HN 46;    NA 55;    KC 44,
                          52;    MN 43, 57;    NP 59;    SF 54;    SE 61;
                          UT 50;    WA 55
                   6   -Saturday Night Waltz    AT 47, 54;    MN 54
                   3   -Hoe Down    DE 69;    MN 54, 59;    SL 52;    UT 55
                  14   Dance Symph arr from Ballet Grogh 1925    AT 69;
                          BU 67;    MN 38, 66
                   6   Danzon Cuban 1942    BN 45;    CL 46;    LA 46;    MN 57;
                          RC 45
                   3   Fanfare for the Common Man 1942    BU 64;    CT 42;
                          DE 69;    WA 45, 57
                  11   Inscape    DT 69;    MN 69;    NP 67;    RC 69;    WA 68
                  10   In the Beginning 1947    SF 67
                  12   Jubilee Var 1944    CT 44, 45
                   7   Letter from Home 1944    CL 46
                  14   Lincoln Portrait, Speaker and O 1942    AT 68;
                          BA 43, 47;    BN 42(2), 48;    BU 44, 65;    CH 44;
                          CT 47, 52, 69;    DE 57, 67;    HN 67;    KC 52;
                          LA 46;    MN 43, 67;    NP 45, 55;    PH 48(2);
                          PT 52, 54;    SL 46, 48, 59;    SE 57, 69; SF 69; UT 52
                          55, 61, 63;    WA 68
```

COPLAND, A. (Cont.)

22	Music for the Theatre 1925 BN 25; CT 33; NP 58; NS 26; PH 31	
25	Music for a Great City Suite BN 64; DA 64; MN 65; PH 65; LA 65; PT 67	
12	Music for Radio: Saga of the Prairie 1937 PH 60	
18	Nonet for Str O CL 63; NP 64; PT 63; SF 65	
11	Old American Songs Set II LA 54	
9	Outdoor Overt 1938 AT 64; BU 40, 46; DA 59; DT 54; ML 66; MN 41; NR 60; NP 49, 57; PT 49, 59; RC 62; SE 40; UT 53, 61; WA 66	
6	Preamble for a Solemn Occasion BN 62; UT 64	
16	Piano Quart SF 66	
9	The Quiet City, Incidental Music AT 52, 63; BN 40, 41, 44, 45, 61; CH 43, 52; CT 41, 69; CL 44, 52, 69; DA 48; DT 69; HN 50, 67; NA 46; KC 45; LA 53; NP 41, 64; PH 52, 57; PT 58; RC 45; SL 42, 53, 55; SF 55, 66, 67; UT 61; WA 66	
15	Red Pony Suite 1948 HN 48; NR 52; NA 60; NP 49	
11	El Salon Mexico 1936 AT 51, 64; BA 42, 43, 56; BN 38, 43, 65; BU 63; CH 54; CT 38, 67; CL 44, 66; DA 49; DE 49, 57; DT 57; HN 41; NA 63, 69; KC 62, 68; MN 39, 45, 57; NR 51, 62, 65; NP 43, 51(3), 54, 60; PH 41; PT 41, 44, 54, 57; RC 44, 60, 69; SL 39, 45, 49, 58; SF 39; UT 49, 54, 58, 67; WA 52, 53, 54;	
5	Scherzo for Large O CT 27; PH 27	
18	Statements 1935 BN 49; MN 35; NP 41; PT 68; WA 55	
25	Symph No 1 for Org and O 1925 BN 24, 34, 59, 63; CH 33; NR 60; NP 66; NS 24	
40	Symph No 3 1946 AT 67; BA 68; BN 46(2), CH 50; CT 63; CL 47, 65; DT 56, 65; KC 62, 66; LA 48; MN 52, 58; NP 47, 57, 65, 67; PT 64; SL 63, 69; SF 50; SE 61; UT 65; WA 67	
15	Short Symph No 2 1933 NP 56, 66; PT 66	
21	Symph Ode 1929 BN 31, 55; CH 69; NP 60	
18	The Tender Land, Suite from Opera BN 58, 59; CH 57; CT 68; CL 60; DE 60; DT 60; KC 68; LA 61; NA 64, 68; NR 68; PH 61; PT 62, 68; SL 58; WA 61	
11	Two Pieces for Str O 1928 BN 28 Var on a Shaker Melody BN 51; CL 69; DA 59; NP 58; PH 60; PT 59; SF 66	

COPPOLA, Carmine	6	Danse Pagane RC 38
COPPOLA, Piero 1888- It	15 13	Burlesque from Suite Intima LA 30; PH 29 La Ronde Sous la Cloche SL 36
CORDERO, Roque 1917- Panama	12	Panamanian Overt MN 45

CORELLI, Arcangelo   4   Adagio for C and Str   CL 69;   SL 44, 50, 57
1653-1713   It   13   Conc for Org arr Malipiero   CH 33;   CT 54
                     12   Conc 2 V, P and C   DE 54
                     CONC GROSSO
                     12   Op 6 No 1 in D for Str and O   CH 38;   CT 53;
                              MN 50;   NP 61;   PH 61
                     13   Op 6 No 2 in F   CT 63;   PT 53
                     13   Op 6 No 3 in c   BN 24
                     15   Op 6 No 8, Christmas, in g   AT 54, 58;   BA 51;
                              BN 25, 34, 46, 68;   BU 40, 47;   CH 27, 48;
                              CT 26, 38, 48, 69;   CL 31, 50, 53, 68;   DA 49;
                              HN 67;   NA 56;   KC 51;   LA 31, 39;   ML 61;
                              MN 59;   NR 52;   NP 23, 27, 30, 37, 45, 52;
                              PH 26, 37, 45, 54, 58, 68;   PT 52;   RC 58;
                              SL 34, 65;   SF 37, 49, 53, 59;   SE 63;   UT 45;
                              WA 42
                     13   Op 6 No 12 in F arr Gemianini   NA 37

                      9   La Folia V and O or Harpsichord and O Op 5 No 12
                              AT 53, 57, 64;   CH 33;   CT 26, 32;   DT 26;
                              NA 49;   MN 32, 41;   PH 27;   PT 46;   SL 50;
                              UT 55;   WA 42
                      8   Pieces for Str   UT 43
                     13   Sonata in D Op 5 No 12   AT 52;   CT 26, 32
                     12   Sinfonia in D   ML 61
                      8   Suite for Str arr Pinelli from Sonata Op 5
                              BA 51;   BN 30, 31, 40, 42, 44, 48;   CH 47;
                              CT 51, 52, 56;   CL 48;   HN 59, 60, 48;   NA 39,
                              43, 53;   LA 44;   MN 37;   NR 53, 57;   NP 45,
                              56;   PH 28, 31, 32, 38, 39, 45, 47, 50, 57;
                              PT 51;   RC 31;   SL 27, 28;   SF 44, 51;   SE 51;
                              UT 43
                      8   Suite arr Kindler   WA 38, 40, 41, 43, 46, 48

CORNELISSEN, Arnold
1895-   US   9   Lilac Bush in Bloom   BU 44;   WA 42
                      8   Serenade Enfantine Op 33   BU 43
                     22   Symph No 1   WA 42

CORNELIUS, Peter   Opera, Der Barbier von Bagdad 1858:
1824-1874   Ger   7   Overt   BA 59;   CT 26;   BN 88, 96, 98, 04, 13,
                              15, 63;   BU 47;   CH 98, 04, 07, 16, 24, 37;
                              CL 48;   MN 29, 42;   NP 18, 40;   PH 06, 27;
                              PT 41
                           Opera, Der Cid 1865:
                      8   Overt   CH 05;   KC 53
                      5   -Siegesmarsch   CH 05
                      4   -Songs: Ein Ton   NS 1893

CORSI, Giuseppe   4   Adoramus te Christe   MN 42, 48
fl 1660-   It

CORTESE, Luigi   7   Canto Notturno   DE 65
1899-   It

CORTEZ, Ramiro   20   Sinfonia Sacra   NP 54
1934-   US   12   Yerma   LA 55

COSTA, Michael   5   Terzetto a Canone Vanne a Colei   NP 1848
1808-1884   Brit

COUPERIN, Francois   6   Aubade Provençale   HN 14
1668-1733   Fr   21   Concert No 8 dans le Gout Theatral arr Cortot
                                 CT 34;   RC 65, 66
                        24   Dance Suite arr Strauss   CL 38;   NP 23, 43
                         4   Juillet for 2 Harpsi from Pieces de Clavecin
                                 CH 32
                         3   Musette de Choise for 2 Fl and 2 Harpsi from Pieces
                                 de Clavecin   CH 32
                        18   Pièce de Concert, C and Str arr Bazelaire   NP 54;
                                 SL 54
                        15   La Sultane, Suite   DE 49;   SL 35
                         7   -Overt or Prelude, and Allegro arr Milhaud for
                                 C and O   BA 52;   BN 49;   CH 47;   CT 41, 45,
                                 48, 53;   CL 51, 58;   DE 61, 63;   DT 51;
                                 NA 49, 55, 57, 61;   KC 45, 54, 63;   ML 66;
                                 MN 41, 44, 47;   NR 50;   NP 42, 44, 51(2), 54,
                                 55, 58;   PH 42, 49, 54;   SL 40, 41, 42, 45,
                                 46, 47(2), 49, 50, 53, 54, 66;   SF 47, 50;
                                 SE 53;   WA 44, 47, 48, 50, 54, 67

COWELL, Henry   4   American Pipers   UT 62
1897-1965   US   5   Ancient Desert Drone 1940   BU 44;   WA 46
                        10   Big Sing 1945   AT 48;   NA 47
                         4   Fanfare to Latin American Allies 1942   CT 42
                         5   Hymn and Fuguing Tune No 1   BN 45, 48;   PH 59;
                                 UT 59
                         7   Hymn and Fuguing Tune No 2 1944   CT 58;   DT 56;
                                 NP 56;   PT 55
                         7   Hymn and Fuguing Tune No 3 1945   CL 54;   DE 56;
                                 MN 54
                         6   Hymn and Fuguing Tune No 16   NP 66
                         9   Music for O 1957   MN 57
                         7   Rondo for O   NA 53
                        19   Symph No 4 Short Symph 1945   BA 52;   BN 47;
                                 NA 50;   LA 48
                        25   Symph No 6   HN 55
                        22   Symph No 11 Seven Rituals of Music   BU 57;
                                 DA 58;   DE 59;   DT 58;   NA 56;   ML 63;   PH 57;
                                 PT 59;   WA 56
                        15   Symph No 12   HN 59;   SF 61
                        15   Synchrony 1930   PH 31;   SF 67
                        13   Tales of Our Countryside 1940   NP 41
                        21   Var for O   CT 56;   HN 59

COWELL, John   8   Cantatum Gloria   SE 50
1920-   US   9   Conc for Koto and O   PH 64
                        15   Conc for O   SE 65

COWEN, Sir   11   Overt Butterfly's Ball   CH 02
  Frederich   35   Symph in C No 3 Scandanavian   BN 1882, 85, 89, 96;
1852-1935   Brit   NP 41, 42

COWEN, SIR F. (Cont.)

37	Symph in b^b No 4 Welsh BN 1887; NP 43	
40	Symph No 6 BN 00	

COWLEY,
US

10	Crazy house suite, 2 dances SF 37

CRESTON, Paul
1906-   US

10	Chant of 1942 Op 33 BU 43; LA 47; PH 45; SE 52
12	Chthonic Ode Op 90 BN 67; CH 67; DT 66
16	Conc Sax and O Op 26 NP 43
21	P Conc Op 43 WA 50
20	V Conc for V and O No 1 Op 65 DT 59
20	V Conc No 2 Op 78 AT 60; LA 60; SE 60
12	Dance Overt Op 62 AT 57; CT 58; CL 56; HN 65; NA 58; KC 62; MN 56, 57, 67; NP 55; RC 33, 55, 57, 61; SL 55; SF 58; SE 62; UT 57
5	Dance Var for Sopr and O Op 30 CT 61
1	Fanfare for Paratroopers, Brass and Percussion 1942 CT 42
10	Fantasy for Tromb and O Op 42 LA 47
10	Frontiers Op 34 BN 43; HN 58; NA 45, 50; KC 58; NR 60; NP 46; UT 50
6	Gregorian Chant for Str Quart Op 8 NA 58
8	Homage for Str O NA 49; NR 52
12	Invocation and Dance Op 58 BA 69; BN 58; DA 68; DT 64; HN 59; NA 56; KC 55; LA 65; MN 64; PH 60; PT 56; RC 54; SF 66
12	Janus Op 77 AT 59; CT 62; DE 59; MN 59; SF 60; WA 59
12	Jubilee Var CT 44, 45
10	Pastorale and Tarentella Op 28 DE 66; PH 44; SL 42; SF 44
6	Pavane, Variations WA 66
10	Pre Classic Suite Op 71 AT 58; DE 60; NR 57
15	Poeme Harp and O Op 39 SF 47
14	Psalm XXIII Op 37 HN 45
5	A Rumor Op 27 CL 42
20	Symph No 1 Op 20 CT 43; DT 47, 57; LA 43; PH 42; SL 44, 53
4	-Scherzo NP 41
24	Symph No 2 Op 35 BA 57; BN 44, 52, 55; BU 57; CH 60; CT 65; DA 56; DE 57; DT 57; HN 56; NA 54; LA 55; MN 54, 56; NR 54; NP 44, 55; PH 46, 49; PT 57; RC 56; SL 57, 58; SF 50, 55, 60; WA 49, 54, 63, 50, 52
27	Symph No 3 Three Mysteries Op 48 AT 59; CH 50; CT 44; DE 55; HN 62; LA 48, 54; MN 52; PH 50; SL 51; SE 55; WA 53
26	Symph No 4 Op 52 DA 57; WA 51
	Symph No 5 Op 64 WA 55
12	Threnody Op 16 CT 40, 47; KC 48; LA 46; PT 38
10	Toccata for O Op 68 CL 57; DE 60; HN 58
10	Toccata for Fl, V and Str O DE 55

CRESTON, P. (Cont.)
24   Two Choric Dances Op 17   BU 42;   CH 52;   CL 49;
      DE 46, 54, 64, 65;   DT 43;   KC 43;   LA 44;
      MN 51;   NR 55;   NP 42;   PH 42, 51;   PT 51;
      SL 50, 56;   WA 40
12   Walt Whitman Tone Poem Op 53   BU 59;   CT 51;
      PT 63

CRISMAN, Merwin   16   Prelude for O   AT 55
          US

CRIST, Bainbridge 13   American Epic: 1620 Tone Poem, 1941   WA 43
1883-   US

CRUMB, George   15   Madrigals Books I and III   SF 67
1929-   US   10   Echoes of Time and the River, Four Processionals
                         for O   CH 68;   CL 68

CUI, Cezar   4   Orientale   BA 26
1835-1918 Russ   4   Song: The Fountain   MN 41
                    5   Statue at Czarskoe-Selo, Song   CL 41

CURRY, Arthur   12   Atala   BN 10
1866-   US

CUSHING, Charles   8   Cereus   RC 60;   SF 60;   WA 60
1905-   US

CUSTER, Arthur   20   Symphony   SL 68

CUTLER, William H. 5   Hymn The Son of God Goes Forth to War   NS 18
1792- ?   Brit

DACHAUER   8   Scene: Margaret at the Spinning Wheel   NP 1870

Dahl, Ingolf   17   Aria Sinfonia   BU 65;   LA 64;   CT 65
1912-   US

DALBY   15   Opus No 18   UT 54
1920-   US   20   Suite Elegrague   UT 49

DALE, Kathleen   5   Romance from Suite for Vla and O   NS 23;   UT 46
  Richards   8   -Romance and Finale   CH 24
1895-   Brit

DALGLEISH, James   7   Statement for O   NP 53
1927-   US

DALL'ABACO, Evaristo 10 Conc da Chiesa Op 2 No 4 arr Bonelli   SL 36
1675-1742 It   10   Conc da Chiesa No 9 arr Kindler   WA 44, 48

DALL'AQUA   6   Villanella   HN 40
          It

| DALLIN, Leon | 5 | Film Overt   UT 49 |
| 1918-   US | 20 | Symph in D   UT 51 |

DALLAPICCOLA, Luigi   15   An Mathilde Cantata   NP 63
1904-   It   23   Marsia, Symphon Fragments from the Ballet 1942
   NR 50;   NP 53
   26   Partita for Sopr and O 1930   MN 56
   8   Piccola Musica Notturna 1939   PT 63
   16   Tartiniana, Divertimento for V and O   BN 67;
   CT 57;   NP 56
   11   Two Pieces for O   BN 65;   LA 50;   PT 55;
   SF 56, 62
   14   Var for O   BN 60;   CT 68;   KC 68;   NP 64(2);
   PH 69

DAMASE, Jean-Michel   15   Concertina for Harp and Str   KC 57
1928-   Fr

DAMROSCH, Leopold   30   V Conc in d   NP 1874
1832-1885   Ger   10   Festival Overt   NS 1885, 89, 93, 09, 27
   5   Romance for Vla and O   NS 23
   15   Serenade for V and O   NS 1884, 86
   SONGS
   4   Dereinst dereinst   NS 1884
   15   Harold Harfrager, Ballad with O   NS 1884
   10   Hymenaen   NS 07
   5   Nilken wind ich und Jasmin   NS 1884
   15   Siegfried's Sword, Ballad   NS 1887

   10   Sulamith, Opera: Overt   NS 1884
   5   -Air   NS 1887(2), 27

DAMROSCH, Walter   STAGE and CHORAL WORKS
1862-1950   US   7-8   Abraham Lincoln for Baritone, Chor and O   WA 38
   15   Canterbury Pilgrims Opera Act II   NS 09
   80   Cyrano Opera, complete   NP 40
   8   -Prelude Act II   CT 03;   RC 32
   10   -Prelude Act II and Letter   NS 12, 16
   4   Dove of Peace, Comic Opera,Song from Act II   NS 11
   15   Electra, Incidental Music   NS 17, 18, 20
   10   Man Without A Country, Comic Opera: Three Midshipmen
   Songs   WA 38
   15   Manila Te Deum: Selections   NS 18
   15   Medea, Incidental Music   NS 17, 18
   60   Scarlet Letter, Opera Three Acts   NS 1894
   SONGS
   4   Danny Deever   NS 23;   SE 48
   4   Death and General Putman   KC 39
   14   Looking Glass Ballad   NP 41;   NS 11, 17, 23
   4   My Wife   NS 17
   4   Peace Hymn of Republic   NS 18

DAN, Ikuma   40   Symph No 4   PH 66
1924-   Japan

DANCLA, Charles   20   Conc for 2 V   NP 1850
  1818-1907   Fr

DANIELS, Mabel W.   7   Exultate Deo for Chor and O 1929   BN 31
  1879-   US   7   Prelude, Deep Forest Op 34   BN 36
                           8   Psalm of Praise for Mixed Chor   BN 55

DANZI, Franz   25   Symphonia Concertante   MN 65
  1763-1826   Ger

DARGOMISZKY, Alexander S.   Cosatchoque or Kazachok Fantasie on Cossack Dance
  1813-1869   Russ   6   NP 15

DAUVERGNE, Antoine   12   Symph in b Op 4   MN 68
  1713-1797   Fr

DAVICO, Vincenzo   10   Polyphemus   BN 22
  1889-   It

DAVID, Félicien   4   Aria, Charmant Oiseau from Le Perle du Bresil
  1810-1876   Fr   Opera 1851   CH 17;   CT 55;   NP 19;   NS 16;
                                  PT 54;   SL 20;   SF 11
                           6   Rain   BA 43

DAVID, Ferdinand   20   V Conc No 2   NP 1850
  1810-1873   Ger   10   Concertino for Tromb   NP 1861
                          10   V Fantasia on Schubert, Lob der Thranen   NP 1856

DAVIDOFF, Karl   8   C Conc No 2 Op 14   CT first mvt only 1897
  1838-1889   Russ   10   C Conc No 3 Op 18   BN 1892
                           8   Russian Fantasy for C and O Op 7   CH 1895

DAVIDOVSKY, Mario   15   Synchronisms No 2 for Fl, Clar, C and Tape
  1934   Arg   Recorder   SF 65

DAVIES, Sir H. Walford 3   Solemn Melody for O 1908   CT 41;   HN 56;   MN 29;
  1869-1941   Brit   PH 19;   RC 32
                          30   Suite: Parthenia, in f Op 34 1911   PH 12

DAVIS, Hilda Emery   15   Symphon Poem: The Last Knight   PH 39;   SF 38
  1890-   US

DAVISON, Archibald   8   Tragic Overt   BN 17;   SL 18
  1883-   US

DAWSON, William Levi   35   Negro Folk Symph No 1 1930   AT 65;   PH 34
  1899-   US

DE BERIOT, Charles A.   5   Aria for Oboe   NP 1846
  1802-1870   Fr   15   V Conc No 3   NP 1852
                          20   V Conc No 4   NP 1845
                          20   V Conc No 6   NP 1851
                          10   Concertino No 2 Op 31 2 mvts Andante and
                                  Rondo Russe   NP 1862

Time in
Minutes

DEBUSSY, Claude   4   Berceuse Héroique 1914   CH 38;   NP 38;   SL 21
1862-1918   Fr   5   Canope No 10 from Douze Préludes for P Book II
                               1910 arr O'Connel   PH 35, 36
                       5   La Cathédrale Engloutie, No 10 of Douze Preludes,
                               Book I 1910   CH arr Stock 32;   DE arr Stokowski
                               50;   HN 56;   KC arr Mouton 48;   MN 46, arr
                               Chardan 47;   NP 48;   PH 25(2), 28, 30, 32, 35;
                               PT arr Stokowski 50;   WA arr Stokowski 50
                      15   Children's Corner 1906 arr Caplet: Suite   CT 24;
                               DA 46;   MN 46;   NP 51;   PT 41;   SL 58;
                               SF 17;   SE 44;   WA 40
                       2   -Little Shepherd   BA 28
                       2   -Serenade of the Doll   PT 39
                       3   -Golliwog's Cakewalk   BA 28;   CT 37;   DA 44;
                               PT 39
                       5   Clair de Lune, No 3 of Suite bergamasque 1890
                               BA arr Klemm 51;   CL 39;   DA 38;   HN arr
                               Kostelanetz 51;   KC 54;   NP 47;   PH arr
                               Stokowski 37, 38;   RC 38, 41;   SL 38;   UT 46
                      21   La Damoiselle élue Soli, Chor and O   Cantata 1887
                               BA 42, 48;   BN 19, 29, 31, 42, 47, 54;   CT 35,
                               46;   CL 20, 27, 43, 55;   DA 48;   DE 65
                               DT 66;   HN 59;   NA 53;   LA 48;   NP 35, 57;
                               PH 16, 43, 46;   RC 47;   SL 66;   SF 37, 62;
                               SE 38;   UT 60;   WA 60
                       6   Danse arr Ravel 1890   BA 51;   BN 24, 27;   CT 62,
                               67;   MN 44;   PH 35, 42, 51, 58;   PT 42, 46;
                               SL 35
                       9   Danse Sacrée et Danse Profane for Harp and Str 1904
                               AT 63;   CH 19;   CT 29;   CL 29, 67;   DA 48;
                               DE 51;   DT 65;   NA 40;   KC 34, 46, 57;   LA 19,
                               41;   MN 49;   NP 17;   PH 17, 30, 51;   PT 41,
                               53;   RC 28;   SL 35;   UT 49
                       5   En Blanc et Noir 1915: Danse arr Goossens   CT 34,
                               42, 44;   CL 44
                      20   L'Enfant Prodigue, Cantata 1884   CT 51;   DE 60;
                               NP 17, 18
                       5   -Recitative and Aria of Lea   CL 19, 23, 26, 43
                       5   -Recitative and Aria, Year follows year   CH 18;
                               HN 58
                       5   -Cortège and Air de Danse   CH 10, 58;   CT 27, 31;
                               HN Air de danse only 58;   PH 41
                       4   -Air de Lia   AT 50;   BA 43, 58;   DA 26, 29;
                               DE 49, 50, 61;   DT 18, 22, 26, 47;   NA 39;
                               LA 19, 22, 36, 38;   MN 36, 44;   SL 17, 22, 25;
                               WA 33, 45
                       5   -Recitative and air d'Azael   LA 22
                      16   Six Epigraphes Antiques arr Ansermet 1915   BN 51;
                               CH 50, 67;   CT 63;   CL 53;   DT 64;   HN 57, 67;
                               NA 62;   LA 66;   RC 49;   SL 44
                      22   Fantasia in e for P and O 1889   BA 51;   BN 19;
                               BU 68;   CH 31;   CT 34, 56;   CL 30;   DA 62;
                               KC 67;   NP 42;   PH 29;   SL 61;   UT 65;
                               WA 64

DEBUSSY, C. (Cont.)

30   Images pour Orchestre 1906   BN 10(3), 11, 13, 16, 18, 21, 22, 25,
     27, 28;   CH 14, 60, 64;   CL 67, 69;   DT 68;   MN 50;   NP 44,
     53, 58, 67;   SL 69

4   -No 1 Gigues   BN 38, 51, 57;   CL 51, 64;   DT 68;   LA 51;
     MN 50;   PH 56;   RC 59;   SF 37

17   -No 2 Iberia   AT 69;   BA 58, 61;   BN 42, 43, 47, 48, 53, 56, 57;
     BU 66;   CH 11(2), 14, 20, 21, 22, 23, 24, 25, 27, 28, 29, 30, 33,
     34, 35, 40, 42, 44, 46, 53, 56, 60, 66;   CT 22, 31, 37, 39, 42,
     61, 69;   CL 20, 22, 23, 28, 32, 35, 37, 41, 45, 51, 60;   DA 50(2),
     53, 55, 57, 63;   DE 50;   DT 21, 31, 39, 51, 54, 68;   HN 57, 64;
     NA 42;   KC 64;   LA 21, 23, 25, 34, 48, 57, 61;   MN 33, 41, 45,
     47, 50, 56, 58, 62, 65;   NP 10, 24, 27, 28, 33, 35, 37, 39, 41,
     42, 46, 51, 53, 62;   PH 27, 30, 35, 38, 41, 46, 50, 56, 58, 63,
     68;   PT 41, 45, 46, 53, 61, 67, 69;   RC 25, 39, 42, 51, 55, 57;
     SL 11, 17, 31, 33, 36, 39, 41, 47, 49, 65, 68;   SF 16, 25, 35, 41,
     43, 49, 55, 62;   SE 29, 50, 58, 63;   UT 50, 61;   WA 62

8   -No 3 Rondes de Printemps   BN 13, 17, 22, 52, 56, 57, 61;   CH 10,
     60, 66;   CT 15, 26, 64;   CL 37, 51, 64;   MN 50;   NP 10, 17, 18,
     24, 34, 62;   PH 44, 50, 56, 59;   PT 60, 63;   RC 27, 48;   SL 37,
     53;   SF 45

16   Jeux, Games, Ballet 1912   BN 19, 57, 68;   CH 62, 68;   CL 64;
     DT 67;   LA 68;   MN 51, 63;   NP 37, 59, 64, 68;   PH 29;   PT 64;
     SL 64;   SF 46, 60;   SE 60

7   L'Isle Joyeuse 1904 arr Molinari   DT 35;   MN 33, 40;   NP 29, 55;
     PH 33, 35;   SL 27

20   King Lear, Incidental Music 1897   BU 64;   RC 52;

5   -Le Sommeil de Lear   CH 40

6   Marches Écossaise 1891   CH 10(2), 17, 23, 26, 32, 38;   HN 51;
     KC 66;   PH 09, 11;   SL 24;   SF 12

25   Le Martyres de St. Sébastien, Incidental Music 1911: Suite for O
     BN 29;   PH 57;   PT 64

4   -La bon pasteur   BU 67;   MN 61;   NP 52;   SL 50, 56, 61

4   -The Council of False Gods   NP 62;   SL 61

5   -La court des Lys   CL 22, 25;   MN 61;   NP 35, 52, 62;   SL 50,
     56, 61

4   -Danse Extatique   BU 67

8   -Danse Extatique and Finale Act I   MN 61;   NP 52;   SL 50, 56

23   -Excerpts   BN 23, 36, 39, 47, 51, 55, 57, 62;   DT 47;   HN 49, 67;
     RC 65;   SL 38, 41, 45;   SF 38, 48, 57

12   -4 Excerpts   PH 27

5   -1 Excerpt   PH 22(2)

4   -The Magic Chamber   NP 62;   SL 61

4   -Paradise   NP 62;   SL 50, 56, 61

5   -Passion   BU 67;   MN 61

10   -Preludes to Acts I and II   CH 12, 37

4   -Prelude   BU 67

4   -The Wounded Lauret   NP 62

20   La Mer, Three Symphonic Sketches 1903
     AT 51, 68;   BA 52, 53, 54, 68;
     BN 06(2), 12, 14, 17, 20, 24, 27, 29, 30, 33, 35, 36, 37, 39, 40, 42,
     43, 46, 48, 49, 51, 54, 56, 58, 60, 61, 62, 69;   BU 43, 58, 61
     CH 08, 09, 18, 19, 20, 22, 25, 28, 31, 33, 36, 39, 41, 42, 44, 47,
     48(2), 49(2), 51, 53, 55, 56, 57, 58, 59, 60, 61, 62, 64, 67, 69;

DEBUSSY, C. (Cont.) La Mer (Cont.)
        CT 21, 26, 28, 30, 31, 36, 37, 38, 43, 45, 47, 55, 57, 60, 62, 64, 65;
        CL 26, 27, 30, 32, 33, 36, 39, 41, 42, 44, 47, 50(2), 52, 54, 56, 57,
        58, 60, 62, 64, 66, 68;
        DA 46, 48, 49, 54, 58, 61, 62, 65;
        DE 49, 51(2), 53, 57, 59, 67, 68;
        DT 36, 37, 45(2), 46, 47, 52, 64, 66, 69;
        HN 47, 49, 55, 59, 62, 64, 67, 68;
        NA 38, 40, 50, 57, 61, 68;   KC 42, 47, 57, 68;
        LA 24, 28, 30, 32, 33, 34, 36, 41, 42, 45, 47, 49, 50, 52, 53, 54, 55,
        56, 59, 61, 62, 66, 69;   ML 65, 68;
        MN 25, 32, 35, 36, 38, 40, 47, 49, 50, 52, 53, 55, 56, 57, 59, 60,
        61, 68;   NR 59, 60(2), 62, 65;
        NP 21, 26, 27, 29, 32, 34, 35, 36, 39, 40, 41, 44, 45, 49, 50, 51(2),
        53, 54, 56, 57, 60, 61, 63, 66, 68;   Ph 10, 26, 27, 28, 31, 33,
        36, 40, 41, 42, 43, 45, 46, 48, 51, 53, 55, 56, 57, 58, 59, 60,
        62, 66, 68;
        PT 39, 47, 48, 50, 54, 57, 58, 62, 64, 66, 68;
        RC 30, 34, 39, 43, 45, 48, 50, 54, 56, 58, 62, 63, 66;
        SL 10, 13, 16, 25, 29, 32, 34, 38, 39, 40, 45, 46, 47, 48, 49, 52,
        53, 55, 56, 57, 60, 64, 67;
        SF 13, 17, 28, 33, 35, 37, 39, 40, 42, 44, 46, 48, 50, 54, 59, 63,
        65, 68;   SE 49, 55, 69;   UT 48, 53, 56, 60;
        WA 50, 51, 53, 55, 58, 63

7   -No 1 De l'aube sur la mer   CT 39
7   -No 2 Jeux de vagues   CT 41
7   -No 3 Dialogue du vent et la mer   CT 39, 41, 46
3   Minstrels No 12 from Douze Preludes, Book I for P 1910 arr O'Connel
        PH 35, 63, 64
14 Three Nocturnes for O 1893   BA 68;   BN 08, 11, 18, 55, 61;   CH 26,
        40, 50, 64;   CT 23, 46, 54;   DA 35;   DE 46, 48, 56, 69;   DT 60;
        HN 61;   NA 36, 39, 43;   KC 50, 56;   LA 35;   ML 61, 59;
        NP 39, 47, 60;   PT 42, 56, 60, 64, 69;   RC 32, 50, 57;   SL 38,
        52, 66;   SF 35, 53, 59;   SE 28;   WA 63;
5   -No 1 Nuages
        AT 50, 60, 63;   BA 41, 54;
        BN 21, 24(2), 26, 28, 31, 33, 37, 40, 43, 50;
        BU 41, 47, 52, 55, 57, 58, 61;
        CH 14(2), 16, 17, 18, 23, 24, 25, 27, 29, 30, 31, 36, 42, 43, 44,
        46, 47, 53, 55, 56, 68;
        CT 09, 16, 29, 34, 52, 57, 60, 64, 68;
        CL 19, 21, 22, 24, 25, 27, 28, 30, 33, 37, 43, 47, 54, 55, 58, 59, 68;
        DA 48(2), 49, 52, 62, 68;   DE 50, 53, 58, 62, 65, 67;
        DT 23, 26, 27, 32, 33, 39, 41, 44, 51, 52, 54, 58, 60, 65;
        HN 47, 53, 61, 64, 65;   NA 48, 54, 60, 68;   KC 39, 46;
        LA 19, 20, 23, 28, 29, 30, 33, 35, 36, 37, 45, 56, 59, 64;
        ML 61, 65, 69;   MN 30, 31, 33, 34, 37, 39, 47, 57, 62;   NR 57, 61;
        NP 16, 22, 30, 31, 32, 35, 36, 43, 45, 51, 54, 56;
        PH 11, 13, 15, 17, 20, 22, 23, 24, 25, 26, 29, 30, 31, 32, 33, 34,
        35, 36, 42, 43, 44, 45, 46, 51, 55, 57, 65;   PT 40, 46, 50, 52;
        RC 32, 34, 36, 38, 43, 46, 50, 53, 55, 61;
        SL 10, 24, 30, 31, 39, 40, 42, 45, 46, 47, 48, 49, 51, 57, 62;
        SF 25, 27, 32, 37, 38, 51, 61, 64;   SE 28, 30, 31, 36, 43, 48, 62;
        UT 44, 45, 51, 55, 63;   WA 35, 38, 45, 49, 50, 57;

DEBUSSY, C. (Cont.)   Three Nocturnes (Cont.)
 5   -No 2 Fêtes
          AT 50, 60, 63;   BA 41, 42, 43, 51, 54;
          BN 21, 24(2), 26, 28, 31, 33, 37, 40, 43, 50;
          BU 41, 47, 52, 55, 57, 63;
          CH 14(2), 16, 17, 18, 23, 24, 25, 27, 28, 30, 31, 36, 42, 43, 44,
          46, 47, 53, 55, 56, 68;
          CT 09, 16, 29, 34, 37, 43, 46, 50, 52, 57, 60, 64, 68;
          CL 19, 21, 22, 24, 25, 27, 28, 30, 33, 37, 43, 47, 50, 53, 54, 55,
          58, 59, 68;   DA 48(4), 49, 52, 62, 68;
          DE 50, 52, 53, 58, 62, 65, 67;
          DT 23, 26, 27, 30, 32, 33, 39, 41, 44;
          HN 39, 44, 47, 50, 53, 61, 64, 65;
          NA 36, 39, 43, 54, 60, 68;   KC 39, 46, 69;
          LA 19, 20, 23(2), 27, 28, 29, 30, 33, 36, 37, 45, 56, 59, 64;
          ML 61, 65;   NR 50, 53, 57, 61, 64;
          NP 09, 16, 22, 23, 27, 30, 31, 34, 35, 36, 43, 45, 47, 51, 54, 56;
          PH 11, 13, 15, 17, 20, 22, 23, 24, 25, 26, 29, 30, 31, 32, 33, 34,
          35, 36, 42, 43, 44, 45, 46, 57, 65;
          PT 40, 46, 50, 52;
          RC 34, 36, 38, 43, 46, 50, 53, 55, 57, 61;
          SL 10, 20, 23, 24, 27, 29, 30, 31, 35, 39, 40, 42, 45, 46, 47, 48,
          49, 51, 57, 62;
          SF 19, 25, 27, 28, 32, 35, 37, 38, 51, 61, 64;
          SE 28, 30, 31, 35, 36, 43, 48, 62;   UT 40, 44, 45, 51, 55, 63;
          WA 35, 40, 45, 49, 50, 57, 69
 5   -No 3 Sirènes with Women's Chor
          AT 67;   BA 41;   BU 57, 63;   CH 68;   CT 43, 68;   CL 43, 54,
          58;   DA 48, 52, 62;   NP 09;   MN 30, 31, 33, 34, 37, 39, 47, 57,
          62;   PH 39, 49, 55, 59, 65;   RC 50, 61;   SF 45, 60;
 90   Pelléas et Mélisande, Opera 1892   BN 56, 62;   DA 50;   SE 50
 15   -Interludes BA 67;   NR 67;   RC 48, 51
 15   -Selections   SF 46
 10   -Preludes and Interludes   CL 45;   HN 61;   PH 56
 10   -Preludes and Interludes 1, 2, and 4   NP 38
 50   -Five Acts. . .Concert Version   NP 58
 15   Petite Suite 1888 arr Busser   AT 51, 61;   BN 19;   CH 13, 53;
          CT 24, 66;   DT 66;   HN 58;   PH 41;   SF 64
 9   Prélude à l'après-midi d'un faune 1892
          AT 52, 61;   BA 51, 54(2), 58, 42, 43;
          BN 04, 05, 08, 11, 14, 16, 19, 23, 25, 28, 32, 33, 35, 38, 41, 45,
          48, 52, 55, 61, 65;   BU 41, 46, 62;
          CH 06(2), 07, 08, 09, 10, 13, 17, 20, 21, 23, 28, 32, 37, 38, 42,
          43, 46, 47, 50, 54, 58;
          CT 04, 05, 11, 13, 18, 25, 27, 28, 30, 33, 34, 35, 37, 38, 42, 47,
          48, 49, 58, 66;
          CL 19, 21, 24, 26, 29, 31, 32, 34, 38, 41, 43, 44, 46, 48, 50, 53,
          58, 67, 69;   DA 32, 48(2), 49, 50, 52, 56, 58, 65, 69;
          DE 45, 46, 47, 51, 53, 55, 57, 59, 62, 63, 67;
          DT 15, 17, 18, 20, 24, 28, 30, 31, 35, 40, 45, 46, 48, 51, 63, 65;
          HN 33, 41, 48, 51, 52;   NA 38, 46, 49, 64, 68;
          KC 34, 39, 40, 49, 54, 61, 65;
          LA 22, 23, 26, 30, 33, 38, 40, 55, 59, 68;   ML 63;
          MN 26, 29, 30, 31, 32, 34, 42, 45, 47, 49, 53, 55, 60, 66, 67;
          NR 50, 52, 59, 63, 68;

DEBUSSY, C. (Cont.) Prélude a laprès-midi d'un faune (Cont.)

	PH 06, 08, 09, 10, 11, 12, 15, 16, 18, 21, 22, 23, 24, 25, 26, 27, 28, 31, 33, 34, 35, 36, 37, 38, 40, 41, 42, 45(2), 46, 47, 52(2), 53, 55, 59, 62, 67;

PT 39, 43, 47, 48, 50, 51, 55, 61, 62;
RC 23, 26, 27, 30, 35, 39, 43, 47, 49, 50, 51, 54, 57, 62, 68;
SL 09, 11, 14, 17, 19, 21, 24, 26, 28, 30, 32, 33, 34, 35, 37, 39, 42, 43, 44, 46, 47, 49, 50, 52, 54(2), 59, 64, 67;
SF 11, 14, 17, 18, 19, 20, 22, 23, 30, 35, 36, 39, 44, 62, 63;
Se 26, 28, 32, 34, 37, 39, 59;   UT 47, 52, 54, 62;
WA 32, 36, 40, 50, 57, 69

8	Printemps for Chor and O 1887 DE 68; DT 68, 69; PH 39, 43
4	Reflets dans l'eau No 1 from Images for P Set I 1905 arr Ormandy PH 40, 45, 46, 53
15	Rhaps for Clar and O No 1 1909 BA 61, 62; BN 25; BU 69; CH 52; CL 68; DA 48; MN 46, 56, 59; NR 68; NP 67; PT 59; SE 29, 45; WA 67
10	Rhaps for English Horn and O BN 31
8	Rhaps for Saxophone and O arr Roger-Ducasse BN 39, 68; CL 57; NA 58; MN 47; PH 26; RC 27; WA 40
6	Sarabande No 2 from P Suite 1896 arr Ravel DE 46; NP 38; WA 33
12	Sarabande and Danse arr Ravel BN 27; BU 63; CH 27; CL 24, 35; NP 23; SF 27, 45;
6	Scottish March CL 40
4	Soirée dans Grenade No 2 from Estampes for P arr Busser HN 60; NP 46; PH 61
	SONGS
8	Chansons de Bilitis for a'capella Chor 1897 arr Delage with O HN 58
3	-No 1 Le Flute de Pan CT 32
3	-No 2 Le Chevelure CT 21, 32; PH 20
4	Fantoches, No 2 from Fêtes galantes, Set I 1892 CT 38
4	Mandoline 1880 NP 11
4	L'Ombre des Arbres No 3 from Ariettes Oubliées NP 19
4	Romance, from Deux Romances PH 17
10	Three Francois Villon Ballades PH 46
27	Twelve Chansons arr Boulez BU 63
26-27	String Quart in g 1893 arr for O Black CL 39
6	-Scherzo DT 32, 34
12	-Two mvts CH 18; SL 26
6	-Third mvt CT 39, 42, 46

DE CURTIS		5	Torna a Surriento DA 48

DELAGE, Charles M.		5	Deux Poèmes Hindus CT 23; PH 22
1879	Fr	8	Tryptique SL 33

DELAMARTER, Eric		10	Cluny, Dialogue for Vla and O CT 49
1880-1953	US	22	Conc No 1 in E for Org and O CH 19, 30; CT 42; DT 26
		22	Conc No 2 in A for Org and O CH 21; CT 49
		20	Dance of Life CH 30
		25	Fable of the Hapless Folktune CH 16, 17, 40

DELAMARTER, E. (Cont.)
10	The Fawn, Overt to a Comedy CH 14, 17; NA 61
6	The Giddy Puritan, Overt AT 47
7	Holiday in Eire AT 49; DT 47
5	June Moonrise CH 31
6	Psalm 144, Baritone and O CH 27
18	Suite: The Betrothal CH 18, 26; LA 45; NP 33; SL 41; SE 55
5	-Overt NP 33
15	Symph No 1 in D CH 13
20	Symph No 2 in g After Walt Whitman CH 25; KC 41; MN 26; DT 43
43	Symph No 3 in e CH 32, 34
9	They too went t'town, Overt KC 39

DELANEY, Robert Mills 20   Night, P, Str O and Chor 1934   WA 52
1903-   US

DELANNOY, Maurice   15   The Glass Slipper, Cinderella, Suite from Ballet,
1898-   Fr   La Pantoufle de vair 1935   CT 40;   SL 35

DE LEEUW, Ton   13   Movements Retrogrades   CT 62
1926-   Neth

DELIBES, Léo   Arioso   NS 1890
1836-1891   Fr   23   Coppelia, ballet in two acts 1870   MN 38
                              -Ballad and Theme Slave   CT 1896
                  8   La Source, Ballet Suite in three acts 1866   HN 17
                  17   Sylvia, Ballet in three acts 1876: Concert Suite
                              CH 04;   DA 29, 54;   NS 14, 17;   SF 11
                  8   -Excerpts   BN 1881, 83;   CT 61
                  7   -3 Movements   CH 1891
                  4   -Pas de Deux   CT 64;   DE 56;   NR 61;   SE 64;
                              WA 58

                  7   Lakmé Opera 1883: Fantaisie aux divine Mensonges,
                              Aria, Act I   CT 48;   MN 48
                  6   -Bell Song: "La Bas dans La Forêt", Act III
                              AT 66;   BA 42, 64;   CH 22;   CT 02, 66;
                              HN 34;   NR 32, 52;   MN 26;   NS 19;   PH 03;
                              PT 51;   SL 11(2);   NP 33, 52
                  6   Naila, Intermezzo, from Divertissemont added to
                              Adam's LeCorsaire 1867   HN 14;   NP 32
                  4   Pizzicato Polka   BA 28;   DA 25;   NA 45
                  4   Valse triste   BA 28;   NP 32
                  4   Song, Maids of Cadiz, Bolero   CH 1894;   CT 31,
                              36, 44, 45;   NP 33;   MN 29;   PH 35;   SL 46

DELIUS, Frederick   45   Appalachia, Var for Chor and O on an old slave
1862-1934   Brit   song 1902   HN 69;   NP 37;   SE 42
                  16   Brigg Fair, An English Rhaps 1907   AT 65;
                              BA 48;   BN 10, 32;   CH 10, 14, 36;   CT 32;
                              CL 49, 53   HN 60, 69;   NA 48;   ML 65;   MN 26,
                              33;   NP 31, 34;   NS 10;   PH 54, 61;   PT 60;
                              RC 28;   SL 28, 43;   SE 29;   WA 50, 62

DELIUS, F. (Cont.)

30	C Conc 1921 NP 27; PH 27
30	P Conc in one mvt in c 1906 BA 43; CH 31; CT 35; DT 41; NP 15; NS 21; PH 41; RC 44; SE 41; WA 42
20	V Conc 1916 HN 67
12	Dance Rhaps No 1 1908 BN 20; CH 16(2), 17, 18, 19, 27; CT 31; DE 51; PH 42, 61; RC 24; SF 25
4	Eventyr: Once Upon a Time, Ballad 1917 NP 35; RC 45
5	Florida, Suite 1886: On the River CH 59; DT 23; PT 59
4	On Hearing the First Cuckoo in Spring, for small O 1912 BA 43; BN 25, 32; CH 30; CT 31, 40, 45, 58; CL 36, 64; DT 23, 46; KC 40; LA 51; ML 61; MN 29; NP 62; NS 13, 22, 25; PH 42, 61; RC 26, 43; SL 22; SF 30, 51; SE 33, 34; UT 43, 61; WA 31, 36, 38, 51, 60
13	In a Summer Garden, Fantasy 1908 BN 11, 17; CH 34, 44, 56; CT 36; DE 60; HN 62; LA 42; NP 11, 17; PH 60; RC 33, 35
7	Late Swallows from Slow mvt of Str Quart 1916 HN 63
12	Life's Dance 1911 CH 13, 14; NP 18, 19
4	-March Caprice BN 51; DT 54; SF 51
26	North Country Sketches 4 parts 1913 CT 37
8	Over the Hills and Far Away, Tone Poem 1895 CH 54; CT 51; CL 51; DE 57; WA 51, 53
20	Paris, Nocturne, The Song of a Great City 1899 BN 09, 40; CH 13, 24, 34; CT 31, 40, 45, 62; CL 38; DA 55; NP 43; PH 55
5	Schlittenfarte, Sleigh Ride 1888 HN 58
30	Sea Drift, Baritone, Chor and O 1903 BA 68; NA 53
15	A Song of the High Hills Chor and O 1911 BN 26; CT 43
7	A Song of Summer 1930 CT 44, 62, 69; DA 61; HN 61, 66; MN 44; NP 42; SL 46, 47, 69
5	Summer Night on the River 1912 BN 51; CT 31; CL 36; LA 40; MN 29, 37; NS 13, 22, 25; RC 43, 55; SL 22, 40; SF 40, 51; SE 59
12	Two Aquarelles NA 46
15	Three Orchestral Pieces, unidentified DT 54

DRAMATIC WORKS

4	Fennimore and Gerda, Opera 1908: Intermezzo HN 61; LA 61; NP 62
4	Irmelin, Opera 1892: Prelude CH 40, 53, 56; CL 52, 55, 57, 58, 60, 67; DA 53; HN 65; MN 56; NR 60; NP 37, 67; PH 55; PT 43
3	Koanga, Opera 1895: Dance, La Calinda NP 35
10	A Village Romeo and Juliet: Ballet MN 43
8	-Intermezzo and Walk to Paradise Garden 1900 AT 62; BN 27, 58, 64; BU 41; CH 33, 40, 45, 47, 58; CT 31, 41, 42, 45, 51, 52;

DELIUS, F. (Cont.) A Village Romeo and Juliet, Intermezzo (Cont.)
                              CL 32, 34, 45;   DA 49;   DE 45, 50, 52;   DT 41,
                              49;   HN 44, 49, 53, 58;   NA 55;   KC 36, 42;
                              MN 42;   NP 27, 31, 38;   PH 27, 41, 58;   RC 32,
                              34, 40, 43, 57;   SL 41, 45, 49, 53;   SE 35, 41,
                              44;   WA 49;   SF 53, 60
                    17   Incidental Music to Hassan, or The Golden Journey
                              1920: Intermezzo   NP 35;   UT 42
                     2   -Serenade   UT 42

DELL 'ACQUA
see D'ALL ACQUA

DELLO JOIO, Norman   24   Antiphonal Fantasy on Theme of Albrici for Brass
1913-   US   and Str   CT 67;   HN 66;   PH 67
                    15   Concert Music for O 1944   NP 56;   PT 45
                    22   Conc for Clar   WA 50
                    18   Conc for Harp 1942   WA 52
                    13   Epigraph in Memory of L.Gillespie   DE 51;   LA 53;
                              PH 54
                    24   Fantasy and Var for P and O   BN 62;   CT 61
                    10   Homage to Haydn   PH 69
                    18   Lamentations of Saul, Voice and O   BA 62
                    22   Meditations on Ecclesiastes   CT 58;   DT 61;
                              NA 60;   WA 57
                    20   New York Profiles   BU 52;   NP 50
                    20   Ricercare, P and O 1946   CL 46;   NP 46
                    16   Serenade for O 1948   CL 49;   NA 61;   SF 52
                    45   Song of Affirmation, Chor and O   DE 53;   NA 57
                    12   Songs of Walt Whitman   ML 67
                     5   The Trial at Rouen, Opera: The Creed of Pierre
                              Cauchon   RC 57
                    30   The Triumph of St. Joan Symph   AT 63;   DA 60;
                              PT 53, 60;   WA 54
                    22   There is a Time   DT 61
                    17   Three Symphon Dances   PT 47
                    12   To a Lone Sentry 1943   BA 44
                    21   Var, Chaconne and Finale, P and O 1947   BN 48, 54,
                              59;   CH 50;   CT 48, 56, 62;   DA 49;   DE 50,
                              56;   HN 53;   NA 65, 69;   KC 56;   LA 51;
                              ML 65;   MN 57;   NR 52;   NP 48, 51, 54, 56;
                              PH 56;   RC 56;   SE 60;   UT 57;   WA 49

DELMAS, Marc   8   Penthesilee,   Overt   BN 25
1885-1931   Fr

DELSART   8   Fantasia for C   CH 1892
              Fr

DEL TREDICI,   12   From a Book of Night   SF 65
1937-   US   8   The Last Gospel   SF 67

DELVINCOURT, Claude 24   Bal Venitien   SL 46
1888-1954   Fr

DENISOV, Edison   6   Crescendo e diminuendo   NP 66
1929-   Russ

DENNY, William	8	Praeludium SF 54
1910- US	20	Symph No 2 SF 50
	20	Symph No 3 SF 62

DE SABATA, Victor	25	Gethsemane, Symphon Poem CH 25, 31; NP 25, 32
1892- It	20	Juventus, Symphon Poem CH 20(2), 25; NP 27

DESPLANES,
  Jean-Antoine
                Fr
	8	Grave SL 51

DESSAGNES, Guntrum Fr	24	Fantasie Concertante for 2 guitars and O DE 62

DESSAUER, Josef 1798-1876 Bohemian	4	Lockung, Song NP 1855

DESSAU, Paul 1894- Ger/US	12	In Memoriam, B. Brecht PT 61

DEUTSCH, Adolph	10	An Essay on Waltzes PH 36
1897- Eng/US	15	Scottish Suite for O and Bagpipes PH 36

DEYO, Ruth L. 1884- US	6	Prelude to the Diadem of Stars PH 30

DIAMOND, David	26	Ahavah for Narrator and O RC 54; WA 54
1915- US	22	Conc for P and Large O NP 65
	7	Elegy in Memory of Ravel, 1937 for Brass, Harps and Percussion BU 61
	10	The Enormous Room 1948 CT 49; SF 49; CL 49
	18	Music for Romeo and Juliet 1947 CH 47; CL 53; NA 63; PH 52; RC 69
	4	Overt to the Tempest 1944 BU 51; LA 49; NP 49; PT 52; RC 52; SL 51
	7	Psalm for Large O 1936 BU 60; DE 69; RC 61; SF 43

	12	Rounds for Str O 1944 BA 64; BN 45, 59;
		  CH 46; CT 62; CL 46; HN 46; MN 43;
		  NP 46; PH 46; RC 44; SL 48; WA 48, 68

	23	Sinfonia Concertante RC 56
	21	Symph No 2, or Symph for O 1943 BN 44
	36	Symph No 3 1945 BN 50; RC 65
	16	Symph No 4 1945 BN 47; CL 51; LA 48; NP 57; RC 48; SF 48; WA 52
	28	Symph No 5 NP 65
	25	Symph No 6 BN 56
	16	Symph No 7 CT 66; PH 61
	28	Symph No 8 CH 65; NP 61
	15	This Sacred Ground, Chor and O BU 63; SF 63
	8	Timon of Athens, A Symphon Portrait DE 50; LA Overt 51; PT 63
	12	The World of Paul Klee, Suite CT 63; NA 65; NP 59

DIAZ, Eugene   4   Benvenuto's Aria from Benvenuto Cellini, Opera
1837-1901   Fr   NA 41

DICK, Marcel,(March)   15   Adagio and Rondo   CL 62
1898-   Austr/US   15   Capriccio for O   CL 56
                        42   Symph No 1   CL 50
                        15   Symph for 2 Str O   MN 68

DIEPENBROCK, Alphonse   6   Overt, The Birds, Incidental Music   NP 21
1862-1921   Neth

DIETER, Christian   25   P Conc in b   CH 32
1899-   US

DIETRICH, Albert   8   Normanenzug,   or Normannenfahrt, Concert Overt
1829-1908   Ger   NP 1874

DIRKSEN,   15   Excerpts from Faith of Our Fathers   WA 51
                 US

DITTERSDORF, Karl von 12   Conc for Harp   UT 69
1739-1799   Ger   11   Conc Double Bass and O No 1 in E arr Jaeger   MN 67
                        22   Symph in a   CT 68
                        25   Symph in C, arr Carse   BN 1896, 17
                        15   The War on Human Passions or Tournament of the
                              Temperaments, Suite arr Kahn   SL 28

DI VEROLI, Donato   13   Theme and Var for O   CT 62
1921-1943   It

DOBROVEN, Issay   30   P Conc   SF 31
  Alexandrovich
1894-1953   Russ

DOHNANYI, Ernst von   5   Andante a la zingaresca, for V   SF 31
1877-1960   Hung   37   P Conc No 1 in e Op 5   BN 00
                        29   P Conc No 2 in b Op 42   DT 48
                        40   V Conc in d No 1 Op 27   BN 22;   CH 22, 36;
                              LA 23;   NS 22;   SL 25
                        30   V Conc in C No 2 Op 53   NP 51
                        26   Concertstück for C and O Op 12   BN 07, 17
                        12   Minutes Symphonique Op 36   CH 35;   NP 39
                        25   Ruralalis Hungarica, Suite Op 32b   CH 33;
                              CT 25, 26, 53;   CL 29, 30, 32, 36;   DT 26, 31,
                              44, 45;   KC 37;   MN 33, 48;   PH 33;   RC 37,
                              46;   SF 27
                        27   Suite en Valse in 4 mvts Op 39   NA 49
                        50   Suite in D   DT 47
                        30   Suite in E   DT 43
                        35   Suite in f# Op 19   AT 59;   CH 15, 16, 21, 22, 23,
                              25, 27, 33, 40, 46, 59;   CT 12, 14, 20, 39, 44,
                              47;   CL 23, 32, 33, 37;   HN 39, 45, 54;   NA 54;
                              KC 34, 35;   LA 25, 31;   ML 66;   MN 25, 30;
                              NP 33;   PH 57;   PT 39(Romanza only);   RC 32,
                              49;   SL 22, 23, 26;   SF 20, 21, 24;   SE 29,
                              31, 46, 63;   UT 40

                                    Time in
                                    Minutes
DOHNANYI, E. (Cont.)

	50	Symph No 2 in d Op 9 BN 03; CH 03, 38; SF 26
	57	Symph No 3 in E Op 40 MN 56, 57
	23	Var on a Nursery Rhyme P and O Op 25 AT 52; CH 23; CT 38; CL 23, 35; DT 45; HN 66; NP 36; UT 62

DONATO, Anthony   6   Prairie Schooner, A Covered Wagon Overt   CT 53
1909-   US   10   Sinfonietta No 2   CH 59
                       24   Solitude in the City, for Narrator and O   CT 54

DONATONI, Franco   29   Concertino for Str O Brass and Solo Timpani   CL 56
1927-   It

DONAUDY, Stephano   5   Aria, O Del Mio Amato Ben   LA 50;   SL arr
1879-1925   It   Warren 55

DONIZETTI, Gaetano   12   Concertina for Horn and O   RC 67
1797-1848   It   OPERAS
                       4   Belisario 1836: Cavatina   NP 03
                            Betly, or La capanna svizzera 1836
                       4   -In questa simplice   NP 30
                       6   Don Pasquale 1843: Overt   CT 66;   DT 38
                       4   -Quel guardo il cavaliere   CT 57, 62, 66; KC 62;   PT 51
                       4   Don Sebastian, roi de Portugal 1844: Deserta in terra   NP 24, 25
                       4   Daughter of the Regiment, La Fille du regiment 1840: Aria   BA 42(2)
                       4   -Chacon le soit   CT 49;   HN 43
                       4   -La dice ognum   AT 65
                       4   -Il faut Partir   CT 42
                       4   Elixir of Love, L'elisir d'amore 1832: Aria   DE 59
                       4   -Quanta amore   NP 03
                       4   -Udite, udite rustici   CT 46
                       4   -Una furtiva lagrima   DT 25, 26, 27, 28, 38, 46; KC 67;   LA 22;   PT 37;   SL 22, 27;   WA 36, 39; MN 26, 31, 35, 64;   NP 63
                       4   La Figlia del' Arciere, or Adelia 1841: Aria Convien partir,   WA 38
                      20   La Favorite 1840, Excerpts   NP 17
                       4   -O Mio Fernando   AT 64;   CH 15;   CT 48;   DA 29; DE 47;   KC 42, 52, 64;   LA 19;   MN 45, 59; NP 13, 24, 45;   SL 20;   SF 43;   UT 58
                       4   Linda di Chamounix 1842:   Aria CT 33, 55
                       4   -Aria and Recitative   SL 11
                       4   -O Luce di quest anima   CT 65;   NP 30;   PT 54
                       4   Lucia di Lammermoor 1835: Aria   BA 50, 67;   DE 57, 60;   PH 19;   PT 44
                       4   -Fra poco a me recovero, Act III   CT 51
                       4   -Mad Scene, Ardon gl'incensi   BA 62;   CT 04, 15, 48, 57, 62, 69;   DA 52;   DE 53;   DT 60;   NA 69; MN 32, 57, 66, 69;   NR 64;   NP 02;   PT 52; SL 46;   SE 63;   UT 67
                       4   -Quando rapito in estasi, Lucy's Cavatina Act I   CT
                       4   -Quartet   NP 07

DONIZETTI, G. (Cont.   Lucia d Lammermoor (Cont.)
    4   -Ragnava nel Silenzio   NP 02;   NR 68
    4   -Sextette   DA 26;   HN 40, 13
    4   -Tomb Scene   AT 50, 52;   SE 60
    4   Marino Faliero 1835:   Tutte or morte   NP 04
    4   Maria di Rohan 1843: Aria, Alma soave e cara   CT 11
    4   Maria Padilla 1841; Romanza, L'amor funesta   NP 20,
              18
    4   Poliuta or Les Martyrs 1840   Di quei soavi
              lagrime   NP 30
            Arias Unidentified
    4   O Gioia che si senti   NA 45;   NP 03 with Rondo,
              Finale de Furioso
    4   Aria Buffa, Conveniensi Teatrali   NP 03
    4   Per questa fiamma   NP 04

DONOVAN, Richard   12   Fantasy on American Folk Ballads, women's Chor and
  1891-   US   O 1940   DT 61

DOPPER, Cornelus   25   Symph No 6, Amsterdam   SF 20
  1870-1939   Neth   20   Gothic Chaconne   DT 25;   NP 21, 27;   PH 25

DORATI, Antal   24   C Conc   MN 57
  1906-   Hung/US   8   Largo Concertato   WA 66
                        35   Madrigal Suite   DA 66
                        31   Symph   LA 68;   MN 59
                        70   The Way of the Cross, Oratorio   MN 56, 58

DORLAY, Georges   20   C Conc, Conc passione   PH 17
              Fr

DOWNEY, John   16   Chant to Michaelangelo   NA 64
  1927-   US

DRAESEKE, Felix   5   Jubliee Overt 1898   BN 1899
  1835-1913   Ger   6   Scherzo from Symph No 1 Op 12   PH 04
                        27   Serenata in D   NS 1889
                        36   Symph No 2 in F Op 25   NS 1884

DRAGOI, Sabin   17   Suite Rustique   NP 38
  1894-   Roum   8   Two Roumanian Carols   PH 38

DRAGONETTI, Domenico   20   Conc for Double Bass in A   PH 39
  1763-1846   It

DUBENSKY, Arcady   12   Conc for 3 Tromb, Tuba and O   NP 49;   RC 52
  1890-   Russ/US   1   Fanfare: Star Spangled Banner 1939   NA 39
                        10   Fantasia, Tchaikowsky Country   NA 39
                         4   Fugue for 18 V 1932   AT 37;   CL 33;   DA 57;
                                DT 32, 34;   NA 37, 40;   MN 33;   PH 31, 32;
                                RC 32;   SL 37;   SE 32;   UT 46
                         3   Gossips for Str 1930   RC 37
                        15   Overt Tom Sawyer 1936   DT 35
                        15   Prelude and Fugue 1932   BN 44
                        15   The Raven, Recitation with O 1931   PH 32

DUBENSKY, A. (Cont.)
	12	Russian Bells, Symph Poem 1928 NS 27 1st mvt only
	14	Suite, Year 1600 SL 51
	15	Theme, Var, Finale on Stephen Foster Themes 1941 CT 41; NA 40, 42

DUBOIS, Theodore
1837-1924   Fr
	30	V Conc in c CH 1897
	15	Fantasie for Harp and O CH 06, 11
	8	Fantasie Truimphale for Org and O CH 1899
	6	Frithjof Overt 1881 BN 03, 18; CT 19
	30	Intermezzo Symphonique de la Notre Dame de la Mer NA 32; LA 21; NP 17; NS 17
	32	Symph Francaise CT 16

DUKAS, Paul
1865-1935   Fr

20   La Peri, A Danced Poeme, Ballet 1912
          BA 62;   BN 18, 23, 24, 27, 35, 56;   CH 19, 22,
          26, 30, 46;   CT 27, 33, 44, 67;   CL 33, 46, 49,
          54, 61;   DE 68;   DT 29, 59, 67;   LA 32;   MN 39,
          48;   NP 33, 38, 57, 65;   PH 29, 52, 58;   RC 57;
          SL 32, 33, 52;   SF 15, 16, 22, 31

5   -Fanfare for Brass   BA 62;   CH 68;   CL 61;
          SL 49

18   Polyeucte Overt 1892   BN 19, 23;   CH 10;   CT 20;
          LA 25;   SL 19

11   Scherzo   PH 50

16   Symphon Poem The Sorcerer's Apprentice, L'Apprenti
          sorcier 1897   AT 50, 52;   BA 42, 44, 59;   BN 04,
          05, 06, 08, 12, 13, 15, 18, 20, 25, 39, 41, 45,
          54, 57;   BU 53, 57;   CH 98, 99, 04, 06, 09, 10,
          13, 14, 16, 17, 18, 19, 21, 22, 27, 43, 47, 55,
          59;   CT 04, 05, 10, 12, 19, 25, 27, 31, 36, 40,
          41, 45, 46, 49, 57, 60, 63;   CL 19, 21, 23, 25,
          27, 31, 34, 39, 49, 58;   DA 27, 34, 38, 56, 59;
          DE 46, 48, 49, 51, 66;   DT 17, 18, 20, 23, 24,
          29, 31, 34, 35, 51, 53, 54, 68;   HN 37, 48, 54;
          NA 38, 48, 56, 61, 65, 68;   KC 34, 35, 46, 51, 61;
          LA 20, 22, 23, 24, 34, 44, 52;   MN 27, 29, 31, 33,
          41, 46, 60;   NR 53, 63;   NP 04, 13, 14, 15, 16,
          17, 20, 23, 28, 31, 35, 40, 44, 47, 49, 53, 54,
          56;   PH 10(2), 11, 12, 14, 15, 16, 22, 25, 26,
          27(2), 28, 30, 35, 37, 44, 46, 59;   PT 37, 38,
          44(2), 48, 49;   RC 24, 31, 33, 37, 51, 61;
          SL 12, 15, 18, 21, 25, 27, 29, 31, 33, 35;
          SF 14, 15, 16, 18, 19, 21, 22, 28, 33, 37, 46,
          51, 53;   SE 28, 52, 56;   UT 47, 68;   WA 37,
          49, 68, 69

38   Symph in C 1896   BN 17;   CH 20;   CT 20;   CL 40;
          MN 42;   NP 36, 48;   NS 10;   PH 09

DUKELSKY, Vladimir
1903-   Russ/US
(non de plume
Duke, Vernon)
	26	C Conc 1943 BN 45
	28	V Conc in g 1942 BN 42; NP 43
	20	Dedicaces for Sopr, P and O 1935 BN 38
	10	Epitaph, Chor and O 1932 BN 31
	6	Ode to Milkyway 1945 MN 63; SL 46
	35	Suite, Zephyr and Flore, Ballet 1925 BN 26
	16	Symph No 1 in F 1928 BN 28
	17	Symph No 2 in D^b 1929 BN 29; CH 32

DUMLER, Martin G.   20   Four Ballet Scenes   CT 43, 46
  1868-1958   US   10   Prelude and Fugue   CT 42

DUNHAM, Henry M.   30   Symph Fantasia for Org   CH 09
  1853-   US

DUNN, James Philip   5   Fantasy-Overt, We   MN 30
  1884-1936   US   5   Overt on Negro Melodies   LA 28

DUPARC, Henri   6   Aux étoiles, Nocturne for O 1910   CT 21;   NS 19
  1848-1933   Fr   15   Lenore, Symphon Poem 1875   BN 96;   CH 96;
                                 CT 18;   SF 19
                               Songs with O
                          4   Chanson Triste 1868   CL 27;   DT 37;   NA 37
                          4   Extase   CT 21;   DT 41;   PH 20
                          4   Invitation au Voyage 1870   BA 44;   BU 44;
                                 CH 17;   CT 40;   DE 46, 48;   DT 15, 18, 41;
                                 NA 38;   LA 27, 45;   MN 22, 29, 46;   PH 17,
                                 18(2), 19, 26;   RC 47;   SL 20, 42, 44, 49;
                                 SF 44
                          4   La Mamoire de Rosamunde   SL 20
                          4   La Vague et le cloche, The Wave and the Bell 1870
                                 BA 44;   CH 05;   CL 26;   NA 48;   NS 22;
                                 RC 26
                          4   Phidylé, Ballad   BA 44;   CT 31, 41;   CL 20;
                                 DE 46;   NA 37;   KC 38;   LA 27, 45;   MN 38
                                 PH 26, 37, 51;   RC 47;   SL 20, 49
                         10   Four Songs unidentified   DT 56

DUPRÉ, Marcel   5   Cortège et litanie Org and O Op 19   CL 27;   RC 24
  1886-1972   Fr   15   Conc for Org and O in e Op 31   UT 46

DUPUIS, Albert   8   Herman et Dorothée Overt   CT 21
  1877-   Belg   8   Jean Michel, Opera 1903: Symphon Fragments CT 20
                         25   Macbeth, Symphon Poem   CT 21

DURAND, August   6   Chaconne   DT 32
  1830-1909   Fr

DURANTE, Francesco   10   Conc Grosso in f No 1 for Str arr Lualdi   BN 59;
  1684-1755   It   NP 59;   PT 69;   SL 52, 53, 63
                          3   Prayer, Virgin, tutto Amor   CH 19, 32

DURHAM, Lowell   20   A New England Pastorale Sketch   UT 55
  1917-   US   7   Prelude Scherzo and Fugue   UT 49

DURUFLÉ, Maurice   7   Andante and Scherzo Op 8   NP 57
  1902-   Fr   Trois Danses Op 6   HN 54
                                 -Two only: Lente, Tambourin   DT 53;   PT 49

DUSSEK, Jan Ladislav   20   Conc for Two P   NP 1847
  1760-1812   Bohemian

DUTILLEUX, Henri   20   Ballet Suite, Le Loup   PH 65
  1916-   Fr   20   Cinq Metaboles   CL 64, 67;   RC 67;   WA 68

DUTILLEUX, H. (Cont.)
                36   Symph   BN 53;   CL 54;   NP 57
                27   Symph No 2 for Large O and Chamber O   BN 59, 62;
                       CH 63, 66;   MN 68;   PH 62

DUVIVIER,   40   Dramatic Symph in f   CH 02, two mvts only 99
        US   15   Grande Valse de Concert   CH 05
               15   The Triumph of Bacchus   CH 1892

DVORAK, Antonin   5   Adagio for C,Waldesruhe Op 68   BN 1894, 14
1841-1904 Czech   4   Aria O grant me from St. Ludmilla Oratorio Op 71
                       CH 1891

  37   P Conc in g Op 33
        BN 69;   CH 51, 57;   CT 52;   CL 53, 66;   DA 63;   DE 58;   HN 59;
        NA 52, 69;   LA 59;   MN 43, 67;   NP 43, 51;   PT 61, 67;   SE 63;
        WA 44, 62

  33   V Conc in a Op 53
        BA 60, 62;   BN 00, 09, 15, 19, 36, 41, 66;   BU 48, 60;   CH 1891,
        95, 04, 19, 31, 41, 49, 54, 61, 65;   CT 04, 24, 31, 39, 62;
        CL 36, 45, 51, 60, 62, 63, 65;   DA 48, 50, 60;   DE 64, 68;
        DT 35, 41, 43, 65, 67;   HN 51, 54;   NA 44, 62, 69;   KC 54, 62;
        LA 51;   ML 63, 68;   MN 39, 41, 47, 50, 63;   NR 55, 64;
        NP 1893, 95, 97, 40, 41, 47, 51, 55, 56, 60, 66;   NS 1893;
        PH 05, 31, 39, 54, 64;   PT 43, 45, 52, 56, 63;   RC 61;
        SL 34, 39, 62, 63, 64;   SF 65, 68;   SE 58;   UT 56, 64;
        WA 38, 45, 68

  39   C Conc in b Op 104
        AT 57, 68;   BA 47, 58, 66;
        BN 1896, 99, 05, 12, 16, 36, 51, 55, 59, 64, 65;
        BU 45, 47, 49, 55, 56, 62;
        CH 1896, 97, 06, 13, 21, 25, 29, 32, 36, 40, 42, 44, 47, 50, 53,
        55, 60, 63, 65, 69;
        CT 10, 15, 17, 24, 26, 27, 31, 32, 39, 48, 53, 60, 64;
        CL 23, 28, 32, 33, 39, 42, 44, 48, 51, 53, 58, 62, 68;
        DA 57, 59, 63, 67;   DE 49, 56, 66;   DT 35, 38, 47, 56, 64;
        HN 37, 47, 49, 54, 66;   NA 63;   KC 44, 50, 60;
        LA 25, 29, 36, 49, 56, 60, 63;   ML 61;
        MN 25, 30, 35, 38, 41, 48, 54, 62, 65;   NR 52, 58, 62;
        NP 1896, 17, 23, 29, 50, 51, 56, 64, 65, 69;
        PH 02, 09, 12, 14, 21, 23, 29, 43, 46, 51, 53, 56, 58;
        PT 11, 45, 50, 53, 55, 58, 60, 63;   RC 23, 51, 62, 68;
        SL 15, 20, 27, 41, 48, 56, 59, 64, 66;   SF 22, 58, 62, 63;
        SE 30, 43, 54, 65;   UT 50, 61;   WA 43, 51, 56, 59, 63, 66
        -Adagio and Allegro   CH 16

   4   Humoresque Op 101   BA 26;   CH 08;   DT 35;   HN 15
  22   Legends Op 59 1st set, nine items   BN 1886, 01
   5   Mazurka in e for V and O Op 49   MN 45
        OVERTURES
  10   Carnival Op 92
        AT 50;   BA 42, 48(2), 51, 59, 65;   BN 1894, 97, 98, 04, 12, 14,
        23, 41;   BU 60
        CH 1893, 97, 98(2), 02, 04, 06, 08, 10, 12, 18, 19, 55;
        CT 06, 07, 08, 30, 31, 36, 39, 42, 45;
        CL 24, 29, 41, 52, 62, 68;   DA 32, 69;   DE 58;

DVORAK, A. (Cont.)   Carnival Op 92 (Cont.)
          DT 24, 30, 39, 61, 66;   HN 46;   NA 39, 41, 66;   KC 35, 41, 51;
          LA 21, 23, 25, 31, 54, 57;   ML 64;   MN 39, 44, 48, 50, 59, 66;
          NR 61;   NP 1894, 03, 10, 12, 14, 17, 19, 20, 40, 54, 65;
          NS 07, 08, 12, 24;
          PH 02, 08, 10, 11, 12, 13, 15, 21, 28, 30, 41, 57;
          PT 40;   RC 24, 25, 31, 33, 34;   SL 11, 15, 20, 24, 29, 68;
          SF 22, 31, 51, 53, 59, 61;   SE 32, 38;   UT 53;
          WA 38, 39, 41, 53, 60, 69
14   Husitzka, Dramatic Overt Op 67
          BN 1892, 01, 06, 11, 13, 15;
          CH 1891, 92, 04, 06, 09, 11, 12, 15, 20, 30, 40;
          CT 1896, 98, 05, 16;   DT 69;   ML 67;   MN 28;   NP 1884, 90,
          96, 04, 25;   NS 1887, 92;   PH 11;   SL 14
12   In der Natur Op 91 in F
          BN 1895, 05;   CH 1894, 95, 97, 98(2), 04, 05, 08, 10, 16, 36, 41;
          NP 1894, 09, 14;   PH 03, 04, 17;   SF 13, 25
10   Mein Heim, My Home from Incidental Music for Josef Kajetan Tyl
          Op 62   CH 01;   NP 12
14   Othello Op 93   BN 1896, 00, 04, 15, 17, 66;
          CH 1898(2), 08, 14, 15, 16, 17, 20, 32, 41;   CT 21;   LA 67;
          NP 1894, 30;   PH 67;   SL 19
 8   The Peasant as Rogue Opera Op 37   BN 1883

 7   Nocturne for Str O Op 40   NS 14
90   Requiem Mass Op 89   SF 69
 8   Romance for V and O in f Op 11   BN 67;   PH 65
 5   Rondo for C and O in g Op 94   BN 1896, 14;   NA 39;   NS 03;   NP 11
12   Scherzo Capriccioso in Db Op 66   BA 53;   BN 1887, 88, 90, 92, 95;
          BU 47;   CH 1891, 94, 95, 96, 99, 03, 05, 08, 10, 12, 17, 18, 23,
          25, 41;   CL 40;   NA 45;   KC 52;   LA 44, 48;   MN 42, 46, 60;
          NP 1885, 89, 15, 17, 30;   NS 06, 13;   PH 03, 33, 43;
          PT 58, 66;   RC 62;   SL 15;   WA 67
30   Serenade for Str in E Op 22   KC 53;   NP 12;   PH 55;   WA 51
      SONGS
 4   Am Bache   CH 32;   MN 27;   SL 31
12   Four Duets for Sopr and Contral Op 32   NS 07
10   Gypsy Songs Op 55   NR 69;   NS 03, 23
 4   O Grant me from St. Ludmilla, Oratorio Op 71   NP 1890;   CH 1891
 4   Songs My Mother Taught Me Op 55 No 4   BU 54;   DT 46;   MN 41;   NP 43
 4   Song to the Moon, from Rusalka Opera Op 114   AT 53, 68;
          DT 46, 47;   HN 55;   ML 62, 64;   NP 43;   RC 47
 8   Songs, unidentified   NS 11

17   Slavonic Dances, series undesignated   UT 41
 4   -1 dance   DT 33, 39
 8   -2 dances   BA 43, 61;   HN 41;   NA 52;   NS 07, 14, 19, 27;
          WA 35
16   -4 dances   NR 62
10   -Excerpts undesignated   BN 1881, 82, 83, 88, 91, 22

24   From Op 46 Series I   CH 23;   LA 49, 63;   UT 41
 3   No 1 in C   CT 1896, 02, 32, 34, 37, 38, 39, 43;   CL 25, 46, 51,
          55(2), 62;   DA 35, 46;   KC 36;   NR 68;   SL 25
 3   No 2 in e   CL 28, 46, 53, 55, 62;   NS 1893, 11

DVORAK, A. (Cont.) From Op 46 Series I (Cont.)
    3   No 3 in D   CH 28, 29, 31, 34, 40;   CT 48, 50, 53, 62;   CL 28,
             46, 51, 53, 55(2), 62, 69;   KC 36;   NR 68;   PH 39;   PT 37; SL 25
    3   No 4 in F   CT 39;   CL 46, 55
    3   No 5 in A   CL 46;   MN 57;   RC 59
    3   No 6 in A^b CL 46;   MN 57;   RC 59
    3   No 7 in e   CT 48, 50, 53, 62;   CL 46, 55;   MN 57
    3   No 8 in g   CH 25, 26, 27, 29, 31, 34;   MN 57;   NR 68;   RC 59

   16   From Op 72 Series II, 8 items   CH 1892(2), 94, 03;   CL 46, 55;
             NP 88
    3   No 1 in B   DA 30, 46
    3   No 2 in e   BN 67;   CL 46, 55, 69;   DA 26, 27, 46
    3   No 4 in D^b NR 68
    3   No 5 in b^b CT 50, 53, 62;   MN 57;   NP 1882
    3   No 6 in B^b BN 67;   MN 57;   NP 35
    3   No 7 in a   CL 53, 62;   MN 57;   NP 1882
    3   No 8 in A^b BN 67;   DA 25, 26, 46;   MN 57
             Slavonic Rhapsodies Op 45
    7   No 1 in D   BN 1886, 01;   CH 03
   13   No 2 in g   BN 1893;   CH 1893(2);   NS 1893, 11
   14   No 3 A^b BN 1896, 00;   CH 1891, 93, 96, 01, 54;   MN 51;
             NP 1898, 18;   PH 35;   SL 17
   25   Stabat Mater Op 58   MN 48
    6   -Inflammatus   CH 02

   21   Suite in D, Czech Suite Op 39   BN 1887, 88, 92, 97, 04;   NS 16,
             20;   SL 10

             SYMPHONIES
   32   B^b Op 4   WA 62
   30   E^b Posthumous Op 10   NP 11;   WA 62
   43   No 1 or No 6 in D Op 60
             BN 1883(2), 85, 89, 63, 67;   CH 1891, 50, 68;   CT 03;   CL 69;
             DE 69;   MN 68;   NR 65;   NP 1882, 87, 92, 31;   PH 58, 66;   RC 46

   30   No 2 or No 7 in d Op 70
             AT 57, 69;   BA 59, 68;   BN 1886(2), 90, 92, 95, 98, 02, 20, 23,
             62, 66, 67;   BU 68;   CH 1893, 03, 14, 15, 19, 20, 28, 32, 34,
             41, 42, 44, 48, 50, 62, 64, 66;   CT 40, 63;   CL 40, 50, 59, 67,
             68;   DA 53, 64, 69;   DE 54, 57, 67;   DT 31, 47, 62, 69;   HN 40,
             43, 60, 62, 66, 69;   NA 60, 65, 69;   KC 59;   LA 58, 62, 65, 67,
             69;   ML 64;   MN 66;   NP 1885, 24, 41, 55, 57, 62, 65, 67;
             PH 64, 68, 69;   PT 49, 55, 65, 66;   RC 58, 67;   SL 10, 61;
             SF 56, 60, 66, 68;   SE 56, 64

   45   No 3 or No 5 in F Op 76
             BN 22, 64;   CH 18;   CL 69;   NP 19;   NS 1890, 24;   UT 69

   35   No 4 or No 8 in G Op 88
             AT 51, 57, 66, 68;   BA 53, 56, 58, 62, 67;   BN 1891, 50, 58, 60,
             65;   BU 60;   CH 45, 52, 57, 60, 66, 67;   CT 32, 46, 49, 50, 51,
             53, 56;   CL 38, 47, 54, 58, 60, 63, 65, 68, 69;   DA 56, 61, 69;
             DE 63, 66, 69;   DT 37, 61, 68;   HN 44, 61, 63;   NA 64, 68;
             KC 52, 56, 62, 68;   LA 41, 52, 56, 60, 61, 64, 66;   ML 62, 67;

DVORAK, A. (Cont.) SYMPHONIES, No 4 or No 8 in G (Cont.)
      MN 41, 51, 57, 65;   NR 51, 56, 59, 62, 66;   NP 1891, 95, 99,
      14, 16, 18, 31, 38, 42, 47, 52, 59, 63, 67, 69;   PH 54, 64, 66,
      68; PT 61, 69;   RC 32, 35, 43, 48, 49, 54, 61;   SL 64, 67;
      SF 30, 49, 52, 59, 66;   SE 32, 41, 53, 61;   WA 50, 59, 63, 66

40   No 5 or No 9 in e Op 95 The New World
      AT 46, 49, 56, 62;   BA 40, 51, 54, 63;
      BN 1893, 95, 96, 97, 00, 02, 04, 08, 10, 12, 17, 19, 29, 34, 38,
      41, 47, 54, 61, 63, 66;
      BU 48, 56, 63;   CH 1894, 95, 98, 99, 01, 04, 06, 08(2), 10, 11,
      12, 13, 16, 17, 18, 20, 32, 41, 43, 46, 47, 51, 57, 60, 65;
      CT 1895, 00, 05, 08, 10, 14, 17, 19, 24, 26, 33, 38, 41, 45, 47,
      49, 57, 59, 65(2);
      CL 19, 20, 22, 24, 25, 29, 31, 33, 36, 41, 42, 43, 46, 51, 53, 58, 63;
      DA 26, 28, 38(2), 49, 57, 60, 62, 66;
      DE 45, 46, 47, 51, 58, 65;
      DT 14, 17, 18, 20, 36, 38, 41, 43, 56, 59, 63, 65;
      HN 32, 37, 40, 46, 52, 54, 55, 56, 60, 65;
      NA 34, 38, 41, 45, 50, 55, 62;
      KC 33, 36, 41, 49, 53, 61, 64, 69;
      LA 19, 21, 24, 36, 43, 57, 62, 68;
      MN 22, 24, 27, 30, 40, 48, 52, 55, 57, 61, 67;
      NR 51, 54, 57, 61, 67;
      NP 1893, 94, 97, 00, 05, 07, 10, 11, 12, 13, 14, 15, 17, 23, 30,
      35, 43, 47, 49, 61, 69;
      NS 1896, 03, 07, 09, 11, 13, 15(2), 16, 18, 19, 21, 22, 23, 25, 26;
      PH 02, 04, 06, 07, 09, 10, 11, 13, 14, 15, 17, 18, 19(2), 20, 21,
      22, 23, 24, 25, 27, 29, 32, 33, 34, 36, 39, 40, 41, 43, 44, 46, 49,
      55, 57, 60, 67, 68;   PT 38, 41, 43, 47, 50, 53, 57, 64;
      RC 25, 31, 38, 40, 50, 60, 65, 67, 68;
      SL 09, 11, 14, 16, 18, 19, 21, 23, 25, 26, 27, 32, 34, 40, 52, 53,
      55, 61, 66, 68;
      SF 12, 17, 19, 21, 23, 25, 52, 53, 55, 61, 66;
      SE 26, 32, 40, 45, 60, 67;
      UT 40, 44, 46, 51, 54, 60, 64;
      WA 31, 34, 35, 36, 48, 53, 54, 61, 63
10   -Allegro con fuoco   CL 18
10   -Largo   CH 1894, 05, 07;   CL 18;   MN 48, 67;   SF 30, 38

   SYMPHONIC POEMS
25   Golden Spinning Wheel Op 109   BA 56;   CH 1896, 56;   NS 10, 19;
      PH 11(2);   PT 56
21   A Hero's Song Op 111   BN 1899;   CH 48;   NP 41;   PH 01
20   The Wood Dove, Die Waldtaube Op 110   BN 05;   CH 1899;   CT 15
13   The Noonday Witch, Die Mittagshexe Op 108   CT 1897
13   The Water Demon Op 107   HN 41

24   Symphon Var on an Original Theme Op 78;   BN 1888, 98, 02;   CH 1892,
      93, 95, 97, 00, 02, 04(2), 08, 24;   CT 99, 01, 33;   MN 24;
      NP 1888, 31, 37;   NS 27;   SE 43;
15   Terzetto for Two V and Vla Op 74   NS 1887, Larghetto and Scherzo NS 07
8   Two Waltzes for Str O Op 54   NP 24

DYKINS,   8   Symphon Suite   DE 52
            US

DYSON, Sir George   12   Overt to Cantata, The Canterbury Pilgrims 1931
1883-   Brit   NP 48

EAMES, Henry P.   5   Pastoral Intermezzo   CH 41
1872-   US

EBANN, W. B.   20   C Conc   PH 01
1873-   US

ECCLES,   8   Sonata en Concert for C and O   DA 50
            US

ECKERT, Carl   4   Aria, Though I Speak, from William of Orange,
1820-1879   Ger   Opera 1846   NP 05
                           25   C Conc in a   BN 1889

EFFINGER, Cecil   35   Christmas Cantata after St. Luke   DE 57
1914-   US   14   Little Symph No 1 Op 31, 1945   NA 60
                           12   Little Symph No 2 1950   CT 48;   DE 50, 56
                            7   Prelude and Fugue Op 14 1942   DE 54
                           20   Symph No 1 Op 40 1946   DE 46
                           30   Symph for Chor and O   DE 52
                           23   Symph No 5   DE 59
                           19   Symphon Prelude in D with Boy's Choir   DE 58
                           13   Tone Poem on Square Dance   DE 55
                            7   Var on a Cowboy Tune   DE 45

EGGE, Klaus   29   V Conc Op 26   NP 56
1906-   Nor   23   Symph No 4   DT 67

EGK, Werner   28   Abraxas, Suite from Ballet 1948   KC 59
1901-   Ger   20   French Suite after Rameau 1949   BA 56;   CH 63;
                                 DT 61;   HN 54;   LA 58;   MN 59;   PH 59;   SL 61;
                                 SF 66;   SE 61;   WA 58
                           15   Georgica, three peasant pieces 1934   NP 34
                            7   Overt to Opera, Magic Violin, Die Zaubergeige 1935
                                 KC 57
                           25   Var on a Caribbean Theme   KC 59

EHRENBERG, Carl   5   Hymes pour toi   NS 27
1878-   Ger

EICHHEIM, Henry   25   A Chinese Legend, Ballet 1924   BN 24;   CL 24;
1870-1942   US   MN 25;   RC 26;   SF 25
                           12   Bali, Symphon Poem   BN 34;   PH 33
                           15   Burma Suite, Four Dances from Ballet 1926   BN 29;
                                 CH 26;   LA 28;   PH 26
                           12   Java, A Symphonic Picture 1929   BN 29;   CT 37;
                                 CL 37;   LA 30;   PH 29
                           10   Japan: Nocturne   CL 22;   PH 24, 28
                           10   Korean Sketch   CL 22, 37
                           12   Malay Mosaic 1924   CL 24

EICHHEIM, H. (Cont.)
              10   Siamese Impression   CL 22
              20   Two Oriental Impressions for Chamber O 1921
                     BN 21;   CH 21;   LA 23;   MN 24;   NR 55;   PH 22;
                     SF 24;   WA 33

EINEM, Gottfried von 14   Ballad for O   CL 57;   MN 65;   PT 65
1918-   Aust 40   Brecht, das Studenlied   AT 64
               8   Capriccio for O Op 2   CH 55;   CT 57;   CL 53;
                     HN 53;   LA 53;   NR 53, 59;   NP 53;   PH 58;
                     SE 61;   UT 57
              20   Conc for O Op 4   PH 55, 56;   PT 54
              15   Danton's Death, Suite from Opera Op 6a   KC 49;
                     NP 62;   RC 64
              45   The Golden Calf Op 27 Rondo Dance, from the Ballet
                     1952   LA 59;   MN 66;   SF 60
              15   Hexameron   SL 69
              20   Meditations for O Op 18   CL 55
              13   Nachstuck   PH 65
              15   Orchestermusik No 1 Op 9   AT 57;   NP 52, 56
              18   Philadelphia, Symph Op 28 3 parts   PH 62
              24   Symphon Scenes Op 22   AT 58;   BN 57
              23   Turandot, Four Episodes from the Ballet 1944   LA 55

EISENHOFER,   5   Waltz   NP 1846
         Ger

EISFELD, Theodore   10   Concertina for Clar   NP 1854, 1857
1816-1882   Ger   6   Elegie Cantabile for Cornet   NP 1860
              10   Nocturne for French Horn, La Solitude   NP 1861
              8   Var de Bravura for Sopr   NP 1863
              10   Scena Italiana de Concerto for Voice   NP 1862

ELGAR, Sir Edward   7   Caractacus Op 35 Cantata for Soli, Chor and O
1857-1934   Eng   CH 11 (selections)
              8   Carillon for Narrator and O Op 75   LA 42;   NS 17;
                     PH 18;   SL 18
              13   Cockaigne Overt Op 40   BA 42, 48;   BN 01;   BU 46;
                     CH 01(2), 02, 04, 07, 15, 23, 24, 45;   CT 31, 63;
                     DE 52;   CL 34;   HN 60, 63;   MN 27, 43;   NP 31,
                     35, 37, 39, 62;   NS 14, 27;   PT 37, 43, 54, 66;
                     RC 23, 27, 40, 50, 61, 63;   SL 19;   SF 47;
                     SE 41, 54
              4   Contrasts: The Gavotte 1700 and 1900 Op 10 No 3 for
                     Small O   CH 02, 04
              50   V Concerto in b Op 61   CH 11, 21, 38, 42, 45;
                     CT 33, 43;   CL 69;   DE 46;   NA 61;   KC 69;
                     LA 46;   MN 42, 63;   NP 33, 37, 49, 67;   NS 21;
                     PT 59, 67;   WA 44, 49, 67
              30   C Concerto in e Op 85   AT 69;   CL 66;   DA 66;
                     DT 67;   HN 62, 68;   LA 68;   MN 68;   NP 66;
                     PT 67;   RC 67;   SL 33;   SF 69
            101   The Dream of Gerontius Oratorio Op 38, Complete   HN 63
             50   -Parts I and II   NP 58
              8   -Prelude   BN 03, 33;   CL 47;   PH 18 with Angel's
                     Farewell

Time in
Minutes

ELGAR, E. (Cont.)

30   Enigma Var on an original theme Op 36
      AT 51, 52, 59, 65;   BA 54, 61, 68;   BN 03(2),
      09, 26, 33, 45, 53, 56, 60, 63, 65;   BU 47, 56,
      69;   CH 01(2), 03, 04, 05, 06, 07, 09, 12, 14,
      19, 22, 27, 31, 32, 37, 39, 40, 42, 43, 53, 59,
      63, 68;   CT 11, 18, 25, 31, 36, 40, 46, 50, 53,
      55, 57, 61, 69;   CL 33, 36, 45, 47, 51, 57, 63,
      67;   DA 48, 50, 56, 57, 63;   DE 47, 48, 51, 55,
      63, 69;   DT 21, 31, 41, 43, 58, 65;   HN 33, 51,
      56, 60, 62;   NA 36, 39, 41, 51, 56, 60, 63, 69;
      KC 36, 56, 59, 69;   LA 32, 39, 44, 49, 51, 53,
      58, 60;   ML 64;   MN 22, 30, 32, 55, 59, 62;
      NR 57, 59, 66;   NP 05, 10, 17, 27, 32, 35, 37,
      38, 40, 42, 51, 64, 68;   NS 06(2), 08, 12, 16,
      20, 21, 27;   PH 04, 12, 16, 19, 21, 29, 33, 35,
      41, 43, 44, 53, 57, 61, 68;   PT 40, 53, 69;
      RC 51, 54, 56, 65;   SL 11, 59, 67;   SF 25, 30,
      44, 47, 57, 61, 66;   SF Nimrod only 64, 69;
      SE 31, 34, 43, 44, 57, 65;   UT 54, 68;   WA 48,
      53, 60

30   Falstaff, Symphon Study in a Op 68   BN 67;
      CT 43;   NP 43, 67;   NS 13, 17;   PH 65;   PT 62,
      65;   RC 52

12   Froissart Overt Op 19   CH 04, 07, 18
10   Grania and Diarmid Incidental Music and Funeral
      March Op 42   CH 03(2), 27, 33
20   In the South, Overt Op 50   BN 05, 06;   CH 04(2),
      06, 13, 24, 28, 50, 65;   CT 32;   NS 04;   SL 17
15   Introduction and Allegro for Quart and Str O Op 47
      BN 30, 40, 56, 65;   CH 05, 13, 30, 38, 63;
      CL 37; DT 55, 69;   HN 58;   LA 31, 41, 55, 65;
      MN 33, 66;   NP 30, 35, 37, 39, 58;   NS 05, 19;
      PH 33, 57, 58;   PT 53;   RC 13, 35;   SF 30;
      SL 44;   SE 55, 66
4   Lullaby from the Bavarian Highlands   CH 08
5   Land of Hope and Glory from Coronation Ode, for
      Soli, Chor and O Op 44 No 6   HN 42
8   Polonia, Symphon Prelude Op 76   CL 40;   NS 16
      Pomp and Circumstance, 5 Marches Op 39
5   March No 1 in D   CH 02(2), 03, 06, 23, 26, 27;
      CL 27, 40;   DT 15, 17;   HN 41;   KC 42;   ML 60;
      MN 42;   NP 19, 44, 55;   PH 12, 15;   WA 33
5   March No 2 in a   CH 02, 03;   NS 07, 12;
      PT 40;   SL 23
6   Saga of King Olaf: Cantata for Soli, Chor and O Op 30:
      The Challenge of Thor   CH 38
12   Sea Pictures for Voice and O Op 37, Five Songs
      AT 55;   CH 02, 03, Nos 2, 4, 5, 05, 13; Nos 1, 2,
      3, 4, 20; Nos 2, 3, 4, 5, 21;   NP 10;   SL 09
8   Serenade for Str O in e Op 20   RC 44;   UT 43, 44
3   Sospiri for Str, Harp and Org Op 70   NA 50, 54;
      NS 16
4   Song, My Love Dwelt   NP 95
13   Three Bavarian Dances Op 27   MN 29
      The Wand of Youth, A Play for Children
18   Suite No 1, Op 1a seven parts   CH 08

ELGAR, E. (Cont.) The Wand of Youth, A Play for Children (Cont.)
                   18   Suite No 2 Op 1b, six parts   CH 10(2), 11; DE 53
                   51   Symph in A^b No 1 Op 55   BN 08, 09;   CH 09(2), 17,
                              33;   CT 34, 41;   NS 09, 13, 17, 19, 24;   PH 12
                   51   Symph in E^b No 2 Op 63   BN 11, 34, 64;   CH 11;
                              CT 11, 38;   CL 49;   HN 66;   NP 34, 38, 65;
                              NS 11;   PT 52, 63

ELKUS, Albert   12   Concertino for C, Timpani and Str on Lezione III of
1884-   Ariosto 1917   SF 19, 37, 61
                       17   Impressions from A Greek Tragedy 1921   LA 23;
                                  SF 19, 37
                        4   Rondo on a Merry Folk Tune 1924   SF 22

ELLIOT, Willard   16   Conc for Bassoon and O   NP 66
1926-   US   8   Elegy for O   DA 59
                       12   Spring Overt   DA 63
                       15   Symph No 2   DA 62

ELMORE, Robert   12   Valley Forge   PH 36
1913-   US

ELOY, Jean-Claude   8   Equivalences SF 66
1938-   Fr

ELSENHEIMER, Nicholas   6   Irrlichter, Scherzo for O   CT 15
1866-1935   Ger

ELWELL, Herbert   20   Concert Suite for V and O   RC 59
1898-   US   25   The Forever Young   CL 53;   SL 53
                       11   Introd and Allegro for O 1942   BU 44;   CL 42;   SL 45
                        9   Ode for O   CL 50;   DT 53;   HN 52;   KC 54;
                                  PT 53;   RC 59
                       34   Pastorale for V and O 1947   BU 50;   CL 47, 56
                       21   Suite from Ballet The Happy Hypocrite 1925   CL 64;
                                  DT 30
                       10   -Overt and Finale   CL 29

EMBORG, Jens L.   4   Norwegian Dances   DE 49
              Dan

ENESCO, Georges   8   Cantabile and Presto for Fl   NS 10
1881-1955   Roum/Fr   9   Concert Overt on Roumanian Motifs   WA 49
                        5   Dance of the Thebans from Oedipus, Opera, 1921-36
                                  CL 24, 25
                       12   Roumanian Rhaps No 1 in A Op 11   AT 49, 56;   BA 41,
                                  42, 43, 44, 45, 47, 49, 54;   BN 37;   BU 45, 53;
                                  CH 12, 16, 24, 34, 36, 40, 47;   CT 12, 19, 33, 46,
                                  47, 56;   CL 20, 23, 24, 27, 28, 35, 39,47;   DA 38,
                                  49, 68;   DE 47, 48, 49, 50, 52, 54, 57, 59;
                                  DT 22, 24, 29, 32, 47, 51, 63;   HN 39, 41, 44, 55;
                                  NA 58, 61, 68;   KC 35, 36, 39, 40, 41, 42, 54, 57;
                                  LA 23, 24, 30, 40, 43, 45, 64;   ML 63;   MN 32,
                                  33, 34, 35, 44, 48, 64;   NR 51, 55, 57, 60;
                                  NP 32, 37, 45, 48, 53;   NS 13, 16, 20;   PH 28,

ENESCO, G. (Cont.) Roumanian Rhaps No 1 in A (Cont.)
                            29, 33, 34, 38, 44, 49, 51, 60;   PT 37, 42, 48;
                            RC 34, 38(2), 42, 44, 46;   SL 14, 16, 27, 44,
                            54;   SF 16;   SE 48, 52, 61;   UT 44;   WA 48,
                            51, 60
                    8   Roumanian Rhaps No 2 in D Op 11   BN 38;   CH 13;
                            CT 12, 31, 32, 48, 50, 52;   CL 23, 38;   DT 51;
                            HN 46;   NA 35, 52, 55;   LA 53;   NS 14;   PH 14,
                            22;   RC 29;   SL 28;   WA 33, 38, 40, 45, 46, 47
                    30   Suite for O No 1 in C Op 9   CH 11, 15, 24, 29, 66;
                            CL 37;   DT 22;   NA 35, 52, 55;   NP 10
                    30   Suite for O No 2 in C Op 20   BN 37;   CH 31;
                            CT 48;   CL 28, 36, 37;   DT 28;   NP 36;   PH 25;
                            RC 47
                    26   Suite for O No 3 in D Op 27   CL 38;   NP 38
                    33   Symph No 1 in E^b Op 13   BN 38;   CH 17, 18, 23, 32,
                            37;   CT 37;   CL 23, 31, 46;   DT 17, 33, 36;
                            HN 47;   NA 47;   NP 36;   NS 11;   PH 12, 22,
                            38;   PT 37;   RC 46;   SF 24;   WA 48

ENGEL, Carl   8   Seashell, Song   SE 48
1883-1944   Ger/US

ENGEL, Lehman   30   The Creation, for Narrator and O 1945   DA 49
1910-   US

ENGLER, Paul   5   Preludium and Toccata   DE 49

ENSOR, Samuel   18   Verses from a Children's Book for Narrator and O
1917-   US   CT 59

EPPERT, Carl   24   Conc Grosso for Fl, Ob, Cl, Bassoon and Str Op 73
1882-   US   PH 60
                    10-11   Escapade, A Musical Satire Op 68   NA 40
                            Symph of the City: Grand Symphonic Cycle in Four Parts
                    9-10   No 1 Traffic Op 50 A Fantasy   CH 32;   CT 32, 41;
                            CL 35;   RC 32;   SL 41
                    8   No 3 Speed Op 53   CH 57
                    23   Symph No 5 in C A Cameo Symphony for Chamber O Op 71
                            NA 49
                    30   Two Symphonic Impressions: Vitamins, Suite No 1
                            Op 69   CH 40

ERB, Donald   20   Conc for Percussion and O   AT 68;   DA 68;   DT 66
1937-   US   12   Christmas Music   CL 67
                       25   Symph of Overtures   AT 67;   CL 65;   DA 66;
                            PH 68;   PT 69

ERDMANNSDORFER, Max   8   Overt Princessin Ilse   NP 1872
1848-1905   Ger

ERICKSON, Robert   10   Introd and Allegro   MN 48
1917-   US

ERK, Ludwig Christian   4   Das Mühlrad, folksong   CT 03
1807-1883   Ger

ERKEL, Ferenc   4   Air from Erzsebet, Opera 1857   CH 1896
1810-1893   Hung

ERNST, Heinrich H.   30   Conc Pathetique in f# Op 23   NP 1878
1814-1865   Moravia   14   Fantasy on Hungarian Airs for V and O Op 22
                        CH 1895;   SE 28
             10   Rondo Papagano Op 30   NP 1856

ERTHEL, Sebastian   15   Symphon Poem Die Nächtliche Heerschan Op 16
17th Cent.   Ger   CH 12

ESPAI, Andrei   35   Symph No 2   WA 66
1925-   Russ

ESPLA, Oscar   20   Don Quijote Velando Las Armes   HN 55;   NS one
1889-   Sp   episode 27
             12   Three Canciones Playeras   RC 37

ESSER, Heinrich   6   Chorus for male Voices, Treue Liebe   NP 1863
1818-1872   Ger

ESTERHAZY, Count Franz   8   Capriccio for O Op 10   MN 32
1895-   Hung/Aust

ETLER, Alvin   20   Conc for Wind Quint and O   BN 62;   CT 63;
1913-   US   MN 67;   NP 62
             12   Conc in One mvt   CL 57, 61
             20   Convivialities   HN 67
             14   Passacaglia and Fugue   CL 49;   PT 47
             25   Symph No 1   CH 53
             14   Symphonietta No 1 1940   PT 40
             20   Symphonietta No 2   1941   PT 42
             16   Triptych for O   BA 69;   HN 66

ETTINGER, Max   18   Old English Suite, Alt-Englische Suite   NP 32
1874-1951   Ger

EVANGELATOS,   22   Coasts and Mountains of Attica   NA 63
  Antiochus
  1904-   Gk

EVERS, Carl   5   Song: An Dem Stürmwind   NP 1864
1819-1875   Ger

EVETT, Robert   25   Anniversary Conc   WA 63
1922-   US   22   Symph No 1   WA 62

FABINI, Eduardo   15   Symphon Poem, Campo, The Country 1923   DT 52
1883-1950   Uruguay

FACCIO, Franco   5   Aria from Hamlet,Opera 1865: Dubita pur che billino
1840-1891   It   CL 20;   DT 20;   PH 20

FAIRCHILD, Blair   25   Ballet-Pantomine, Dame Libellule, Lady Dragon-Fly,
1887-1933   US   Suite Op 44   NS 22
                       8   Chants Negres   BN 29;   SL 31
                      20   A Persian Legend, Shah Feridoun, Symphon Poem Op 39
                             NS 25

FALLA, Manuel de   20   Conc for Harpsi, Fl, Ob, CL, V and C 1926   BN 26;
1876-1946   Sp   CL 60;   PH 26
                      26   El Amor Brujo, Love the Sorcerer, Ballet with Voices
                             1915   BN 24, 27, 30, 33, 47;   DA 50, 64;
                             RC 34;   SE 26, 37, 59
                       3   -El Aparecido   CT 48
                       4   -Aria, Love the Magician   CH 65;   PT 51;   WA 67
                       3   -Caucion del fuega fatua, Aria   CT 43, 45
                       5   -El Circulo Magico   CT 48
                       3   -Dance of Terror   CT 46, 48;   RC 37
                       3   -Introd   CT 46, 48;   WA 32
                       3   -Pantomine   CT 46, 48;   KC 34;   RC 39
                       5   -Ritual Fire Dance   CT 42, 43, 48;   KC 34;
                             RC 39, 40, 42;   SF 51;   WA 32
                       4   -Romance of Fisherman   WA 32
                      20   -Suite for O   AT 57;   BA 42, 48, 56;   BN 54;
                             BU 64, 69;   CH 53, 62, 68;   CT 30, 56;   CL 30,
                             40, 49, 51;   DE six parts 51, 58;   DT excerpts
                             28, 52, 65;   HN 52;   NA 51;   KC 43, 52, 63;
                             LA 29, 32, 48, 59;   ML 64;   MN excerpts 25, 33;
                             NR 51, 54, 60, 67;   NP 27, 33, 46, 47, 56, 69;
                             NS 27;   PH 21, 30, 32, 34, 43, 59;   PT 44, 45,
                             50, 53;   SL 28, 33, 34, 47, 52, 61, 63;   SF 27,
                             52, 53, 57;   UT 58;   WA 34, 50, 53, 60, 64
                       5   Gypsy Suite   DT 34
                      19   Homenajes, Homage   CH 65;   NP 53
                       5   La Vida Breve.Life is Short, Opera in three acts,
                             1923: Aria, Alli esta riyendo   WA 67
                       7   - -Aria: Vineus los que Rien   PT 57;   WA 54, 67
                       5   -Dances   BA 43;   KC 36;   RC 43, 44;   SL 35;
                             SF 43;   WA 33
                       7   -Interlude and Dance   CH 40, 54, 57, 58;   CL 37;
                             DE 47, 62;   DT 46, 48;   KC 42;   MN 49;   NR 58;
                             NP 53;   PH 28, 37, 42, 43;   PT 47;   RC 33;
                             SF 58, 60
                      25   Nights in the Gardens of Spain P and O Impressiones
                             Sinfonicas, 1913   BA 65;   BN 23, 29, 46;   CH 25,
                             45, 57;   CT 25, 31, 39, 44, 50, 65;   CL 28, 54,
                             66;   DA 67;   DE 50;   DT 26, 39, 46, 56;
                             HN 43;   KC 34, 52;   LA 47;   MN 29, 50, 65;
                             NR 51, 64;   NP 26, 38, 56, 65;   NS 25;   PH 26,
                             30, 36;   PT 46, 60;   RC 27, 55, 69;   SL 27,
                             29; 34, 37, 40, 45, 49, 52, 55, 62;   SF 26, 30,
                             52, 56, 62;   SE 28, 52, 57, 68;   UT 52;
                             WA 34, 45, 53, 62, 67
                      30   El retable de Maese Pedro, Master Peter's Puppet
                             Show, Opera 1923   SL 64;   SF 56

FALLA, M. (Cont.)

14	Seven Spanish Songs 1922 arr for O by Halfter AT 52; DT 64; LA 58; NR 55
4	-Jota RC 43; SL 46
30	El sombrero de tres picos, The Three-Cornered Hat, Ballet 1919 AT 57; KC 69; LA 68; PH 68; SE 41, 47, 52
3	-Fandango CT 33
3	-Dance Finale CT 44; RC 56
4	-Miller's Dance RC 42, 43, 56
4	-Neighbor's Dance RC 56
15	-Suite, unspecified BA 49, 55, 56; BN 61; DE 64; KC 50
14	-Suite No 1 CH 63; CT 25, 31, 35, 38, 40, 41, 42, 58, 61; DA 62; SF 43
12	-Suite No 2 CH 22, 44, 45, 47, 49, 53, 55, 57, 59, 63 67, 68; CT 25, 31, 35, 38, 40, 41, 42, 58, 61, 67; CL 32, 35, 36, 43, 49, 50, 53, 63; SL 56, 62; SF 43
12	-Three Dances AT 66; BA 50, 58, 64, 67; BN 21, 25, 28, 29, 33, 40, 46, 51, 55; BU 50, 52; DA 34, 46, 53, 57, 65; DE 50, 56, 68; DT 27, 35, 41, 51, 55, 62, 64, 69; HN 47, 51, 54; KC 62, 64, 69; LA 27, 35, 45, 57; ML 62, 67; MN 24, 28, 32, 34, 35, 39, 41, 44, 48, 50, 52, 55, 57, 59, 66; NR 50, 56, 64; NP 25, 29, 31, 36, 37, 39, 44, 49, 52, 53, 54, 55, 61; NS 23; PH 27, 28, 32, 33, 34, 37, 42, 45, 57, 64; PT 41, 46, 51, 61, 66; RC 28, 31, 35, 38, 39, 49, 56, 61; SF 35, 39, 41, 45, 52, 56, 58, 60; SE 41, 47, 54, 63; UT 51, 66; WA 40, 54, 62

FANELLI, Ernest 1860-1917 Fr	15	Tableaux Symphoniques, Thebes NS 13
FARBERMAN, Harold 1929- US	10 20	Elegy Fanfare and March DE 67 Symph for Str and Perc, 3 mvts HN 59
FARNABY, Giles 1560-1640 Brit	6 18	Quodling's Delight from Fitzwilliam Virginal Book, arr Bantock CT 11; NS 09 Suite of XVI Cent arr Rabaud BN 18
FARNON, Robert 1917- Brit	27	Symph No 1 in D^b PH 41
FARWELL, Arthur 1872-1952 US	18 18	Suite The Gods of the Mountain Op 52 1927 MN 29 Symbolistic Study No 3 for P and O after Walt Whitman 1922 PH 27
FAURÉ, Gabriel 1845-1924 Fr	20	Ballade for P and O in F# Op 19 BA 62; BN 59; CH 43; CT 42; CL 58, 60, 64; DE 57; HN 51; MN 54; NP 44, 47, 61; SF 48, 51; UT 53; WA 46
	17 7	Dolly, Suite for O Op 56 arr Rabaud BN 52 Élégie for C and O Op 24 BN 24, 28, 35; BU 64; DE 68; NS 08; RC 27

FAURÉ, G. (Cont.)

18	Fantasie for P and O Op 111 CL 60
14	Masques et berga masques: Suite for O Op 112 NS 20
5	Nocturne for Str NS 18
7	Pavane for Chor and O Op 50 CT 21; DE 45, 49, 55; DT 52, 61, 64; HN 49, 63, 68; NS 23; PH 39; PT 50, 64; SL 56; SF 64
20	Pelleas and Mélisande Incidental Music for Drama, Suite for O Op 80 AT 59; BA 53; BN 04, 05, 10, 23, 37, 39, 58, 60, 62; BU 67; CH 24, 40, 43, 45, 46, 62; CT 19, 58, 63; DA 53; DT 51, 53; HN 53, 59, 68; KC 59; LA 47, 58; MN 42, 47, 66; NR 53, 59, 60; NP 37, 56, 58, 65, 66, 69; PH 40, 45, 48, 50, 58, 62, 68; PT 49, 61; RC 49; SL 25, 31, 34, 47, 49, 50, 59, 69; SF 48, 58, 63, 67, 69; SE 64, 69; WA 49,54, 69
4	-Adagio BN 49
4	-Allegretto NS 27
7	-Pavane NS 25
5	-Prelude CL 20; NS 23, 27; SL 38, 43
8	-Prelude and Andante BN 44, 45, 51, 66
4	-Spinning Women, Fileuses CT 38; CL 20; DA 29; NS 19, 23, 25; RC 37; SL 38, 43
	Pénélope, Lyric Drama, 1913
8	-Prelude BN 18, 24, 50, 59; CH 44
40	Requiem Soli, Chor and O Op 48 BN 37, 55, 60; CH 62, 67; CL 62; DT 60; NP 61; SL 54; SF 55
20	Shylock Incidental Music Suite Op 57 BN 18; DT 57; SE 50
8	-Nocturne and Entr'Acte SF 37
4	Sicilienne for C and O Op 78 DA 29

FEBVRE-LONGERAY, A.
1900-   Fr

8	Stèle pour le Pecheur de Lune PH 28

FELDMAN, Morton
1926-   US

11	Out of Last Pieces NP 63; SF 66
14	The Swallows of Salangan BU 64

FERGUSON, Howard
1908-   Brit

25	P Conc with Str O in D Op 12 NP 52

FERGUSON, Donald
1882-   US

6	Evening Landscape MN 41
8	The House Beautiful MN 41

FERIR, Emile
1879-1949   US

10	Caprice Basque for Vla and O LA 20
4	Song LA 20

FERNANDEZ, Oscar L.
1897-1948   Brazil

4	Batuque fr Opera, Malazarte 1933 BA 48, 50; BU 41; DE 53; DT 44; HN 51; KC 43; PH 44; WA 45
5	Batuque fr Suite, Reisado do Pastoreio 1930 DE 53; NP 43
35	Symph in b BN 48; WA 43

FERRARI, Benedetto   6   La Vita Nuovo   CT 25
1597-1681   It

FERROUD,   11   Foules, Crowds, Symphon Poème 1926   CH 28;
  Pierre-Octave   NP 27;   SL 32
1900-1936   Fr   20   Symph in A 1935   CH 31;   PH 31
                          20   Types: Suite in 3 mvts 1924   CH 35

FESCA, Friedr. Ernst   10   Ballad, Winged Messenger   NP 1854
1789-1826   Ger   4   Song, Remember Me   NP 1852, 53
                          4   The Wanderer   NP 1853

FETLER, Paul   12   Cantus tristes   MN 64
1920-   US   22   Contrasts for O   DT 67;   MN 58;   RC 60;   SF 68;
                                 WA 59
                         10   Gothic Var   MN 52
                         21   Soundings Symph in 5 mvts   MN 62
                         20   Symph No 3   MN 55

FIBICH, Zdenek   7   A Night at Karlstein, or Karlun-Tyn, Overt Op 35
1850-1900   Czech   BN 02;   NP 19
                          8   At Twilight, Idyl Op 39   CH 00;   DT 37;   NP 15
                          5   Three Miniatures for Str   NS 11

FICHER, Jacobo   20   Suite Op 78 for Chamber O   NA 53
1893-   Russ/Arg

FIEDLER, August Max   4   Song: The Tambourin Player   NP 09
1859-1939   Ger

FIELD, John   4   Nocturne   NP 1858
1782-1837   Ir

FILTZ, Anton   15-20   Symph in E^b SL 50
1725-1760   Ger

FINE, Irving   14   Nocturne for Str and Harp   BN 62;   NP adagio only 62
1914-1966   US   9   Serious Song, Lament for Str   BN 65;   BU 64;
                                 CH 58;   NP 58
                         24   Symph 1962   BN 61;   NP 66
                         11   Toccato Concertante 1947   BN 48, 64;   SE 68

FINNEY, Ross Lee   23   Conc Perc and O   MN 66
1906-   US   18   P Conc in E 1934   WA 54
                          5   Slow Piece for Str O 1940   DT 56;   MN 40
                         23   Symph No 1, Communiqué 1943   WA 64
                         21   Symph No 2   DT 61;   PH 59;   PT 62
                         22   Symph No 3   PH 63;   MN 63
                         16   Symph Concertante   KC 67
                         12   Var, Fugue and Rondo 1943   MN 65
                         20   Hymn, Fugue and Holiday: CT 67;   RC 68

FISCHER, Anton   5   Tarantelle for C and O   NS 1879
1778-1808   Ger/Aust

FISCHER, C.A.   4   Song of Mary, A Christmas Carol from the Spanish
  and Kranz, Albert   of Lope de Vega   AT 48, 54(2)

FISCHER, Irwin   5   Ariadne Abandoned   AT 48
  1903-   US   15   Choral Fantasy for Org and O   SL 54
                         5   Lament for C and O   WA 44

FISCHER, C. L.   10   Chorus: Meeresstille und Glückliche Fahrt   NP 1850

FISER, Lubas   12   Fifteen Prints after Durer's Apokalipsis   LA 67
              US

FITELBERG, Jerzy   15   Nocturne for O 1946   NP 46
  1903-1951   Pol/US

FITELBERG, Gyzegorz   15   Polish Rhaps Op 25   CH 25, 37;   LA 31;   PH 21, 31
  1879-1953   Pol   4   Song of the Falcon for O Op 18   SL 12, 18

FLANAGAN, William   10   A Concert Ode   DT 59;   PH 60
  1926-   US   18   Narrative for O   DT 64

FLETCHER, Percy   4   Walrus and Carpenter   BA 42
  1879-1932   Brit

FLOERSHEIM, Otto   15   Consolation   BN 1886
  1853-1917   Ger/US   10   Elevation   BN 1887
                        10   Prelude and Fugue   BN 1891
                         8   Scherzo for O   BN 1889

FLORIDIA, Pietro   4   Song: Madrigale   CH 07
  1860-1932   US   30   Symph in d   CT 07

FLOTOW, Friedrich von   9   Martha, Opera 1847: Overt   BA 26, 28;   DA 52;
  1812-1883   Ger   HN 42;   PT 38
                         4   -Aria, M'appari   BU 48;   DA 52;   DT 28, 46;
                                SL 46;   SF 38

FLOYD, Carlisle   8   Introd, Aria, Dance   NR 67
  1926-   US   17   The Mystery: Song Cycle 5 songs for Sopr   HN 61;
                                PT 61
                        10   Pilgrimage   NR 68

FOERSTER, Josef B.   20   Symphon Suite Cyrano de Bergerac Op 55   CH 07
  1859-1951   Czech

FOGG, Eric   17   Conc for Bassoon and O in D 1930   KC 38
  1903-1939   Brit

FONT y DE ANTA,   6   Jota de Alcaniz arr Manuel Infante   CT 42, 44;
  Manuel   RC 39, 40, 42
  1895-   Sp

FOOTE, Arthur   15   Aria and Fugue for Str   NA 38, 40, 51
  1853-1937   US   30   C Conc in D Op 33   CH 1894
                        16   Clarinet Pieces   BN 11, 18

FOOTE, A. (Cont.)

16	4 Character Pieces after Omar Khayyam Op 48 CH 07, 13; CT 13, 22; PH 17; SL 12
8	In the Mountains Overt Op 14 BN 1886, 87
4	Irish Folk Song CT 1896; DA 32
8	Night Piece for Fl and Str 1914 BN 22, 32, 36; CL 46; DT 34; NP 58; RC 36
10	Serenade in D Op 25 BN 1889; SL 10
15	Suite in E Op 12 BN 08, 20, 24, 28, 36, 44; CL 43, 45, 52
15	Suite in d Op 36 BN 1895, 02; CH 1898; CT 00
15	Suite in E for Str O Op 63 CH 11; DA 57; DT 47; NA 44, 52; NP 41; WA 54
20	Symphon Prologue Francesca de Rimini Op 24 BN 1890, 94; CT 1895
18	Skeleton in Armour, Chor and O Op 28 BN 1892
12	Theme and Var Op 32 CH 01

FOOTE, George   25   Suite fr Praise of Winter 4 mvts 1936   BN 39
1886-   Fr/US

FORSYTH, Cecil   6   Chant Celtique O and Vla   BN 11
1870-1941   Brit/US 4   Song: O Red is the English Rose   PH 18

FORTNER, Wolfgang 12   Impromptus   PH 63
1907   Ger   30   Symph 1947   PH 65
                   25   Triplum   BU 67

FOSS, Lukas   11   Baroque Var   BU 67
1922-   US   22   C Conc   BA 68
                   21   Conc for Improvising Solo Instruments   PH 60
                   39   P Conc No 2   BN 51;   CH 54;   CT 53;   CL 60;
                         DT 57;   MN 58;   PT 56;   SL 55
                   11   Elytres   LA 64;   NP 65;   RC 65;   SL 66
                    9   Introductions and Goodbyes   NP 59
                   10   Ode for O, To Those Who Will Not Return 1944
                         LA 46;   NP 44;   PH 58;   PT 45;   SL 63;
                         SF 47
                   16   Pantomime for O   BA 46;   HN 46
                   31   Parable of Death, Cantata   BU 59;   NR 64;
                         NP 61;   SF 63
                   15   Pharion   NP 66;   PT 69;   SF 67
                   54   The Prairie, for Soli, Chor and O   BN 43;   NP 44
                   13   Psalms for Chor and O   NP 56
                   10   Recordare   BN 48
                   19   Song of Anguish, Baritone and O 1945   BN 49
                   23   Song of Songs, Biblical Cantata 1946   BN 46;
                         DA 52;   LA 54;   NP 55
                   32   Symph in G 1944   PT 44
                   31   Symph of Chorales   BN 58;   NP 58;   PT 58;   CL 60
                    6   -Choral Prelude No 2   BU 59
                    6   -Choral Prelude No 3   CT 62
                   22   Time Cycle, four Songs for Sopr and O   BN 61;
                         BU 64;   CL 65;   DE 60;   KC 60;   LA 62;
                         NP 60;   SF 66

	Time in Minutes	

FOSTER, Stephen
1826-1864   US

SONGS with O

4	Jeannie with the Light Brown Hair DT 43; NA 34; KC 41
4	Old Black Joe HN 42; NA 32(2)
4	Swanee River NA 32
4	Old Dog Tray NA 34
4	Jennie Comes Over the Green NA 34

FOURDRAIN, Felix
1880-1923   Fr

SONGS

4	Chevauchée Casaque CT 41; DT 40
4	Carneval NS 17; PH 19
4	Le Papillon SL 45

FOURESTIER, Louis
1892-   Fr

| 8 | A Saint Valéry for Voice and O   SL 34 |

FRANCAIX, Jean
1912-   Fr

18	P Conc 1936 PH 38
10	Concertino for P and O 1932 NR 52
11	Serenade for Small O 1934 CL 63; NR 52
16	L'Horlage de Flore Ob and O MN 68; PH 60, 68
4	Solo Dance A la Francaix DE 56

FRANCHETTI, Alberto
1860-1942   It

| 26 | Symph in e   NP 1886 |

FRANCHETTI, Arnold
1906-   US

| 10 | Largo for Str In Memoriam   NP 60 |

FRANCK, Cesar
1822-1890   Fr

15	Les Béatitudes Oratorio, 1869 NS 16
6	-First Beatitude, Part I CT 41
4	-Aria Where'er We Stray CL 24
13	Le Chausseur Maudit, Symphon Poem 1882 AT 66; BN 00, 03, 10, 19, 22, 40, 59, 61; CH 97, 00, 01, 05, 12, 17, 19, 27, 34, 37, 42, 45, 64; CT 98, 18, 31, 35; CL 24, 38; DT 41, 56; KC 54, 65; ML 64; MN 29, 46; NR 50; NP 12, 16, 38, 47; NS 19; PH 09, 11; PT 50; RC 27, 36, 39, 40; SL 32; SF 18, 35; SE 56
13	Three Chorales for O 1890 No 1 in E arr Loesser CT 47; CL 34; NP 36; WA arr Potter 39 No 2 in b for Org and O BN 21, 22; DT 33 No 3 in a DT 24
12	Chorale and Var CH 46
13	Les Djinnes, Symphon Poem after V Hugo for P and O 1884 BN 20; NS 16, 21
11	Les Éolides, Symphon Poem 1875 BN 99, 02, 13, 18, 22, 31, 34; CH 1895, 97, 00, 02, 05, 11, 18, 27, 28, 36, 39, 43; CL 22; DT 33; HN 34; LA 34, 56; MN 44; NP 17, 29, 35; SL 16, 19, 22; SF 16, 35
4	Ninon, Song, words by de Musset 1842 WA 45
5	Nocturne for Sopr and O 1884 CT 38; CL 31; SL 29

FRANCK, C. (Cont.)

8   Panis Angelicus, for Tenor, Org, C, Harp and
        Double Bass 1871   AT 46;   DT 46

8   Pièce Héroique 1878   NR 44;   SF 40

5   Prelude, Air and Finale 1886 arr Gui from P Solo
        DT 32;   MN 39;   SF 49

     Prelude, Chorale and Fugue for P and O arr Pierne
        1884   BN 20;   CL 43;   NP 32, 51(2);   NS 13,
        14, 18;   PH 26;   SF 37

10   The Procession, Voice and O 1888   NP 18;   NS 17

13   Psyche, Symphon Poem for O and Chor 1886   BN 18,
        36;   CH 43, 44, 45, 64;   WA 52, 61

9   -Excerpts   BN 05, 06, 21;   NP 02, 30, 60

4   -Psyche enlevee par les Zyphes   CT 27;   NS 16, 19

6   -Psyche and Eros   CH 55, 68;   CT 27;   CL 35, 55;
        DT 53, 60;   PT 49, 69;   RC 69

9   -Suite   BN 53;   PH 27;   SF 37, 42, 45

4   -Sommeil de Psyche   CT 27;   NS 16

10   Psalm 150 for Chor, O and Org 1888   BN 18, 28;
        KC 50

13   Redemption, Symphon Poem for Sopr, Chor and O 1871
        HN 31(2);   PH 06, 18(2)

4   -Aria Les rois dont vantez la gloire   CH 17

7   -Morceau Symphonique piece   BN 07, 16, 18, 21, 51;
        CH 01, 31;   CT 19, 31, 36, 62;   DT 52, 61;
        NP 11, 31, 37;   NS 06, 17, 18, 20, 24, 27;
        PT 49;   RC 27, 38;   SL 26, 35;   SE 43

6   -Prelude, Part II   CL 38;   MN 32, 40, 46;
        NP 27, 51;

6   Str Quart in D 1889 Poco Lento and Allegro   CH 33,
        46;   MN 38

40   Str Quint in f with P 1889   CL 25;   NS 20

34   Symph in d 1886
        AT 46, 47, 50, 53, 58, 61, 62;
        BA 28, 36, 38, 40, 42(2), 43, 45(2), 46, 48(2),
        54, 65;
        BN 1898, 99, 39(2), 41, 44, 45, 50, 55, 56, 60,
        62, 66;   BU 41, 42, 43, 49, 56, 62;
        CH 1899, 03, 06, 07, 08, 09, 10, 11, 12, 13, 14,
        16, 17, 18, 19, 20, 21, 22, 23, 24, 25, 26, 29, 30,
        33, 34, 35, 36, 39, 43, 44, 45, 49, 51, 60, 63;
        CT 06, 11, 15, 17, 18, 20, 21, 24, 25, 27, 31, 34,
        36, 38, 39, 41, 43, 46, 49, 52, 53, 60;
        CL 21, 22, 24, 25, 26, 28, 29, 31, 32, 33, 35, 36,
        37, 39, 40, 41, 43, 45, 47, 49, 51, 52, 53, 55, 57,
        59, 62;   DA 30, 38, 49, 51, 52, 56, 60, 62, 64;
        DE 45, 46, 50, 53, 57, 63;
        DT 15, 18, 19, 21, 24, 27, 29, 32, 40, 47, 52, 55, 66;
        HN 35, 38, 39, 41, 43, 45, 46, 51, 54, 56, 58, 61,
        63, 66;   NA 33, 36, 37, 39, 41, 43, 49, 52, 56, 60,
        64, 65, 68;   KC 33, 34, 35, 37, 39, 48, 51, 65, 69;
        LA 20, 22, 24, 25, 27, 29(2), 30, 32, 33(2), 34, 37,
        41, 47, 49, 56, 59, 63;   ML 60, 65, 69;
        MN 22, 24, 25, 26, 30, 32, 33, 34, 35, 36, 39, 42,
        44, 46, 49, 62, 68;   NR 50, 53, 55, 57, 61;

FRANCK, C. (Cont.)   Symph in d 1886 (Cont.)
                    NP 11, 15, 17, 19, 20, 21, 23, 24, 26, 27, 28, 29,
                    30, 33, 37, 38, 39, 43, 45, 46, 47, 49, 50, 51(3),
                    53, 55, 58, finale only 62, 69;
                    NS 10, 11, 16, 19(2), 21(2), 23(2), 24, 25, 26;
                    PH 04, 05, 06, 07, 09, 10, 11, 12, 13, 15, 16, 17,
                    18, 19, 20, 21, 22, 23(2), 24(2), 25(2), 26, 27,
                    28, 29(2), 30, 31, 32, 33, 34, 35, 36, 37, 39, 40,
                    41, 42, 43, 44(2), 45, 46, 47, 48(2), 49, 50, 51,
                    52, 53, 55, 57, 58, 60, 62, 63, 65, 67, 69;
                    PT 37, 39, 43, 47, 48, 49, 54, 57, 60, 62, 67, 69;
                    RC 23(2), 28, 30, 32, 35, 36, 38, 42, 44, 50, 59,
                    65;   SL 10, 11, 13, 15, 17, 18, 20, 21, 23, 25,
                    27, 30, 31, 32, 34, 36, 38, 39, 41, 43, 52, 54, 58,
                    64;   SE 27, 28, 30, 35, 38, 42, 44, 47, 48, 51, 57,
                    64;   SF 13(2), 19(2), 20, 22, 23, 24, 28, 40, 42,
                    44, 46, 49, 56, 62, 63, 66;
                    UT 40, 44, 45, 50, 58, 62;
                    WA 33, 36, 54, 56, 62, 68

          15   Symphon Var for P and O 1885
                    AT 59, 65, 68;   BA 50, 51, 57, 64;
                    BN 16, 18, 54, 59, 68;   BU 46;
                    CH 05, 13, 21, 22, 28, 30, 32, 35, 37, 43, 57, 61, 6
                    CT 18, 21, 24, 31, 39, 47, 50, 58, 64;
                    CL 24, 28, 33, 44, 47, 53, 56, 60, 64;
                    DA 34, 49, 58;   DE 68;
                    DT 18, 21, 24, 37, 39, 43, 47, 52, 57;   HN 69;
                    NA 43, 47;   KC 37, 49;   LA 43, 48, 57;   ML 65;
                    MN 24, 30, 43, 46, 48(2), 51, 52;   NR 67;
                    NP 14, 15, 21, 28, 36, 51(2), 52, 54, 56, 57;
                    NS 10, 16, 18, 20, 22;
                    PH 05, 10, 14, 17, 24, 43, 58;
                    PT 42, 55, 59, 63, 69;
                    RC 23, 26, 30, 37, 38, 47, 53, 55, 66, 69;
                    SL 21, 22, 29, 38, 43, 56, 60, 67, 68;
                    SF 24, 40, 51, 53, 59, 61;
                    SE 30, 39, 42, 46, 55;   UT 49, 53;
                    WA 33, 36, 40, 46, 47, 52, 55, 64, 67

FRANCKENSTEIN,   8   Var for O on a theme by Meyerbeer Op 45
  Clements von   DT 25;   MN 28
  1875-1942   Ger

FRANKLIN, Benjamin   7   5 Pieces for Str   MN 55
  (attributed to)
  1706-1790   US

FRANZ, Robert   8   (Songs with Piano accompaniment)   CH 09;
  1815-1892   Ger   NP 1890(2), 98(2), 99;   NS 1888

FRAZZI, Vito   10 Preludio Magico   CH 49;   NP 49
  1888-   It

FREDERICK the Great   12 Symph No 3 in D   BN 28;   BU 42;   CT 29
  1712-1786   Ger 15 Symph in G   DT 31;   KC 66

FREED, Isadore   12   A Festival Overt 1944   BN 55;   DE   49;   SF 46
1900-   Russ/US   20   Jeux de Timbres Symphon Suite 1931   SF 35
                           12   Pastorales, Suite of Miniatures 1936   SF 43; WA 38
                           23   Symph No 2 for Brass O   PH 52;   SF 50

FREEDMAN, Harry   10   Tangents   DE 69;   RC 67
1922-   Can

FRESCOBALDI, Girolamo 12   Bergamesea arr Stoessel from Fiori Musicali   NP 53
1583-1643   It   22   Four Pieces arr Ghedini   BN 52;   NP 51
                          15   Frescobaldiana arr Giannini from three Org Pieces
                                    HN 59
                           5   Gagliarda arr Stokowski   HN 58;   PH 35, 37
                           6   Toccata arr Kindler   AT 63;   BN 53;   PH 48;
                                    PT 49;   SE 52;   WA 37, 43, 45, 48, 50
                           8   Two Canzoni arr Ghedini   RC 50

FREY,   6   Song: Wie Kann die Liebe for Chor   NP 1871

FREYRE   4   Serenade Criolla--Ay! Ay! Ay! HN 42
                 Chile

FRICKER, Peter R.   11   Dance Scene for O Op 22   BU 62
1920-   Brit   27   Symph No 1 Op 9   CT 59

FRID, Geza   17   Paradou Symphon Fantasy Op 28   MN 51
1904-   Hung/Neth   15   Suite for O Op 6   BN 31

FRIED, Oskar   9   Adagio and Scherzo for Wind Inst, Harps, Kettledrum
1871-1941   Ger   Op 2   BN 14;   CH 05
                          10   Prelude and Double Fugue for Str   BN 06, 14

FRISCHEN, Josef   8   Ein Rheinische Scherzo Op 14   CT 03
1863-   Ger

FROBERGER, Johann J.   12   Suite in e arr De la Marter   CH 31
1616-1667   Ger

FÜCHS, Ferdinand K.   15   Conc for Horn and O   NP 1850
1811-1848   Aust   10   Guttenberg Opera 1846, Rec and Aria   NP 1854, 58

FUCHS, Robert   Serenades for Str O
1847-1927   Aust   22   No 1 in D Op 9   BN 1884, 99;   CH 1894;   CT 15;
                                    NP 1876, 78, 82;   NS 1885, 14, 3 mvts only 16
                          16   No 2 in C Op 14   BN 1884, 86
                          23   No 3 in e Op 21   BN 1887, 88;   DT 17
                          35   Symph in C Op 37   BN 1885

FULEIHAN, Anis   21   P Conc No 2, 1937   CH 39
1900-1970   US   20   Conc P, V and O 1944   NA 48
                          12   Conc for Theremin and O 1944   PH 47
                           5   Fanfare for Medical Corps, for Brass   CT 42
                           8   Fiesta, Overt 1939   NA 39
                           7   Invocation to Isis 1940   NA 40;   SL 41
                          12   Jubilee Var on Theme by Goossens   CT 44, 45

FULEIHAN, A. (Cont.)
13-14	Mediterranean Suite 1930 BA 37; SL 35
14	Mediterranean Suite No 2 DE 55; CT 34; DT 35
4	Melody for Winds WA 46
8	Pastorale MN 41
27	Symphonie Concertante for Str Quart and O 1939 NP 39
23	Symph No 1 1936 NP 36
24	Symph No 2 NP 66
13	Three Cyprus Serenades 1943 LA 47; PH 46

FURSTENAU, Moritz   20   Conc in A^b Fl and O Op 52   NP 1845
1824-1889   Ger

FURTER, Virto   5   Song: Mensage   CL 27
1887   Sp

GABRIELLI, Andrea   9   Aria Della Battaglia for Winds arr Ghedini
1510-1586   It   BN 53;   CH 61;   NP 52
                        10   Music for Brass Choirs: LA 69

GABRIELLI, Giovanni   6   Canzoni duo decimitoni a 8 arr Ghedini   CL 51, 58;
1557-1612   It   ML 69
                         6   Canzoni septimitoni a 8 arr Ghedini   NP 49;   WA 53
                         6   Canzon quartitoni a 15 arr Stokowski   BN 63;
                               BU 63;   NP 49;   SL 63, 66
                         8   Canzon a 6   CH 01
                         5   In Ecclesiis Benedicte Domino, Motet   CH 69;
                               HN 58;   SF 59;   NP 49
                         5   Jubilate Deo for Chor, Brass Choir and Org
                               DE 57;   WA 59
                         6   Sonata, Pian e Forte, arr Stokowski for double
                               brass choir   BN 34, 50;   CH 01(2), 31, 35, 37;
                               HN 59;   LA 69;   MN 57;   PT 54, 59;   SF 56;
                               UT 61

GABRILOWITSCH, Ossip S.4   Song, Good Bye   DT 34, 40
1878-1936   Russ/US

GABURO, Kenneth   13   Elegy   NP 58
1926-   US   15   On a Quiet Theme   NP 54

GADE, Niels W.   23   V Conc in e Op 56   CT 1896
1817-1890   Dan   30   Napoli, Ballet 1842 Act III   WA 56
                        15   Novelletter for Str O Op 53   BN 1887
                              OVERTURES
                         5   Echoes from Ossian Op 1   BN 1882, 84, 86, 90;
                               NA 31;   NP 1852, 54, 62, 69;   NS 1883, 90
                         5   Hamlet Op 37   NP 1868
                         6   In the Highlands or Scottish Op 7   BN 1881, 87;
                               NP 1852, 56, 63, 70
                         6   Michaelangelo Op 39   BN 1888;   NP 1873
                              SYMPHONIES
                        25   No 1 in c Op 5   BN 1886, 89;   NP 1848, 49, 55,
                               62;   PH 02

GADE, N. (Cont.) Symphonies (Cont.)
                  20   No 4 in B^b Op 20   BN 1882, 88, 91;   DE 51;
                              NP 1853
                  25   No 5 in d Op 25   NP 1858
                  25   No 8 in b Op 47   NP 1872

GAERTNER, Louis   12   Tone Poem, Macbeth   PH 10
1866-   US

GÁL, Hans   9   Pickwickian Overt Op 45   CL 48
1890-   Aust/Brit

GALLICO, Paolo   15   Symphon Episode, Euphorion 1922   DT 25;   LA 22;
1868-1955   It/US   NP 23

GALLIARD, Johann E.   5   Sonata in G for Chamber O   BN arr Steinberg 25,
1687-1749   Ger/Brit   29;   NA arr Sevitzky 41, 46

GALUPPI, Baldassare   4   La Calamita de' cuori Opera 1752;Aria.Euttiva
1706-1785   It   Rosa Bella   SF 38

GALYNIN, Herman   20   P Conc in C   DE 56;   SF 60
1922-   Russ

GANDOLF, Riccardo   5   Marche Héroique de Don Quichotte   HN 13
1839-1920   It

GANZ, Rudolph   23   Animal Pictures, Suite of 20 1932   CH 33;   CT 36;
1877-   Swiss/US   DT 32;   WA 38
                  23   P Conc in E^b Op 32   CH 40;   RC 2nd and 3rd mvt
                            only 40
                  15   Conzertstück in b for P and O Op 2   CH 11;   DT 32
               7-10   Overt to an Unwritten Comedy, Laughter-Yet Love,
                            Op 34   CH 51, 56, 66;   CT 50;   DE 51;   ML 62;
                            SL 51;   SF 51;   WA 52

GARAT, Pierre Jean   4   Song, Dans le Printemps de mes annees   MN 42
1762-1823   Fr

GARDINER, Henry B.   7   A Comedy Overt   NS 21
1877-1950   Brit   5   Shepherd Fennel's Dance 1911   CH 13;   CT 33, 45;
                      CL 29;   RC 32

GARDNER, Samuel   17   Broadway, Tone Poem 1924   BN 29
1891-   Russ/US   25   V Conc in C Op 18   NP 24
                  10   New Russia, Tone Poem   DT 20;   PH 19;   SL 21

GARNIER, Louis   10   Vision, Poem for O   DT 19;   PH 18
1885-   Fr

GAROFALO,   20   Romantic Symph   SL 35

GARRIDO-LECCA, Celso   8   Elegia á Machu Picchu   NP 66
1926-   S Amer

GASPARINI, Francesco   4   Aria, Lasciar d'Amarti   CH 19
1668-1727   It

GASSMAN, Remi   6   Symphon Overt in G   CH 40
              US

deGastyne, Serge   14   Atata, Portrait for O   HN 58
1930-   Fr/US   17-19   Hollins Hall, Symphon Ode in memory of Honegger
                               CT 56
                     29   L'Ile Lumière   CT 55

GATES, Crawford   12   Overt to Spring   UT 55, 61
1921-   US   6   Promised Valley   UT 47, Interlude only 49, 56
                     12   Portrait of a Great Leader Op 40   UT 64
                     20   Symph No 1   UT 53
                     14   Symph No 3   UT 65
                     15   Symph Allegro   UT 51

GAUBERT, Phillipe   13   Conc in F for O   SL 34
1879-1941   Fr

GAUL, Harvey   14   Suite Ecclesiasticus for Str   PT 39
1881-1945   US

GEBHARD, Heinrich   20   Fantasy for P and O   NP 25
1878-   US

GEMINIANI, Francesco   5   Andante for Str, Harp and Org   BU 44;   DT 37;
1687-1762   It/Brit   NP 27, 51;   PH 31, 38
                     10   Conc Grosso No 1 for Str and Cembalo   DT 38
                     11   Conc Grosso No 2 in c Op 2   NP 32
                     12   Conc Grosso No 2 in g Op 3   BN 60;   CL 56, 66;
                               MN 60;   NP 33
                     11   Conc Grosso No 3 in B^b Op 3   DA 46, 60;   CT 33
                  11-15   Introd and Allegro   MN 52
                     12   Largo for Str   SL 27

GENZMER, Harold   8   Prologue for O   PH 68
1909-   Ger

GEORGES, Alexander   5   Hymne au Soleil   PH 18(2)
1850-1938   Fr

GEORGE, Earl   20   V Conc   MN 54
1924-   US   8-9   Introd and Allegro   MN 50
                      5   Thanksgiving Overt   MN 56

GERAL,   30   C Conc   NS 18

GERARD, Louis   4   Rice Fight Song   DA 49
              US

GERHARD, Roberto   37   Symph No 1 1952   NP 62
1896-   Sp   35   Symph No 4   NP 67

GERICKE, Wilhelm   4   Chor of Homage   BN 1885
1845-1925   Aust   18   Conc Overt   BN 1885
                         15   Suite for Str,3 mvt only   BN 1885

GERMAN, Sir Edward   9   Henry VIII Suite, Suite of Dances 1892
1862-1936   Brit   CH (three dances) 1895, 98;   HN 14, 39
                          4   -Morris Dance   BA 42
                         16   Welch Rhaps 1904   NS 07

GERNSHEIM, Friedrich   20   V Conc in D   BN 1897
1839-1916   Ger   25   Symph in E^b No 2   BN 1882
                          8   Tone Poem, To A Drama Op 82   BN 10;   CT 12

GERSHWIN, George   16   An American in Paris 1925
1898-1937   US   AT 52, 54, 69;   BU 46;   CT 28, 59, 64;
                                CL 42, 50;   DA 46, 48, 49;   DT 57;   HN 45, 51;
                                NA 51;   LA 30, 42, 48;   MN 29, 49, 57, 58, 63;
                                NR 56, 68;   NP 28(2), 43, 53, 54, 56, 58;
                                PH 57;   PT 48, 49;   RC 29, 55;   SL 29, 48, 58;
                                SF 51, 54, 55, 66;   SE 37, 54;   UT 48, 51, 56(2),
                                66;   WA 49, 50
                         30   P Conc in F 1925
                                AT 49, 54;   BU 50, 52;   CH 44, 51, 63;
                                CT 26, 43, 46, 66;   CL 39, 53;   DA 48, 49;
                                DT 65;   HN 46;   NA 40, 50, 66;   KC 43;
                                LA 42, 64;   MN 49, 63;   NP 45, 47, 48;
                                NS 25, 26;   PH 36, 43, 51, 66(2);   PT 39;
                                RC 48;   SL 45, 54, 58;   SF 36, 66;   SE 48;
                                UT 51, 68;   WA 36, 45, 50
                         11   Cuban Overt 1932
                                AT 54;   NA 66, 69;   NP 56, 59;   RC 42;
                                SL 45;   SF 55;   WA 49
                         16   Rhaps in Blue for P and O 1923
                                AT 49, 54;   BA 39;   BU 50;   CT 26, 44, 50;
                                DA 48, 49;   DE 45;   DT 43;   NA 45, 66;
                                KC 41;   LA 42;   MN 49;   NP 42, 58, 54;
                                PH 36, 43, 51, 66;   RC 43;   SL 45, 46, 58;
                                SF 55, 66;   SE 48;   UT 41, 51, 58, 66;
                                WA 49, 50
                         12   Rhaps in Blue for 2 P and O arr Iturbi   CT 45
                         12   Second Rhaps for P and O 1923   BN 31
                         24   Porgy and Bess, Opera 1935, A Symphonic Picture
                                arr R.R. Bennett
                                AT 54, 60;   BN 43;   CH 47;   CL 43;   DA 48,
                                49;   DT 43, 65;   NA 43, 45;   KC 43;   LA 43;
                                MN 43, 46, 49;   NP 42, 45, 53, 54, 56;   PT 42,
                                44, 49;   RC 41, 46, 51;   SL 44, 45, 58;
                                SE 44, 56;   UT 67;   WA 36, 46, 49, 50
                         24   -Suite arr Gould   AT 65;   NA 66;   LA 42;
                                RC 55;   SF 36, excerpts 55, 66;   UT 58, 63
                          4   -The Man I Love   HN 51;   NP 54
                          4   -It Ain't Necessarily So   DE 45
                          4   -I Got Plenty O'Nuttin   DE 45
                          4   -Summertime   BU 42, 43
                          4   -Of Thee I Sing   ML 65
                          4   -My Man's Gone Now   BU 42, 43

GERSHWIN, G. (Cont.)
                    40   Three Scenes from The New Yorker, Ballet   SE 41
                    4   Lady Be Good arr Mundy   LA 42
                    6   Two Preludes   SL 45

GERSTER, Ottmar   7   Capriccietto for Timpani and Str O 1932   MN 43
1897-   Ger

GESENSWAY, Louis   26   Conc Fl and O   PH 46;   NP 65
1906-   US   28   Four Squares of Philadelphia, for Narrator and O
                           PH 54
                    10   Now Let The Night Be Dark For All Of Me, Tone Poem
                           PH 56
                    26   Suite, 3 mvts for Str and Per   PH 44
                    10   Symphon Poem No 2 Ode to Peace   PH 59

GHEDINI, Giorgio   16   Architetture, Conc for O 1940   LA 60
1892-   It   23   Conc dell' Albatro, for the Albatross, for Narrator,
                           Str, Percussion 1945   NP 52
                    20   Conc for O in F   BN 50
                    17   Marinaresca e Baccanale, 1933   CH 49;   NP 49;
                           PH 49;   PT 48
                    14   Pezzo Concertante 2 V, Vla and O 1931   CH 57;
                           DE 54;   DT 51;   NP 54;   PH 48;   PT 49;   SL 51
                    15   Sonata da Concerto for Fl, Str and Perc   BN 61
                    12   Score for Un Credo   CH 64;   PT 64

GHIONE, Franco   15   Soul d'aleromo, Suite   DT 37
1889   It/US

GIANNINI, Vittorio   28   Canticle of Christmas, Baritone, Chor and O   CT 51
1903-   US   15   Frescobaldiana: Toccata, Aria and Fugue   CT 48;
                           DA 57;   DE 57;   RC 57;   SE 57, 68
                    40   The Medead   AT 60;   DA 62;   DT 61
                    20   Psalm 130   NA 64
                    25   Sinfonia for O in one mvt   CT 50

GILARDI, Gilarado   10   Gaucho with the High Boots   RC 15
1889-   Arg

GILBERT, Henry F.B.   9   Comedy Overt on Negro Themes   BN 10;   CH 12, 17;
1868-1928   US   CL 51;   NP 58;   PH 42;   PT 43;   RC 35, 45
                    15   Dance in the Place Congo, Symphon Poem Op 15   BN 19
                    7   Indian Sketches   BN 20;   NP 21
                    7   Negro Rhaps   BN 23
                    15   Nocturne for O, Symphon Mood   PH 27
                    6   Suite for Pilgrim Centenary   BN 21
                    20   Symphon Piece   BN 25
                    5   Symphon Prologue, Riders to the Sea   BN 18;
                           KC 42;   NP 34;   PH 19;   WA 43

GILCHRIST, Wm. W.   20   Symphon Poem, in G   PH 20
1846-1916   US   40   Symphon No 1   PH 01, 02, 09, 25

GILLIS, Don   22   Atlanta Suite   AT 51
1912-   US   4   January, February, March   NA 50
                         18   Portrait of a Frontier Town   CT 47;   DA 49;   RC 48
                          4   Short Overt to an Unwritten Opera 1945   AT 46;   HN 46
                         14   Symph No 5 1/2   DA 50;   DE 48;   NA 51;   KC 47;   LA 47
                         22   Thomas Wolfe, Narrative Poem with Music   CT 50

GILSON, Paul   12   Canadian Rhaps   CT 1898, 19
1865-1942   Belg   5   Cavatine   CT 1898
                          7   Fanfare Inaugurale   CH 1896, 05, 10, 17
                         35   La Mer, 4 Symphon Sketches   BN 1892, 98;   NP 1892
                         20   -3 Excerpts   CH 06

GINASTERA, Alberto   22   Conc Harp and O   NR 68;   PH 64;   WA 67
1916-   Arg   25   P Conc   BN 67;   DA 68;   NA 66;   KC 67;   MN 66;
                               UT 69;   WA 61, 66
                         25   V Conc   CH 63;   CT 67;   LA 66;   MN 64;   NP 63;
                               SL 64;   WA 64
                         16   Conc per Carde   BU 67;   CL 67
                         30   Estancia, Ballet   AT 66;   DE 65;   NA 53, 66;
                               SE 59;   WA 59
                         12   -4 Dances   ML 66;   NP 68;   RC 62
                         15   Estudios Sinfonicos Op 35   BN 57;   NR 69;   SE 68
                          9   Overt Creole Faust   DE 54, 68;   HN 54;   NR 64;
                               NP 56;   WA 56
                         17   Pampeana No 3 Pastoral Symphony   CL 56;   NP 64;
                               MN 56
                          8   Psalm 150   PH 68
                         22   Symph Don Rodrigo Sopr and O   PT 68;   WA 65
                         12   Variaciones Concertantes   BA 66;   CH 58;   CL 69;
                               DA 67;   DE 56;   HN 59;   MN 53;   NA 54, 63;
                               NR 54, 63;   NP 54;   PH 65;   SL 56;   SE 61;
                               WA 57

GIORDANI, Giuseppe   4   Canzonetta Caro mio ben   DT 47;   BU 43
1753-1798   It   (attributed to Giordani; possibly to Pacchierotti)

GIORDANO, Umberto   Andrea Chénier, Opera 1896: Arias
1867-1948   It   4   -Colpito qui m'avete, Act I   CH 19;   CL 19, 24
                          4   -Come un beldi di maggio, Act IV   NA 42;   LA 32
                          4   -Improviso   DT 28
                          4   -La mamma morta   WA 45
                          4   -Nemico della patria, Act III   BA 42, 50, 67;
                               CH 49;   CT 36, 38, 40;   NA 52, 56, 69; KC 53;
                               MN 38;   NS 05;   RC 30;   SL 55;   SE 35, 48
                               Fedora, Opera 1898
                          4   -Amor te vieta, Act II   CT 33;   CL 21

GIURANNA, Barbara   11   Apina, Stolen by the Dwarfs of the Mountain,
1902-   It   Suite   CH 28
                         10   Legio, Tone Poem   DT 37
                          7   Marionette   CH 28
                          7   Toccata   DT 38

```
                    Time in
                    Minutes
GLAZUNOV, Alexander          BALLETS
1866-1936    Russ    40      Raymonda Suite Op 57a    BN 01;    CH 02
                      6        -Pas de deux    DE 56;    NR 60
                     40      Ruses d'Amour, Suite Op 61    CH 01(2), 04, 06, 09
                      4        -Finale    CH 26
                     12        -Introd, Valse, Grand Pax, Finale    CH 22, 27, 40
                     12        -Introd, Valse, Finale    CH 00, 20, 34
                     10        -Valse, Ballabile, Finale    CH 29
                      8        -Valse, Finale    CH 09
                      8      The Seasons Op 67    DA 46;    RC Baccanale 27

                     20      Concerto-Ballata for C and O Op 108    CH 32
                     20      V Conc in a Op 82
                                AT 54;    BA 56;    BN 11, 26, 29;    BU 41;
                                CH 11, 21, 25, 29, 30, 34, 35, 37, 39, 46;
                                CT 61;    CL 23, 30, 53, 60, 67;    DA 54, 57;
                                DE 50;    DT 22, 47, 51, 54, 58;    HN 51;
                                NA 64;    KC 62;    LA 26, 29, 45, 50, 53, 57;
                                MN 25, 33, 48, 49, 64;    NR 55;    NP 11, 53, 56;
                                NS 19, 22, 23;    PH 11, 23, 29;    PT 42, 50, 56;
                                RC 35;    SL 15, 22, 24, 29, 36, 52, 55, 65;
                                SF 35;    SE 64;    UT 50;    WA 32, 44, 60
                     15      Conc for Saxophone, Fl and Str    RC 37
                      6      Cortège solennelle Op 50    CH 1896;    LA 19
                     15      Finnish Fantasy Op 88    CH 12
                     15      Fantasy Op 53    CH 1899
                      7      Incidental Music to Salome Op 90    LA 21, 23
                      5      Love, for mixed Chor Op 94    NP 07
                     11      Lyrique Poem Op 12    BN 1897;    CH 14, 28, 32;
                                CT 96
                     22      Oriental Rhaps Op 29    CH 1896
                             OVERTURES
                      9      Carnival Op 45    BN 03;    CH 09, 10, 16;    DA 35;
                                NA 52
                     15      On Greek Themes No 1 Op 3    NP 41, 56
                     11      Solennelle Op 73*    BN 01, 12;    CH 01(2), 03, 05,
                                07, 09, 18;    CT 36, 54;    CL 19, 26;    PH 08;
                                SL 25;    WA 38
                     12      Scène dansante Op 81    CH 14(2)
                      6      Serenade in A Op 7    NP 03
                     12      Spring, Tableux Musicale Op 34    BN 08;    BU 49;
                                CH 1898, 04, 06, 09, 18, 24, 28, 34, 35;
                                NP 10;    SL 49
                             SUITES
                     14      Chopiniana Op 46    DA 52
                     20      Moyen Age Op 79    CH 03;    CT 19;    NA 44, 48
                      4        -Prelude    BN 25;    CH 29
                      4        -Serenade    DT 38, 39
                     29      Scenes de Ballet Op 52    CH 1897(2), 02, 05, 10,
                                13, 26, 40;    CT 1898;    PH 04, 06;    SF 15
                      5        -Marionettes and Valse    CH 08;    RC 27
                      8        -Preamble, Valse, Polonaise, Pas d'action
                                CH 38
```

*Groves assigns Op 73 to the V Conc in A

GLAZUNOV, A. (Cont.)   SYMPHONIES
                        40   No 3 in d Op 33   CT 22
                        32   No 4 Eb Op 48   AT 52;   BN 03(2), 22, 48;   CH 05,
                                   19, 22, 27, 35, 38;   CT 31;   CL 31, 34, 48;
                                   DT 23(2), 26, 29, 32, 36, 40;   KC 58, 64;
                                   LA 21, 22, 23, 30, 52;   NP 22;   NS 21;   PH 26,
                                   28;   RC 29;   SL 29;   SF 29;   WA 43
                        36   No 5 Bb Op 55   BN 06, 13;   CT 29, 40;   NP 1897,
                                   21;   NS 22, 23, 25;   PT 46;   SL 09
                        38   No 6 in c Op 58   BN 1899(2), 29;   CH 00, 20, 29;
                                   CT 00, 21, 32;   DT 19, 29;   LA 24;   NP 04;
                                   NS 24;   SL 12;   SE 29, 36
                        30   No 7 in F Op 77   PH 10, 11, 18;   SF 28
                        40   No 8 in Eb Op 83   BN 24, 35;   CH 18;   CT 33, 35
                                   4th mvt;   SL 13, 16

                        16   Symphon Picture, The Kremlin Op 30   BN 05;
                                   CH 07, 08, 22, 31;   SL 13, 16
                        16   Symphon Poem, Stenka Razin Op 13   BN 19, 22, 29,
                                   38;   CH 22, 25, 36;   CL 25, 41;   NP 35;
                                   RC 29;   SL 15;   SF 42
                        8   Symphon Prelude in Memory of Gogol Op 87   CT 46
                        16   Triumphant March for Chicago World's Fair Op 40
                                   CH 24, 29
                        9   Valse de Concert No 1 in D Op 47   CH 1896, 99,
                                   02, 06(2), 08, 37;   CT 02, 50;   DA 27;   DT 15;
                                   PH 02;   SL 10, 23
                        10   Valse de Concert No 2 in F Op 51   CH 1897, 12, 19,
                                   23, 25, 37

GLEASON, Fred. Grant   5   Romanzo, Deep in my Heart, from Otho Visconti,
1848-1903   US   Opera 1907   CH 1891
                        12   Symphon Poem, Edris Op 21   CH 1895, 97
                        12   Symphon Poem, The Song of Life   CH 00

GLIÈRE, Reinhold   26   Conc for Horn Op 91   PH 60
1875-1956   Russ   4   March Héroique Op 71   CT 41
                                OVERTURES
                        8   Fête Ferganaise Op 76   CH 40, 41
                        9   The Friendship of the Peoples Op 79   NA 46
                        8   Hulsara, Uzbeck drama 1936   KC 39

                        13   Two Poems for Sopr and O Op 60   NR 64
                        20   The Red Poppy, Ballet Op 70   MN 43
                        5   -Ribbon Dance   NR 57
                        3   -Sailor's Dance, Jablockko   BA 42, 45;   CH 33;
                                   DA 34, 37, 38;   HN 40:   KC 34;   MN 33;   PH 33,
                                   40;   RC 33;   SE 38;   WA 35
                        35   Symph No 1 in Eb Op 8   CH 09
                        45   Symph No 2 in C Op 25   DT 31
                        45   Symph No 3 in b Ilia Muromets Op 42   BN 41;
                                   CH 17, 19, 21, 23, 24, 28, 30, 31, 32, 33, 34,
                                   35, 37, 39, 41, 49, 57, 62;   CT 45;   CL 38;
                                   DA 65;   HN 56;   MN 67(2),   NP 43, 49;   PH 33,
                                   39, 56;   PT scherzo 42;   WA 56

GLIÈRE, R. (Cont.)

15   Symphon Poem, The Sirens Op 33 BN 23;   CH 13(2),
      14, 16, 17, 18, 22, 24, 25, 27, 35; CT 17;
      CL 21; DT 19, 22, 28, 36; LA 21, 22, 23, 25;
      MN 27; PH 12, 16, 18, 29;   SF 26

GLINKA, Mikhail I.   9   Capriccio Brilliante on the Jota Aragonese, or
1804-1857   Russ   Spanish Overt No 1 1845 LA 42; MN 42

7   Fantasia, Kamarinskaya 1848 BN 1883, 89, 93, 18;
      CH 1898, 43; CT 30; DE 54; HN 34; NA 32;
      KC 57; LA 44; NP 30; NS 1878; PH 29, 33;
      PT 43, 45; SL 13, 28; SF 36; WA 43

10   A Life for the Tsar Opera 1836: Overt CH 08, 16;
      CT 31; CL 32, 39; DT 25; NA 30; PT 40

4   -Cavatina and Rondo CH 16; LA 24; PH Cavatina 16

4   -Finale BN 26

4   -Orphan Song DA 28

8   -Pas de Trois WA 59

5   Old Russian Boat Songs arr Stravinsky NS 20

10   Russian and Ludmilla, Opera 1838 Overt AT 61;
      BA 41, 42, 43, 44, 45, 50, 55, 64; BN 1893, 24;
      BU 46, 50; CH 16, 17, 19, 22, 28, 47, 54, 58;
      CT 1896, 00, 01, 10, 21, 30, 42, 45, 46, 49, 57;
      CL 21, 27, 31, 36, 38, 42, 62; DA 68; DE 45,
      49, 52, 53, 54, 56, 57, 59, 63, 68; DT 20, 24,
      25, 30, 44, 62; HN 32, 33, 40, 43, 46, 56;
      NA 40, 54, 55; KC 33, 34, 35, 36, 54; ML 60,
      63; MN 31, 36, 41, 43, 47, 62; NR 56, 67;
      NP 06, 19, 23, 26, 44, 45, 55, 63; NS 1895,
      20, 21, 22; PH 16, 22, 23, 26, 31, 32, 33, 40,
      53, 67; PT 38, 42, 47; RC 23, 26, 31, 35, 40,
      42, 44; SL 22, 26, 36, 40, 48, 60, 61, 67;
      SF 20, 41, 55; SE 29, 34, 38, 47, 53; UT 46,
      47, 56, 67; WA 32, 42, 45, 48

GLUCK,   9   Alceste, Opera 1767: Overt
  Christoph Willibald   BA 39, 57; BN 46, 54, 59; CH 03, 12; CT 33;
1714-1787   Ger   DE 51, 54; DT 39; KC 37, 52, 59; MN 40, 42;
      NP 12, 42, 51, 56; PH 15, 16, 17, 18, 23, 28,
      31, 35; PT 52, 57, 62; RC 52, 54; SF 48, 55;
      WA 53

4   -Aria, Act I, Sopr, Divinites du Styx BA 42;
      BN 52; CH 05, 13, 17; CT 13, 15, 29, 48;
      CL 26; DT 15, 31; HN 41, 44; NA 42; KC 40;
      LA 50; MN 41, 45, 46; NP 1893; NS 1889, 04;
      PT 40; SL 18, 50, 52; UT 50; WA 48

4   -Aria unidentified BA 51; DE 52, 53; PH 12,
      13, 17

4   Armide, Opera 1777: Aria, Ah That my Heart NP 1881

4   -Aria, Enfin il est dans ma puisance NP 1891

18   Don Juan, Ballet, 1761 Ballet Music CH 41; NP 37

25   Selections arr Kretzschmar four mvts BN 1896

4   Iphigenie en Aulide, Opera 1774: Aria unidentified
      CL 18; NP 30; PH 15; SF 47

GLUCK, C.W. (Cont.) Iphigénie en Aulide, Opera (Cont.)
```
  4      -Aria, Diane impetoyable   CH 01;   DT 17;   MN 25;   NS 10, 25;
         SL 16, 17
 18      -Ballet Suite   NS 85, 86, 10, 14, 20, 26
 10      -Overt arr Wagner   AT 64;   BN 1883, 88, 91, 93, 96, 99, 02, 11,
         19, 23, 33, 40, 57, 67;   CH 1891, 93, 96, 99, 01, 06, 07, 11, 13,
         17, 23, 30, 35, 36, 38, 41, 43, 52, 53, 63;   CT 12, 17, 19, 28,
         51, 66;   DA 49, 59;   DE 65;   DT 14, 16, 17, 19, 26, 32, 36, 40;
         HN 33, 60;   NA 57;   LA 24, 25, 29, 33(2), 38, 44, 50;   MN 26,
         29, 41, 46, 49, 64;   NP 1855, 64, 68, 71, 76, 85, 88, 00, 04, 11,
         14, 18, 28, 30, 36, 54, 60, 64, 65;   NS 1885, 88, 95, 08, 10, 12,
         20, 24, 27;   PH 01, 07, 08, 09, 10, 11, 13, 15, 19, 27, 34, 38,
         43, 68;   PT 46, 53;   RC 62;   SL 16, 29, 31, 33, 34, 35, 37, 38,
         43;   SF 16, 19, 20, 28, 39, 43, 48, 56, 59;   SE 47;   WA 34, 39,
         40, 47
 10      -Passacaglia and Minuet   NS 91
  4      Iphigénie en Tauride, Opera 1779: Aria   PH 15
  4      -Le Calme, rentre dans mon coeur, Tenor, Act II   CT 05
  4      -Ihr die das Laud   CH 30
  4      -Ihr die ihr mich verfolgt, Act II, Baritone   CH 30
  4      -Nur einen Wunsch, nur ein Verlangen   CH 91
  4      -O Lasst mich tief Geben   NS 1884
  4      -O Malheureuse Iphegénie, Act II Sopr   NS 1888
  4      -O Toi qui Pidongeas mes Jours   SL 40
  5      -Recitative and Aria, De noirs pressentiments   CH 07;   WA 39
  4      -Unis dès la plus tendre enfance, Tenor, Act II   CT 48;   NP 01
 90      Orfeo ed Euridice, complete Opera 1762   SF 49, 67
 75      -Concert form   NP 34
  4      -Adagio   CH 97, 00, 02
  4      -Aria   DE 45, 52, 58;   NR 53, 56
 26      -Ballet Music   SL 21, 29
  4      -Can I Bear this Anguish?   CH 01
  4      -Che faro senza Euridice, Ach ich habe sie verloren, I have lost
         my Euridice   BN 52;   BU 69;   CH 14, 16, 48, 64;   CT 1899, 15,
         47;   DT 48, 53, 56, 63;   LA 31, 41;   MN 41;   NP 1869, 73, 99;   NS 10,
         17, 20;   PH 08, 10, 19;   SL 17, 21, 29;   SF 57;   UT 56;   WA 35
  4      -Che puro ciel   CH 64
  5      -Dance of the Blessed Spirits, Reigen seliger Geister Act II,
         Scene II   BN 63, 64, 67;   CH 1897, 00, 01, 02, 16, 29, 34, 35,
         40;   LA 25;   MN 45;   NS 1884, 21;   RC 51, 54;   SF 62;
         SE 26;   UT 51;   WA 36
  5      -Dance of the Furies, Act II Scene I   BN 1888, 91;   CH 1897, 00,
         02, 34;   NS 1884, 21
  6      -Dances   DE 52
 10      -Excerpts   BU 69
  5      -Overt   CH 64;   SF 58
  5      -Recitative and Aria of Orpheus,O, My Consort   CH 01
  5      -Scene for Fl   NS 25
 10      Paride ed Elena, Opera 1770  Ballet Music arr Reinecke   RC 54
         -Aria, O del mio dolce ardor   CH 1891, 32;   CT 14, 22, 33, 41;
         DT 35, 38;   NA 39;   NP 1898, 36;   PH 12
 15      Ballet Suite No 1   arr Mottl   BA 49(2);   BN 32;   DT 15, 17(2),
         23, 32;   LA 20;   PH 12, 16, 24, 29, 32, 33;   SE 29
 12      Ballet Suite No 2   arr Mottl   BN 27;   LA 26;   NP 27;   WA 32,
         37, 39
         La Rencontre Imprévue, or Les Pèlerins de la Macque, Opera 1764
  5      Ariette   NS 08
```

GLUCK, C.W. (Cont.)
   12   Ballet Music No 1 arr Gevart   BN 1881
   15   Ballet Music No 2 arr Gevart   BN 1886, 99
    7   -Excerpts   BN 1894, 13, 15
    8   Chaconne   LA 33, 38
    6   Sinfonia in G major   CT 31

   15   Suite in D No 1 arr Mottl   CT 08, 31, 39, 44, 45;   SE 34, 59
   30   Suite in Six Parts, Air Gai, Lento, Graziozo, Musette, Air Gai and
           Sicilienne   SE 29

GNATTALI, Radames   30   P Conc No 2   PH 42;   WA 43
1906-   Brazil

GOCKEL, August   10   Caprice Burlesque   NP 1852
1831-1861   US

GODARD, Benjamine   24   V Conc in a No 1, Op 35   BN 1883, 01;   CT 1897
1849-1895   Fr   24   V Conc No 2 in g, Romantique   Op 131   CH 1892;
                     NP 1892
                    Le Tasse, Dramatic Symph for Soli, Chor and O 1878
          4   -Aria of Leonora   DT 18, 19;   SL 17
          4   -Bohemian Dances   BN 1883
         18   Scènes Poétiques Suite Op 103   HN 13
          6   -Mazurka   PH 02
          6   Scènes Ecossaises: March of the Highlander, with Oboe
               Soloist   SE 45
         20   Suite No 1 from Opera Jocelyn 1888   BN 1895
         30   Symphonie orientale Op 84   BN 1890
          7   -Chinoiserie   CH 05

GODEFROID, Dievdonne   5   Marche Triomphale du Roi David, Harp Solo   CH 02
1818-1897   Belg

GODOWSKY, Leopold   8   Java Suite, Phonoramas arr M. Press   CT 32;   DT 33
1870-1938   Pol/US

GOEB, Roger   25   Symph No 4 in b   PT 55
1914-   US

GOEHR, Alexander   35   V Conc   SL 69(2)
1932-   Brit 17   Pastorals   LA 66

GOEPP, Philip   5   Academic March in C   PH 08
1864-1936   US   5   Heroic March   PH 17

GOETZ, Hermann   25   P Conc in B^{b} Op 18   NP 1881
1840-1876   Ger   Opera, Taming of the Shrew, Der Widerspänstigen
or GÖTZ   4   Zahmung 1874: Aria My Strength is Spent   CH 11;
                CT 11;   NA 37;   NP 35;   PH 14
          8   Overt, Spring, in A Op 15   BN 1894, 14
         35   Symph in F Op 9   BN 1886, 89, 93, 95, 01, 07, 13;
                KC 66;   NP 1883   PH 01;   SL 14
          5   -Intermezzo   CH 1899

GOLD, Ernest   10   Audubon, An Overt   UT 54
1921-   Aust/US

GOLDBECK, Robert   6   Forest Devotion   CH 1894
1839-1908   US   6   Leaping Marionettes   CH 1894
                        20   Deux Morceaux Symphoniques for P and O   NP 1861
                        10   Morceaux Symphonique No 4, Le Songe, for P and O
                              NP 1863
                         8   Two Mexican Dances   CH 1894

GOLDMARK, Karl   33   V Conc No 1 in a Op 28
1830-1915   Aust   BN 1890, 94, 98, 01, 05, 10;   BU 57;
                              CH 01, 10, 14, 32, 44, 56;   CT 10, 20, 27, 30,
                              43;   CL 21, 36, 51;   DT 19, 41, 57;   HN 59
                              KC 44, 59;   LA 21, 58;   MN 42, 68;
                              NP 1894, 10, 44, 56;   NS 10, 15, 23;   PH 10, 15,
                              26, 35, 42;   PT 45;   RC 44, 59;   SL 23, 32;
                              SF 26;   WA 57, 65;
           OVERTURES
    10   In Days of Youth, Aus Jugendtagen Op 53   LA 25
    11   In Italy Op 49   BN 04;   CH 04, 07, 11;   NP 04, 07, 11;   PH 04,
           07, 11
    10   In the Spring Op 36 Overt
              BN 1888, 92, 98, 01, 05, 07, 12, 14, 16, 21;   CH 1892, 95, 98, 02,
              06, 08, 09, 10, 12, 14, 15, 16, 18, 21, 25, 56;
              CT 15, 18, 32, 36, 41, 53;   CL 27, 39;   DA 34;   DE 57;
              HN 45;   NA 36;   KC 34, 36, 41;   LA 30, 45;   MN 30, 39;
              NP 00, 01, 02, 04, 07, 13, 15, 16, 20, 25, 30, 40;
              NS 1889, 96, 07;   PH 00, 01, 04, 07, 20, 25, 40;   PT 40;
              RC 30;   SL 09, 15, 19, 21;   SF 12;   SE 26
    18   Penthesilia Op 31   BN 1885, 88, 01;   CH 1893;   NS 1879(2), 85
    16   Promethus Bound,Der gefesselte Prometheus Op 38   BN 1890, 91, 99;
              CH 1893, 96;   CT 14;   NP 1890, 92, 96, 99, 19;   NS 1890, 93
    19   Sakuntala Op 13   BN 1882, 84, 86, 89, 91, 95, 96, 98, 00, 03, 05,
              06, 10, 14, 17, 19, 23;   CH 1891, 99(2), 00, 04, 10, 13;
              CT 96, 11, 12, 18;   CL 21, 23, 24, 27, 30;   DA 35;   DE 59;
              DT 15, 23, 26;   HN 33, 41;   NA 31, 47;   KC 39;   LA 19, 31;
              NP 1869, 70, 73, 77, 83, 94, 02, 04, 05, 06, 07(2), 08(3), 09(2),
              10(2), 11(2), 12(2), 15, 21, 33, 50;   NS 1878, 81, 87, 11; PH 02, 04,
              05, 06, 07(2), 08(3), 09(2), 10(2), 11(2), 12(2), 15, 21, 33;
              SL 10, 11, 15, 17, 20, 26, 30;   SF 11, 14, 45;   SE 35;   WA 39
    13   Sappho Op 44   BN 1894, 99, 04, 15, 17;   CH 1894, 95, 97, 00, 05,
              07, 14, 21;   LA 21;   MN 22;   PH 01, 08;   NP 01, 08
           OPERAS
     5   Merlin 1886 Chor of Spirits   BN 02;   CH 1893
     8   Cricket on the Hearth, Das Heimchen am Herd, 1896   Prel Act III
              BN 1896;   CH 1896;   DT 32;   MN 29
    11   Queen of Sheba, Die Königen van saba, Op 27 1875: Ballet Music
              CH 1892;   HN 39
     4   -Aria Lift Thine Eyes   SL 40
    10   Scherzo in A Op 45   BN 00;   CH 1894, 95, 11;   LA 26;   NS 09,
              12(2);   PH 02;   NP 02
           Scherzo in e Op 19   PH 02
     4   SONG: Die Quelle   NS 1890

GOLDMARK, K. (Cont.)
```
  40    Symph No 2 in E♭ The Rustic Wedding Op 35    AT 55;    BA 39;
           BN 1887, 88, 00;    CH 1891, 94, 95, 97, 00, 01, 04, 06, 09, 10,
           11, 14, 15, 21, 24, 36;    CT 04, 15, 17, 19, 21;    CL 26;
           HN 34, 41, 54;    NA 31, 35, 43;    KC 34, 39;    LA 28;
           NP 1888, 01, 03, 05, 06, 08, 09, 10, 11, 14, 17, 30, 3 mvts 36;
           NS 1892, 03, 10, 17;    PH 01, 03, 05, 06, 08, 09, 10, 11, 14, 17,
           30, 36;    SL 10, 14, 17, 22;    SE 28;    UT 62
   8    –Wedding March and Var    CH 1896, 05, 14;    NS 91
   4    –Bridal Song    HN 17
   4    –Serenade    HN 17
```

GOLDMARK, Rubin   15   Call of the Plains 1919   NS 23
1872–1936   US   8   Hiawatha Overt 1900   BN 99, 05
                      15   A Negro Rhaps   BN 28;   CH 23, 28;   DT 24;
                               LA 24;   NP 22, 23, 27;   NS 25;   RC 30;   SF 24
                      25   Requiem, After Gettysburg 1919   CH 19, 42;
                               DT 34;   NP 18, 19;   SL 19, 21
                      22   Tone Poem, Samson 1914   BN 13;   CH 17;   NP 16,
                               20;   PH 17;   SF 21

GOLDSCHMIDT, Berthold 24   C Conc 1933   PT 57
1903–   Ger/Brit

GOLESTAN, Stan   11   First Rhaps, Roumania   CL 31;   PH 31
1875–1956   Roum

GOLTERMANN, Georg   6   Contilena for Cello   BN 1897
1824–1898   Ger   30   C Conc in à Op 14   BN 1889;   CH 1899;   CT 18;
                               DA finale 48;   NP 1857, 71
                      25   C Conc in d Op 30   CH 1896
                      25   C Conc in b Op 51   CH 09

GOMBAC,(or GOMBAU)   8   Escena Charra   RC 42
               Sp   6   Segovianos   RC 40

GOMER, Lleweln   8   De Frundis for O and Chor   CT 47
1911–   Brit

GOMEZ, Antonio Cailos   OPERAS
1836–1896   Brazil 4   The Slave, O escravo Opera 1889: Aria Como
                               Seremamente   CT 40
                       8   –Interlude, Alvarado   CH 47;   CL 48
                       4   O Guarani 1870: Ballad, There was a Prince   CH 1894
                       8   –Overt   DE 59

GOOSSENS, Eugene   5   By The Tarn,Sketch for Str Op 15 No 1   CH 20;
1893–   Brit/US   CT 34, 45;   CL 20;   NS 25;   PH 39;
                               RC 23, 26, 30, 36;   SL 27
                       7   Concertino for Double Str O Op 47   BN 29;   CT 34,
                               46;   DT 29;   SL 29, 38
                      11   Conc for Ob and O Op 45   CL 42
                      23   Concerto-Fantasy for P and O Op 60   CT 43
                       4   Don Juan de Manara, Opera Op 54 1937: Aria Act I
                               CT 38
                       5   –Intermezzo   CT 37;   RC 36;   NP 37
                       5   –Serenade Act II   CT 38

GOOSSENS, E. (Cont.) 18   Eternal Rhythm, Symphon Poem Op 5   CH 22;   RC 25
                     4   Fanfare for the Merchant Marine   CT 42
                     4   Fanfare for Victory   CT 45;   NA 45
                     7   Four Conceits Op 20   NS 21
                     8   Fantasie for Strings Op 2   CT 41;   NP 41
                     12   Jubilee Var on a Theme, Theme and Finale   CT 44, 45
                     4   Judith, Opera Op 46: Prayer   CT 32
                     5   -Ballet Music   RC 29
                     10   Kaleidescope, Suite Op 18   MN 32;   RC 32
                     3   -No 3 Hurdy-Gurdy Man   MN 28
                     15   Lyric Poem V and O Op 35   CT 43;   RC 29
                     8   Rhythmic Dance Op 30   BN 28;   CT 34;   RC 26, 27
                     15   Sinfonietta Op 34   BN 25;   CT 33;   CL 44;
                            NP 29;   RC 23, 30;   SF 30
                     38   Symph No 1 Op 58   BN 40;   CT 39, 40, 42;   CL 43;
                            NP 2nd and 3rd mvts 40
                     3   Tam O Shanter, Scherzo Op 16   BN 22;   CT 39;
                            CL 24;   MN 24;   RC 24;   SF 24
                     15   Two Nature Poems Op 52   BN 38;   CT 37

GORIN, Igor   4   Caucasian Melody, Song   CT 38;   SL 40
  1908-   Russ   4   Lament, Song   CT 39
                     4   Ukrainian Folk Song   CT 39

GOSSEC, Francois   14   Symph in D   NP 54
  1734-1829 Neth/Fr

GOTOVAC, Johov   8   Kolo Symphonie Op 12   DT 38
  1895-   Yugo

GOTTLIEB, Jack   18   Articles of Faith for O and Memorable Voices
  1930-   US   DT 65

GOTTSCHALK, Louis   22   Cakewalk Suite arr Kay   NR 52
  1829-1869   US   8   Escenes Campestres   NR 68
                     6   Grand Tarantella P and O   NR 69
                     4   Marche Triumfel, with Band   NR 69
                     20   Montivideo Symph   NR 68
                     9   Var on Portuguese Hymn P and O   NR 69

GOUDOEVER,   20   Suite for C and O   NP 21
  Henry D. van
  1898   Neth

GOULD, Morton   12   American Concertette Interplay for P and O
  1913-   US   AT 60;   NP 60;   WA 44
                     5   American Salute: When Johnny Comes Marching Home
                            CH 54;   CT 43;   CL 43;   LA 43;   MN 43
                            PT 43;   UT 50, 52, 63;   WA 44, 46
                     9   American Symphonette No 1   NP 42
                     9   American Symphonette No 2   LA 41, 55;   PT 38
                            -Pavane   HN 43
                     18   American Symphonette No 4 Latin America   BA 45;
                            RC 41;   UT 56, 62
                     10   -Guaracha   HN 43;   WA 42
                     5   -Rhumba   MN 44;   WA 42
                     6   -Tango   WA 42

GOULD, M. (Cont.)

5	Anniversary Quadrille SL 54	
8	Columbia Broadsides for O WA 67	
18	Conc for O 1944 CL 44; MN 45, 47, 3rd and 5th mvt 57	
12	Cowboy's Rhaps CT 44; DA 41; MN 43	
22	Dance Var 2 P and O AT 54; DT 55; NP 53; SF 53	
30	Declaration for Narrator, Soli and male Chorus WA 56	
24	Fall River Legend, Ballet Suite 1948 NP 51; SF 48	
11	Festive Music AT 66	
2	Fanfare for Freedom CT 42	
33	Foster Gallery PT 39	
12	Harvest 1945 SL 45	
5	Homespun Overt RC 40	
17	Inventions 4 P and O CT 54; DT 56	
22	Jekyll and Hyde Var AT 60; DA 63; HN 68; NP 56; SE 67; WA 57	
18	Lincoln Legends 1942 DE 46	
8	Minstrel Show 1946 NA 46; MN 46; PT 49; SF 47	
3	Night Song AT 46	
9	Philharmonic Waltz MN 48	
5	Red Cavalry March PT 43	
15	A Serenade of Carols BA 54; CH 53; DE 49, 60; HN 49; NA 49, 53	
18	Show Piece NP 54	
8	Soundings AT 69; CL 69	
17	Spirituals for Str O 1941 BA 53; BN 44, 45; BU 52; CT 44; CL 41; DA 46; DT 51; NA 53; KC 44; LA 52; MN 43, 56; NR 50; NP 42, 45, 49; PH 49; PT 49, 51; RC 43, 51; SL 43(2), 46, 48, 54; SF 52; SE 55; WA 54	
19	Suite of Christmas Hymns NA 53	
32	Symph No 1 1936 PT 42	
31	Symph No 2 on Marching Tunes 1944 CT 44; MN 44	
35	Symph No 3 1946 DA 46; NP 48	
45	Vivaldi Gallery SE 67	

GOUNOD, Charles
1818-1893   Fr

	OPERAS	
5	La Colombe 1859: Entr'acte BN 1882	
4	Faust 1852: Aria DA 34; DE 57	
4	-Aria, Avant de quitter NA 56; SL 55	
4	-Aria, Salue demeure chaste et pace DT 22, 41; NP 11	
6	-Ballet Music BA 49; DA 26, 52; HN 14, 38, 58	
4	-Cavatina DT 46; SE 36	
	-Excerpts HN 38	
6	-Finale SE 51	
4	-Jewel Song AT 53; CT 44; DA 26; HN 15, 55; KC 34; ML 64; SL 46; SE 58	
8	-The King of Thule, Ballad for Sopr from Act III CT 44; KC 34	

GOUNOD, C. (Cont.)   Faust (Cont.)
                4   -Mefistophelis Serenade, Vous qui faites
                        l'endormie   AT 68;   KC 60, 64
                        -Soldier's Chor   HN 42;   NR with waltz 68
                6   Mireille 1863: Valse Ariette   DT 58
                4   Philémon et Baucis 1859: Aria, He has lost my trace
                        BN 83;   CH 97
                4   -Vulcan's Song   NA 34
                5   Queen of Sheba, La reine de Saba 1861: Ballad   DE 59
                        -Inspirez moi, race divine   CT 07
                        -Lend me your aid   CH 1892, 99
                        -Plus grande dans son obsurite   CT 95;   CL 26;
                        HN 44;   MN 24, 43;   PT 37;   SL 25
                        -Sous les pieds, Cavatina de Soliman   CT 00
                4   Romeo and Juliet 1864: Aria Ah! leve-toi soleil
                        DT 18
                        -Je veux vivre, Waltz   AT 51;   CT 40, 44, 46,
                        64;   HN 14, 40;   SL 15;   SF 11;
                        -unidentified aria   NS 13;   DA 34
                        -Wedding Feast   PH 05
                4   Sappho 1850: Aria O ma lyre immortelle   CH 1899, 10
                        -Stances de Sappho   NS 22

                6   Funeral March of a Marionette 1873   BN 1882;
                        CH 02;   HN 42
               12   Psalm 137, Chor and O   CH 08
                4   Serenade for Voice and O, Barcarolle   NP 24
                6   O Sing to God, Chor and O   NS 16
                3   Symph for Wind Instruments, Scherzo   NS 07
                5   Vision de Jeanne d'Arc, for V and O   BN 1891

GRÄDENER, Hermann   10   Cappriccio for O Op 4   BN 1888;   NP 1883
1844-1929   Ger   20   C Conc in e   BN 08
                6   Lustspiel Overt   BN 1887

GRAENER, Paul   8   Comedietta   DT 30;   PH 30
1872-1944   Ger   15   Suite Op 88 The Flute of Sans Soci   CH 38;
                        DT 38;   NP 38

GRAINGER, Percy   7   Children's March: Over the Hills and Far Away for
1882-   Austr/US   Winds, Double Bass and Percussion   CH 27;
                        NS 19(2)
                6   Colonial Song Voices and O   BU 43;   DT 15, 24;
                        HN 33
               17   Danish Folk Music Suite 4 mvts 1937   CH 31;   WA 42
                3   -Nightingale   SE 31
                3   -Two Sisters   SE 31
               10   English Dance for 2 P, Org and O   CH 25;   MN 29
                8   Green Bushes, Passacaglia   CT 35, 41;   DT 29;
                        RC 29;   SE 32
                4   Gumsucker's March   WA 32
                4   Handel in the Strand, P and Str, Clog Dance
                        CH 27, 35;   SE 31;   WA 32
                3   Harvest Hymn 1933   CH 40
                7   Hill Song No 2 for P, Cymbals, Org, Harmonium 1929
                        CH 35

Time in
Minutes
GRAINGER, P. (Cont.)

14	In A Nutshell Suite for P, Perc and O 1916	
	CH 16; CT 40, 42; NP 16; SL 16; SF 15;	
	WA 42	
8	Irish Tunes, British Folk Music Settings Suite	
	BU 41; DA 25; DT 21; LA 19; NS 14, 15,	
	16; SL 21, 27; WA 32	
2	-Country Gardens MN 47	
4	-Londonderry Air BA 42; CT 42; RC 23, 24,	
	26, 38; UT 53	
6	-My Robin is to the Greenwood Gone, Chamber O	
	CH 27; SF 15	
2	-Shepherd's Hey BU 43; CH 14; DT 24;	
	MN 47; NS 21; RC 23; SF 15	
5	Mock Morris for Str O CH 13, 14; DT 16	
3	-Molly on the Shore HN 16; MN 47; NS 21;	
	PH 15; RC 23, 38; SL 21, 27; SF 15	
5	-Irish Reel HN 16	
5	Spoon River, P and O CH 35; SE 31; WA 32	
9	To A Nordic Princess Org and O CH 35	
18	The Warriors, Music to an Imaginary Ballet 1916	
	CH 19; MN 26; NS 16	
22	Youthful Suite, 5 mvts WA 46	
10	Walking Tune for Woodwinds CT 40	

GRAMMANN, Carl   6   Prelude, Melinine   BN 1881, 82
1844-   Ger

GRAMATTÉ, Sonia Marie 20   Élégie and Danse Marocaine for V and O   CH 29;
c 1890   Russ/Fr   PH 29
                          25   Konzertstück for P and O   CH 29;   PH 29

GRANADOS, Enrique   18   Dante, Symphon Poem Sopr and O Op 21   CH 15, 23
1867-1916   Sp   12   Dances, Spanish: Three dances arr Grignon
                              CT 42;   CL 39;   RC 36
                     4   No 10   PT arr Byrnes 39
                     4   No 11 Amor gitano   CT 43, 44;   RC 43, 50;
                              SF 43
                     4   -Rondalla   CL 30;   SL 30
                     4   -Orientale   RC 37, 40, 41
                     4   -Andalusia   RC 37
                     4   -Dance for Guitar   DE 54
                     4   Goyescas, Opera 1916: Aria   DE 57;   DT 19;   SE 58
                     4   -Dance Enbozados   CT 43
                     4   -Epilogue   PH 33
                     4   -Fandango   CT 43, 44;   RC 44
                     4   -Intermezzo   CH 57, 62;   CT 38, 42, 43;
                              CL 29;   DT 35;   MN 36, 48;   NP 56;   NS 27;
                              PH 33;   RC 34, 39, 40, 42;   SL 28;   WA 36
                     17   -Suite arr Dorati   RC 43
                     4   Jota Aragonesa   CT 43;   SF 43
                     4   Jota Valenciana   CT 43;   SF 43

de Grandval,   10   Ob Conc in d Op 7   CH 07
  Nicholas R.
1676-1753   Fr

GRANZ	6	Trumpet Solo, Brilliant Var NP 1848
GRAUN, Karl	8	Der Tod Jesu, Cantata, Selections CH 67
1704-1759 Ger	4	Montezuma, Opera 1755: Aria, Non ancalma AT 66
GRAY	4	Syllogism BA 39
US		
GRECHANINOV,	10	Elegy Op 175 BN 45
Alexander	8	Festival Overt 1942 NA 46
1864-1956 Russ/US	90	Missa Oecumenica Op 142, for Soli, Chor, Org and O
		BN 45
	12	Motet, O God Hear My Prayer CH 32
	8	Russian Folk Songs Op 186: two only DT 43
		SONGS
	4	Over the Steppe CT 32, 36; DA 30; DT 29;
		HN 41; LA 32; PH 28; SL 40
	4	Berceuse DA 35; NS 22
	4	Only Begotten Son MN 43
	4	Cherubic Hymn NS 16
	4	Lord's Prayer KC 34
	4	Praise the Lord MN 42
	4	My Native Land NS 22
	30	Symph No 1 Andante and Scherzo only Op 6 CH 13
	30	Symph No 4 Op 102 NP 41
	30	Symph No 5 in g 1939 PT 47
	6	Theme and Var DT 39
	10-12	Triptiche, Suite for Str Op 163 NA 51
de GREEF, Arthur	12	Three Old Belgian Folksongs NS 18
1862-1940 Belg	16	Four Old Flemish Folk Songs CH 19; SF 23
	8	Two Old Flemish Folk Songs NS 23
GREENSWAY, L.	24	Five Russian Pieces I-V SE 47
US		
GRÉTRY, André	5	Anacréon Opera 1797 Overt NS 27
1741-1813 Fr	15	Céphale et Procris, Opera 1775: Aria Naissantes
		fleurs NP 14
	6	-Dances SF 52
	4	-Menuetto, arr Johnson CT 50
	15	-Suite arr Mottl AT 46; BN 40; CH 07, 09, 16,
		23, 38; CL 24, 25, 28, 31, 44; DA 46; DE 66;
		DT 21, 28, 35; HN 34, 50; NA 59; KC 56;
		LA 49; MN 28, 50; NR 57; RC 35, 58; PH 15,
		17, 29, 43, 46; SL 35, 37, 38, 42, 48, 49, 50,
		51, 55; SF 36, 46; SE 38, 61; WA 33, 38, 45
	4	-Tambourine CH 19, 25, 26, 31, 36; CT arr
		Johnson 50
	7	-Three pieces BN 08, 21
	10	L'Épreuve villagoisie Opera 1782: Overt CH 10;
		CT arr Johnson 50; NR 62; NP 25; NS 16
	12	Franko, Little Ballet CL 31; MN 30
	8	Gavotte and Danse Legero KC 40
	14	Zémire et Azor Opera 1771, Suite CH 58; HN 58
	6	-Aria La Femmette BN 43; NP 1886

GRIEG, Edvard   15   Aruljeit Gelline, At the Cloister Gate, Soli,
1843-1907   Nor   women's Chor and O Op 20   NS 1878
              5   Ave Maris Stella, Chor and O 1899   CH 08
             10   Bergliot,Declamation with O Op 42   NA 31
             30   P Conc in a Op 16
                        AT 48, 58, 66;   BA 44, 54, 64;   BN 1881, 99, 01,
                        04, 05, 06, 18, 19;   BU 43;   CH 1896, 97, 99,
                        01, 03, 07, 11, 15, 55, 63;   CT 1896, 01, 02, 03,
                        13, 15, 34, 39, 44, 68;   CL 22, 25, 29, 48, 50,
                        56;   DA 28, 29, 49, 56, 58;   DE 45, 49;   DT 14,
                        16, 24, 27, 62;   HN 31, 44;   NA 41, 43, 45, 55;
                        KC 48, 52, 66;   MN 24, 43, 47;   NP 1897, 98,
                        05, 06, 07, 12, 14, 16, 18, 22, 25, 27, 50, 56;
                        NS 1878, 03, 07, 09, 11, 16, 19;   PH 03, 04, 05,
                        07, 09, 13, 15, 42, 53;   PT 61;   RC 23, 25, 29,
                        43, 60;   SL 12, 16, 24, 27, 45, 46, 61;   SF 16,
                        22, 43, 59;   SE 31, 47;   UT 52, 55, 68;
                        WA 32, 42, 62, 67
              6   Dance Algerienne, Dutch Dance   NS 16
              9   Two Elgiac Melodies for Str Op 34   BN 1882, 90, 91;
                        CH 34;   CT 42;   DT 17, 33;   HN 13;   KC 33;
                        NP 11, 19;   NS 1881;   PH 29, 35;   SL 21
              5   Heart Wounds or the Wounded One   CH 1892, 04, 11;
                        CT 32, 35;   DA 27, 29, 37
              5   Last Spring   CH 1892, 04, 11;   CT 1890, 03;
                        DA 27, 29;   MN 42;   PT 38;   UT 43
              6   Funeral March   NS 13, 19
             20   Holberg Suite for Str O, 5 parts Op 40   BN 1888,
                        94, 17;   CT 18;   CL 28;   DT 47;   NS 1892;
                        PH 01;   SL 44, 59
             16   Lyric Suite arr for O by Maddy from P Suite Op 54
                        CH 07;   NP 06;   PH 11, 17;   SF 15
              4   No 3 Nocturne   DT 32
             12   Norwegian Dances Op 35   BA 42;   DT 48;   HN 14
                        NS 06, 14
              6   No 1 in d   DT 40, 47;   HN 33, 39
              6   No 2 in a   HN 33, 39;   SE 27
             20   Old Norwegian Romance with Var Op 51   BN 11;
                        CH 08;   CT 16
              8   2 Norwegian Melodies Op 63   CH 1898, 06;   NS 1881
             11   Overt In Autumn, Concert Overt Op 11   BN 06, 13;
                        CH 08, 18;   CT 18, 19, 43;   CL 43;   DT 15;
                        NA 32;   MN 43;   NP 11;   NS 25;   PH 08, 09,
                        10, 11;   PT 44
              9   Olaf Trygvason, Scenes from the Opera Op 50   CH 96
             15   Peer Gynt Suite No 1 Op 46   BA 43;   BN 1889, 92,
                        96, 97, 99, 09;   CH 1891, 93, 95(2), 98, 01, 02,
                        03, 10;   CT 1896, 01;   DA 28;   HN 31, 36;
                        NA 30, 31;   MN 23, 46;   NP 07;   NS 07, 19, 20;
                        PH 08(2);   RC 26;   SF 33;   WA 32
              4   No 1 Morning   BA 28
              4   No 3 Anitra's Dance   BA 42;   DA 27, 35
              4   No 4 In the Hall of the Mountain King   BA 28,
                        43;   CT 95, 98
              8   -Selections   HN 67(2)

GRIEG, E. (Cont.)

14	Peer Gynt Suite No 2, Op 55 BN 09; CH 1892; HN 37	
4	No 1 Ingrid's Lament UT 58	
4	No 3 Return of Peer Gynt UT 58	
4	No 4 Solvejg's Song CT 1895; HN 31; MN 44; UT 58	
4	Storm at Sea UT 58	
18	Quart for Str in g Op 27 CH Romance and Intermezzo 19; MN 38	
20	Sigurd Jorsalfar Op 56 Suite from Incidental Music to the Opera CH 1893, 10; PH 10, 11, 14; SL 11; WA 34	
8	-March of Homage DT 17	
35	Symphon Dances Op 64 BN 1899; CH 1898	
	Nos 2, 3 and 4 CH 18, 26	
	Nos 2 and 4 CT 16; NP 19	
	No 2 PH 1733	
	No 4 CH 32; LA 42; PH 02, 03, 33; SE 27	
6	Symphon Dances Op 68, Evening in the Mountains and At the Cradle CH 02	

SONGS

4	Autumn Storm Op 18 No 4 CT 1899
4	A Dream Op 48 No 6 CL 49; DE 47; LA 40; MN 37, 40, 48; NS 25; NP 19
4	Eit Syn Op 33 CH 1892; PH 37
4	Eros Op 70 No 1 BA 47; CT 36; DT 48; KC 38; MN 38; PH 37
4	God's Son Has Made Me Free MN 48
4	Ich Liebe dich, I Love Thee Op 5 No 3 MN 48
4	Lauf der Walt Op 48 No 3 NS 25
4	From Monte Pincio Op 39 No 1 MN 44
4	The Swan Op 25 No 2 DT 48; LA 40; MN 40
4	Varen, Spring Op 33 No 2 DT 48; LA 40; MN 37, 40

GRIFFES, Charles
1884-1920   US

5	Bacchanale for O PH 19
12	Five Old Chinese and Japanese Songs, Voice and O Op 10 AT 51
4	Lament of Ian the Proud Sopr and O Op 11 No 1 CL 21
7	Nocturne for O PH 19
14	The Pleasure Dome of Kubla Khan, Symphon Poem 1920 BN 19, 20, 30; BU 40; CH 19, 32, 41; CT 31, 48; CL 38, 47, 53; DT 63; NA 37; MN 24, 43; NP 24; PH 31; PT 41; SL 20; SF 38
9	Poem for Fl and O 1918 AT 62; BA 65; BN 31; CT 25; CL 62; NS 19; PH 43; WA 54

Roman Sketches Op 7

6	No 1 The White Peacock AT 54, 64; BA 39; BN 22; BU 47; CH 22, 48; CT 47, 49, 53, 56, 57; CL 28, 29, 30, 45, 57; DA 62; DE 63; DT 43, 44; HN 47; NA 48, 50, 57; LA 48; KC 40, 63; ML 61; NP 35, 45, 47; NS 20; PH 19, 44, 48; SE 40, 63; UT 47, 53, 62, 68
5	No 4 Clouds BN 22; CH 22; PH 19

GRIGNON, Lamote de   8   Tone Picture, Andalusia   RC 27(2), 39
           Sp

GRIMM, Carl Hugo   15   Abe Lincoln, Tone Poem for O   CT 31
1890-   US   10   An American Overt   CT 45
                      15   Christmas Conc Op 52   CT 51
                      15   Erotic Poem for O   CT 27
                      20   Montana, Two impressions   CT 42

GRIMM, Julius Otto   10   Suite in Canon Form for Str   NP 1873
1827-1903   Ger   30   Symph in d   BN 1883

GRISON, Jules   4   Fantasy on O Come All Ye Faithful   SL 54
           US

GROFÉ, Ferde   32   Grand Canyon Suite, 5 mvts 1932   PT 54;   UT 58;
1892-1972   US   WA 50, 54
                       6   -Cloudburst   NP 53
                       6   -On the Trail   DE 45;   NP 53
                       6   -Sunrise   DE 45
                       6   -Sunset   NP 53
                       9   Hudson River Suite   NP 55
                      12   Mississippi Suite 1925   NP 54
                      20   San Francisco Suite   SF 59
                      20   Tabloid Suite 1933   PH 36

GRONDAHL, Launny   17   Conc for Bassoon   CH 51
1886-1960   Dan

GROSZ, Wilhelm   15   4 Love Songs Op 10   CT 27
1894-1939   Aust/US 10   Prelude to Comic Opera Op 14   CT 24

GRUBER, Franz X.   6   Christmas Day, Chor and O   DE 47
1787-1863   Aust   7   Silent Night, arr Roy Ringwald   DE 47

GRUENBERG, Louis   39   V Conc Op 47   CT 44;   PH 44;   SF 44
1884-   Russ/US   4   Emperor Jones, Opera 1933: Aria, Lawd Jesus Heah
                             My Prayer   PH 40
                      20   Enchanted Isle, Symphon Poem 1918   BN 29;   CH 30;
                             LA 31;   NP 30
                      10   Hill of Dreams, Symphon Poem   NS 21;   SL 21
                      18   Jazz Suite Op 28   BN 29;   CH 29;   CT 28;
                             LA 29;   RC 33
                      11   Moods, 9 parts 1929   PH 31
                      10   Serenade To a Beauteous Lady 1939   CH 34;   LA 42
                      45   Symph No 1 1926   BN 32

GUARNIERI, Camargo   12   Albertura Concertante Overt   BN 42;   NP 56
1907-   Brazil   11   Dances, 3 Brazilian   DA 49;   LA 44;   NP two
                             only 43;   PH 43;   SL 52
                       3   -Dance Brasiliera   NP 43
                       4   -Dance Negra   HN 55;   NA 57;   NP 43
                       4   -Dance Selvagem   NP 48
                       8   Prologue and Fugue   BN 47;   NP 57
                      13   Suite IV Centenario   NA 62
                      25   Symph No 2   BN 46;   CL 51;   DA 50;   NP 62

GUERRINI, Guido	6	La Citta Perduta for two voices, Chor and O NA 47
1890-1965 It	80	Enea, Opera 1948: Trittico for O NA 50
	35	Nativitas Christi NA 54
	9	Six Ancient Dances, Vinci NA 48
	20	Trifons, 1932 NA 38

GUILHAUD, George   5   Conc for Ob in g   CH 03, 17;   SE 38
1883-   Fr

GUILMANT, Alexandre   6   Adoration for Org and O   CH 1896
1837-1911   Fr   6   Allegro for Org and O   CH 1896
                       5   March Fantasie for Org and O   PH 11
                      24   Symph No 1 in C Org and O   BN 02, 18;   DA 25
                      25   Symph No 2 in d Op 42   CH 1893, 97;   DE 52;
                            MN 27

GUION, David   48   Texas, Symphon Suite   HN 51
1895-   US   4   Turkey in the Straw   DA 25

GUIRAUD, Ernest   5   Caprice, V and O 1884   CT 02;   NP 1899
1837-1892   Fr/US   5   Carneval in F   CT 1898
                      8   Chasse Fantastique, Symphonic Poem 1887   CH 1893

GUMBERT, Ferdinand   4   Song: Spielman's Lied   NP 1852
1818-1896   Ger

GUNGL, Joseph   4   Amoretten Valse   AT 64
1810-1889   Hung

GUSIKOFF, Michael   14   American Conc for V and O   WA 32
(GUZIKOW)
1895-   US

GUTCHE, Gene   8   Epimetheus, U.S.A. Op 46   DT 69
1907-   US   9   Genghis Khan   NA 66;   MN 63
                    7   Holofernes Overt Op 27 No 1   MN 59;   NP 65
                   15   Hsiang Fei Op 40   CT 66;   MN 66
                   20   Symph No 5, Op 34   CT 63

HAASE, C.   8   Trumpet Solo with Var, Carneval of Venice   NP 1851
             US

HADLEY, Henry K.   14   The Culprit Fay, Rhaps Op 62   BN 10;   CH 09;
1871-1937   US   CT 18;   NP 10, 20;   NS 11;   PH 10;   SL 14;
                         SF 13
                   14   In Bohemia, Overt Op 28   CH 12, 29, 40;   CT 20,
                         46, 50, 52;   NA 44, 50;   SL 18, 22;   SF 31;
                         SE 39;   UT 42
                   15   Koncertstück C and O in b Op 61   CH 10;   SF 12
                    8   Lucifer, Tone Poem Op 66   BN 15;   CL 25;   NP 14;
                         PH 18
                         Ocean, Tone Poem Op 99   BN 23;   CH 22;   DT 25;
                         NA 37;   NP 21, 33;   SL 21
                   12   Othello, Dramatic Overt Op 96   PH 19
                   24   Salome, Tone Poem Op 55   BN 06, 30;   CH 17;
                         CT 17;   DT 19;   NP 08, 24;   SF 14

HADLEY, H.K. (Cont.)
    6   Scherzo Diabolique Op 135   CH 34;   CT 34
   16   Streets of Pekin, Chinese Suite 1932   BN 30;
          CH 30;   CT 30;   DT 31;   RC 31
   11   Symphonia Fantasia Op 46   BN 18;   NA 38;   LA 19;
          NP 16;   SL 09;   SF 18
   30   Symph No 1 Op 25   NP 20
   30   Symph No 2, The 4 Seasons in f Op 30   BN 04;
          CH 01;   NP 01, 19;   SF 11
   30   Symph No 3 in b Op 60   BN 07;   CH 10;   CT 26;
          NS 10;   PH 11
   40   Symph No 4, North, South, East, West in d Op 64
          BN 24;   CH 14;   NP 17;   PH 13;   SF 12;
          SL 17, 20

HAGEMAN, Richard   10   Capansacchi, Opera 1931: Carneval Music   CH 35
1882-   Neth/US   5   -Prelude and Last Scene   LA 44
   55   Crucible, Concert Drama for Soli, Chor and O 1942
          LA 42
    5   In a Nutshell, Overt   LA 44
   10   Miranda   KC 43
    4   Song, At the Well   CT 38;   LA 19;   NP 19;
          PH 40;   SL 42
    4   Song, Do not go, my love   CT 41

HAHN, Aug.   15   Symph for Str O   BN 09
         Fr

HAHN, Reynaldo   4   Merchant of Venice, Opera 1935: Aria   DE 59
1875-1947   Fr   4   Song, If my songs had wings   CL 20;   HN 42;
          SF 44

HAIEFF, Alexei   24   P Conc No 1   BN 52;   DA 55;   SL 58;   UT 68
1914-   Russ/US   12   Divertimento for small O 1944   BN 46;   BU 63;
          DE 54;   UT 69
   21   Symph No 2   BN 57, 58;   CH 58;   NP 63
   22   Symph No 3   BN 61;   BU 61;   SF 63

HAINES, Edmund T.   20   Concertino for 7 Solo Instruments and O   SF 58;
1914-   US   WA 60

HAIRSTON, Jester   6   Negro Spirituals   AT 54
1901-   US

HALÉVY, Jacques F.   4   Jaguarita l'Indienne, Opera 1855: Aria Le grand
1799-1862   Fr   guerrier est fache   CH 22;   PH 22
    4   La Juive, Opera 1835: Aria   LA 64;   NS 13
    4   -Aria, Si la rigueur   CT 20;   DE 49
    4   -Aria, Rachel!   UT 51

HALFFTER-ESCRICHE,   12   Deux Esquisses Symphoniques 1923   PH 32
  Ernesto   20   Rapsodia Portuguesa   P and O   DA 53;   SF 53
  1905-   Sp   35   Sinfonietta in D 1927   BN 28;   CL 29;   DT 28, 37;
          LA 29;   NS 27;   SL 28
    4   Song of the Lamplighter for O   SL 28
   10   Sequences   HN 69
    8   Yes, Speak Out, Yes   MN 68

HALL, Reginald   12   Elegy for O   NP 55
1926-   US

HALLE, Jens   18   Whims of Cupid, Ballet   WA 56
1786-   Dan

HALLÉN, Andreas   12   Rhaps No 1 in F Op 17   CT 01
1846-1925   Swed

HALLSTROEM, Ivar   4   Den bergtagna, The Bewitched One, Opera 1874: Aria
1826-1901   Swed   Spin, Spin   MN 26

HALVORSEN, Johan   2   Boyard's March   CH 1895
1864-1935   Nor   20   Vasantasena, Suite for a Hindu Drama   CT 1899

HAMERIK, Asger   12   Suite No 1 Op 22   CH 1892
1843-1923   Dan   12   Tovelille, Opera, Interlude for O Act II   CT 1896
                         4   La vendetta Opera 1870 Overt   BA 63

HAMM, Chas.   20   Sinfonia for O   CT 53
1925-   US

HAMMERBACHER   6   Phantom Knight, Overt   BA 26

HANDEL,   12   Allegro, Sarabande, Gigue arr Sevitzky   NA 44
   George Frederick   4   Andante from Sonata da Camera in b Op 1 No 9
1685-1759   Brit   arr Ormandy   HN 43;   PH 41
                        15   Conc for Vla and O in b arr Casadesus   AT 49;
                                BA 54, 67;   BN 49;   CH 46;   CT 30;   CL 28;
                                HN 48;   NA 41, 56;   MN 45;   PH 26;   PT 38;
                                SL arr Barbirolli 49;   UT 46, arr Barbirolli 62
                        12   Conc for Oboe in B^b SE 42
                        12   Conc for Oboe No 3 in g   BA 67;   BN 1887, 09, 58;
                                BU 40;   CH 04;   CT 60;   CL 58;   DE 54;
                                DT 45, 55;   HN 58;   LA 49;   SE 36;   PH 31, 43
                        10   Conc for Oboe, Org and Str in E^b NP 14
                        10   Conc for Oboe and Harpsi Op 21   AT 67
                         8   Double Conc for 2 Wind Choirs and Str in F   BN 1891(2),
                                07, 13, 15, 21, 34, 53;   CH 16, 32, 42;   CT 50;
                                CL 45;   NS 07, 17, 20   PH 08, 09, 10, 11
                        12   Conc for 2 Vla and O arr Lorenz from Sonata Op 2
                                No 8   CT 48
                        13   Conc for 2 V, C and Str   NS 14
                        15   Conc for 2 Oboes and Str in F Op 3 No 4a   DA 63;
                                NS 1878
                        18   C Conc Op 101   MN 36;   PT 54
                        14   Conc in g for Org Op 4 No 1   NP 58;   PH 67
                        12   Conc in B^b for Org or Harpsi Op 4 No 2   CH 23;
                                CT 39;   DT 23;   NP 35, 49;   NS 24;   PH 23,
                                49;   WA 2 mvts 66
                        15   Conc in g for Org Op 4 No 3   NP 51
                        17   Conc in F for Org Op 4 No 4   BN 00, 19, 24;   PH 67
                        16   Conc in F arr for Org or Harpsi Op 4 No 3   BN 50;
                                CH 07;   CL 26, 31;   DA 49;   DT 47, 58, 63;
                                NP 58(2),   PH 43, 52, 63;   RC 29

HANDEL, G.F. (Cont.)

14   Conc in B^b arr for Harp Op 4 No 6   CH 65;   DE 66;   DT 56;   HN 48,
        53;   LA 41;   UT 64;   PT 59;   RC 66
16   Conc in d arr for Org or Harpsi Op 7 No 4   BN 42, 49;   CT 37;
        DT 25, 60;   NS 24
8   Conc in D arr Harty   CH 42;   CT 48;   NA 48;   NP 34, 43;   RC 34
14   Conc for Harp unidentified   KC 47;   SL 24, 27
15   Conc for Org unidentified   CH 1897;   UT 48;   SF 49
        Concerti grossi
8   Op 3 No 1 in B^b and g   BN 63;   NP 60;   SF 20
12   Op 3 No 2 in B^b NP 56
12   Op 6 No 1 in G   HN 51;   NS 12
14   No 2 in F   BU 67;   CH 1895, 14, 15, 20, 24, 30, 31, 36
17   No 3 in e   NP 31;   WA 34
17   No 4 in a   AT 67;   LA 52;   MN 49, 58;   NP 47;   NS 26;   SE 34
8   No 5 in D   BN 1890, 19, 22, 24, 27, 33, 54;   CH 38, 54, 59;
           CT 25;   CL 58;   DT 45;   LA 35, 59;   NR 56;   NP 04, 24, 25,
           33;   NS 11;   PH arr Ormandy 27, 40, 42, 44, 47, 49, 51, 55, 61,
           62, 65;   PT 46;   SL 56;   SF 36, 47, 51, 60
20   No 6 in g   BN 1894, 23, 26, 30, 34, 36, 43;   CH 1893, 39, 45, 49,
           52;   CT 12, 21, 59;   CL 40, 57;   HN 54;   LA 40, 57;   NP 31,
           38, 40;   NS 1889, 23;   PH 03, 43;   RC 57, 65;   SL 30, 31, 34;
           SF 52;   WA 33, 49
14   No 7 in B^b BA 62;   BN 1883;   CH 40;   CT 14;   HN 33, 61;
           NP 37, 39, 40;   RC 55;   SL 33;   WA 46
14   –arr Schoenberg for Str Quart   CH 35;   LA 37;   NP 34
13   No 8 in c   MN 51
16   No 9 in F   BN 31, 52, 63;   MN 55
16   No 10 in d   BN 1893, 16, 17, 21, 24, 27, 29, 32, 38, 39, 42, 46,
           51;   CH 1894, 18, 30, 33, 40, 43, 45, 65;   CT 15;   CL 34;
           DA 59;   DT 26, 30, 31, 40, 48, 53;   LA 27, 30, 50;   MN 38,
           43;   NP 24, 29, 32, 38;   PH 32;   PT 61, 63;   SL 29, 40, 48;
           SF 33, 55;   UT 53;   WA 31
5   No 11 in A   BN 56;   CH 63;   MN 67
17   No 12 in b   BN 1884, 04, 26, 28, 30, 33, 39, 41, 43, 47, 57;
           BU 49, 58, 60;   CH 50, 54;   CL 52, 59;   NP 29, 33, 41, 58;
           PH 42;   PT 50;   RC 59;   SL 25, 26;   SF 26;   WA 50
16   No 21 in d   BA 47;   BU 48;   WA 35, 36

14   Conc Grosso in C arr Mottl   CT 35;   DT 32;   LA 25;   NP 13, 21;
        SE 30

8   Fantasia in C arr Cailliet   PH 37
12   Hornpipe, Larghetto, Allegro Molto   CH 1894
7   Introd and Rigaudon arr Harty   PH 47
60   Ode to St. Cecilia's Day, Secular Choral Work   NP 58

8   Overt No 1 in D arr Wüllner   BN 1896, 10;   CH 05, 06, 11, 23, 26,
        28, 38, 54;   DE 49;   NR 58;   NP 36, 38;   RC 35, 36, 44;   SL 35
8   Overt to Occasional Oratorio from Milton's Psalms   BN 38;   CT 01,
        04, 07, 34, 36;   NP 34
6   Overt in d for Org from Chandos Anthems arr Elgar   CT 47;   DA 50;
        DE 51, 55, 58;   DT 37, 45, 46;   HN 60;   KC 45;   ML 66;   MN 32;
        PH 25, 26(2), 28, 29, 32, 35, 37;   PT 37;   RC 33, 41;   WA 34
        –arr Stokowski   HN 56;   PH 39;   PT 51
        –arr Ormandy   PH 41, 45, 53, 57

HANDEL, G.F. (Cont.)

10	Passacaglia in g arr Akon KC 45; SF 44; WA arr Aleinkoff 31, arr Harty 48
6	Prelude and Fugue in d from Concerto Grosso Op 35 arr Kindler UT 56; WA 38, 44, 47, 50
	SONGS
4	Aria, No Oh dio DE 60; PT 59; UT 51
8	Two Arias DE 60; LA 43
4	Aria SF 47
4	But Who may abide WA 67
6	Dank sei dio, Hymn of Praise, Arioso from a Cantata CH 30; CT 40; DE 59; LA 23, 31, 45; MN 33, 35; NP 36; SE 35, 38, 48; WA 33
4	Da quel giorno fatale SE 67
4	Invocation WA 46
4	Recitative and aria from Act II, Siroe NP 39
4	The Seasons, Air NS 1893
4	O Sing unto the Lord a New Song, Anthem CT 67; CL 67
4	Skylark PH 00
8	Songs NS 1894
4	Thus saith the Lord WA 47
6	Te Deum, Dettingen WA 32
4	Tra le fiamme NA 60
14	Suite of Dances from the Opera Alcina 1735 arr Whitaker BA 51; NP arr Wood 37; PH 64; SF 58
6	-Excerpts NP 28, 29
14	Suite Amaryllis arr Beecham CT 43; CL 43; NA 60, 64; PT 59; RC 44; SL 44
11	Suite in e for Clavier arr Skilton CT 43; CL 43; KC 39; PH 45; SE 46
25	Suite from The Faithful Shepherd arr Beecham AT 63; BN 55; CH 58; CT 41; CL 42; DE 64; DT 40; NA 57; LA 40; MN 42; NP 42; PH 43, 58; RC 43, 61; SL 40, 41, 42, 52, 54, 55, 62; SF 40; UT 42; WA arr Kindler 43, 45, 47, 51, Beecham 62
4	-Bourrée NP 27
4	-Musette BN 27, 51; NP 27; PH 27
21	Suite, The Gods Go A-Begging, for Ballet,arr Beecham from Alcina et al NP 31; PH 46
16	Suite, The Great Elopement arr Beecham CH 56; DA 55; DE 49; HN 54; NR 56; PH 55; RC 44; UT 44; WA 49
4	Suite, The Harmonious Blacksmith from Harpsi Suite No 5, E DT 23
12	Suite, Polonaise, Ariette, and Passacaglia arr Harty CL 32; DT 28; ML 63; RC 32; SE 40; WA 39
6	-Ariette and Passacaglia only PH 40, 44
18	Suite, Love in Bath, Ballet arr Beecham CH 59; PT 59; SF 59; SE 59
12	Suite, The Origin of Design, Ballet arr Beecham DT 41; MN 42; PH 41
14	Suite from the Music of the Royal Fireworks arr Harty in D Op 3 No 26 AT 56; BA 65; BN 40, 50; BU 51; CH 31, 35, 64; CT 27, 36, 67; CL 52; DA 69; DE 55; DT 60, 65; LA 46; ML 65; MN 36; NR 59, 64; NP 34; PH 27, 36, 44, 54, 58; PT 51; RC 35, 58; SL 65; SF 27, 54, 60; SE 53; UT 54; WA 50, 53, 58

HANDEL, G.F. (Cont.)   Suite from the Music of the Royal Fireworks (Cont.)
                    -arr Johnson   CT 54, 56
                    -Overt B^b BA 37;   CH 30;   PT arr Wullner 39
16   Suite, The Water Music arr Harty Op 3 No 25   AT 52;   BA 43, 46;
            BN 1885, 87, 00, 26, 49, 51, 57, 61, 65, 67;   BU 61;   CH 27, 28,
            29, 33, 36, 46(2), 47, 48,   arr Ormandy 50;   CT 22, 25, 38, 41,
            42, 47, 49, 51, 53, 57;   CL 26, 30, 33, 36, 41, 50, 67;   DA 51,
            52, 64;   DE 45, 50, 52, 55, 56, 60;   DT 34, 38, 43, 56;   HN 53,
            59, 61;   NA 37, 54, 55, 57, 61, 64, 69;   KC arr Stokowski 40, 51,
            58;   LA 30, 37, 47, 53, 60, 63;   ML 63;   MN 27, 29, 34, 35, 39,
            41, 45, 50;   NR 51, 54, 60;   NP 35, 36, 41, 44, 46, arr Stokowski
            49;   PH 26(2), 31, 34, 37, 40, 43, 50, arr Ormandy 58;   PT 45,
            48, 58, 63;   RC 33, 34, 37, 40, 48, 56;   SL 31, 33, 39, 42, 43,
            47, 48, 53, 58, 66;   SF 37, 50, 52, 53;   SE 27, 33, 34, 43, 51,
            64;   UT 44, 51, 64;   WA 49, 53, 61
4   -Air   AT 55, 59
6   -Allegro and Allegro Deciso   CH 25
8   -Excerpts   HN 38
8   -Overt, Hornpipe, and Allegro   CH 01
6   -Suite No 1   CL 67

        DRAMATIC WORKS
4   Acis and Galatea, Secular Choral Work 1718: Aria   DA 58
4   -As When the Dove, for Sopr   CT 46
4   -Heart, The Seat of Soft Delight   CT 46
4   -O, ruddier than the cherry, air for Bass   CT 97
18   Alceste Secular Choral Work 1751; Enjoy the sweet Elysian Grove,
               Incidental Music   DT 64
4   Admeto, Opera 1727 Aria, A Passing Pleasure   CH 17
5   Agrippina Opera 1709 Overt   CH 62;   CL 58;   DT 47, 61;
               LA 58, 68;   RC 66
4   Amadigi di Gaula, Opera 1715, Aria Ah spietato   CH 18;   MN 37
4   Alessandro, Opera 1726, Aria Calm Thou My Soul   CT 43
4   -Lusinghe piu care, for Sopr   CH 53;   CT 1896, 29;   DT 29
6   Alexander's Feast, Secular Choral Work 1736   DT scene 32;
               NS scene 1880
           L'Allegro, Il Penseroso, ed Il Moderato Ode, Secular Choral Work
4   1741: Air   NS 1891, 20, 22;   PH 02;   SL 13
             -Two Choruses   MN 47
4   -Let Me Wander Orpheus!   NP 35
4   -Sweet Bird   CH 22;   CT 1896, 03, 53, 61;   WA 63
8   Arminio, Opera 1737 Overt   PH 14
4   Atalanta, Opera in Italian 1736: Aria Care selve for Sopr   AT 49,
               52;   CH 18;   CT 31;   DE 48;   SL 18;   SF 42
4   -Say to Irene   BA 67
4   Berenice Opera in Italian 1737: Aria   SL 43
9   -Overt   CH 61;   SL 61;   UT 67
4   -Si, Tra i ceppi   BU 43;   CL 58
4   Belshazzar, Oratorio 1745: Aria of Nitocris   DT 43
4   -Thy God Most High   BA 43;   CT 44
4   Esther, Oratorio 1732 Overt   NP 31
4   Giulio Cesare, Julius Caesar, Opera in Italian 1724: Air   NS 13
               PH 41
4   -Air of Empio   NS 20
4   -Breite aus   RC 59
4   -Piangero la sorte mia   CH 26, 52;   PH 12

HANDEL, G.F. (Cont.)
	Semele, Secular Choral Work 1744 CL 67
4	-Hence Iris, hence away CT 1898
4	-Oh Sleep why dost thou leave me, for Sopr BU 51; CT 29;
	DE 50; DT 29, 45, 52; MN 40; SL 53
4	-Where'er you walk for Tenor AT 50; BA 43; CH 17; CT 31;
	DE 54; HN 43; NA 42; SL 20, 35; SE 35; UT 56
	Solomon, Oratorio 1749 Entrance of the Queen of Sheba CH 53, 56;
	PT 44; SF 56
4	Serse or Xerxes, Opera in Italian 1738: aria DA 58; NS 78, 16;
	WA 52
4	-Frondi tenere e belle CT 51; NA 56
6	-Largo, Ombra mai fu, for Tenor AT 52; CH 16; KC 43, 52;
	SL 17, 55; WA 46
4	-arr for O BA 26(2); BN 1884, 85, 95; CH 1891, 93, 98, 99,
	01(2), 03; CT 43, 51; CL 27; DT 21, 34; HN 31, 36, 39, 43;
	NA 56; MN 22, 31, 35, 37, 41; NP 54, 55; NS 14; RC 28;
	SF 33; UT 57; WA 32, 46
4	Sosarme, Opera 1732 Rend il sereno CH 13
4	Susanna Oratorio 1749, Overt NP 35
6	Teseo, Opera 1713 Overt BN 27; NP 27; PH 27; WA 1896
4	Theodora, Oratorio in English 1750: Defend her, Heaven MN 39
13	-Overt arr Jacob CT 55; RC 56
4	Tolomeo, Opera 1728 Aria PH 23

HANDY, W. C.	5	St. Louis Blues arr M. Gould CT 44; MN 44;
1873- US		PH 36

HANSON, Howard	27	Bold Island Suite CL 61
1896- US	12	-Summer Seascape NA 61; NR 58
	10	Cherubic Hymn, Chor and O Op 37 AT 61
	18	Conc for Org, Str and Harp Op 22 NP 54
	20	P Conc Op 36 BN 48; DA 66; HN 55; RC 49
	18	Conc for Org No 5 Op 27 RC 26, 31
	12	Elegy To Memory of Koussevitzky Op 44 BN 55,
		61; CH 56; DE 56; DT 60; NR 56; UT 56
	10	Exaltation, Symphon Poem with P obligato Op 25
		RC 25
	12	Fantasy Var on a theme of youth RC 51, 52
	3	Fanfare for the Signal Corps CT 42
	20	For the First Time, Suite RC 63
	16	Heroic Elegy, Chor and O Op 28 RC 27
	6	Jubilee Var on theme of Goossens CT 44, 45
	20	Lament for Beowulf Chor and O Op 25 CL 28; RC 27
	15	Lux Aeterna, Symphon Poem, with Vla obligato Op 24
		CL 25; NA 48; LA 24; NS 25; RC 24; SF 28
	10	Mosaics AT 69; CL 57, 58; CT 66; PH 58;
		RC 61
	18	North and West Symphon Poem, Op 22 NS 23; RC 24
	11	Pan and the Priest, Symphon Poem with P obligato
		Op 26 CH 26; MN 27; NP 26; RC 26, 31, 47;
		SL 27
	6	Pastorale for Ob and Str CL 51; MN 53; PH 50;
		RC 50
	12	Song of Democracy Chor and O RC 57; WA 56

HANSON, H. (Cont.)

	12	Song of Human Rights WA 63
	6	Serenade for Fl, Harp and Str Op 35 BA 47; BN 46; CT 62; CL 35, 60; DE 48; PH 47; RC 48; SL 51
	16	Suite from Opera, Merry Mount Op 31 CL 48; DT 36; LA 48; PH 35; RC 36, 46; WA 49
	28	Symph No 1 Nordic in e Op 21 BA 26; BN 28; CH 30; CL 54; NA 47; LA 25; MN 25; RC 23; SL 24; SF 25
	16	-2nd mvt DT 30
	6	-Andante RC 28, 29
	24	Symph No 2, Romantic Op 30 AT 52, 56, 61; BN 40; BU 59; CH 33; CT 30; CL 52; DA 34, 64; DT 30, 68; NA 39; KC 58; NR 58; NP 32, 45; PH 62; RC 30, 56; SL 33; SE 35, 55; WA 40, 50, 66
	36	Symph No 3 Op 33 BN 39(2), 44; BU 47; CT 42; CL 39; DA 66; DE 54, 62; MN 41; RC 57
	20	Symph No 4 Requiem Op 34 BN 43, 45; CT 50; DE 59; DT 45; LA 48; RC 43
	16	Symph No 5 Sinfonia Sacra in one mvt AT 59; CT 59; CL 55; PH 54; RC 55, 66; WA 58, 65
	25	Symph No 6 NP 67; RC 68
	8	Three Songs from Drum Taps, Baritone, Chor and O Op 32 SE 52

d'HARCOURT, Marguerite 1884- Fr	36 8	Symph Neo-Classique in F CH 16 Tasso Overt BN 05

HARKNESS, Rebekah 1915- US	12	Macumba Suite NR 63

HARLINE, Leigh 1907- US	30 20	Centennial Suite UT 46 Civic Center Suite 1941 CL 41; RC 41

HARMATI, Sandor 1892-1936 Hung/US	5	Prelude to a Dance PH 28

HARRIS, Roy 1898- US	9 18 8 11 9 25 20 18 5 6 11 5 6	Acceleration 1941 NA 41; WA 51 American Creed 1940 CH 40; NP 58 American Overt When Johnny Comes Marching Home 1934 CT 38; ML 60; NP 35; SL 47; CH 25 Celebration on Hanson Themes 1946 BN 46 Chorale for Str O Op 3 1933 CH 44; CL 37; LA 32; NP 34 Conc 2 P and O 1946 DE 46 Conc for Amplified P, Brass and Percussion ML 69 Cumberland Conc for O CT 51 Elegy and Paean for Vla and O 1938 HN 48 Evening Piece 1941 DE 45 Farewell to Pioneers 1935 BA 63; PH 35 Folk Rhythms of Today 1942 MN 42; SF 44 Jubilee Var on Goossen's Theme CT 44, 45

HARRIS, R. (Cont.)
                              10   Kentucky Spring 1940   BN 49;   NP 62

	10	Kentucky Spring 1940 BN 49; NP 62
	6	March in Time of War 1943 NP 43
	11	Memories of a Child's Sunday 1945 DA 46; DE 47; NP 45
	10	Ode to Consonance DT 58; NA 57
	5	Overt from Gayety to Sadness LA 32
	14	Prelude and Fugue for Str 1935 PH 35, 59; SL 37; SE 36
	28	Symph No 1 1933 BN 33
	25	Symph No 2 1934 BN 35
	18	Symph No 3 1937 AT 58, 69; BN 38, 39, 41, 48, 59; BU 58; CH 39; CT 41, 55; CL 39, 59; DA 59; DT 44, 55; HN 67; NA 58, 64; KC 51; LA 43, 53, 69(2); MN 62; NP 44, 56; PH 42, 56, 69; PT 50; SL 40, 44, 58; SF 47, 67; UT 48, 61; WA 55, 66
	44	Symph No 4 Folksong with Chor 1939 BN 40; CL 40; NP 42; PT 49, 53
	28	Symph No 5 1942 BN 42; CH 51; SF chorale only 62
	28	Symph No 6, on Gettysburg Address 1944 BN 43
	19	Symph No 7 1951 BN 54; CH 52; NP 61; PH 55; PT 52; SL 54
	22	Symph No 9 PH 62
	30	Symph No 11, Pere Marquette ML 67; NP 67
	20	Symph San Francisco SF 61
	12	Symphon Epigram NP 54
	15	Three Pieces for O PH 41

HARRIS, Victor
1869-1943   US

	4	Night Song CT 1895
	4	Song: A Madrigal CT 1895

HARRISON, Lou
1917-   US

	17	Suite for Str O 1948 DA 60

HARSANYI, Tibor
1898-1954   Hung/Fr

	17	Danses Variées 1951 SL 52
	25	Divertimento No 2 Sérénade for Str O and Trump 1943 SL 47
	12	La Joie de Vivre SL 34
	30	Symph in C BN 52

HART, Fred
1898-   US

	20	Happy Valley, 3 Pastorales for Woodwind Quart and Str O 1945 SF 47

HART, Weldon
1911-1957   US

	25	Symph No 1 1946 CT 47; PT 52

HÄRTEL, A.
             Ger

	5	Chor, Mein, for men's Voices NP 1859

HARTLEY, Walter
1927-   US

	7	Concert Overt WA 55

HARTMANN
fl 1871   US

	4	Song: Swan's Song NS 1886

HARTMANN, Emil   10   Overt The Vikings, a tragedy, Eine nordische
1836-1898   Dan   Heerfahrt a Northern Campaigne in f Op 25
                            BN 1893;   CH 07;   CT 1897, 98

HARTMANN, Karl A.   35   Symph No 3   SF 59
1905-   Ger   35   Symph No 4 for Str O   BA 58
                     17   Symph No 5 Symph Concertante for Winds, Perc, C
                            and Double Bass   MN 63
                     26   Symph No 6 for O   BN 61;   PH 58

de HARTMANN, Thomas A. 26   C Conc Op 57   BN 37
1886-1956   Russ/Fr 10   Dances from Esther, Opera Op 76   DA 54;   HN 55

HARTY, Sir Hamilton   27   An Irish Symphony 1925   RC 34
1879-1941   Ir   18   John Field Suite   BA 40
                     18   With the Wild Geese, Symphon Poem 1910   CL 32;
                            RC 33

HARVEY, Vivien   8   A Box of Toys   RC 38
             US

HATTON, Gaylen   10   Music for O   UT 57
1928-   US

HAUBIEL, Charles   15   Rittrati 3 Portraits   CH 35
1892-   US

HAUFF, Wilhelm   20   Symph No 2   UT 67
             Ger

HAUG, Hans   11   Passacaglia from Michelangelo, Oratorio 1937
1900-   Swiss   PH 51

HAUSEGGER, Siegmund   50   Barbarossa, Symphon Poem 1900   BN 01;   CH 02;
von   NP 01
1872-1948   Aust   30   Symphon Var on Nursery Song, Aufklaenge 1919
                            DT 30;   PH 30
                     12   Symphon Poem, Wieland der Schmidt 1904   PH 13

HAUSSERMANN,   20   Conc for Voice and O Op 25   BU 44;   CT 41;
John, Jr.   PH 45
1909-   US   15   Eclogue Romanesque   CT 58
                     12   Rondo Carnavalesque   CT 44
                     30   Symph No 1, Op 16   CT 40
                     25   Symph No 2, Op 22   CT 43
                     25   Symph No 3   CT 48

HAVELKA, Svatopluk   10   Pena   KC 68
c1925-   Czech

HAYDN, Franz Joseph   CONCERTOS
1732-1809   Aust   25   Cello in D Op 101
                            AT 46;   BA 42, 45, 62;   BN 1890, 00, 13, 14, 20,
                            25, 31, 35, 39, 42, 45, 49, 51;   BU 41, 49, 68;
                            CH 00, 03, 08, 14, 15, 20, 26, 35, 36, 40, 45, 52,
                            69;   CL 24, 26, 30, 37, 45, 52;   DA 68;

HAYDN, F.J. (Cont.) CONCERTOS, Cello in D Op 101 (Cont.)
        DE 46, 62, 64;   DT 32, 34, 37, 39, 43, 48, 65;   HN 34, 53;
        NA 36, 41, 43, 49;   KC 36, 43, 56;   LA 20, 30, 35, 37, 51, 57,
        59, 63;   MN 40, 68;   NR 57;   NP 15, 24, 34, 36, 44, 51, 54,
        62, 69;   NS 09, 19, 25;   PH 27, 34, 36, 41, 60, 64;   PT 38,
        42, 47, 55, 61;   RC 36, 46;   SL 11, 16, 22, 34, 39, 42, 46, 60,
        67;   SF 22, 28, 67;   SE 45, 49, 57, 68;   UT 48;   WA 41, 64

25   Cello in C
        BA 68;   BN 65;   CH 64;   PH 25;   LA 66;   PT 68;   SL 68;   SF 69
20   Flute in D   PT 61
13   Harpsichord in D Op 21   BA 26;   NP 25, 44;   NS 26;   SF 24, 57;
        UT 45
21   Oboe in C   BU 62;   HN 61
21   P in D Op 42   BU 68;   CH 30, 31;   LA 48, 64;   MN 45;   SL 34,
        40, 60;   WA 54
14   Trumpet in E^b DT 46, 67;   NR 62;   PH 67;   PT 61, 67;   SF 66;
        SE 61
18   Violin No 1 in C   CH 52;   CL 54;   DE 49;   NS 09, 20;   PT 54;
        RC 54;   SE 40;   WA 54
22   Symph Concertante for V, Oboe, C and Bassoon in B^b Op 84
        BA 65;   BN 50, 68;   BU 67;   CH 31, 59, 66;   CT 61;   CL 36,
        67;   DE 55;   DT 60;   HN 60;   NA 58;   LA 57;   MN 30, 37, 45,
        54;   NP 31, 36, 50, 58;   PT 54, 60, 66;   RC 29, 51, 60;
        SL 52, 59, 63, 67;   SF 27, 66
15   V, P and Str in F   CT 57;   NA 51
18   V in g   DT 69
100   The Creation, Oratorio, complete   BN 67;   CT 69;   CL 58;   LA 59;
        NP 57, 65;   SL 60;   SF 65;   SE 60;   UT 55
4   -Air   NS 1897
6   -The Heavens are telling   NA 32
4   -On Mighty pens Auf starken Fittige   NP 1856, 75
4   -In native worth   NP 21
4   -Recitative and Aria   SL 43
6   -Rolling in foaming billows Rollend in Schaumenden Wellen   CH 1897;
        NP 1887, 93
6   -With verdure clad   AT 58;   CH 52, 54;   CT 1895, 02, 52, 69;
        DE 60;   DT 54;   NP 1871, 06;   NS 1882(2)

12   Divertimento in B^b LA 48;   PT 60

15   Fantasia in C arr Kephal   LA 53

8   Grand March for Royal Society of Musicians   BN 65;   RC 69
      MASSES
45   in d Lord Nelson   CL 63, 69
50   in B^b, Schöpfungsmesse, The Creation Mass   BN 66
5   -Kyrie   NA 32
25   Pauken Messe, Mass in Time of War in C 1796   CL 67

5   Orfeo and Eurydice, Opera 1791: Overt   HN 51
        -Reudele o questo, cara speme: HN 49;   KC 46;   WA 47
        -Recitative and Aria   WA 52

HAYDN, F.J. (Cont.)
OVERTURES
6   Armida B^b No 14   LA 44, 52
6   L'isola dishabitata in g No 13   BN 49;   NA 40, 41, 44, 68
5   Manx Overt arr Wood   AT 47
5   Overt to an English Opera in C probably Overt for Covent Garden
       NP 53
QUARTETS arr for O
20   Unidentified   NS 1891
20   in G Op 3 No 3   CT 58
8   in D, Emperor No 42 Var Op 33, No 6   NA 32, 35;   SF 61
7   No 50 Op 51 No 1 Largo   NA 34
6   No 68 Op 64 No 6 Andante Cantabile NA 31, 32(2);   PH 24
6   in C Op 76 No 3: 2nd mvt   CT 20
6   -Theme and var   CH 01, 03, 16, 33
6   in D Op 76 No 5   2nd mvt   CT 18
6   -Largo   NA 53

96   The Seasons, Die Jahreszeiten, Oratorio, complete   BN 64;   CH 64;
       CL 65;   NP 64
4   -At Last the Beauteous Sun   CT 08
20   -Excerpts   NA 32
6   -Oh How Pleasing to the Senses, Welche Labung fur die sinne
       AT 58;   CH 53
4   -Simon's Aria   DT 59
4   -Summer   WA 54

6   Serenade for Str   BA 42, 50

60   The Seven Words of Jesus, Die Sieben Worte
5   Es ist vollbracht, It is Finished No 6   CT 51
5   Vater in Deine Hande   No 7   CT 51
5   Das Erd beben   CT 51
5   Elegy   PT 45, 65

SONGS and ARIAS
4   Al Tuo seno fortunato   UT 67
4   Aria   NP 1872
From Twelve English Canzonettas
4   No 31 Sailor's Song   NA 61
4   No 34 She Never Told Her Love   NA 61;   NP 1846;   WA 46
4   No 33 Sympathy, Canzonetta   NP 1841
9   Te Deum for Chor and O   BN 63
8   The Tempest for Chor and O   NP 1876
8   Var on Austrian National Hymn   BN 1884, 88

HAYDN, F.J.
SYMPHONIES

8	No 1 in D 1759 BN 1898, 02, 17, 31; SL 65
12	No 4 in D DT 32, 39
30	No 7 Le Midi BU 44; CH 18, 34; HN 32; NA 65; NS 26; PH 49, 65; SL 62; SE 60, 62
15	No 8 in G La Tempete CL 62; NS 78, 82, 88
9	No 12 in E DT 68
20	No 21 in A BN 64
20	No 22 in E^b The Philosopher BU 65; CT 40; NA 48; LA 62; NP 61; PT 60
15	No 24 in D BN 67; MN 24
14	No 26 in d Lamentations BA 40; DE 51; NA 46; SL 65
20	No 31 in D Horn Signal BN 29(2), 33, 66, 69; CH 66; CT 34, 48; CL 28, 30, 53, 64; KC 50; LA 52; ML 66; MN 50; NS 16; PH 39, 45; PT 45
15	No 39 in g BN 63; SL 64
15	No 44 in e Mourning CT 61; CL 60; MN 66; RC 63
30	No 45 in f# Farewell BA 51; CT 29; CL 35, 64; KC 59; NS 06; PH 25, 54; SL 67; SF 59, 62; DT 69; NR 68
20	No 46 in B WA 39
15	No 48 in C Maria Theresa CT 43; MN 51; NP 68
26	No 49 in f La Passione BA 40; CH 31; DA 50; KC 42; NR 63; NP 64; PT 62
19	No 52 in c AT 68; BN 62; CL 62
17	No 53 in D Imperiale AT 52, 63; BN 54; NA 51, 62; WA allegro only 35
15	No 55 in E^b Schoolmaster CT 43; NP 66; PT 66
22	No 57 in D CT 64; HN 52
17	No 60 in C Il distralto CH 65
20	No 61 in D DT 69
16	No 64 in A NP 33
27	No 67 in F CH 68; PH 64, 66
25	No 73 in D, La Chase DT 51; NA 42, 44, 46, 49; MN 42; PT 62
25	No 75 in D SF 68
24	No 77 in B^b AT 60
26	No 79 in F BN 67
17	No 80 in d BN 43; NA 45; MN 40; NP 51, 53
17	No 82 in C L'Ours, The Bear BN 32; CH 50; CT 36; DA 66; HN 67; ML 65; MN 25; NR 61, 64; NP 61; SL 38, 53; WA 40
18	No 83 in c La Poule, The Hen CH 68; CT 35; HN 67; ML 64, 69; NP 1860, 68, 1961; LA 69
17	No 84 in E^b NP 65
20	No 85 in B^b La Reine, The Queen BN 19(2); CH 09; CT 35, 44; CL 37, 66; DE 67; HN 52, 68; NA 56, 69; ML 68; MN 50; 58; NP 60; NS 06; PH 03; PT 58; RC 58; SL 22, 58; SF 40, 46, 56, 62; SE 53
16	No 86 in D BA 63; BN 02, 30, 38, 45; CH 48, 51; CT 51, 58, 64, 69; CL 52; DA 54; DE 69; MN 27, 31, 42, 57, 64; NP 56, 66; NS 24; PH 54; PT 65; RC 61, 65; SL 25, 43; SF 66, 69
29	No 87 in A CL 67; DA 69; NP 66, 68; WA 51
22	No 88 in G AT 50; BA 52, 54, 56, 63, 67; BN 1889, 91, 94, 97, 06, 10, 12, 14, 19, 24, 27, 34, 37, 40, 43, 60; BU 40, 53, 61; CH 1891, 97, 04, 06, 32, 40, 48, 59, 64; CT 07, 42, 48, 50, 51,

HAYDN, F.J. (Cont.)   Symphony No 88 in G (Cont.)
        54, 57;   CL 30, 34, 42, 48, 51, 52, 54, 58, 64;   DA 49, 56;
        DE 52, 55, 58, 65;   DT 15, 18, 28, 31, 35, 36, 38, 53, 62, 64;
        HN 14, 46, 47, 49, 55, 57, 58, 60, 69;   KC 43, 54;   NA 32(2),
        47, 59;   LA 26, 29, 34, 45, 55, 58, 69(2);   MN 44, 67;   NR 50,
        58, 62, 69;   NS 23, 25;   NP 1871, 01, 08, 22, 25, 27, 29, 33,
        35, 43, 46, 52, 53, 54, 55, 58, 62;   PH 07, 14, 16, 19, 21, 24,
        28, 31, 35, 42, 44, 47, 56;   PT 43, 49, 57;   RC 44, 50, 57, 69;
        SL 11, 29, 31, 34, 39, 41, 44, 46, 59;   SF 15, 28, 37, 49, 52,
        55, 61, 62;   SE 30, 45, 54;   UT 47, 58, 64;   WA 36, 53, 62

20   No 89 in F   NP 68
16   No 90 in C   CH 58;   CL 67;   HN 64;   RC 68
15   No 91 in E^b CH 68;   CT 68;   NP 68
27   No 92 in G Oxford   AT 67;   BA 69;   BN 45, 57, 64;   BU 56, 62;
        CH 1898, 07, 13, 22, 26, 29, 32, 34, 35, 46(2), 48, 56, 61, 68;
        CT 41, 45;   CL 27, 46, 48, 61, 66;   DA 62;   DT 56, 66;   HN 50,
        52, 64;   LA 20, 40, 69;   ML 63;   MN 23, 40, 62;   NR 65;
        NP 1872, 16, 37, 40, 41, 46, 47, 50, 52, 65;   PH 45, 64;   PT 55,
        61, 65;   RC 28, 58;   SL 18, 19, 33, 51, 52, 56, 60;   SF 54, 57,
        59, 61, 62, 67;   UT 51, 67
21   No 93 in D   BN 00, 52, 66;   CH 52;   CT 16, 37, 65;   CL 53, 58,
        66, 67;   DA 62;   LA 38;   MN 31;   NR 61;   NP 54, 63;   PH 41,
        57;   PT 50;   RC 43, 63;   SF 50, 53;   SE 43, 66;   UT 44;
        WA 60
20   No 94 Surprise   AT 64;   BA 66;   BN 1895, 00, 07, 12, 14, 17, 22,
        25, 28, 31, 36, 45, 55, 61, 69;   BU 49, 52;   CH 29, 39, 54, 55,
        66;   CT 26, 49, 52;   CL 52, 66;   DA 65;   DT 31, 41, 61, 63;
        KC 44, 56;   NA 30, 33;   HN 16, 69;   LA 56;   MN 22, 33, 55, 62;
        NR 55, 57;   NP 1850, 89, 12, 19, 30, 63, 68;   NS 03, 11, 15;
        PH 26, 34, 37, 48, 59, 67;   PT 47, 51, 56, 57, 59;   RC 27, 34,
        36, 52, 54, 62;   SL 21, 55, 69;   SF 24, 53, 59, 64;   UT 49, 65;
        WA 67
        -Minuet and Finale   MN 49
20   No 95 in c   BN 1888, 92, 96, 03, 16, 42, 45, 47, 51, 59;   CH 30,
        53, 57, 61;   CT 1899, 04, 25, 53;   CL 45, 68;   DA 60;   DE 63;
        MN 30, 58;   NA 37, 53;   LA 67, 69(2);   NP 1874, 06, 11, 14, 36,
        39;   NS 25;   PH 05, 23, 29, 31, 66, 67;   PT 39, 44, 50, 64;
        RC 62;   SF 66
26   No 96 in D   BN 62, 67;   CH 60;   CT 62;   CL 61, 68;   DA 67;
        DT 35, 55, 60, 65;   KC 52, 59, 63;   LA 55, 64, 69(2);   ML 67;
        MN 49, 64;   NP 54, 56;   PH 53, 55, 61;   PT 68;   SF 54, 57;
        WA 54
30   No 97 in C   AT 61;   BA 56;   BN 1882, 87, 01, 03, 23, 44, 63;
        CH 47, 51, 56, 62;   CT 1897, 00, 05, 23, 58;   CL 43, 47, 49,
        54, 57, 69;   DT 25, 26, 30;   LA 33;   MN 34, 49;   NR 56;
        NP 28, 36, 44;   NS 27;   PH 27, 28, 38, 52;   PT 41, 56, 62;
        RC 56;   SL 30;   SF 40;   SE 42;   WA 43, 52
25   No 98 in B^b and b^b BN 05, 60, 69;   BU 66;   CH 02, 05, 08, 14,
        37, 43, 49;   CT 14, 27, 35, 55;   CL 69;   DA 53;   DT 29;
        KC 45;   HN 49, 54, 61;   LA 37, 61;   MN 53;   NP 1879, 31;
        PH 27;   PT 62, 63;   SF 68;   WA 47, 59
16   No 99 in E^b AT 62;   BA 54;   BN 85, 26, 32, 35, 37, 48, 59;
        BU 47;   CH 03, 45, 58, 64;   CT 03, 15, 33, 59;   CL 48, 57,
        65;   HN 58;   KC 65;   LA 68;   MN 56, 64;   NA 63;   NR 65;
        NP 1863, 75, 85, 29, 31, 42, 57, 64;   PH 41, 64, 65;   PT 52;
        RC 48;   SL 63, 68;   SF 48, 59, 66;   SE 41;   UT 48;   WA 64

Time in
Minutes
HAYDN, F. J. (Cont.) SYMPHONIES (Cont.)

25   No 100 in G Military   BA 64;   BN 83, 86, 99, 20, 53, 59;   CH 39,
        47, 58, 67;   CT 09, 12, 31, 42;   CL 32, 37;   DA 63;   DE 53, 64;
        DT 26, 58;   MN 54, 62;   LA 19, 65;   MN 42;   NP 13, 21, 42, 52,
        56;   NR 66;   NS 12, 14, 25;   PH 13, 32, 41, 44, 53, 58, 60, 64;
        PT 40, 61, 66;   RC 24, 41, 54, 69;   SL 13;   SF 19, 57, 60;
        SE 45, 63;   UT 57;   WA 57

25   No 101 in d and D The Clock   AT 63;   BA 43, 53, 55;   BN 1894,
        48, 53, 57, 65;   BU 61;   CH 36, 41, 58, 62, 65;   CT 16, 28,
        30, 32, 41;   CL 39, 64;   DE 55, 60, 62;   DT 30, 57, 66;   HN 54;
        NA 36, 61;   KC 37;   LA 31, 35;   MN 31, 35, 39, 59, 65;   NR 51,
        59;   NP 25, 28, 35, 49, 69;   NS 13, 17, 20;   PH 29, 32, 40, 47,
        58, 61;   PT 50, 60;   RC 37, 59;   SF 55;   SE 69;   UT 44, 53;
        WA 34, 50, 65

30   No 102 in B♭   BA 65;   BN 1881, 84, 92, 94, 08, 13, 22, 30, 36, 38,
        41, 55, 57, 66;   BU 48, 63;   CH 1894, 50, 55, 60, 66;   CT 1896,
        02, 12, 22, 39, 50, 68;   CL 39, 41, 50, 60;   DA 48, 52, 55;
        DT 23, 27, 33;   HN 48;   KC 46;   LA 41, 48, 69(2);   MN 22, 55,
        62;   NR 54;   NP 23, 31, 42, 52, 56, 59, 62;   NS 23;   PH 29,
        43, 46, 55, 65, 69;   PT 42, 54, 60, 62, 65;   RC 13, 22, 24, 35,
        44, 46, 51, 56;   SL 68;   SF 52, 56, 67;   SE 36, 52, 59, 67;
        UT 56;   WA 58, 59

26   No 103 in E♭ Drum Roll   BN 1891, 04, 10, 15, 21, 30, 32, 35, 37, 50;
        BU 50;   CH 01, 42, 56, 66;   CT 40, 63, 67;   CL 31;   DA 55, 68;
        DE 47;   DT 19, 67;   NA 57, 66;   LA 51, 69;   MN 44;   NP 1864,
        76, 82, 27, 30, 34, 55, 69;   PH 17, 31;   PT 53, 63, 67;   RC 49;
        SL 35, 59;   SF 51, 53;   SE 61;   UT 50, 68;   WA 51

7   -1st mvt   MN 43

38   No 104 in D and d London Toy Symphony   BA 50, 51, 55, 57, 61;
        BN 1884, 88, 90, 93, 96, 01, 05, 06, 10, 15, 21, 31, 37, 41, 49,
        54, 58;   BU 64;   CH 1896, 38, 43, 57, 61, 63, 67;   CT 1896, 01,
        11, 13, 32, 47, 56;   CL 20, 33, 43, 51, 53, 60, 68;   DA 46, 69;
        DE 50, 68;   DT 21(2), 25, 43, 52, 64;   HN 13, 38, 45, 60, 62;
        NA 40, 61;   LA 40, 44, 46, 51, 60, 69(2);   MN 37, 46;   NR 51,
        60, 68;   NP 1854, 81, 11, 28, 35, 37, 39, 51(2), 57;   NS 24;
        PH 08, 10, 12, 15, 22, 28, 30, 55;   PT 46, 55;   RC 26, 45, 50,
        52;   SL 23, 36, 43, 57, 60, 66;   SF 12, 52, 62;   SE 34;
        UT 54, 66;   WA 49, 61, 69

      Unidentified Symphonies
20   in C   BN 1889, 97
20   in G   BN 1886, 99, 04, 09
20   in A   CH 31

HAYDN, Michael   4   Carol, Silent Night   DA 49
1737-1806   Aust

HAYNES, Walter B.   4   Song, Weep ye no more   NS 1893
1859-1900   Brit

HAZELMAN, Herbert   8   Moronique Danse   WA 32
1913-   US

HEAD, Michael   4   Song, When I think upon the Maidens 1918   DA 34
1900-   Brit

HECKSCHER, Céleste   20   5 Dances of the Pyrenies   PH 10
Mrs.
1860-1928   US

HEFTI, J.C.   12   Mystic Pool   PH 37
1914-   US

HEIDEN, Bernard   12   Euphorion, Scene for O   CH 55;   DT 56;   NP 56;
1910-   Ger/US   PT 53
                          8   Envoy for O   NA 65, 66, 67, 68
                         10   Prelude for O 1935   DT 38
                         24   Symph No 2   NA 57

HEIDER, Werner   8   Divertimento   CT 60
1928-   Ger

HEINEFETTER   5   Overt Macbeth in C Op 13   NP 1871
               Ger

HEINEMYER, Ernest W.   10   Var for Fl   NP 1850
1827-1869   Ger

HELFER, Walter   8   Overt In Modo Giocoso   CH 43
1896-   US

HELLER, James G.   20   Four Sketches for O   CT 45
1892-   US   15   Little Symph for small O   CT 40
                         12   Pastorale and Scherzo   KC 37
                               Rhaps for O   CT 49

HELLER, Stephen   10   Promenades d'un solitaire Op 80 No 2   NP 1862
1814-1888   Hung/Fr   10   Phantasie on Halevy's Opera Charles VI Op 37
                               NP 1845

HELLMESBERGER, Joseph   6   Ball Scene   PH 56
1855-1906   Austr   5   Valse   HN 15

HELM, Everett   8   Ballad on the Times of Man Chor and O 1943   CT 43
1913-   US   14   Conc for 5 Solo Instruments   KC 59;   MN 62
                         24   P Conc No 1 in G   NP 53
                         14   Divertimento for Str O   MN 57
                         23   Symph for Str O   SF 60
                         12   Three Gospel Hymns 1942   CL 55

HELPS, Robert   8   Saccade   SF 67
c 1920   US

HELY-HUTCHINSON,   8   3 Fugal Fancies   SE 34
  Christian
1901-1947   Brit

HEMMER, Eugene   8   Fountain Square, from Cincinnati Profiles Suite
1929-   US   for O:4th mvt   CT 52

HENDL, Walter   10   Conc for Toys and O   DA 49
1917-   US   5   Cotton Bowl March   DA 49
                          3   Fanfare for Peace   DA 57
                          5   Song and Dance   DA 49
                          5   The Little Brass Band   DA 49

HENIOT, Hans 1902- Ger	8	A Mountain Legend for O CT 29; DT 29

HENKEMANS, Hans 1913- Neth	10	Barcarolle Fantastica LA 66

HENSCHEL, Sir George   15   P Conc in E^b BN 1882
1850-1934   Ger/Eng   4   Morgen-Hymne for Chor and O Op 46 No 4   WA 38
                          6   Serenade, Canon for Str in D Op 23   BN 1883
                          6   Songs   NS 1883
                         10   Suite from Incidental Music to Hamlet Op 50
                                   BN 1891
                          5   Te Deum, Soli, Chor and O Op 52   BN 1882
                          8   Ballad in f# for V Op 39   BN 1883

HENSELT, Adolf von   38   P Conc in f Op 16   BN 1881, 84, 86, 97, 03;
1814-1889   Ger   CH 04;   NP 1857-58, 72, 81, 88;   NS 1887;
                                   PH 04, 06
                          15   Var de concert on Le Philtre Op 1   NP 1862

HENZE, Hans Werner   8   Ariosi   DT 68
1926-   Ger   16   Being Beauteous   SF 66
                      20   P Conc No 2   CH 68
                      15   Conc for Double Bass   CH 67
                      15   Double Conc for Harp and Ob   RC 67
                      15   Five Neapolitan Songs   CH 60, 65
                      12   Musen Siziliens   CH 67
                       9   Quattro Poemi   CL 66
                      25   Symph No 1   PT 68
                      23   Symph No 2   PH 61;   SF 60, 62;   LA 69
                      25   Symph No 3   CH 63;   PH 68;   UT 69
                      18   Symph No 5   DA 67;   NP 62;   SL 69;   KC 68
                      21   Suite No 2 from Undine, Ballet   CH 68;   CL 68;
                               PH 64;   SF 67
                      13   -Three Pas de Tritons   KC 59
                      12   Telemanniana   CH 68;   DT 68;   KC 68;   SL 69

HERBECK, Johann   10   Dance mvts for O;Tanz-Momente   BN 1884
1831-1877   Aust

HERBERT, Victor   8   American Fantasy   CL 28;   UT 57
1859-1924   Ir/US   25   C Conc No 2 in e Op 30   CH 10;   CT 03;   DA 56;
                               NP 1893, 06;   PH 05, 44;   SL Andante, Serenade,
                               Tarantelle 19;   NS 86
                      12   Hero and Leander Tone Poem Op 33   DT 20;   NP 03
                      10   Irish Rhapsodie   CH 17, 18, 24;   CT 17;   DA 30;
                               PH 23;   RC 34;   SF 12
                       4   Mdme. Modiste, Operetta: Aria Kiss Me Again   HN 51
                       4   Natoma, Opera 1911: Aria I list the trill   DE 48
                       4   -Prelude Act III   BA 39;   CH 13;   PH 11, 19;
                               SL 11
                      20   Serenade for Strings 1888   CT 95
                      15   Suite Romantique, Op 31   CT 02;   NP 05
                       6   Suite for C 1886: Andante, Serenade, Tarantelle
                               NS 86
                       8   Woodland Fancies Op 34   CH 18;   CT 17;   NP 20

HERDER, Pablo   20   Mvts for O   BA 66
            US

HERMANN, Hans   4   Die Wand'rer Song with O arr Saar   CT 14, 20
1870-1931   Ger   4   Salome, Song with O arr Saar   CT 14

HERRMANN, Bernard   20   The Devil and Daniel Webster, Suite, concert
1911-   US   version 1944   NP 48;   PH 43
                         8   For the Fallen, Berceuse 1943   BU 43;   HN 61;
                                   NP 43;   WA 53
                        45   Moby Dick, Cantata, for Soli, male Chor and O
                                   1937   NP 39
                        40   Symph No 1   NP 42
                               -Scherzo   BA 39
                        18   Welles Raises Kane divertissement for O from
                                   Film Music for Citizen Kane 1944   DA 46;   SL 45

HERNANDEZ, Pablo   5   Serenata Regionale   HN 43
1834-1910   Sp

HÉROLD, Louis Joseph   16   Pas de deux from La Fille mal Gardée, Ballet 1828
1791-1833   Fr   arr Lanchbery   AT 59;   NR 58
                         4   Le Pré aux Clercs, Opera 1832, Aria   NP 1874
                         8   Zampa, Opera 1831, Overt   BN 1881;   NP 1843

HEUBERGER, Richard F.   8   Overt Cain   BN 1886
1850-1914   Aust   30   Var on Schubert Theme   BN 1890

HIER, Ethel Glenn   7   The Bells of Asolo, Tone-Picture 1938   CT 44
1889-   US

HIJMAN, Julius   8   March and Tarantelle   HN 42
1901-   US

HILDACH, Eugen   4   Song, Will Niemond   NS 04
1849-1924   Ger

HILL, Alfred   5   Waiati Poi arr Verbrugghen Maori Song-dance   MN 28
1870-   Austr

HILL, Edward B.   15   American Ode   BN 30
1872-1959   US   12   Concertina for P and O 1931   BN 33
                        25   V Conc Op 38   BN 38;   WA 39
                        10   Fall of the House of Usher   BN 20
                        19   Lilacs, Poem for O 1926   BN 26, 29, 35, 41;
                                   CH 39;   CL 31, 45;   SL 33
                         8   Music for Eng Horn and O Op 50   BN 44, 48
                         8   Parting of Lancelot and Guinevere, Symphon Poem
                                   BN 15;   SL 15
                        12   Scherzo for 2 P and O   BN 24;   PH 24
                        15   Sinfonetta for Str Op 37   BN 32
                        15   Sinfonetta for Str Op 40a   BN 35;   CL 36;   SL 39
                        16   Sinfonetta for Str Op 46   BN 39;   PH 39
                        15   Stevensoniana Suite No 1 Op 24   BN 18;   CH 20;
                                   CT 18;   NS 17;   PH 19;   SL 19

HILL, E.B. (Cont.)
    11   Stevensoniana Suite No 2 Op 29   BN 23;   LA 28;
          PT 41
    18   Symph No 1 in B^b Op 34   BN 27, 28, 34, 42;
          CH 31;   LA 38
    24   Symph No 2 in C Op 41   BN 30
    28   Symph No 3 in G   BN 37;   CL 38
     8   Waltzes for O   BN 21

HILLER, Ferd.   8   Concert Overt   NP 1846
  1811-1885   Ger   20   P Conc in f#   BN 1883;   NP 1863
                      4   Song, Ein Traum in der christnacht   NP 1862
                      4   Song, Prayer   NP 1872
                      4   Song, The Sentinel   BN 1881, 82
                     30   Symph in E   NP 1857

HINDEMITH, Paul   15   Chamber Music No 1 for small O Op 24 No 1   CH 37
  1895-1963 Ger/US 20   Chamber Music No 2 P and O Op 36 No 7   CH 25;
                          NS 25
                     16   Chamber Music No 3, C and small O Op 36 No 2
                          BU 64;   CH 27;   MN 51, 62
                     23   Chamber Music No 4 V and O Op 36 No 3   CL 54;
                          RC 51
                     17   Chamber Music No 5 for Vla and large Chamber O
                          Op 36 No 4   BN 37;   MN 64
                     18   Concert Music for Str and Brass Op 50   BA 67;
                          BN 30, 31, 37, 40, 45, 59, 65;   CH 62, 65, 69;
                          CT 62;   CL 49, 61;   DA 69;   NA 55, 60;
                          LA 49, 69;   MN 45, 64;   NP 47, 55, 60, 68;
                          NS 26;   PH 49, 53;   PT 55;   SF 38
                     15   Concert Music for Wind O Op 41   CT 29
                     28   C Conc 1940   BN 40;   CH 41, 57, 67;   NA 52, 59;
                          MN 52;   NP 52, 57, 59;   PH 42;   PT 63;   SL 66
                     17   Conc for O Op 38   BN 25, 28;   CH 58;   CT 28;
                          CL 51;   DT 67;   NA 26, 60;   NP 60;   PH 27,
                          57;   SL 29, 30;   SE 64;   MN 66
                     30   P Conc 1924 Op 29   CL 46;   PH 26, 32
                     26   V Conc Op 14   BN 39, 46, 63;   CT 40, 66;   CL 40,
                          62;   DA 52, 63;   NA 63, 67;   LA 48, 66;
                          NP 63;   PT 54, 58, 63, 66;   CH 48, 57, 66
                     25   Conc for Org and O Op 46 No 2   BN 52;   NA 62;
                          NP 62
                     24   Conc for Woodwinds, Harp and O   BN 65;   CL 60;
                          NA 50
                     21   Conc for Cl and O   RC 68
                     16   Conc for Trump, Bassoon and Str   MN 68
                      6   Cupid and Psyche, Ballet, Overt 1944   CL 67;
                          DA 49;   DE 49, 50;   DT 69;   NA 61;   LA 44
                          PH 43, 50;   WA 44
                     28   The Four Temperaments, Theme and Var   BN 44;
                          BU 65;   CH 50;   CT 64;   CL 63;   DT 45, 62;
                          PH 64;   PT 47, 66;   SL 49
                     22   Heriodiade, for small O 1944   MN 56;   SL 66;
                          WA 66
                     14   Das Marienleben Song cycle for Sopr and O   BN 56;
                          CH 54

HINDEMITH, P. (Cont.)

26   Mathis der Maler, Symph fr the Opera 1934
    AT 64;   BA 62, 67;   BN 34, 36, 39, 43, 47, 51,
    56, 58, 65;   BU 41, 44, 49, 61;   CH 35, 36, 44,
    49, 52, 56, 60, 63, 67;   CT 34, 52, 57, 63, 67;
    CL 35, 41, 48, 54, 56, 59, 64;   DA 49, 54, 61, 68;
    DE 55, 69;   DT 45, 56, 63;   HN 50, 52, 55;
    NA 34, 41, 44, 51, 55, 56, 61, 64;   KC 40;
    LA 34, 47, 55, 58, 62, 67, 68;   ML 65;   MN 38,
    41, 54, 59, 63, 67;   NR 52;   NP 34, 41, 44, 51,
    55, 56, 61, 64, 67;   PH 34, 40, 42, 48, 49, 51,
    54, 56, 59, 61, 64, 65, 66, 69;   PT 46, 50, 52,
    56, 60, 62, 66;   RC 41, 50, 59, 65;   SL 42, 56,
    61, 62, 66;   SF 48, 50, 60, 64, 68;   SE 60, 68;
    UT 50, 57, 64;   WA 49, 53, 54, 57, 59, 62, 69

12   -3 Duets from Opera   NA 59;   NP 59

19   -Entombment   BU 63

9   -1st mvt   CT 49

8   News of the Day, Overt from the Opera 1929
    BA 53;   CH 30, 41, 43, 64;   CT 30;   DA 38;
    HN 52, 63;   NA 30;   MN 43;   NP 30, 48;   PT 41,
    50, 60;   SL 32, 36, 52, 68;   SF 35, 47

20   Nobilissima Visone from St. Francis Ballet Suite
    1938   AT 67;   BN 42, 51, 58, 62;   CH 55, 64,
    passacaglia only 42, 67;   CT 61;   CL 63;   DA 55,
    64;   DT 61;   HN 48, 59;   LA 38, 63;   MN 61,
    complete St. Francis Ballet 38;   NR 63, 68;
    PH 38, 46, 50, 56, 66;   PT 67;   RC 49;   SL 47,
    67;   SF 54;   UT 60

8   Nusch-Noschi, Dances from Marionette Opera Op 20
    CH 33;   CT 31;   NS 25;   PH 24;   RC 32

21   Philharmonic Concerto, Var for O 1932   BN 58;
    CH 60;   CT 58;   DA 59;   DT 65;   NA 48, 56;
    NP 48

26   Pittsburgh Symph   BN 59;   NA 63;   NP 66;
    PT 58, 59

25   Der Schwanendreher   Var, small O and Vla 1935
    BN 66;   BU 69;   CH 37;   DE 57;   NA 36, 68;
    LA 38;   MN 40;   PH 35;   PT 40;   SF 38, 67

21   Sinfonetta in E   BN 54;   CH 62

18   Symphonia Serena   BN 47, 63;   CH 58;   CL 55;
    DA 46, 49, 50, 55, 65;   NA 47;   KC 64;
    LA 50, 61;   MN 50;   NP 47;   PH 49;   SL 55;
    SF 47;   WA 64

18   Symphon Metamorphoses on theme of Weber 1945
    AT 64, 67;   BA 52, 61;   BN 42, 44, 48, 51, 52,
    63, 65;   BU 60, 66;   CH 44, 45, 48, 51, 52, 56,
    60;   CT 44, 50, 51, 53, 56, 57;   CL 44, 47, 52,
    59, 64, 65, 69;   DA 48, March only 50, 53, 57,
    61, 66;   DE 53, 68;   DT 44, 53, 61, 64, 68;
    HN 46, 49, 53, 66, 69;   NA 43, 47, 56, 60, 63,
    67;   KC 44, 55;   LA 54, 65;   ML 68;   MN 49,
    56, 60, 65;   NR 50, 56, 59, 60, 64;   NP 43, 56,
    60, 63;   NP 67, 69;   PH 55, 59, 61, 68;   PT 44,
    57, 61, 64;   RC 55;   SL 45(2), 61;   SF 49, 52,
    63, 64, 66, 68;   SE 52, 63, 69;   UT 52, 66;
    WA 50, 56, 64, 67

HINDEMITH, P. (Cont.)
	27	Symphon Dances BN 38, 50; CH 37, 41; LA 39; WA 60
	19	Symph in B^b for Concert Band LA 52; RC 54
	34	Symph The Harmony of the World, 1951 BN 57, 62; CH 53; CL 53; NA 53; LA 53; MN 52, 53; NP 53; SF 56
	33	Symph No 1 in E^b 1941 BA 46, 47, 51; BN 41; CT 44; NA 41, 46, 66; KC 61; MN 41; NP 41, 46, 66; RC 60; WA 52; SF 63
	20	Symph No 2 CL 68
	6	Trauermusik, Funeral Music for Vla and Str 1936 BU 64; LA 37; PT 53
	60	When Liacs Last in the Dooryard Bloomed, an American Requiem for Mez Sopr, Bar, mixed Chor and O 1946 CL 62; NA 62; NP 62
	5	-Prelude CH 54

HINES, Jerome   75-100   I Am the Way, Music Drama   NP 67
1921-   US   39   Twenty-Third Psalm   AT 53

HINTON, Arthur   20   P Conc in d   BN 07;   PH 07
1869-1941   Brit

HODEIR, Andre   9   Around the Blues   CT 60
1921-   Fr

HODGSON, Walter   12   P Conc   AT 48
1904   US

HOFMANN, Josef   30   P Conc No 1 in a Op 16   NP 07
1877-   US   35   P Conc No 2 in A^b PH 23
(pseudonym,   10   Chromaticon, Symphon Dialogue, P and O   CH 17,
Dvorsky, Michael)   18, 37;   CT 16, 27;   CL 27;   DT 30;   PH 16, 23, 30
                25   Haunted Castle, Symphon Narrative P and O
                    CH 19;   DT 25;   PH 18, 19, 23, 28

HOIBY, Lee   22   Hearts, Meadows and Flags, Suite   NR April Fool
1926-   US   only 52;   RC 52;   SF 52
            6   Suite No 2 Op 8   BA 59
            7   Two Pastoral Dances for Fl and O Op 4   NR 56

HOLDEN, David   Rhaps, Say, Paw, on Kentucky folk tunes   CL 43
1911-   US

HOLBROOKE, Josef   17   Queen Mab 1904   BN 12;   CT 36
1878-1958   Brit   20   Rhaps on Three Blind Mice Op 37a   RC 16

HOLLER, Karl   32   Hymns on 4 Gregorian Melodies for O Op 18   CH 38
1907-   Ger   23   Var on Theme by Sweelinck Op 56   WA 59
            25   Symphonic Fantasie on Frescobaldi Theme 3 parts
                Op 20   NR 60

HOLMES, Augusta   15   Au pays bleu, Symphon Suite 1891   NA 36
1847-1903   Fr

HOLMES, Paul   12   Adagio and Allegro   WA 53
1923-   US   8   Fable   HN 55

HOLST, Gustav   14   Ballet Music fr the Opera The Perfect Fool Op 39
1874-1934   Brit   BN 31;   CT 31, 61;   DT 69;   HN 58;   NS 23;
                                 PH 45;   SF 30
                       16   Beni Mora, Oriental Suite Op 29 No 1   CH 22, 25,
                                 29, 37;   SL dance only 28;   SF 23
                       12   Christmas Day mixed Chor and O 1910   DE 47
                       10   Choral Hymns fr Rig Veda group Op 26 No 1   CT 42;
                                 DT 48
                       15   Egdon Heath, Op 47 for O   NS 27
                       10   Fugal Concert Fl, Ob and O Op 40 No 2   BN 34;
                                 NS 23
                        6   Fugal Overt Op 40 No 1   NP 34
                       16   Hammersmith Prelude and Scherzo Op 52   BN 31
                       20   Hymn of Jesus Op 37 2 Chor and O   NA 52
                    11-12   Japanese Suite Op 33   CH 25;   PH 25
                        6   Ode to Death Op 38 Chor and O words fr Walt
                                 Whitman   BN 27
                       55   The Planets Suite in 7 mvts Op 32   BA 68;   BN 22,
                                 31, 45;   CH 20, 26, 28, 34;   CT 67;   DT 66;
                                 HN 60, 69;   NA 48;   ML 69;   MN 24, 27, 67;
                                 NR 69;   NS 21, 3 mvts 27;   PH 34;   PT 63;
                                 RC 32;   SF 29, 64;   UT 69
                       30   -Mars, Venus, Jupiter   CH 20
                       35   -Mars, Venus, Mercury, Jupiter   CT 34;   RC 55;
                       42   -Mars, Venus, Uranus, Mercury, Jupiter   NP 58;
                                 RC 24
                       42   -Jupiter, Saturn, Uranus, Mercury and Mars   RC 24
                       12   St. Paul's Suite for Str 1913   BN 31;   BU 53;
                                 CH 37, 40;   CL 42;   LA 46;   MN 27, 45;
                                 NP 34, 40;   SE 42
                       11   Suite No 1 in E^b Op 28a for Military Band   AT 46

HOMER, Sidney   SONGS
1864-1953   US   4   From the Brake, the nightingale Op 17 No 2   CH 14
                        4   Sheep and Lambs   NS 17
                        4   Sing to me, Sing, Op 28   CH 14
                        4   The Song o' Shirt, Op 25   CH 14
                        4   Thy Voice is Heard   NS 17

HOMMANN, Charles   8   Sinfonie E^b CT 52
c 1825-c 1857   Ger

HONEGGER, Arthur   13   Amphion, Narrative and Chor 1926, Prelude, Fugue
1892-1955   Fr   and Postlude   BN 50;   DA 48
                       28   Christmas Cantata   BN 54, 57;   CH 58;   PH 60
                        7   Chant of Joy 1923   BN 55;   CH 28
                       11   Chant of Nigamon 1917   BN 38, 61;   CH 28
                       13   Concertino for P and O 1925   BN 28;   CH 28;
                                 CT 26;   NP 32, 49, 57;   RC 33;   SL 52;   SF 52
                       17   Conc for Chamber O Fl, Horn, and Str 1949   BU 62;
                                 CL 50;   LA 59, 66;   PH 59;   SF 65;   RC 33

HONEGGER, A. (Cont.)

15	C Conc in C 1934 CH 30
20	V Conc DE 59
35	Dance of Death, La Danse des morts, Soli, Chor and O 1938 BN 52
20	Horace Victorious, Mimed Symph 1920 BN 22, 28; CH 22
18	Incidental music for Phaedre 1926 BN 27; CH 28
80	Jeanne d'Arc au Bucher, Stage Oratorio 1934 CH 66; CL 67; DA 57; MN 53, 64; NR 62; NP 47, 57; PH 52; SE 61; UT 56
23	Jour de Fête Suisse, Suite for O, 7 parts 1943 CT 48
50	Judith, Biblical Drama 1926 UT 64
60	King David, Symphon Psalm for Soli, Narrator and Chor 1921 AT 54; BA 53; CH 29; CL 33, 63; DE 52; KC 53; PH 35, 51; RC 36; SF 64; UT 51, 61;
15	Monopartita for O BN 51; CL 52
10	Mouvement Symphonique No 3 1932 BN 33
9	Nocturne for O 1936 NA 56
8	Pacific 231, Mouvement Symphonique No 1 1923 BN 24, 26, 28, 51; CH 24, 27, 28; CT 24(2), 50; DA 34; DE 54; KC 57; LA 24; MN 24, 50; NP 27, 29, 30, 62; PT 60; RC 26; SL 24, 31, 68; UT 65; WA 34
6	Pastorale d'été, Symphon Poem for Chamber O 1920 BA 60; BN 28; CH 23, 29, 36, 38, 40, 42, 44; CT 65; DE 67; LA 24, 52; MN 29, 36; NP 27, 29, 51, 62; PH 49; RC 37, 57; SL 22, 30, 53, 55; SF 55; SE 28, 37
8	Prelude to the Tempest of Shakespeare 1923 CH 43; DT 37, 48; LA 25; NP 26; SF 37
6-8	Prelude, Ariosa and Fughetta on B.A.C.H. 1936 PH 50
8	Rugby, Mouvement Symphonique No 2 1928 BN 28, 56; CH 28; MN 32; NP 62; PH 32; SF 54
20	Suite from L'Imperatrice aux Rochers, Incidental Music 1925 CT 63
22	Symph No 1 1930 BN 30, 53, 60
25	Symph No 2 for Str and Trump, 1941 BN 46, 47, 48, 51, 52, 56, 59, 62, 66; BU 60; CH 46, 47, 49, 62, 66; CT 57; CL 47, 68; DA 58; DE 61; DT 68; KC 47; LA 47, 58, 61; MN 60, 66; NP 47, 57, 61, 66; PH 47, 56, 57, 62; SL 57; SF 52; SE 63; WA 50
30	Symph No 3, Liturgique, 1945 BN 47, 55, 65; BU 58; CH 61; CL 61; DA 60; DT 67; LA 48; MN 61; NR 63, 68; NP 46; PH 56; PT 50; SF 57, 68; RC 62
32	Symph No 4 Delicae Basiliensis 1946 BN 48, 55, 58, 64; CH 48, 63; NP 48
27	Symph No 5, Di Tre Re for three Kings 1951 BN 55 first mvt, 58, 61; CH 52, 53; CT 60; HN 51, 63; LA 63; MN 52, 62; NP 66; PH 65; PT 52, 66; SL 58, 59
8	Toccata CT 57

HOPEKIRK, Helen   20   P Conc in d   BN 03
  1856-1945   Brit/US

HOVEY, Serge   32   Sholem Aleichem Suite for Soli, Chor and O   CT 57
              US

HOVHANESS, Alan   12   Ad Lyram Op 143 for Solo Quart and O   HN 56
  1911-   US   4   As on the Night, Song for Sopr, C and Str from
                                 Triptych Op 100   HN 56
                       22   Conc No 1 Op 88, Arevakl, Music for Lent   NA 56
                       11   Concertina for Accordian and O Op 174   KC 62
                       10   Elibtis Op 50 for Fl and Str   SF 49
                       20   Floating World   SE 69
                        8   Fra Angelico Op 220   BA 69;   DT 67;   NR 68
                       14   Meditation on Orpheus Op 155   HN 58;   ML 66;
                                 NR 63
                        9   Meditation on Zeami   PT 64
                       10   Mountain of Prophesy Op 195   SL 61
                       10   Pel-el-Amarna City of the Sun   UT 52
                        7   Prelude and Quadruple Fugue Op 128   BN 63;
                                 DT 58, 64;   NA 57;   ML 63
                       21   Symph No 1, Op 17 Exile   LA 42
                        7   Symph No 2 Mysterious Mountain Op 132   AT 57, 62,
                                 69;   BN 57;   CH 57;   CT 55;   CL 57;   DA 60;
                                 DE 57;   HN 55, 62;   KC 59;   NR 64;   RC 58;
                                 PT 59;   SE 59;   WA 59
                       27   Symph No 11 Op 186   NR 60, 69
                       30   Symph No 19 Vishnu Op 217   CT 68;   PT 68
                       11   Vision from a High Rock Op 123   DT 54

HOWE, Mary   8   Agreeable Overt   WA 61
  1882-   US   14   Castellana for 2 P and O   WA 35, 39
                       11   Dirge, In Memoriam H. Randolph   WA 32
                        3   Liebeslied   WA 46
                       11   Paean   WA 43
                       12   Poema, Voices and O 1924   BA 26
                        6   Spring Pastorale 1936   SE 42;   WA 36
                       12   Three Pieces for O   WA 55
                        4   Stars and Whimsy 1937   BA 44;   WA 45, 64
                        3   Sand 1932   PH 34
                        3   To an Unknown Soldier   WA 46

HOWLAND, Russell   15   Tribute to Fighting Men   CH 44;   PH 44
  1908-   US

HUBAY, Jeno   12   Carmen Fantasie   PH 01
  1858-1937   Hung   26   V Conc No 3 in g Op 99   CH 17;   NS 17;   SL 20

HUBER, Hans   30   Symph No 1 Op 63 William Tell   NP 1881
  1852-1921   Swiss   40   Symph No 2 in e Op 115   BN 02, 04;   CH 13, 16, 26

HÜE, Georges   8   Fantasy for Fl and O   NS 13;   PH 42
  1858-1948   Fr   15   Theme Varie, Vla and O   PH 25
                       12   Titania, Symphon Suite from the Opera 1903   BN 21

                    Time in
                    Minutes

HUFFMAN, Walter S.   22   March, Chorale, Var   MN 59;   RC 61;   WA 59
  1921-   US   6   Overt No 1   BA 46
                     12   Overt No 2   WA 50
                     20   Symph No 2   BA 50
                     20   Symph No 4   WA 53
                  25-28   Symph No 8   BA 59

HUGGLER, John   6   Music in Two Parts   BN 65
  1928-   US   18   Sculptures Op 39   BN 64

HUGHES, Herbert   4   Song, Has Sorrow Thy Young Days Shaded?   CT 40
  1882-1937   Brit

HUGHES, Kent   8   Paean, Overt for O   HN 50
              US

HUMMEL, Johann N.   Concertos for P and O
  1778-1837   Hung   15   in A^b Romanza and Rondo with V and C Op 113
                               NP 1842, 50
                     30   in a Op 85   NP 1859, 63
                     32   in b Op 90   BN 83;   NP 1st mvt 43, 52;
                               NS 1893
                     10   Fantasia on Oberon Op 116   NP 1844, 49
                     20   Quintet in d   NP 1842
                     15   Septet in d Op 74   NP 1848
                               2 mvts   NP 1843

HUMPERDINCK,   6   Overt to The Forced Marriage, Die Heirat wider
  Engelbert   Willen, Opera 1905   BN 07, 15
  1854-1921   Ger   90   Hänsel and Gretel Opera 1893 Complete   AT 62;   DT 43
                     60   -Concert form   PH 54
                      4   -Cradle Song   DT 23;   NS 22, 25
                      8   -Dream Pantomine   AT 50, 54;   BA 40, 51;
                               BN 1895;   CH 1895, 98, 32;   DE 48, 53;   DT 24;
                               HN 33, 37, 52;   KC 34;   NP 1895, 97;   NS 08;
                               PT 38;   SE 29;   WA 33, 37, 45
                      3   -Evening Song   WA 38
                      8   -Prelude   BA 40, 43;   BN 1897, 10, 13, 21;
                               CH 1894, 98, 01, 04, 08, 11, 21, 24, 29, 32, 33,
                               39, 41, 43, 54;   CT 06, 29;   DA 27;   DE 51,
                               61;   HN 40, 45;   NA 37;   ML 61;   MN 29;
                               NP 1886;   NA 1894;   PT 46;   RC 27;   SL 23,
                               26, 42, 43(2), 48;   SF 60;   SE 44, UT 45, 49
                      5   -Prayer and Slumber   AT 46
                     10   -Selections   DA 49
                      4   -Waltz   BA 40;   HN 41
                      6   -Witch's Ride   HN 41
                     10   The King's Children, Königskinder,   Opera Selections
                               BN 1896, 05;   LA 29
                     18   -Children's Dance, Death, Hellafast, Minstrel's
                               Song, Ruin   CH 10, 11, 16, 22
                     20   -Hellafast   CH 1897, 31
                      7   -Prelude   CH 10, 11, 16, 22, 31, 41;   NP 1897,
                               22;   CT 55;   DA 46;   PH 10(2), 27;   SF 13
                      5   Humoresque for O 1880   BN 1892, 05

HUMPERDINCK, E. (Cont.)
```
                       34    Moorish Rhapsody 1898    BN 1899, 01, 10;    CH 1899,
                                 13;    NP 1899;    PH 00
                        4    Song, Wiegenleid    CH 21
                       10    Thorn Rose, A Tone Picture    CH 02
```

HUMPHREYS, Henry   8   A Christmas Fantasy Overt   CT 59
1909-   Brit   20   The Waste Land, Narrator and O   CT 57

HURÉ, Jean   12   Nocturne with P Obligato   SL 09
1877-1930   Fr

HUSA, Karel   15   Mosaiques pour orchestre   BN 67
1921   US   15   Serenade for Woodwind Quintet   BA 63
                       28   Symph No 1   BA 65;   BU 67;   CT 67

HUSS, Henry H.   10   Cleopatra's Death, Dramatic Scene   NP 1897
1862-1953   US   30   P Conc in B   BN 1894, 03;   NP 00
                        6   La Nuit, Poem for O 1938   WA 42
                       20   Rhaps for P and O   BN 1886

HUSTON, Scott   12   Four Phantoms   CT 67
1916-   US   5   Abstract   CT 54
                        5   Toccata for P and O   CT 64

HUTCHESON, Ernest   12   Fantasie for 2 P and O   MN 26
1871-1951   Austr/US

IBERT, Jacques   10   Capriccio for small Orchestra 1938   CH 50
1890-1962   Fr   13   Chant de Folie for 4 Sopr, 2 Contral, Chor and O
                                 BN 25
                       16   Concertina de Camera for Saxophone and Chamber O
                                 1934   BN 39, 57;   CL 57;   DT 46;   NA 58;
                                 KC 47, 55;   WA 40
                       11   Conc for C and Wind Instruments 1925   CH 26;
                                 PH 30;   PT 68
                       17   Conc Fl and O   BN 53;   CH 51;   DT 58;   LA 48;
                                 PT 57;   SL 53
                        8   Divertissement   DT 47;   HN 42;   NA 55;   KC 47,
                                 55;   LA 47;   MN 44;   NP 69;   SE 65;   WA 51, 67
                       18   Escales, Ports of Call, 3 mvts 1922   BN 25, 56;
                                 BU 53;   CH 25, 28, 32, 42, 44;   CT 28, 42, 63;
                                 CL 32, 34, 49, 59, 65;   DA 50, 56, 60, 68;
                                 DE 50, 60, 66;   DT 54, 61;   HN 58;   KC 66;
                                 LA 31;   ML 65;   MN 26, 35, 46, 66;   NR 56;
                                 NP 28, 35, 44;   PH 36, 38, 43, 46, 47, 49, 51,
                                 60;   PT 48;   RC 47, 61;   SL 31, 37, 50, 52,
                                 54;   SF 45, 68;   SE 53, 63;   UT 67;   WA 47
                        8   Féerique, Scherzo for O 1925   BN 28
                       15   Festival, Overt, Overt de Fête 1942   CH 45; NP 45
                       10   Gold Standard Suite, Ballet   DT 35
                       11   Impressions of the Day, Suite   DT 32
                       13   Movement Symphonique, Bostoniana   BN 62
                       12   Les Rencontres, Ballet Suite, 1925   BN 26; NS 26
                       50   Suite Symphonique, Le Chevalier Errant, Don
                                 Quixote, Ballet   CH 52
```
```

IENNI   30   Passion According to St. John   SF 61

ILLIASHENKO,   12   Dance Suite   DT 31
  Andre S.   20   Danses Antiques, Suite   PH 26
  1884-   Russ   10   Dyptique Mongol, 2 parts   PH 31

IMBRIE, Andrew   6   Ballad in D 1947   SF 56
  1921-   US   6   Dandylion Wine   SF 67
                         15   Legend   SF 59, 60;   BU 67
                         20   Symph No 1   SF 65
                         35   V Conc   SF 64
                         20   Symph No 2   SF 69

d'INDY, Vincent   30   Conc for P, Fl, C and Str Op 89   NA 54
  1851-1931   Fr   12   Fantasy on Popular French Themes, Ob and O Op 31
                                 BA 28;   BN 14;   CH 15;   DT 47
                               Fervaal,Opera in 3 acts Op 40   CT 1899, 19, 20
                          7   -Intro Act I   BN 49;   CH 07, 08, 12, 21, 27,
                                 28, 37;   DT 38;   KC 38;   MN 29;   SL 22, 31;
                                 SF 35;   UT 51;   WA 39
                          5   -Prelude Act III   CH 33;   SL 51
                               La Foret Enchantée, Legende Symphonie Op 8
                                 BN 03;   CH 01, 18, 40
                         33   Jour D'Ete, Summer Day in the Mountains, Op 61
                                 BN 07, 13, 23;   CH 07, 16, 31, 36;   CL 29, 32;
                                 MN 47;   NP 34;   NS 07
                         14   Lied, for C and O Op 19   BN 17;   NS 08, 10;
                                 RC 27;   SF 15
                         16   La Legende de St. Christophe Op 67, La Queste de
                                 Dieu Symphon Interlude   BN 20;   CH 19(2), 21,
                                 37, 39;   CL 20, 24, 31;   NS 20
                         15   Legende for O Saugefleurie Op 21   CL 19
                         24   Medea, Suite, Incidental Music Op 47   BN 99;
                                 CH 99;   NP 17
                         22   La Poeme des Rivages, Symphon Suite Op 77   BN 21;
                                 PH 21
                          6   L'etranger, Opera Op 53, Entr'acte   BN 03
                                 -Prelude   NS 08
                         36   Symph No 2 in B^b Op 57   AT 57;   BN 04, 05, 09,
                                 19, 22, 24, 31, 39, 50;   CH 05, 12, 19, 20, 21,
                                 23, 24, 27, 28, 29, 31, 34, 35, 37, 38;   CL 22,
                                 23, 27, 31, 38, 43, 46;   NP 34;   PH 03, 52;
                                 PT 48;   SF 41, 50
                         28   Symph No 3 Sinfonia Brevis de bello gallico, Op 70
                                 BN 19;   CH 26;   CT 18;   NS 19
                         25   Symph on French Mountain Air, P and O Op 25
                                 AT 52;   BA 51;   BN 01, 05, 18, 23, 32, 49, 57;
                                 CH 02, 13, 20, 28;   CT 20, 40, 48;   CL 24, 25,
                                 30, 49;   DT 21, 47, 55;   KC 38;   LA 45, 58;
                                 MN 24, 39;   NR 59, 65;   NP 22, 35, 40, 46, 48,
                                 55, 67;   NS 05, 13, 18, 20;   PH 16, 58;
                                 PT 48, 58;   RC 49, 59;   SL 17, 24, 37;   SF 38,
                                 68;   SE 39, 58, 67;   UT 51;   WA 43

d'INDY, V. (Cont.)

17   Symphon Var, Istar Op 42   BN 1898, 00, 05, 11,
      19, 31, 33, 36, 39, 44, 55;   BU 56;   CH 97, 16,
      21, 37, 42, 44, 66;   CT 17, 18, 20, 66;   CL 28;
      DA 49;   DT 19, 24, 31;   HN 46;   LA 35;   MN 25,
      35;   NP 27, 30, 31;   NS 16, 17, 18, 19, 21, 24;
      PH 15, 31;   SL 16;   SF 25, 49

33   Wallenstein Triptych, 3 Symphon Overtures Op 12
      BN 07, 18, 21;   CH 00, 15;   CT 20;   LA 23;
      NP 51

8   -The Camp   CH 00, 06, 19, 20, 29, 31, 34, 44;
      CT 04, 06;   DT 56;   MN 27;   PH 02;   SL 38;
      SF 45, 50

45   Symphon Poem, On Shores of Seas, Tableux de voyage
      Op 36   NS 21

INFANTE, Manuel   15   Danses Andalouses for 4 P and O   RC 40;   SF 41
1883-   Sp   6   Ruta de Seville   RC 44

INGEGNERI, Marc A.   8   Tenebrae Factae Sunt   MN 44
1545-1592   It

INGHELBRECHT,   15   For the Day of First Snow in Old Japan   CH 28
  Desire-Emile   15   Sinfonia Breve di Camera   SL 38
1880-   Fr   10   Symphon Poem: La Valse Retrouvée   MN 38

IPPOLITOV-IVANOV,   6   Armenian Rhaps Op 48   DT 29
  Michael   22   Caucasian Sketches Op 10   BA 41;   CT 09, 10;
1859-1935   Russ   DA 29;   HN 34, 41;   NA 35;   MN 42;   NP 18,
                             52;   PH 12, 15, 62;   WA 31
                       4   -In the Village   CL 18, 26, 29;   HN 41;
                             SE 26
                       6   -March of the Sardar   CL 18, 26, 29;   HN ·39, 41;
                             MN 48;   RC 28;   UT 29;   WA 31
                       4   -Mosque   MN 48
                       8   -In the Mountain Pass   CH 11;   HN 41;   PH 33

IRELAND, John   20   Concertino Pastoral for Str 1939   CT 39
1879-   Brit   9   Epic March 1942   NP 42
                       8   The Forgotten Rite, Prelude 1913   BN 45;   CT 33
                       11   A London Overt 1936   CH 38;   HN 53

ITURBI, Jose   20   Fantasy for P and O   DE 56;   KC 55;   NP 42;
1895-   Sp   SF 42;   HN 42
                       5   Solioquy for O   CT 41

ITZEL   Ballet for Sultan   BA 28

IVES, Charles   8   America, Var   BA 67;   BU 64;   CL 64;   DA 69;
1874-1954   US   WA 66
                       17   Central Park in the Dark   NP 61;   SF 69;   UT 69
                    20-23   Holidays, Symphony No 2 1911   BN 62;   BU 69;
                             CL 66;   DA 68;   HN 50;   NA 65;   KC 69;   MN 53;
                             NR 65;   NP 50, 58, 60, 67;   PT 69;   PH 62, 68;
                             SF 54;   SE 63;   WA 62

IVES, C. (Cont.) Holidays, Symphony No 2 (Cont.)
                  6   -Decoration Day   DT 69;   MN 65;   NR 68;
                           NP 62;   SF 67;
                  5   -Fourth of July   AT 68;   SF 67
                  6   -Thanksgiving, Chor and O   NP 67
                  6   -Washington's Birthday   CT 68;   DA 66
                  12   Orchestral Set No 1 1914, 3 of 6 parts   RC 69
                  11   Over the Pavement, Scherzo   CL 65
                  5   The Housatonic at Stockbridge   DT 59
                  12   Steeples and Mountains   SF 67;   UT 68
                           -Allegro   CL 65
                  45   Symph No 1 1896   AT 66;   HN 68
                  25   Symph No 3, Camp Meeting 1911   AT 60;   CH 68;
                           MN 67;   NP 65;   PH 68;   SF 51, 60;   UT 66
                  40   Symph No 4, 1916   BN 66, 69;   MN 65;   NP 65,
                           68;   PH 66;   RC 66;   SF 67
                  25   Three Places in New England, Orchestral Set No 1
                           1915   BN 47;   DA 52, 62;   DT 66;   LA 32, 68;
                           MN 62;   NP 68;   PH 63;   PT 60, 66
                  8   The Unanswered Question   BA 61;   CT 58;   CL 56,
                           65;   DA 59;   DE 69;   DT 62;   HN 55;   MN 60;
                           NR 62;   NP 59;   PH 69;   RC 62, 67;   SL 58,
                           67;   SF 65;   UT 62

JACOB, Gordon   13   William Byrd Suite from the Fitzwilliam Virginal,
1895-   Brit   3 mvts arr for O 1939   RC 40

JACOBI, Frederick   15   California Suite 1917   LA 21;   SF 17
1891-1952   US   18   C Conc 1932   CL 35
                    25   The Eve of St. Agnes, Symphon Poem 1919   SF 22
                    28   Indian Dances 1927   BN 28;   PH 28;   SF 28
                    6   Music Hall Overt 1948   CL 49;   SL 50
                    12   Ode for O 1941   BN 42;   SF 42
                    12   Pied Piper, Symphon Poem 1915   SF 15
                    10   Serenade for P and O   NA 52
                    21   Symph in C No 1 1922   RC 24;   SF 24, 47
                    10   Two Pieces in Sabbath Mood 1946   NA 47

JAMES, Philip   13   Bret Harte Overt No 1 1926   PH 37;   SL 37;   SF 36
1890-   US   8-9   Overt in Olden Style on French Noels 1923
                           BU 40;   DA 32, 49;   NA 59;   WA 34
                    15   Station WGZBX, Suite 1931   BN 32;   MN 35

JANÁCEK, Leos   50   Glagolitic Mass 1926   CH 69
1854-1928 Czech   25   Sinfonetta 1926   BA 61;   BN 34, 45, 54, 61, 66(2);
                           CH 50, 66;   CT 65, 69;   CL 46, 54, 61, 65;
                           DA 61, 68;   DT 67;   KC 64;   MN 66;   NS 26;
                           RC 49, 61;   SL 68;   SF 59;   WA 66
                    48   Slavonic Mass   BN 62;   BU 67;   CL 65
                    16   Suite from the Opera 1921 Cunning Little Vixen,
                           Das Schlau Füchslein   BN 66;   CH 69;   CT 69;
                           DA 69
                    23   Taras Bulba, Slavonic Rhaps after Gogol 1918
                           BN 33;   CH 49;   CT 60;   CL 58, 68;   LA 66

JANIN, Jacques   20   Symph Spirtuelle with Org   BN 28
  c 1890-   Fr

JANSSEN, Werner   18   New Year's Eve in New York 1930   CH 31;   CL 29;
  1899-   US   RC 31

JACQUES-DALCROZE,   15   V Conc   BN 05
  Émile   6   Overt to Sancho Panza Opera 1897   CT 19
  1865-1950   Swiss   5   Tableaux Romands Suite for O Op 66, Kermesse only
                                  CT 21

JARECKI, Tadeusz   30   Symphon Poem, Chimere Op 26   PH 25
  N. de
  1889-   Pol/US

JÄRNEFELT, Armas   4   Berceuse   CH 05, 09, 12;   HN 41
  1869-1958 Fin/Swed   15   Korsholm, Symphon Poem, 1894   CH 02
                         5   Kchtolaulau, Song   CL 19
                         3   Praeludium for small O   CH 12;   HN 38;   PH 12,
                                  17, 25;   RC 23, 27;   WA 32, 35

JAROCH, Jiri   10   The Old Man and the Sea   KC 68;   WA 68
  1920   Czech

JAUBERT, Maurice   20   Sonata a Due, C, V and Str   BN 46
  1900-1940   Fr   18   Suite Francaise 1935   SL 33

JENKINS, Joseph   12   5-Part Fantasy No 1 in D for 5 Str arr Cailliet
  1592-1676   Brit   PH 38
                         9   Fantasy in D for 5 V arr Grainger   SE 35

JENKINS, Joseph W.   14   Sinfonia Concertante for two Str Quart and Str O
  1928-   US   WA 58

JENSEN, Adolf   4   Song Am Ufer   NP 16
  1837-1879   Ger   4   Song Murmelndes Lüftchen   NP 1891

JENSEN, Ludwig Irgens   15   Passacaglia   NP 32;   PH 32
  1904-   Nor

JIMENEZ-MABARAK,   8   El Baile de Luis Alonso   NP 42
  Carlos
  1916-   Mex

JIRAK, Karel B.   20   Symphon Var Op 40   CL 50
  1891-   Czech/US   30   Symph No 5 Op 60   CH 51

JOACHIM, Josef   28   V Conc in D   BN 1881, 04, 09, 15
  1831-1907   Ger   6   -1st mvt   BN 1886, 01
                        17   V Conc No 2 in d Op 11 The Hungarian   CT 06;
                                  MN 26;   NS 26
                         6   -1st mvt   CH 10, 38
                        25   V Conc in G   NP 1890
                        30   Theme and Var for V and O   NS 1894

JOACHIM, Otto   15-20   Contrastes   BN 67
1910-   Can

JOHANSON, S.E.   8   Fetia   RC 67
1919-   Swed

Johns, Clayton   15   Berceuse and Scherzo for Str   BN 93
1857-1932   US

JOHNSON, Horace   14   Imagery: Suite on Hindu Themes   CT 38;   HN 38;
1893-   US   KC 38;   SF 38
                        10   Streets of Florence, O Suite   PH 41
                         8   Witness   DE 69

JOHNSTON, Benjamin   18   Quint for Groups for O   SL 66
                US

JOLIVET, André   10   Concertina for Trump, Str and P 1948   CH 64
1905-   Fr   22   Conc for ondes Martinot and O 1947   BN 49
                        23   P Conc 1951   PH 56;   SF 59;   WA 57
                        12   Conc No 2 Trump and O   MN 62
                        12   Les Amants Magnifique, Var on a theme of Lully
                                    CL 61;   DE 65;   ML 66
                        30   Symph of Danses 1940   CL 58
                        27   Symph No 2   DT 60

JOMMELLI, Niccolo   5   Air, La Calendrina   NS 1879
1714-1774   It

JONES, Charles   4   Cowboy Song and Gallop for Ob, P and Str 1940
1912-   US   SL 43
                         4   Little Symph for the New Year   SL 55
                         4   Overt for O 1942   WA 45
                        12   Suite for small O 1937   SL 41

JONES, George T.   8   Overt to an Imaginary Drama   WA 52
1917-   US

JONGEN, Joseph   25   C Conc   NP 05
1873-1953   Belg   15   Fantasy on 2 Popular Walloon Carols 1902   MN 24
                        19   Impressions d'Ardennes Op 44   CT 33
                        14   Rondes Wallone Op 40   MN 25
                        33   Symphonie Concertante for Org and O Op 81
                                    DT 58;   NP 54;   PH 64

JORA, Michel   5   Marche Juive   NP 36
1891-   Roum

JORDAN, Sverre   4   Song,Drick   CT 49
1889-   Nor

JOSEPHS, Wilfred   50   Requiem Op 39   CT 66
1927-   Brit   23   Symph   2   CT 67

JOSLYN, Henry   20   Pagan Symph   NP 31
1884-1931   US   8   War Dance, Symphon Suite   PH 24

JOSTEN, Werner   22   Conc Sacro No 1   Str and P 1927   BN 28;   PH 33
  1888-   Ger/US   16   Conc Sacro No 2 P and Str 1927   CT 33;   CL 32
                      14   Jungle, Symphon mvt 1928   BN 29;   CH 31;   PH 32
                      17   Serenade for O 1934   CL 34
                      17   Symph in F 1936   BN 36

JUON, Paul   30   Vaegtervise: Fantasy on Danish Folk Songs Op 31
  1872-1940 Russ/Ger   BN 13;   PH 06;   SF 20

JUST, Robert   15   Two Symphon Poems for 2 P and O   MN 27
  c 1900   Ger/US

KABELAC, Miloslav   6   Mirrors   LA 65
  1908-   Czech

KABALEVSKY, Dmitri   18   Colas Breugnon Suite in four mvts Op 24   DA 67;
  1904-   Russ   SL 43, 55
                       5   -Overt   AT 59, 64;   BN 43, 56;   BU 47, 48, 55,
                             56, 60, 61;   CH 45, 47, 48, 54, 58;   CT 44, 49;
                             CL 44, 63;   DA 48, 52;   DE 47, 48, 51, 52, 54,
                             56, 58, 61;   DT 56, 67;   HN 45(2), 48, 52, 55,
                             61, 63, 69;   NA 44, 46, 57, 62, 65, 68;   KC 43,
                             53, 63, 66;   LA 43;   ML 61;   MN 44, 47;
                             NR 52, 58, 63;   PH 43, 51, 56, 59;   PT 43, 44,
                             46, 51, 62;   RC 47, 58;   SL 43, 56, 69;   SE 57;
                             UT 46, 56, 62, 63, 69;   WA 51, 56, 63;   NP 44,
                             46, 54, 55
                       4   -Peoples' Fete   PH 47
                      15   Comedians, Suite for small O Op 26   KC 52
                      40   C Conc Op 49   BN 53, 59;   DA 54;   LA 68;   PH 62;
                             PT 49, 56;   RC 63
                      23   P Conc No 2 in g Op 23   NP 45
                      18   P Conc No 3 Youth Op 50   KC 56
                   13-15   V Conc Op 48   DE 56;   SE 54
                      25   Symph No 1 Op 18   NR 59
                      25   Symph No 2 in e Op 19   AT 58;   BN 45;   BU 59;
                             CT 44;   DE 65;   DT 65;   NA 55;   KC 44;   LA 44;
                             NP 42;   PH 42, 60;   PT 45;   RC 60;   SL 57;
                             WA 44, 45
                      39   Symph No 4   NR 57, 67;   NP 57;   PH 67

KAGEL, Mauricio   15   Diaphonie   BU 64
  1931-   Sp

KAHN, Robert   6   Overt Elegy, in c   BN 94
  1865-1951 Ger

KALINNIKOV, Vassili   27   Agnus Dei   KC 34
  1866-1901 Russ   7   Fir Tree and the Palm   NP 19
                      42   Symph No 1 in g   AT 47, 49, 57;   BN 20, 36;   CH 10;
                             CT 34;   CL 20;   DA 32;   HN 45;   NA 37, 40, 46;
                             KC 41;   MN 28;   NP 18, 40;   NS 15, 16, 21, 25;
                             PH 10, 11, 14, 17, 25;   PT 43;   SF 14, 19, 26,
                             44;   WA 32, 39, 45
                      45   Symph No 2 in A   NS 17;   SL 16

KALKBRENNER,   10   Rondo for P and O Le Gage d'amitié   NP 1851
Friedrich W.
1785-1849   Ger

KALLIWODA, Johann W.   8   Conc Overt No 11 Op 143   NP 1847
1801-1866   Bohem   20   Duet for 2 V and O Op 109   NP 1847
                      12   Overt in D   NP 1842
                       8   Overt in F   NP 1843
                      20   Symph No 1 in f 1826   NP 1845

KALMAN, Emerich   4   Czardas   KC 64
1882-1953 Hung/US

KAMINSKI, Heinrich   30   Conc Grosso for Double O 1922   CH 26;   PH 26
1886-1946   Ger   25   Magnificat for Sopr, Chor and O 1925   CT 30

KAMINSKI, Josef   11   Israeli Sketches   PT 68
1903   Russ/Is

KANITZ, Ernest   11   Ballet Music for small O   SL 38
1894-   US   22   Conc for Bassoon and O   DT 67;   SF 63;   NP 67;
                               PH 67
                      21   Sinfonia Seria 1963   SL 64
                      20   Symph No 2   SF 68

KAPER, Bronislaw   14   Tone Poem, Bataan   SE 43;   UT 43
1902-   US

KARLOWICZ, Mieczslaw   30   V Conc in A Op 8   MN 62;   NP 24;   NS 21
1876-1909   Pol   8   Returning Waves Symphon Poem Op 9   CL 33

KASSERN, Tadeusz Z.   15   Conc for Voice and O 1928   CL 34
1904-1957   Pol   Adagio from Conc for Str O   NP 53

KATWIJK, Paul van   5   Gavotte and Air   DA 28
1885-   Neth   10   Hollandia Suite for C   DA 30
                       4   Idyll, Roest   DA 26, 35
                       4   Kermesse   DA 26

KAUFMANN, Walter   7   Dirge for O   UT 47
1907-   US   5   Madras Express   NA 60

KAUN, Hugo   8   Fantaisiestück for V and O Es war einmal Op 66
1863-1932   Ger/US   CH 16
                      10   Festival March and Hymn to Liberty Op 29   CH 1897(2),
                               99, 03, 08
                      30   Four Pieces for small O Op 70   CH 07
                      20   Sir John Falstaff.Humoresque Poem Op 60   CH 05, 27
                      12   Maria Magdelena, Symphon Prologue Op 44   CT 05
                       9   On the Rhine, Overt Op 90   CH 12
                       6   Overt Der Maler von Antwerpen   CH 1898, 99
                       8   Rondo and Joyous Wanderings   NS 10
                      12   Suite for O.EinKarnevalsfest Op 28   RC 05
                      30   Symph No 1 in d Op 22 An mein Vaterland   CH 1897
                      38   Symph No 2 in c Op 85   CH 10
                      39   Symph No 3 in e Op 96   CH 15

KAUN, H. (Cont.)
                    27   Symphonic Poems, Hiawatha, Minnehaha Op 43 Nos 1 and
                              2   CH 02, 11;   BN only No 2 03
                    22   Three Pieces for small O Op 76   CH 08

KAY, Hershey   5   Stars and Stripes Ballet: Pas de deux   SE 64
    1919-   US 27   Western Symph for NYC Ballet   WA 60
                    15   Theatre Set   AT 68

KAY, Ulysses S.   12   Covenant for Our Times   DT 69
    1917-   US 14   Markings   CL 66;   DE 69
                     9   Saturday Night   NP 55;   SF 55
                    18   Serenade for O   NP 66
                    18   Suite   AT 65
                    20   Symph in E   CL 53
                    12   Umbrian Scene   KC 67;   NR 63;   RC 66

KEATS, Donald   18   Elegy   CT 64
    1929-   US

KECHLEY, Gerald   45   Daedalus and the Minataur, Dramatic Oratorio for
    1920-   US   Narrator, Soli, Chor and O   SE 62

KELEMEN, Milko   12   Improvisations Concertantes for Str   DT 67
    1924-   Yugo 18   Sub-Rosa   RC 65

KELKEL, Manfred   7   Ostinato   DE 64
    1929-   Ger

KELLER, Homer   16   Symph No 2   WA 50
    1915-   US

KELLEY, Edgar S.   28   Aladdin Suite Op 10 4 mvts   SL 16
    1857-1944   US   5   -At the Wedding   CL 19
                     5   -In the Palace Garden   CL 19
                    10   California Idyll for Sopr and O   BN 18;   NS 18
                    10   Defeat of Macbeth, Symphon Poem Op 7   CH 13;
                              CT 12;   PH 37
                    12   Pit and the Pendulum, Symphon Suite 1930   CT 27,
                              39;   NA 38
                    30   Symph No 1 Voyage to Lilliput 1935   CT 36
                 40-42   Symph No 2 in b^b New England Op 33   BN 15;   CT 14,
                              21, 28, 41;   CL 21;   DT 26;   NP 17;   PH 17;
                              SL 14;   SF 16;   SE 38

KELLY, Robert   15   Emancipation Symph   WA 62
    1916-   US 10   A Miniature Symph   CL 51

KENNAN, Kent   5   Andante for Ob and O 1939   PH 45, 58
    1913-   US   4   Night Soliloquy for Fl, P and Str O 1936   CL 50;
                              DE 45, 51, 60;   NR 58;   PH 42, 48;   UT 55;
                              WA 46, 47

KENNEDY, John B.   22   Symphony in 2 mvts   SF 65
                US

	Time in Minutes	

KERN, Jerome   4   All the Things You Are   HN 51
1885-1945   US   20   Mark Twain, Portrait for O   NR 60
                    20   Scenario for O on Themes fr Showboat   AT 50;   BA 45;
                              CL 41, 42;   DA 46, 49;   DT 43;   NA 50;   KC 42;
                              MN 43;   NP 41, 45, 55;   SF 51, 55;   UT 41
                     4   -Smoke Gets in Your Eyes arr Gould   CT 44; MN 44
                     4   -Old Man River   UT 56
                    20   -Fantasie fr Showboat   RC 42
                    10   -Medley fr Showboat arr Kastelanitz   HN 51
                     5   Waltz, Springtime   PH 36

KESSLER, John   10   Intro and Fugue Op 51   SL 36
1904-   US   12   Poem for O Op 36   SL 31
                    18   Soliloquy Op 58   SL 44
                    15   Symphonic Sketches, Avalon Op 47   SL 33

KHATCHATURIAN, Aram   Conc Fl and O   DE 69
1903-   Russ   31   C Conc   BN 47;   CH 49;   HN 51;   KC 67;   NP 60;
                              PT 64;   SL 59;   WA 67
                    29   P Conc 1936   AT 57;   BA 57;   BN 43(2), 45;
                              BU 44;   CH 43, 62;   CT 42, 56, 67;   CL 45, 55;
                              DE 60, 67;   DT 58;   HN 46, 63;   KC 44, 51;
                              LA 45;   MN 44, 58;   NR 57, 65;   NP 46, 49, 60;
                              PH 43, 48;   RC 46;   SL 43, 48, 55;   SF 61, 68;
                              SE 49, 66;   WA 45
                    35   V Conc 1940   AT 50, 63;   BA 64;   BN 55;   BU 50;
                              DE 46;   DT 59;   HN 58;   KC 66;   NR 68;   PH 45;
                              PT 61;   RC 68;   SL 48;   SE 60;   WA 65
                    30   Concert Rhaps for C and O   CH 67;   KC 67;
                              PH 69;   WA 67
                    10   Festive Poem   HN 55
                           Gayne Ballet 1942
                     8   -Suite No 1   AT 51, 58;   CH 47
                    17   -Suite No 2   KC 45
                     8   -Three Dances   KC 44, 67;   LA 45;   MN 45
                     4   -Polka Coquette   DE 59
                     5   -Saber Dance   DA 49;   DE 49, 51;   HN 45;
                              PT 50
                     8   -Dance of the Rose Maidens   CT 47;   DE 49, 51;
                              HN 45
                     4   -Lullaby   DE 49, 51;   HN 45
                    20   -Dances   NA 67;   NP 48;   PH 47;   WA 67
                    15   Dance Suite in Five mvts 1933   WA 67
                    15   Masquerade Suite in five mvts   AT 48, 49, 59;
                              BU 49;   NP 47, 54;   SE 51;   WA 48
                     8   -Gallop and Waltz   DA 49
                     5   Russian Fantasy   BU 49;   NP 47
                           Spartacus, Ballet in six mvts
                     4   -Grand Adagio   NA 67
                    20   -Suite No 1   CH 67
                    25   Symph No 2 1942   CH 67;   HN 58;   NA 67;   KC 67;
                              NP 48;   PH 46;   WA 67
                    28   Symph No 3   CH 67

KHRENNIKOV   22   Symph No 1 in b Op 4   BA 53;   BN 59;   CL 45;
  Tikhon N.   DE 49;   DT 41;   PH 36, 42, 59;   SL 45
1913-   Russ   38   Symph No 2 in g Op 9   WA 68

Kilar, Wojciech   6   Riff 62   BU 64;   CL 64;   NP 65(2)
1932-   Pol

KILPATRICK, Jack F. 10   Cherokee Legends, Suite   BU 45
1915-   US   8   Encore Overt   NA 48
                      6   Invocation and Ritual   DA 54
                      8   Ozark Dances   SL 42;   WA 45
                     10   Prelude and Indian Dance fr Golden Crucible   DA 62
                      4   Romanza for Ob and Str   DA 49
                     14   Symph No 5 in f#   DA 52

KIM, Earl   10   Three Songs   SF 67
1920-   US

KINDLER, Hans   5   Pacific Nocturne   PH 48
1892-   Neth/US   16   The Seven Provinces   WA 45
(Philip Henry, Pseudonym)

KINKEL, Charles   4   Song   NP 1867
1832-   US

KIRCHNER, Leon   30   P Conc No 1   BN 62;   NP 55;   PT 63;   SF 60
1919-   US   30   P Conc No 2   CL 63;   NP 64;   SE 63
                     19   Sinfonia for O   BN 60;   NP 51
                     14   Toccata for Str, Winds and Perc   BN 59;   DE 64;
                            SF 55
                     20   Str Quart with Electronic Tape No 3   SF 67
                     14   Music for O   NP 69

KIRK, Theron   Symph in 1 mvt   HN 63
1919-   US

KJERULF, Halfdan   4   Von Liebe, Song   CT 1895
1815-1868   Nor

KLAMI, Uuno   27   Kalevala Suite Op 23   CT 51, 52;   MN 53
1900-1961   Fin   29   Karelian Rhaps Op 15   WA 53
                     10   Tone Poem, Three Beaufort, A sea pastorale   SE 32
                     36   Vipusessa Kaynti for Baritone, male Chor and O
                            BN 53;   CT 53

KLEBE, Gisellher   13   Zu Zwitschermaschine Op 7   CH 64
1925-   Ger

KLEIN, Bruno   20   Conzertstueck for P   PH 04
1858-1911   US   20   Suite for C and O in F   NP 03

KLEIN, Joseph   6   Music a Go-Go   SE 68
1936-   US

KLEINSINGER, George   12   Archie and Mehitabel, A Back-Alley Opera   CT 57
1914-   US   20   Jesse James, Fanfare for O   DE 50
                        9   Street Corner Conc for Harmonica or Sax and O   AT 59

KLENAU, Paul von   18   Orchestral Phantasy, Hampstead Health for O and
1883-1946   Dan   boys Voices   DT 25, 30;   LA 26;   PH 30
                        9   Overt Klein Idas Blumen, from the Ballet   DT 31

KLENGEL, Julius   6   C Capriccio   BN 1894
1859-1933   Ger

KLOSE, Freidrich   6   Dance of the Elves   CH 14;   SL 11
1862-1942   Swiss   10   Prelude and Double Fugue for Org, Trump and Trombones
                                  on a Theme of Bruckner   BN 14;   CH 08

KLUGHARDT, August   20   C Conc in a Op 59   BN 12;   CH 05;   NP 16
1847-1902   Ger   30   Symph No 3 in C   BN 1890;   NP 1892

KNIPPER, Lev   18-20   Maku Suite, Iranian Themes, 1942   PT 44
  Konstantinovitch   20   Marchen eines Gyps-Gottes   PH 28
1898-   Russ

KNORR, Ivan   8   Var on Ukraine Folk Song Op 7   BN 1894
1853-1916   Ger

KNUSSEN, Oliver   20   Symph No 1   HN 68
1953-   Brit

KOCH, Erland Von   15   Conc Piccolo for two Saxophones and O   RC 65
1910-   Swed

KOCH, Franz   12   Symphon Fugue Op 8   NP 1891
1862-1927   Ger

KODALY, Zoltan   5   Ballet Music 1925   BN 37
1882-1967   Hung   19   Conc for O Op 1   CH 40;   NA 67;   PH 44, 66;
                             SF 56
                       15   Dances of Galanta 1933   BA 68;   BN 55;   CH 53,
                             63;   CT 37, 47, 58;   CL 36, 44;   DA 55, 63;
                             DE 54, 64, 67;   DT 38, 51;   HN 60;   LA 47, 66;
                             MN 36, 58, 67;   NP 36, 43, 51, 53;   PH 36, 57,
                             62;   PT 43, 44, 46, 63;   RC 22, 44, 57;   SL 37,
                             44, 48, 61;   SF 53, 59;   SE 55, 65;   UT 64;
                             WA 37, 61
                       21   Hary Janos Suite from Opera 1926   AT 64;   BA 59,
                             67;   BN 28, 62, 64;   CH 28, 29, 30, 34, 38,
                             39, 42, 55, 60;   CT 27, 29, 52, 66;   CL 33, 68;
                             DA 46, 52;   DE 50, 53, 55, 63;   DT 45, 61, 65;
                             HN 54, 58, 60;   KC 37, 38, 48, 54, 63, 68;
                             LA 28, 30, 43, 46, 56, 61;   ML 66;   MN 31, 33,
                             49, 50, 56;   NR 66;   NP 27, 28, 42, 46, 55;
                             PH 28, 31, 33, 37, 42, 50, 61;   PT 45, 66, 69;
                             RC 33, 57, 62, 67, 69;   SL 29, 38, 50, 56, 61;
                             SF 29, 52, 58;   SE 30, 66;   WA 65
                        4   -Intermezzo, Entrance of the Emperor   NP 55

KODALY, Z. (Cont.) Hary Janos Suite (Cont.)
4 -Defeat of Napoleon   CT 46
8 -Musical Clock and Dance   DA 46
12 Marosszek Dances 1930   BU 55;   CH 30;   CT 30;
      KC 63;   MN 56;   NP 30;   SF 69
24 Peacock, Var on 2 Hungarian Folksongs 1938   BA 69;
      BN 64;   CH 46, 53, 59;   DE 56, 62;   DT 46, 67;
      HN 61;   LA 61;   MN 50;   NR 58, 61;   NP 59;
      PH 46, 64;   PT 64;   RC 54, 62, 66, 69;   SL 65;
      SE 67;   SF 68
23 Psalmus Hungaricus, for Tenor, Chor and O Op 13
      CH 40;   DA 48, 59;   DT 68;   NA 37, 52;
      LA 29, 63;   MN 52;   NP 29, 51, 67;   WA 58
20 Summer Evening 1906, revised 1926   CT 31;
      NP 29, 33
21 Te Deum, Soli, Chor and O 1936   CL 41;   NA 67;
      WA 59
30 Symph   CH 63;   CT 62;   CL 61;   SF 61;   SE 62

KOECHLIN, Charles   8 3 Chorales for O Op 76   BN 22
1867-1950   Fr   4 L'Hiver, Symphon Poem Op 47 No 2   CT 36;   PH 35

KOENEMAN, Theodore   5 When The King Went Forth   NA 41, 43;   PT 45
                Russ

KOESSLER, Hans   16 Symphon Var in c#   BN 01
1853-1926   Ger

KOETSIER, Jan   36 Symph No 1   SF 50
1911-   Neth   28 Symph No 3, Op 40   NP 60

KOHN, Karl   6 Sensus Spei for a cappella Chor   SF 66
1926-   Aust/US

KOHS, Ellis B.   6 Legend for Ob and Str 1946   SF 47
1916-   US   14 Life with Uncle Sam 1943   BU 45
         16 Symph No 1   SF 51

KOKKONEN, Joonas   8 Opus Sonorum   HN 65
1921-   Fin

KOLAR, Victor   4 Bagatelle for Fl and O   DT 34
1886-   US   5 Fairy Tale   NS 12
         6 In Memory of a Friend, Victor Herbert   DT 24
         6 Slovakian Rhaps   DT 22
         30 Symph No 1 in D   CL 29;   DT 20, 24, 28;   NS 17
         15 Symphon Suite   NS 13
         15 Symphon Poem, Hiawatha   NS 10

KOMZAK, Karel   5 Waltz, Badner Mad' In Op 257   MN 28
1850-1905   Czech

KONOYE, Hidemaro   10 Etenraku   KC 52;   NP 55;   SF 55
1898-   Japan

KONSTANTINOFF, K.   12   Wien, paraphrase on J. Strauss Melodies   SL 34
           Fr

KORBAY, Francis   4   Hungarian Song: Where The Torjas Torrents   NS 92
1846-1913   Hung   6   Nuptiale for O   BN 1887

KORESCHENKO, Arseny   4   Ode to Terpsichore   DA 32
1870-1921   Russ

KORN, Peter   3   Overt In Medias Res   PT 63
1922-   Ger   30   Symph No 3 in 1 mvt   LA 57

KORNAUTH, Egon   8   On the Death of a Friend   SL 24
1891-1959   Aust

KORNGOLD, Erich   22   V Conc Op 35 in D   CH 46;   DT 53;   LA 52;
1897   Aust/US   NP 46;   SL 46
                             Einfache Lieder, A Set of Songs Op 9
                        4   No 4 Liebesbriefchen   CH 22;   CT 30;   PH 22
                        4   No 6 Sommer   CH 22;   CT 30;   PH 22
                       25   Much Ado About Nothing, Incidental Music Op 11
                               CT 23;   DE 5 excerpts 60;   DT 22, 31;   LA 29,
                               40;   PH 28, 41;   PT 60;   RC 52;   SL 30;
                               SF 27, 29;   SE 3 excerpts 27
                       16   Schauspiel Overt to a Comedy Op 4   CH 12, 14;
                               CT 13;   NP 12;   PH 13;   SF 20
                       45   Sinfonetta Op 5   BN 14;   CH 13;   NP 14
                       27   Symphon Serenade Op 39   PT 55
                        5   Die tote stadt Opera Op 12: Mariotta's Aria, Glueck
                               das mir verblieb   AT 59;   CT 37;   DA 49;
                               HN 55;   NA 53;   KC 52, 64;   LA 65;   ML 63
                       18   Vorspiel, Sursum Corda   DT 27;   NP 22

KORNSAND, Emil   18   Metamorphosis   BN 56
1894-   Ger

KOSHETZ   4   Bells of Home   DA 30

KOSTELANETZ, Andre   15   Roumanian Fantasy   SF 51
1901-   Russ/US 15   Roumanian Folk Dances   BA 45;   KC 44

KOCHETOV, Nikolay R.   4   Song, A la Balalaika   DT 29
1864-   Russ

KOUSSEVITZKY, Serge   10   Passacaglia on Russian Theme   BN 34
1874-1951   Russ/US

KOUTZON, Boris   25   V Conc   PH 51
1901-   Russ/US 12   Conc for 5 solo instruments and str O 1934   BN 39
                        8   Concert Overt from American Folklore 1943   PT 56
                        7   Morning Music for Fl and Str   NP 50
                       14   Solitude, Poem-Nocturne 1927   PH 26;   SF 28
                       12   Valley Forge, Symphon Poem 1931   CH 43;   CL 41

KOYAMA, Kiyoshige   4   Kobiki Uta,Woodcutter's Song   CT 64;   SF 67
  1914-   Japan

KOZELUCH, Leopold   10   Andante, Allegro   NP 35
  1752-1818   Aust

KRAFT, Anton   24   C Conc formerly attributed to Haydn Op 101
  1752-1820   Aust   CT 00, 16, 19, 22, 35, 42, 49, 54

KRAFT, Leo   20   Conc for Percussion and O   BN 67;   BU 68;
  1922-   US   DE 69;   MN 69;   SF 69
                        20   Contextures   LA 67
                        20   Var for O   CT 60

KRAMER, A. Walter   6   Intermezzo for Str   SE 30
  1890-   US   Nocturne   NP 19

KRASA, Hans   10   Marche for C   PH 23
  1899-   Czech 10   Pastoral and Marche fr Symph for small O   BN 26

KREIN, Gregory   5   Ode to Lenin   PH 29(2)
  1880-1955   Russ   8   Vocalise   CT 33

KREIN, Alexander   10   Funeral Ode or Threnody in Memory of Lenin Op 40 LA 30
  1883-1951   Russ   20   The Rose and the Cross, A Symphon fragment Op 26
                                CL 30

KREISLER,   8   In the Novgorod Forest for Str O   CT 36
  Alexander von
  1893-   Russ

KREISLER, Fritz   8   V Conc   NP 42;   MN 44
  1875-1962   Aust/US 5   L'Ephemere   NS 16
                         4   Liebesfreud   HN 43
                         6   Prelude and Allegro for V and O arr Sevitsky
                                NA 41, 45, 48;   MN 47
                         6   O Salutaris Hostia, Song   PH 15

KRENEK, Ernest   12   Cantata for Wartime, Sopr, Chor and O Op 95   MN 43
  1900-   Aust/US 22   C Conc   HN 57
                        30   Conc Grosso No 2 Op 25   CH 26;   NS 25
                        19   Conc for Harp and Chamber O   AT 52;   PT 53
                        22   P Conc No 2 Op 81   BN 38;   CH 38
                        17   P Conc No 3 1946   NA 49;   MN 46
                        18   V Conc Op 29   LA 53
                        30   Conc for 2 P and O 1951   NA 53;   MN 66
                        15   Little Symph Op 58   BN 30;   CH 30;   CT 31;
                                NA 30;   RC 32;   SF 31
                        22   Medea, Monologue, Sopr and O 1951   AT 52
                        12   Symphon Elegy for Str 1946   BU 50;   CL 5p;
                                DT 51;   NA 50;   PT 52;   SL 51
                        16   Symphon mvt Var on I Wonder, Op 94   BN 44;
                                NA 42;   MN 42

KRETCHMER, Edmund   7   American Festival Overt   HN 15
  1830-1908   Ger

KREUTZ, Arthur 1906- US	19-20 5	Music for Symph O 1940 NP 44 Winter of the Blue Snow from Paul Bunyan Suite 1941 CH 43

KREUTZER,
   Konradin
1780-1849   Ger
	4
	
	8
		Das Nachtlager von Granada, Opera 1834, Aria,
		    Seine fromme Liebes Gabe NP 1844
		Fruelingshahen Chor NP 1860

KREUTZER, Rudolph 1766-1831 Fr	4	Perpetuum Mobile arr Schonherr CH 38; CL 38
KROEGER, Ernest 1862- US	8 6 6 6	Endymion Overt SL 19 Hiawatha, Symphon Overt SL 12 Mississippi, Father of Waters SL 25, 28, 35 Thanatopsis, Overt SL 10, 17
KRUG, Arnold 1849-1904 Ger	19	Othello Symphon Prologue Op 27 BN 1886, 87; CH 1893; NP 1886, 88, 93
KRULL, Frederic US	5 10	Native Moods 3 NA 30 Synfonietta in C NA 32
KUBELIK, Jan 1880-1940 Czech	20	V Conc No 4 CT 34
KUBIK, Gail 1914- US	5 22	Bachata, Cuban Dance Piece NA 56 Symph No 3 NP 56
KUMMER, Friedrich 1797-1879 Ger	15	Grande Fantasie, Air Russe for C NP 1860, 69
KUPFERMAN, Meyer 1926- US	8 19	Comicus Americanus, Cantata, Soli and Chor KC 69 Little Symph DT 53; LA 52
KURKA, Robert 1921-1957 US	15 21 9 21 8	Concertina for 2 P, Trump and Str CT 60 Good Soldier Schweik, Suite in 6 mvts BA 63; PT 66 Julius Caesar, Symphon Epilogue CT 66; NP 61 Symph No 2 BN 58; CL 58; NA 59, 66; NR 66 Serenade on Poems of Whitman NR 61
KURTH, Chas 1860- Hung/Ger	20	Almausor, Symph Poem for O CT 00
KURTHY, Zoltan 1901- Hung/US	8 8 15	American Overt BA 40 Overt MN 40 Symph Rhaps, Puszta CH 37
KURTZ, Edward F. 1881- US	15	Suite Parisienne AT 68

KYSER, Kay
    US
	4	Tar Heels on Hand, U. of N. Carolina Fight Song
		    DA 49

LABATE, Bruno   4   Reminisce   BA 43
                US   12   Theme and Variant   BA 43

LABROCA, Mario   17   8 Madrigals by Tommaso Campanella arr for Baritone
1896-   It   and O   BA 58;   MN 57

LABUNSKI, Felix   9   Canto di Aspirazione   BU 67;   CT 63;   DE 65;
1892-   Pol/US   SL 43
                       38   P Conc in C Op 16   KC 38
                       20   Polish Renaissance Suite   CT 66
                       16   Symphon Dialogues   CT 60
                       15   Suite for Str O 1935   CT 45;   SL 47
                       18   Symph in g Op 14: 1st mvt   KC 44
                        9   -Canzone and Scherzo   SL 43
                       14   Var for O   CT 50;   SL 51

LABUNSKI, Wiktor   20   Conc for 2 P   KC 67
1895-   Pol/US

LACALLE   4   Song Amapola   DT 28

LACHNER   10   Festival Overt in D (Vincenz)   NP 1849
brothers: Ger   10   Serenade for C and Str Quart   NP 1870
Franz 1798-1890   20   Symph: Passionata   NP 1848
Ignaz 1807-1895   SONGS
Vincenz 1811-1893   4   Weep Not for Sorrows (Vincenz)   NP 1847
                        4   Überall, Du (Ignaz)   NP 1858
                        4   Bewüsstein (Franz)   NP 1858
                        5   Krieger's Gebet   NP 1871
                       30   Suite d Op 113 (Franz)   BN 88, 94
                        5   -1 mvt   BN 81, 84
                       30   -Var and March   CH 01
                       20   Introd and Fugue   CH 1894

LADMIRAULT, Paul E.   10   Var sur des Airs de Biniou   NP 54
1877-1944   Fr

LA FORGE   4   Into the Light, Song   NA 39
1879-1953   US   4   Song of the Open   NA 33

LAJTHA, Laszlo   29   Symph No 5 Op 55   CL 59
1892-   Hung

LALANDE, Michel R. de   Chaconne gracieuse   BN 21
1657-1726   Fr   15   Music While the King Dines   MN 51;   NS 21;   PH 21

LALO, Edouard   4   Arlequin: esquisse, fr Sonata for P and V   NS 09,
1823-1892   Fr   10, 13
                       23   C Conc in d 1876   BN 1899, 00, 11, 14, 17, 26, 50;
                             BU 67;   CH 1897, 99, 09, 13, 14, 19, 23, 26, 29,
                             30, 34, 43, 45, 63;   CT 1898, 06, 12, 18, 21, 30;
                             CL 22, 25, 40;   DA 35;   DE 50, 69;   DT 24, 26,
                             44, 48, 51, 57, 69;   HN 69;   KC 37;   LA 19, 23,
                             65;   MN 27;   NR 57;   NP 1897, 02, 07, 22, 24,
                             53;   NS 1892 2 mvts, 15, 19;   PH 02, 14, 18, 20,
                             24, 26, 61, 66;   PT 37, 44;   RC 69;   SF 13, 19,
                             24, 1 mvt 31

LALO, E. (Cont.)
<table>
<tr><td>30</td><td>V Conc russe, Op 29 1883   CH 18</td></tr>
</table>

```
30    V Conc russe, Op 29 1883    CH 18
31    Conc in f Op 20    BN 10;    CH 00, 28;    CT 19;    MN 28;    NP 03, 38;
         NS 1895, 24;    PH 12, 14, 17
10    Intermezzo V and O in B^b    NS 20
40    Namouna, Ballet Suite 1882    BN 1895, 22;    CT 07;    DE 61;
         DT excerpts 57;    NR 67;    NP 67;    NS 05;    PH 02;    SL 19
         -Fete Foraine    CT 20
 4    -Introd    NS 1887
         -Serenade    NS 1887, 92, 19
16    Norwegian Fantasie V and O in A 1880    BN 1884
16    Norwegian Rhaps in A 1881    BN 1888, 90, 18, 33;    CH 00, 06, 07, 09,
         18;    CT 18;    NS 1885;    PH 02, 04, 10, 18;    SL 13;    SF 17
11    Roi d Ys Overt to Opera 1888    BA 41, 42;    BN 1891, 92, 07, 13, 18,
         20, 49, 68;    CH 07, 47, 55;    CT 16, 21, 54;    CL 20, 21, 25, 29,
         44, 66;    DA 25, 67;    DE 62, 68;    DT 52, 54, 60, 63;    HN 65;
         MN 22, 28, 38, 39, 42, 44;    NP 02, 04, 26, 46, 48, 53, 56;
         NS 1889, 97, 18, 19, 22;    PH 23, 64;    PT 48;    RC 43;    SL 13,
         27, 33, 40;    SF 41, 55;    UT 59;    WA 34, 43
 5    Scherzo 1884    DA 34;    NS 1885, 13
34    Symph in g 1885    NP 31
30    Symphonie Espagnole, V and O Op 21    AT 50, 56, 64;    BA 46, 55, 66;
         BN 1887, 89, 96, 99, 03, 07, 10, 14, 19, 23, 44, 53;    CH 1899, 05,
         07, 10, 17, 20, 40, 44, 58, 66, 3 mvts: 13, 15, 19, 31;    CT 08, 15,
         17, 39, 49, 68;    CL 20, 22, 38, 44, 47, 57, 67;    DA 49, 56;
         DE 48, 50, 52, 55, 59, 67;    DT 19, 23, 28, 40, 44, 53, 56, 59, 67,
         69;    HN 40, 50, 58;    NA 45, 56, 66;    KC 38, 42, 44, 50, 52, 58,
         66, 69;    LA 44, 50, 54, 56, 67;    ML 67;    MN 22, 30, 32, 36, 38,
         43, 44, 47, 58;    NR 51, 54, 57, 60, 68, 69;    NP 36, 46(2), 47,
         50, 51, 53, 54, 56, 57, 69;    NS 10, 12, 18, 19;    PH 20, 21, 22,
         28, 38, 56, 66;    PT 37, 41, 44, 47, 54, 60, 69;    RC 50;    SL 43,
         46, 51, 54, 59, 67;    SF 11, 21, 25, 27, 29, 38, 41, 46, 47, 54;
         SE 35, 45, 50, 56, 65;    UT 41, 49, 55
         -First mvt    DA 28
 5    Theme and Var    NS 1892
      SONGS
 4       Aria fr Roi d Ys    AT 52;    CT 51;    LA 21;    NP 10;    PH 17, 35
 4       The Slave    CT 1896
```

```
LAMBERT, Constant    16    The Rio Grande, Chor, O and P 1927    BN 30, 33;
1905-1951    Brit             CH 31;    CL 31;    LA 31;    RC 15

LAMBRO, Phillip     5    Miaflores for Str O    BA 63
1935-        US

LA MONACA, Joseph    9    3 Dances fr Hindu Opera, The Festival of Gauri
1872-       It/US           PH 32

LAMOND, Frederic     5    Overt, from the Scottish Highlands 1892    CH 1894;
1868-1948    Scot           NP 1895

LA MONTAINE, John    35    P Conc Op 9    BN 54, 59;    MN 58;    SF 59, 64;
1920-        US             CT 60;    WA 58
                     30    Songs fr Song of Songs Sopr and O Op 29, 7 songs
                              NP 63;    SF 64;    WA 60
                  13-15    Songs of the Rose of Sharon Op 6    UT 67
```

LAMOTE DE GRIGNON,   11   Andalusia, Symphon Picture from Hispanicas
  Juan   CT 43, 44
  1899-   Sp

LAMPE, Johann F.   23   Serenade for Winds in A^b Op 7   CH 08
  1703-1751   Ger

LANDOWSKI, Marcel   14   Poéme Symphonique, Edina   SL 47
  1915-   Fr

LANDRE, Guillaume   12   Anagrammen 1916   MN 62
  1905-   Neth   15   Caleidoscopic Symphon Var   LA 57
                      14   Symph No 3   CH 51;   DT 63;   PH 53

LANG, Henry Albert   25   Symphon Fantasies of a Poet 4 parts   PH 13
  1854-1930   US

LANG, Margaret R.   8   Dramatic Overt   BN 1892
  1867-   US   15   Winds,Chor and O   NP 13

LANGENDOEN, Jakobus   19   Improvisation for 0,4 parts   BN 38
  1890-   US   18   Var on Dutch Theme   BN 26

LANGE-MULLER, Peter   4   Serenade, Kornmodsglandsen, Song   CT 49
  1850-1926   Dan

LANGER, Ferdinand   4   Introd,Dornroschen   BN 1894
  1839-1905   Ger

LANGSTROTH, Ivan   8   Scherzo 1931   LA 42;   PH 42;   SF 47
  1887-   US   10   Symphon mvt   BU 45
                      30   Symph in C Op 31   SF 51

LANNER, Josef   15   Die Mozartisten Waltzes Op 196   BN 63
  1801-1843   Aust   5   Pesth Waltz Op 93   CL 43
                       8   Die Schönbrunner Waltz Op 200   MN 58;   PH 41, 48

LAPARRA, Raoul   Dimanche Basque, P and O   BN 18
  1876-1943   Fr

LARKIN, John   22   Mass for the Popes, Voices, Str, Org and O   CT 57
  1927-   US   8   Mountain Adams fr Cincinnati Profiles, Suite for O
                             2nd mvt   CT 52, 54

LARSSON, Lars-Erik   13   Pastorale Suite Op 19 Scherzo   HN 45
  1908-   Swed   8   -Overt and Romance   HN 45
                      20   Sinfonetta   Str O Op 10   CL 35

LASSEN, Eduard   3   All Soul's Day, Song   NS 1886
  1830-1904   Dan/Belg 12   Beethoven Overt   CH 07
                      25   V Conc   NP 1892
                       6   Festival Overt Op 51   NP 1874

	Time in Minutes	
LASSUS, Orlando di or LASSO	8	Cantiones Duarum Vocum Sancti Mei-qui Vult Venire BU 63
1532-1594 Neth	3	Madrigal, Matonna, Lovely Maiden Op 28 NP 1889
	4	Surrexit Pastor Benus, Motet No 295 MN 43
LASZLO, Alexander 1895- Hung/US	11	Improvisation on Oh Susannah HN 42
LATHAM, William P. 1917- US	12	The Lady of Shallot, Tone Poem CT 40
LAUCELLA, Nicola 1882- US	10	Symphon Impressions, Whitehouse NP 1917
LAUDENSLAGER (LAUTENSCHLAGER) 1903- Ger	6	Overt to The Strait DT 66
LA VIOLETTE, Wesley 1894 US	4 20 12	Chorale for O SL 36 Dedications, V Conc CH 31 Penetrella for Str O MN 28; CH 28; SF 28
LAVRY, Marc 1903- Latvia/Is	18	Israeli Dances DT 52
LAYTON, Billy Jim 1924- US		Str Quart in 2 mvts SF 65
LAZAR, Filip 1894-1936 Roum/Fr	30 22 15 4 18	P Conc No 3, Op 23 BN 34 Conc Grosso No 1 in the old style Op 17 BN 29; SL 32 Music for an O BN 27 The Ring, a four minute round of boxing CL 30; RC 38; WA 34 Tziganes, Scherzo for O BN 26; CT 30
LAZAROF, Henri 1932- Fr		Mutazione UT 68
LAZARUS, Daniel 1898- Fr	28	Symph with Hymn in 5 mvts, excerpts SL 32
LAZZARI, Sylvio 1857-1944 It/Fr	15 8	Impressions of Night, Symphon picture NP 19 Prelude to the Opera Armor 1898 CH 98
LE CLAIR, Jean Marie 1697-1764 Fr	20 15 4	V Conc in d NP 12 Conc Grosso for Str O arr Dubensky PH 45 Musette and Gigue for Fl NS 15
LEE, Dai-Keong 1915- US	6 9 24	Hawaiian Festival Overt 1940 CT 45; DE 46; MN 42 Prelude and Hula 1939 WA 42 Symph No 2 SF 51
LEHMANN, Elizabeth 1862-1918 Brit	4 4	Ah, Moon of My Delight DT 28; KC 43 Spinning Song for Voice and O PH 04

LEIBOWITZ, Rene   4   Overt   PT 59, 61
1913-   Fr

LEICH, Roland   10   Prelude and Fugue   PT 55
            US

LEIGHTON, George   4   I'm Wantin' You Jean, Song   CT 12
1886-1935   US

LEITERMEYER   10   Polyphony   SF 65

LEKEU, Guillaume   10   Adagio for Str O Op 3   BN 41;   CH 20, 43, 47;
1870-1894   Belg   CT 18;   DT 41;   MN 22, 30, 37;   NP 28;
                           NS 13, 17, 20, 21, 24
                     9   Contrapuntal Fantasy on a Cramignon of Liege 1890
                           BN 25;   PH 25
                     8   Symphon Fantasia on two Folk Songs of Anjou 1892
                           BN 20;   CT 21;   NS 18;   RC 52;   SF 42

LENDVAI, Erwin   Symph in D Op 10   BN 12
1882-1949   Hung

de LEON, Javier   100   Mexican Fiesta   WA 69

LEONCAVALLO,   7   Pagliacci, Opera 1892: Prologue   AT 51;   CH 1897;
  Ruggiero   CT 1899, 48, 52;   DA 27;   DE 50;   DT 16;
1858-1919   It   HN 31;   NA 52;   ML 60;   MN 20;   PH 01;
                           RC 23, 57;   SL 18;   SF 36;   WA 49
                     4   -Decidi il mio destin, aria   HN 31
                     4   -Duet   SF 56
                     4   -Harlequin's Serenade   AT 52
                     5   -Mattinatta, aria   DA 48
                     4   -Vesti la guibba, aria   AT 64;   RC 24;   UT 51

LEES, Benjamin   20   Conc for O   RC 61
1921-   China/US   23   P Conc No 1   NA 56;   LA 69
                    22   P Conc No 2   BN 67;   DT 68;   SE 68
                    21   V Conc   BN 62;   NA 64;   PT 63
                    17   Conc Str Quart and O   BA 65;   CH 66;   CT 65;
                           CL 66;   DT 66;   KC 64
                    18   Divertimento Burlesca in four mvts   SE 58
                    11   Interlude for Str   BA 63
                     7   Profile for O   NP 64
                    22   Symph No 2   BN 69;   CH 64;   CT 63;   CL 59;
                           KC 65;   PT 69;   WA 61
                    20   Symph No 3   DT 68
                    10   Spectrum for Chamber O   PH 68

LEEUW, Ton de   21   Mouvements retrogrades   CL 60
1926-   Neth

LE FLEM, Paul   10   Magicienne de la Mer, Opera:Two Interludes   HN 57
1881-   Fr   10   Symphon Poem, To the Dead   NS 21;   PH 21

LEGINSKA, Ethel   4   Old King Cole   DA 32
1886-   Brit   10   Symphon Poem, Beyond the Fields   NS 21
                         15   Two Short Pieces for O   BN 23

LEGLEY, Victor   10   Dyptique   SL 66
1915-   Belg   12   La Cathédrale d'Acier Op 52   SL 63

LE GUILLARD, A.   20   Prelude a la Conte de Fées   AT 56
               Fr

LEHAR, Franz   3   The Merry Widow Operetta 1905: Overt   KC 64
1870-1948   Hung   4   -Villia   NA 66;   KC 64
                         5   Gold and Silver Waltzes   PT 38
                         4   Liebe du Himmel auf Erden from Paganni   AT 59

LEPLIN, Emanuel   11   Comedy for O   SF 46
1917-   US   43   Symph No 1   SF 61
                         36   Symph No 2   SF 65
                         23   Two Pieces for O, Landscapes and Skyscrapers   SF 59

LEPS, Wassili   15   Andon, Japanese Reincarnation Theme, Sopr, Tenor and
1870-   Russ/US   O   PH 05(2)
                         5   Overt, In the Garden of the Gods   PH 07
                         10   Symphon Illustration, Loretto   PH 25

LEROUX, Xavier   4   Le Nil, song   CT 42
1863-1919   Fr   15   Suite, Les Perses, Incidental Music after Aeschylus
                                   1896   NS 16

LESSMAN, W. J. Otto   4   The Red Red Rose, arr van des Stucken   CT 97
1844-1918   Ger

LESUR, Daniel   8   Sarabande et Farandole   CT 57
1908-   Fr

LEVANT, Oscar   32   P Conc in One mvt 1936   PH 43
1906-1970   US   5   Dirge in Memory of Gershwin   CL 39;   PT 39

LEVIDIS, Dimitri   15   Symphon Poem for Electric Instrument and O   PH 30
1886-   Gk/Fr

LEVY   30   Twenty Four Var on an Original Theme   CH 41

LEVY, Marvin David   23   Symph No 1   LA 60
1932-   US   12   Electronic Piece with O   ML 69

LEWIS, H. Merrils   12   Requiem: The Blue and the Grey, for Chor, 2 P,
1900-   US   Percussion and O   HN 66
                         16   Symph in One mvt   HN 53

LEWIS, Robert Hall   15   Designs for O   BA 63;   BN 64
1926-   US

LEWIS   5   The Spiritual: Donnie's Theme   CT 66

LIADOV, Anatol   4   Baba Yaga, A Musical Picture Op 56   BN 40;   CH 08,
1855-1914   Russ   09, 16, 25, 26, 28, 29, 32, 34, 38, 39, 41;
                           DA 53;   NA 33;   LA 20, 22;   MN 28;   PH 05, 10;
                           RC 25;   SF 18
                      5   Ballad   NS 09
                      4   Dance of the Amazons Op 65   PH 24
                      6   The Enchanted Lake, Tone Poem Op 62   BN 35, 40,
                           44;   CH 11, 17;   CL 25, 26, 28, 32, 49, 63;
                           DA 34;   DE 50, 58;   DT 45, 68;   HN 34, 49;
                           KC 37, 42, 45;   LA 26, 48;   ML 61;   NP 45, 54,
                           56;   PH 29, 32;   PT 38;   RC 31, 40, 55;   SL 61;
                           SF 19, 23;   SE 27, 38;   UT 44;   WA 34, 36
                      7   Kikimora, Tone Poem Op 63   BA 40, 55, 60;   BN 35;
                           CH 11, 25, 28, 33;   CT 15, 31, 36;   DA 46;
                           DE 62;   DT 46;   HN 49;   KC 35;   LA 20;
                           PH 32;   PT 45, 62;   RC 23, 31;   SL 11, 23
                      6   A Musical Snuff Box Op 32   BA 43;   NA 33;   WA 32
                     18   8 Russian Folk Songs, Suite for O Op 58   BN 27;
                           CH 33, 35;   CT 49, 56;   DA 35;   HN 57;   NA 38,
                           42;   KC 36;   MN 33, 35, 42;   NS 13, 21;   PH 32,
                           33, 36, 40, 44;   PT 39;   RC 32, 33;   SL 29, 32,
                           34;   SE 36, 37;   NA 45;   WA 45
                     20   From the Book of Revelation, Poem Op 66   BN 25,
                           27, 36, 42;   LA 25;   NS 22;   SF 22
                     12   Three Pieces for O   BN 10, 21, 24, 51

LIAPOUNOV, Sergei   25   P Conc No 1 in E^b Op 4   BN 17;   CH 07;   CT 17;
1859-1924   Russ   NS 16
                     18   P Conc No 2 in E Op 38   CH 19;   PH 19
                     15   Rhaps for P and O on Ukranian Songs Op 28   BN 21

LIDHOLM, Ingvar   17   Ritornello   CT 59;   DT 64;   MN 62
1921-   Swed   10   Rites, NR 68

LIEBERMANN, Rolf   15   Conc for Jazz Band and Symph O   BA 55;   CH 54;
1910-   Swiss   CL 55;   DE 58;   KC 55;   NP 54;   PT 56;   SF 55
                      8   Furioso for O   BA 56;   BU 65;   CT 55;   HN 54;
                           KC 55, 68;   MN 60;   NP 53;   RC 66;   SE 59;
                           UT 57;   WA 50
                     12   Geigy Festival Conc for Side Drum and O   CL 58
                     21   Musik for Narrator and O   NP 55

LIEBERSON, S.A.   25   In A Winter Garden Suite of four mvts   CH 34, 35;
1884   Russ   CT 40

LIGETI, Gyorgy   9   Apparitions   BU 66
1923-   Hung   7   Atmospheres   DE 69;   NP 63, 69;   PH 65;   RC 65;
                           SF 66

LINDNER, August   20   C Conc in e Op 34   BN 1888;   CH 00;   NS 06
1820-1878   Ger

LINDPAINTNER, Peter 15   Concertante with O No 1   NP 1847
1791-1856   Ger   15   Concertante, Sinfonia No 2   NP 1844, 45, 49
                      6   Abraham's Sacrifice Overt   NP 1854

LINDPAINTNER, P. (Cont.)
	8	Faust Overt in f# NP 1851, 1857
8	Vampyre Overt NP 1847, 50
8	War Jubilee Overt NP 1844, 48

LIPATTI, Dinu   15   Chef cu lautari   BN 38;   CL 38, 47;   PH 38
1917-1950 Roum/Swiss 6   Satrarii Suite, Rejoicing with the Gypsy Band   RC 47

LIPINSKY, Karl   15   Conc Militaire No 2   NP 1861, 69, 78
1790-1861   Pol

LISZT, Franz   6   Angelus from Annees de pelerinage, Troisieme
1811-1886   Ger   Annee, Op 163 No 1   CH 1891
                         11   Christus, Oratorio, Op 3 for Soli, Chor, Org and O:
                                Excerpts   BN 02, 06, 14
     10   No 2 Pastorale and March   PH 09
     6   No 4 Hirtengesang Shepherds' Song   NP 1872
     12   No 5 March of the Three Kings   NS 1880
     18   P Conc No 1 in E^b Op 124   AT 47, 59, 63, 66;   BA 60;   BN 1885,
            86(2), 96, 02, 03, 05, 06, 07, 08, 11, 12, 29, 48, 60, 64, 68;
            CH 1893, 95, 98, 03, 05, 06, 08, 09, 11, 17, 18, 24, 28, 30, 31,
            33, 41, 43, 45, 55, 59;   CT 1896, 03, 07, 09, 17, 22, 29, 36, 40,
            42, 43, 47, 58, 60;   CL 20, 24, 30, 31, 35, 40, 45, 60, 61, 66;
            DA 27, 29, 38, 46, 49, 50, 56, 57, 60;   DE 45, 52;   DT 20, 23,
            31, 39, 58, 61, 64, 69;   HN 37, 46, 47, 49, 61;   NA 37, 45, 47,
            52, 68;   KC 33, 39, 46, 52, 60, 62, 68;   LA 20, 22, 28, 62, 65;
            MN 22, 27, 38, 48, 60, 63, 66;   NR 68;   NP 1866, 69, 74, 78, 93,
            99, 04, 16, 19, 21, 22, 30, 43, 51, 56, 58, 59;   NS 1886, 89, 95,
            96, 05, 11, 18, 22, 23, 26;   PH 01, 05, 06, 07, 08, 09, 10, 12,
            15, 17, 18, 19, 21, 24, 40, 43, 50;   PT 52, 64, 65, 66;   RC 24,
            26, 34, 38, 47, 65;   SL 10, 13, 14, 18, 22, 26, 30, 60;   SF 12,
            14, 27, 30, 40, 51, 59;   SE 34, 40, 48, 66, 69;   UT 45, 63, 69;
            WA 38, 41, 48, 57, 61, 68
     19   P Conc No 2 in A Op 125   BA 28, 64;   BN 1883, 89, 90, 92, 98, 00,
            03, 05, 07, 11, 16, 21, 23, 60, 64;   BU 62;   CH 00, 05, 07, 11,
            12, 17, 18, 21, 37, 38, 44, 51, 63, 68;   CT 03, 07, 15, 17, 21(2),
            39, 57, 64, 67;   CL 51, 68;   DA 30, 54;   DE 50, 60;   DT 19, 27,
            45, 54, 57;   HN 33, 52, 54, 64;   KC 44, 55, 65;   LA 21, 45, 62;
            MN 22, 43, 45, 49;   NR 67;   NP 1870, 84, 03, 11, 15, 27, 51, 63;
            NS 05, 09, 10, 12, 17;   PH 07, 10, 15, 19, 30, 35, 49, 57, 58,
            65, 69;   PT 42, 45, 48, 53, 60, 66;   RC 27, 52, 60;   SL 09, 11,
            21, 37, 61, 64;   SF 17, 21, 28, 42, 44, 45, 50, 55, 67;   SE 49,
            59;   UT 54, 65;   WA 35, 55, 61, 65, 67
     20   Conc for 2 P and O Op 365 Pathetique arr Gabor   AT 57;   BN 01;
            CH 21;   CT 1899;   DT 24;   NP 39;   NS 21;   RC 39, 50
            Concert Paraphrases
     15   Midsummer Night's Dream Op 410   NP 1858, 75
     10   Rigoletto Op 434   NP 1860
     8   Gounod's Faust Op 407   NP 1863
     16   Dance of Death, Totentanz Op 126 Var on Dies Irae for P and O
            BN 01, 03, 21, 41;   CH 10, 25, 28, 32, 39;   CT 46, 47, 62, 68;
            CL 44;   DA 52, 62;   DE 48;   DT 21, 26;   HN 48, 60, 66;   NA 45;
            KC 46;   LA 44;   MN 39;   NP 01, 30;   NS 1888, 11, 22;   PH 22,
            49, 60;   PT 50, 60;   SL 11;   SE 29, 62;   WA 50
     20   Fantasy and Fugue for Org Op 259   CH 1896, 10, 11
     14   Fantasy on Beethoven's Ruins of Athens Op 122   CT 1895;   NP 1867

LISZT, F. (Cont.)
15   Fantasy on Hungarian Themes for P and O Op 123   AT 51;   BA 60;
          BN 1881, 01;   CH 1891, 96, 13, 14, 16, 21, 24, 28, 32;   CT 1897,
          20, 23, 42, 60;   DT 16;   HN 69;   KC 43, 54, 60, 65;   MN 27, 45,
          48;   NR 64;   NP 29, 58;   NS 1896, 14, 25;   PH 14, 51;   SL 11,
          23, 30, 44;   SF 19, 42, 60;   UT 57;   WA 31, 36, 37, 47, 63
 8   Goethe Festival March Op 115   CH 1899
 5   Grand Galop Chromatique arr Byrnes Op 219   KC 43;   PH 42
 8   Graner Messe Op 9 Credo   NP 1864
        HUNGARIAN RHAPSODIES Op 244
15   No 1 in f   BN 1886(2), 90, 99;   BU 47;   CH 1891, 04;   CT 01,
          13;   CL 25;   DA 32, 34, 37;   NA 37;   NP 13, 14, 16, 18, 19,
          22;   NS 22(2);   PH 02, 03, 04, 07, 09, 14, 21, 22, 24;   RC 28,
          38, 39
10   No 2 in c#   BA 38, 49;   BN 1883, 86, 87, 95, 00;   CH 1892, 95,
          02, 09, 10, 21;   CT 1896, 12, 18, 20;   CL 27;   DE 50;   DT 16,
          17, 20, 24, 26, 29, 31, 33;   HN 31;   NP 48;   PH 01, 16, 19, 20,
          24, 29, 36;   RC 37, 45 arr 4 P and O;   SL 25;   SF 48;   WA 32
 6   No 3 in D   BN 1883, 94, 98;   CH 55;   CL 32
11   No 4 in d   NS 03, 04
10   No 6 in D♭, Carnivale of Pest   BN 1896;   CH 08;   CT 03, 21; WA 44
 9   No 7   CT 1897, 02, 04
 6   No 10   NP 1875
10   No 12   CH 06;   DA 30
14   No 14   CH 1892;   NS 1885;   SE 29
10   Undesignated   NS 1892
 9   For V and O   CL 33
        Legend of Elizabeth, Oratorio Op 2, for Soli, Chor, Org and O
 8   Crusaders' March   CT 00;   NP 1869
 6   -Prelude   CH 10
 9   Legend of St. Francis Preaching to the Birds Op 4   BN 04;   CH 1892;
          CL 22, 41;   MN 46;   NS 11, 14, 16, 27
 5   Liebestraume Nocturne No 3, arr Verbrugghen   MN 27;   SF 11
10   Mephisto Waltz Op 110   AT 63;   BN 1887, 92, 93, 96, 01, 06, 12, 19,
          23, 27, 35;   CH 1892, 94, 95, 00, 02, 05, 07, 12, 15, 20, 28, 35,
          39, 55;   CT 11, 24, 30;   CL 48;   DT 25;   NA 57;   KC 38, 64;
          LA 46;   ML 62;   MN 24;   NP 1898, 06, 23, 30, 44, 54;   NS 1889,
          14, 17;   PH 57;   PT 51;   RC 59;   SL 10;   SF 41;   SE 28, 47;
          WA 37, 69
 6   O Salutaris hostia for women's Chor, Org and O Op 40   NS 1887
 9   Polonaise No 2 in E♭   BN 1887;   CH 1892, 93, 06, 07, 11;   CT 07,
          18;   DT 15;   NP 1861, 21;   SF 12
10   Psalm XIII Op 13   BN 25;   NP 17
10   Psalm 137 for Sopr, Chor, O, Org, V and Harp Op 17   NS 1887
        SONGS Die Drei Zigeuner Op 320   CT 1898, 02;   NP 01, 16;
 4   NS 1889;   PH 10, 17, 27
 4   Der Fischer Knabe from Schiller's Wilhelm Tell Op 292 No 1   NP 15
 4   Gretchen Op 375   NP 1890
 4   Lorelei Op 273   CH 06, 09;   CT 07;   DT 25;   NP 1877, 82, 15;
          NS 1896, 10, 21;   PH 05;   SF 14
 4   Jeanne d'Arc au bucher, aria from Dumas Op 293   KC 48;   MN 49;
          NS 94
 4   Mignon's Lied after Goethe Op 275   NP 1885;   NS 1882
 4   O quand je dors after Hugo Op 282   CT 1896, 11, 37;   LA 38
 4   Am Rhein, im schoener strom Op 272   CT 07
 4   Uber allen Gipfeln ist Ruh Op 306   NP 16
10   Wanderer's Nachtlied   PH 17

LISZT, F.(Cont.)
12   Spanish Rhaps arr Busoni Op 254   BN 1893;   CH 23, 25, 32;   MN 39;
      NS 13;   PH 14
      SYMPHONIC POEMS
38   No 1 Ce qu'on entend sur la montagne, Berg Symphonic Op 95   BN 15;
      CH 1893;   NP 1868, 75;   PH 05;   SL 20
19   No 2 Tasso Op 96   BN 1882, 86, 90, 92, 95, 02, 05, 11, 16, 20, 23,
      24;   CH 1892, 99, 01, 03, 05, 08, 13, 18, 19, 20, 21, 27, 30, 35,
      45;   CT 03, 10, 15, 19;   DA 26, 50;   DT 18, 25;   HN 32, 34;
      LA 21;   NP 1859, 62, 66, 70, 74, 76, 78, 97, 03, 11, 13, 14, 22,
      24;   NS 1879, 82, 86, 95, 11, 20, 23;   PH 06, 07, 08, 09, 11,
      12, 13, 14, 16, 17;   SL 12, 14, 17;   SF 12, 16, 22;   SE 27, 50;
      WA 33
20   No 3 Les Préludes Op 97   AT 57;   BA 38, 40, 43;   BN 1881, 85,
      86, 89, 91, 94, 98, 99, 03, 08, 11, 13, 15, 19, 22, 31, 38;
      CH 1891(2), 93, 96, 98(2), 99, 01, 02, 03, 04, 05, 07, 08, 13, 17,
      18, 19, 21, 30, 36, 38;   CT 1895, 00, 02, 04, 06, 09, 12, 14, 19,
      21, 26, 27, 37, 39, 46, 48, 54, 67;   CL 22, 24, 26, 29;   DA 25,
      26, 28, 32, 35, 49, 52;   DE 45, 56;   DT 16, 17, 18, 20, 23, 26,
      28, 29(2), 35, 36, 40, 52, 55, 60, 64;   HN 40, 43;   NA 30, 35,
      38, 42, 44(2);   KC 33, 34, 36, 41, 42, 47, 48, 57;   LA 19, 20,
      21, 22;   ML 60, 64;   MN 27;   NR 53, 59, 64, 68;   NP 1858, 61,
      64, 71, 73, 75, 89, 94, 03, 05, 09, 12, 18, 19, 20, 23, 35, 54,
      56;   NS 1878, 11, 13, 18, 19, 24;   PH 04, 05, 06, 07, 08, 09,
      10(3), 11, 12, 13(2), 15, 17, 18, 20, 21, 25, 27, 29, 30, 36, 44,
      47, 51;   PT 38;   RC 23, 24, 25, 30, 32, 36, 38, 41, 48;   SL 11,
      13, 16, 19, 21, 23, 25, 33;   SF 11, 15, 27, 38, 47, 61;   SE 26,
      27, 32, 37, 40, 42, 67;   UT 41, 42, 44, 49, 52, 61;   WA 32, 36,
      40, 45, 47, 67
13   No 4 Orpheus Op 98   BA 39;   BN 1884, 93, 05, 20, 62;   CH 1899,
      06, 09, 11, 19, 44, 58;   CT 1897, 38;   CL 28;   DT 25,
      39, 52, 63;   LA 19, 20;   NP 1861, 85, 15;   RC 26;   SL 23;
      SF 25, 39
12   No 5 Prometheus Op 99   BN 17;   CT 34;   NP 1891
16   No 6 Mazeppa Op 100   BN 1899, 12, 14, 16, 18, 21, 27;   CH 1891,
      97, 00, 07, 15, 47;   CT 03, 14;   DT 20, 53;   HN 37;   MN 40;
      NP 1865, 67, 71, 77, 09, 21;   NS 1880, 83, 88, 10, 11, 24;
      PH 10, 11;   SL 12;   SF 17
18   No 7 Fest Klänge Op 101   BN 1889, 01, 04;   CH 02;   NP 1860, 87,
      02;   NS 1879, 90, 92
22   No 9 Hungaria Op 103   BN 13;   SF 42
18   No 11 Hunnenschlacht, Battle of the Huns Op 105   BN 00, 04, 06,
      12, 22;   CH 1893, 95;   CT 19;   NA 51;   NP 1878, 04, 12, 15;
      NS 1881, 84, 91, 09, 18;   PH 11;   WA 51
30   No 12 Die Ideal, after Schiller Op 106   BN 1888, 03;   CT 02;
      NP 1868, 86, 11, 16;   PH 02

      SYMPHONIES
46   Dante Symph on the Divine Comedy Op 109   BN 1885, 02, 11, 15, 21;
      CH 02, 11;   CT 01;   LA 52;   MN 27;   NP 1869, 72, 11, 13, 14,
      16, 17, 20(2);   NS 1884;   PH 06;   SL 15
72   A Faust Symphony in Three Character Pictures Op 108 I Faust,
      II Marguerite, III Mephistopheles, with final Chor   BN 1898,
      09, 14, 16(2), 22, 25, 31, 36, 40, 48, 58;   BU 48;   CH 1898,
      99, 11(2), 30, 46;   CT 05;   CL 20; 21, 25, 30, 40, 49;
      DA 46;   DT 22, 53, 66;   HN 55;   NA 49, 61;   MN 35;   NP 63,
      80, 96, 01, 04, 12, 49, 60;   NS 1883, 07, 11, 20;   PH 01, 03,

LISZT, F. (Cont.) A Faust Symphony (Cont.)
        05, 07(2), 16, 22, 49;   PT 53;   RC 29, 45, 49;   SL 11, 17, 29;
        SF 23, 47, 60, 68;   SE 39, 49, 67;   WA 36, 42
  30   -2 Parts   NP 1866, 81
  52   -Without Chor   BN 1893, 05, 53
  10   -Excerpts   BN 1885, 88
  12   -II Marguerite   CH 1895, 05, 22;   CT 42;   DA 54;   HN 38;   SE 29
  12   -III Mephistopheles   CH 38;   CT 42;   RC 24

  14   Weeping and Wailing, Var on Bach Theme Op 180 arr Wiener   CH 54;
       NP 36
   6   Will of the Wisps   MN 35;   PH 44

LITOLFF, Henry   8   Chant des Belges   NP 1856
1818-1891 Brit/Fr 18   P Conc No 3   BN 1889, 97
          15   Conc Symphonique for P and O on Dutch Airs Op 45
               No 3   NP 1857
          25   Conc Symphonique for P and O No 4 in d Op 102
               NS 1887
           6   -Scherzo   CT 1896;   PH 03
           6   Overt, King Lear   BN 02
          10   Overt, Robespierre   NP 1850, 52
           8   Souvenir de Hartzburg Op 43   NP 1859
           5   Spinnlied, Solo P Op 51 in A^b NP 1858

LOBE, Johann C.   5   Reiselust Overt   NP 1852
1797-1881   Ger

LOCATELLI, Pietro 16   Conc for 4 V, Str O and Org Op 1 No 12   NR 55;
1695-1764   It   PH 51
          15   Elegiac Symph   BN 32

LOCKE, Matthew   12   Music for Sackbuts and Cornets, Rescored by
1630-1677   Brit   Anthony Baines   HN 62

LOCKWOOD, Normand 109 Children of God Oratorio for 5 Soli, Chor,
1906-   US   Children's Chor and O
          60   Part I, Am I My Brother's Keeper?   CT 56
          30   Light out of Darkness   BU 57
          10   Erie, Symphon Poem   CL 35
          25   Psalm 150, Soli, Chor and O   CT 52
          20   Suite, Odysseus   CH 28
          20   Symph: A Year's Chronicle   CH 34

LODER, George   6   Concert Overt, Marmion   NP 1845, 50
1816-1868   US

LOEFFLER, Charles 10   Beat! Beat! Drums   CL 32
1861-1933   US 18   Canticle of the Sun, St. Francis of Assissi
              Voice and O   BN 29, 30;   CH 29;   CL 35; PH 25
          15   C Conc   BN 93, 97
          10   Divertissement in a for V and O or Sax and O
               BN 94, 96
          17   La Bonne Chanson after Verlaine   BN 01, 02, 18,
               20, 24, 28;   CH 02, 25;   CT 24;   CL 24;
               NP 24;   PH 24

LOEFFLER, C. (Cont.)

	10-12	Evocation, women's Chor and O 1930 BN 32, 33; CL 30, 32
	30	Five Irish Fantasies for Voice and O CL 29; DE 56; DT 58; BN Nos 2, 3, 5 in 21
	10	Hora Mystica, Symph in One mvt with men's Chor Op 6 BN 16; DT 35
	14	Memories of My Childhood, Poem 1925 BN 25, 26; CL 25; NS 25(2); PH 26; CH 34, 39
	10	Morceau Fantastique for C and O PH 04
	25	La Mort de Tintagiles, Symphon Poem Op 6 Vla and O BN 1897(2), 00, 03, 13, 15, 22, 31; CH 14, 15, 41; CL 22, 27, 31; LA 53; NP 21, 32; NS 05, 14; PH 25; SL 18
	10	Nights in the Ukraine, Suite, V and O BN 91, 99
	22	A Pagan Poem, after Virgil Op 14 BN 07(2), 12, 23, 27, 30, 35, 38, 42, 59; CH 09, 17, 29; CT 16; CL 24, 30, 35, 42, 52; LA 29; MN 28; NP 22, 25, 29, 30, 45; NS 09; PH 19, 31; RC 30; SL 20, 29; SF 30
	10	La Villanelle du Diable, Symphon fantasy for Org and O Op 9 BN 01, 02, 05, 09; CL 21; NP 10; NS 13, 18, 20; PH 12

LOEWE, Karl 1796-1866 Ger	8	Ballad, Archibald Douglas for Bar and O CH 99; PH 11
	4	Ballad, Edward 1818 NP 00
	4	Song Canzonetta NS 08

LOEWE, Fredrich 1904- US	10	My Fair Lady, excerpts SF 56

LOPATNIKOV, Nicholas 1903- Russ/US	12	Concertina for O Op 30 BN 44; CT 52; DA 62, 66; HN 66; KC 67; PT 45, 67; RC 52; SL 46
	19	Conc for O Op 43 PT 63
	20-22	Conc for 2 P and O Op 33 CT 53; DE 52; MN 52; PT 51, 64; RC 52; WA 53
	23	V Conc Op 26 BN 41; CH 47; PH 45; PT 48
	25	Danton, Suite from Opera Soli, and O Op 20 PT 66
	20	Divertimento for O Op 34 BN 53; DT 55; PT 52
	11	Festival Overt Op 46 CH 62; DT 68; NP 60; PH 63; PT 62
	8	Introduction and Scherzo Op 10 NP 30
	4	-Scherzo BN 27
	14	Music for O Op 39 BN 59; MN 61; PT 60
	11-12	Opus Sinfonicum Op 21 CL 43
	16	Sinfonetta, Op 27 BN 42; PT 47
	25	Symph No 1 Op 12 DT 31; PH 31; NP 33
	25	Symph No 2 Op 24 BN 39
	36	Symph No 3 PT 54
	8	Two Russian Nocturnes DA 46
	24	Variazioni Concertante Op 38 CT 62; NP 64; PT 58

LORCA, Federico G. ? -1936 Sp	20	Sierra Granada and Fiesta RC 43
	10	Zorongo Gitano CT 43; RC 43

LORENZITI, Luigi | 20 | Conc for Vla d'amour and Double Bass   PH 19
1740-1794   It | 20 | Suite in 4 parts for Vla d'amour and O   NS 18;
PH 18;   SL 18
| 12 | Venetian Symph for Quinton Vla, Harpsi and O   BN 27

LORTZING, Gustav A. | 4 | Aria from Peter the Great, Opera 1837   NP 1853
1801-1851   Ger

LOTTI, Antonio | 4 | Aria, Pur dicesti   NS 1882
1667-1740   It | 4 | Crucifixus, double Choir a capella   CH 08;   KC 34

LOUREGLIO, Fleuthere | 8 | Spectres   SL 35
1900-   It

LOURIÉ, Arthur | 20 | Sonata Liturgique, 4 Chorales with Voices   BN 30
1892-   Russ/US | 20 | Suite from the Blackamoor of Peter the Great
Opera,   SL 61
| 26 | Suite, Feast During the Plague 1943   BN 44
| 15 | Symphonia Dialectica 1930   BN 33;   PH 30
| 18 | Symph No 2, Kormtchaia   BN 41

LUALDI, Adriano | 6 | Overt for a Comedy   DT 37
1887-   It

LUCAS, Clarence | 5 | Overt Macbeth Op 39   CH 00
1866-1947   Can

LUCKHARDT, Hilman | 10 | Two Choral Preludes   SE 44, 46
1914-   US | 12 | Var and Finale for O on British Folksong, Beneath
the Willow Tree, 9 parts   SE 44

LUDLOW, Ben | 7 | Christmas Overt   PH 50
1910   US | 12 | Fantasy on Christmas Carols   DT 47

LUEBECK, Ernest | 5 | Grand Polonaise   NP 1861
1829-1876   Neth

LUENING, Otto | 20 | Concert Piece with Ussachevsky, for Tape Recorder
1900-   US | | and O   NP 59
| 14 | Poem in Cycles and Bells, with Ussachevsky   LA 54
| 10 | Serenade for Three Horns and Str   RC 27
| 8 | Synthesis for O and Electric Sound   ML 63
| 8 | Two Symphon Sketches   CH 35;   NP 36

LUIGINI, Alexander | 7 | Ballet Egyptian   HN 14
1850-1906   Fr

LULLY, Jean-Baptiste | 10 | Ballet Suite arr Stokowski   PH 14, 18, 31
1632-1687   Fr | 10 | Ballet Suite arr Mottl   BN 22, 32;   CT 39;
CL 22, 30, 39;   MN 40;   PH 16, 17, 18, 22, 31;
SF 33, 53;   WA 45
| 10 | Ballet Suite, Nopces de village 1663 arr Rosenthal
NP 46;   PH 48
| 4 | Opera, Thésée 1675: Air de Venus   CT 40
| 4 | -Revenez, Revenez, amours   HN 40
| 12 | Te Deum, Selections   SF 56

	Time in Minutes	
LUTOSLAWSKI, Witold 1913- Pol	29	Conc for O BA 68; BN 67; CH 63; CL 58; DA 65; DT 64; LA 64; ML 66; MN 61; NR 67; NP 60; PT 59; RC 66; SF 60, 65
	12	Funeral Music CH 67; CL 59; MN 66; NP 63, 68; SF 66
	8	Jeux Venetiens BN 65; CL 66; MN 62; RC 67; SL 64
	14	Trois Poems d'Henri Michaux BU 65; CL 69
	5	Prelude No 1 WA 69
LYNN, George 1915- US	8	The Gettysburg Address DE 62
	21	Symph No 1 1963 DE 63
MAAS, Louis 1852- US	32	P Conc in c BN 1881, 89
MACCUNN, Hamish 1868-1916 Scot	8	Overt, The Land of the Mountain and Flood Op 3 CH 1892; RC 07
MACDOWELL, Edward 1861-1908 US	30	P Conc No 1 in a Op 15 BN 92; CH 93, 20; SL 14; SF 47; UT 60
	23	P Conc No 2 in d Op 23 BA 28, 66; BN 1888, 97, 98, 07, 19, 36; BU 66; CH 1898, 07, 13, 17, 18, 19, 29, 60; CT 1895, 14, 29; CL 53; DA 52; DT 61; NA 63; LA 50; NP 1894, 30, 39, 65(2); NS 15; PH 13, 18, 38; PT 64; RC 24, 31; SL 18, 43; UT 59; WA 65; KC 53
	4	Eight Songs Op 47 No 7, The Sea CT 09
	4	Four Songs Op 56 No 3 A Maid Sings Light CT 09; NP 10
	12	Sea Pieces Op 55 8 parts arr Barrymore NA 41
	10	Song of Roland, two fragments Op 30 NP 10; NS 05 No 1 The Saracens DT 16; NP 10
	35	Suite No 1 in a Op 42 BN 91, 95, 07, 15, 18; CH 91, 11, 12, 17, 20; SL 18; SF 12; CT 00
	31	Suite No 2 Indian Op 48 in e BN 1894, 97, 01, 06, 07, 12, 14, 17, 22; BU 54; CH 1897, 22, 32; CT 09, 17, 23; DT 15, 16, 18, 60; NA 32; LA 20; NP 1897, 16, 58; PH 01, 10, 18; PT 43; SL 15, 32; SF 13
	6	No 1 Legend CH 12, 17; MN 32
	6	No 2 Love Song CH 12, 17; RC 23
	6	No 3 In War Time CT 32; MN 32; PH 32; RC 23
	6	No 4 Dirge CT 32; NP 21, 39; NS 20; PH 32
	6	No 5 Village Festival CH 12, 17; NS 20
	10	Symphon Poem Op 25 Lancelot and Elaine BN 1889, 98, 05; CH 99, 05, 07; NP 15
	15	Symphon Poem Op 22 Hamlet and Ophelia BN 1892, 32; CT 1898; NP 17; PH 05
	35	Symphon Poem Op 29 Lamia BN 08
	29	Sonata Tragica Op 55 DT 46
	12	Woodland Sketches Op 51, Three numbers arr Winstead KC 40
	4	No 1 To A Wild Rose arr Victor Herbert BA 28
	5	No 3 Trysting Place arr Brasch DT 43
	5	No 7 Uncle Remus DT 43

MACHEDO, Augusto   3   Gran Fandango   DE 59
1845-1924   Sp

MACINNIS, Donald   6   Intersections for Tape Recorder and O   AT 68
1923-   US

MACKENZIE, Sir Alex C.20   La Belle Dame Sans Merci Op 29 Ballade for O
1847-1935   Scot   BN 1886, 90;   NP 1883
                        7   Brittania Overt Op 52   CH 1894; NS 1894, 17
                       17   Burns, Scottish Rhaps No 2 Op 24   CH 1892
                       12   From the North, Three Scottish Pieces Op 53   CH 1897
                       12   The Little Minister, Incidental Music Op 57   Three
                              Dances   CH 1898
                        5   Twelth Night Overt Op 40   NP 1888
                       25   Pibroch, V and O Op 42   BN 1886, 90

MACMILLAN, Sir Ernest 7   Two String Sketches on Fr. Canadian Airs
1893-   Can   -Our Lord As A Beggar   NA 48
                                 -In St. Malo   NA 48

MADERNA, Bruno   8   Amanda   PT 69
1920-   It   10   Quadrivium   CH 69

MADETOJA, Leevi   15   Sammon ryosto, The Capture of Sampo, for Baritone,
1887-1947   Fin   male Chor and O Op 24   BN 53
                        4   -The Capture of Sam   CT 53

MAEKELBERGHE, August   6   Scherzo Impromptu   DT 45(2)
1909-   Belg/US

MAGANINI, Quinto   8   Cuban Dance, La Rumba 1926   NS 26
1897-   US   6   Pastoral Scene from Tuolumne, A California Rhaps for
                              Trump and O 1924   NS 24

MAGNARD, Alberic   14   Hymne a la Justice Op 14   BN 18;   PH 23
1865-1914   Fr

MAHLER, Gustav   25   Kindertotenlieder 1902
1860-1911   Aust   BA 56;   BN 58;   BU 54;   CH 49, 65;   CT 25,
                                53, 69;   CL 69;   DA 54;   DE 66;   DT 65, 69;
                                NA 65;   KC 52;   LA 41, 65;   MN 49;   NR 69;
                   NP 59, 64, 68;   PH 16, 34, 40;   PT 55, 64;   SF 49;   WA 37
        51   Das Knaben Wunderhorn, Songs from Youth's Magic Horn 1882   NP 67;
               PT 68
        20   -Selections, with Soli   CH 67
        16   -Four Songs   PH 21
         4   No 1 Der Schildwache Nachtlied   DT 30;   PH 30
         4   No 4 Wer hat dies liedlein erdacht?   CH 53;   CT 24, 27, 29;
               CL 27;   DT 21, 25;   HN 68;   MN 34;   NP 52
         4   No 5 Das irdische Leben   LA 21;   NP 59;   NS 25
         4   No 6 Des Antonius von Padua Fischpredigt   RC 58
         4   No 7 Rheinlegendchen   CH 30;   CT 27, 29;   CL 28;   DT 21, 30;
               HN 68;   NP 10;   PH 27, 30;   RC 58;   SL 30(2)
         4   No 9 Wo die schönen Trompeten blasen   CH 53;   HN 68;   LA 56;
               NP 52, 56;   RC 58
         4   No 12 Urlicht from Symphony II   CT 29;   SL 30

MAHLER, G. (Cont.)

60   Das Lied von der Erde, Song of the Earth for O, Contral and Tenor
        Soli 1908   AT 55;   BA 64;   BN 28, 30, 36, 43, 49, 60, 69;
        BU 46, 61, 67;   CH 38, 50, 52, 57, 59, 64;   CT 23, 49, 54;
        CL 40, 47, 59, 66, 69;   DA 46, 59, 66;   DE 65;   DT 55, 63;
        HN 60;   NA 44, 67;   KC 51;   LA 46, 56, 61, 67;   ML 67;
        MN 41, 54;   NR 66;   NP 28, 29, 34, 40, 41, 44, 47, 52, 59, 63, 66;
        PH 16, 37, 54, 67;   PT 41, 53, 59, 67, 69;   RC 41, 68;   SL 57;
        SF 41, 49, 63, 65, 69;   SE 62;   UT 52, 67

14   Lieder eines fahrenden Gesellen, Songs of a Wayfarer Four Songs 1883
4   No 1   AT 56;   BA 53;   BN 52, 58, 68(2);   CH 15, 37, 66;
        CT 22, 29, 46, 52;   CL 58, 63;   DA 46, 60, 67;   DE 56, 64;
        DT 48, 53;   HN 49;   NA 49, 59;   KC 46;   LA 58, 68;   MN 35,
        40, 43, 50;   NR 53;   NP 45, 64;   NS 15;   PH 33, 36;   PT 45;
        RC 51;   SL 50, 63;   SF 64, 67;   SE 47;   UT 56;   WA 47, 60
4   No 2 Ging Heut' morgen übers Feld   CL 27;   NP 10
4   No 6 Um schlimme Kinder artig zu machen   DT 21
4   No 7 Ich ging mit lust durch einen grunen Wald   CT 27
        Songs to Poems by Ruckert 5 songs 1902
4   No 1 Ich atmet' einem linden Duft   CH 28, 53;   CT 24;   DT 25;
        HN 68;   LA 56;   MN 34;   NP 52, 56, 59;   PH 16;   RC 58
4   No 2 Liebst du um Schönheit   CT 27, 29;   CL 27;   SL 30
4   No 3 Blicke mir nicht in die Lieder   RC 58
4   No 4 Ich bin der Welt abhanden gekommen   CT 29;   LA 56;   NP 52,
        56, 59;   RC 58;   SL 30
4   No 5 Um Mitternacht   NP 59
12   Three Songs Unidentified   DE 62
4   The Song Birds Contest before the Donkey   DT 21
24   Six Songs for Sopr and O   PT 67
        Der Tamburg'sell 1910   CH 30;   CL 28;   SL 30

        SYMPHONIES

52   No 1 in D Titan 1888
        BA 47, 48, 49, 51, 67;   BN 23, 35, 42, 55, 59, 62, 67;   BU 57, 59;
        CH 14, 35, 49, 51, 56, 59, 62, 64, 68;   CT 30, 42, 47, 67;
        CL 41, 49, 62, 67;   DA 49, 54, 58, 69;   DE 67, 69;
        DT 22, 32, 41, 66;   HN 47, 50, 52, 59, 67;   NA 52;
        KC 46, 54;   LA 27, 40, 55, 58, 61, 63;
        MN 37, 40, 48, 52, 61, 64;   NR 50, 56, 64, 69;
        NP 09, 20(2), 33, 40, 42, 45, 46, 49, 51, 53, 58, 59, 61, 66;
        NS 23;   PT 51, 52, 63, 68, 69;   PH 46, 49, 53, 59, 63, 66;
        RC 50, 58, 65;   SL 46, 51, 63;   SF 21, 42, 53, 63;   SE 66;
        UT 53;   WA 49, 53, 60, 65
4   -Feirlich und Gemessen   CH 37, 38
4   -Kraftig und Bewegt   CH 37, 38
75   No 2 in c, Soli and Chor, Resurrection 1894
        AT 65;   BA 69;   BN 17, 19, 48, 59;   BU 51;   CH 48, 50, 54, 68;
        CT 51, 60;   CL 35, 68;   DA 52, 63, 69;   DT 22(2), 33;
        HN 61, 68;   KC 67;   LA 34, 37, 50, 64;   MN 34, 53;   NR 68;
        NP 25, 32, 35, 41, 43, 48, 56, 60, 63;   NS 08;
        PH 20, 34, 52, 55, 67, 69;   PT 52, 57, 66, 67;   RC 60;
        SL 54, 65;   SF 25, 47, 67;   SE 59;   UT 59, 65, 66;   WA 54
        -Second mvt   PT 38
        -Fourth mvt   NP 59

MAHLER, G. (Cont.) Symphonies (Cont.)
94   No 3 in d 1895
          BN one mvt 42, 61, 66;   CH 66;   CT 13;   CL 69;   DA 64;
          HN 66;   LA 64;   MN 49;   NP 21, 55, 60;   PH 68
52   No 4 in G Ode to Heavenly Joy Sopr and small O 1900
          AT 53, 68;   BA 55, 66;   BN 3rd and 4th mvts 41, 44, 53, 56, 62,
          65;   BU 56, 60, 68;   CH 15, 16, 23, 28, 36, 46, 51, 58, 64, 67;
          CT 25, 50, 51, 62;   CL 36, 46, 50, 55, 60, 62, 65;   DA 48, 61;
          DT 24, 51, 65;   HN 64, 69;   NA 47;   KC 49;   LA 31, 49, 56, 60,
          68;   MN 37, 51, 56, 59, 65;   NP 10, 15, 41, 43, 52, 59, 61, 64,
          67, 69;   NS 04;   PH 45, 60;   PT 44, 58, 67;   RC 47, 69;
          SL 23, 26, 60, 68;   SF 52, 65;   SE 49;   UT 50, 61, 67;
          WA 43, 58, 64
65   No 5 in c 1902   BN 05(2), 12, 13, 31, 37, 39, 48, 50;   CH 06, 50;
          CT 55, 66;   CL 52, 69;   DA 56(2);   DT 22, 59, 69;   HN 65;
          LA 28;   ML 69;   MN 66;   NR 65;   NP 11, 26, 31, 39, 59, 62,
          67;   PH 64;   PT 55;   SL 69;   SE 57
          -Adagietto for Str and Harp   AT 62;   CH 45, 47;   CT 41;
          DE 63, 65;   DA 20, 21, 25;   MN 44;   PH 42;   RC 66;
          SL 53, 65, 66;   SF 69;   UT 59, 61, 65;   WA 39
          -Allegretto only   DA 29
          -Funeral March only   NP 46
75   No 6 in a 1904   BN 64;   CH 67;   CL 67;   LA 68;   NP 47, 54, 64,
          66, 69;   PH 68;   PT 60, 68;   SL 64;   SE 67
78   No 7 in D Song of the Night 1905   BN 48;   CH 20, 21, 22, 32;
          CT 30;   HN 69;   LA 3 mvts only 51, 62;   NP 22, 48, 61, 65;
          PT 61, 67;   RC 3 mvts only 31, 53, 57;   UT 64;
          -Nachtmusik I   BU 49, 66;   CL 45, 51;   NP 31;   PT 56;   SL 30
          -Nachtmusik II   BU 49, 66;   CL 45, 51;   NP 31;   PT 45, 56;
          SL 30
90   No 8 in E^b Symph of a Thousand, Soli, Chor and O 1907   CT 68;
          NP 49, 65;   PH 15;   SL 66;   UT 63
72   No 9 in D^b 1909   BN 31, 33, 35, 39 adagio only, 40, 51, 66, 69;
          BU 62;   CH 49, 52, 59, 62, 68;   CL 48, 63, 68;   DT 69;   LA 69;
          NP 45, 59, 62, 65;   PH 69;   PT 68;   SF 64;   UT 68
71   No 10, Unfinished 1910   CH 65, 68;   CT 59;   CL 58;   DT 68;
          NA 59;   MN 63;   NR 58;   NP 67;   PH 67;   SL 68;   SF 66, 68
          -Andante   NP 57, 59
          -Allegretto   BN 59

MAILLART, Aimé Louis   6   Overt Les Dragons de Villars, Opera 1856   AT 66
1817-1871   Fr

MAKRIS, Andreas   8   Symphon Overt   WA 67
1930   Gk

MALATS, Josquin   5   Serenade for O   CT 43
1872-1912   Sp

MALIPIERO, Gian F.   10   A Claudio Debussy arr O'Connel   PH 35
1882-   It   12   La Cimarosiana 1921   BN 27;   KC 55
                       14   C Conc 1937   SL 50
                       15   P Conc No 1 1934   BN 36;   MN 38;   NP 50
                       18   V Conc 1932   BN 34;   CH 34
                       20   Concerti, Seven Short Concerti 1931   PH 31
                       8   Ditrambo Tragico 1917   PH 20

MALIPIERO, G. F. (Cont.)
	18	Grottesco, Piccola and small O 1918 SL 21

MALIPIERO, G. F. (Cont.)

18   Grottesco, Piccola and small O 1918   SL 21
8   Impressioni dal Vero, Suite No 1 1910   BN 20;
      KC 37;   LA 24;   MN 26
20   Impressioni dal Vero, Suite No 2 1914   CT 38;
      RC 25
8   Impressioni dal Vero Suite No 3 1923   CH 24;
      CT 29
14   Oriente Imaginario for small O 1920   PH 25
14-16 Pause del Silencio, Seven Symphonic Expressions 1917
      BN 18, 19;   CH 22;   CT 20;   DT 34;   NP 29;
      PH 19;   SL 28
32   La Passione, for Soli, Chor and O 1935   SF 61
16   San Francesco d'Assissi, Mystery for Baritone,
      Chor and O 1920   PH 28;   SF 30
5   -Finale   CH 38
8   -Fragments   PH 28;   SF 30
10   Study per Orchestre   RC 67
30   Sul Fiume del Tempi   PH 26
30   Symphon Suite on Knightly Story   CH 21
20   Symphon Suite on Three Plays   NS 24
23   Symph No 1 in 4 Tempi as the Four Seasons 1934
      BN 34;   CH 35;   DT 35;   SE 34
20   Symph No 2 Eligiaca 1936   BN 37;   NP 37;   SE 36
18   Symph No 3 The Bells 1944   NR 47
25   Symph No 4 In Memoriam 1946   BN 47
18   Symph No 5 for 2 P and O 1947   NA 50
20   Symph No 7 delle canzoni 1948   SF 55
15   Vivaldiana   NP 53

MALOTTE, Albert   4   Song, Lord's Prayer   NA 36, 40
1895-   US

MANCINELLI, Luigi   14   Cleopatra Overt 1877   HN 35;   SL 27
1848-1921   It

MANCZYK, Fritz   10   Six Var on a Sarabande by J.S. Bach   CT 58
1916-   Ger/US

MANDL, Richard   9   Overt to a Gascon Chivalric Drama   BN 10;   CH 14;
1862-   Czech/Fr   SL 12

MANFREDINI, Francesco 8   A Christmas Pastorale for Str   CT 31, 42, 43;
1688-1748   It   CL 44;   MN 32
                       8   Conc for 2 Trumpets and Str   CH 54
                       6   Prelude and Fugue arr Tinayre   SL 39
                      12   Sinfonia No 10 in e arr Ehrmann   CH 51

MANHEIM, Ernest   20   Symph in b   KC 50
1900-   Ger/US

MANN, Robert   5   Entr'acte: Excerpts from Attitude No 1   AT 64
1902-   US   5   Fantasie   AT 64
                       9   Innocence and Spring Attitude No 2   AT 64
                       7   Mexican Folk Dance, arr La Golondrina for Ballet
                             AT 64

MANUEL, Roland 1891- Fr	4	Pena de Francia SL 37
MAQUARRE, Andre 1875- Belg/US	8 10	On the Sea Cliffs BN 08 Two Songs PH 19
MARAIS, Marin 1656-1728 Fr	14	Five Old French Dances arr Cooley CL 31
MARCELLI, Nino 1892- Chile/US	6	Ode to A Hero LA 42

MARCELLO, Benedetto
1686-1739   It
	5
	
	10
	
	16
	
	5
	
	4
		Adagio in a arr Manczyk WA 33
		Conc in c for Ob and Str O arr Bonelli
		   AT 58; DT 47, 66; LA 53; PH 58; PT 57
		Conc Grosso in F Op 1 No 4 for Str O and Cembalo
		   arr Bonelli NP 39
		Introd, Air and Presto for Str and Cembalo arr
		   Bonelli CL 44; SL 39, 40, 42, 43, 44, 46, 49,
		   50, 55
		Aria, Il Mio Del Fuoco CT 22; DT 23; PH 12

MARGUMA, Pasquale 1873-1941 Sp	10	Espagna Cani NP 56
MARKEVITCH, Igor 1912- Russ/Swiss	12 20 24	Introd and Hymn for O 1932 BN 33 L'Envoi d'Icare Ballet 1933 NP 57 Rébus, An Imaginary Ballet 1931 BN 32

MARSCHNER, Heinrich
1795-1861   Ger
	8
	
	4
	
	8
		Opera, Hans Heiling, 1833 Overt BN 1894, 99;
		   NP 1855
		-Aria, An jenem Tag CH 05, 32; CT 1898, 03;
		   MN 30; NP 1889; NS 1890; PH 04, 05, 27
		Opera, Der Vampyr 1828, Overt NP 1844, 48, 53,
		   58, 61

MARTELLI, Henri 1895- Fr	15 15	Bas-reliefs Assyriens, Symphon Suite 1928 BN 29, 37 Conc for O Op 31 1931 BN 31
MARTIN, Easthope 1887-1925 US	4	Roll Along Home SE 48

MARTIN, Frank
1890-   Swiss
	17
	7
	7
	20
	30
	25
	22
	
	21
	22
	17
		Ballade, C and O 1949 CL 67
		Ballade, Fl, P and Str O 1939 PT 53
		Ballade, Tromb, Sax and O 1940 RC 65
		Conc Harpsi and O CH 47
		V Conc 1951 CT 52; CL 52; DA 52; NP 52
		P Conc No 2 1934 NP 68
		Conc for 7 Wind Instruments, Timpani, Percussion
		   and Str 1949 BN 51; CL 50; DA 63; LA 52;
		   MN 66; NR 59, 68; NP 50; PH 58; PT 56
		Etudes for Str O BN 61; PH 66; PT 59
		The Four Elements CH 66; PT 65
		Six Monologues from Jedermann for Baritone and O
		   1943 CL 65

MARTIN, F. (Cont.)

                          9   Overt Athalie, Incidental Music for women's Chor
                                 and O 1946   BU 57
                       22   Petite Symphonie Concertante for Harp, Harpsi,
                                 P and small O 1945   BN 48;   BU 69;   CL 48;
                                 DT 58, 68;   LA 51;   MN 61;   NP 57;   PH 49;
                                 SF 53;   SL 68
                       22   Symphonie Concertante for large O 1915   BN 28

MARTINEZ, Ambrosio   5   Brisas de Marbella, Dance   DE 58
1916-   Cuba

MARTINI, Giovanni   9   Prelude, Adagio and Fugue arr Read   NA 44
1706-1784   It

MARTINI, Jean Paul   4   Song, Plaisir d'amour   NS 1894;   SF 38
1741-1816   Ger

MARTINON, Jean   19   Conc Lyrique, Str Quart and O Op 38   CH 64
1910-   Fr   26   V Conc No 2 Op 51   CH 63
                       12   Overt to a Greek Tragedy 1951   BN 65;   CH 67;
                                 RC 58
                       10   Prelude and Toccata   BN 59
                        8   Rose of Sharon   CH 66
                       30   Symph No 2 Hymn à La Vie Op 37   BN 56;   CH 61, 68
                       25   Symph No 4   PH 67;   SF 69

MARTINU, Bohuslav   9   La Bagarre 1927   BN 27
1890-1959 Czech/US 22-24 P Conc No 2 1935   CH 64;   DE 69;   PH 44
                       25   P Conc No 3   CL 50;   DA 49;   MN 51;   NP 64;
                                 SF 52, 64
                       20   Conc No 4 Incantation   DA 59;   WA 62
                    23-24 Conc for 2 Str O P and Timpani 1938   BN 66;
                                 CH 49, 51, 52;   MN 63;   PH 65;   PT 49;   WA 68
                       22   Conc for 2 V and O in d   CH 52;   DA 50
                       27   V Conc No 1 1931   BN 43;   CH 44;   CL 45;   RC 48
                       25   Conc for Fl, V and O 1936   CH 63
                       22   V Conc for Str O and Timpani   WA 68
                       26   Conc for 2 P and O 1943   BN 44, 60;   CH 48;
                                 CT 52;   DE 51;   DT 54;   NA 54;   HN 56;   MN 50;
                                 NR 55;   PH 43, 49;   PT 55;   RC 44;   SL 48, 51;
                                 UT 57
                       25   Conc for V, P and O   NA 55;   PH 55
                       27   C Conc No 1 in D 1944   NP 52
                       20   C Conc No 3   NA 48
                       17   Conc for Str Quart and O   BN 32;   BU 52;   ML 60;
                                 NP 35;   PT 53;   SE 56;   WA 39, 63
                       14   Conc Grosso for O 1938   BN 41, 46;   CH 47;
                                 LA 50;   PT 43
                            Fantasia Concertante for P and O   BN 59
                       20   Frescoes of Piero della Francesca   CL 56;   DA 57
                       10   Intermezzo   SF 57
                       15   La Symphonie   BN 28
                        8   Memorial to Lidice 1943   CL 65;   NP 43;   PH 43;
                               SL 48

MARTINU, B. (Cont.)
22   Parables for O   BN 58, 59;   DT 66
28   Rhapsodie Conc Vla and O 1928   CL 52;   PT 53
14   The Rock, Prelude Symphonique   CL 57
35   Symph No 1 1942   BN 42, 52;   DA 54
25   Symph No 2 1943   CL 43;   MN 43;   NP 43;
          PH 44;   PT 43
30   Symph No 3 1944   BN 45;   NP 47
34   Symph No 4 1945   DA 69;   PH 45;   RC 47
29   Symph No 6, Fantaisies Symphoniques   BN 54, 55,
          61, 65;   CL 55;   DA 55(2);   SF 69
23   Suite Concertante for V and O 1944   SL 45
18   Toccata and Two Canzones   BA 47;   DE 67
12   Tre Ricercari, 1948   CH 50
12   Three Frescoes   PT 65

MARTIRANO, Salvatore   9   Contrasts   NP 66;   MN 69
1927-   US   9   Octet   SF 67

MARTUCCI, Guiseppe   30   P Conc in b^b Op 66   NP 10;   CH 12
1856-1909   It   9   Danza Tarantelle   NP 30
                        6   Quattro Piccoli Pezzi Op 70 No 1: Notturno   NP 27,
                                35;   CT 04, 37, 56;   CH 18, 58;   DT 36, 51;
                                KC 34;   PH 42;   PT 56;   RC 57;   SL 24, 27
                        6   Novelletta-Nocturno Op 82   BN 35;   CT 37, 27;
                                HN 32;   PH 42;   SL 24, 27;   RC 09, 31, 57
                       30   Symph No 1 in d Op 75   NP 32;   PH 12
                       39   Symph No 2 in F Op 81   NP 27

MARX, Adolph B.   12   Theme, Var and   Passacaglia   DT 41
1795-1866   Ger

MARX, Burle Walter   8   Samba Concertante   PT 61;   WA 62
1902-   Brazil

MARX, Joseph   30   P Conc, Castelli Romani 1931   CT 34
1882-   Aust 24   Symphon Nightmusic   CT 26
                          Songs
                        4   Ach, Gestern hat er mir Rosen gebracht   BU 45;
                                CT 45, 52;   DT 45;   LA 27;   CH 32
                        3   Hat dich die Liebe   CT 25;   CL 29;   DT 45;
                                LA 27;   MN 27, 35;   SL 31
                        3   Marienlied, arr La Violette   BU 45;   CT 25;
                                DT 25
                        4   Der Ton   CT 34;   LA 31;   SL 31
                        3   Waldsligheit   CT 52
                        3   Venetianisches Wiegenlied   CT 25;   CL 29
                        4   Gebet   LA 45

MASCAGNI, Pietro   4   L'Amico Fritz, Opera 1891: Intermezzo   CH 1892;
1863-1945   It   DA 35
                        4   Cavalleria Rusticana, Opera 1889: Addio Alla Madre
                                AT 53;   BA 67;   KC 67;   MN 60;   NA 68
                        4   -Aria   DE 59;   HN 55;   SE 58
                        4   -Fantasie   HN 13
                        4   -Intermezzo   CH 1893; 95,   HN 36;   MN 46;
                                DA 28

MASCAGNI, P. (Cont.)   Cavalleria Rusticana (Cont.)

4   -Prelude, Voice and O   BN 91
4   -Santuzza's Aria   RC 23
20   -Synthesis Suite   DA 55
4   -Vio La Sapete   CT 47;   DT 63;   HN 42;
     KC 35, 63;   LA 31;   SL 62;   UT 45
4   Iris, Opera 1898: Aria, Inno al Sole   HN 31
4   William Ratcliffe, Opera 1895, Dream   SL 27

MASETTI, Enzo   6   Ora di Vespro for O 1936   DT 38;   MN 61
1893-   It

MASON, Daniel G.   5   Cape Cod Pageant, Prelude 1915   NS 15
1873-1953   US   8   Chanticler, Festival Overt Op 27   CH 30;   CT 28;
     CL 30;   DT 29, 30;   LA 30;   MN 30;   NP 28;
     PH 30
3   Fanfare for Friends 1942   CT 42
12   Prelude and Fugue for P and O Op 20   BN 22;   CH 20;
     DT 21;   NP 21;   PH 22
16   Russians, Songs for Baritone and O Op 18   BN 20;
     CH 18;   CT 49;   DT 18;   NS 19;   PH 19
20   Suite, after English Folk Songs Op 32   CH 41;
     CT 34, 41;   DT 34, 45;   NP 34;   PT 37, 39;
     SF 39;   SE 47
38   Symph No 1 in c Op 11   BN 27;   CH 24, 25;   DT 20,
     27;   NP 22;   NS 24;   PH 15
32   Symph No 2 in A Op 30   CH 31;   CT 30;   NP 31
34   Symph in f No 3 A Lincoln Symphony Op 35 1937
     CT 39;   LA 38;   NP 37;   SE 45
10   Three Pieces for Fl, Harp and Str Op 13   NS 26

MASON, Stuart   4   Bergerie 1923   BN 23
1883-   US   8   Rhaps on Persian Air for P and O 1920   BN 20

MASON, William   6   Ballade in B   NP 1863
1829-1908   US   4   Serenade, Slumber Sweetly   NP 1852

MASSENET, Jules   INCIDENTAL MUSIC
1842-1912   Fr   20   Les Érinnyes 1873   BN 1883, 97;   CH 1896(2), 97,
     98, 99, 03, 04, 12;   CT 1896, 98, 06;   DA 30;
     DT 16, 17;   HN 34;
5   -Overt   CH 00
6   -Scene Religiuese   CH 00, 06, 08
9   Phèdre 1900 Overt   BN 1881, 89, 91, 21;   CH 1892,
     93, 01, 04, 17;   CT 1895, 97, 04, 17, 53;   CL 18,
     22;   DA 27, 32;   DT 61;   NA 32;   MN 44;
     NS 1888, 12;   PH 09, 10;   SL 26;   SE 29, 65;
     WA 34

4   La Vierge, Legende Sacrée 1880: Oratorio, Angelus
     DA 28
4   -La dernier Sommeil de la vierge   CT 1896;
     DA 28;   PH 06
      SUITES
23   Alsaciennes Scenes Suite No 7   BN 1881;   CH 4
     items 1894   MN 45
5   -Sous les Tilleuls   CH 07, 08, 11;   NS 06

MASSENET, J. (Cont.)   Suites (Cont.)

17	Esclarmonde, from Drama-Lyrique 1889 BN 1891, 00; CH 1891; CT 01; NS 1895
16	Pittoresque Scenes BN 1885; CT 1898; HN 17, 32; NA 34; NS 12
8	-March, Festival NS 20

OPERAS

4	Cindrillon Fairy Tale Opera 1899: Minuet, Le Sommeil, Les Mondores CT 01
8	El Cid: Aria NP 50; PH 20; SL 11
4	-Ballet Music, Dances from Spain, Act II CT 1897 02; HN 38; KC 35; NS 14; SL 10
4	-March Héroique CH 1894, 99; DA 28
4	-Moorish Rhapsody CH 1894
10	-Prelude CH 1894; HN 38
4	-Pleurez, Pleurez, Aria BU 42; CH 1893, 94, 18; DT 17, 18, 45; LA 19; MN 41
5	Don César de Bazan, Opera Comique 1872: Entr'acte Act II CT 00
4	Don Quichotte: La mort du Don Quichotte CT 49; HN 49
4	Grisélidis 1901: Aria Revoir Griselidis DT 17
4	Hérodiade 1881: Aria NS 26
4	-A Dieu Donc PH 11
4	-Il est Doux, Il est Bon, Act I AT 50; CH 08, 16, 20; CT 00, 40; CL 20; DT 44; HN 41; NA 40; LA 22, 37, 45; MN 24; NS 18; PH 46; WA 43
4	-Ne me Refuse Pas, Act I CT 48; MN 43
4	-Romance NP 43, 47
8	-Salome! KC 38; MN 38; PH 37
4	-Vision Fugitive, Act II CH 1895, 97, 18; CT 38, 40; CL 24; DT 16, 18, 29; KC 37; MN 29; PH 01, 05; RC 43; SL 17, 18
6	Jongleur de Notre-Dame 1902: Legend of the Sagebrush NS 05; PH 15
6	Le Mage 1891: Overt NP 10
8	Manon 1894: 2 Arias DE 54
	-Adieu, notre petite table, Act II HN 42; KC 42; WA 43
4	-Aria: Ah fuyez douce image CT 21, 37 DT 18, 20, 28, 40; HN 42; KC 42; LA 22; SE 37; WA 43
4	-Ah si les fleurs avaient des yeux CL 19; NP 19
5	-Gavotte, Act III BU 43; CT 10; CL 19; NA 66; KC 46
4	-The Dream, Le Rêve AT 52; CT 37, 48, 51; CL 27; DT 26, 27; HN 16; NA 39; LA 21, 50; MN 48; NP 10; NS 12; SE 39
4	Roi de Lahore 1877: Aria Act IV CT 36
4	-Aria BA 42; CL 18; PH 07
4	-Arioso NS 18
4	-Promesse de mon avenir Act IV CT 36; LA 20; MN 25; NS 14; SL 12, 16
4	-Recitative and Aria CH 07
6	Roma 1912: Overture SL 26

MCCOLLOH, Byron US	6	Two Pieces for O PT 57
MCCOY, Wm. J. 1848- US	4	Prelude, Act III to Egypt DT 23; LA 25
MCDONALD, Harl 1899-1955 US	23-24	Conc for 2 P and O 1936 CT 42; DE 45; NA 47; NR 52; PH 36; PT 43
	22	V Conc 1943 PH 44
	8	Daybreak WA 41
	3	Fanfare for Poland 1942 CT 42
	27	Lament for the Stolen,women's Chor and O 1939 PH 38
	4	Legend of the Arkansas Traveller for O 1939 DE 46
	4	Lullaby, Gott Weiss Alles PH 51
	10	Miniature Suite, three mvts BA 41
	25-26	My Country at War, Suite 1944 NA 43; PH 44
	10	-Bataan, Tone Poem BU 42; LA 42; PH 42
	10	Overt 1941 NA 41; PH 51
	15	Saga of the Mississippi 1948 PH 47
	8-9	San Juan Capistrano, Two Nocturnes NA 39; LA 39; PH 39, 48; RC 40, 51; SF 40

	24	Scenes From Childhood, Suite, Harp and O 1941
		    AT 57; CL 42; DE 46; NA 54; PH 40, 52;
		    RC 52

	23	Symph No 1, The Santa Fe Trail 1932 PH 34, 40, 50
	32	Symph No 2, Rhumba 1934 PH 35; UT 42, 44
	5	-Rhumba CH 37; CL 38; HN 40; KC 37; RC 40; DA 38
	33	Symph No 3, Tragic Cycle, for Sopr, Chor and O 1935 DE 45, 50, 60; PH 35, 56
	30	Symph No 4, Cakewalk 1937 PH 37
	11	Three Poems on Aramaic and Hebraic Themes for O 1938 NA 38, 44, 46; PH 36
	8	-Two Only BA 43; SF 41
	12	Two Pieces for O from the Damariscotta PH 59
MCEWEN, Sir John 1868-1948 Scot	13	Grey Galloway, A Border Ballad 1905 CH 29
MCKAY, George 1899- US	12	Fantasy on a Western Folksong 1931 NA 38; SE 35, 42
	9	Lyric Poem for Str 1938 SE 30
	21	Sinfonetta No 3 1933 SE 48
	11	Sinfonetta No 5,3 parts, short, in small form SE 44, 51
	12	Song Over the Great Plains 1953 NA 53
	11	Symph Miniature, Op 40, 1937 NA 52
	24	Symph No 5 for Seattle SE 51
	10	To A Liberator or A Lincoln Tribute, Symphon Poem 1940 NA 39
MCKINLEY, Carl 1895- US	10	Masquerade, An American Rhaps 1925 BN 30; CH 26; CL 32; DT 29, 46; PH 29
	15	Symphon Poem, The Blue Flower 1920 CH 25

MCLAUGHLIN, John   4   March from Scottish Sketches   DA 49
or M'LACHLAN
fl 1776-82   Scot

MCPHEE, Colin   17   Tabuh-Tabuhan, Toccata for 2 P and O 1936   CL 57;
1901-1964   Can/US   DE 57;   LA 57;   NP 57

MEACHAM, Frank W.   4   American Patrol March, arr Marquardt for Iturbi
              US   RC 42

MECHEM, Kirke   20   Symph No 1 Op 16   SF 64
1925   US   20   Symph No 2 Op 29   SF 66, 68

MEDNIKOFF, Nikolai   5   The Hills of Gruzia, Song   CT 46;   CL 41
1890-1942   Russ/US

MEDTNER, Nicholas K.   30   P. Conc in c Op 33   CH 24;   CT 24;   DT 24;   PH 24
1880-1951   Russ   6   Serenade for Voice and O after Pushkin Op 52 No 6
                              CT 51;   MN 41, 48

MEEKER   4   Primitive Rhythm   DA 34

MEHUL, Etienne N.   8   Le Jeune Henri Opera 1797: Overt, La Chasse
1763-1817   Fr   CH 13;   NP 1845, 14;   NS 1888;   RC 27;   SF 38
                        8   Les deux Aveugles de Toledo, Opera Comique 1806:
                              Overt   NP 36
                        8   Joseph, Opera Comique 1807: Aria, Champs paternels
                              CT 67
                              -Overt   BN 1881;   NP 1851
                              -Theme and Var from Trio   NP 1852

MELAMET   6   Cantata Columbus   BA 26

MELLERS, Wilfred   20   Alba in 9 metamorphoses for Fl and O   PT 62
1914-   Brit

MENDELSSOHN, Felix   13   Athalie Op 74 Incidental Music   BN 1881, 83, 87,
1809-1847   Ger   01;   DT 23
                        5   -War March of the Priests   CT 18, 20
        10   Bohemian March for 2 P and O arr Moscheles   NP 1851
        12   Calm Sea and Prosperous Voyage Meeresstille und gluckliche Fahrt
               Overt Op 27   BN 1885, 88, 89, 93, 97, 00, 04, 05, 07, 10, 13, 15;
               CH 1892, 05, 28, 44, 54, 59;   CT 06, 08, 13, 25, 66;   DT 21;
               NP 1849, 53, 60, 67, 75, 33, 53;   PH 46;   PT 46;   SL 12
        12   Capriccio Brilliant in b for P and O Op 22   BA 65;   BN 1882, 59,
               67;   CL 64;   MN 48;   NP 1849, 59, 55, 62, 65;   NS 08;   WA 67
        18   P Conc No 1 in g Op 25   AT 53, 58, 63;   BA 64, 67;   BN 12;   BU 58;
               CH 07, 17, 23;   CT 47, 68;   CL 47, 54, 57;   DA 49, 69;   DE 47,
               57;   DT 55, 57;   HN 52, 69;   NA 49;   KC 36, 49;   ML 61;
               MN 34, 44, 57, 63;   NP 1845(2), 47, 51, 65, 12, 37, 50, 53, 54,
               64, 67;   NS 1883, 08;   PH 02, 07, 49, 53;   PT 47, 53, 57, 68;
               SL 39;   SF 13, 56, 60, 62, 68;   SE 61;   UT 54;   WA 57, 64, 67
        25   P Conc No 2 in d Op 40   NP 1851, 58, 62, 68, 1964;   PH 57;   SL 57

MENDELSSOHN, F. (Cont.

30   V Conc in e and E Op 64   AT 48, 53, 59, 68;   BA 28, 45, 46, 47, 54, 61, 62;   BN 1881, 85, 86, 94, 99, 03, 05, 13, 14, 18, 22, 35, 36, 37, 44, 45, 49, 55, 60;   BU 47, 53, 57, 59, 61;   CH 1895, 96, 98, 01, 02, 08, 14, 17, 19, 22, 35, 37, 41, 42, 43, 45, 46(2), 47, 48, 50, 56, 62, 65;   CT 1895, 07, 14, 16, 19, 36, 38, 46, 54, 59; CT 67, 69;   CL 19, 24, 25, 37, 38, 41, 43, 44, 45, 46, 47, 49, 51, 54, 58, 61, 64, 68;   DA 46, 48, 50, 51, 52, 56, 60, 62, 64; DE 49, 54, 58, 59, 64, 66, 69;   DT 15, 24, 34, 46, 53, 59, 61, 67, 68;   HN 32, 46, 54;   NA 36, 45, 53, 61, 66;   KC 36, 37, 40, 43, 49, 51, 55, 60, 63, 67;   LA 19, 21, 25, 27, 36, 46, 57, 59, 61, 65;   ML 60;   MN 27, 30, 42, 43, 45, 46, 48, 52, 53, 55, 56, 58, 61, 63;   NR 51, 52, 56, 62, 68;   NP 1849, 51, 55, 58, 62, 64, 65, 66, 67, 73, 75, 95, 01, 02, 08, 09, 13, 19(2), 20(2), 21, 25, 32, 35, 37, 38, 39, 58, 62, 63;   NP 67, 68;   NS 1883, 18, 19, 24, 25;   PH 01, 03, 05, 13, 19, 27, 39, 42, 53, 57, 61, 67; PT 40, 45, 47, 49, 54, 58, 59, 64, 65, 67;   RC 39, 45, 46, 54, 66, 69;   SL 11, 13, 23, 25, 27, 30, 32, 35, 37, 43, 44, 50, 55, 58, 60, 61, 62, 63, 68;   SF 14, 17, 46, 48, 49, 53, 54, 61, 63, 64, 65;   SE 46, 47, 51, 64, 67;   UT 40, 44, 46, 50, 62;   WA 32, 33, 38, 60, 64, 67

8   -Andante and Finale   CH 03;   DA 27

8   -First mvt   SF 24

24   V Conc in d Op 40   CL 52;   SL 53

20   Conc for 2 P and O in A^b probably from Op 38 No 18 Duetto   CT 58; HN 67;   NP 57;   PH 65;   PT 56;   SE 62

20   Conc for 2 P and O in E   DT 62

96   Elijah, Oratorio Op 70   AT 52, 60;   DA 49;   HN 53;   KC 52; MN 24, 48;   NP 51, 65;   NS 08;   PH 68;   UT 59

4   -Aria   DE 54;   HN 55;   UT 51

4   -Hear Ye, Israel Sopr   NP 1856;   NS 1897

4   -It is Enough, Baritone   NP 1851, 61

4   -Lift thine Eyes   NP 1854

4   -Lord God of Abraham, Bass   KC 53;   MN 42

4   -If With All Your Heart, Tenor   CT 56;   HN 43;   NA 55;   LA 54

4   -Thanks be to God   NS 1897

4   -Watching Over Israel   NP 1854

4   -Yet doth the Lord   NP 1854

4   St. Paul Oratorio Op 36: Aria   NP 1853

4   -Oh God Have Mercy Upon Me   CT 14;   KC 53;   NP 1855

4   -Overt   BN 1882;   MN 46

12   The Fair Melusine, Die schöne Melusine Concert Overt   Op 32   BN 1884, 87, 89, 94, 99, 03, 05;   CH 1891, 95(2), 99, 01, 03, 06, 10, 25, 41, 45, 49, 51, 58;   CT 03, 15, 28, 29, 33;   DA 50, 53, 55, 58, 61;   DE 60;   DT 20;   HN 55;   LA 49;   MN 60;   NP 1844, 47, 55, 59, 65, 68, 73, 76, 85, 89, 96, 10, 12;   PH 58;   PT 52, 60; SF 16, 29;   SL 37

40   Festgesang or Lobgesang, for Chor O Hymn of Praise , Symph Cantata Op 52   HN 37

4   -Hark the Herald Angels Sing   DA 49

4   -An die Kunstler   NP 1864

35   First Walpurgis Night, Cantata after Goethe Op 60   DA 53;   NP 1860

6   Fugue in e Op 35 No 1   BA 42, 47;   DT 41

MENDELSSOHN, F. (Cont.)

9   Hebrides, Fingal's Cave, Concert Overt Op 26   AT 49;   BA 37, 39,
          42, 43(2), 45, 55;   BN 1882, 85, 88, 89, 90, 92,   93, 95, 98, 01,
          08, 19, 22, 25, 51, 56;   BU 45, 48;   CH 1892, 98, 02, 04, 05, 08,
          09, 12, 14, 16, 17, 19, 20, 21, 33, 36, 44, 52, 55, 59, 62, 68;
          CT 09, 14, 21, 28, 31, 32, 36, 45, 49, 50, 52, 53, 55, 69;   CL 28,
          34, 41, 47, 50, 59, 62;   DA 50, 53, 55, 58, 61;   DE 52, 68;
          DT 15, 17, 18, 28, 30, 32, 45, 47, 52, 53, 61;   HN 35, 51, 63;
          NA 45, 55;   KC 34, 40, 58;   LA 19;   ML 62;   MN 29, 40, 45, 48,
          50;   NR 50, 58, 62, 69;   NP 1844, 47, 52, 57, 61, 66, 71, 90, 07,
          13, 15, 18, 20, 21, 22, 29, 47, 50, 53, 59, 61, 64, 67;   NS 1878,
          85, 05, 07, 12, 16, 18, 24;   PH 02, 09, 10, 11, 12, 14, 15, 22,
          26, 61, 66;   PT 47, 50, 51, 55, 63, 66;   RC 40, 44, 45, 48, 51,
          56, 59, 68;   SL 15, 17, 21, 24, 29, 32, 33, 34, 50, 52, 57, 61, 68;
          SF 20, 54, 60;   SE 28, 50, 58;   UT 43, 58;   WA 32, 40

10   Lorelei Op 98 Opera, Unfinished: Finale of Act I   NP 1854, 64

14   Midsummer Night's Dream Incidental Music Op 61   AT 48, 51, 58, 62,
          65;   BA 43, 46, 59;   BN 1893, 51, 53, 62;   BU 65;   CH 59, 66;
          DA 62, 67;   HN 32;   KC 40;   LA 21, 35, 48;   MN 63;   NP 1842,
          43, 45, 47, 48, 99, 05, 10, 23, 27, 31, 38, 45, 50, 51, 52, 55,
          58, 63, 66;   NS 1883, 86, 08, 20;   PH 47, 50, 55, 63, 66, 69;
          PT 52, 59;   RC 61;   SF 55, 65;   SE 66;   UT 40

10   -Excerpts   BN 1881, 82, 83, 84, 86, 87, 90, 96, 00, 03, 06, 08,
          09, 11(2), 12, 14, 15, 17, 19, 23, 24, 30, 35;   HN 54;   KC 34,
          52(2), 62;   LA 21, 35, 48;   NP 1849, 50, 56, 65, 67, 69, 70,
          79, 93, 08, 13, 20, 23, 27, 29, 41, 42, 45, 46, 50, 51;   PH 01,
          08, 13, 15, 17, 19, 25, 26, 27, 31, 33, 41, 45, 47, 56

5   -Intermezzo   HN 36;   NA 33, 48, 51;   RC 47, 50;   WA 49, 60

4   -March of Faries   RC 25

6   -Nocturne   AT 48, 62;   BA 47;   CH 1893, 97, 08, 15(2), 22, 46,
          48, 50;   CT 1897, 23, 27, 31, 34, 64;   CL 26, 31, 34, 41, 66;
          DE 46, 55, 59;   DT 14, 18, 51, 62;   HN 34, 36, 41, 50;   NA 33,
          48, 51;   MN 31, 48;   NR 51, 54, 63;   NP 59;   NS 26,   PT 45,
          49, 57;   RC 08, 25, 28, 30, 47, 50;   SL 32, 54;   SF 41;
          SE 27, 34;   WA 32, 40, 49, 60

10   -Overt Op 21   AT 69;   BA 38, 43;   CH 1893, 94, 96, 97, 98, 01,
          03, 06, 14, 22, 32, 46, 48, 50, 51, 69;   CT 1897, 12, 16, 17, 23,
          27, 34, 39, 59, 64;   CL 27, 34, 41, 47, 51, 53, 55, 60, 61, 66;
          DA 49, 54, 56, 68;   DE 48, 53, 54;   DT 14, 18, 21(2), 22, 25,
          26, 29, 54;   HN 16, 36, 41, 52;   NA 32, 38;   KC 38, 56;   LA 56,
          58;   MN 22, 31, 42, 46, 53, 56;   NR 54, 63;   NS 22, 24, 25;
          PH 02, 06, 07, 11, 20, 30;   PT 41, 47;   RC 25, 26, 29, 32, 35,
          37, 38, 45, 47, 52, 56;   SL 13, 15, 29, 47;   SF 12, 37, 51, 52;
          SE 26, 41, 44, 48, 66;   WA 49, 52, 60, 67

4   -Pas de Deux   SE 66

4   -Scherzo   AT 48, 62;   BA 43;   CH 1893(2), 97, 01, 04, 08, 15,
          22, 26, 28, 39, 46, 48, 50;   CT 1897, 23, 27, 34, 64;   CL 26,
          31, 34, 41, 66;   DA 29, 49, 50;   DE 46, 55, 59;   DT 18, 23, 28,
          34, 45, 51, 54, 60, 62;   HN 36, 41, 50;   NA 33, 48, 51;   KC 33,
          57;   LA 19, 25;   MN 31;   NR 51, 54, 57, 59, 63;   NS 26;   PH 02,
          05, 28, 31;   PT 45, 49, 57;   RC 25, 30, 31, 37, 47, 50;   SL 15,
          28, 29, 32, 34, 43, 46, 48, 52, 54, 55;   SF 19, 41, 46;   SE 21,
          30, 34, 47;   WA 40, 49, 60

4   -Song with Chor   RC 35

MENDELSSOHN, F. (Cont.)   Midsummer Night's Dream (Cont.)
6   -Wedding March   BA 26, 43, 47;   CH 1893, 97, 01, 08, 48;   CT 1897,
         22, 23, 27;   DE 59;   DT 14;   HN 41;   NA 48, 51;   MN 31;
         NR 54, 63, 67;   NP 59;   NS 08;   PT 45;   RC 32, 47, 50;   WA 60
30   Octet for Str in E^b Op 20   BA 51;   BN 1885, 20, 60
5   -Scherzo   BA 47;   BN 34, 36;   NA 60;   KC 45;   MN 38;   NP 37,
         38, 43, 51, 64;   NS 08;   PH 44, 69;   PT 39;   SL 37, 43
9   Overt in C Op 101 for Trump and O   BN 1883;   LA 60
12   Ruy Blas Overt after V. Hugo Op 95   BA 47, 50, 64;   BN 1882, 84,
         87, 88, 91, 97, 02;   BU 50;   CH 08, 40, 53, 57;   CT 04, 20;
         CL 50;   DA 64;   DE 67;   DT 14, 24, 26, 54;   HN 16, 39, 55, 64;
         NA 51;   KC 38, 67;   LA 22, 26, 64, 68;   MN 41, 44, 47;
         NP 1854, 70, 11, 15, 37, 44, 48, 49, 53, 55, 60;   PH 13, 28; PT 45,
         65;   RC 36, 48;   SL 14, 16, 18, 31, 63;   SF 37, 47, 49, 61;
         SE 55
11   Serenade and Allegro for P and O Op 43 in b   NP 1858
6   Son and Stranger Heimkehr aus der Fremde Op 89, Opera: Overt   BN 1884;
         CT 66;   CL 61
4   -I am a Roamer Bold   DA 34
         SONGS
4   Auf Flugeln des Gesanges on the Wings of Song Op 34 No 2   NS 04
4   Hunting Song for Quart   NP 1852
4   Infelice Op 94 for Sopr and O   CT 1898, 01;   HN 45;   KC 46;
         NP 1859, 60, 61, 65, 66, 08, 17;   PH 17;   SL 17
4   In Grunen Op 8 No 11   NP 1878
4   Jager's Abschied Op 50 No 3   NP 1846
4   Maybell Flowers   NP 1852
4   Psalm 43 Chor acapella Op 78   CH 08
4   Psalm 114 Op 51   CH 1897
4   Spinning Song Op 67 No 4   NS 08, 18
4   Through the House Give Glimmering Light   CH 1897, 48
4   Voyager's Song, Duet   NP 1852
4   Wood Minstrels Op 63 No 4   NP 1889
4   You Spotted Snakes with Chor   CH 1897, 48
12   Songs Without Words Op 62   NS 08
4   No 6 Spring Song   BA 28;   CH 1895(2), 04, 06;   CT 1895, 02, 08,
         69;   NA 33;   NS 1883, 09
9   Str Quart in g Op 20: Allegretto   NS 19
4   -Canzonetta   NS 08, 10
5   -Scherzo   CH 56;   CL 38, 47
37   Symph No 1 in c Op 11   CL 66;   SE 63
36   Symph No 3 in a Scotch Op 56   AT 50, 54, 65;   BA 37, 58;   BN 1882,
         84, 90, 91, 93, 95, 96, 97, 99, 01, 03, 07, 08, 13, 20, 32, 37, 43,
         44, 51, 59, 64, 67;   BU 68;   CH 1891, 95, 08, 19, 25, 42, 47, 54,
         58, 60, 63;   CT 1895, 11, 13, 19, 32, 36, 42, 46, 51, 65;   CL 35,
         42, 47, 50, 55, 59, 69;   DA 46, 52, 58;   DE 51, 67;   DT 15, 20,
         25, 46, 55, 69;   HN 33, 35, 41, 51, 53;   NA 30, 32, 43;   KC 58;
         LA 22, 65;   ML 63;   MN 23, 29, 32, 36, 41, 43, 46, 48, 50, 52,
         54, 56, 60, 65;   NR 56, 65, 69;   NP 1845, 47, 49, 57, 64,
         70, 74, 99, 12, 26, 34, 47, 48, 50, 53, 56, 57, 63;   NS 1881, 83,
         97, 03, 05, 08, 19, 23;   PH 05, 12, 15, 18, 20, 21, 26, 29, 45;
         PT 37, 47, 52, 56, 61;   RC 28, 36, 39, 51, 56, 60;   SL 12, 26,
         32, 47, 53;   SF 21, 39, 45, 50, 57, 62, 65;   SE 27, 43, 49, 54,
         63, 69;   UT 53, 59;   WA 67, 69
8   -Scherzo and Finale   MN 46

MENDELSSOHN, F. (Cont.)
25   Symph No 4 in A Italian Op 90   AT 47, 52, 59, 63, 64, 66;   BA 44,
          45, 46, 50, 57, 63;   BN 1884, 89, 92, 94, 96, 98, 02, 03, 15, 18,
          21, 25, 27, 34, 40, 42, 46, 52, 55, 57, 65;   BU 49, 56;   CH 1892,
          98, 05, 13, 17, 20, 25, 35, 36, 38, 50, 53, 59, 60, 61, 65;
          CT 1899, 19, 31, 35, 37, 42, 43, 49, 51, 60, 68;   CL 23, 29, 40,
          47, 49, 57, 58, 62;   DA 46, 49, 51, 63;   DE 49, 56, 62, 63, 64;
          DT 16, 21, 32, 38, 49, 54, 57, 60, 63, 67;   HN 44, 49, 52, 65;
          NA 34, 38, 39, 41, 53, 56, 64;   KC 36, 43, 51, 53, 62;   LA 47,
          54, 56, 59, 65;   ML 61, 65;   MN 30, 33, 42, 48, 51, 54, 57, 61;
          NR 50, 52, 53, 57, 59, 64;   NP 1851, 54, 59, 67, 73, 78, 86, 06,
          08, 10, 16, 25, 32, 36, 37, 39, 43, 53, 54, 57, 60, 64, 69;
          NS 1889, 08, 10, 14, 20(2);   PH 01, 04, 14, 16, 22, 29, 33, 40,
          43, 46, 47, 48, 51, 56, 58, 62, 63;   PT 40, 45, 47, 49, 51, 54,
          59;   RC 25, 36, 39, 49, 53, 56, 59;   SL 10, 19, 20, 28, 30, 31,
          37, 41, 42, 45, 49, 50, 54, 55, 61, 63;   SF 17, 25, 29, 36, 41,
          44, 46, 48, 53, 58, 64, 68;   SE 35, 42, 45, 48, 51, 59, 67;
          UT 41, 42, 47, 56, 59, 62, 65;   WA 38, 49, 53, 55, 57
6   -First mvt   DA 30
6   -Third mvt   MN 48
25   Symph No 5 in D Reformation Op 107   AT 49, 57;   BA 39, 59;
          BN 1881, 83, 85, 88, 19, 44, 49, 57, 61, 64;   BU 67;   CH 48, 67;
          CT 21, 45, 54, 63, 66;   CL 59;   DA 56, 65;   DT 56;   HN 40, 41,
          42, 43;   NA 62, 66;   LA 52;   ML 67;   MN 44;   NP 1868, 31, 32,
          44, 48, 53, 54, 62;   PH 42, 44, 55, 59, 65, 69;   PT 48, 62;
          RC 48;   SL 48, 66;   SF 49;   SE 65;   UT 60;   WA 51, 63
23   Symph No 9 Str Symph from 11 Str Symphonies in Manuscript only
          BA 47;   DT 17;   LA 48
15   Var Serieux   Op 54   NS 08
6   Wedding at Camacho Die Hochzeit des camacho, Opera Op 10: Overt
          BN 1881, 86, 04;   NP 1954

MENGELBERG, Rudolph   30   Missa Pro Pace, Chorale   WA 49
1892-   Neth   8   Prelude   NP 1923
                       10   Scherzo Sinfonica   PH 26
                        8   Symphon Elegy   DT 24;   NP 23

MENNIN, Peter   9   Canto for O   BA 65;   BU 66;   CT 65, 68;   DA 63;
1923-   US   DE 67;   PH 64, 65;   PT 64;   RC 65;   SL 63
                       12   Concertato for O, Moby Dick   BA 61;   CT 67;
                                 CL 62;   DA 52;   DE 56;   DT 62;   NA 60;
                                 LA 53, 60;   PH 58;   SL 62
                       26   P Conc   CT 56
                       27   V Conc   CL 57
                        8   Folk Overt   BA 63;   CL 52;   DT 54;   HN 47, 65;
                                 ML 63;   MN 55;   WA 49
                        9   Fantasia for Str in 2 mvts   BA 48
                        5   Sinfonia for Chamber O 1946   CT 47
                       20   Symph No 3 1946   BA 58;   CL 47, 64;   DA 64;
                                 NA 65;   LA 55;   NP 46, 53, 61;   PT 46;
                                 RC 65;   SL 64;   WA 55
                       22   Symph No 5   BA 59;   BN 50;   DA 49, 50, 56;
                                 MN 57;   SF 51
                       22   Symph No 6   CH 61;   CT 62;   DA 55;   DE 62;
                                 LA 54;   NP 54;   PH 61
                       25   Symph No 7 in 1 mvt Variation Symph   AT 69;
                                 CH 67;   CL 63;   MN 64;   NP 63

MENNINI, Louis   16   Andante and Allegro Energico   PH 48
1920-   US   6   Arioso for Str O   PH 50
                        8   Restful Composition   NR 62

MENOTTI, Gian-Carlo   120   Amahl and the Night Visitors 1951   AT 65;   BU 53;
1911-   It/US   CT 56, 62;   DE 53, 54, 60;   DT 59;   HN 53;   NR 67
                        20   -Excerpts   HN 52
                        5   Amelia Goes to the Ball, Opera 1937: Overt   CL 38;
                               DE 46, 56;   DT 52;   MN 50;   NP 61;   PH 37,
                               41;   PT 47;   SE 53, 61
                        24   Apocalypse, in three mvts   BN 66;   BU 51;   CT 52;
                               DT 51;   MN 66;   NR 67;   NP 64;   PH 51;   PT 51;
                               SF 52;   SE 66
                        8   -Three Excerpts   LA 52
                        50   The Counsul, Opera 1950   CT 57
                        28   P Conc in F 1945   AT 53;   BN 45;   CT 61;   CL 50;
                               DA 53;   DE 52;   HN 58;   NA 51;   NP 48, 51;   PH 53
                        30   V Conc in d   BN 54;   HN 65;   NP 53;   PH 52;   SL 57
                        30   Death of the Archbishop of Brindisi, Dramatic
                               Recital   AT 65;   BA 64;   BN 64
                        8   The Island God, Tragic Opera 1942: Two Interludes
                               NP 55;   RC 56;   SL 55;   SF 56
                        80   The Medium, Opera in one act 1964: Aria, Am I
                               Afraid   SE 59
                        30   The Old Maid and the Thief, Radio Opera in one act
                               1939   LA 43
                        4   -Overt   NP 41, 64;   SL 44
                        20   Suite from Sebastian, Ballet 1944   BA 58;   DT 55;
                               HN 47;   MN 46;   WA 49
                        35   The Telephone, Opera in one act 1947   SL 57
                        4   -Lucy's Aria   AT 51;   WA 51

MERCADANTE,   4   Aria, Se M'abbaudoni   NP 1845
  Guiseppe Saverio   4   Aria from Il giuramento, Opera 1837   NP 1878
1795-1870   It   4   Cavatina from Il Bravo, Opera 1839   NP 1857
                        4   Elle Piaugea aria from I Normanni a Parigi, Opera
                               1832   NP 1855

MERCER, John H.   6   Laura   WA 67
1909-   US

MERIKANTO, Oscar   4   Song: Jag Lefver   CL 19
1868-1924   Fin   4   Song: Hell Dig Lif   CT 49

MERO, Yolanda   15   Capriccio Ungarese P and O Op 2   CH 28;   CT 28;
1887-   Hung/US   CL 27;   NS 27;   SL 28

MESSAGER, André   6   Entr'acte aud Passepied from La Basoche, Opera
1853-1929   Fr   Comique 1890   NS 18

MESSIAEN, Oliver   30   L'Ascension, 4 Meditations 1934   BN 59, 62;
1908   Fr   CT 60;   CL 49, 65;   KC 52;   LA 46, 50;   MN 49,
                               62;   PH 59;   SL 48;   SF 46, 47;   WA 54
                        15   Chronochromie for O   BN 68;   CL 66
                        6   Et Exspecto Ressurectionem mortuorum   AT 68; CH 68
                        12   Hymne au Saint Sacremont for large O 1932 CH 59; NP 46

MESSIAEN, O. (Cont.)

11	Les Offrandes Oubliées, Meditation Symphonique 1930	
	BN 36; DT 69; MN 54; RC 66; WA 40	
14	Oiseaux Exotiques for P and small O CH 66; MN 64;	
	SL 68; WA 68	
16	Reveil des Oiseaux HN 55	
35	Sept Haiki for P and O PH 69	
30	Trois Petites Liturgies de la Présence Divine, for	
	women's Chor and O 1944 NP 49, 61	
70	Turangalia P, O and Ondes Martenot 1937 BN 49	

METZDORFF, Richard   30   Symph No 1 in F   NP 1875
1844-1919   Ger

METZL, Vladimir   15   Symphon Poem, The Sunken Bell   NP 07
1882-   Russ

MEYERBEER, Giacomo   OPERAS
1791-1864   Ger/Fr   4   L'Africane 1865: Aria O Paradiso   AT 53;   BU 48;

	CT 43; DE 54; HN 55; NA 55; KC 44, 67;	
	LA 25, 26, 32, 50, 54; ML 63; MN 29, 35;	
	SL 24	
4	Il crociato in Egitto, Opera 1824: Scene and	
	Cavatina NP 03	
4	Dinorah 1859: Ombre légère, Shadow Dance BA 66;	
	CT 43, 65; DA 29; HN 31; ML 61; NP 14;	
	NS 14; PT 52; SL 23; SE 67	
4	-Slumber Song NS 15	
4	L'Étoile du Norde 1854: Aria, C'est bien l'air,	
	O Happy Days CT 1898; KC 35; UT 67	
4	Les Huguenots 1836: Aria, Au beau pays ML 64, 65;	
	NP 17; UT 67	
4	-Aria Nobil Signor NS 1882	
8	-Overt NP 08	
4	Le Prophete 1849: Aria Ah Mon Fils CT 13, 18;	
	DT 31; MN 24; NP 16, 27, 29; PH 07, 11, 14;	
	SL 11, 13, 18, 23	
4	-O Pretes de Baal CT 04, 34; DT 29; MN 24, 30	
4	Robert le Diable 1831: Aria Grace NP 03	
10	-Ballet Music CH 1892	
4	-Cavatina NP 05	
4	-Invario il fato, Aria NP 15, 32	
4	-Va Dit elle, Aria NP 19	
4	Overt from Incidental Music for Struensee 1846	
	BN 1889	
	Miscellaneous	
4	Coronation March 1863 MN 46	
4	Melodie, Le Moine NP 12	
4	Neluskas Ballad MN 35	
12	Les Patineurs, Ballet Suite, arr Lambert DE 65	
5	Polanaise BN 1882, 97	
5	Torch Dance No 1 for the King's silver Wedding	
	1846 CT 1899	

MEYEROWITZ, Jan	18	Conc for Fl and O BA 62
1913- US	11	Homage to Peter Breughel, Flemish Overt CT 61; CL 59
	22	Six Pieces for O PT 66
	21	Symph Midrash Esther NP 56
MIASKOVSKY, Nicolas	7	Overt of Homage, Greetings, in C Op 48 CH 45
1881-1950 Russ	24	Sinfonietta for Str in b Op 32 No 2 BN 34; NP 43; SL 37
	5	Slavic Rhaps in b^b Op 58 NP 49
	45	Symph No 5 in D Op 18 CH 25, 34; CT 30; PH 25; SL 30; SF 26

	75	Symph No 6 in e^b for Chor and O Op 23 CH 26, 27,
		  29, 30, 33, 35, 36, 38, 39; CL 35; LA 29;
		  MN 26; NP 36; PH 26

	23	Symph No 7 in b Op 24 CH 27, 28, 31, 38; NP 26
	56	Symph No 8 in A Op 26 BN 28; CH 29
	20	Symph No 10 in f Op 30 CH 30; PH 29
	29	Symph No 12 in g Op 35 CH 32
	20	Symph No 13 in b Op 36 CH 34
	40	Symph No 15 in d Op 38 CH 38

	20	Symph in f# No 21 Symphon Fantasie in one mvt Op 51
		  BN 42; CH 40; DT 43; HN 49; NR 60;
		  NP 42; PH 44, 47, 53

MIČA, František	20	Symph in D Op Posth CH 49; ML 69
1694-1744 Czech		
(or cousin, after 1750)		
MIDDELSCHULTE,	20	Conc for Org in a CH 05
Wilhelm	10	Passaglia CH 1898, 12
1863-1943 Ger		
MIERSCH, Paul	20	Elegy for Str O CT 01
1868-1956 Ger/US	15	Indian Summer Op 19 CT 02
MIGNONE, Francisco	15	Brazilian Fantasy No 1 for P and O LA 44

1897- Brazil	9	Congada, Dance Afrobrasileria from the Opera,
		  O Contratador dos Diamantes 1924 BA 42, 46, 49;
		  DE 53; NP 48

	14	Four Church Festivals, Symphon Poem CL 43; DT 45; LA 52; NP 51; PH 45
MIHALOVICI, Marcel	10	Capriccio Roumanian NP 38
1898- Roum/Fr	7	Cortège des Divinities Infernales from the Opera L'Intransigeant Pluton Op 27 SL 31
	15	Musique Notturno, Nocturne MN 65
	15	Sequences, Suite for O SL 48
	16	Symphonies pour le temps present Op 48 NP 66
	8	Tragic Overt DE 66; MN 62
MIKESHINA, Ariadna	8	Kozatchok Op 30 RC 33
MILHAUD, Darius	12	Ballade for P and O 1920 NS 26
1892- Fr	10	Le Bal Martiniquais for O 1944 MN 46; NP 45; SF 46

                         Time in
                         Minutes
MILHAUD, D. (Cont.)

      13   Le Boeuf sur le Toit, Ballet 1919   CT 66;   DE 51;
              MN 44;   SL 45, 53, 57;   SE 60

       5   Cain and Abel for Narrator and O 1944   UT 46

      23   Le Carnaval d'Aix for P and O 1926   BN 26;   DE 53;
              NP 26, 51(2), 54;   PT 67;   SF 54;   UT 66

      60   Les Choephores, Music for a Play, The Libation
              Bearers, Soli, Chor and O   NP 50, 61

       6   Chants Populaire Hebraiques for Voice and O 1938
              CL 62

           Christopher Colombe, Opera in 2 parts, 1928   NP 52

      18   Concertina de Hiver for Tromb and Str O   CT 61

      15   C Conc No 1 1935   BA 50;   BN 48;   BU 64;   MN 50;
              NP 46;   PH 48;   PT 54;   RC 65;   SL 50;   WA 64

      18   Conc for Fl, V and O 1938   BA 43

      28   Conc for Marimba, Vibraphone and O 1947   SL 48

       7   Conc for Percussion 1929   PH 31;   PT 58;   SF 56

      12   P Conc No 1 1933   BN 49;   MN 38

  13-20   P Conc No 2 1941   CH 41;   CT 41;   SL 41

           P Conc No 4 1949   SL 50

      18   Conc for 2 P and O 1941   AT 67;   NP 67;   PT 42;
              WA 46

      15   Conc No 1 for Vla and O 1929   CT 30

      15   Conc No 2 for Vla and O   BN 62;   KC 56, 59

      10   V Conc No 1 1927   KC 56, 59

      20   V Conc No 2 1946   CH 50

      14   Cortège Funèbre from Espoir, Film Music after
              Malraux 1939   BN 40, 42;   NP 43

      15   La Création du Mond, Ballet 1923   BN 53, 60;
              CH 42, 60;   CT 69;   CL 65;   DT 59;   DE 69;
              NA 60;   NP 58;   PT 69;   SL 55;   SF 39, 66;
              UT 61

      30   David, Opera in 5 acts, 1954   SF 62

       3   Fanfare for O 1941   CT 41;   SL 39

       3   Fanfare for Liberty 1942   CT 42

      10   Fantasie Pastorale P and O 1938   BN 40

       9   Les Funerailles de Phocion, Homage a Poussin PT 62

      20   Jeux de Printemps, Ballet in 6 mvts 1944   CT 50

       9   Kentuckiana   LA 47;   SF 48

      20   L'Homme et son Désir, Ballet 1921   UT 65

       6   Two Marches, In Memoriam and Gloria Victoribus
              DE 48;   MN 47

       8   Music for Indiana 1966   NA 66

      30   Opus Americanum No 2 Ballet Suite 1940   CH 45

       9   Overt Philharmonique 1962   NP 62

      15   Pacem in Terris   SF 64;   UT 64

       8   Psalm CXXI male Chor and O   CH 38

      45   Protée, Chor and O Suite No 2 Incidental Music 1929
              BN 51;   SF 44

      10   Quatre Chansons de Ronsard, Voice and O 1941
              BN 43;   DT 58

       5   2 Chansons   BA 50

      40   Saudades Do Brasil, Suite of dances 1920   BN 45;
              NP 46;   PH 3 dances only 22;   SL 34, 42

      17   Suite Concertnte for P and O   BN 53

MILHAUD, D. (Cont.)
            16   Suite Francaise in 5 mvts 1944   AT 55;   CH 45;
                  CT 63;   NA 63;   KC 48;   ML 66;   MN 45;
                  NP 45;   PH 55;   PT 45, 56, 63;   SL 53;
                  SF 45;   SE 45;   UT 47
            16   Suite Provençale 1936   BN 40, 43, 60;   BU 68;
                  CH 44;   CT 41, 47, 49, 52, 56;   CL 63;   DT 43,
                  55;   NA 61, 68;   KC 62;   LA 37, 46, 50;   MN 41,
                  43, 52;   NR 64;   NP 41, 54;   PH 43;   SL 40;
                  SF 38, 60;   UT 50;   WA 49
            17   Suite Symphonique for V and O   PH 45
            22   Suite Symphonique No 2 for O   BN 20;   CH 23, 28;
                  NP 44, 47
            28   Symph No 1 Le Printemps 1917   CH 40, 41;   PH 50;
                  SL 41;   SF 40
             4   -Introd and Marche funèbre   BN 52;   SL 44;
                  SF 48
            27   Symph No 2 Pastorale 1918   BN 46
            31   Symph No 3 for Chor and O, Serenade 1921   LA 25;
                  PH 22;   SF 48
            30   Symph No 4 Overt, Chorale and etude for Str 1922
                  LA 47
            26   Symph No 5 for small Wind O 1922   SF 55
            27   Symph No 6   BN 55;   SF 56
            26   Symph No 7   CH 55;   NA 58
            21   Symph No 8   PH 59;   SF 58
            22   Symph No 10   SF 68
            26   Symph No 11 Romantique   DA 60
            17   Symph No 12   SF 61

MILLER, Charles   12   Folk Rhaps, Appalachian Mountains   CH 39;   DT 48;
1914-   US   MN 44

MILLER, Edward   6   Anti-Heroic Amalgam   MN 69
1930-   US   8   Orchestral Changes   SF 67

MILLS, Charles   17   Crazy Horse Symph   CT 58
1914-   US   8   Prologue and Dithyramb for Str O   DT 58
                    12   Theme and Var Op 81   CT 62;   CL 54;   NP 54(2)

MILLS, Sebastian B. 6   Tarantella, P. Solo   NP 1862
1838-1898   US   6   Tarantella No 2   NP 1865

MINKUS, Leon   14   Grand Pas de Deux from Don Quixote, Ballet 1869
1827-1890 Aust/Russ   AT 59;   DE 59;   NR 57
                    10   Revel of Maenads and Fauns, excerpt from Ballet
                          DA 32

MITROPOULOS, Dmitri 12   Conc Grosso for O   NP 67
1896-1965   Gk/US

MIYAGI, Michio   7   Sea of the Spring   NP 55;   SF 55
1894-1956   Japan

MIYOSHI, Akira   18   Symphon Three mvts   CT 64
1933-   Japan

MLYNARSKI, Emil   40   Symph in F Op 14   MN 28
1870-1935   Pol

MOE, Daniel   50   Coventry Nativity, Christmas Opera   DE 55
               US

MOERAN, Ernest John   8   In the Mountain Country, Symphon Impression 1921
1894-1950   Brit   NP 48
                        42   Symph No 1 in g 1937   CT 37

MOEVS, Robert   20   Attis for O, Chor and Tenor solo   BN 59
1920-   US   15   Et Occidentem Illustra   BN 66
                        20   Fourteen Var for O 1955   BN 55
                        20   Symph in 3 mvts 1957   CL 57

MOHAUPT, Richard   20   V Conc 1953   NP 53
1904-1957   Ger/US   8   Overt to the Opera Die Wirten von Pinsk 1936
                                   PT 44
                        10   Lysistrata, Ballet Suite   KC 46;   PT 46
                        25   Symph No 1 Rhythm and Var   NP 41, 51
                        14   Town Piper Music   BA 58;   LA 57;   MN 57;   NP 49

MOLIQUE, Bernhard   35   C Conc in D Op 45   CH 35
1802-1869   Ger   4   -Andante   NS 1883, 03
                         8   -Andante and Allegro   CH 14
                        20   V Conc No 5   BN 1888, 93

MOLLENHAUER, Edward   10   Concerto for 2 V in C, First mvt, Grand Duo   NP 1855
1818-1885   Ger/US   25   V Conc in A   NP 1860
                        10   La Sylphide for V   NP 1855, 56

MOMPOU, Federico   4   Spanish Song and Dance for C and P   MN 47
1893-   Sp   18   Var on Euclid   KC 33

MONCAYO, José Pablo   7   Huapango for O 1941   CT 43, 44, 45;   MN 63;   PT 46
1912-1958   Mex

MONDONVILLE, Joseph   8   Le Carneval du Parnasse, Opera-Ballet 1749
1711-1772   Fr   CL 29, 30, 32, 37

MONHARDT, Maurice   6   The Trumpet Shall Sound, Overt   MN 58
1929-   US

MONIUSZKO, Stanislaw   OPERAS
1819-1872   Pol   6   La Comtesse 1858; Overt   DT 47
                         8   Flis, the Raftsman, Opera 1858: Overt   BU 61
                         8   Halka, 1847: Mazurka and Mountaineer's Dance
                                   CL 33;   LA 31
                         4   -Overt   MN 64

MONSIGNY, Pierre   8   Chaconne et Riguadon from Aline, Opera 1766
1729-1817   Fr   BN 1882, 94, 10;   NP 26

MONTEMEZZI, Italo   25   Lyric Poem for O, Paul and Virginia   LA 41;   NP 40
1875-1952   It

MONTEVERDI, Claudio	4	L'Arianna, Opera 1608: Aria, Lament CT 16; MN 36,
1567-1643 It		41, 47; NP 14; PH 13
	4	Coronation of Poppea, Opera 1642: Seneca's Farewell
		NA 34
	14	Madrigals, three unspecified arr Malipiero
		BU 52; SL 54
	4	L'Asciatemi Morire PH 38; WA 39
	4	Illustratev, O Cieli PH 38; WA 39
	4	Lamento della Ninfa PH 38; WA 39
	4	Maledetto sia L'aspetto NA 61; LA 60; WA 39
	15	T'amo mia vita 5 items PH 38; WA 39
	80	Orfeo, Opera 1607 Complete arr Respighi NP 51
	6	-Excerpts PH 31, 38
	5	-Overt NS 21; PH 21
	8	-Sinfonie and Ritornelli arr Malipiero BN 35
	10	-Two Sinfonie SL 54; WA 38
	20	-Suite arr David CT 50; DA 48, 49
	10	Sonata Sopra, Sancte Marie arr Molinari for Chor
		and O NR 63; NP 27
	5	Vespers of 1610: Fanfare arr Foss BU 66; SF 66
	25	-Magnificat complete arr Ghedini with Chor
		HN 52; NP 51, 55; LA 60
MONTZAROS, N.	3	The Greek National Anthem UT 42
1795-1873 Gk		
MOOR, Emanuel	20	P Conc No 3 in D^b Op 57 BN 07
1863-1931 Hung	30	Conc for Str Quart and O in E 1916 CH 20; MN 24
	25	Triple Conc for P, V and C Op 70 1907 DE 62;
		ML 61
MOORE, Douglas	12	The Emperor's New Clothes, One Act Operetta 1948
1893-1969 US		DA 49
	12	Four Museum Pieces 1922 CL 23
	11	In Memoriam 1943 NP 44
	8	Overt on An American Tune 1931 NA 53
	18	The Pageant of P. T. Barnum, Suite 1924 CL 25, 26;
		DA 34; RC 29
	22	Symph No 2 in A 1945 DE 59; LA 46; NP 47;
		RC 47; SE 46
MORALES, Petro		Malaguena arr Reinisch RC 40
1879- Sp		
MORAWETZ, Oskar	15	P Conc No 1 MN 63; SL 69
1917- Czech/Can	8	Passacaglia on a Bach Chorale NA 65
MORENO, Torroba	12	Sonatina for Guitar, Str and Fl SF 59
1891- Sp		
MORGAN, Arthur		SONGS
1915- Brit	4	Devotion KC 34
	4	All Souls Day KC 34
	4	Dream in the Twilight KC 34

MORLEY, Thomas   4   Fire, Fire My Heart from Ballets for five Voices
1557-1603   Brit   No 14 1595   CH 31
                       4   My Bonny Lass, She Smileth from Ballets for five
                                  Voices No 7 1595   NP 1895

MOROSS, Jerome   30   Symph No 1 in 4 mvts 1942   LA 44;   SE 43
1913-   US

MORRIS, Harold   27   Conc on two Negro Themes for P and O   BN 31
1890-   US   10   Overt Joy of Youth 1938   DE 53
                      16   Tone Poem after Rabindranath Tagore's Getanjali
                                  1918   CT 18;   LA 20;   NP 18
                      15   Suite for O in 3 parts 1937   SL 43

MOSCHELES, Isador   28   P Conc No 3 Op 58   NP 1847, 59
1794-1870 Czech/Ger 15   Duo for P on Praciosa   NP 1851
                       6   Overt Maid of Orleans   BN 1881

MOSSOLOV, Alexander   10   Symph of Machines, Steel Foundry Op 10   CH 31;
1900-   Russ/Aust   CT 31;   CL 30;   DA 37;   DT 37;   NP 32;
                            PH 31;   SF 61;   WA 32, 34

MOSZKOWSKI, Maurice   25   Boabdil, Opera Op 49 Suite 7 items   CH 1892
1854-1925   Ger   8   -Prelude and Malaguena   NS 07
                      34   P Conc in E Op 59   CH 06, 23, 35;   DT 23;   NS 07,
                                  09;   PH 06;   SL 09
                      30   V Conc in C Op 30   BN 1888, 95;   CT 02
                      20   From Foreign Lands Suite Op 23   SF 12
                       4   -Italian   CH 33
                       4   -Hungarian   CH 33
                       3   Serenate Op 15 arr Rehfield   MN 27
                      10   Spanish Dances   HN 14
                      30   Suite No 1 in F Op 39   BN 1887, 88, 90, 92, 93;
                                  NP 20;   PH 01, 03, 05
                       4   -Intermezzo   CH 04, 08, 21, 24;   NS 19(2)
                       4   -Perpetual Motion   CH 04, 08, 21, 24;   NS 19(2),
                                  21, 23
                       6   -Excerpts   BN 1892
                      30   Suite No 2 in g Op 47   NP 1849;   NS 1890
                      15   -2mvts   NS 09
                       4   -The Obstinate Note   NS 10
                      15   Symphon Poem, Jeanne d'Arc   PH 03
                       5   Torchlight Dance Op 51   CH 1893

Mouquet, Jules   15   Sonata, The Pipes of Pan Op 15   CH 15;   NS 18
1867-1946   Fr

MOWREY, Dent   30   P Conc   SE 36
1896-

MOYZES, Alexander   7   Overt to Jánošik Op 21 1934   DA 38;   NA 38
1906-   Czech

MOZART, Leopold   14   Conc for Trump   AT 57
1719-1787   Aust   12   Toy Symph   SF 60

MOZART, Wolfgang A.   7   Adagio and Rondo K 617   HN 57
  1756-1791   Austr   8   Adagio and Fugue for Str in c K 546   BN 10, 52, 55,
                             60;   BU 46, 67;   CH 65;   CT 64;   CL 68;
                             KC 62;   ML 65;   NR 65;   NP 1879, 29, 47;
                             PH 62;   PT 67;   RC 60
                     5   Fugue only arr Thomas   CH 1893
  5   Adagio or Rondo in E for V and O K 261   CH 68;   CL 65;   DT 54;
         SL 57;   NP 50, 53, 55;   PH 66;   PT 50, 66, 69;   SL 69;   WA 55
  3   Andante for Fl and Str K 315   MN 38, 52
  8   Cantata for Tenor, male Chor and O, Die mauerfreude K 471   CH 38
  8   Cantata, Eine Kleine Freimaurer Kantate K 623   CH 38
 10   Cantata or Oratorio, Davidde Penitente for Chor and O K 469   CT 55
 15   Cassation No 1 in G, K 63a: Andante   BN 43;   SL 69;   WA 39
 14   Cassation No 2 in B^b K 99   SL 35

      CONCERT ARIAS
      Unidentified arias   DE 58(3), 62(2);   HN 52, 53(2), 61(3)
  8   Ah le previdi, A t'invola,Recitative and aria, Sopr and O K 272
         CT aria only 24, 40
  5   Ah, se in Ciel aria, Sopr and O K 538   DA 68;   ML 61
  5   A questo seno deh vieni, Recitative and aria, Sopr and O K 374
         CH 18
  5   Bella mia fiamma, Scene and Aria for Sopr with P Obbligato K 528
         BA 44, 63, 66;   DE 60;   SL 67
  6   Ch'io mi scordi, Scene and Rondo K 505   CH 55;   CL 58;   DE 51;
         KC 42;   LA 50;   MN 44;   SL 42;   SF 59;   WA 50, 64;   DT 51
  5   Ma che vi fece o stello K 368
      Mandina amabile Trio for Sopr, Tenor, Baritone and O K 480 CT 51
  8   Mentre ti lascia, o figlia Bass and O K 513   CT 43;   DA 63;
         KC 47;   MN 44, 58;   PT 46
  5   Mia speranza adorata Scene and Aria, Sopr and O K 416   BU 68;
         CH 21, 57;   CT 54, 65;   CL 20;   DA 63;   DT 20, 22, 60;   MN 47,
         66;   NP 1882, 90;   NS 18;   PH 21;   PT 53, 60;   SL 19, 20, 22;
         SF 23;   WA 48, 63
  5   Misero, O sogno Recitative and Aria, Tenor and O K 431   CT 67;
         ML 68;   NA 68
  5   Misera dove son K 369   CH 35, 67
  4   Nehmt meinen Dank for Sopr K 383   CT 62;   ML 61;   SF 59
  6   Ombre Felice, Recitative and Aria for Contralto and O K 255 KC 52
  6   Per questa bella mana for Bass and O K 612   CH 23, 36;   BA 63;
         PH 20
  6   Popoli di Tessaglio Recitative and Aria for Sopr and O K 316   CT 59
  4   Rivolgate a lui lo squardo, Aria for Bass and O K 584   MN 58
  6   Si nostra la sorte, Aria for Tenor and O   K 209   CH 67;   PH 25
  6   Vorrei spiegarvi for Sopr, O and solo Oboe K 418   CL 55;   NP 69
  6   Voi avete un cor fidele for Sopr and O K 217   CT 62;   CL 55

      CONCERTOS
      for Piano
 16   K 246 No 8 in C   NP 19, 20, one mvt 25, 26
 31   K 271 No 9 in E^b BA 55;   BU 67;   CH 02, 05, 56;   CT 67;   CL 30,
         49, 58, 65, 68;   DE 49;   DT 51, 56;   KC 55;   NP 51, 53, 68;
         SF 49, 56, 66;   WA 56, 68
 23   K 413 No 11 in F   NP 44
 28   K 414 No 12 in A   AT 49;   CH 50;   CL 54;   PT 59
 18   K 415 No 13 in c   DE 50;   NP 46;   PH 50

MOZART, W.A. (Cont.) Concertos, for P (Cont.)
16   K 449 No 14 in E^b CH 51;   CT 62;   CL 51, 65;   DE 59;   DT 31, 65;
     ML 64;   NR 60;   NP 53, 59;   PH 59;   SL 62
17   K 450 No 15 in B^b BA 61;   CH 66;   CT 65;   CL 47, 63;   NP 61,
     66;   PH 65;   PT 47, 48;   SE 48
18   K 451 No 16 in D   BN 55;   DA 53;   NP 55;   PT 57, 60
31   K 453 No 17 in G   AT 52;   BN 58;   CH 36, 51, 61, 67;   CT 56, 64;
     CL 47, 54, 56, 60, 65;   DE 55, 57;   DT 47;   KC 34;   MN 49;
     NP 36, 50, 52, 53, 55;   PH 69;   PT 53, 62;   SL 68;   WA 53, 55
29   K 456 No 18 in B^b BN 49, 52, 66;   CH 51, 69;   CT 61;   DE 52;
     CL 49, 61, 65;   DT 43, 60;   NP 69;   SF 66
25   K 459 No 19   CH 32, 52;   CT 65;   CL 51, 57, 68;   DA 59;   LA 65;
     MN 39;   NR 46;   PH 64;   PT 44, 61;   RC 69;   WA 68
30   K 466 No 20 in d   AT 66;   BA 60, 65;   BN 1885, 14, 60;   BU 43,
     50, 59;   CH 15, 33, 35, 43, 51, 54, 60;   CT 20, 21, 40, 46, 57,
     60, 69;   CL 32, 49, 50, 61, 63, 65;   DA 49, 63;   DE 61;   DT 18,
     22, 29, 58, 67;   HN 16, 42;   NA 47;   KC 43, 53, 67;   LA 57,
     62, 69;   MN 27, 30;   NR 67;   NP 1884, 05, 29, 33, 34, 36, 52,
     55, 56, 60, 65, 66, 68;   NS 16, 22;   PH 14, 18, 21, 24, 30, 37,
     38, 39, 59;   PT 46, 52, 63, 67;   RC 09, 17, 65;   SL 17, 30, 34,
     38, 44, 59, 66;   SF 15, 30, 33, 50, 58, 65;   SE 31, 49, 61;
     UT 57, 60, 65;   WA 32, 37, 52, 60, 64, 69
6   -Third mvt   CT 30
20   K 467 No 21 in C   BA 57, 59;   BN 26, 32, 37, 49;   BU 63;   CH 31,
     43, 48, 68;   CT 26, 31, 37, 55, 66;   CL 47, 54, 58, 61, 64, 66;
     DA 48;   DT 26, 55;   HN 50;   LA 37, 55;   MN 31, 46, 55, 64;
     NR 67;   NP 33, 50, 58, 53, 54, 58, 64;   NS 26;   PT 56, 61, 69;
     RC 39, 60;   SL 42, 43(2), 54, 60, 66, 67, 69;   SF 55, 66, 68;
     SE 69;   UT 54, 68;   WA 52, 55
20   K 482 No 22 in E^b BN 33, 40, 61;   BU 54;   CH 23, 37, 41, 45;
     CT 24, 34, 44, 47;   CL 47, 54, 60, 63, 66;   DE 56;   DT 36;
     LA 42, 48, 60;   NR 64, 67;   NP 24, 26, 27, 55;   PH 55, 60;
     PT 53;   RC 56;   SL 24, 60;   SF 23, 38, 62;   UT 66;   WA 63
25   K 488 No 23 in A   AT 51, 62, 63;   BA 48, 51, 62;   BN 28, 33, 47,
     54;   BU 51, 56;   CH 20, 25, 37, 41, 45, 54, 58, 61, 64;   CT 20,
     25, 42, 51, 62;   CL 28, 33, 34, 44, 51, 60, 67;   DA 23, 46, 49,
     52, 67;   DE 61, 63, 66;   DT 38, 54, 59;   HN 53, 58, 67;   NA 37,
     40, 43;   KC 37, 46;   LA 57, 69;   ML 65;   NP 30, 49, 55, 56, 59,
     65;   NS 14, 21;   PH 19, 24, 46, 67;   PT 54, 58, 63;   RC 53, 61;
     SL 23, 29, 36, 46, 47, 49, 52, 58, 68;   SF 43, 50, 53, 60, 61, 64,
     66, 67;   SE 46;   WA 63
31   K 491 No 24 in c   AT 47, 56, 67;   BA 68;   BN 62, 69;   BU 55, 57,
     69;   CH 10, 50, 59, 60, 67;   CT 58, 60, 66;   CL 31, 47, 54, 61,
     63, 69;   DA 58, 62;   DE 51, 60;   DT 48, 52, 58, 68;   HN 49, 55,
     60, 61, 64, 66, 69;   NA 63;   KC 46;   LA 45, 67;   ML 61;
     MN 53, 60, 63;   NR 59;   NP 24, 44, 53, 55, 56, 58, 64, 65, 67, 69;
     PH 14, 57;   PT 47, 49, 54, 59, 65, 66;   SL 50, 57, 64, 65, 66;
     SF 47, 54, 60, 64, 66, 68;   SE 53;   UT 63;   WA 50, 52, 68
31   K 503 No 25 in C   BN 1882;   BU 50;   CT 41, 59;   CL 50, 58, 64;
     DE 55, 59, 62, 69;   LA 61, 68;   MN 57, 68;   NP 44, 55;   PT 52;
     RC 66;   SF 56;   SE 60
20   K 537 No 26 in d, Coronation   BN 44, 69;   BU 59, 62;   CH 44;
     CT 39, 60;   CL 49, 62, 67;   DE 62;   DT 43;   HN 35;   LA 64;
     NP 25, 39, 54, 69;   MN 44;   PH 26, 56;   PT 41, 55, 65;   RC 41,
     52;   SL 35, 56;   SE 55, 68

MOZART, W.A. (Cont.) Concertos, for P (Cont.)
29   K 595 No 27 in B^b AT 68;   BN 68;   BU 40;   CH 52;   CT 52, 63;
         CL 47, 52, 64, 68;   DA 59;   DT 31;   NA 66;   KC 35, 41, 54;
         LA 38, 66, 68;   ML 69;   MN 59, 62, 66;   NP 35, 41, 51, 59, 65,
         67;   NS 12;   PH 61, 63;   PT 55, 64, 67;   RC 61;   SF 39, 47,
         55, 66;   WA 52, 68

 4   Concerto for Harpsichord in D   NP finale only 27
24   K 242 Conc for 2 or 3 P in F   AT 65;   BA 56;   BU 65;   CH 67, arr
         for Harpsi 32;   CT 53, 67;   CL 56, 62, 65;   DE 51;   HN 68;
         NA 57, 69;   MN 67;   NP 39;   NS 20;   PT 54, 66
23   K 365 Conc for 2 P in E^b AT 49, 50, 55, 67;   BA 43;   BN 1883, 09,
         20, 44;   BU 45, 58, 65;   CH 11, 16, 20, 27, 47, 51, 57;   CT 37,
         42, 45, 50, 62, 68;   CL 21, 41, 55, 56, 59, 61;   DA 49;   DE 45,
         68;   DT 30, 44, 45, 68;   HN 54;   NA 47, 50, 58;   KC 44, 55, 60;
         LA 22, 65;   MN 26, 34, 47, 50, 59, 67;   NR 50, 52, 65;   NP 50,
         55, 59;   PH 10, 17, 23, 30, 39, 47, 60;   PT 42, 43, 49, 52, 62;
         RC 39(2), 44, 61;   SL 21, 42, 43(2), 61;   SF 38, 56;   SE 41, 55,
         68;   UT 47, 55, 57, 67;   WA 35, 39, 46, 58, 64
20   K 191 Conc for Bassoon in B^b BN 57;   CT 67;   DA 60;   DE 52;
         LA 47;   NS 19;   PH 49;   PT 58;   SL 66
 5   -Allegro   MN 38
20   K 412, Conc for C in D, adapted from Horn Conc   CH 33
20   K 447 Conc for C in E^b, adapted from Horn Conc   BN 32
27   K 622 Conc for Clar in A   AT 68;   BN 56;   CH 62;   CL 55, 61;
         DT 65;   LA 59;   MN 57;   NR 50, 67;   NP 13, 40;   PH 43, 55;
         RC 62;   SF 59, 67;   SE 42, 49;   UT 65
25   Conc for Clar, unspecified   BN 18, 30;   BU 66;   NS adagio and
         finale 17
20   K 313 Conc for Fl and O in G   CT 30;   DE 68;   KC 62;   NR 69;
         PH 47, 52, 59;   PT 66
19   K 314 Conc for Fl in D   BA 43;   PH played as Oboe Conc 62;
         SL 69;   SF 60, 65;   NP 64;   UT 62, 64;   WA 42
26   K 299 Conc for Fl, Harp and O in C   AT 58;   BA 64;   BN 1883, 86,
         91, 13;   CH 03, 10, 41, 62;   DT 36, 48, 62;   NA 36;   KC 37,
         56, 64;   PH 18, 31, 50, 57;   PT 51, 65;   RC 53;   SL 42;   SF 64
20   Horn Conc, unspecified   BN 1888, 28
15   K 447 Conc for Horn in E^b No 1   BU 60;   CH 15;   CL 67;   HN 52,
         69;   NR 51;   NP 12;   SL 13, 44;   SE 49
15   K 495 Conc for Horn in E^b No 4   CH 04;   HN 59;   PH 56;   SE 47
16   K 417 Conc for Horn No 3 in E^b SL 50, 66;   MN 59
12   Conc for Oboe in D   CH 14
12   Conc for Oboe in C   CH 66
27   Conc for Accord, Oboes, Horns and Str, arr for Oboe and O   PH three
         mvts 19
20   K 297 or K 9 Sinfonia Concertante or Quart Concertante for Oboe,
         Clar, or Fl, Horn, and Bassoon   BA 60;   BN 55, 60, 63, 65, 69;
         BU 45, 61;   CH 1898, 10, 15, 55;   CT 26, 62;   CL 33, 45;
         DT 46;   HN 62, 67;   NA 69;   KC 50;   LA 33, 50;   ML 64;
         MN 49, Theme and Var only 44, 49;   NR 66;   NP 23, 36, 55, 57,
         66;   PH 27, 40, 47, 51, arr Stokowski 39, 69;   PT 39, 47, 53, 58,
         61;   SL 52, 58, 66, 67;   RC 61;   SE 48, 57;   WA 68
         -Two mvts   SL 32
15   K 207, Conc No 1 in B^b for V and O   DT 34;   NP 61;   SL 59;   SF 61

MOZART, W.A. (Cont.) Concertos (Cont.)
27   K 216, Conc No 3 in G for V and O   BA 68;   BN 51, 54, 56;   BU 44,
        50, 63;   CH 12, 41, 46, 51, 59, 65, 68;   CT 58;   CL 51, 55, 69;
        DA 48, 54;   DT 21, 60, 63, 65;   HN 50, 51;   KC 52;   LA 34, 53,
        55;   ML 68;   MN 60, 66;   NR 58, 60;   NP 41, 52, 55;   PH 12, 56;
        PT 52, 65, 66;   NA 47, 53, 63;   RC 40, 61, 68;   SL 50, 59;
        SF 46, 58, 60, 61, 65, 69;   SE 59;   UT 63;   WA 49, 63
27   K 218 Conc No 4 in D for V and O   BA 48, 53;   BN 11, 13, 31, 32,
        41, 48, 59;   BU 44, 47, 55;   CH 11, 31, 33, 46, 51;   CT 27, 38,
        44;   CL 26, 29, 48, 55, 56, 59, 63;   DE 59, 66, 67, 68;   DT 24,
        26, 44, 55, 56, 68;   KC 61;   LA 32, 38, 43, 69;   MN 29, 32, 44,
        46, 53, 56, 67;   NR 50, 65;   NP 40, 69;   NS 13;   PH 36, 40, 55,
        69;   PT 39, 49, 57, 62, 69;   RC 07, 29, 53;   SL 38, 48, 68;
        SF 35, 48, 56, 59;   SE 41, 47;   WA 34, 39, 52, 56, 69
29   K 219 Conc No 5 in A for V and O   BA 49, 63;   BN 07;   BU 55;
        CH 15, 18, 46, 49, 52, 55, 63, 64, 67;   CT 25, 63;   CL 39, 49,
        52, 53, 57, 61, 62, 68;   DA 38, 62;   DE 56;   DT 47, 53, 59;
        HN 64;   NA 56;   KC 42, 43;   LA 23, 46, 52, 59, 60, 62, 69;
        MN 42, 54, 57, 64, 67;   NP 40, 46, 47, 54, 55, 56, 62;   PH 06,
        35, 42, 47, 54, 65, 68, 69;   PT 43, 55, 68;   RC 51;   SF 35, 42,
        64, 67;   UT 48;   WA 31, 37, 52, 55, 67
26   K 268, Conc in E^b for V and O No 6   AT 59;   BN 20;   BU 63;   CH 03,
        18, 26;   CT 98, 04, 18, 28;   DT 18;   LA 29;   MN 29;   NS 12;
        PH 03, 18;   RC 25;   SL 22, 59;   SF 18
35   K 271a, Conc in D No 7 for V and O   BN 42, 50, 51, 59;   CH 37;
        CT 32, 37, 48;   CL 28, 31, 36;   NA 47, 48;   MN 51, 67;   LA 57,
        66;   NP 34, 50, 55;   PH 24, 25;   PT 48;   SL 28, 41;   WA 66
27   K 364 Sinfonia Concertante in E^b for V and Vla   AT 58;   BA 61;
        BN 15, 19;   BU 51, 63;   CH 04, 27, 41, 43, 55, 63;   CT 07, 27,
        41, 50, 55;   CL 24, 43, 50, 55, 63;   DA 46, 48, 66;   DE 51, 59;
        DT 55, 61;   HN 66;   NA 38, 58;   KC 49, 55(2);   LA 48, 56, 62,
        65;   MN 56;   NR 53;   NP 18, 52;   NS 16, 24;   PH 21, 48, 64;
        PT 60;   RC 53, 59;   SL 67;   SF 40, 65, 66, 67;   SE 41, 55, 67;
        UT 53, 60, 67;   WA 49, 55
        -One mvt   BN 1891
6   -Adagio only   CH 29
24   Conc for V in D, Adelaide   BN 33
24   Conc for V unidentified   BN 31;   NS 03

5   Contra Dances   DA 49;   NP 50, 52
8   German Dances K 64   BN 07, 12;   RC 62;   WA 2 dances 35
        -K 611   NP 10, 30, 41, 48
8   -3 German Dances K 605   BN 67;   CT 49;   DE 58;   HN 42;
        NA 31;   SL 30;   WA 67
4   -No 3 Sleigh ride only HN 36;   UT 69
9   -6 German Dances K 571   CH 46;   MN 50
8   -4 German Dances   PH 38, 42, 61

19   Divertimento No 2 in D K 131   CL 48, 55, 62;   DA 64;   MN 66;
        NP 3 mvts 31, 56(2);   PH 55
4   -Minuet arr Goossens   CT 41
18   Divertimento No 3 in D K 136   AT 66;   BN 53, 58, 64;   CL 66, 69;
        DA 65;   HN 60;   KC 69;   LA 61;   PH 67;   RC 69;   SF 58, 69;
        UT 67;   WA 69
4   -Adagio   SE 41
16   Divertimento in C K 187   NP 31(2)

MOZART, W. A. (Cont.)
15 Divertimento in d No 7 K 205 BN 67; CH 61; NP 28, 37; WA 39
16 Divertimento No 10 in F K 247 BN 63; CT 58; PH 37, 41
18 Divertimento in D No 11 K 251 CH 56, 66, 68; DT 60; KC 69;
     NP 68; PT excerpts 66
16 Divertimento in D for Str K 449 RC 39, 62
27 Divertimento in B♭ No 15 for Str and Horns K 287 BN 38, 44, 47, 64;
     CH 64; DA 53; HN 61; LA 55; MN adagio 26; NP 53; NS 24;
     RC 60; SE 41
15 Divertimento No 17 in D K 334 CH 34, 54; CL 65; MN 35;
     NR 56; NP Theme and Var 1898; PH 36, 56, 67; PT 4 mvts 45
8 -Andante and Var BN 1895

15 Eine Kleine Nachtmusik Serenade K 525 AT 48, 51, 55, 66; BA 42,
     43, 49(2), 54, 58; BN 23, 24, 26, 29, 32, 43, 55, 62; BU 55,
     60; CH 09, 15, 27, 33, 35, 42, 47, 48, 54, 66; CT 15, 25, 39,
     53, 63, 68; CL 25, 39, 44, 53, 60, 68; DA 37, 46, 49, 58, 63;
     DE 51, 59, 63, 65; DT 27, 41, 48, 57, 62, 66; HN 34, 51, 62;
     NA 37, 57; KC 43, 48, 52; LA 36, 47, 65; MN 23, 37, 45, 49,
     52, 67; NR 51, 56; NP 06, 22, 25, 54, 63; NS 20; PH 05,
     28, 33, 47, 50, 58; PT 38, 42, 49, 54, 64; RC 33, 39, 43(2),
     53, 55, 63; SL 27, 29, 32, 33, 37, 39, 40, 42, 52, 55, 67, 68;
     SF 39, 55, 56, 64, 66, 67; UT 55; WA 35, 36, 39, 45, 52;
     SE 45, 63;
6 -Minuet and Finale RC 10

14 Fantasia in c for P K 396 BN 1881; CT 40; RC 38
11 Fantasy for a Musical Clock K 608 CH 42
5 Marches in D K 335 CL 67; MN one only 56, 57; NP 67
4 March No 3 in C K 408 BN 65; CL 67; NP 67
4 March in D K 249 MN 59
4 Turkish March from P Sonata in A K 331 BA 43; BN 1885, 95;
     CL 53; DT 23; NS 24(2); SL 52
4 Masonic Funeral March Mauerische Trauermusik K 477 BN 1881, 91,
     08, 13, 51, 55, 58, 61, 69; BU 67; CH 50, 64; CT 00, 29,
     64; CL 50, 52; DA 54; HN 58; LA 57; MN 49, 61; NR 63;
     PH 68; NP 1891, 29, 68; NS 11; SL 61, 63; SF 53; SE 28;
     WA 37
80 Mass in c K 427 BU 69; CH 55; CL 66; DA 62; MN 63; PH 55;
     RC 65
6 -Qui Tollis RC 45, 65
6 -Et incarnatus est BA 66; CT 51; CL 55; DT 63; LA 57;
     NP 53, 55; NS 20; PH 46; RC 47; SL 59
15 Missa Brevis in B♭ for Voices, Str and Org K 275 PH 53
17 Motet, Exultate Jubilate K 165 AT 56; BA 53; CL 53, 62;
     DA 52 excerpts 35; DE 53, 57; DT 52, 58, 63; HN 66;
     NA 57; LA 53, 57, 65; NP 53, 63; PT 60; SL 58; SF 65,
     67; SE 57; WA 69
4 -Alleluia BU 51, 60; CH 18, 26, 46; CT 34; DE 54, 66;
     DT 26; HN 42, 48; NA 45, 65; KC 52; LA 27; NR 66;
     PH 26; PT 51; SF 36; WA 38
6 Motet Ave Verum Corpus K 618 BN 55; CH 68; DE 64; MN 49;
     NP 53; RC 45; SL 36; 52, 58, SF 64
8 Motet, Regina Coeli for Chor, Sopr and O K 276 BN 55
18 A Musical Joke K 522 CH 57; DA 49; PH 69

Time in
Minutes

MOZART, W.A. (Cont.)

10	Offertory Alma Dei Creatores K 277 PH 53
20	Overt in the Italian Style K 318 NP 27
6	Overt in B^b K 311a PH 26
20	Quart in F for Oboe and Str K 370 NR 53
11	Quintet in g for Str K 516 NP 50; WA 41
15	Quintet with Clar K 581 SE andante only 27
57	Requiem in d K 626 AT 64; BN 1887, 31, 41, excerpts 59; BU 67; CH 50, 57, 63; CL 64, 67; DA 50, 65; NA 38; KC 55; LA 66; MN 60, 65; NR 55; NP 41, 55, 63; RC 45; SL 58; SF 64; SE 50
5	Rondo for Harpsi BN 26
5	Rondo for P and O K 382 CT 65; DA 59; NP 50; MN 45; SF 68; SE arr Bellison for Clar 54
7	Rondo Allegretto or Adagio for V and O K 373 CH 68; MN 45, 47; NP 50; PH 66; PT 50, 66, 69; SL 69; WA 55

Serenades

25	No 3 in D LA 32
11	No 6 in D, Serenata Notturna K 239 AT 54; BN 21; CH 43, 45, 52; CT 62; CL 39; DE 55; HN 68; NA 40, 59, 60; KC 66; MN 55, 65; NP 40; NS 21; PH 28; PT 54; RC 63; SF 54; UT 50
23	No 7 in D, Haffner K 250 BN 1885, 93, 97, 13, 21, 66; CH 29; CT 56; HN rondo only 46; MN 24, 53; NP 27; LA 25; NS 22; PH 27; RC 32, 54; SF 29
15	No 8 in D K 286 for 4 O's BN 1881, 13; DA 54; KC 50, 68; NP 62; PH 53; SL 28, 29; SF 57; SE 58
25	No 9 in D, Posth K 320 BA 53, 63; BN 36, 62; CH 62; CT 60, 65, 69; CL 40, 45, 50, 60; LA 41; NP 30, 47; RC 40, 45
25	No 10 in B^b for Wind Instruments K 361 BN 1894, 32, 52, 55; BU rondo only 63; CH 5 parts 14, 63, 2 parts 63, 68; CL 69 DA excerpts 63; DE 53; HN 53; NP adagio and Rondo only 61, 69; PT 69; RC 55; SL excerpts 65
19	No 12 in E^b K 375 SF 57, 66
	-in c K 388 for 8 Wind Instruments CH 43
	Songs
4	The Violet K 476 CH 1894
4	Wehe mir! Ist's Wahrheit oder Traum ich? CH 28
4	Wiegenlied K 350 MN 34

SYMPHONIES

	Symphony in C NP 52
8	K 16 No 1 in E^b CH 43; HN 57; LA 69; MN 55; NP 32; SL 52, 63
10	K 45 No 7 in D BN 1886, 97, 02
22	K 114 No 14 in A DA 55; DT 68
14	K 133 No 20 in D HN 69
13	K 134 No 21 in A MN 59
7	K 162 No 2 in C SL 64
8	K 181 No 23 in D HN 61; NR 60; PH 53; SL 65; SF 61
8	K 182 No 24 in B^b HN 62; NP 62; SE 49
18	K 183 No 25 in g BA 68; BN 1899, 47; CH 31, 42, 50, 56, 65; CT 41, 66; CL 62; DA 68; DE 66; DT 69; HN 59; LA 42, 59, 68; ML 67; MN 44, 55, 59; NR 69; NP 41, 55; RC 54; SL 69; SE 28

MOZART, W.A. (Cont.)   Symphonies (Cont.)

10   K 184 No 26 in E^b BN 66;   CH 50;   NA 60

11   K 199 No 27 in G   DA 46

16   K 200 No 28 in C   BN 23, 63;   CH 66;   CT 59, 65, 66;   CL 41, 65;   NP 32, 33;   NS 24;   PH 41

18   K 201 No 29 in A   BN 36, 37, 40, 43, 55, 60, 65;   CH 45, 52, 55, 61, 63;   CT 29, 39, 54, 61;   CL 56, 59, 69;   DA 58, 68;   DE 63, 68;   DT 64;   HN 56;   KC 57, 67;   LA 41, 50, 56, 63;   ML 68;   MN 57, 60;   NR 56, 58, 65;   NP 31, 40, 54, 55, 60, 69;   PH 48, 55, 61, 66, 69;   PT 41, 60, 66;   RC 55, 62;   SF 60, 67;   UT 69;   WA 38, 42, 47, 55

14   K 202 No 30 in D   NA 44, 66;   PH 61, 64

19   K 297 No 31 in D, Paris   BN 1887, 92, 95, 97, 45, 53, 56, 65;   CH 59, 60, 63, 67, 69;   CT 40, 67;   HN 65;   NA 61, 69;   LA 19, 46, 52, 63;   MN 49;   NP 35, 64;   PH 60, 68;   PT 69;   RC 28, 29, 45, 55;   SL 64;   SF 40, 51, 66;   SE 41;   WA 41, 52, 62

10   K 318 No 32 in G   BN 67;   CH 55, 64;   CT 69;   CL 60;   DA 46;   NP 69;   SF 55

22   K 319 No 33 in B^b BA 57, 69;   BN 64;   CH 50, 65;   CT 58, 59, 64, 68;   CL 50, 58, 62;   DA 49, 65;   DT 56, 61, 63;   HN 48, 51;   KC 47;   LA 58;   ML 60;   MN 53, 57, 62;   NP 51;   PH 66, 68;   RC 55;   SL 69

22   K 338 No 34 in C   BA 65;   BN 1898, 04, 23, 27, 29, 31, 36, 39, 42, 51, 68;   CH 51, 52, 55, 59, 66;   CT 35, 63;   CL 50, 57, 63, 68;   DA 46, 62;   HN 63;   NA 57, 68;   LA 49, 57;   ML 67;   MN 49, 58, 67;   NP 27, 37, 39, 41, 60, 67;   PH 27, 59, 62, 63, 69;   PT 57, 63, 67;   RC 59, 63;   SL 48;   SF 54;   WA 57

17   K 385 No 35 in D Haffner   AT 51, 58, 60, 66, 69;   BA 42, 44, 53, 55;   BN 1884, 08, 16, 22, 25, 32, 38, 41, 48, 55, 68, 69;   BU 39, 43, 47, 52, 54, 58, 60, 63, 67;   CH 15, 31, 36, 42, 46, 47(2), 48, 54, 56, 60, 64, 67, 69;   CT 31, 36, 42, 46, 47, 49, 52, 54;   CL 30, 34, 41, 43, 45, 46, 54, 59, 68;   DA 52, 63, 67;   DE 46, 47, 53, 54, 55, 58, 63, 64, 66, 69;   DT 22, 25, 35, 37, 54, 60, 65, 69;   HN 47, 53, 69;   NA 42, 46, 54, 55, 58, 65;   KC 38, 63, 68;   LA 40, 45, 50, 53, 55, 64;   ML 66;   MN 28, 40, 42, 45, 47, 51, 54, 56, 59, 61, 65;   NR 52, 55, 60, 61, 64;   NP 1861, 70, 28, 32, 34, 44, 49, 50, 51, 57, 64, 68;   NS 16, 22, 26;   PH 29, 30, 37, 40, 43, 44, 45, 47, 50, 51, 52, 53, 57, 59, 60, 62, 65, 67;   PT 42, 45, 48, 52, 62;   RC 36, 40, 44, 50, 53, 58;   SL 33, 34, 36, 40, 42, 45, 46, 48, 52, 57, 58, 62;   SF 26, 39, 42, 52, 60, 63, 67;   SE 38, 48;   UT 43, 49, 61, 67;   WA 44, 48, 49, 53, 58, 68

26   K 425 No 36 in C Linz   BA 67;   BN 1882, 20, 46, 57, 67;   BU 57;   CH 13, 40, 43, 46, 49, 51, 53, 57, 62, 65;   CT 43, 47, 50, 62;   CL 43, 54, 61;   DA 48, 60, 64, 67;   DE 55;   DT 40, 51;   HN 47, 66;   LA 40, 67;   MN 50, 63, 65;   NR 57, 63, 69;   NP 31, 36, 60, 63, 68;   PH 42, 45, 54, 57, 58, 63, 69;   PT 47, 54, 59, 65, 68;   RC 21, 43, 51, 58, 60;   SL 40;   SF 55, 57, 62, 64;   SE 41, 64;   UT 51, 60

15   K 444 No 37 in G   MN 52

27   K 504 No 38 in D Prague   AT 48, 68;   BN 1881, 94, 04, 07, 13, 18, 21, 36, 31, 47, 49, 54, 59, 64, 67;   BU 49, 55, 66;   CH 1894, 99, 04, 11, 16, 22, 25, 30, 32, 34, 36, 38, 50, 52, 54, 55;   CT 14, 22, 27, 34, 48, 61;   CL 36, 48, 55, 56, 59, 65;   DA 49, 56, 64;   DE 66;   DT 46, 62, 67;   HN 49;   NA 55, 62, 66;   KC 68;   LA 46, 59, 62, 69;   ML 62, 69;   MN 54, 58, 60, 62;   NR 54, 61;   NP 1865, 74, 77, 81, 29, 31, 35, 37, 53, 56, 62, 69;

MOZART, W.A. (Cont.) Symphonies, K 504 (Cont.)
    NS 17, 24(2); PH 27, 41, 46, 47, 48, 55, 63, 65; PT 67;
    RC 48, 53, 58; SL 29, 35, 39, 44, 51, 55, 69; SF 39, 44, 52,
    59, 65; SE 62, 69; UT 56, 66; WA 52, 55, 59
29 K 543 No 39 in E^b AT 50, 64, 68; BA 59; BN 1883, 85, 88, 89,
    91, 94, 96, 01, 03, 09, 13, 15, 17, 22, 27, 29, 33, 35, 36, 40, 43,
    50, 52, 54, 59, 68; BU 48, 53, 55; CH 1891, 97, 00, 03, 07, 13,
    14, 15, 18, 19, 22, 24, 29, 33, 37, 41, 45, 48, 51, 53, 54, 56, 58,
    60, 62, 65, 66, 68; CT 1896, 13, 19, 21, 22, 27, 30, 33, 40, 45,
    53, 56, 60; CL 21, 35, 42, 45, 46, 51, 55, 59, 64; DA 48, 52,
    59, 61, 63, 64; DE 54; DT 14, 20, 48, 51, 52, 57, 62, 63, 66;
    HN 49, 52, 61, 68; NA 32, 59; KC 51; LA 20, 23, 30, 38, 41,
    47, 52, 54, 61; MN 24, 37, 41, 48, 51, 58, 61, 64; NP 1846,
    69, 89, 95, 96, 24, 28, 31, 35, 50, 53, 60; NS 1883, 94, 12, 21,
    23; PH 02, 12, 15, 19, 21, 24, 33, 39, 58, 63, 64; PT 41, 45,
    49, 54, 58, 61, 66; RC 24, 26, 37, 49, 52, 59, 69; SL 13, 21,
    30, 31, 49, 59, 66; SF 13, 17, 21, 22, 28, 37, 48, 54, 61, 65;
    SE 31, 41, 54, 60, 63, 67; UT 50, 54, 65; WA 39, 49, 51, 56
6 –Menuetto CH 01; HN 43
29 K 550 No 40 in g AT 47, 62; BA 41, 42, 43, 44, 48, 50, 58, 66;
    BN 1881, 84, 86, 89, 91, 93, 95, 96, 00, 05, 07, 11, 12, 14, 18,
    19, 22, 24, 30, 34, 40, 46, 49, 52, 55, 57, 61, 65, 66; BU 43,
    46, 55, 61, 63; CH 1892, 94, 97, 00, 02, 05, 09, 14, 16, 17, 18,
    20, 21, 25, 27, 36, 38, 45, 47, 49, 54, 56, 58, 61; CT 1895, 01,
    10, 13, 16, 17, 23, 28, 32, 38, 40, 48, 55, 59, 64, 69; CL 19,
    23, 26, 27, 29, 33, 37, 39, 40, 41, 42, 44, 46, 48, 53, 55, 57, 58,
    59, 61, 66, 69; DA 56, 61, 66; DE 45, 48, 53, 56, 60, 64, 67;
    DT 19, 38, 40, 45, 47, 51, 55, 58, 64, 67; HN 33, 49, 51, 53, 55,
    64, 67; NA 35, 39, 56, 62, 67; KC 34, 36, 44, 49, 64; LA 21,
    24, 29, 35, 37, 39, 43, 48, 53, 57, 59; ML 64; MN 25, 30, 31,
    33, 41, 43, 46, 48, 51, 53, 62; NR 30, 53, 55, 59, 67; NP 1845,
    48, 49, 50, 54, 60, 67, 80, 83, 85, 90, 97, 02, 10, 12, 15, 17, 21,
    25, 30, 32, 33, 35, 38, 39, 40, 43, 46, 48, 49, 52, 59, 62, 68, 69;
    NS 1881, 89, 92, 06, 10, 13, 18, 20, 22, 25, 26; PH 01, 04, 05,
    07, 09, 11, 13, 16, 17, 18, 19, 20, 21, 22, 23, 25, 26, 28, 31, 33,
    38, 39, 42, 43, 45, 48, 50, 55, 60, 63, 67, 69(2); PT 44, 46, 48,
    51, 53, 57, 63, 64; RC 27, 32, 50, 52, 55; SL 12, 17, 22, 24,
    29, 31, 33, 34, 38, 41, 43, 46, 47, 49, 51, 53, 54, 57, 61;
    SF 15, 18, 20, 24, 27, 31, 37, 43, 46, 47, 49, 53, 60, 64, 66;
    SE 27, 30, 36, 41, 43, 45, 52, 56, 65; UT 41, 47, 52, 63; WA 33,
    40, 50, 52, 61, 63, 69
28 K 551 No 41 in C Jupiter AT 46, 54, 57; BA 26, 55, 62; BN 1884,
    88, 90, 93, 96, 98, 01, 02, 05, 10, 12, 14, 16, 18, 20, 28, 34, 41,
    43, 47, 51, 52, 55, 60, 62, 65, 68; BU 51, 52, 55, 58, 59;
    CH 1892, 96, 98, 01, 04, 06, 12, 13, 16, 18, 21, 23, 26, 28, 38,
    41, 43, 47, 48, 50, 53, 55, 57, 61, 62, 64, 67, 68; CT 1897, 12,
    15, 19, 20, 24, 27, 31, 32, 36, 41, 44, 45, 58; CL 22, 24, 31,
    40, 47, 49, 55, 57, 63, 66; DA 46, 50(2), 59, 69; DE 52, 65;
    DT 16, 30, 39, 44, 45(2), 46, 52, 59, 65, 68; HN 40, 43, 50, 55,
    56; NA 41, 50, 58, 63, 69; KC 35, 39, 46, 53, 60; LA 22, 33,
    51, 55, 57; MN 22, 29, 36, 39, 42, 44, 47, 52, 55, 63, 68;
    NR 69; NP 1843, 45, one mvt 56, 62, 66, 73, 78, 82, 88, 91, 96,
    01, 03, 11, 17, 19, 29, 32, 33, 36, 38, 39, 41, 45, 47, 52, 58, 60,
    62, 63, 66, 67; NS 1879, 05, 09, 14, 19, 20, 23, 24, 27; PH 03,
    06, 10, 14, 17, 19, 20, 21, 22, 23, 25, 33, 34, 35, 41, 44, 49, 53,
    62, 65, 67; PT 40, 43, 46, 48, 51, 52, 55, 60, 66; RC 23, 25,
    30, 38, 40, 46, 51, 53, 61; SL 10, 27, 32, 35, 37, 39, 43, 56,

MOZART, W.A. (Cont.) Symphonies, K551 (Cont.)
        60, 62, 64, 67, 68;   SF 19, 22, 29, 31, 38, 41, 46, 50, 51, 53,
        56, 63, 64, 66, 67;   SE 29, 32, 35, 50, 66;   UT 48, 58, 64, 68;
        WA 37, 50, 52, 54, 65, 68

10   Var arr La Forge on the aria Ah vous dirai-je-maman K 265   BA 42;
        BN 43;   CT 41
        -arr Adam   CT 21
        Vesperae Solemnes de confessore, 4 C, Org and O K 339   CT 66

DRAMATIC WORKS
4   La Clemenza di Tito Opera K 621: arias, unidentified   NS 12;
        SL 11;   SF 47
4   -Ach nur einmal   NS 22
4   -Air di Sexto   CT 04
4   -Deh per questo   CT 32;   NP 1844, 83
4   -Ecce il Punto   NP 1898
4   -Jetzt, vitellia, Recitative and Nie Soll mit Rosen, aria   CH 03,
        06, 12, 20;   LA 21;   NS 06;   PH 01, 06, 13, 17;   SF 13
4   -Nie wird mich Hymen   CT 02
4   -Non piu dei fiori   MN 23;   NS 23
4   -Parto, Parto   CT 18, 34;   DE 66;   NA 65;   MN 33;   LA 54;
        NP 1856, 58, 66, 70;   SE 56
5   -Overt   BN 1883;   CH 43, 52;   CT 48;   CL 34;   HN 61, 64, 66;
        NA 53, 62;   NP 34, 38, 39, 56;   SL 33;   SF 61;   SE 49;   WA 50
120   Cosi Fan Tutte Opera K 588: Complete   AT 58;   BA 56;   DE 64;
        MN 55;   PT 55;   SL 55;   WA 54
4   -Arias, unidentified   BA 57(3);   DA 35;   DE 50;   NR 60;   NS 07
4   -Come scoglio immoto resta for Sopr   BU 51;   DE 49;   DT 52, 63;
        NA 64;   KC 57, 62;   PT 57;   RC 59;   SL 53, 59;   WA 59
70   -Concert Version   CT 55
4   -E amore un ladroncello for Sopr   CT 32;   ML 63;   SF 51;   SE 58;
        WA 64
4   -Ei parte senti   CT 52
4   -Fior di legi   DT 24;   NS 15
4   -Forgive me dearest   NA 53
4   -I will choose the handsome one   AT 61
4   -In uomini, in soldati   NA 52;   WA 51
5   -Overt   BU 64;   DT 56, 64;   NA 50, 59, 64, 68;   MN 28, 48, 54;
        NR 66;   NP 1853, 1953, 66;   PT 65;   RC 48, 59;   SF 64, 67;
        SE 69
4   -Per Pieta ben mio, Recitative and Aria   BN 50, 54;   BU 54;
        CH 33, 50, 52;   DT 54;   KC 57;   ML 61, 63;   NP 1854, 1957;
        NS 1886;   PT 57;   RC 59;   WA 59
4   -Un aura amorosa for Tenor   DT 58;   MN 32;   NP 37
120   Don Giovanni Opera K 527, Complete   AT 65;   BU 56;   SL 56;   WA 55
4   -Aria, unidentified   DE 54, 59;   HN 34, 54;   ML 62;   NP 1850, 58,
        70;   SE 46, 63
4   -Ah Pieta signor miei Bass   WA 49, 60
4   -Batti, batti o bel Musetto Contralto   AT 51:   CT 42, 51, 64, 66;
        DT 23, 38;   KC 45;   MN 66;   NP 1846;   MS 22;   WA 51
4   -Crudele? Ah no mio bene, Recitative   NS 1897, 17
4   -Dalla sua pace for Tenor   LA 50;   NS 87;   SF 39;   SE 38, 39, 58, 63
4   -Deh vieni alla Finestra serenade   BA 47, 67;   CT 38, 51;   CL 26;
        NA 41, 53, 69;   LA 45;   ML 60, 64;   NS 06, 14;   RC 43, 53;
        SL 13, 17, 38

MOZART, W.A. (Cont.)   Dramatic Works, Don Giovanni (Cont.)
4   -Donna Anna's Aria   NP 1845;   NS 1888, 93;   PH 02, 06, 11, 12,
        16, 40
4   -Funeral Music   SF 38
4   -Il mio Tesoro for Tenor   AT 50;   BU 48;   CL 23;   DT 46, 58;
        NA 39, 55;   KC 43;   LA 22, 33;   MN 28, 35, 48;   NP 1859, 66,
        11;   NS 1881;   PT 37, 59;   SL 21;   UT 51;   WA 36, 43
4   -In quali eccessi, Recitative   CH 55;   SE 55
4   -La ci darem la nono   CT 51;   NA 66;   SL 48
4   -Madamina, Catologue, Leporella's Aria   CT 19, 20, 39, 43, 45, 46,
        51;   DA 63;   DT 46, 52;   HN 46;   NA 66;   KC 47;   MN 34, 41,
        44, 56;   NS 22;   SL 41;   SE 40, 46, 63;   UT 40;   WA 49
4   -Mi tradi quell'alma ingrata   DT 46;   NA 64;   SF 54
5   -Music for 3 O's   BU 63, 68
4   -Non mi dir for Sopr   AT 66;   CT 1895, 21, 45;   DT 51, 60;
        KC 45;   MN 43;   NP 1853, 56, 57, 63, 68, 74
4   -Or sai che l'onore for Sopr   WA 60
6   -Overt   AT 49;   BA 28;   BN 1885, 94, 96, 01, 20, 67;   BU 48, 63,
        68;   CH 1898, 05, 16, 23, 25, 41, 46, 47, 58, 66, 68;   CT 28, 38,
        43, 51, 66;   DA 34, 38, 51;   CL 35, 38, 40, 43;   DE 55, 65;
        DT 15, 19, 20, 26, 35, 39, 40, 51, 53, 55, 58, 60, 62, 64, 67;
        HN 69;   KC 46, 59, 69;   LA 37, 42, 62;   ML 64;   MN 26, 40, 43,
        46;   NP 46, 50, 55;   NS 22;   PH 13, 14, 15, 16, 19, 20, 35, 48,
        63, 65;   PT 47, 50, 59, 66;   RC 38, 58;   SL 22, 28, 31, 33, 40,
        41, 43, 48, 51, 53, 54, 68;   SF 55, 64, 66;   SE 51;   UT 50, 63;
        WA 33
4   -Verdrai carino   CT 64;   DT 62
       Die Entführung aus dem Serail, The Abduction from the Seraglio,
          Musical Play   K 384
4   -Arias unidentified   DE 57;   NS 13;   PH 14;
4   -Aria, Bravura   NP 1842
4   -Ach ich liebte, Constanza's Aria Sopr   CT 19, 55, 62, 66;   MN 46;
        NS 16, 20;   PT 54
90   -Concert form   BA 52
4   -Constance, Constance for Tenor   CT 28, 30;   CL 31, 32, 34
4   -Con vezzi   LA 21
4   -Dances   DE 52
4   -Durch zartlichkeit und Schmeicheln Sopr   CH 14;   NS 14
4   -Finale, Act II   NS 1888
4   -Hier soll ich denn schon Tenor   CT 28, 30;   MN 31
4   -Martern aller Arten for Sopr   CH 1898;   CT 63;   NA 62;   KC 64;
        LA 24;   MN 22;   NS 15, 22
4   -Nur ehrem frieden   MN 37
4   -Osmin's Aria   NP 50
5   -Overt   BN 1882, 94, 20, 51, 56, 66, 68;   CH 09, 31, 69;   CT 16,
        31, 33, 51, 53, 57;   CL 34, 39;   DT 30, 31, 52, 54, 55;   DE 69;
        HN 54, 62;   NA 38;   KC 57, 63;   LA 32, 47;   ML 63, 68;
        MN 26, 40;   NR 62;   NP 11, 41, 51, 53, 55, 63, 68;   NS 1888;
        PT 38;   RC 40, 46, 52;   SL 38, 68;   SF 56, 58, 63;   SF 69;
        SE 54;   UT 53;   WA 51, 55
4   -Solche hergelauf'ne laffen   CH 1894;   CT 46;   WA 49
4   -Trastet die Heissgeliebte   MN 37
4   -Wer ein Liebchen hat gefunden for Bass   CH 1894
4   -O Wieling wie feurig   MN 31
4   -O wie will ich triumphieren Bass   WA 49

MOZART, W.A. (Cont.)   Dramatic Works (Cont.)

20   L'Epeuve d'amour, full Ballet   MN 38

La Finta giardinera, Opera   K 196 Finale to Overt   NP 1869, 62, 07, 21, 26

Idomeneo, rè di Creta, Opera   K 366

    -Arias unidentified   DE 48, 58;   HN 52, 54;   NS 27(2)

10   -Ballet Music   K 367   NP 1851;   NS 1887, 12

15   -Concert Version Suite   CT arr Busoni 19, 41;   CL 50;   MN arr Busoni 42;   NP 37, 51, 55;   NS 87

15   -Excerpts   BU 64

4   -Gavotte   DT 32;   PH 27

4   -Non temer amato ben, Scene and Rondo   BN 54;   CH 26;   CT 27; CL 27, 58;   KC 56;   LA 58;   NP 03;   PH 56

5   -Overt   BN 44, 66, 68;   CH 43, 45, 51;   DA 64;   NA 61' MN 50;   NP 1870;   PH 57;   RC 60;   SL 46, 58;   SF 57;   SE 64

    -Zefferetti Lusinghiere for Sopr   DT 51;   NA 48;   KC 55; NP 63;   WA 32

Il re pastore, Dramatic Festival Play   K 208

4   -Arias unidentified   DE 58;   HN 32;   NS 12, 19;   PH 03, 04, 11, 16, 39

4   -Air tranquillo   NP 63

4   -L'amero saro costante   AT 59;   CH 12, 21, 22;   CT 01, 20, 24, 45, 62;   CL 22, 24, 43;   DE 46;   DT 16, 21, 40;   KC 37, 45, 52;   ML 61;   MN 22, 29, 31;   NP 31;   RC 26;   SL 16, 31; SF 40;   WA 51

7   Lucia Silla Opera   K 135 Overt   BA 40;   CT 59;   MN 68;   SE 69; WA 41, 53

120   Zauberflaute Magic Flute   K 620 Complete   SE 49

    -Arias unidentified   BA 43, 44, 51(2), 54, 64, 66, 67(3);   DA 46; MN 45(2);   NP 22, 33;   NS 05;   ML 62;   SL 09, 11(2), 46; WA 52

4   -Ach ich fuhl's, or Ah lo so, I feel grief and sadness   CT 49; CL 25;   DT 25;   KC 65;   LA 21, 25;   MN 32;   NS 18;   SL 20; WA 60

4   -Ah cien est fait   SL 14;   ML 62

4   -Be not afraid   CH 19;   MN 23

4   -Der Holte rache   The pangs of hell, Queen of the Night's Aria BU 68;   CT 10, 57, 64;   DT 26, 46, 60;   KC 54;   MN 28, 32, 57;   PT 44, 51;   NP 1889;   NS 24

4   -Dies Bildnis ist bezaubered schon, O angel like image   CT 31, 42, 48;   KC 43;   MN 48;   NP 1847, 57, 59

6   -Grand Scene   NP 1891

    -In diesen Heilgen Hallen, In these hallowed halls for Bass CT 39;   DE 49, 62;   DT 44;   HN 46;   MN 56;   SE 46;   UT 40

    -Isis and Osiris Sorastro's Aria, Invocation, Bass and Chor Act II DE 49, 55;   DA 49

    -My happiness has flown   CL 18

    -Non paventar   NP 1859

    -Overt   AT 50, 67;   BA 37, 62;   BN 1881, 82, 84, 86, 91, 93, 98, 00, 06, 09, 11, 12, 14, 15, 16, 19, 23, 25, 29, 30, 32, 40, 44;   BU 55;   CH 1892, 95, 00, 03, 05, 07, 08, 09, 10, 12, 14, 15, 16, 18, 19, 20, 23, 24, 27, 29, 34, 36, 44, 46, 55, 56, 62, 63;   CT 06, 09, 12, 18, 21, 26, 31, 35, 37, 41, 46, 47, 49, 52, 56, 57, 60, 61, 64;   CL 21, 26, 27, 28, 30, 37, 48, 53, 61, 69; DE 47, 48, 52, 54, 56, 57, 58, 61;   DT 15, 19, 20, 26, 35, 39, 40, 51, 53, 55, 60, 62, 64, 67;   HN 41, 44, 49;   NA 60;   KC 34, 36, 37, 38, 40, 41, 42, 44, 58, 65;   LA 23, 27, 37, 51, 55, 57, 58;

MOZART, W.A. (Cont.) Dramatic Works, Magic Flute: Overt (Cont.)
        ML 61, 65;   MN 22, 23, 25, 30, 36, 38, 41, 43, 49, 55, 62;
        NR 52, 59, 62, 65;   NP 1843, 45, 47, 51, 59, 64, 66, 69, 00, 04,
        11, 16, 18, 19, 49, 52, 53, 54, 59, 61, 63, 66;   NS 1880, 10;
        PH 05, 07, 12, 14, 15, 16, 17, 23, 25, 35, 43, 50, 51, 52, 55,
        56, 60;   PT 40, 42, 48, 49, 50, 51, 63, 68;   RC 31, 42, 51, 55,
        69;   SL 14, 16, 19, 21, 24, 28, 32, 34, 35, 37, 45, 47, 63, 67,
        69;   SF 19, 24, 37, 51, 55, 59, 61, 66;   SE 32, 35, 36, 39,
        44, 57, 67;   UT 49;   WA 32, 35, 49, 56, 59
4   -Pamina's Aria   PH 05, 07, 13(2), 15, 23, 40(2), 41, 46;   RC 42
4   -Papageno's Aria, Baritone   HN 44;   NS 10
4   -Se vuole ballare   MN 56
4   -Tamina's Aria   NA 45
4   -Thy Magic shall Speak   MN 42
100   Le nozze di Figaro The Marriage of Figaro Opera K 492 Complete
        BU 52
        -Arias unidentified   DA 35;   DE 48, 62;   HN 32, 34, 54;   ML 62,
        3 arias 65;   NR 3 arias 64;   NP 1847, 75, 88;   SE 55;   SL 10,
        45, 46, 47, 48, 49
4   -Al deseo di chi t'adora   DA 48;   NA 48
4   -Almaviva's Aria   SL 13, 17
4   -Aprite unpo quegli ecchi   CH 18
4   -Come My heart's delight   CL 18
4   -Crudele! perche finora, Act III   NP 38
4   -Deh vieni non tardar   BN 50;   BU 54, 68;   CH 20, 22;   CT 20,
        32, 38, 39, 40;   CL 26;   DT 17, 21, 23, 62;   NA 47;   KC 42;
        ML 64;   MN 34, 35;   NP 26, 28;   NS 82, 16, 18, 24;   RC 55;
        SL 20, 23, 30, 42;   WA 31
4   -Die ihr die Triebe   NP 90
4   -Dove sono   AT 54, 57;   BU 49; 60;   CH 91, 93, 08, 09, 46, 55;
        CT 05, 14, 29;   DT 18, 45, 58, 63;   HN 48;   NA 57, 64;   KC 55;
        MN 25, 41, 58;   NP 1845, 63, 71;   RC 55;   SL 18, 48, 49, 59;
        SF 54, 69;   SE 69;   WA 69
4   -Duet   NP 1852
20   -Excerpts   LA 20, 22, 26
4   -La Vendetta for Bass   MN 41
4   -Non piu Andrai for Baritone   BU 45;   CT 44, 45, 47, 49;   DT 47;
        HN 49;   NA 53;   KC 47;   LA 26;   MN 35, 56;   NP 21;   NS 10,
        12;   RC 43
4   -Non so piu cosa son for Sopr   AT 58;   BU 52;   CT 38;   DA 29,
        32, 34;   DT 53;   HN 44;   NA 54;   KC 42;   LA 26;   NS 89;
        RC 55;   SL 42
4   -Overt   AT 66, 68;   BA 38, 43, 49, 50, 53, 58, 66;   BN 1886,
        87, 93, 04, 07, 11, 16, 22, 24, 31, 39, 40, 43, 49;   BU 41, 44;
        CH 02, 05, 06, 07, 08, 09, 18, 19, 22, 24, 28, 30, 37, 39, 44, 45,
        46, 48, 53, 56, 61, 69;   CT 13, 16, 29, 31, 32, 33, 34, 35, 37,
        39, 40, 41, 43, 44, 45, 46, 48, 49, 51, 55, 62;   CL 27, 29, 31,
        33, 35, 40, 50, 51, 57, 60, 63;   DA 46, 49, 51, 58, 66, 68;
        DE 46, 47, 52, 53(2), 55, 57, 60, 62, 65;   DT 14, 20, 22, 26, 27,
        29, 40, 44, 47, 52, 53;   HN 32, 39, 40, 46, 47, 50, 61;   NA 37,
        44, 60;   LA 19, 20, 23, 25, 29, 34, 37, 41, 45, 56, 58, 61, 66;
        ML 62, 64;   MN 22, 25, 27, 28, 29, 31, 37, 39, 41, 43, 45, 46,
        47, 48, 49, 56, 57, 58, 59, 64, 65;   NR 56, 59, 64;   NP 12, 13,
        23, 25, 31, 43, 48, 49, 50, 51, 54, 56, 65;   NS 07, 10, 20, 21,
        24, 27;   PH 13, 14, 15, 16, 23, 28, 29, 35, 39, 40, 55, 56, 59,

MOZART, W.A. (Cont.) Dramatic Works, Le nozze di Figaro: Overt (Cont.)
        60, 67;   PT 37, 39, 48, 49, 53, 61;   RC 24, 30, 33, 34, 36, 43,
        44, 45, 46, 68;   SL 13, 15, 17, 18, 20, 22, 25, 28, 30, 31, 32,
        34(2), 37, 38, 39, 40, 41, 42, 44, 45, 46, 47, 49, 51, 53, 54, 57,
        60, 63, 67;   SF 12, 23, 30, 36, 50, 52, 55, 62, 63, 65, 69;
        SE 34, 35, 43, 45, 51, 69;   UT 44, 46, 48, 51, 54, 57, 63, 65;
        WA 31, 37, 42, 48, 65, 66, 69

4   -Porgi amori, Cavatina for Sopr   BA 45;   BN 91;   BU 60;
        CH 55;   MN 42, 44, 46;   NP 1898
4   -Procession and Tarantelle   DE 52
4   -Susanna's Air   NS 14
4   -Susanna non vien   KC 35;   LA 29;   WA 41
4   -Voi che Sapete Sopr   AT 58;   BU 52, 60;   CH 1891, 07, 19;
        DT 18;   HN 44;   LA 26;   MN 34;   NP 16, 33, 49;   NS 1882,
        08, 12;   UT 56;   WA 38
5   -Wedding Procession   WA 35, 41
4   -Wuntess   PH 05, 12, 14(2), 16, 18(2), 27(2), 40(2), 45
        Les Petits Rien, Ballet K 299b or K supplement No 10
16   -Ballet Suite   CH 10, 28, 34;   NA 57;   MN 22, 28;   NS 09, 12,
        18, 21, 24;   RC 41;   SL 10
5   -Overt   CH 60;   SL 58
4   -Pantomime   DT 33
        Der Schauspieldirektor, The Impressario, Comedy in one act, K 486
4   -Bester jungling   AT 54;   DT 51;   MN 48;   NS 18
5   -Overt   BA 59, 65;   BN 44;   BU 66;   CH 14, 15, 16, 17, 19, 22,
        25, 28, 39, 53, 57;   CT 20, 39, 44;   CL 42, 47, 57, 59, 65, 68;
        DA 50, 60;   DE 53, 62, 69;   DT 47;   HN 67;   NA 48, 60, 67;
        LA 46, 53, 60;   ML 67;   NR 58;   NP 38, 40, 67;   NS 04, 07;
        PH 35, 65;   PT 45, 46, 50;   RC 56, 63;   SL 62;   SF 67;
        SE 66, 68;   WA 37, 68
4   Thamos, King in Egypt Opera K 345, Entr'acte   BN 65
40   -Incidental Music   PH 55
5   -Overt   NA 60
        Zaida, Opera K 344
4   -Ruhe sanft   CH 21, 53

MRACZEK, Joseph   10   Slavonic Dances   DT 30;   PH 30
1878-1944 Czech/Ger 26   Symphon Burleske, Max and Moritz 1912   BN 12;
                CH 12(2)
          13   Symphon Poem, Eva 1922   CH 21

MUCZYNSKI, Robert   14   Dance mvts Op 17   WA 64
1929-   US   4   Dovetail Overt for O Op 12   BA 62
           7   Symphon Dialogues Op 20   WA 65

MUELLER, Otto   10   Carneval Overt, Schlaraffiade 1921   PH 21
1810-1907   Ger/US 10   Dramatic Overt   PH 13
          15   Five Symphon Studies on the American Folk Song,
                El-A-Noy   CH 41, 48
          8   Two Symphon Sketches: Enigma and Awakening   CH 31

MULÈ, Guiseppe   6   Prelude to Liola, Opera 1935   DT 37
1885-1951   It   8   Singing Sicily, Excerpts 1924   SL 28

MURADELY, Vano   8   Georgian Symphon Dance 1936   NP 48
  1908-   Russ   35   Symph No 1 in b In Memory of Kirov 1938   CH 39

MURAVLEV, Alexei   12   The Legend of Azov Mountain, Tone Poem Op 10   HN 58
  1924-   Russ

MURRAY, Dom Gregory   4   Song, O Bethlehem, Christmas Carol   AT 54

MUSSORGSKY, Modeste 120   Boris Gudunov, Opera 1868 Complete   BA 54
  1839-1881   Russ   10   -Act I, Scene I   CT 35;   SL 65
                       6   -Clock Scene   BA 59;   HN 61;   SL 60;   WA 53, 55
                      90   -Concert Form   PH 29
                       8   -Coronation   CT 35, 49;   DA 30;   DE 52, 58;
                              NA 41, 46;   ML 49;   MN 43, 49;   PH 35;   PT 45;
                              RC 27, 39, 41, 52;   SL 60;   SE 40, 50;   WA 35,
                              36, 37, 39, 41, 53, 55
         6   -Death Scene   AT 53;   BA 44, 64;   CT 29, 35, 39, 44, 51;
                DA 30;   DE 52;   DT 44, 52, 56;   HN 53, 61;   KC 45;   MN 43,
                56;   PT 45, 57;   RC 40;   SL 60;   SE 40, 50;   WA 53, 55
         6   -Entrance of Boris   BA 44, 64
        20   -Excerpts   BN 67;   KC 51;   MN 43;   NR 65;   NP 52;   PH 36,
                37, 38, 47;   SF 52, aria only 63;   DE 55;   NA 41, 43, 46;
                PH 40
         6   -Farewell and Prayer   BA 59;   DE 52, 58;   MN 42, 43;   RC 39;
                SF 52, 63;   WA 53, 55
         6   -Hallucination   BA 44, 64;   DT 44, 56;   KC 45;   MN 43, 56;
                PT 45;   UT 40
         6   -Monologue   AT 53;   BA 59;   CT 39, 43, 45;   DA 30;   DT 44,
                56;   HN 46, 61;   KC 45;   MN 43;   PT 45;   RC 18, 25, 40;
                SL 41, 43, 60;   SE 40, 50;   UT 40;   WA 53, 55
         4   -Pilgrim's Chorus   WA 55
         4   -Polonaise   BA 44;   CL 28;   DA 26, 27;   KC 45;   LA 25;
                MN 43;   SL 60;   WA 53, 55
         6   -Prologue   NA 41, 46;   LA 25;   PH 35;   RC 52;   WA 35, 36,
                37, 39, 41, 53, 55
        30   -Scenes   BU 66;   CL 62;   LA 4 scenes 62;   SE 5 scenes 46,
                3 scenes 50, 53
        30   -Suite   PH 52
         5   -Varlaam's Aria   BA 46;   CT 20, 46;   MN 41;   WA 31, 32, 34,
                45, 46
                The Fair At Sorotchinski Opera, Unfinished 1874-80: Ballet   MN 43
         4   -Overt   CL 29
         6   -Reverie and Dance of Parissia   CT 32;   CL 21;   DA 30;   DT 21;
                HN 45;   LA 32;   NS 27;   PH 22
         9   Khovantschina, Opera, Unfinished 1872-80: 2 Excerpts   BA 41
        30   -Act III   BN 34
         4   -Aria, Martha's Fortune Telling: PT 64
         3   -Entr'Act Act IV   CT 37;   CL 53;   HN 58;   KC 33;   MN 35;
                NP 33;   PH 22, 23, 25, 28, 29, 32, 36, 39;   SE 29, 39;   WA 33,
                43, 55, 64
        20   -Four Choruses   NP 69
         8   -The Great Gate at Kiev   NP 65
         4   -Introd Act IV   WA 35, 38

MUSSORGSKY, M. (Cont.)   Khovantschina (Cont.)
5   -Overt   BN 24, 29, 34, 38, 40, 42, 45, 54, 56, 61;   CH 29, 50,
         53, 57(2);   CT 26, 36, 39, 64;   CL 29, 30, 31, 32, 33, 37, 42,
         46, 54, 56, 57, 62, 64, 67, 69;   DA 53;   DE 46, 55;   DT 22,
         24, 25, 28, 30, 35, 45, 48;   NA 36;   KC 36, 45;   LA 31, 43,
         48, 56, 62, 68;   MN 25, 36, 41, 44, 47;   NR 53;   NP 34, 36,
         53, 55, 65;   PH 25, 28, 30, 32(2), 44, 45, 49, 65;   PT 64, 42;
         RC 33, 36, 39, 42, 59, 62, 69;   SL 24, 27, 29, 30, 32, 35, 38,
         41, 42, 43, 46, 47, 48, 53, 55, 60, 62, 67;   SF 42;   SE 38;
         WA 35, 67
6   -Persian Dances   BN 25;   CT 28;   CL 23;   DA 27;   NS 16;
         PH 32;   PT 42, 64;   SL 53;   WA 64
4   -Tableux, Act IV   WA 64
13   A Night on Bald Mountain St. John's Eve (Gogol) 1867   AT 48, 56,
         61;   BA 41, 42, 44, 51;   BN 19, 23, 25, 33, 44, 52;   CH 18,
         24, 28, 31, 33, 34, 38, 54, 56, 58, 61;   CT 21, 27, 34, 35, 47,
         49, 51, 55, 58;   CL 20, 25, 35, 53;   DA 55;   DE 45, 48, 53,
         57;   DT 24, 52, 54, 58;   KC 33, 40, 52, 57;   MN 28, 34, 42;
         NR 58;   NP 19, 22;   NS 24;   PH 06, 09, 21, 22, 28, 38, 40, 44,
         46;   PT 41, 42, 44, 46, 49, 55;   RC 35, 62;   SL 27, 28, 31,
         34, 35(2), 42, 54, 61;   SF 18, 25, 57;   SE 27, 34, 35;
         UT 44, 65;   WA 45, 47
4   Peep Show Song, 1870 arr Wood for O   NS 24
29   Pictures at an Exhibition 1874 arr Ravel   AT 52, 67;   BA 53, 55,
         63, 69;   BN 24, 26, 28, 30, 32, 34, 38, 41, 45, 48, 52, 54, 56,
         59, 61, 64, 66;   BU 50, 59, 63, 68;   CH 19, 29, 47, 50, 52, 55,
         57, 59, 62, 64;   CT 29, 30, 38, 42, 51, 54, 58, 60, 63, 65, 69;
         CL 31, 32, 34, 40, 43, 50, 54, 58, 60, 63, 64, 67;   DA 46, 48,
         52, 57, 58, 61, 68;   DE 52, 63, 68;   DT 27, 30, 35, 38(2), 43,
         51, 53, 57, 60, 62, 64, 68;   HN 52, 53, 57, 59, 63, 69;   NA 56,
         62, 64, 68;   KC 39, 49, 55, 60, 66;   LA 29, 32, 34, 38, 39, 46,
         49, 53, 56, 61, 65;   ML 62, 65;   MN 30, 32, 35, 39, 42, 44, 49,
         51, 53, 57, 62, 65, 67;   NR 50, 55, 57, 59, 62;   NR 66, 69;
         NP 29, 34, 35, 41, 42, 44, 51, 52, 54, 56, 57, 58, 59, 60, 62,
         64;   NS 24;   PH 29, 31(2), 36, 37, 38, 39, 41, 42, 45, 46, 51,
         52, 54, 57, 58, 61, 64, 65, 66, 67;   PT 39, 42, 45, 50, 56, 58,
         62, 64;   RC 30, 33, 38, 40, 48, 51, 54, 56, 59, 61, 63, 65, 68;
         SL 30, 33, 47, 51, 56, 59, 60, 61, 62, 66;   SF 29, 31, 35, 38,
         41, 43, 45, 48, 53, 60;   SE 28, 49, 56, 60, 68;   UT 52, 63, 68;
         WA 49, 51, 55, 57, 63
6   Promenade to the Old Castle, from Opera-Ballet, Mlada 1880   WA 32
5   Scherzo in B^b 1858   NP 33
       Songs
4   After the Battle   NS 25
4   After Years, The Old Man's Song 1863   NS 25
4   The Classicist 1867   CH 23;   CT 25;   DT 21, 23;   LA 21, 27;
         MN 26
       Death Songs and Dances   Song Cycle
4   No 1 Cradle Song of Death, Death's Lullaby 1875   DT 21, 29; PH 28
4   No 2 Death's Serenade 1875   CH 18, 23;   CT 32;   CL 32;   LA 32;
         NS 19;   PT 64
4   No 3 Trepak 1875   PH 22;   PT 64
4   No 4 Death of the Field Marshall or Commander 1877   DT 21;
         PH 22;   RC 23
       Hopak 1866   BA 46;   CH 16, 17;   CT 32, 38;   CL 32;   DA 32;
         DT 15, 29;   HN 41;   NA 40;   KC 40;   PH 18, 28;   RC 30;
         SL 40;   WA 42

MUSSORGSKY, M. (Cont.)

4	Humoresque CT 33; PH 22	
4	My Little Room, Within Four Walls 1874 NS 25	
4	On the Dneiper 1879 CH 18, 23; CT 25; CL 23; DT 21, 23; LA 19, 27; MN 26; NS 19; PH 27	
4	Pain CH 23; CL 23; DT 21, 23; LA 21; MN 26; PH 14	
4	Ruin CT 25	
4	Song of the Flea 1879 CH 32; CL 23; DT 52; NS 25; RC 24	
	Songs by the Don 1867 CH 18, 23; LA 19; NS 19	
	To a Little Star 1857 BA 46; NA 61; SL 40; WA 46	

MYROW, Frederic   25   Symphon Variations   LA 65
1939-   US

NABOKOV, Nicolas   22   C Conc Les Hommages   PH 53
1903-   Russ/US   30   La Vita Nuova, Conc for Sopr, Tenor and O 1949
                                          BN 50
                              30   Little Symphony   CL 31
                              19   Return of Pushkin, Elegy for Sopr and O   BA 48;
                                          BN 47
                              25   Sinfonia Biblica 1939   BA 44;   MN 58;   NP 40
                              15   Studies in Solitude, 4 Moods for O   PH 61;   SL 63
                              17   Symboli Christinai, Baritone and O   BA 57;   PH 58
                              15   Symph Lyrique   BN 30
                              25   Symph No 3   NP 67
                              28   Suite, La Vie di Polichinelle 1934   CL 36;   MN 37
                              12   Two Portraits   CH 69

NADELMANN,   5   Lamentation   DT 47
          US

NAPOLEAO, Arthur   8   Grand Caprice on Martha for P   NP 1859
1843-1925   Brazil

NAPRAVNIK, Eduard   4   Nocturne in D^b, Piano Solo   CH 1893
1839-1916   Czech/Russ

NARDINI, Pietro   13   V Conc in e   CH 31
1722-1763   It

NAVARRO, Juan   4   Danza Castellana arr Infante   CT 42, 44;   RC 39,
1530-1580   Sp   41, 46
(pseudonym for José Iturbi)

NEGRO SPIRITUALS   4   Balm of Gilead   MN 42
US Folk Music   4   By-An-By   MN 32;   NS 24
                      4   Camp Meeting   MN 32
                      4   Deep River   NS 25
                      4   Go Down, Moses   NS 24
                      4   Hear the Lambs   MN 32
                      4   Heav'n, Heav'n   MN 47;   NS 25
                      4   My Good Lawd Done Been Here   MN 48

NEGRO SPIRITUALS (Cont.)
<table>
<tr><td></td><td>4</td><td>My Soul's Been Anchored in the Lord   MN 47</td></tr>
<tr><td></td><td>4</td><td>Sit Down   NS 25</td></tr>
<tr><td></td><td>4</td><td>Trampin`   MN 47</td></tr>
</table>

NELHYBEL, Vaclav   12   Etude Symphonique   CT 63;   MN 64
1919-   Czech

NELSON, Ron   8   Fantasia, Savannah River Holiday   DE 59;   HN 63
1929-   US   8   Overt for Latecomers   RC 61;   WA 61
        10   Two Contrasts for O Andante and Presto   DE 62

NEUKIRCHNER   8   Bassoon Solo, Fantasie from Landliche Scene
        Ger   NP 1861

NEVIN, Ethelbert   Songs
1871-1901   US   4   At Twilight Op 12 No 5   CH 1891;   CT 1895
        4   Nocturne Op 20 No 7   CT 1895
        4   The Merry Merry Lark 1894   CT 1894, 95
        4   The Rosary   BA 28

NICHOLSON, Charles   8   Piece for Fl and O   NP 1849
1795-1837   Brit

NICODÉ, Jean Louis   6   Fantasiestück, Die Jagd Nach dem Glück Op 11
1853-1917   Ger   CH 10
        3   March Jubilee Op 20   CH 06
        53   Symphon Ode, The Sea, for Soli, men's Chor, Org and
            O Op 31 seven mvts   NP 1891
        8   -Introd, Phosphorescent Lights   CH 09
        20   Symphon Var Op 27   BN 1889;   CH 1891;   CT 1898;
            NP 1884, 87, 93

NICOLAI, Carl Otto   4   Merry Wives of Windsor, Opera 1849: Aria   PH 49
1810-1849   Ger   4   -Mistress Ford's Aria   CT 45
        4   -Frau Fluth's Aria   DE 46, 49
        9   -Overt   AT 65;   BA 39;   BN 1881, 92;   CH 1893,
            02, 05, 08, 12, 15, 22;   CT 1898, 48;   CL 26;
            DA 25, 26;   DE 59;   DT 45, 48;   HN 17, 34, 36,
            39, 41;   NA 32(2), 33, 63;   KC 33, 36, 40, 44,
            62;   MN 42, 49;   NP 1857;   PH 17, 30;   PT 45,
            60;   RC 49, 52;   SF 65;   SE 29;   UT 40, 43,
            44, 47, 57;   WA 38
        5   Religious Festival Overt, Ein Feste Burg, Op 31
            BN 08;   CH 1896

NICOLAI, Philippe   10   Chorus, Awake, Awake arr Christiansen   CH 31
1556-1608   Ger

NIELSEN, Carl   34   V Conc   Op 33   NP 68
1865-1931   Dan   27   Conc for Clar and O Op 57   CT 67;   NP 66
        20   Conc for Fl and O 1926   BN 66;   NP 65
        12   Overt for O Helios Op 17   CH 66;   DT 68;   WA 56
        4   Overt to Opera, Masquerade 1906   BA 66;   CT 59,
            62, 65;   CL 66;   DE 68;   DT 65;   NA 64;
            NP 61;   SL 55

NIELSEN, C. (Cont.)

	6	Prelude, Act II Saul and David Opera 1900 CL 64
	15	Little Suite for Str O in a Op 1 BA 67; DT 62
	34	Symph No 1 in g Op 7 CH 06; HN 67; NR 69; PH 66
	30	Symph No 2 The Four Temperaments Op 16 DE 55; SE 67
	32	Symph No 3 Sinfonia Espansiva Op 27 BN 68; CL 65; DA 66; DT 63, 67; MN 69; NP 65
	36	Symph No 4 Inextinguishable Op 29 CH 66; CT 65, 68; DT 66; SF 69; WA 53
	37	Symph No 5 Op 50 BA 67; BN 53, 67; CH 67; CL 50, 66, 69; DT 64; HN 62, 69; NA 66; LA 67; MN 65; NR 66; NP 61, 69; PH 50, 64; PT 64; SF 57, 68; UT 68; WA 50, 65, 69
	32	Symph No 6 Sinfonia Semplice 1924 BN 65; CH 64; CT 56; DT 68; PH 65

NIGG, Serge
1924-   Fr

    30   V Conc   MN 67

NIKOLSKY, Yuri
1895-   Russ

    20   The Earth is the Lord's   KC 34

NIN-CULMELL, Joaquin
1908-   Cuba

    10   El Burlador de Seville   SF 68
    12   Differencia for O   SF 62
     9   Three Old Spanish Pieces 1930   SF 60, 64

NINI, Alexander
    -1880   It

     6   Cavatina from Ida della Torre   NP 1843

NIXON, Roger
1921-   US

     7   Air for Str   SF 62
    20   Mooney's Grove, Suite 1967   SF 67
    25   Conc Vla and O   SF 69

NOBLE, Tertius
1867-1953 Brit/US

    15   Introd and Passacaglia in g   CH 36;   CL 45; DT 34;   NP 34, 39;   SE 33

NOELTE, Albert
1885-1946   Ger/US

     8   Night Song for 8-part Chor Op 30   CH 38
    10   Prologue to a Romantic Drama Op 35   CH 40
    15   Suite for Str and Kettledrums   CH 27, 41
    20   Suite for Winds, Percussion and Harp Op 27   CH 30
    25   4 Symphonic Impressions   CH 36

NONO, Luigi
1924-   It

    15   Due Espressioni   PT 59
    10   Epitaph for Federico Garcia Lorca   BU 67
     7   Incontri   SF 60
     6   Liebeslied   BU 67
    13   La Victoire de Guernica   LA 64

NORDEN, N. Lindsay
1887-1956   US

    Clouds of the North   RC 21

NORDHEIM, Arne
1931-   Nor

    12   Epitaffo for O and Magnetic Tape   SE 69

NORDOFF, Paul	25	P Conc 1934 WA 39
1909- US	22	Conc for P, V and O 1951 DE 54; NA 51
	5	Fugue 1936 PH 36
	5	Lento NR 55
	35	Secular Mass for Soli, Chor and O 1934 MN 34

NOREN, Heinrich	37	Kaleidescope Theme and Var Op 30 BN 08; CH 08,
1861-1928 Aust/Ger		11; NP 13
	30	V Conc in a Op 38 CH 13
	25	Vita, Symph for Modern O BN 16

NORTH, Alexander	7	The Little Indian Drum DA 49
1910- US	7	The Waltzing Elephant for Narrator and O DA 49

NORTON, Spencer	6	Prologue to Dance Suite MN 41
1909- US		

NOSKOWSKI, Siegmund	18	Symphon Poem, The Steppe Op 66 BN 06; NP 1843;
1846-1909 Pol		PH 12, 25; SL 10

NOVACEK, Ottokar	5	Perpetuum Mobile 1897 NS 97
1866-1900 US		

NOVAK, Vitezslov	26	Serenade Op 36 SL 20
1870-1949 Czech	25	Symphon Poem, In the Tatra Mountains Op 26 NP 19

NUSSIO, Otmar	9	Danze d'Majorca PT 53
1902- It/Swiss	6	Overt to Escapades of Scapin KC 52

NYSTROEM, Gosta	20	Hommage a la France, for Vla and O CT 53
1890- Swed	31	Sinfonia Expressiva, Symph No 2 1935 DT 69

OFFENBACH, Jacques	20	Blue Beard Operetta 1866: Ballet MN 42, 43
1819-1880 Fr	7	Gaieté Parisienne Operetta 1866: Ballet Suite arr
		Rosenthal AT 59; CT 48; DT 40, 41; HN 55;
		MN 38; NR 67; NP 55, 67; SF 56; SE 54
	20	Helen of Troy, Ballet Suite DA 48; MN 42, 49
	10	Offenbachianna arr Rosenthal AT 57; DE 56;
		HN 52
	4	La Périchole Operetta 1868: Aria Tu n 'es pas beau
		KC 50
	4	Pierrot Dance NS 16
	10	Tales of Hoffman Opera Posth Excerpts NA 60

OHANA, Maurice	18	Conc for Guitar CH 65
1914- Sp/Brit		

OLDBERG, Arne	25	P Conc in A No 2 Op 43 CH 32
1874- US	23	V Conc Op 46 CH 46, 49
	10	Fantasy At Night Op 38 CH 16, 17, 46; ML 62
	15	Festival Overt Op 29 CH 11
	13	Paola and Francisca, Dramatic Overt CH 07, 19, 58
	12	Rhaps, June, Op 36 CH 14; PH 16
	30	Rhaps No 2 Op 39 CH 21
	23	The Sea, Symphon Poem Op 47 CH 36, 40
	10	St. Francis Assissi, Prayer-Hymn CH 55

OLDBERG, A. (Cont.)
	22	Symphon Mvt Op 50 CH 38
	25	Symphon Var for Org and O Op 35 CH 13
	40	Symph No 2 in c Op 34 CH 15
	36	Symph No 3 in f Op 41 CH 16, 30
	36	Symph No 4 in b Op 50 CH 42
	30	Symph No 5 in e Op 54 CH 49
	20	Theme and Var for O Op 19 CH 12

OLDROYD, George   4   Prayer to Jesus   MN 42
1886-1951   Brit

ONDERDONK,   18   Sonata for P   SF 65

O'NIELL, Charles   8   Prelude and Fugue in G   AT 47
1882-   Brit/Can

ORBON, Julian   23   Conc Grosso for Str Quart and O   PT 60
1925-   Cuban 23   Three Symphon Version of Ancient Music   MN 57;
                                 SL 64

ORFF, Carl   65   Carmina Burano, Scenic Cantata 1937   BA 54, 57, 62;
1895-   Ger   CH 68;   DA 55, 66;   DE 56;   DT 60;   NA 68;
                                 HN 55, 57;   KC 56, 60;   LA 54, 65;   PH 56, 59;
                                 PT 55, 56, 68, 69;   RC 58;   SL 60;   SE 58, 66;
                                 WA 54, 55, 61, 57, 66
                         25   Introd and Part III   CT 57
                         45   Catulli Carmina, Scenic Cantata, 1943   PH 66
                         11   Naenie und Dithyrambe, Chor and O   HN 57
                         45   Trionfo di Afrodite Opera 1952   HN 55;   PH 56;
                                 WA 57

ORNSTEIN, Leo   10   A la Chinoise   PH 18
1895-   Russ/US 35   P Conc No 2 1923   PH 24
                         10   Marche Funèbre   PH 18
                         13   Nocturne and Dance 1936   SL 36
                          5   Tribal Dance   SF 38

ORREGO-SALAS, Juan   12   Festive Overt Op 21   BA 63;   NA 63;   MN 54
1919-   Chile   22   Symph No 2 1955   MN 55

OSHER   12   Jarl Hakon   KC 38
                         10   Overt The Bride of Baboad   KC 34

OTESCU, I. Nonna   10   Two Excerpts from De la Matei Citire   CL 36;
1888-1940   Roum   DT 36

OTEY, Wendell   10   Var for O   PT 40
               US

OTIS, Philo Adams   5   Benedictus   CH 30
1846-1930   US

OTT, Joseph   15   Premise for O   WA 63
1930-   US

OTTERSTROM, Thorwald 15   Elegy, Chorale and Fugue   CH 12, 28, 33, 45
1868-   Dan   21   Suite American Negro   CH 16, 17;   NS 16

OWEN, Jerry   20   Symph   NA 68
1944-   US

PACHELBEL, Johann   7   Canon and Gigue   CH 63
1653-1706   Ger   7   Praeudium, Chorale and Fugue arr De Lamarter   KC 55

PACINI, Giovanni   5   Niobe, Opera 1826: Aria I tuoi frequenti   NP 1856,
1796-1867   It   61
                      10   Introd Theme and Var for Voice and V   NP 1857

PADEREWSKI, Jan   30   P Conc in a Op 17   BN 1890, 91, 92, 97, 13;
1860-1941   Pol   CH 1892, 13;   MN 30;   NS 13, 22, 23, 24
                      21   Fantasie Polonaise for P and O Op 19   CH 1895,
                            16, 29, 35;   KC 56;   NP 15
                       3   Minuet, from Pieces Op 1   HN 15
                      26   Symph in b Op 24   BA 36;   BN 08;   DT 30;   PH 14,
                            30;   CH 08, 35
                      10   -Andante con moto and vivace   CH 37

PAER, Ferd   8   Overt to Il Sargino, Opera 1803   NP 29
1771-1839   It

PAGANINI, Nicolo   5   Caprice for V Op 1 No 24   AT 14;   BN 1897;
1782-1840   It   HN 14;   MN 47
                            Caprice No 9 arr Dubensky   PH 39
                      12   V Conc No 1 Op 6 in E^b BA 65;   BN 1884, 44;
                            CH 09, 18, 21, 29, 39, 41, 48, 61;   CT 11, 40,
                            42, 47, 53;   CL 41, 47, 49, 59, 67;   DA 52, 61;
                            DT 52, 62;   HN 45, 50, 67;   NA 42, 50, 62, 69;
                            KC 48;   LA 45, 67, 69;   ML 68;   MN 42;   NR 53,
                            58, 61, 67;   NP 44, 50, 51, 58;   PT 40, 45;
                            RC 40, 62;   SL 16, 41, 43, 46, 50, 51, 59;
                            SF 52, 61;   SE 47, 55;   WA 62, 68
                       6   -Allegro Maestoso   CH 40;   CT 39;   SL 43
                      14   V Conc in one mvt Op 7 in D   CT 64;   PH 14, 19
                             -arr Wilhelmj   BN 1891;   PH 23
                             -arr Francescatti   DE 47;   PH 49, 58, 43
                      20   V Conc No 2 in b   BU 45, 64;   MN 66
                      20   V Conc No 4   DT 43
                       6   Grand Fantasie, V and O   CH 1894
                       7   Introd Theme and Var on a Rossini Theme from
                            Cenerentola Op 12   CH 1896
                       8   Il Papiti Introd and Var on Rossini Theme from
                            Tancredi Op 13   DA 57;   MN 49;   WA 65
                       6   Konzertstück, V and O   CH 36;   MN 44
                       8   Moses in Egypt, Fantasie on Theme Rheinehagen
                            MN 67
                       4   Perpetual Motion Op 11 for V and O   AT arr Sopkin
                            53, 60;   BN 1889;   CH arr Stock 34, 36, 37, 39,
                            40, 41;   MN 34, 35;   NP 33, 54;   PH arr
                            Ormandy 34, 39;   PT 35;   SF 39
                             -arr Molinari   CL 35;   DE 49;   DT 35, 36;
                            NA 37;   RC 38;   SE 58
                       4   Le Streghe, Hexendanz Op 8   NP 1852

PAINE, John K.   5   Azora, Opera 1901: Music from Azora   BN 1899, 03
1839-1906   US   4   -Aria   NP 1890, 18
                        4   -Moorish Dances   CH 00
                        6   The Birds, Prelude to Incidental Music 1901
                               BN 05;   CH 02
                        4   Columbus March and Hymn 1892   BN 1892;   CH 1892
                       15   Island Fantasy, Tone Poem, Op 45   BN 1888, 94;
                               NP 1889
                        8   Oedipus Tyrannus, Incidental Music 1881   BN 1881,
                               93, 98, 06, 23;   CL 53
                        4   St. Peter, Oratorio 1873: Aria O God forsake me not
                               CH 1891
                       36   Symph No 2, In Frühling in c Op 23   BN 1883, 91;
                               CH 1891
                       15   The Tempest, Symphonic Poem after Shakespeare Op 31
                               BN 1882, 85;   CH 1898;   HN 36

PAISIELLO, Giovanni   6   Overt Barber of Seville Opera 1782   KC 42;   WA 41
1741-1816   It   4   Overt Nina,o sia La pazza per amore, Opera 1789
                               DT 36;   PH 35

PAKHMUTOVA, Alexandra 13   Trump Conc in E^b DT 65
1929-   Russ

PALAU, Manul   26   Triptico Catedralicio   DA 57;   RC 57
1893-   Sp

PALESTER, Roman   14   Passacaglia   MN 62
1907-   Pol/Fr   12   Symphon Fragments from Death of Don Juan Opera
                               in one act   MN 64
                       20   Symph No 4 in 1 mvt   MN 61

PALESTRINA, Giovanni   4   Adoremus te, 4 part motet 1581   CH 11;   CT 25;
1525-1594   It   PH arr Stokowski 35, 37
                        8   Exultate Deo, 5 part motet 1584   CT 25
                        8   Fratres Ego Chor Mixed Voices   NP 1864
                        5   Gloria Patri, Double Chor   CH 11
                        4   Hodi Christus Natus Est   MN 48
                        3   Sanctus from Mass   CH 31
                        4   Tu es Petrus, six part Chor   CH 11

PALMGREN, Selim   23   P Conc No 2 in E The River Op 33   CH 17, 25;
1878-1951   Fin   , MN 28;   PH 17;   SF 31
                        4   Elégie   RC 23
                       18   Metamorphoses, P Conc No 3 Op 41   RC 23, 25
                       17   Symphon Pictures,from Finland Op 24   CH 24
                        4   Wiegenleid Op 17 No 9   RC 24

PANIZZA, Hector   29   Tema con Variazioni   CH 23
1875-   Arg

PANUFNIK, Andrzej   26   Sinfonia Elegiaca, Symph of Peace   DT 54;   HN 57
1914-   Pol   5   Tragic Overt 1942   NP 48

PAPAIOANNOU, Yannis   46   Symph No 5   CT 65
1909-   Gk

PARAY, Paul	14	Fantaisie for P and O DT 61
1886- Fr	50-70	Mass commemorating 500th Anniversary of Jeanne d'Arc DT 53, 56, 62; RC 58
	25	Seven Songs DT 62
	31	Symph No 1 in C DT 62
	40	Symph No 2 in A DT 54, 60, 67
PARCHMAN,	15	Concerto for Marimba and O CT 67
Gen Louis	14	Concerto for Percussion and Str CT 69
1929- US	21	Symph for Str CT 61
	12	Winsel Overt 1962 CT 63
PARISH-ALVARS, Elias	5	Conc for Harp in One mvt NP 1855
1808-1894 Brit/Aust	12	Harp Fantasie on Arias NP 1853
	4	Reverie Harp Solo CH 03
PARKER, Horatio	23	Conc for Org and O in E^b Op 55 BN 02; CH 02
1863-1919 US	12	Cahal Mor of the Wine-Red Hand, Op 40 for Baritone and O BN 1894; CL 25; NS 25
	30	Fairyland, Opera Op 77: Prelude, Intermezzo and Ballet CH 15
	12	A Northern Ballad, Op 46 BN 1899; CH 1899, 13; DT 18; NP 00
	10	Red Cross Hymn, Contral and O Op 83 NS 17
	10	Robert of Paris, Overt Op 29 CH 1893; CT 1895
PARRIS, Robert	15	Conc for 5 Kettledrums and O The Phoenix DT 69; SE 59; WA 57
1924- US		
PARRY, Sir Charles	12	Anacreontic Ode, Song 1880 NS 1892
1848-1918 Brit	4	King Saul's Dream from Oratorio, King Saul 1894 CT 1896; NP 1895
	12	Symphon Var 1897 CH 1898
PARTOS, Odon	15	V Conc NP 65
1907- Ger/Is	15	Ein Gev, Symphon Fantasy KC 58
PASCAL, Claude	25	C Conc CL 61
1921- Fr		
PENDERECKI, Krzysztof		Capriccio for V BU 67
1933- Pol		De Natura Sonoris BU 67; DT 69; LA 68
	120-60	Passion According to St. Luke AT 60; MN 67
	15	Stabat Mater SF 65

	8	Threnody: To The Victims of Hiroshima AT 68;
		   BU 64; DA 69; HN 68; MN 66; NR 68;
		   PH 68, 69; RC 69; UT 69

	10	Tren BU 64
PENDLETON, Edmund	21	Alpine Conc Fl and O SL 50
1905- US		
PERAGALLO, Mario	27	P Conc RC 63
1910- It	33	V Conc BN 54

PERGOLESI, Giovanni   15   Concertina No 2 for Str in G   BA 67;   CL 58;
1710-1736   It   DT 62;   MN 57, 59;   NR 65;   SL 62;   WA 52, 61
                 16   Concertina in f for Str and O arr Franko   NP 17,
                      35, 59
                 12   Concertina No 3 in A for Str arr Hinnenthal   NP 59
                 15   Conc for 2 P or Harpsichords and Str   SL 59
                 16   Salve Regina, Contr and O   CH 19
                 4   La Serva Padrona, Opera 1733: Aria, son imbrogiato
                      io gia   BU 45;   WA 49
                 4   -Aria, Stizzoso, mio stizzoso, Act I   BA 47;
                      CT 42
                 40   Stabat Mater, for Sopr, Alto, Chor and O arr Scott
                      CH 65;   DA 62;   DT 37;   NP 41, 59;   WA 38
                 4   Song, Nina   MN 31

PERI, Jacopo   4   Euridice, Opera 1600: Invocation of Orfeo   CT 40
1561-1633   It

PERINELLO, Carlo   10   Symphon Poem, The Dying Swan   CH 23
1877-   It

PERKINS, John   7   Music for O   SL 64
1935-   US

PERLE, George   16   Three mvts for O   NP 65
1915-   US

PEROTINUS or Perotin   15   Sederunt Principes, for four part song arr DeCarvalho
1180-1230   Fr   for modern O   BN 65;   SL 65

PERPESSA, Harilaos   12   Prelude and Fugue for O   NP 48
1907-   Ger/US   35   Christus Symph   NP 50;   PH 56

PERRY, Julia   10   Study for O   NP 64
1924-   US

PERSICHETTI, Vincent   8   Dance Overt Op 20   MN 49
1915-   US   22   Fables for Narrator and O Op 23   PH 44
                 10   Serenade No 5 Op 43   PH 63;   WA 65
                 30   Symph No 3, Op 30   PH 47
                 23   Symph No 4 Op 51   AT 59;   DT 65;   PH 54
                 25   Symph No 7 Op 80 Liturgical   NA 60;   SL 59
                 18   Symph for Str Op 61   PH 59

PESCARA, Aurelio   10   Tibet, Symphon Sketch 1943   CT 43;   WA 45
1900   US

PETERSON-BERGER, Olaf   45   Symph No 3 Laxland   PH 26
1867-1942   Swed

PETERSON, Wayne   22   Exaltation, Dithyramb and Caprice 1960   MN 60
1927-   US   20   Free Var for O 1955   MN 58

PETRASSI, Goffredo   25   P Conc 1936   SL 66
1904-   It   20   Conc for O No 1 1933   AT 64;   CT 61;   DA 58;
                      MN 52;   NP 57;   PH 61;   SF 57

PETRASSI, G. (Cont.)
22	Conc No 4 for Str O NP 66
24	Conc No 5 for O NP 55
7	Introd and Allegro for V and Str AT 58
17	Partita per O 1932 NP 67
18	Il Ritratto di Don Chisciotte, Suite from Ballet 1947 RC 61

PETRIDIS, Petro
1892-   Gk
| 8 | Two Greek Folk Songs arr for Voice and O   LA 54 |

PETZOLD, Johann
1639-1694   Ger
| 15 | Turm Musik, Brass Suite   PT 57 |
| 10 | Three Pieces for Brass   HN 40 |

PFEIFFER, Theodore
1853-1929   Ger
| 4 | Song, Liebesbotschaft   NP 1875 |

PFITZNER, Hans
1869-1949   Ger
12	Overt, Little Christ Elf Op 20 BN 07, 12, 54; CH 08, 25, 34
10	Kathchen von Heilbronn Incidental Music Op 17: Overt CH 14; NP 10; NS 24; PH 13
15	Palestrina, Opera in 3 Acts 1917: Three Preludes BN 49; KC 52; NP 45, 51; RC 55
8	Prelude Act III PH 34

PHELPS, Norman
         US
| 8 | Noel arr for O   NA 48 |

PHILLIPS, Burrill
1907-   US
7	Scena for Small O WA 47
12	Suite, Courthouse Square 1936 PH 36
16	Suite, McGuffey's Reader 1934 BU 42; DA 46; PT 42
9	Tome Paine Overt CH 51; LA 47

PHILLIPS, Montague
1885-   Brit
| 15 | Violin Phantasy   CL 25 |

PHILLIPS, Van
         US
| 4 | Thank You, Mr. Bach   PH 36 |

PIATAGORSKY, Gregor
1903-   Russ/US
| 10 | Var on a Theme from Paganini for C and O arr Cohen   DE 45;   MN 46 |

PIAZZOLLA, Astor
1921- Latin Amer
| | Buenos Aires   NA 53 |

PICKHARDT, Ione
1900-   US
| 10 | Mountains   PH 33 |

PICK-MANGIAGALLI,
  Riccardo
1882-1949   It
6	Dance of Olaf PT 48
12	Notturno and Rondo Fantastique Op 28 CH 21; MN 45; NP 29
9	Piccola Suite, 1927 CT 27, 29
9	Prelude and Fugue Op 47 BN 29
8	Scene Carnevalesche, Ballet Suite 1931 BN 31
12	Symphon Poem, Sortilegi for P and O Op 39 CH 22, 29; NP 22; PH 22

Time in
Minutes

PIERNÉ, Gabriel   10   Les Cathédrales, Prelude for Chor and O   NS 19
1863-1937   Fr   80   Cantata Les Enfants de Bethlehem 1907   BU 40;
                                CH 30, 40;   NS 10, 25
                        5   Cantata La Croisade des enfants 1902   CL 31;
                                KC 50;   BN 10
                       13   Concertstück, Harp and O Op 39   CH 08;   KC 42;
                                NS 19;   RC 28;   SF 25
                       19   Cydalise et le chèvre-pied, Ballet Suite 1923
                                DT 54;   NS 23
                        5   -Entrance of the Fauns   CL 27;   MN 26;   NS 25(2);
                                WA 33
                        6   -Parts 2 and 3   NS 23
                       13   Divertissement on a Pastoral Theme Op 49   BN 33
                        8   Le Marriage de Marion, Chor and O   NP 13
                        6   Ramuntcho, Incidental Music 1908   BN 21
                        8   Serenade for Str   DA 26
                        8   Sur La Route de Poggio-Bristone, Song 1896
                                PH 24

PIJPER, William   16   Symph No 3 1926   BN 51;   CH 48;   LA 56;   PH 27,
1894-1947   Neth   47;   SF 39, 47

PIKET, Frederick   20   Conc for O   NA 51
1903-   Turkey/US   6   Curtain Raiser to an American Play   MN 48
                       10   The Funnies   NP 55

PILATI, Mario   9   Prelude, Aria and Tarentella   CH 38
1903-1938   It   15   Suite for P and Str O   BN 30

PINGOUD, Ernest   15   The Prophet, for O   PH 26
1890-1942   Fin

PINSUTI, Ciro   4   Song of the Ocean Isle, Voice   NP 1872
1829-1888   It

PISK, Paul   13   Three Ceremonial Rights Op 90   SL 65
1893-   Aust/US

PISTON, Walter   14   Concertino for P and Chamber O 1937   BN 39;
1894-   US   DE 47;   HN 43
                       14   Conc for O 1933   BN 33;   CT 57;   CL 39;   MN 46;
                                NP 58;   RC 62
                       19   Conc for Vla and O   BN 57;   BU 62;   LA 58;
                                NP 64;   SF 63
                       23   V Conc for V and O No 1 1939   BA 64;   BN 40;
                                BU 60;   CH 53;   HN 66;   PT 47
                       23   V Conc No 2   DT 60;   NP 61;   PT 60
                        8   Divertimento   SF 67
                       10   Fantasy for Horn, Harp and Str   BN 53
                        3   Fanfare for the Fighting French 1942   CT 42
                       17   Incredible Flutist, Ballet Suite 1938   CT 43;
                                CL 40, 44, 53;   DT 55;   HN 55;   KC 52;   LA 40;
                                NR 62;   NP 45;   PT 40;   RC 48;   SL 40;   SF 41;
                                UT 63;   WA 46, 63
                       10   Jubilee Var on a Theme by Goossens 1944   CT 44, 45
                       12   Lincoln Center Festival Overt for O   NA 64;   PH 62

PISTON, W. (Cont.)

	15	Three New England Sketches BN 60; DT 59
	12	Prelude and Allegro for Org and Str 1943 BN 43, 44, 68; DA 49; UT 53
	13	Prelude and Fugue for O 1934 BU 61; CT 52; CL 35
	6	Ricercare NP 67
	17	Sinfonietta 1941 BN 41; DE 67; NR 53; SL 51
	15	Suite for O No 1 1929 BN 29; CT 35; LA 32; NP 33, 37; PH 31
	24	Suite for O No 2 1946 BN 49; DT 56
	24	Symphon Piece 1927 BN 27
	9	Symphon Prelude BU 61; CL 60, 67; DT 62; HN 61; NA 62; RC 68; NR 62; PH 62; SL 61; SE 55, 62;
	27	Symph No 1 1937 BN 37
	26	Symph No 2 1943 BN 43, 54; CL 45; LA 47, 56; NP 45; PH 45; PT 46; RC 46, 59; WA 44
	30	Symph No 3 1947 BN 47, 48, 58; RC 63; SF 54
	23	Symph No 4 1949 BN 63; CL 63; DA 53; DE 54; LA 53; MN 50, 51; NP 64; PH 53; WA 56
	22	Symph No 5 BN 56
	25	Symph No 6 BN 55, 59, 61; BU 56; CH 58; CL 56; HN 68; LA 63; PT 67; RC 66
	19	Symph No 7 BN 62; CH 62; MN 63; PH 60
	20	Symph No 8 BN 64
	9	Toccata 1948 AT 69; BN 51; CH 48; CL 48; NA 49; KC 54; LA 68; NR 54, 55, 66; NP 54; PH 55, 65, 69; PT 54, 69; RC 60 SL 52; SF 53; SE 57

PITT, Percy   6   Interlude to Act II, Paola and Francesca, Incidental
1870-1932   Brit   Music 1902   CT 03

PITTALUGA, Gustavo   6   The Cuckold's Fair   MN 43;   RC 39
1906-   Sp

PIZZETTI, Ildebrando 30   P Conc Canti dalla stagione alta 1930   CT 51;   PH 35
1880-   It   25   Conc dell'estate 1928   BN 37;   CH 29;   DT 37, 46;
                          NP 28, 31;   PH 29;   RC 30, 52;   SF 54
             9   Fedra Opera 1905: Prelude   CH 55;   PH 18
             18   Introd to Agamennone, Chor and O Incidental Music
                          1930   NP 30
             4   Il Pastori, Song 1908   CL 21;   WA 33
             16   Pisanella, Ballet Suite for play by d'Annunzio 1913
                          CT 22;   NR 50;   NP 27;   NS 22;   PH 23, 27
             11   Prelude a un altro giorno, to Another Day 1951
                          NP 52;   PT 53
             5   Requiem Mass 1922: Sanctus   CT 25
             23   Rondo Veneziano 1929   CT 32;   CL 35;   NP 29;
                          RC 51;   SF 52
             43   Sinfonia in A 1940   MN 52

POENITZ, Franz   12   Nordische Ballade Op 33, Harp Solo   CH 05
        Brit

POHLIG, Carl   15   Suite, Impressions of America   PH 09(2)
1858-1928   Ger   30   Symphon Poem, Per Aspera ad Astra   PH 07, 11

PONCE, Manuel M.   15   Chapultepec, 3 Symphon Sketches 1934   HN 42; PH 34
1886-1948   Mex   20   Conc del sur, Guitar and O 1940   BA 59;   CH 55;
                              PT 55;   SF 54;   WA 46
                       4   Estrellita, Song 1913   CT 48;   HN 42
                       8   Gitanilla, Poem for Voice and O   HN 42
                      20   V Conc 1942   WA 68

PONCHIELLI, Amilcare   4   La Giocanda, Opera 1876: Aria   DE 54;   LA 43
1834-1886   It   4   -Aria, Act IV, Suicido   CT 32, 37, 42;   ML 65;
                              MN 49;   SL 18
                       4   -Aria, Voce di Donna   CT 41;   KC 35;   NS 27
                       4   -Aria, Cielo e Mar, Act II   CT 17, 56;   LA 54
                       6   -Ballet   BA 26, 28
                       9   -Dance of the Hours, Act III   DE 60;   HN 31;
                              NR 57;   SE 51

PONS, José   8   Seguidillas   DA 57
1768-1818   Sp

POOT, Marcel   9   Allegro Symphonique   CH 38, 45;   DT 38
1901-   Belg   11   Ballade for Str Quart and O 1939   WA 39
                       5   Overt, Joyeuse   BN 39;   CH 42;   MN 36;   WA 56
                      20   Symph No 1 1935   BN 37;   CH 37

POPPER, David   25   C Conc in e Op 24   CH 02
1843-1913   Czech

PORRINO, Ennio   11   Overt Tartarin de Tarascon 1933   PT 57
1910-1959   It   16   Sardegna, Symphon Poem 1934   RC 37

PORTER, Cole   5   Night and Day   UT 56
1892-1964   US

PORTER, Quincy   24   Conc for Harpsi and O   CL 60
1897-   US   13   The Desolate City, Baritone and O 1950   CT 50
                      20   New England Episodes   SE 64

POTJES   4   Le Coffret de Salome: Intermezzo   Se 27
               Fr   20   Symph Poem, Easter Morning   SE 30

POTTER, Edward C.   10   Elegiac Overt, Chatterton   WA 36
1860-1940   US   12   Montana Sketches   WA 34

POULENC, Francis   16   Les Biches, Suite from the Ballet 1939   CH 67;
1899-1963   Fr   DE 68;   PH 66
                      25   Concert Champétre, for Harpsi or P and O 1927
                              NP 48, 49;   SF 58;   WA 67
                      21   P Conc   BN 48;   CT 51
                      17   Conc Org and O 1 mvt   BA 48;   BN 48, 60;
                              BU 65;   ML 69;   WA 66

POULENC, F. (Cont.)

21	Conc for 2 P and O 1932 in d	AT 54, 64; BA 46, 62; BN 60; BU 67; CH 41; CT 37, 48; CL 39; DA 49; DE 49, 64, 65; DT 52, 64; HN 52, 63, 67; NA 53, 55; KC 49, 57, 60; NR 62; NP 37, 61; PH 35; PT 50, 56; RC 50; SL 47, 64; SE 62; UT 47, 67; WA 37
17	Conc Org, Str and Tympani in G	DT 60; NA 63; MN 66; NR 63; NP 62; PH 62; RC 69; UT 63
24	Gloria for Sopr, Chor and O	AT 64, 68; BN 60; CL 62; DA 69; NA 69
3	Movement Perpetual P and O	CT 31
8	Matelote Provençale	CT 57
5	Overt	PH 22
25	Sept Répons des Ténèbres	NP 62
8	Sonata for 2 Clar and O, 1st mvt 1918	NS 25
12	Suite Francaise	CL 60
29	Sinfonietta	CL 49; DA 50; MN 49
2	Valse fr Album des Six	DA 38

POUSSEUR, Henri
1929-   Belg/US

15	Rimes, pour differentes sources sonores	BU 66; SL 63

POWELL, John
1882-   US

35	Conc V and O in E	CH 12; NP 23
12	In Old Virginia, Overt Op 28	CH 27; LA 28, 32; NS 21
7	Natchez-on-the-Hill, 3 Virginia Country Dances Op 30	CH 32; DT 32; HN 34; PH 31; SE 39; WA 32
14	Rhapsodie Negre for P and O 1918	BN 22; CH 20; CT 20; CL 21; DT 18, 21; LA 25; NS 20; PH 22; SF 25; WA 34, 39
5	A Set of Three 1935: Green Willow	WA 36
	Symph in A 1937	WA 51, 63

POWELL
         US

8	Immobile V for O and Tape	MN 69

POZDRO, John
1923-   US

23	Symph No 3	WA 61

PREVIN, Andrew
1929-   Brit

20	C Conc 1967	HN 67; MN 69

PREYER, Gottfried
1807-1901   Aust

20	Konzertstueck for P and O	KC 35

PRINCE, Robert
1929-   US

40	New York Export, Opus Jazz, 5 parts	NR 63

PRINZ, Leonhard
1899   Ger/Brit

30	Symph No 2 1967	SF 67

PROCH, Heinrich
1809-1878   Aust

5	Theme and Var	DE 53; NA 45; PT 44

PROHASKA, Felix   15   Concertina for Jazz Quart and Str   CT 66
   1912   Aust

PROKOFIEFF, Sergei   40   Alexander Nevsky Op 78 Cantata for Sopr, Chor and O
   1891-1953   Russ   From the Film music   BN 64;   CH 58, 68;   DA 50;
                                   DT 62;   NP 60;   PH 44, 53;   RC 62;   SL 49
                 Three Ballet Suites for O   NR 61
      16   Summer Day, Op 65a arr for O from Children's Suite for P   CH 45;
                 NP 45;   SF 45
      35   Chout, The Buffoon, Ballet Suite Op 21   BN 26, 34, 37, 46, 51, 62;
                 CH 64;   LA 65;   PH 44;   PT 48;   SL 53
      12   -Four dances   PT 69
      30   Cinderella Suite Op 87   DE 65;   HN 54
                 CONCERTOS
   16-17   P Conc No 1 in D^b Op 10   BN 37;   CH 18, 60, 66;   CT 64;   CL 29,
                 59, 65;   DA 50;   NA 63;   MN 46;   PH 44;   SL 61(2)
      32   P Conc No 2 in g Op 16   BA 55, 60, 67;   BN 29, 56, 61, 65;   BU 59;
                 CH 29, 58, 65;   CT 53, 63, 64;   CL 61;   DA 55;   DT 44, 59, 60;
                 NA 58, 64;   LA 63;   MN 58, 63, 68;   NP 54, 58, 61, 64;   PH 66;
                 RC 53;   SL 59;   SF 52, 58, 63, 68;   SE 67;   WA 56, 62
      26   P Conc No 3 in C Op 26   AT 49, 57, 63, 65, 69;   BA 56, 62;   BN 25,
                 36, 42, 52, 54, 60;   BU 58;   CH 21, 36, 44, 46, 50, 52, 59, 60,
                 62, 65, 68;   CT 35, 46, 54, 57, 61, 69;   CL 52, 62, 64, 65, 69;
                 DA 48, 53, 61, 66, 68;   DE 55, 57, 61, 64, 66;   DT 53, 61;
                 HN 59, 69;   NA 53, 59, 62, 67;   KC 69;   LA 29, 49, 54, 58, 60,
                 62, 64, 67;   ML 63;   MN 37, 51, 64;   NR 52, 54, 59, 62, 67;
                 NP 32, 42, 43, 50, 52, 53, 54, 55, 60, 64, 65;   PH 46, 58, 61,
                 63;   PT 43, 45, 50, 61, 63, 64;   PT 68, 69;   RC 36, 58, 63;
                 SL 36, 40, 44, 46, 51, 53, 56, 59, 62, 64;   SF 48, 49, 60, 63,
                 64, 67;   SE 47, 57;   UT 53, 61, 66;   WA 53, 59, 61, 63
      27   P Conc No 4 in B^b Op 53 for left hand alone   BN 67;   CL 64;   NP 66;
                 PH 57
      23   P Conc No 5 in G Op 55   BN 32, 63;   CH 32, 68;   CT 48;   CL 65;
                 HN 65;   MN 60;   NP 60;   NS 21;   PT 69;   SF 65
      20   V Conc No 1 in D Op 19   AT 68;   BA 51, 53;   BN 24, 28, 35, 47, 63;
                 BU 50, 67;   CH 25, 43, 56, 59, 61, 65, 67, 68;   CT 26, 56, 65;
                 CL 28, 36, 49, 54, 57, 60;   DA 48, 52, 56, 65;   DE 49, 53, 56;
                 DT 54, 63;   HN 50, 65;   NA 63;   LA 30, 48, 65, 69;   MN 53, 56,
                 63, 66;   NR 58;   NP 26, 44, 52, 55;   NS 25;   PH 27, 42, 61,
                 62;   PT 43, 57, 69;   RC 24, 61, 67;   SL 45, 53, 56, 60, 65, 69;
                 SF 38, 54, 61;   UT 55;   WA 62
      24   V Conc No 2 in g Op 63   BA 67;   BN 37, 39, 48, 55, 56;   BU 48, 63,
                 69;   CH 42, 51, 58, 66;   CT 38, 51, 62;   CL 45, 49, 52, 60, 68;
                 DA 46, 59, 69;   DE 59, 69;   DT 38, 66;   HN 56;   NA 48;   KC 45,
                 57, 65;   LA 61, 66;   ML 68;   MN 48, 50, 64;   NR 67;   NP 48, 50,
                 52, 55, 56, 59, 61;   PH 48, 69;   PT 38, 62, 66;   RC 53, 61;
                 SL 38, 48, 50, 52, 57, 66, 69;   SF 39, 48, 51, 66;   SE 53, 61, 69;
                 UT 54, 67;   WA 53, 57
      35   C Conc No 1 in e Op 58   BN 39, 62;   CH 54;   CT 37;   NP 55;
                 PT 61;   WA 65;
                 C Conc No 2 also called Sinfonia Concertante for C and O Op 125
                 CH 61, 64, 68;   CT 37, 66;   DA 64;   NA 66;   NP 55;   SL 66;
                 SF 55;   SE 64;   WA 65
      12   Diabolic Suite arr Byres   PH 45;   SF 44
      14   Divertimento Op 43   CH 29;   CT 31

PROKOFIEFF, S. (Cont.)

33	The Gambler,Le Jouer, Opera: Four Portraits Op 49 BN 32; CH 32; NP 32
90	Ivan the Terrible Op 116 SL 67
20	Lieutenant Kiji Suite Op 60 AT 58, 62; BA 61; BN 37, 42, 67; BU 64; CH 43, 54, 56, 62; CT 69; CL 38, 44, 68; DA 64 DE 53, 57; DT 62; HN 44, 51; KC 51; LA 38; MN 41, 47; NR 67; NP 43, 55; PH 39, 62, 65; RC 43, 48, 59; SL 38, 40, 44; SF 41; SE 64; UT 47; WA 45
20	The Love of Three Oranges Opera Op 33: Suite BN 26, 36; BU 61; CH 65, 67; CT 26, 53; DA 37, 56; DE 52, 55; NA 55, 67; LA 30; MN 30, 33, 43, 54; NR 63; PH 27, 33, 36, 48, 59, 62; PT 62; SL 28, 36, 49, 59; SF 54, 61; SE 28; WA 37, 52
3	-March AT 58; BA 45; BN 36, 53; HN 44; NA 61; LA 39, 54; MN 52; NR 51; PH 28
3	-Scherzo AT 58; BN 36, 53; NA 61; LA 39, 54; MN 52; NR 51
18	Nuits d'Egypt, Suite Op 61 MN 54
15	Ode to the End of the War for Chor and O Op 105 PH 46
9	Overt on Hebrew Themes for Cl, Str Quart and P Op 34 CL 39; DE 54; KC 40; SE 26, 30; UT 67
8	Overt in e^b Op 42 PH 29 revised version
14	Le Pas d' acier Op 41 Age of Steel, Ballet BN 27; CH 29; CL 29; PH 30; UT 63
24	Peter and the Wolf for Narrator and O Op 67; BA 42; BN 37; BU 41; CH 39; CL 39, 43; DE 47; HN 40; KC 41; MN 39, 42; PH 40; PT 41; RC 52; SL 39, 53, 63; SE 43; UT 49; WA 42
35	The Prodigal Son, Ballet Suite Op 46 NP 31
20	Romeo and Juliet, Ballet Op 64: Excerpts BN 66, 68; CH 69; DT 62; KC 3 excerpts 43; ML 69; NR 50, 8 excerpts 58; NP 5 excerpts 42, 52, 9 excerpts 57, 6 excerpts 64; PT 69
25	-Suite No I BA 52, 53, 56, 60, 63, 66; BU 47; CH 36; CT 69; CL 45, 59, 67, 69; HN 58; MN 61; PH 44, 51, 63, 64, 66; PT 40, 48, 61; RC 52; SF 51, 59, 60
32	-Suite No II BN 37, 41, 47, 56; CT 61; DE 65; DT 56, 66; LA 48, 63; MN 60; PH 66; PT 48, 61; RC 52; SL 48, 59; WA 54, 62
2	-Dance CH 63; RC 56
5	-Dance of the People CH 55
2	-Dance of the Young Maidens from the Antilles CH 57, 63
4	-Death of Tybalt CH 42, 55; RC 47, 54, 55
4	-Friar Laurence CH 42
3	-Juliet, The Young Maiden CH 63; RC 33, 55
3	-Masks CH 55; RC 47, 54, 55
4	-Montagues and Capulets CH 42, 63; RC 54, 55
5	-Romeo and Juliet CH 55, 57; RC 54
4	-Romeo at the Tomb of Juliet CH 57, 63; RC 46, 52, 54, 55, 57
12	Russe Overt Op 72 BN 37; CT 42; MN 42; SL 42; SF 53
40	Semyon Kotko Opera Op 81 Suite PT 45
7	Sept ils sont sept We are Seven Tenor,Chor and O Op 30 BN 25, 26, 33
	The Stone Flower, Ballet Suite Op 128: Three parts DE 54
5	-Ural Rhaps PH 65
15	-Wedding Suite BU 53; CT 55; HN 55; NP 53; SF 55

PROKOFIEFF, S. (Cont.)
        SYMPHONIES
    15   No 1 in D Op 25 Classical
            AT 49, 53, 61;   BA 42, 43, 45, 48, 50, 56;   BN 26(2), 28, 31, 35,
            37, 41, 42, 52, 57, 62, 65;   BU 49, 52, 57, 62;   CH 21, 30, 44,
            52, 54, 58, 62, 68;   CT 29, 37, 41, 44, 49, 50, 66;   CL 33, 37,
            41, 43, 44, 55, 61, 68;   DA 48, 49, 63, 67;   DE 48, 51, 52, 54,
            56, 62, 69;   DT 34, 36, 39, 41, 43, 44, 46, 48, 51, 57, 61, 62,
            63, 66;   HN 49, 51, 52, 60, 67;   NA 42, 46, 49, 53, 60, 65;
            KC 40, 42, 45, 53, 57, 61, 68;   LA 27, 55;   MN 31, 34, 39, 41,
            43(2), 46, 49, 52, 64;   NR 50, 51, 57, 59, 62, 67;   NP 28, 34,
            39, 41, 53, 56, 57, 64;   PH 30, 31, 32, 33, 36, 39, 41, 42, 44,
            46, 47, 49, 50, 57, 60, 66, 68;   PT 42, 44, 46, 48, 51, 53, 60,
            64;   RC 31, 33, 41, 42, 50, 54;   SL 28, 35, 36, 40, 41, 43, 51,
            67;   SF 35, 41, 50, 51, 65, 67, 69;   SE 44, 48, 52, 63;   UT 48,
            53, 60, 69;   WA 42, 49, 53, 60, 64
    35   No 2 Op 40   BN 67;   PH 29
    33   No 3 Op 44   BN 65;   CH 34, 66;   DT 60, 68;   MN 57, 67;   PH 31;
            SF 60;   UT 63, 64
    36   No 4 Op 47 (revised Op 112)   BN 30;   PH 57
 40-42   No 5 in B^b Op 100
            BA 64;   BN 45, 48, 55, 58, 60, 63;   CH 46, 47, 54, 57, 60, 63, 67;
            CT 54, 60, 62, 64, 68;   CL 46(2), 52, 54, 59, 64, 67;   DA 46, 49,
            55, 60, 61, 62;   DE 64, 66, 69;   DT 46, 51, 55, 58, 64;   HN 52,
            57, 61;   NA 54, 59;   KC 49, 52(2);   LA 58, 65;   ML 64;   MN 46,
            47, 51, 55, 59;   NR 57, 61;   NP 45, 46, 50, 52, 53, 54, 56(2),
            57, 60, 64, 65;   PH 46, 57, 63, 67;   PT 47, 48, 57, 64, 69;
            RC 46, 54, 56, 60, 63, 68;   SL 46(2), 47, 52, 56, 63, 65, 67;
            SF 46, 68;   SE 59;   UT 51, 58, 66, 69;   WA 49, 55, 60, 64, 69
 43-45   No 6 in e^b Op 111
            BN 50, 62, 64;   CH 50;   DA 52;   DT 65;   HN 49;   NA 64;
            LA 56;   MN 68;   NP 49;   PH 49, 51, 59, 61, 69;   PT 68;
            RC 49, 55
    30   No 7 in c# Op 131
            BN 53;   CH 53;   CT 58, 67;   CL 53;   DA 53;   DT 67;   NA 53;
            KC 55, 62;   LA 54, 61;   MN 53;   NP 61;   PH 52, 53, 58, 64,
            67;   SL 66;   SF 55, 62;   SE 58;   WA 55, 61

    21   Scythian Suite, Ala and Lolly Op 20   BA 68;   BN 24, 27, 29, 36,
            41, 47, 57, 66;   CH 18, 44;   CT 28;   CL 65;   DT 60, 67;   KC 66;
            MN 50, 63;   NR 54;   NP 28, 46, 54, 63;   PH 24, 26, 33, 43, 47,
            63;   SL 58;   SE 61
    31   Waltz Suite Op 110   KC 58, 67
   120   War and Peace Op 91, Complete Opera   BA 60
     8   -Overt   BN 62
    20   Winter Holiday for Narrator and O Op 122   AT 65
            Vision Fugitive Op 22 from P Solo arr Susskind   SL 68

PROTO, Frank   20   Conc for Double Bass and O   CT 69
1941-   US

PRUME, Jehin   10   Fantasie Brillante for V   NP 1865
(Jehin-Prume)
1839-1899   Belg

PRYDATKEVYTCH   5   Mountains and Plains   DE 50

PSAHOS   5   Mediterranean Serenade arr Vrionides   UT 42

PUCCINI, Giacomo   6   Crisantemi, Poem for Str   MN 58;   SF 61;   SE 26
1858-1924   It   OPERAS
                            100   Bohème 1896 complete   AT 64;   HN 44
                              4   -Arias unidentified   BA 51;   HN 17, 58;   SL 47;
                                       SE 3 arias 51
                              4   -Aria: Addio   KC 62
                              4   -Aria: Che gelida manina   AT 53;   CT 10;
                                       DT 28;   LA 26;   PT 37;   WA 35
                              4   -Aria: O silane Fanceulla   AT 53
                              4   -Aria: Si, mi chiams Mimi   AT 49, 51, 53, 56;
                                       DE 48;   NA 67;   KC 65;   WA 43, 51
                              4   -Duet   DA 55;   KC 68
                             10   -Excerpts   SL 46;   SF arr Kostelanetz 56
                              4   -Musetta's Waltz   ML 63;   MN 46
                              4   -Rudolfo's recitative   DA 30;   PH 35
                            100   Madama Butterfly 1904   HN 36
                              4   -Aria unidentified   HN 55, 56;   SL 47
                              6   -Overt Act III   DA 55
                              4   -Un bel di vedremo, aria   AT 49, 52, 55;   CT 11;
                                       DE 53;   DT 67;   NA 67, 69;   LA 31;   MN 46
                              4   Gianni Schicchi 1918: Aria   O mio babbino caro   KC 52
                              4   Manon Lescaut 1893: Aria   HN 58
                              8   -Finale, Act IV   WA 62
                              4   -In quelle trine morbide   LA 37;   ML 65
                              5   -Intermezzo, Act III   DA 55;   MN 46;   NS 11
                              4   La rondine 1917: Aria Che il bel sogno   AT 65;
                                       DT 67
                              4   -La Canzone di Doretti   NA 66
                              4   Suor Angelica 1918: Aria, unidentified   HN 58
                              4   -Intermezzo   CL 18
                              4   -Senza Mamma   DT 67;   NA 67
                              4   Il Tabarro 1918: Aria, Scorri fiume eterno   CT 40
                            100   Tosca 1900 complete   AT 63;   BA 55;   DT 35;
                                       HN 43;   SE 50
                              4   -Aria unidentified   BA 51;   DE 60;   HN 36, 51,
                                       56;   NP fr ACT III 20;   NS 07;   SE 50
                              4   -E Lucevan le Stelle   AT 50;   LA 25;   RC 25;   SL 21
                              4   -Prayer   CH 08
                              4   -Recondita armonia   CT 48
                              4   -Vissi d'arte   AT 52, 55;   CT 20;   DT 18, 26;
                                       NA 66;   KC 68;   MN 46, 49, 58, 64;   RC 56;
                                       HN 36
                              4   Turandot, Posth: Aria unidentified   DA 55
                              4   -Il questa Reggia   AT 56, 58;   DA 69;   DT 69;
                                       WA 61
                              4   -Nessun Dorma   KC 68;   ML 68

PURCELL, Henry   4   Song: My Amphytrite from Incidental Music to
1659-1695   Brit   Amphitryon 1690   DE 59
                                     Abdelazer, or The Moor's Revenge, Incidental Music
                             15   1695: Suite   CH 63;   ML 65
                              4   -Pavanne   CT 58;   DT 61;   NP 56;   RC arr
                                       Sadoff 56

PURCELL, H. (Cont.)

17	Dido and Aeneas, Opera 1689: Suite CL arr Stoessel 38; LA arr Cailliet 51; PH 39 SF 60; SE 62
9	-Prelude and Final Air BN arr Mitropolis 36; KC 44; MN 41, 46; NP 41, 52; PH arr Kindler 35, 60
4	-When I am laid in earth, Dido's Lament, Act III BA 42, 44, 47; CT 11, 12, 42, 44; CL 54; DE 54, 64; DT 51; KC 39; LA 36; ML 62; MN 31; NP 61; PT 51; SL 39; WA 50, 61
8	Chaconne in g arr Barbirolli from Sonata No 6 CH 40, 45; NP 40
16	Dioclesian Opera 1690 Incidental Music LA 48
18	-Suite, arr Hanson RC 55; SE 55
13	Fairie Queene Opera 1695: Suite arr Byrnes DE 61; NA 48; SF 66
12	-Dances, arr Barbirolli NP 37, 39
4	-Echo, Pastoral and Largo WA 50
5	-Hornpipe CL 54; WA 50
20	Fantasias for Str, 5 parts BN 59; MN 69; NP 68 -Three parts CH 45; CT 35; NP 35; PT 67; SL 67
	Golden Sonata, 5 mvts AT arr Mann 65
4	King Arthur, Opera 1691: Air, Ye Blust'ring Brethren of the Skies CH 01
10	-Chaconne, The Grand Dance CH 01
4	-Trumpet tune BN 45; CH 01; WA arr Stokowski 50
6	Nymphs and Shepherds BA 44; SL 39
17	Orpheus Suite of 6 Songs arr Britten LA 49
	Set of Tunes and Dances arr Bliss LA 24
	St. Cecelia's Ode 1683 Overt LA 49
11	Suite BN arr Wood 33; NS arr Coates 20, 22; RC arr Coates 24; WA 37, 45, 47
14	Suite from Dramatic Music arr Barbirolli BN 64; CL 40; NA 37; MN 51; NP 36, 37, 38; PT 57; SL 38, 42, 48, 53, 59; WA 39, 49, 50, 52, 59
4	The Tempest, Opera 1695: Aria DE 59
4	Trumpet Voluntary arr Wood in D BN 25; CT 47; CL 54; DA 56; DE 56; HN 56; LA 51; MN 49, 54, 59; NR 52, 62; NP 37; PH 24(2), 31, 33; SE 63; UT 53, 60; WA 51, 53, 54
4	-Prelude arr Luck NR 55, 57, 59
10	Three Pieces for V and O arr Reed DT 45

QUANTZ, Johann 1697-1773 Ger	16	Conc for Fl in G CT 35
QUILTER, Roger 1877-1953 Brit	13 4	Children's Overt CL 36; MN 28; PH 20 Song, Blow, Blow Thou Winter Wind MN 41
RABAUD, Henri 1873-1949 Fr	15 5	Divertissement sur des Chansons Russes Op 2 CT 21 Eclogue, after Virgil Symphon Poem Op 7 NP 22; SF 23

RABAUD, H. (Cont.)
   6   Marouf, Opera 1914 Dances   BN 21
   7   Suite Anglaise   NS 25
  16   Symphon Poem, Nocturnal Procession Op 6   BN 18, 19, 24, 38, 40, 43,
         49;   CH 19, 30, 37, 51;   CT 01, 04;   CL 18, 21, 27, 29;   DA 34;
         DT 56, 67;   HN 41;   LA 24;   MN 48;   NP 26, 49;   SL 11, 18, 30;
         SF 18, 47;   SE 38;   WA 35
  50   Symph No 2 Op 5   BN 18;   CH 18;   PH 13, 15, 16, 18;   NS 17, 20

RACHMANINOFF, Sergei   Air for Choir of Solo V   PH 18
1873-1943   Russ   26   P Conc No 1 in f# Op 1   BN 04;   CH 11, 56;   CT 49,
               56;   CL 39;   DT 59;   HN 50;   ML 63;   MN 38,
         50, 65;   NR 50, 67;   NP 38, 56, 68;   NS 11, 21;   PH 18, 38, 47,
         49, 56, 62;   PT 50;   RC 43, 50;   SL 11, 38;   SF 40;   SE 62;
         WA 69
  33   P Conc No 2 in c Op 18   AT 49, 55, 61, 65;   BA 26, 42, 44, 47, 56,
         65;   BN 09, 16, 18, 21, 24, 34, 45, 49, 53, 61, 66;   BU 44, 53,
         61, 67;   CH 09, 12, 21, 27, 32, 33, 42, 44, 45, 46, 47, 48;
         CT 14, 19, 22, 26, 29, 30, 33, 36, 42, 43, 44, 47, 49, 51, 56, 60,
         62, 65, 68;   CL 20, 22, 29, 33, 40, 41, 42, 44, 49, 55, 61, 67;
         DA 32, 50(2), 51, 57, 60, 62, 64;   DE 46, 54, 56, 57, 58, 61, 63,
         68;   DT 20, 21, 25, 27, 32, 36, 57, 60, 64, 67, 68;   HN 39, 43,
         47, 49, 54, 59, 61, 65;   NA 34, 42, 44, 46, 54, 63, 66, 67;
         KC 34, 38, 45, 52, 63;   LA 27, 31, 39, 44, 50, 54, 60;   ML 66;
         MN 22, 25, 31, 33, 36, 42, 49, 57, 58, 60, 67;   NR 51, 56, 59, 63,
         66;   NP 21, 26, 37, 41, 43, 45, 51, 53, 56, 59;   NS 14, 18, 20,
         22;   PH 20, 25, 27, 29, 36, 39, 45, 46, 48, 51, 53, 54, 55, 60, 62,
         66;   PT 39, 49, 56, 60, 62, 67;   RC 27, 30, 42, 44, 49, 59, 63,
         69;   SL 14, 19, 22, 26, 29, 32, 36, 42, 43(2), 46, 47, 49(2), 53,
         54, 56, 59, 61, 62;   SF 25, 27, 29, 39, 42, 44, 46, 49, 54, 57;
         SE 46, 50, 51, 64, 69;   UT 46, 53, 64;   WA 49, 55, 61, 65, 69
  35   P Conc No 3 in d Op 30   AT 51, 56, 58;   BA 44, 45, 56, 60, 63, 65,
         68;   BN 19, 27, 35, 40, 43, 47, 48, 51, 57, 63;   BU 47, 52, 57,
         62, 68;   CH 60, 61, 67;   CT 27, 34, 36, 46, 50, 52, 54, 57, 61,
         66, 69;   CL 28, 31, 55, 59, 62;   DA 49, 54, 56, 57, 58, 61, 69;
         DE 45, 47, 48, 54, 55, 65, 69;   DT 19, 22, 28, 31, 33, 53, 59, 63,
         65, 68;   HN 45, 50, 55, 56, 63, 69;   NA 48, 59, 62, 65;   KC 48,
         54, 59, 66;   LA 29, 41, 46, 48, 55, 61, 65, 69;   ML 65, 69;
         MN 32, 34, 43, 44, 47, 54, 59, 63;   NR 58, 68;   NP 20, 31, 32,
         38, 39, 43, 48, 51, 53, 55, 58, 61, 63, 66;   NS 09, 19(2), 24(2),
         27;   PH 19(2), 27, 37, 39, 40, 43, 49, 50, 53, 55, 66;   PT 40,
         42, 44, 48, 50, 51, 60, 66;   RC 11, 25, 61, 68;   SL 27, 31, 35,
         39, 44, 58, 62, 63, 68;   SF 40, 45, 51, 59, 69;   SE 39;   UT 52,
         63, 67, 69;   WA 49, 52, 60, 62, 64, 66
  34   P Conc No 4 in g Op 40   AT 60;   CH 30, 33, 41;   NP 53, 69;
         PH 26, 41;   PT 64
  18   Fantaisie, The Rock Op 7   HN 67
   5   Fate, Theme for V and O on Beethoven's Symph No 5 Op 21   LA 27, 30;
         PH 27
  22   Rhapsodie on a Theme of Paganini for P and O Op 43 1934   AT 55, 58,
         62, 67;   BA 48, 54, 58, 61, 62, 65;   BN 37, 47, 55;   CH 35, 38,
         40, 42, 44, 49;   CT 39, 41, 44, 47, 50, 53, 59, 63;   CL 37, 44,
         46, 53, 56, 60, 62, 68;   DA 46, 48, 52, 57, 62, 69;   DE 53, 59, 62;
         DT 39, 48, 51, 52, 56, 62, 64, 66;   HN 53, 57, 64, 67;   NA 63,
         65;   KC 46, 56;   LA 41, 47, 49, 53, 59, 62, 68;   ML 62, 64;

Time in
Minutes
RACHMANINOFF, S. (Cont.) Rhapsodie on a Theme of Paganini (Cont.)
      MN 35, 43, 44, 49, 50, 56, 57, 62;   NR 50, 54, 58, 64;   NP 34,
      40, 42, 45, 49, 53, 54, 55, 60, 63;   PH 35, 44, 48, 50, 55, 58,
      59, 65;   PT 37, 41, 46, 53, 57, 63, 67;   RC 35, 55, 61, 67;
      SL 34, 43, 48, 51, 53, 67;   SF 40, 45, 50;   SE 52, 60;   UT 49,
      54, 65;   WA 52, 56, 58, 63, 68

25   Five Picture Studies arr Respighi for O from P Solos Op 33 BN 31;
      CH 31;   CT 31;   CL 39
4   Georgian Melody   DA 32
22   The Isle of the Dead, Die Toteninsul Symphonic Poem Op 29
      AT 55;   BN 09(2), 10, 15, 17, 21, 24, 42, 44;   CH 09, 11, 21,
      31, 41, 56;   CT 10, 15, 43, 56;   CL 34, 41;   DE 52;   DT 19,
      32, 45;   HN 43;   NA 60, 66;   KC 37;   LA 31;   MN 44;   NP 18,
      19, 21, 24, 46;   PH 12, 24, 28, 32, 42, 47, 54, 65;   RC 28, 41;
      SL 10, 43;   SE 29;   WA 49, 51
6   The Miserly Knight, Opera Op 24 Scene   DA 53;   PH scene 2 53
3   Prelude in c# Op 3 No 2 arr Stokovski HN 17, 58;   MN 42, 43
6   Three Preludes arr Cailliet   PH 38, 49, 62;   RC 50
   Songs
4   Diese herrliche Nachte, Midsummer Night Op 14 No 5   CH 16
4   Eti letnia Notchi   CL 19
4   Floods of Spring Op 14 No 11   CT 46;   DE 45;   MN 43;   NR 57;
      WA 46
4   Glory to God   PT 49
4   Hopak   DE 45
4   In the Silent Night Op 4 No 3   CT 42;   DE 45;   HN 44;   KC 43;
      MN 48
4   Keen the Pain   PH 19
4   O, Cease thy Singing Maiden Fair Op 4 No 4   CT 33
4   Peasant Song, or The Drooping Corn, or Oh, the Billowing Harvest,
      or The Harvest of Sorrow, Op 4 No 5   CH 14;   NP 14;   PH 14;
      CT 43;   WA 46
4   Praise the Lord from Heaven KC 34
4   Sorrow in Spring Op 21 No 12   CT 30
4   Springtide Op 6 No 11   NP 11
      Three Russian Songs for Chor and O Op 41   PH 26
4   To the Children Op 26 No 7   DT 40

15   The Spring, Cantata for Baritone, Chor and O Op 20   NA 40
36   Three Symphon Dances Op 45   CH 41;   CT 64;   CL 41, 44;   DA 58,
      65;   DE 53;   DT 57;   HN 59;   LA 42;   MN 42, 48;   NP 42, 53,
      65;   PH 40, 57, 59, 65;   PT 61, 65;   RC 44, 50, 51;   SL 67;
      SF 67;   SE 61
35   Symphon Poem for O, Chor and Solo, The Bells after Poe Op 35   CH 40;
      DT 66;   HN 43;   NA 58;   PH 19, 36, 39, 53
40   Symph No 1 in d Op 13   PH 47, 65;   RC 26
47   Symph No 2 in e Op 27   AT 53, 56, 63, 66;   BA 52, 54, 55, 64;
      BN 10(2), 11, 13, 17, 23, 35, 42, 44, 58;   BU 50, 66;   CH 11(2),
      12, 16, 17, 19(2), 20, 21, 22, 24, 26, 28, 29, 31, 33, 35, 36, 38,
      39, 42, 44, 46, 47, 62, 66;   CT 17, 27, 31, 48, 61;   CL 19, 20,
      21, 22, 25, 27, 28, 30, 32, 36, 39, 44, 49, 54, 65;   DA 54, 62,
      67;   DE 49, 53, 56, 63, 64, 68;   DT 21, 28, 30, 33, 43, 44, 46,
      52, 56, 63, 69;   HN 37, Scherzo only 43, 44, 47, 49, 59, 65, 67;
      NA 45, 52, 56, 67, 68;   KC 37, 40, 42, 50, 55, 66;   LA 23, 32,
      41, 44, 47, 50, 53;   ML 63;   MN 26, 31, 32, 35, 42, 43, 46, 47,
      67;   NR 50, 52, 54, 56, 59, 61, 66;   NP 17, 19, 20, 23, 24, 40,

RACHMANINOFF S. (Cont.) Symphony No 2 in e (Cont.)
    44, 50, 51, 53, 55;   NS 11, 12, 21, 27;   PH 09, 30, 32, 39, 41,
    44, 46, 47, 48, 49, 50, 51, 52, 55, 57, 58, 60;   PT 42, 51, 53,
    58;   RC 02, 20, 60, 63;   SL 15, 16, 18, 20, 23, 25, 28, 45, 47,
    49, 50, 51, 53, 55, 56, 65, 69;   SF 12(2), 14, 17, 23, 30, 31,
    40, 52;   SE 33, 38, 47, 52, 60, 65;   UT 59;   WA 45, 50, 54

46	Symph No 3 in a Op 44 AT 55; BN 46; CH 36, 40, 41, 65; CL 37; DT 45; HN 68; KC 38; MN 39; NP 41; PH 36, 38, 39, 54, 62, 67; PT 67; RC 43, 52; SL 36; SF 52; SE 58; UT 61	
6	Vocalise for Voice or V and O Op 34 No 14 AT 57; BN 43, 44; CH 31, 41; DE 56, 57; DT 20; KC 35, 43, 57; LA 26, 44; NR 59, 66, 69; NP 54; NS 27; PH 49, 48, 55, 57, 60; RC 50	
15-20	Youth Symphony and Scherzo NA 51	

RAFF, Joachim	24	V Conc No 1 in b Op 161 NS 1878
1822-1882 Swiss/Ger	24	C Conc in d Op 193 CH 1898, 05
	25	P Conc in c Op 185 BN 1883, 91, 95; CH 1892; NP 1874; NS 1883
	10	Dream King and His Love NS 1885
	8	Ein feste Burg, Overt to a Drama Op 127 BN 03
	10	La Fée d'Amour for V and O Op 67 BN 1892; CT 1896
	30	Suite for V and O Op 180 CH 04
	8	-Adagietto BN 1883
	15	Suite P and O in E^b Op 200 NP 1877
	30	Symph No 1 Op 96, Vaterland BN 1889
	30	Symph No 2 in C Op 140 NP 1869, 75
	31	Symph No 3 in F Op 153 In Wald BN 1885, 87, 90, 91, 94, 97, 01; CH 1891, 95, 00, 12; NP 1871, 77, 82, 88, 91, 98, 05; NS 1885, 17; PH 07, 09; SL 12, 20
	30	Symph No 4 in g Op 167 NP 1872
	34	Symph No 5 in E Op 177, Lenore BN 1882, 85, 88, 91, 95, 02; CH 1893, 96, 02; CT 1896, 98, 02; MN 24; NP 1873, 84, 94; NS 1883, 88, 16(2), 19
	10	-Excerpts BN 1894
	4	-March CH 1895, 07; CT 1895
	30	Symph No 6 in d Op 189 NP 1874
	30	Symph No 8 Op 205 Walpurgis Night NS 1879, 85
	30	Symph No 9 in e Op 208, Im Sommer CT 21
	34	Symph No 11 Op 214 Der Winter, unfinished BN 1883

RAINGER, Ralph	8	La Bomba PH 36
c 1915 US		

RAKSIN, David	5	Montage PH 36
1912- US		

RAMEAU, Jean-Philippe		OPERAS
1683-1764 Fr	15	Acanthe et Céphise 1751, Suite NS 1895
	25	Castor and Pollux 1737, Suite for small O arr Rameau CT 33; NS 24; SF 57
	4	-Air Gaie CH 01, 09
	4	-Gavotte CH 01, 09
	4	-Nature, amour DT 54
	5	-Overt PH 31
	3	-Tambourine CH 01, 03, 09

RAMEAU, J.P. (Cont.)   Operas (Cont.)
15   Dardanus 1739 Suite arr D'Indy   BN 47, 57, 61, 62;
        CH 30, 36, 48, 62;   CT 25, 34;   HN 38;   MN 50;
        NP 34, 47;   PT 62;   SF 54, 63;   WA 62
4   -Amour   SF 38
4   -Overt arr De La Marter   CH 30(2);   LA 58;   RC 58
16   -Suite No 2   NP 47;   SL 31, 33, 37, 53;   WA 62
10   -Air de Ballet, four parts   NS 20;   PH 62
20   Fêtes d'Hébé, 1739: Ballet Suite   CT 64
4   -Ariette: arr Mottl, Accourez, riante, jeunesse
        CH 18
4   -O mort, aria   CH 18
6   -Musette, arr Mottl   KC 35
3   -Tambourine   SE 29
8   Hippolyte and Aricie 1733: airs   BN 18
4   -Air de Thésèe   MN 46
18   -Suite No 2   PH 06
15   Les Indes Galantes 1735 Ballet Suite No 1 arr Rameau
        CT 39
4   -Aria   SL 48, 49
7   -Invocation and Hymn to the Sun   CH 48;   NA 48;
        PH 51;   SL 48, 49;   SF 48
20   Les Paladins 1760: Suite No 1   CH 63;   SF 48
3   Platée 1745: Overt and Gavotte   NS 14
10   Ballet Suite arr Mottl, Three Ballets   BN 1899,
        30;   CH 00, 11, 30, 32, 36;   DT 28;   HN 38;
        NA 60;   SE 29
10   -arr Kretzscher   BN 16, 17
15   -arr Cailliet   PH 37
3   Minuet arr Segovia for Guitar   DE 54;   SL 54
12   Six Concerts en Sextuor for Str No 3   BU 68;   CL 64
12   No 6   BU 68;   CL 64;   DA 68
8   2 Items   SL 66

RANGSTRÖM, Ture   4   Song, Pan   MN 49
1884-1947   Swed

RATHAUS, Karol   10   Adagio for Str 1941   SL 41
1895-1954 Pol/US   12   Prelude for O Op 71   SL 54
6   Polonaise Symphonique Op 51   SL 44
15   Salisbury Cove Overt for O Op 65   SL 49
18   Serenade Op 35   CT 35
18   Suite for full O Op 29   SL 32
15   Uriel, Acosta, Incidental Music   WA 39
12   Vision Dramatique Op 52   NP 48

RATNER, Leonard   6   Harlequin   SF 57
1916-   US

RAVEL, Maurice   10   Alborado del Gracioso arr Ravel from Miroirs Suite
1875-1937   Fr   for P 1905   AT 55;   BA 42, 43, 47, 51;   BN 28,
        35, 41, 44, 56;   BU 55, 67;   CH 24, 25, 29, 37,
    40, 46, 56, 60, 61, 67;   CT 29, 37, 43, 44, 46, 68;   CL 35, 37,
    41, 44;   DE 50, 64;   DT 28, 30, 37, 41, 55, 57, 61, 68;   HN 45,
    57;   KC 48, 67;   LA 26, 28, 33, 43, 47, 49, 52, 59;   MN 33, 43,

RAVEL, M. (Cont.)   Alborado del Gracioso (Cont.)
51;   NR 60;   NP 35, 36, 50, 53, 55;   NS 24(2), 26, 27;   PH 25, 33, 37, 42, 57;   PT 41, 54, 60;   RC 39, 44, 52, 53, 56;   SL 28, 35, 39, 46, 48, 52;   SF 37, 41, 46, 55, 60;   SE 28, 46, 65; UT 69;   WA 56

11   Bolero 1927   AT 54, 57, 63;   BA 36, 39, 47, 50, 60;   BN 29(2), 30, 37, 52, 55;   BU 45, 63;   CH 29(2), 30, 32, 33, 47, 49, 54, 65;   CT 29(2), 30, 34, 36, 37, 38, 39, 40, 42, 43, 44;   CL 30, 32, 39, 42, 45, 53, 59, 68;   DA 30, 46, 48, 50;   DE 63;   DT 29, 34, 52, 58, 61, 64, 67;   HN 36, 41, 49, 51, 55;   NA 32, 39, 40, 45, 52, 55, 67;   KC 33, 38, 39, 41, 49, 52(2), 54, 58, 61;   LA 30(2), 32;   MN 29, 30, 31, 32, 35, 45, 49, 60;   NR 50, 56, 62, 65, 68; NP 29, 53, 57, 61;   PH 29, 30, 31, 37, 39, 40, 42, 57, 59;   PT 37, 39, 47, 48, 58, 63, 64;   RC 29(2), 36, 37, 40, 41, 46, 48;   SL 29, 30, 31, 32, 34, 40, 45, 46, 52, 54, 61, 67;   SF 33(2), 37, 62, 64;   SE 30(2), 48, 50, 58;   UT 40, 47, 53, 65;   WA 32, 33, 34, 39, 60, 65

20   P Conc in G 1931   AT 62, 63;   BA 58, 68;   BN 31, 37, 48, 57, 59, 63;   BU 66;   CH 50, 51, 57;   CT 32, 39, 45, 63, 66;   CL 54; DA 48, 63, 66;   DE 52, 62;   DT 32, 60, 66;   HN 47, 51, 64; LA 32, 49, 63, 69;   MN 37, 54;   NR 53, 67;   NP 33, 53, 65; PH 31, 37, 48;   PT 48;   RC 32, 45, 56;   SL 44, 49, 50, 52, 60, 64;   SF 52, 57, 60;   UT 54, 69;   WA 50, 63, 68

18   P Conc in D for Left Hand alone 1931   AT 51;   BA 61, 69;   BN 34, 37, 60;   BU 43, 48, 56, 65;   CH 44;   CT 34, 60, 68;   CL 38, 53, 59, 63, 69;   DA 49, 59;   DE 55, 59;   DT 55;   HN 49, 66; KC 49;   LA 46;   MN 44, 57, 59, 65;   NR 60, 64, 68;   NP 37, 41, 56, 59;   PH 46, 56, 60;   PT 41, 57, 63;   RC 59, 68; SL 42, 43, 58, 67;   SF 42, 46, 54;   SE 46, 67;   UT 50;   WA 54, 58, 69

50   Daphnis and Chloé Ballet Suite 1909   BN 54, 60;   CH 48, 67; CT 51;   CL 69;   DT 67;   HN 50, 62, 65;   NA 67;   MN 54; NP 42, 60;   NS 14(2), 15, 16, 19, 22, 25;   PH 67;   SL 63; SF 40, 55

15   -Excerpts   CH 39, 64;   MN 30, 31, 32, 34, 35, 37, 41, 44, 47, 48;   NS 26;   SL 27, 29, 30, 32, 34, 35, 36, 37, 38, 41

17   -Suite No 1   BN 18, 23, 24, 34;   CT 31, 41;   CL 38, 62; DE 50;   HN 61;   LA 26, 27, 41;   MN 58, 60;   NR 64;   NP 58; PH 32, 38, 44, 49, 50, 51, 52, 62;   PT 58;   RC 2 mvts 26, 58; SF 37, 45, 47, 51, 2 mvts 43;   WA 52, 61

16   -Suite No 2   AT 62, 66, 67;   BA 43, 44(2), 45, 46, 47(2), 49, 51, 53, 54, 56, 57, 59, 62, 67;   BN 17(2), 21, 25(2), 27, 29, 31 33, 34, 37, 38, 41, 42, 44, 47, 49, 50, 51, 53, 59, 61, 64, 67; BU 56, 61, 65, 69;   CH 23, 27(2), 30, 32, 33, 37, 40, 41, 42, 43, 45, 46(2), 47, 48, 54, 56, 57, 59, 60;   CT 25, 28, 30, 33, 39, 40, 41, 42, 43, 44, 45, 46, 48, 50, 53, 58, 61, 64;   CT 66, 68; CL 24, 25, 31, 33, 35, 36, 37, 39, 40, 41, 44, 47, 50, 53, 54, 55, 56, 58, 59, 61, 62, 64, 65, 66;   DA 46, 48, 49, 50, 60, 62, 69;   DA excerpts 54, 57, 68;   DE 47, 48, 49, 52, 53, 55, 57, 60, 63, 65;   DT 28, 31, 39, 40, 41, 43, 44, 45, 46, 48, 51, 52, 55, 59, 62, 63;   HN 47, 48, 52, 53, 55, 60, 61, 69; NA 37, 43, 46, 48, 53, 55, 57, 63;   KC 35, 36, 37, 40, 41, 42, 46, 51, 56, 61, 63;   LA 29, 31(2), 34, 37, 41, 43, 46, 47, 49, 50, 52, 54, 62, 63, 65;   MN 24, 50, 52, 58(2), 59, 60, 63, 66, 68;   NR 50, 52, 54, 55, 58, 60, 62;   NP 27, 28, 30, 34, 35, 36, 39, 40, 41, 43, 44, 45, 46(2), 47, 49, 52, 54, 56, 57, 58, 61, 63, 69;   NS 20, 28;   PH 26, 27, 32, 33, 35, 36, 38, 39, 41, 43, 44, 45, 46, 47, 48, 55, 58, 59, 60, 62, 65;

RAVEL, M. (Cont.) Daphnis and Chloé (Cont.)
     PT 37, 39, 44, 49, 50, 51, 54, 57, 58, 61, 64, 67;   RC 36, 38,
     41, 43, 45, 51, 53, 55, 56, 58, 65, 69;   SL 45, 46, 48, 50, 52,
     53, 54, 56, 57, 60, 61, 66;   SF 35, 37, 39, 42, 44, 46, 49, 50,
     56, 61, 64, 65, 69;   SE 47, 56, 68;   UT 47, 54, 59, 62, 67;
     WA 38, 45, 49, 51, 52, 53, 55, 57, 61, 63, 66, 68
     -Danse Guerriere only   CT 34, 35

7   Deux Melodies Hebraiques 1914   V and O   CT 23;   PH 22, 58
      No 2 Kaddisch   SL 49
12   Don Quichotte a Dulcinee, 3 Songs for Baritone and O 1932   BA 46;
      BN 52;   CH 45, 67;   CL 65;   DA 53;   DT 48, 54;   NA 48;
      MN 46;   PH 51;   SL 49;   SF 48
4   No 1 Chanson Romanesque   DA 58
45   L'Enfant et les sortilèges, Opera in one act 1908   NR 63;   MN 68;
      PT 50
5   Fanfare for the Ballet L'Éventail de Jeanne 1927   HN 55
      Gaspard de la nuit 1908, Le Gibet arr Goossens   CT 42, 54;   CL 44
      L'Heure Espagnole 1907 one act comic Opera   NP 50
      -Air de Concepsion   CT 32
12   Introd and Allegro for Harp and Chamber O 1905   AT 56;   BA 43;
      BN 31, 42, 55;   CH 19, 23, 27, 43, 67;   CT 28, 44, 57;   CL 25,
      28, 63, 68;   DA 57;   DE 46, 66;   DT 30, 43;   HN 49, 51, 54;
      NA 43;   KC 36, 40;   MN 38, 53;   NR 54;   NS 16;   PH 17;
      PT 41;   RC 38;   SL 47;   UT 64
      Menuet Antique 1895   CT 36;   CL 31;   NP 31
14   Ma Mère L'Oye, Mother Goose Suite Ballet 1908   AT 60;   BN 13(2),
      15, 19, 25, 27, 29, 34, 36, 37, 40, 47, 51, 57;   BU 45;   CH 12,
      29, 41, 44, 55, 58, 63, 67;   CT 23, 28, 69;   CL 27, 50, 66;
      DA 32, 62, 68;   DT 56, 63;   HN 34, 56, 63;   NA 49;   KC 38;
      LA 21, 32, 35, 45, 46, 69;   MN 27, 37, 55, 57, 64;   NR 60;
      NP 24, 37, 50, 53, 57, 66;   NS 12, 15, 18;   PH 25, 56;   PT 40,
      56;   RC 30, 56, 58;   SL 13, 26, 30, 31, 56, 58;   SF 18, 51,
      56;   UT 51, 61;   WA 34, 61
4   -Beauty and the Beast   NS 26;   SF 37
4   -Empress of the Pagoda   CL 20;   NS 26;   RC 24;   SF 37
4   -The Fairy Garden   WA 44
4   -Lai deronnette   RC 24;   SF 37
4   -Prelude and Dance of the Spinning Wheel   DT 27
7   Pavane pour une Infante défunte 1899   AT 55;   BA 42, 43;   BN 37,
      45, 56;   BU 67;   CH 54;   CT 27, 29, 34;   CL 37, 48, 62;
      DA 53;   DE 47, 49, 54, 67;   DT 31, 54, 68;   HN 44;   NA 37, 40;
      KC 57, 67;   LA 37;   MN 22, 37, 43, 48, 51;   NR 57, 65;   NP 36,
      50, 54, 55;   PH 27, 35, 37, 42, 43, 66;   PT 38, 47, 51;   RC 24,
      34, 37, 38, 39(2);   SL 24, 34;   SF 42, 64;   UT 67;   WA 41
14   Rhapsodie Espagnole in four mvts 1905   AT 61;   BA 57;   BN 14, 15,
      18, 22, 27, 29, 31, 35, 36, 37, 43, 44, 50, 52, 55, 64;   BU 49,
      63;   CH 09(2), 18, 29, 31, 33, 40, 42, 45, 47, 49, 56, 61, 64,
      67;   CT 26, 31, 35, 40, 44, 46, 47, 52, 59, 62, 65;   CL 27, 34,
      37, 40, 42, 50, 51, 55, 58, 62, 68;   DA 52, 59, 64, 68;   DE 48,
      53, 57, 65, 67;   DT 51, 53, 54, 61;   HN 52, 60, 64, 67;   NA 40,
      58, 65;   KC 49, 54, 60, 67, 69;   LA 22(2), 24, 29, 33, 49, 56;
      ML 63;   MN 25, 35, 36, 40, 49, 55, 56, 61;   NR 53, 61, 63, 67;
      NP 23, 25, 28, 34, 36, 43, 50, 53, 57, 58;   NS 09, 21, 27;
      PH 17, 26(2), 33, 34, 37, 39, 42, 45, 46, 49, 50, 53, 55, 57, 58,
      61, 62;   PT 42, 51, 55, 59, 62;   RC 27, 36, 40, 49, 52, 58, 66;
      SL 22, 24, 29, 32, 40, 43, 45, 46, 47, 51, 60, 63, 67;   SF 23,

RAVEL, M. (Cont.)   Rhapsodie Espagnole (Cont.)
         27, 35, 39, 43, 46, 48, 51, 56;   SE 59, 69, 64;   UT 54;   WA 49, 64, 68

3   No 4 Feria   CT 42

10   Scheherazade, Three Songs for Sopr and O 1903   AT 57;   BA 43, 51, 57;   BN 23, 27, 33, 37, 42, 50;   BU 68;   CH 27, 50, 53; CT 46, 50;   CL 27, 34, 62;   DA 48, 67;   DE 51;   DT 45, 51, 56, 62;   HN 62, 67;   NA 46, 59;   KC 55;   LA 50, 65;   ML 62, 66;   MN 65;   NR 63;   NP 58, 64, 68;   PH 26, 39, 45;   PT 60; RC 24;   SL 35, 63;   SF 27, 39, 48;   SE 66;   WA 50, 54

3   No 1 Asie   BU 51

3   No 2 La Flute Enchantee   CT 39;   SL 35

19   Le Tombeau de Couperin, Suite 1914   AT 58;   BA 51;   BN 20, 27, 33, 34, 37, 38, 41, 46, 50, 53, 60, 67;   BU 68;   CH 27, 32, 43, 50, 54, 61;   CT 30, 39, 47, 58;   CL 27, 30, 37, 43, 51, 59, 65, 68;   DE 49, 50, 53, 57;   DT 44, 53, 58, 66, 69;   HN 53;   NA 42, 58, 64;   LA 31, 37, 49;   MN 33, 37, 41;   NR 58;   NP 35, 58; NS 21, 25, 26, 27;   PH 20, 31, 33, 37, 41, 50, 56, 58;   PT 46, 65;   RC 31, 37, 69;   SL 29, 37, 40, 42, 50, 51;   SF 27, 36, 38, 45, 50, 61, 68;   SE 45, 49;   UT 49, 56;   WA 58, 64

12   Three Songs   DT 48

8   Tzigane, Rhapsodie for V and O 1924   AT 60;   BN 27, 31, 51, 59; BU 68;   CH 25, 28, 30, 32, 41, 43, 65;   CT 28, 61;   CL 31, 44, 51, 64;   DA 57, 61;   DE 53, 67;   DT 52;   HN 49;   NA 47, 50;   KC 42, 47;   LA 31;   NP 40, 41, 48, 52, 54, 63;   NS 26, 27;   PH 57, 65;   SL 47, 51, 66;   SF 41, 58;   SE 61;   UT 67; WA 37, 49

18   La Valse Choreographic Poem 1919   AT 53, 66;   BA 36, 56, 67; BN 21, 23, 24(2), 26, 27, 28(2), 30, 33, 35, 40, 44, 45, 48, 49, 51, 52, 57, 58, 61, 62, 66, 68;   BU 48, 59, 64;   CH 22(2), 23, 24, 25, 26, 27(2), 28, 29, 30, 31, 32, 34, 35, 36, 37, 38, 39, 40, 41, 44, 47, 48, 50, 53, 58, 59, 60, 61, 62, 64, 67;   CT 27, 30, 36, 42, 46, 49, 56, 66;   CL 22, 27, 33, 39, 43, 45, 48, 53, 56, 59, 65, 66;   DA 34, 46, 48, 49, 50, 52, 55, 61, 66;   DE 47, 48, 49, 50, 51, 52, 53, 54, 56, 58, 64, 65, 67;   DT 24, 35, 44, 47, 51, 53, 54, 57, 61, 65, 68;   HN 51, 53, 56, 60, 63, 65, 67; NA 48, 57, 62, 68;   KC 51, 55, 60, 65, 68;   LA 24(2), 26, 30, 33, 40, 41, 44, 48, 50, 53, 55, 57;   ML 61, 64;   MN 26, 31, 33, 37, 51, 53, 60, 65, 68;   NR 54, 59, 60, 66;   NP 21, 22, 24, 27, 29, 30, 33, 40, 41, 44, 46, 50, 52, 54, 55, 56, 57, 58, 65; NP 67(2), 69;   NS 24, 27;;   PH 22, 23, 27, 30, 31, 34, 35, 37, 39, 40, 44, 46, 47, 49, 50, 51, 53, 54, 55, 56, 58, 63, 66; PT 46, 47, 48, 49, 51, 53, 65, 66, 67;   RC 26, 33, 38, 40, 46, 48, 51, 55, 57, 59, 63, 67, 69;   SL 21, 23, 28, 30, 31, 33, 38, 39, 43, 45, 46, 47, 48, 49, 50, 51, 55, 56, 57, 60, 61(2), 64; SF 21, 23, 27, 37, 39, 51, 54, 59, 63, 68;   SE 29, 44, 45, 50, 53, 57, 62;   UT 48, 49, 61, 64, 68;   WA 57, 63, 67, 69

14   Valses Nobles et Sentimentales 1913 also called Adelaide or Le Language des fleurs   BN 20, 49, 58, 62;   BU 55;   CH 21(2), 48, 56, 58, 62;   CT 33, 37, 41;   CL 27, 43, 54, 66;   DA 50; DE 69;   DT 51, 58;   LA 57;   ML 64, 69(2);   MN 42, 68;   NP 19, 48;   NS 16;   PH 43, 62;   PT 45, 66;   SL 28, 53, 54, 55; SF 45, 63;   SE 50;   WA 49

RAWSTHORNE, Alan   25   P Conc No 2 1951   BU 56
1905-   Eng   5   Overt, Street Corner 1944   HN 67;   NP 67

READ, Gardner   10   Fantasy for Vla and O Op 38   SL 43
1913-   US   8   Overt No 1 Op 58   NA 43;   RC 46
                    15   Pennsylvania, 3 folksongs for O   PT 47
                     7   Prelude and Toccata Op 43   BN 58;   DE 47;
                            NA 59;   KC 43;   PT 45;   WA 43
                    15   Sketches of the City, Suite Op 26   CH 34;   SL 42;
                            SF 45
                    13   Suite for Str O Op 33a   BN 38
                    38   Symph No 1 Op 30   CH 37;   NP 37
                    25   Symph No 2 in b^b Op 45   BN 43
                    25   Symph No 3, Op 75   PT 61
                    22   Symph No 4 Op 92   CT 69
                    35   The Temptation of St. Anthony, A Dance Symph Op 56
                            BN 53;   CH 52
                     6   Toccata Giocoso Op 94   NP 56;   RC 69

RÉBEL, Jean-Féry   15   Suite fr Ballet The Elements, 1737   CH 62
1661-1747   Fr

REDDICK, William   5   Espanharlem   LA 41;   RC 38, 40;   SF 42
1890-   US

REED, H. Owen   20-22   La Fiesta Mexicana   DT 64
1910-   US

REGAMEY, Constantin 18   Variazioni e Tema 1948   MN 64
1907-   Russ/Swiss

REGER, Max   20   Ballet Suite in D Op 130   LA 26;   NP 13, 14;
1873-1916   Ger   PH 28
                    48   Concertino for P and O in f Op 114   BN 63;
                            MN 45;   NP 49;   PH 58
                    57   V Conc in A Op 101   NP 41
                    21   Concert in Older Style for O Op 123   BN 12;
                            CH 29;   DT 30;   SL 12
                    12   Fantasy and Chorale on Wie schön luechtel Op 40,
                            No 1   MN arr Fritz Busch 50
                    10   Introd and Passacaglia arr Harrison   RC 19
                     9   Overt to a Comedy in D Op 120   BN 11
                    29   A Romantic Suite three parts   Op 125   BN 52;
                            CH 13(2), 16, 22, 26, 35, 37, 49;   CT 16;
                            LA 37;   PH 27;   SF 39, 46;   NP 12
                    25   Requiem, Contral, Chor and O Op 114b
                     9   Scherzo No 2 in d   CH 24
                    40   Serenade Op 95 Standchen in G   BA 65;   BN 06;
                            CH 3 mvts 06, 14;   CT 14
                     4   Song, an die Hoffnung Op 124   CH 31
                     4   Song, Maria Wiegenlied Op 76 No 52   CH 22;
                            CL 22;   KC 35;   LA 23;   PH 22;   SL 54;   SF 29
                    35   Symphon Prologue to a Tragedy Op 108   BN 09;
                            CT 15
                    26   4 Tone Pictures after Böcklin Op 128   BN 14; CH 29;
                            CT 30, 49, 51, 52;   DT 51;   LA 50;   MN 39;
                            NS 27;   PH 47, No 3 Toteninsel 65;   SE 60

REGER, M. (Cont.)

35	Var and Fugue on Theme of Bach in b for P and O	
	Op 81 CT 41; CH 27	
20	Var and Fugue on Theme of Beethoven in B^b Op 86	
	NP 32	
39	Var and Fugue on Theme of Hiller in E Op 100	
	BN 07, 10, 16; CH 10, 65; CT 25; CL 34;	
	LA 68; NP 11, 23, 34, 62; NS 16; PH 07,	
	16; PT 58	
5	Var and Fugue on Theme of Mozart in A for P and O	
	Op 132 BN 39; BU 62; CH 22, 40; CT 23,	
	26, 32, 47; CL 37; DT 60, 64; NA 59;	
	LA 28, 34; MN 30, 36; NP 15, 16, 19, 22, 66;	
	NS 26, 27; PH 26; PT 56, 66, 69; RC 13, 66;	
	SL 55; UT 55	

REICHA, Antonin   8   Quintet for Fl, Ob, Clar, Horn and Bassoon
1770-1836 Czech/Fr   NP 1844, 51

REINECKE, Karl   20   C Conc in d, 2 mvts   BN 1890
1824-1910   Ger   8   -Allegro No 1   NS 1893
                     10   Conc for Harp and O Op 182, Adagio, Scherzo, Finale
                           CH 14
                      6   -Adagio   CH 1892
                     30   P Conc in f# No 1   NP 1871, 75
                     30   P Conc in e Op 120 No 2   NP 1875
                      8   Der Gouveneur von Tours, Opera 1891, Entr'acte
                           BN 1894
                      8   King Manfred, Opera in 5 Acts 1867: Overt   BN 1892
                      6   -Entr'acte BN 1882, 89;   NA 30
                      6   -Introd to Act V   CT 01;   NA 31
                           Overtures
                      8   Aladdin   NP 1870
                      8   Dame Kobold   BN 1882

REINHOLD, Hugo   8   Concert Overt in A Op 32   BN 1886, 88;   NP 1882
1854-1935   Aust 15   Prelude Menuet and Fugue for Str O Op 10   BN 1885,
                           86, 02;   NP 1879, 84

REISER, Alois   35   C Conc in d Op 14   LA 32
1887-   Czech/US

REISSIGER, Karl   10   Concert Overt Op 128   NP 1845, 46
1798-1859   Ger

RENIÉ, Henriette   25   Harp Conc in c   CH 27;   CT 29;   NA 40
1875-1956   Fr

RESPIGHI, Ottorini   5   Aria for Org and Str   CH 46
1879-1936   It   23   Ancient Airs and Dances
                    15   Suite I   BA 54;   BN 23, 24;   CH 21, 32, 33, 40;
                           CT 22, 26;   DA 46;   NS 20, 21, 27;   PH 27, 43,
                           45, 52;   SF 24, 36, 44
                    20   Suite II 1924   BN 26;   CH 25;   CT 25, 52;
                           CL 26, 37;   DE 52, 59;   DT 38, 44, 62;   MN 53;
                           NP 18, 25, 30;   PH 25, 31;   SL 24, 28;   SF 28

RESPIGHI, O. (Cont.) Ancient Airs and Dances (Cont.)
    16   Suite III 1932   BN 42, 55;   BU 44;   CH 64;   HN 55, 65;   NP 37;
            PH 64;   PT 43;   SL 45, 56;   SF 52
    18   Ballata delle Gnomidi 1920   BN 22;   CH 21;   CT 22;   NP 32;
            SF 18, 24
     7   Belfagor, Opera 1921 Overt   BN 26;   CT 26;   CL 26;   NS 25;
            PT 56;   RC 34, 56
    20   Brazilian Impressions 1927   HN 65;   NA 50;   RC 24
    30   V Conc Gregoriano 1922 in a   BN 24;   CH 24;   CL 25, 28;   LA 30,
            51;   MN 24, 45;   NP 29;   PH 37;   RC 04;   SL 31
    36   Conc in Mixolydian Mode for P and O 1924   BN 26;   CH 25;   CT 25;
            CL 25;   LA 31;   NP 25;   PH 25
    23   Feste Romane, Symphon Poem 4 mvts 1929   BA 62;   BN 29, 67;   BU 62;
            CH 29, 58, 63;   CT 29, 63;   CL 31, 66;   DA 55;   DT 37, 59, 63;
            HN 60;   KC 55, 60, 67;   LA 29, 55, 59;   MN 30, 54, 63;   NR 64;
            NP 28, 29, 54, 67;   PH 40, 41, 45, 47, 60;   RC 07;   SL 28;
            SF 29, 52;   SE 30, 58, 64;   WA 66(2)
    18   Fountains of Rome Symphon Poem 1917   BA 55;   BN 20, 22, 26, 35,
            54, 59;   BU 56;   CH 19, 20, 23, 35, 38, 43, 48, 54, 59;   CT 23,
            26, 28, 33, 38, 45, 60;   CL 21, 25, 30, 36, 51, 61;   DA 52, 66;
            DE 47, 48, 50, 53, 54, 56, 61, 62, 63, 64, 67;   DT 22, 26, 27,
            30, 34, 35, 44, 55, 63, 68;   NA 48, 69;   KC 39;   LA 27(2), 39,
            52, 58;   ML 65;   MN 28, 32, 35, 39, 52, 55, 56;   NR 63;   NP 18,
            28, 29, 38, 39, 54, 66;   NS 20, 22;   PH 31, 35, 39, 43, 46, 48,
            50, 51, 54, 56, 60;   PT 50, 66;   RC 01, 07, 19, 27, 59;   SL 23,
            25, 27, 32, 36, 49(2), 53, 55, 57;   SF 29, 39, 45, 50, 62;
            SE 28, 39, 66;   UT 43
    20   Gli Uccelli, The Birds, Suite for small O 5 mvts 1927   BA 67;   BN 41,
            68;   CH 28, 34, 43, 44, 55, 62;   CT 50;   CL 28, 35, 59;   DE 57,
            66;   DT 30, 33, 41;   HN 50;   NA 57, 62;   KC 52, 63;   LA 29;
            ML 63;   MN 51, 63;   NR 60, 68;   NP 28, 31, 36;   PH 30, 44, 52,
            64;   PT 59, 66;   RC 28, 50;   SL 30;   SF 32, 49
    52   Maria Egiziaca Mary in Egypt, Mystery in one Act, 3 episodes, for
            Chor, O and Soli 1930   NA 54;   KC 49;   NP 31
    25   Laud to the Nativity 1930   LA 60
    23   Metamorphoseon modi XII, Theme and Var 1930   BN 30;   PH 31
    20   Pines of Rome, Symphon Poem 1924   AT 60, 65;   BA 53, 55, 58, 61,
            64;   BN 25, 26, 29, 35, 54, 60;   BU 66;   CH 25(2), 26, 27, 29,
            32, 34, 35, 36, 39, 42, 45, 49, 56, 59;   CT 25, 26, 27, 32, 43,
            45, 47, 48, 51, 52, 57, 62, 68;   CL 26, 33, 50, 53, 55, 62;
            DA 48, 52, 56, 61, 67;   DE 49, 51, 62, 65;   DT 28, 29, 32, 34,
            36, 39, 43, 44, 46, 48, 51, 58, 61, 66;   HN 35, 47, 52, 54, 56,
            59;   NA 37, 39, 42, 44, 46, 48, 50, 53, 56, 63, 64, 65, 68;
            KC 54, 59, 65, 68;   LA 26, 27, 30, 31, 59, 64;   ML 62, 66;
            MN 26, 27, 29, 31, 33, 37, 47, 50, 62, 64;   NR 51, 56, 60,
            66, 68;   NP 25, 27, 35, 38, 40, 44, 46, 54, 61, 69;   PH 25,
            27, 28, 31, 32, 38, 42, 44, 45, 57, 59, 61;   PT 37, 49, 61, 64;
            RC 05, 06, 08, 09, 15, 17, 21, 23, 33, 35, 55, 57, 61, 63, 68;
            SL 26, 27, 28, 31, 34, 46, 51, 54, 62;   SF 26, 28, 33, 36, 38,
            43, 48, 50, 51, 52, 53, 68;   SE 27, 54, 62, 68;   UT 46, 51, 55,
            64;   WA 32, 35, 43, 50, 52, 55, 58, 61, 64, 69
    13   Poema Autumnale for V and O   CH 27
    25   Rossinianna Suite from Rossini's Riens 1925   CT 59;   DE 67;
            NP 30;   RC 33, 55;   SL 55, 56;   SF 33
    60   Sinfonia Drammatica 1915   NP 24;   PH 23

RESPIGHI, O. (Cont.)
```
    18    Toccata, P and O 1928   BN 36;   CH 28;   CL 28;   MN 36, 44;
              NP 28;   SF 28
    20    Three Virgins and the Devil, Ballet    MN 42, 43
    16    Il Tramonto, Sopr and small O 1918    BN 26;   CT 26
    16    Trittico Botticelliano for small O 1927   CT 28, 66;   CL 28, 66;
              DT 69;   NP 31;   SL 65;   SF 28
    27    Vetrate di Chiesa,Church Windows, Symphon Impressions 1927   BA 61,
              65;   BN 26, 64;   CH 27, 28, 43;   CT 27, 28;   CL 28;   DT 29,
              30, 33, 58;   LA 29;   MN 54;   PH 63;   RC 05
```

```
RETI, Rudolph              30    P Conc in two mvts 1947   DT 47
1885-1959  Serbia/US    5    Overt and Dance from David and the Giant Goliath
                                 KC 37
```

```
REVUELTAS, Silvestre   10    Caminos, Paths, Tone Picture 1934   CT 43
1899-1940       Mex     11    Cuauhnahuac 1930   RC 56
                        15    Janitzio, Symphon Poem 1936   HN 51, 57;   ML 68;
                                 NR 68;   PT 41, 46;   RC 40
                        18    Redes, Waves 1935   SE 66
                         7    Sense maya, Symphon Poem 1938   HN 62;   KC 65;
                                 MN 63;   NP 63;   PH 46, 65;   PT 66;   WA 67
```

```
REYER, Ernest            6    Song, The Waking  of the Valkyrie from Sigurd,
1823-1909       Fr             Opera 1887   NP 1888
```

```
REYNOLDS, Roger         18    Graffiti   SE 65;   WA 68
1934-           US
```

```
REYNOLDS, Verne          4    Fanfare for Brass Choir    CT 49
1926-           US
```

```
REZNIČEK, Emil           5    Donna Diana, Comic Opera 1894, Overt   AT 51, 69;
  Nikolaus von                   BA 43, 51;   BN 1895;   BU 59;   CH 1895, 08,
1860-1945  Czech/Ger            09, 10, 20, 26, 32, 34, 37, 39, 45;   CT 1896,
                                23, 51, 68;   CL 30;   DE 50, 54;   DT 19, 22,
                                55, 65;   HN 45, 50, 61, 65;   KC 49, 54, 60,
                                66;   LA 45;   NP 21, 38, 64;   NS 07, 19;
                                PH 09, 10, 11, 30, 38, 48, 49, 54, 59;   PT 39,
                                42;   UT 43;   WA 50, 64
                         7    -Waltz Interlude   CH 1895
                        12    Overt to a Comedy 1903   CH 38;   PH 03
                        40    Schlemilhil, A Symph for O, Tenor and Org   BN 13, 14
                        28    Symphon Suite in e   BN 07
                        20    Three Symphon Dances   NP 31
```

```
RHEINBERGER, Josef      25    Conc for Org and O in F No 1 Op 137   BN 07, 15;
1839-1901       Ger             CH 1898
                        25    Conc for Org and O in g No 2 Op 177   CH 1894, 09
                         4    Night Song, Chor and O   CH 31
                        40    Symph Wallenstein Op 10   BN 1885;   CH 1892;
                                 NP 1884
                         5    -Scherzo   PH 02
                         8    Overt, Demetrius Op 110   NP 1880
```

```
RIBAUPIERRE, André de   4    Swiss Lullaby arr Sopkin for V   AT 47
1893-           Swiss
```

	Time in Minutes	
RICE, Wilham	15	Conc for Wind and Percussion Instruments HN 56
1921- US	10	In Memoriam, The Alamo HN 53
	5	Overt, Androcles and the Lion HN 52
RICKARD, Truman	3	Hail Minnesota MN 48, 49
US		
RIEF, Paul	8	Fanfare and Fugue CT 69
1910 Czech/US		
RIEGAL, Heinrich J.	15	Symph in D BN 24
1741-1799 Ger/Fr		
RIEMENSCHNEIDER, George	4	Todtentanz for O BN 1892
1848-1913 Ger		
RIES, Franz	5	Perpetuum Mobile from Suite Op 34 CH 11
1846-1932 Ger		
RIES, Ferdinand	10	Overt Grosse NP 1844
1784-1838 Ger	8	Overt Triumphal NP 1848, 51
	6	Overt Festive in E^b Op 172 NP 1851, 58
RIESENFELD, Hugo	10	Overt Romantic Style NP 19
1879-1939 US		
RIEGGER, Wallingford	8	Canon and Fugue in d Op 33a BU 45; CT 54;
1885- US		NP 49; PH 55; WA 43, 47
	8	Dance Rhythms Op 58 CT 54; HN 55; NA 58, 69;MN 56;
		UT 58; WA 56
	12	Dichotomy Op 12 NP 65
	7	Music for O Op 50 CL 55, 56; DA 58; NP 58
	5	New Dance Op 186 DE 59; PT 41
	10	Overt for O Op 60 CT 56
	8	Passacaglia and Fugue Op 34a WA 44
	12	Rhaps for O Op 5 NP 31
	9	Study in Sonority Op 7 for 40 V BN 58; NP 61,
		69; PH 28
	23	Symph No 3 Op 42 PT 50; SF 57; WA 50
	24	Symph No 4 Op 63 BN 58; CL 58
	18	Var for P and O Op 54 NP 60
RIETI, Vittorio	20	Conc for 2 P and O CT 51; DA 54; PT 52
1898- It/US	15	Conc Woodwind Quintet and O 1923 CT 24; DT 26;
		NP 27
	15	C Conc No 2 NP 54; SL 54
	65	Don Perlimplin, Opera in a Prologue and Three
		Scenes CH 51
	15	Sinfonia Tripartita Symph No 4 1944 DE 68; SL 44
	20	Suite from Barabou, Ballet 1925 SL 42
	17	Suite Noah's Arc, Ballet Suite CH 33; CT 26;
		LA 31; PH 27
	15	Symph No 5 1945 CH 50
	12	Waltz Academy, Ballet 1944 DT 44

RIETZ, Julius   8   Concert Overt in A Op 7   BN 1883, 86;   NP 1856, 64
1812-1877   Ger   10   Quintet for Woodwinds and Horn   NP 1870

RIISAGER, Knudaage   10   Concertina for Trumpet and Str Op 29   DT 69
1897-   Dan   12   Fool's Paradise, Ballet Suite No 2   PT 40
                       9   Quarrtsiluni, Silence Op 36   DT 67;   WA 48
                       5   Torgot Dance   PT 51;   UT 51

RIMSKY-KORSAKOF,   35   Antar Op 9 Symph No 2   BN 1897, 12, 15, 18, 67;
  Nikolay A.   CH 01, 16;   CL 24, 45;   DA 35;   DT 25, 53;
1844-1908   Russ   NR 69;   NP 31;   NS 08, 21, 22;   PH 06;
                            RC march only 05;   SL 30;   SF 45
                            -March   CT 32
        15   Capriccio Espagnole Op 34   AT 48, 52(2), 55, 59;   BA 37, 41, 42,
              43, 45;   BN 07, 09, 13, 15, 18, 24, 30, 32, 34, 37, 40, 42, 43,
              45;   BU 40, 41, 42, 45;   CH 00, 04, 06, 07, 08, 10, 11, 12, 13,
              16, 18, 21, 22, 23, 28(2), 30, 31, 32, 33, 38, 40, 61;   CT 1899,
              19, 21, 30, 35, 36, 43, 44, 46, 47, 49, 60, 64;   CL 20, 21, 26,
              29, 33, 41, 42, 44, 51, 57, 66;   DA 27, 34, 46, 49;   DE 45, 49,
              54;   DT 14, 17, 18, 22, 25, 26, 30, 32, 36, 39, 43, 45, 52, 60;
              HN 33, 38, 42;   NA 37, 41, 50, 53, 64, 67;   KC 36, 39, 40, 48,
              53, 64;   LA 19, 20, 23, 24, 37;   ML 59;   MN 32, 33, 34, 36,
              39, 47;   NR 57, 64;   NP 03, 13, 14, 15, 17, 20, 24, 51, 53, 55,
              58;   NS 24;   PH 08, 09, 10, 11, 14, 16, 17, 18, 25, 28, 30;
              PT 40, 47, 48;   RC 23, 25, 31, 35, 37, 39, 41, 42, 44, 45;
              SL 11(2), 14, 16, 18, 19, 21, 29, 30, 31, 33, 38, 52, 54;   SF 12,
              17, 62;   SE 27, 33, 35, 36, 37;   UT 42, 48, 56(2), 65;   WA 33,
              34, 48, 50, 52, 64
        19   Christmas Eve, Opera after Gogol 1894: Suite   BN 24;   CH 25, 26,
              31, 39, 40;   CL 27;   NP 06, 33;   PH 25, 37
        10   -Introduction and Polonaise   WA 34, 45, 47, 48
         5   -Polonaise   BA 51;   CT 31, 41;   MN 32;   RC 28;   WA 33, 45
        19   -Scenes arr Ormandy   DE 47
        15   P Conc in c# Op 30   CH 19;   CT 32;   LA 21;   NS 23;   PH 04
        12   V Conc in b Fantasie on Russian Themes Op 33   CH 40;   NP 00;
              NS 23
        27   Coq d'Or, The Golden Cockeral, Opera 1906: Suite   BN 19, 27, 29,
              34, 36, 42, 51, 63;   CH 19, 32;   CT 31, 68;   DA 49, 57;   DT 53;
              HN 42, 63;   KC 57;   NP 37;   NS 21;   PH 06, 12, 13, 16, 17, 18,
              19, 20, 21(2), 22, 23(2), 24(2), 25(2), 27, 28, 30, 31, 32, 33,
              41, 44, 47, 48, 50, 62;   PT 52;   RC 02, 12, 18;   SF 51;   WA 51, 61
         4   -Aria of the Queen   DT 20
        27   -Concert Form   MN 37;   SE 39
        10   -Excerpts   DT 36;   PH 25, 29;   SL 23, 33, 35;   SF 54, 62;
         4   -Hymn to the Sun   CH 19;   CT 19;   CL 20;   LA 21;   NS 18
         5   -Introd and Wedding March   BN 34, 36, 42;   CT 27, 29, 34, 40;
              CL 20, 23, 25, 27, 29, 31, 42, 43;   DA 32, 35;   DT 60;   LA 24;
              MN 44, 50;   NP 55;   PT 40;   RC 50;   SF 58;   WA 32, 37, 48
         8   -Overt   BN 34, 36, 42;   CT 27, 29, 34, 40
         4   -Wedding March, Cortège des Noces   CT 27, 29, 34, 40;   HN 37;
              NS 16(2), 18, 21, 27;   UT 44
         4   The Czar's Bride, Opera 1898: Aria Dearest Mother   CH 16;   DT 20, 35
         4   -In Novgorod   CT 28
         4   -Martha's Aria   PH 22
         6   -Overture   BN 02, 03, 06, 15;   DT 27, 39;   NA 66;   SL 09
         4   -Song of Lubasha   CL 65;   PT 64

RIMSKY-KORSAKOF, N.A. (Cont.

5   Dubinushka, Russian Folk Songs for Chor and O Op 62   BN 39, 43;
      DA 28;   NR 54;   NS 09, 16, 25;   RC 23;   SL 29

4   The Invisible City of Kitezh, Opera 1903 The Battle of Kershenetz
      BN 39

10   -Excerpts   BN 25;   PH 2 excerpts 23

10   -Tone Pictures   BN 26

4   -Oriental Romance, Nightingale and the Rose Op 2 No 2   AT 52;
      CT 32;   DA 30;   DE 48;   DT 29, 46;   LA 32;   PH 22

10   The Maid of Pskov or Ivan The Terrible, Opera 1868: Overt   CT 33;
      NP 39

4   -Overt to Act III   PH 38

4   May Night, Opera 1877, Midnight Sun   DT 35

8   -Overt   BN 27;   CL 28, 34;   DT 27;   LA 31;   PH 25;   PT 47;
      RC 44, 45;   SL 33;   SE 43

4   -Quel Calme   CT 23, 30

4   Mlada, Fairy Opera-Ballet, 1872: Aria   PH 22

4   -Cortège des Nobles   LA 39;   UT 42

17   -Dance Suite   CH 1896
      -Act III Night on Mt. Triglaff arr for O   BN 21, 33, 35, 42

23   Overt on Russian Themes Op 28   BN 1897, 19, 21, 23, 27, 30, 32, 35,
      42, 44;   CT 31, 36;   CH 40;   CT 32;   DT 28;   HN 58;
      PH 1 mvt 28

14   Russian Easter Overt, Le Grande Paque Op 36   AT 47, 54;   BA 36, 38,
      40, 44, 46, 47, 48;   BU 41, 44, 65;   CH 11, 18, 24, 27, 28, 29,
      30, 33, 36, 39, 43, 50;   CT 25, 27, 30, 41, 43, 47, 54, 58, 63;
      CL 21, 22, 27, 29, 31, 39, 48, 52, 55;   DA 35, 54, 57, 64;
      DE 48;   DT 20, 27, 28, 32, 52, 58;   HN 40, 57, 58;   NA 38, 41,
      47, 64, 68;   KC 33, 36, 37, 40;   LA 32, 44, 54, 59;   ML 63;
      MN 28, 30, 38, 42, 46, 49, 66;   NR 54; 60, 62, 64;   NP 07, 19,
      46, 47, 53;   PH 12, 16, 17, 18, 19, 20, 21, 23, 24, 25, 26, 27,
      28, 29, 30, 32, 35, 38, 39, 42, 45, 46, 56, 58;   PT 45, 51, 62,
      66;   RC 26, 39, 57, 65;   SL 20, 27, 31, 32, 35, 39, 67;
      SF 20, 21, 33, 35, 38, 47, 52, 56;   SE 28, 39, 55, 64;   UT 41,
      46;   WA 38, 47, 64

35   Sadko, Suite from Opera Op 5 in Seven Scenes 1894   BN 04, 18, 21,
      26, 29, 33;   CL 27, 31, 38;   DT 21, 29;   LA 20;   PH 27, 29,
      33;   RC 33;   SL 29;   SF 18

4   -Berceuse   CL 31

4   -Song of the Guest Viking   DT 46;   NA 43

4   -Song of the Indian Guest   CH 14;   MN 35;   NP 14, 20;   PH 14

42   Scheherazade Symphon Suite Op 35   AT 49, 52, 63;   BA 28, 36, 42;
      BN 1896, 97, 99, 04, 08, 11, 16, 18, 21, 25, 26, 27, 31, 33, 36,
      40, 42, 43, 46, 67;   BU 41, 47;   CH 1897(2), 01, 06, 17, 20, 23,
      27, 34, 42, 59;   CT 09, 15, 18, 25, 28, 51, 69;   CL 19, 21, 23,
      26, 29, 31, 32, 33, 38, 39, 42, 44, 48, 50, 53;   DA 25, 30, 46,
      48, 52, 63;   DE 51, 56;   DT 18, 19, 21, 25, 31, 33, 35, 38, 44,
      55, 62, 67;   HN 36, 40, 63;   NA 38, 42, 49, 53, 63;   KC 35, 39,
      42, 43, 50, 55, 63;   LA 20, 22, 29, 50;   ML 67;   MN 22, 26, 32,
      37, 39, 43, 45, 58, 68;   NR 52, 58, 61, 66;   NP 05, 14, 18, 19,
      20, 22, 24, 54, 58, 67;   NS 05, 11, 12, 17, 20, 21, 22, 23;
      PH 06, 12, 13, 16, 17, 18, 19, 20, 21(2), 22, 23(2), 24(2), 25(2),
      27, 28, 30, 31, 32, 33, 41, 44, 47, 48, 50, 62;   PT 38, 54;
      RC 3 mvts 06, 23(2), 24, 28, 31, 37, 49, 59, 69;   SL 09, 13, 15,
      17, 19, 21, 23, 25, 26, 30, 32, 38, 39, 41, 44, 49, 50, 51, 55;
      SF 14, 16, 17, 20, 22, 53, finale 55;   SE 26, 35, 69;   UT 49,
      58;   WA 33, 34, 40, 49, 50, 53, 60

RIMSKY-KORSAKOF, N.A. (Cont.)   Scheherazade Op 35 (Cont.)
  4   No 4 Festival of Bagdad   DA 48
  4   No 2 Tale of Prince Kalemdar   CT 26;   DA 48
 10   -Excerpts   SE 43
 13   Snow Maiden, Snegourochka, Opera 1880: Suite   DT 67;   NP 30;   SL 25
  4   -Aria   DA 35;   DT 35, 43
  4   -Aria, Aller du bois, Through the Woods   CH 14;   CT 28
  4   -Dance of the Buffoons or Tumblers   BA 28, 43, 44;   DE 47;
       HN 42;   PH 22, 23, 29, 33;   PT 39;   UT 40
  5   -Introduction and Dance   WA 39
  4   -Song of Lei   BU 44;   PT 64
      The Fairy Tale of the Czar Sultan Opera Op 57 1898
       -Excerpts   PT 47
  4   -Flight   of the Bumble Bee   BN 24;   CL 25;   DA 26, 27, 30, 35,
       49;   DT 31;   KC 34;   MN 26;   NS 24;   Ph 29, 33;   SL 26, 31;
       SE 27;   WA 31
  4   -Lament of the Banished Czaritsa   MN 26
  4   -March   CL 30
 18   -Musical Pictures, Suite   BN 22(2), 32, 36, 44;   CL 48;   CT 25,
       28, 42;   DT 32, 39, 54;   MN 26;   NP 46;   NS 09, 22, 24;
       PH 32;   RC 24
      Songs
  4   Song of the Lark from   Cycle, Spring Op 3 No 1   MN 41
  4   Shepherd Lehl   NP 14;   PH 14

RITTER, Alexander   6   Overt to Der Faule Hans Opera 1885   CH 05
1833-1896   Russ/Ger 10   Symphon Poem, Good Friday and Corpus Christi   CT 00
                      14   Symphon Waltz, Olaf's Wedding Dance   Op 22   BN 06;
                             CH 02;   NP 12

RITTER, Frederic L.   20   C Conc   NP 1864
1834-1891   Fr/US   8   Overt Otello   NP 1867
                       30   Symph in e No 2   NP 1871

RIVIER, Jean   28   Conc Brass, Timpani and Str   WA 64
1896-   Fr   21   P Conc No 1 in C 1940   MN 52;   NP 51
                       18   V Conc 1942   BN 50
                       10   Overt for a Don Quixote 1929   BN 35;   CL 29
                        6   Overt for an Imaginary Operetta 1930   SL 34
                       21   Symph No 3 in G for Str 1938   PH 52;   NP 46;
                             SL 47
                       23   Symph No 5 1950   NP 60, 67;   PH 67
                       25   Symph No 6   NP 66

RIZZO   4   Song, Salvo Maria with P   NP 1868
              It

ROBB, John Donald   12   Symph No 3 in 1 mvt   SL 62
1892-   US

ROBERTS, Arthur   11   Overt for the Dedication of a Nuclear Reactor
1912-   US   RC 53

ROBERTSON, Leroy   17   American Serenade for Str 1944   UT 56
1896-   US   27   C Conc   UT 56
                       20   P Conc   UT 66
                       23   V Conc   UT 49, 61

ROBERTSON, L. (Cont.)

	59	Oratorio from Book of Mormon UT 52, 53, 54, Pastorale only 60
	6	Festival Overt UT 41, 65
	6	Saguaro Overt UT 64
	12	Passacaglia DE 61; PH 59; UT 58, 55
	30	Prelude Scherzo and Ricercare 1941 UT 48
	6	Punch and Judy Overt 1945 HN 47; PT 51; UT 47, 49, 53, 63, 68
	17	Rhaps for P and O DT 47; UT 44, 51
	33	Trilogy for O 1940 DT 47; UT 47, 54

ROCCA, Lodovico   5   Dance from Opera, Il Dibuk 1934   DT 38
1895-   It

ROCHBERG, George
1918-   US

	11	Night Music BN 65; KC 64; MN 63; NP 52; PH 61
	39	Symph No 1 BA 60; PH 57
	25-28	Symph No 2 in 1 mvt CT 62; CL 58, 59
	10	Time Span II for O BU 63; SL 60
	10	Waltz Serenade CT 57
	14	Zodiac for O 12 Pieces PH 67

RODE, Pierre   12   Conc Var in G for Voice   NP 1856
1774-1830   Fr

RODGERS, Richard
1902-   US

	8	Ballet, Ghosttown MN 39
	6	Carousel Waltzes AT 51; CH 54; DA 49; MN 48
	10	King and I, Selections UT 56
	4	Medley ML 65
	35	Oklahoma Suite arr M. Gould KC 44
	4	-O What a Beautiful Morning CT 44; MN 44
	4	-Surrey with the Fringe on Top CT 44; MN 44
	5	Slaughter on 10th Avenue from On Your Toes DA 49
	4	Serenade from No Strings ML 64
	10	South Pacific: Selections AT 51; SE 51

RODRIGO, Joaquin
1902-   Sp

	20	Conc Andaluz for 4 Guitars AT 69; BU 68; NA 68
	21	Concierto de Avanjuez in A for Guitar and O CL 59; DA 67; NA 67; LA 66; HN 68; ML 67; MN 67; SE 67
	8	Con Certa Serenata for Harp and O NA 64; ML 67; PH 63; RC 66; SE 64; UT 69
	22	Fantasia para un Gentilhombre SF 57
	13	Los Ayes, 3 arias for Voice and O CT 48
	6	4 Madrigals Amatorios WA 67
	8	Zarabanda Lejana y Villancico RC 37, 41; SF 58
	3	-Zarabanda only RC 37
	10	Music for a Garden WA 67

ROEMHELD, Heinz   4   Menuet   SE 38
1901-   US

ROGALSKI, Theodore   10   Burial at the Cemetary of the Poor   NP 37
1901-1954   Roum   8   Three Roumanian Dances   CL 60;   PH 60

ROGER, Kurt George 1900- Aust/US	18	Conc Grosso for Trump, Timpani and Str O Op 27 CH 50; RC 51; WA 52
ROGER-DUCASSE, Jean Jules 1873-1954 Fr	11	Interlude from Au Jardin de Marguerite, Symphon Poem for Double Chor and O 1901 NS 18
	15	La Julie Jeu de Forêt, Scherzo CH 15; NS 14; SL 17, 20
	12	Nocturne de Printemps 1919 CT 32; NS 20; PH 23
	6	Petite Suite 1897 LA 19
	19	Sarabande for Voices and O Symphon Poem 1911 BN 25; NP 18, 25, 29, 33; PH 37; PT 42
	20	Suite Francaise in D 1909 BN 09, 20; CH 27; CT 20; NP 37; NS 21
	12	Var Plaisantes for Harp and O 1909 NS 13, 23
ROGERS, Bernard 1893- US	14	Africa, Symph in 2 mvts CT 58; RC 63
	8	Anzacs, March for O RC 42
	10	Apparitions CT 67
	10	The Colors of Youth DT 51
	6	The Colors of War, March for O 1939 RC 42
	9	Dance of Salome 1938 CT 40; CL 41; MN 45
	8	Elegy in Memory of F.D. Roosevelt 1945 NP 45
	10	Fantasia for Horn, Timpani and Str RC 54
	12	Five Fairy Tales, Once Upon a Time 1935 CH 36; NP 35
	8	Fuji in the Sunset Glow 1925 NS 26
		Jubilee, Var on a Theme of Goossens CT 44, 45
		Platte Valley, Fantasy on Cowboy Tunes and Rhythms Arr Max di Julio DE 50
	24	Portrait for V and O CL 56
	5	Soliloquy for Fl and Str 1922 CT 43; NA 37, 44; PH 45; RC 26; WA 32
	19	Song of the Nightingale, Symphon Poem 1939 CT 39; RC 41
	12	Three Dance Scenes CT 63; CL 54
	12	Three Japanese Dances with Mezzo-Soprano Solo 1928 CL 52; DA 62; DT 67
	8	To The Fallen, A Dirge 1918 NP 19
	11	Two American Frescoes 1933 PH 36
	24	Var on a Song by Moussorgsky RC 60
ROGERS, M. Robert 1913- US	5	The President's Prayer WA 69
ROHE, Robert K. 1920- US	8	Mainescape NR 65
ROLAND-MANUEL, Alexis 1891-1962 Fr	2	Caharie CT 57
	6	Overt, Isabella and Pantalon, Comic Opera 1922 BN 24
ROLDAN, Amedeo 1900-1939 Cuba	5	Fieste Negra from Tres Pequenos Poemas 1926 CL 27
ROLLINS, Mary Lynn US	5	Spanish Dance DA 25

ROMBERG, Bernhart 1767-1841 Ger	5	Cello Elegie NP 1842
ROMBERG, Sigmund 1887-1961 US	50 8	Program of His Popular Music MN 45 Selections from The Student Prince DA 25
RONALD, Sir Landor 1873-1938 Brit	4 4 4	Songs, An April Birthday PH 00 A Southern Song AT 49, 52 O Lovely Night CT 41
RONTGEN, Julius 1855-1932 Neth	8 20	Ballad on a Norwegian Folk Song Op 36 BN 00; CH 1896, 99 C Conc in g NS 16
ROPARTZ, Joseph Guy 1864-1955 Fr (or GUY-ROPARTZ)	30 14 15 15 35 10	Conc for 2 P CH 20 Divertissement BN 20 Fantasia in D BN 49; CH 19 Pastorale et Dances NS 20 Symph No 4 in C BN 14, 17; CH 14; NP 14; PH 20; SL 14, 18 Symphon Etude, La Chasse du Prince Arthur NP 13, 48
ROREM, Ned 1923- US	17 8 14 23	Design for O CH 59; CT 63; HN 65; MN 65; PH 57; PT 65; SL 56, 65; WA 61 Eagles, after Walt Whitman BN 63; BU 60; PH 59; UT 63 Lions, A Dream CT 68; DT 65; NR 67; UT 66, 67 Symph No 3 BU 59; DT 60; LA 59; NP 58; PT 61; UT 68; WA 63
ROSALES, Antonio 1740-1801 Sp	10	Three Spanish Dances CH 32
ROSEN, Milton 1906- US	15 8	Fantasie Americana for P and O CT 36 Vintage 1939 PT 42; RC 42
ROSENBERG, Hilding 1892- Swed	27 23 12 6	Conc for O CH 52 Conc for Str O 1946 DT 65 Orpheus in Town, Dance Suite 1938 CT 49; NA 49 Overt to Marionettes Suite from the Opera 1939 CL 66; DT 69
ROSENTHAL, Laurence 1926- US	15 13	Horas RC 54 Ode NP 56
ROSENTHAL, Manuel 1904- Fr	19 30 12 22 18 55 15	La Fête du Vin 1937 NP 46 Jeanne d'Arc for Narrator and O, Symphon Suite 1938 CT 38; SL 53; SF 49; SE 49 Magic Manhattan CH 63; NA 49; SL 49 Musique de Table, Suite 1941 NP 46; SL 46 Les Petits Métiers 1933 NA 47; SL 35; SE 48 St. Francis D'Assise, Narrator, Voice, Chor and O 1939 PH 46; SL 53 Symphonie de Noel 1947 PH 48

ROSSEAU, Norbert   12   Var for O   SE 64
1907-   Belg

ROSSELLINI, Renzo   5   Canto di Palude   BA 52;   NP 53;   PH 45
1908-   It   4   Lullaby   BA 55

ROSSI, Francesco   4   Aria from Opera, Mitrane 1689   CT 1896;   DA 28,
1645-1689   It   35;   NS 80
                        20   Symphonia for Double O arr Sinzheimer   CH 44

ROSSINI, Gioacchino   Stage Work
1792-1868   It   4   Armida, Opera 1817: Duet   NP 01
                       120   Barber of Seville Opera 1816 Complete   BU 67
    4   -Aria   DA 52;   DE 63;   NP 13, 27, 39;   PH 02, 19, 36
    4   -Bartollo's Aria, Act II   MN 41
    4   -Don Basilio's Aria   MN 34
    4   -La Columnia, Aria   BU 45;   DE 57;   NA 41;   WA 49
    4   -Largo al Factotem, Aria   BA 42, 46, 47;   CT 39;   DE 45;   DT 17,
                    47;   HN 36, 41;   NA 40, 52;   KC 36, 37;   LA 34;   MN 36;
                    NP 06, 27;   NS 06, 27;   RC 26;   SL 17, 35;   SF 36
    7   -Overture   AT 46, 50, 62, 65;   BA 28(2);   BN 23;   BU 62;   CH 57;
                    CT 10;   CL 34, 62;   DA 52, 68;   DT 33;   HN 36, 63;   NA 51, 63,
                    69;   KC 55;   LA 29;   ML 66;   MN 26, 32, 41, 44, 56;   NR 60, 66,
                    67;   NS 02, 19, 26, 36;   PH 19, 26;   RC 28, 39, 61;   SL 21, 26,
                    45, 49, 56, 59;   SF 61;   SE 51;   UT 40, 51;   WA 60
    4   -Di Piacei mi balza   NP 28
    4   -Une Voce, Aria   AT 58, 65;   CT 40, 45, 46, 52, 57;   CL 68;
                    CT 69;   DT 37, 60, 65;   HN 40;   NA 48, 69;   MN 59, 64, 69;
                    NS 04;   PT 51;   RC 23;   SL 49;   SF 67
    4   Cenerentola Opera 1817: Arias unidentified   NA 46;   KC 40;   PT 43:
                    WA 33
    4   -Eccomi al Fine   DT 67
    4   -Nacqui all affano   CT 52;   DT 29, 65;   MN 33, 44, 59
    4   -Non piu Mesta   CT 52;   DT 43, 65
    8   -Overt   BA 55, 57;   CH 58;   CT 26;   DT 36, 44;   HN 56;   NA 59,
                    64, 69;   KC 37, 40;   LA 45;   MN 49, 66;   NP 30, 53;   NS 26, 63;
                    PH 26, 63;   PT 43;   RC 59;   SE 58;   SL 66, 69
    4   -Recitative and Rondo   DA 48, 50;   DE 48;   RC 44;   SF 48, 67
    4   -Rondo   BU 44
    4   La Donna del Lago, Opera 1819: Aria, Lanti affettl   SF 67
    9   La Gazza Ladra Opera 1817: Overt   AT 52, 61, 65;   BA 64, 67;
                    BN 39, 53;   CH 49(2);   CT 62;   CL 41, 52, 56, 61, 64;   DA 46,
                    48, 52, 61;   DE 50, 63;   DT 40, 51, 59, 63;   HN 41, 54, 61;
                    NA 57, 63, 69;   KC 43, 60, 65, 67;   LA 45, 52, 58;   ML 66;
                    MN 28, 35, 46, 62;   NP 40, 49, 50, 59;   NS 41, 63;   PH 41, 63;
                    PT 40, 45, 48, 51, 59, 69;   RC 21, 43, 57, 69;   SL 51, 60;
                    SF 52, 56;   SE 56, 59;   UT 50, 58, 67;   WA 66
    4   Italian in Algiers Opera 1813: Aria of Isabella   SF 67;   WA 52
    7   -Overture   AT 47, 53, 57, 64;   BA 41;   BN 21, 49, 61;   BU 52,
                    69;   CH 42, 55, 58;   CT 42;   CL 51, 55, 60;   DA 67;   DE 48;
                    DT 37, 62;   HN 40, 61;   NA 55, 66;   KC 55;   LA 42, 47, 58;
                    MN 51, 55;   ML 68;   NP 29, 40, 42, 44, 53, 54, 55;   NS 27, 42;
                    PH 27, 42;   PT 47, 56;   RC 47, 56;   SL 60;   SF 38, 53, 56, 67;
                    SE 47, 54
    9   The Journey to Rheims, Opera 1825: Overt   AT 57;   CH 54, 63;
                    CL 58;   HN 60;   NP 69

ROSSINI, G. (Cont.)
```
  4     Othello, Opera 1816: Willow Song and Prayer    SF 67
  6     La Scala di Seta, The Silken Ladder, Opera 1812: Overt    AT 50, 54, 61;
        BA 52, 56;   BN 64;   BU 63;   CH 45, 54, 58, 60, 61;   CT 36, 43,
        58, 66;   CL 44, 50, 55, 58, 59, 61;   DA 67;   DE 49, 54, 61, 65;
        DT 37, 60, 62;   HN 54, 62;   NA 60, 67;   LA 55;   ML 60;
        MN 47, 60;   NR 50;   NP 33, 50, 51, 55, 60, 62;   NS 56;   PH 56;
        PT 43, 46, 57;   SL 67;   SF 64, 67;   SE 60, 64
 12     Semiramedi Opera 1823
  4     -Ah quel Giorni   CH 18;   ML 65;   NS 19;   SL 19;   NP 29, 31, 33
  4     -Aria unidentified   NR 64;   SF 67
  4     -Bel Raggio Lusing Hier   AT 66;   DT 39, 66;   LA 54;   NP 29, 31,
        33;   SL 52;   SE 56
 12     -Overture   BA 55, 59, 65;   BN 22, 37, 52;   BU 53, 60;   CH 52,
        62;   CL 49, 64;   DA 49, 53;   DE 46, 51, 53, 57, 59, 63, 68;
        HN 33, 39, 40, 45, 52, 54, 60, 65;   NA 33, 55, 60, 62, 67;
        LA 35, 60;   ML 65;   MN 36, 45, 52, 59;   NR 51, 54, 61, 64, 69;
        NP 02, 27, 32, 39, 46, 51, 53, 55;   PH 35, 44, 51, 68;   PT 37,
        41, 50, 64, 68;   RC 26, 31, 37, 56, 66;   SL 28, 62;   SF 33,
        54, 56, 62;   SE 46, 52, 67;   WA 55, 62
  5     Il Signor Bruschino, Opera 1813: Overt    BA 61;   BN 63;   CH 54;
        CT 63;   NA 58, 65;   KC 58;   ML 62;   MN 50;   NP 29;   PT 39,
        45;   RC 33, 48;   SF 59;   SE 49, 55, 66:   UT 60;   WA 50
  9     Siege of Corinth Opera 1826: Overt    BN 68;   CL 55;   DT 38;   NP 17,
        30, 36, 54, 58;   NS 67;   PH 67;   PT 56, 69;   RC 26, 55;
        SF 58, 67
  9     The Turk in Italy, Opera 1814: Overt    CL 65;   MN 58;   NA 69
  4     Tancredi, Opera 1813: Aria    NP 32
  4     -Di tanta palpiti   SF 67
  4     -Il conte ory   NP 61
 11     William Tell Opera  1829, Overt    BA 40, 42;   BU 54;   CH 1892, 50,
        65;   DA 28, 49, 50, 69;   DT 26, 30, 38, 46, 58;   HN 34, 38;
        NA 35;   LA 31;   ML 62;   MN 26, 27, 30, 48, 56;   NP 01, 05,
        08, 28;   NS 11, 20, 24;   PH 22;   PT 42, 58, 66;   RC 23, 24;
        SL 22, 27;   SF 53, 67;   SE 61;   WA 37
  6     -Ballet Music   DA 50, 69
  4     -Passo a sci   ML 60
  4     -Prayer   NP 14;   NS 06
  4     -Selva Opaca   NP 24
  4     -Sombre foret   CL 68
  4     -Tarantella   CT 42;   NS 25
 25     Dances of the 16th Century, La Boutique Fantastique arr Respighi
        CH 22;   DT 67;   MN 39;   NS 29;   SL 55
  5     La Danza from Les Soirées musicales 1835   HN 43;   NP 14;   WA 46
 75     Missa Solemnis 1863   NP 38
  6     -Prelude Religioso   NP 40
 25     Rossiniana, Suite  See also Respighi, arranger    CT 59;   DE 67;
        NP 30;   RC 33, 55;   SL 55, 56;   SF 33
 19     Sonata for 2 V, C and Contrabass arr Casella    CH 62
 12     Sonata No 3 in C for Str    CH 69;   WA 64
        -Var   PT 56
 40     Stabat Mater 1842   KC 54;   LA 27;   NP 64;   SE 63
        -Fac ut Pirtem   NP 04
  5     -Inflammatus   NA 50;   NP 01
 15     Symphony for Str O   HN 54
  6     The Venetian Regatta   WA 66
```

ROTA, Nino   15   Variazioni Sopra un Tema Gioviale   NP 57;   PT 57
1911-   It

ROTHWELL, Walter H.   8   Songs: Bacchanale and Midsummer's Night   LA 19, 22
1872-1927 Brit/US

ROUSSEAU, Jean Jacques 3   Overture Le devin du Village arr Schwartz   PH 15
1712-1778   Fr

ROUSSEL, Albert   17   Bacchus et Ariane, Op 43 Suite No 1 from Ballet
1869-1937   Fr   BN 46, 51, 52, 56, 59, 61;   CH 63;   CT 61
                         4   -Padmavati   BN 25
                        20   Suite No 2 from Ballet Op 43   BN 50;   CH 46,
                                47, 54, 60, 63, 66, 67;   CT 54, 61;   CL 47, 63;
                                DA 55, 57, 66, 69;   DE 64;   DT 62;   HN 51, 53,
                                62, 67;   LA 46, 51, 58, 66;   MN 67;   NR 62;
                                NP 57;   PH 56, 58, 59, 65, 67;   PT 65;   RC 54,
                                57, 62, 66;   SL 52, 53, 56;   SF 57, 66;   SE 57,
                                67;   WA 52, 54, 60, 64
                        17   P Conc in G Op 36   BN 51;   CH 51;   NA 48;   NP 52;
                                PH 28
                        14   Conc for small O Op 34   NR 53;   PH 28, 46
                        38   Le Festin de l'araignée, The Spider's Feast,
                                Ballet Op 17   BN excerpts 52;   CH 25, 46, 58,
                                65;   CT 33, 58;   CL 57;   DT 38, 45, 53, 65;
                                KC 67;   MN 23, 43;   NP 30, 33, 56;   NS 24;
                                PH 51;   PT 50;   SL 28, 36;   SF 53;   SE 27;
                                WA 50, 55
                         9   Flemish Rhaps Op 56   BN 36, 38, 58;   HN 46
                        12   Pour un féte de printemps Symphon Poem Op 22
                                BN 24;   CH 37, 65;   NP 22
                        30   Psalm 80, Tenor, Chor and O   PH 29
                         9   Sinfonietta for Str Op 52   BN 35;   CH 51;   SL 36
                        15   Suite in F Op 33   BN 26, 32, 43, 48, 54, 57;
                                CH 38, 42, 52, 60;   CT 38, 59, 67;   CL 39, 52;
                                DE 52, 56, 59, 67;   DT 33, 56;   LA 32, 65;
                                MN 48, 61;   NP 27, 31, 47;   PH 33, 50, 57;
                                RC 55, 62;   SL 31, 34, 43(2);   SF 28, 33, 48,
                                60;   UT 67
                        45   Symph No 2 in B^b BN 24
                        25   Symph No 3 in g Op 42   AT 66;   BA 59;   BN 30,
                                34, 37, 41, 47, 50, 53;   CH 50, 61, 64, 66;
                                CL 47;   DE 66;   DT 69;   HN 49;   NA 69;   LA 49;
                                MN 47, 63, 66, 69;   NR 51;   NP 34, 43, 54, 61,
                                66;   PH 56, 66;   RC 55, 65;   SL 51, 63, 69;
                                SF 54, 61;
                        22   Symph No 4 in A Op 53   BN 35, 49, 59, 64;   CH 48,
                                66;   CT 63;   NP 35, 48;   PH 62, 64;   PT 55;
                                RC 52;   SF 64;   WA 51
                        43   Trois Evocations, Op 15   BN 28
                        15   -Excerpts   BN 23
                        15   -La Ville Rose No 2   CH 19;   PH 13;   SL 33, 37
                        15   -Les Dieux No 1   NP 20;   NS 21;   PH 21

ROYCE, Edward   7   Far Ocean   RC 15
1886-   US

	Time in Minutes	
ROZSA, Miklos 1907- Hung/US	18	Capricio, Pastoral and Danza for large O Op 14 CH 42; PH 42
	24	Conc for Str O Op 17 CH 45; LA 44; PH 57
	25	P Conc Op 31 HN 67; LA 66; PH 68
	28	V Conc Op 24 CL 57; DA 55; PH 57; SL 61
	21	Notturna Ungherese, Op 28 PH 63
	10	Overt to a Symphon Concert Op 26 DA 57; LA 57
	20	Rhaps for C and O Op 3 NA 61
	17	Theme, Var and Finale Op 13 CH 37; DE 52; NP 43; LA 54; PH 47
	10	Three Hungarian Sketches LA 59
	15	The Vintner's Daughter, Var PH 55
RÓŻYCKI, Ludomir 1884-1953 Pol	8	Symph on Scherzo, Stańczyk, The Jester MN 36
DE RUBERTIS, Orestes 1893-1930 It	15	Fior di Lotto, Leggenda Indiana LA 25
RUBINSTEIN, Anton 1829-1894 Russ	8	Antony and Cleopatra, Symphon Overt Op 116 BN 1890; CH 1894; NP 1890, 94; NS 1890

	31	Bal Costumé, Suite No 2, Op 103 CH 29, 30, 31,
		    33, 40
		    -2 Dances CH 1899
		    -Wedding March CH 40

	30	P Conc in G Op 45 No 3 BN 1882, 89; CH 1891;
		    CT 37; NP 1889, 37, 43; NS 04; PH 04, 14;
		    PT 43

	30	P Conc in d Op 70 No 4 BN 1882, 85, 87, 91, 92,
		    94, 96, 98, 01, 05, 07, 09, 10; CH 1891, 95,
		    96, 97, 99, 01, 05, 09, 17, 20, 38; CT 1896,
		    99, 02, 03, 10, 13, 16, 18; CL 25; DA 32, 35;
		    DT 25; HN 33; NA 30; LA 24; MN 28; NP
		    1870, 72, 83, 92, 96, 01, 06, 16, 18; NS 1885,
		    87, 91, 10, 17; PH 05, 07(2), 09, 17, 32;
		    SL 14, 25, 33; SF 26

	30	P Conc in E^b Op 94 No 5 BN 08; CH 21; CT 07, 19; DT 19; NP 11; NS 08; PH 06; SL 19
	25	C Conc Op 96 No 2 BN 02
	30	V Conc in G Op 46 No 1 BN 1887; NP 1887
	8	Concert Overt in B^b Op 60 NP 1862
	6	Dance Satanique NS 16
	8	Demetrius of the Don, Overt BN 1895; CH 1894
	4	The Demon, Opera 1875: Aria NP 1891
	14	-Ballet Music BN 1885, 93, 97; CT 1895
	8	-Toreador and Andalonse, Two Dances NA 34; NS 22; RC 24, 44
	15	Don Quixote, A Musical Portrait Op 87 BN 1893; NS 16
	4	Etude in C for P and O Op 23 NP 17
	20	Fantaisie in C Op 84 NP 08; PH 08
	20	Fantaisie for 2 P in f BN 1885
	5	Feramors, Opera 1863: Ballet Music BN 1882, 85, 93, 96; CT 18
	4	-Candle Dance NA 34
	4	-Hochzeitung CT 1895, 18

RUBINSTEIN, A. (Cont.)

	4	Hecuba, No 1 of Two scenes for Contral and O Op 92 NP 1877, 80
	10	Ivan the Terrible, A Musical Portrait Op 79 NP 1890
	4	Moses, Opera Op 112: Scene NS 1888
	6	Nero, Opera 1879: Ballet CH 1893
	6	-Scene from Act III NP 1886
	4	Scene and Aria, E dunque ver for Sopr and O Op 58 NP 1870, 84, 92
	14	Symphon Poem, La Russe 1882 NS 1882, 87
	30	Symph No 1 in F Op 40 NP 32
	40	Symph No 2 in C Op 42 Ocean BN 1883, 85, 88, 91, 94, 96, 02; CH 1891; NP 1870, 72, 77, 82, 88, 96, 99, 07, 19; NS 1881, 86, 89, 94, 11
	40	Symph No 4 in d Op 95 Dramatic BN 1893, 95; CH 1893; NP 1879, 83, 86, 91
	30	Symph No 5 in g Op 107 BN 1882, 94; NP 1881
	30	Symph No 6 in a Op 111 BN 1887, 03
	8	Str Quart in F Op 59 Adagio NP 03
	5	The Vine, Opera 1882: Ballet Music BN 1884, 87, 01
		Songs
	4	Since First I Met Thee arr from Romance for P Op 44 No 1 CT 1896
	4	The Dream DT 20
	4	O Frage Nicht NP 1873
	4	Nachfall NP 1873
	4	Wenn es doch NP 1878
	4	Der Page NP 1883
	4	Es Blinkt der Than NS 1882
RUBINSTEIN, Beryl 1898- US	30 15	P Conc in C 1935 CL 36 Scherzo for O 1926 CL 26
RUDIN, Herman US	6 4	Legende RC 17 Parade RC 23
RUFTY, Hilton 1909- US	5	Hobby on the Green arr Bales WA 43
RUGGLES, Carl 1876- US	15 8 6 15	Men and Mountains, Symphon Ensemble 1924 NP 35, 58; SF 59 Organum CL 50; HN 51; NP 1890 Portals 1926 BN 64; ML 69 Sun-Treader 1933 CH 66
RUSSO, William 1928- US	12 21-22	Three Pieces for Blues Band and O NP 69 Symph No 2 in C Titans NP 58
Rybner, Cornelius 1855-1929 Dan/US	8	Festival Overt PH 10
RYCHLICK, Charles V. fl 1897- US	6	Spring Overt RC 19

SAAR, Louis V.   8   Ganymed, Contral and O   NP 1899
  1868-1937 Neth/US   16   Mountain Kingdom of Great Northwest, Suite
                               4 items 1922   CH 22
                       15   Suite Rococo Op 27   CH 18;   SL 18

DE SABATA, Victor   20   Juventus, Symphon Poem 1919   CT 27, 31;   DT 34;
  1892-   It   NS 20;   PT 49
                       20   Symphon Suite 1902   NS 18(2)

SACCHINI, Antonio   6   Oedipe a Colone, Overt arr Franko   NP 34
  1730-1786 It

SAEVERUD, Harald   8   Galdreslatten Danza Sinfonica con Passacaglia Op 20
  1897-   Nor   CT 53;   KC 61
                        6   Kjempevise-Slatten Song of Revolt   MN 53
                       33   Minnesota Symph Op 40   MN 58
                       17   Peer Gynt Suite No 1 Incidental Music Op 28
                               PH 59

SAINTON, Prosper   8   V Fant on Lucretia Borgia   NP 1854
  1813-1890 Fr   15   Two Tone Pictures   SE 33

SAINT-SAENS, Camille   11   Africa, Fantasie for P and O Op 89   NS 06;   SF 23
  1835-1921 Fr   16   Algerienne Suite Op 60   CH 1892;   CT 1897, 07,
                               21;   NA 33;   NP 52;   NS 19;   SL 10;   SF 37;
                               SE 35
       4   -3rd mvt, Reverie du Soir   DA 26
       4   -4th mvt, March Militaire Francaise   CT 42;   DA 26;   DT 57
      10   Allegro Apassionata for P and O Op 70   NS 06
       8   Andantino, for V and O   NP 02
      17   Ascanio Opera 1890 Ballet Suite   MN 28
       5   The Barbarians 1901 Opera Comique: Overt   BN 03;   CH 02;   CT 19, 21
      38   Christmas Oratorio for Soli, Chor and O Op 12   AT pts I and II 48;
                    CT 51, 56;   HN 66
      18   C Conc in a Op 33   AT 47, 59, 61, 66;   BN 1881, 98, 02, 03, 05, 10,
                    15, 19, 20, 38, 48;   CH 1893, 00, 06, 11, 18, 22, 34, 35, 40, 43,
                    56, 59;   CT 02, 05, 09, 13, 19, 22, 31, 35, 52;   CL 23, 28, 37,
                    38, 40, 52, 57;   DA 60, 69;   DE 45, 47, 52, 59, 68;   DT 27, 46,
                    66, 69;   NA 35, 45;   KC 46, 61, 68;   LA 35;   ML 62;   NR 52,
                    54, 56, 60;   NP 1892, 01, 22, 46, 50, 51, 55, 69;   NS 1879, 94,
                    21;   PH 01, 06, 07, 11, 18, 29, 48, 53, 63, 66;   PT 43, 64;
                    RC 23, 29, 39, 56, 65;   SL 10, 26, 28, 35, 43, 50, 55, 56;
                    SF 16, 56, 69;   SE 55, 60, 67;   UT 56, 69
      22   P Conc No 2 in g Op 22   AT 46, 47;   BA finale 42, 43, 59, 68;
                    BN 1882, 83, 92, 94, 95(2), 00, 02, 07, 17, 18, 20, 61;   BU 63;
                    CH 1898, 01, 03, 05, 06, 15, 17, 18, 19;   CT 02, 04, 07, 11, 17,
                    18, 32, 35, 59, 63;   CL 33, 35, 61;   DA 38, 49, 53, 69;
                    DE 61, 65;   DT 19, 65;   HN 66;   LA 20, 31, 53, 64;   ML 60;
                    MN 26, 46, 48, 68;   NP 1876, 02, 16, 19, 20, 55;   NS 1880, 85,
                    15, 16, 18;   PH 07;   PT 62;   RC 26;   SL 15, 17, 32, 36;
                    SF 18, 21, 37;   SF 36, 43, 56, 69;   WA 33, 39, 41, 47, 60, 64,
                    67
      29   P Conc No 3 in E^b Op 29   BN 53, 62;   HN 60
      12   -Excerpts   BN 04
      24   P Conc No 4 in c Op 44   BA 51, 62;   BN 1881, 92, 97, 08, 22, 35,
                    42;   CH 1892, 08, 16, 18, 19, 22, 24, 37, 46, 58;   CT 1895, 99,

SAINT-SAËNS, C. (Cont.)   P Conc No 4 in c Op 44 (Cont.)
        04, 06, 13, 16, 18, 22;   CL 26, 32, 57, 64;   DE 51, 62, 69;
        DT 17, 18, 27, 47, 54;   HN 44, 62;   KC 40, 60;   LA 55;   MN 25,
        41, 57;   NR 58;   NP 02, 10, 53, 61;   NS 1881, 90, 19, 22, 24;
        PH 16, 22, 27, 60, 69;   PT 43, 67;   RC 28, 59, 69;   SL 20;
        SF 28, 29, 48, 55;   UT 51;   WA 54, 62
30   P Conc No 5 in F Op 103   AT 68;   BA 63;   BN 03, 19;   CH 14, 22,
        23, 29, 34;   CT 07, 36, 58, 68;   CL 22, 61;   KC 67;   MN 27;
        NP 51, 64;   PH 06, 07, 19, 68;   PT 56;   RC 61;   SL 11;
        SE 61;   WA 38;   SF 68
10   V Conc No 1 in a Op 20   BN 1884, 92;   CH 1894(2), 02, 08, 13, 18,
        23, 49, 54, 62;   DE 45, 47, 52, 59;   MN 43, 46, 66;   NP 22;
        NS 08, 10
28   V Conc No 3 in b Op 61   BA 28;   BN 1889, 97, 01, 03, 09, 12, 17,
        18, 29, 49;   CT 1896, 01, 03, 05, 12, 15, 17, 18, 19, 25, 28,
        48;   CL 22, 25, 48, 62;   DA 35, 55;   DE 51;   DT 25, 26;
        HN 34, 52;   KC 37, 52;   LA 21, 26, 32, 33, 42, 50, 51, 65;
        MN 23, 68;   NR 54, 62;   NP 1894, 03, 08, 17, 18, 19, 49, 55;
        NS 14, 18;   PH 10, 12, 26, 47, 63;   PT 38, 53, 63;   RC 27, 60;
        SL 12, 18, 19, 26, 33, 47, 61;   SF 19;   SE 34;   WA 33, 34, 50
25   Conc for Harp and O, Morceau de Concert in G Op 154   SF 20
15   Concert piece in e for V and O Op 62   BN 1893
8   Coronation March Op 117   CH 02, 03, 06;   LA 19, 22
25   Carnaval of Animals, Fantasie 1886   AT 49;   BN 22;   CH 39;
        CT 26, 41;   CL 35, 62;   DA 63;   DT 64;   HN 55;   NR 56;
        NP 22, 55;   NS 22, 25;   PT 54;   SL 22;   SF 23, 55;   SE 35,
        53, 63;   UT 57;   WA 55
4   -The Swan   BA 26, 28, 42;   DE 56, 59;   HN 31;   NR 57
4   -The Elephant   BA 42
5   Dance Macabre, Tone Poem No 3 Op 40   BN 1882, 84, 87, 10, 35;
        CH 1892, 95, 98, 03, 06, 17;   CT 07, 25, 49;   CL 26, 35;
        DA 38;   DT 15, 17, 37, 54, 58;   HN 34, 37, 42, 49;   KC 40;
        MN 46;   NP 19, 30, 35, 50;   PH 01, 06, 07, 08, 09, 10, 17, 22,
        24, 25, 37, 58;   PT 37;   SL 04, 16;   SF 17;   SE 38;   WA 32
8   The Deluge, Oratorio Op 45: Overt   CH 05, 21;   DT 24, 53;   HN 17,
        35, 37;   NA 35;   MN 23, 46;   NP 50;   NS 19;   PH 06;   SL 24;
        SF 21, 25
9   Fantasie for Harp Op 95   CH 1893, 94
8   Fantasie for Org Op 101   CH 1896
13   La Fiancée du Timbalier, Voice and O   BN 1899, 09;   CH 04;
        CT 05, 09;   SL 23
10   Havanaise for V and O Op 83   BN 17;   CT 04;   DE 68;   NA 47;
        MN 28, 44
4   Henry VIII, Opera 1883: Aria   NS 19
10   -Ballet Music   BN 1883(2);   PH 01, 06
8   -Dances   NS 03
4   -Dance of Gypsy   NS 16, 19
4   -Qui donc commande   CT 28;   SL 19
4   -Scotch Idyl and Gigue   NS 19
6   Hymn to Pallas Athène Sopr and O Op 98   NS 11
10   Introd and Rondo Capriccioso for V and O Op 28   AT 58;   BA 51;
        BN 1883;   CH 1895(2), 15, 17, 25, 28, 45, 61;   CT 1895, 04, 14,
        18, 59;   CL 56, 58;   DA 50, 51, 57, 65;   DE 51, 67;   DT 18,
        24, 25, 56, 65;   HN 40, 51;   NA rondo only 53;   KC 57;
        LA 60(2), 65;   ML 68;   MN 44, 67;   NR 51;   NP 63;   NS 1896,
        04, 13, 16, 25;   PH 05, 16;   PT 40;   RC 39;   SL 16, 22;
        SF 11;   SE 38, 48, 51;   UT 51

SAINT-SAËNS, C. (Cont.)

16   Jeunnesse d'Hercules, The Youth of Hercules, Symphon Poem Op 50
          BN 1883, 90, 94, 00, 04, 18;   CH 01, 04;   CT 1898, 07, 17, 20,
          21;   NP 55;   PH 08
10   La Lyre et la Harpe for Solo, Chor and O Op 57   BN 18
4   -Forth the Eagle   NP 1885
7   March Hérioque, March Militaire Op 34 CH 1895, 10;   CT 1899, 18;   HN 37
5   March Occident and Orient Op 25   NS 10
6   A Night in Lisbon, Barcarolle Op 63 HN 39; NS 1884, 09, 18; SE 26
9   Omphale's Spinning Wheel, Le Rouet d'Omphale, Tone Poem Op 31   BA 64;
          BN 1888, 91, 93, 95, 98, 02, 10, 18, 35, 57;   BU 45;   CH 1891,
          93, 96, 97, 99, 02, 03, 04, 13, 14, 18;   CT 1895, 00;   CL 35, 49;
          DT 16, 17, 18, 23;   HN 33;   KC 38;   MN 47, 48;   NP 49;
          NS 1887, 92, 06, 08, 16, 19;   PH 10, 11, 14, 18, 30;   SL 13, 20,
          23;   SE 43;   WA 33, 39, 40, 41
8   Phaeton, Tone Poem No 2, Op 39   BN 1887, 98, 18;   CH 1891, 96, 98,
          99, 01, 02, 04, 06, 13;   CT 07;   DA 50;   DT 59;   MN 29;
          NP 11, 19, 55;   NS 1893, 18;   PH 02, 07, 09, 10, 11;   SL 14,
          18, 23;   SF 16;   SE 50
6   La Princesse Jeune, Opera in one Act Op 30: Overt   AT 66;   BN 50,
          57;   DA 52;   NA 60, 66
4   Phryne, Opera Op 98: Aria of Pallas Athene CH 18;   CT 1896;   NS 11
8   Rhapsody Amerique 1895   BN 1895
8   Romance for V in C Op 48   BN 1881
6   Romance for Fl Op 37   NS 11
5   Romance for Fr Horn Op 36   CH 03
4   Samson and Delilah Opera Op 47: Aria unidentified   DE 58, 61;
          PH 03, 07, 15
          -Two Arias   DA 58;   KC 41, 61
4   -Amour, viens aider   CH 1891, 94;   CT 1898;   DA 35;   NA 50;
          KC 33, 63;   MN 36, 43;   NP 1898;   NS 1897;   SL 21
4   -Bacchanale   CH 07;   CT 18, 20;   DE 56, 60;   HN 32, 39, 41;
          NA 50;   KC 33, 58;   NS 17;   WA 33
4   -Ballet   NS 14
45   -Concert Version   DE 49;   DT 61;   SE 30
4   -Dance   NA 50;   NS 1893
15   -Excerpts   BN 1882;   NA 50;   RC 49
4   -Fair Spring is returning   CH 1899, 19;   CL 21;   NA 50;   MN 36;
          NP 12;   NS 1891, 93
4   -Finale   NA 50
4   -Mon Coeur s'ouvre a ta voix AT 50, 56, 64;   CH 10, 18;   CT 1895,
          07, 10, 18, 47;   DA 27;   DE 69;   DT 17, 22;   NA 41, 50, 55;
          KC 42;   LA 21, 31;   MN 36;   NP 03, 15;   NS 1894;   PT 55;
          WA 32, 35, 46
5   -Overt   NA 50
4   -Prelude to Act II   NA 50
4   -Samson soon will be in my power   CH 1897
8   Scherzo for 2 P and O Op 87   CH 20
8   Septet in E^b for P, Trumpet and Str Op 65 BN 1886; NS 18, 24; SE 28
10   Serenade Bacarolle for V, C, P and O Op 108   NS 1888, 15
      Songs
4   La Cloche after Hugo   CT 00
4   Le bonheur est chose legere   DA 35

SAINT-SAËNS, C.(Cont.)

33	Suite No 1 for O in D Op 49 BN 1896; CH 1895	
31	Symph No 1 in E^b Op 2 BN 04	
25	Symph No 2 in a Op 55 BN 1892, 18; CH 00, 04, 17, 21; CT 48; DT 15, 35; NP 04, 16, 26, 51; NS 1878, adagio only 87, 90, 18; PH 17; SL 21; SF 23, 44; WA 43	
36	Symph No 3 in c with 2 P and Org Op 78 BA 53, 64; BN 00, 01, 13, 17, 18, 22, 25, 27, 29, 34, 37, 45, 49, 53, 58, 65; BU 67; CH 1891, 95, 11, 21, 28, 29, 33, 34, 35, 37, 54, 62; CT 38, 41, 66; CL 26, 58, 66; DT 38, 57, 60, 65, 68; HN 46, 66; NA 44, 61, 65; KC 49, 56, 59, 66; LA 35, 53, 57, 67, 69; ML 69; MN 27, 45; NR 50, 63, 69; NP 1886, 12, 27, 30, 43, 58, 65; NS 1893, 95, 11, 14, 16, 20, 25; PH 10, 11, 60, 62; PT 69; RC 04, 27, 60, 69; SL 64, 68; SF 49, 60, 68; SE 59; UT 57, 63; WA 51, 53, 64	
7	Tarantelle for Fl, Clar and O Op 6 CH 1891, 96, 03; KC 34	
12	Var on Beethoven Theme for 2 P and O Op 35 CH 16	
6	Wedding Cake, Valse Caprice for P and Str Op 76 CT 07; NS 06	

SAKNOWSKY or	4	Song, The Clock PH 19
SACHNOVSKI Russ		

SALIERI, Antonio	5	Axur Re d'Ormus, Overt NP 64
1750-1825 It	15	Conc for Fl, Ob and O KC 65

SALTZMAN, Eric	7	Night Dance MN 60
1933 US		

SALVIUCCI, Giovanni	10	Introduzione, Pasacaglia and Finale CH 69
1907-1937 It	10	Italian Symph in 1 mvt NA 50

SALZEDO, Carlos	17	Conc Harp and Winds 1926 CT 28; PH 49
1885-1961 US	13	The Enchanted Isle, Symphon Poem, Harp and O 1918 BN 22; CH 19; CL 28; NA 43; PH 25

SAMAZEUILH, Gustave	13	Étude Symphonique 1907 CH 25
1877- Fr	9	Naiades au Soir, Symphon Poem SL 35
	9	Nuit, Poem for O 1925 BN 52

SAMINSKY, Lazare	18	Ansonia, Italian Pages Op 39 CL 35
1882- Russ/US	30	Rachel, Lament and Triumph, Ballet Op 14
	10	-2 Excerpts BN 21
	10	-Final scene NS 24
	9	Stilled Pageant Op 48 in 4 mvts DT 47
	30	Symph No 3 The Seas Op 10 NS 27
	8-9	Three Shadows, Poems for O Op 42 CH 43; NP 35
	12	Vigiliae, Three Short Songs DT 21; NS 23

SAMMARTINI,	9	Sinfonia in D CT 37
Giovanni B.	9	Symph No 3 in G CH 58; NP 51, 57; PT 56;
1698-1775 It		RC 56

SANDBY, Herman	3	Bridal March WA 48
1881- Dan	20	C Conc in D PH 15
	5	Elfhill WA 48
	12	Vikings at Helgoland, Opera Prelude, Act IV PH 12

SANDBY, H. (Cont.)
                5   Woman the Fiddler Prelude to a Play   PH 11
              15   -Suite   PH 14

SANDERS, Robert L.   14-15   Little Symph in G 1937   CH 42;   NA 39, 43;   MN 39;
1906-   US   NP 39;   SL 41
               5   Saturday Night Barn Dance   MN 41;   NP 33;   UT 49
              27   Symph in A   WA 59
              22   The Tragic Muse, 5 Impressions   CH 35

SANDERSON   4   Song, Green Pastures with P   NA 36

SANDIFUR   10   Suite for Str O   DE 52
        US

SANJUAN, Pedro   8   Black Liturgy Liturgia Negra, Afro-Cuban   Suite
1886-   Sp/US   for O 1934   CT 41;   HN 42;   RC 41;   SL 41
              25   Castilla, Poem de Ambiente 3 pts 1942   PH 31
              11   Ritual Symph, La Mocumba 1945   SL 51

SANTA CRUZ, Wilson   15   5 Short pieces for Str   SF 42
1899-   Chile

SANTOLIQUIDO,   4   Nel Giardino, Baritone Solo   DE 50;   WA 49
  Francesco   8   The Perfume of the Oasis in the Sahara   CH 22
1883-   It   10   Twilight on the Sea   CH 22

SANTORO, Claudio   9   Music for Str O   DA 49
1919-   Brazil   30   Symph No 3 in g Op 42   SL 63
              16   Symph No 8 with Sopr   SL 64

SAPERTON   5   Midway Plaisance   DA 38
        US

SAPIO, Romualdo   4   Primavera, Song   CT 1896
1858-1943   US

SAPP, Allen D.   12   Colloquies   BU 63
1922-   US   13   Overt, The Women of Trachis   BU 62

SARASATE, Pablo de   20   Fantasie on Carmen   V and O   CH 22
1844-1908   Sp   8   Gypsy Tunes for V and O   NS 05

SARMIENTOS, Jorge 15   Conc for 5 Timpani and O   WA 65
   Guatamala

SASONKIN, Manus   15   Symph Op 4   SL 64
1930-   US

SATIE, Erik   8   2 Gymnopédies, Nos 1 and 3 arr Debussy 1888
1866-1925   Fr   BN 25(2), 36, 40, 43, 54;   CH 23, 29, 59;   CT 49;
                   CL 67;   DE 52, 57, 66;   HN 65;   NA 68;   KC 33;
                   MN 42;   NP 31;   PH 21, 22, 35, 37, 43, 51, 63;
                   RC 46, 49;   SL 50, 52, 57
               4   No 1 only   KC 40, 57;   SL 30, 39, 46

SATIE, E. (Cont.)

	7	Jack in the Box, Music for a Pantomime 1899 SF 48
	8	Messe des Pauvres, Mass for the Poor 1895 arr
		Diamond CT 50; NP 51; RC 51
	3	Passacaglia 1906 NP 51
	13	Parade, Ballet 1916 CH 59; KC 68; MN 66;
		NP 61; PH 22; SF 69
	5	-Excerpts SL 66
	9	2 Preludes, Posth arr Poulenc MN 52

SATTER, Gustav   10   Festival Polonaise for P   NP 1859
1832-1879 Aust/US

SAUER, Emil   30   P Conc No 1 in e   BN 08;   CH 08;   PH 08
1862-1942   Ger

SAUGUET, Henri   10   Variation   CT 57
1901-   Fr

SAVINE, Alex   15   Golgotha   NP 22
1881-   Yugo/US

SAXE, Serge   12   Symph for Str   HN 66
         Russ/US

SCALCOTAS
see SKALCOTAS

SCALERO, Rosario   7   The Divine Forest, Symphon Poem   PH 40
1870-1954   It/US   15   Suite for Str Quart and Str O   NS 22

SCARLATTI, Alessandro 10   Exultate Deo 4 pa Chor   CH 11
1660-1725   It   4   Sedecia, King of Jerusalem, Oratorio 1796, Aria
                             SL 29
                       12   Sonata in A for Fl and Str arr Benjamin   CT 03
                        5   Toccata Nona arr Stein   CH 46
                        2   The Violet, Sopr with Str O arr Molinari   CL 31
                             SL 29

SCARLATTI, Domenico 12   Cantata, Su La sponda del mare for Voice and Str DE 60
1685-1757   It   16   Ballet Suite fr Good Humored Ladies arr Thommasini
                             BN 26;   CH 53;   CT 25, 45;   PH 63;   PT 57;
                             SL 30, 51;   SF 23;   SE 64;   DE 46
                     10   Conc No 5 in c for Str O   SL 36
                     16   Conc Grosso in f   SF 61
                     15   Five Sonatas arr Thommasini   CH 21;   NP 27
                     20   Six Pieces for O arr Byrnes   CL 42, 44
                      6   Sonata for Cross Keyboards   NS 23
                   8-10   Suite fr Sonata for Str arr Saluaggi   CL 38
                     11   -arr Byrnes   CH 42;   PH 42;   SL 44;   NP 43
                     11   Three Pieces for small O arr Roland-Manuel   BN 26;
                             CL 29
                     12   Toccata, Bourrée and Gigue arr Casella   SL 34

Schaefer, Ferdinand 10   Forest Scene, An O Study   NA 31, 40
1861-1953   US   10   Introd and Scherzo Str O   NA 37, 42

SCHARWENKA, Philipp 1847-1917 Ger	12	Frühlingswogen, Symphon Poem Op 87 BN 1892; CH 1891; NP 1892
SCHARWENKA, Xaver 1850-1924 Pol/Ger	35	P Conc in b^b No 1 Op 32 BN 1890, 98, 68; CH 1892; NS 1878, 92, 06; PH 06
	30	P Conc in c No 2 Op 56 CH 10; NP 1892
	35	P Conc in f No 4 Op 82 BN 10; CH 10; CT 10; SL 10
	6	Prelude to Metaswintha, Opera 1896 CH 1892; SL 10
	30	Symph in c Op 60 NP 1886
SCHEDRIN, Rodion 1932- Russ	20	Conc No 2 for O Zvony, The Chimes NP 67
	12	Mischievous Folk Ditties or Naughty Limericks Conc for O NP 66
	20	The Humpbacked Horse, 9 parts Ballet HN 57
SCHEIDT, Sam. 1587-1654 Ger	4	Vater unser in Himmelreich, Choral Prelude arr Leonardi SL 36
SCHEINPFlUG, Paul 1875-1937 Ger/US	9	Overt to a Comedy of Shakespeare Op 15 BN 08, 14; CH 09(2), 10, 13, 16, 23; SL 15; MN 27, 29, 39; SF 15
SCHEINFELD, David 1910- US	10	Adagio and Allegro SF 46
	20	V Conc PH 64
	10	Etudes for O PT 60
SCHELLING, Ernest 1876-1939 US	25	V Conc 1916 BN 16; PH 28; CH 26
	25	Fantastic Suite P and O 1905 BN 07; CH 08, 20, 22, 38; DT 23; NP 22; NS 07; PH 21; SL 21
	40	Impressions of an Artist's Life, Var for P and O 1915 BN 15; CH 15, 16, 21, 36; NP 25, 28, 32; PH 16; MN 25
	15	Légend Symphonique for O 1904 CH 13; DT 47; PH 13
	20	Morocco, Symphon Poem 1927 BN 28; CH 29; CT 33; NP 27; PH 29
	26	Suite Varié CH 36, 38; NP 38
	20	A Victory Ball,Fantasy for O 1923 BN 23; CH 22, 23, 26, 27, 45; CT 23; CL 25, 26; DA 34; DT 23; MN 23, 24, 25, 27, 32; NP 22, 26, 45; PH 22, 38; RC 44; SL 25, 26, 33; SF 25, 36; SE 39
SCHENCK, Elliott 1868- US	10	In a Withered Garden, Tone Poem BN 23; CH 22
SCHIASSI 1690-1754 It	12	Christmas Symph AT 57; MN 44
SCHIBLER, Armin 1920- Swiss	17	Passacaglia Op 24 PH 57
	20	Metamorphoses Op 75 DT 68
SCHIDLOWSKI, Leon 1931- Chile	5	Llaqui, Elegy for O PT 65

SCHILLINGER, Joseph	8	1st Airphonic Suite 1929 CL 29
1895-1943 Russ/US	4	March of the Orient 1921 CL 28
SCHILLINGS, Max	24	Hexenlied Op 15 Ballad, Narrator and O CH 05;
1868-1943 Ger		CT 09; NS 05; PH 04, 08, 20; SL 09
	5	Ingwald, Opera Op 3: Intermezzo NS 1895
	6	-Prelude, Act II BN 1896; CH 1896, 03, 04,
		09; CT 1896, 00
	5	Moloch Opera Op 20: Harvest Festival BN 08;
		CH 09, 10, 15, 23, 25
	14	Oedipus, Symphon Prologue Op 11 BN 01; CH 00;
		NP 01; PH 03, 05, 13
	11	Pfeifertag, The Piper's Holiday Opera Op 10: Prelude
		Act III BN 05; CT 01; NP 10
	30	2 Symphon Fantasies Op 6
	15	No 1 Meergruss BN 13
	14	No 2 Seemorgen BN 13; PH 10
SCHIMMERLING, Hanus	11	Toccata and Chromatic Fugue NA 49
1900- Czech/US		
SCHINDELMEISSER,	6	Overt for O Uriel Acasto NP 1856
Louis		
1811-1864 Ger		
SCHINDLER, Kurt	5	Song, El Pono CL 27
1882-1935 US		
SCHIPA, Tito	4	Song, I shall Return DT 28
1896- It		
SCHJELDRUP, Gerhard	11	Opferfeuer, Summer Night on the Fjord BN 07;
1859-1933 Nor		SL 10
	7	Sunrise over Himalayas BN 07
SCHMIDT, Franz	56	Symph No 2 E^b PH 40
1874-1939 Aust	46	Symph No 4, Requiem Symph LA 68
	25	Var on Hungarian Hussar's Song NP 31
SCHMITT, Florent	20	Antony and Cleopatra Op 69 Incidental Music NP 24
1870-1958 Fr	6	-Le Camp de Pompée CH 26, 28, 33, 37; CL 24
	4	-Nuit au Palais de la Reine CH 28
	10	Chant de Guerre Op 63 Chor and O CL 22
	17	Feuillets de Voyage Op 26 CH 22
	8	Musique de Plein Air Op 44 BN 18
	35	Psalm 47 Sopr, Chor, Org and O BN 27, 37;
		DA 54; SF 61
	15	Pupazzi Op 36 Suite LA 19; NS 15; SE 26
	8	No 2, Scaramouche MN 28
	8	Rêves for O No 1 Op 65 BN 24
	8	3 Rhapsodies Op 53, No 3, Viennese CH 13, 25;
		DT 24; NP 19; PH 13; SF 17
	15	Salammbo Op 76, Suite No 2 NP 56
	12	Symph Concertante P and O Op 82 BN 32
	25	Symph No 2 Op 137 BN 60
	8	-Theme and Var DT 47

SCHMITT, F. (Cont.)

	17	Symphon Fragment Op 10 En Ete SE 35
	10	Tragédie de Salomé, Ballet Op 50 BN 13, 19, 30, 31, 35, 38; CH 19(2), 45; CT 20, 46; CL 28, 37; DT 52, 57; LA 32; MN 40; PH 18; PT 51; SL 19, 31

SCHMITZ, H.   6   Horn Solo with Echo   NP 1848
fl 1848   US

SCHNABEL, Arthur   10   Rhaps for O 1946   CL 47;   NP 48
1882-1951   Ger/US   25   Symph No 1 1939   MN 46

SCHNEIDER, Fr.   20   Symph No 20 in B   NP 1854
1786-1853   Ger

SCHNEIDER, Edward F.   15   Sargasso   SF 21;   SL 25
1872-   US   15   Thus Spake the Deepest Stone   SF 37

SCHOENBERG, Arnold   8   Accompaniment to a Chinese Cinema Op 34   BN 52;
1874-1951   Aust/US   CH 60;   MN 62

	26	Chamber Symph No 1 Op 9b BA 64; BN 47, 50, 65; CH 60; DT 60; LA 65; NP 59; NS 15; PH 15, 22; SL 58, 62
	18	Chamber Symph No 2 Op 38 LA 44; NP 66; SF 44
	20	C Conc LA 35
	28	P Conc Op 42 AT 69; BN 67; CL 59; LA 64; NP 53, 57; SF 62
	30	V Conc Op 36 BN 64; MN 45; NP 66; PH 40; CH 68
	30	Erwartung, Monodrama for Sopr and O Op 17 NP 51; SE 65; SL 68
	30	Five Pieces for Op 16 BN 14, 57; BU 66; CH 13, 25, 33, 51, 58, 66; CT 66; CL 63; DA 63; DT 65; LA 62, 65; ML 68; MN 61, No 3 only 65; NR Excerpts 63; NP 48, 60; NS 25; PH 21, 63, 65; PT 62, 65; SL 64, 69; SF 51; WA 69
	13	Four Songs with O Op 22 PT 65
	9	Friede auf Erden, Chor and O Op 13 CL 66; LA 69
	130	Gurre-lieder for Soli, Chor and O 1900 CT 50; LA 2 pts 49, 67; PH 31, 60
	13	-Song of the Wood dove BN 64; CH 32; MN 50; NR 51; NP 49
	20	Gluckliche Hand Opera Op 18 PH 29
	18	Ode to Napoleon for Narrator and O Op 41b NP 44
	45	Pelléus and Mélisande Symphon Poem Op 5 BN 33; BU 68; CT 16, 29; HN 67; LA 65; NP 15, 33; PH 20; PT 65
	8	Pillar of Fire DT 44
	5	Prelude for Chor and O Op 44, Genesis Suite UT 46
	20	Psalm No 1 MN 56
	20	Suite for Str O NP 35
	29	Str Quart arr for Str O No 2 Op 10 BN 65; MN 44
	10-12	A Survivor fr Warsaw, Narrator and Chor Op 46 BN 68; BU 63; LA 68; MN 68; NP 49, 66; SL 63

SCHOENBERG, A. (Cont.)

14   Theme and Var Op 43b   BN 44;   BU 49;   CH 48;
                CL 46;   DT 44;   NP 45;   PH 48;   PT 43, 65;
                SL 49;   SF 49

22   Transfigured Night for Str O Op 4   BA 60;   BN 21(2),
                33, 62;   BU 58;   CH 21, 25(2), 28, 33, 44, 46,
                47, 54, 57, 60;   CT 22, 28, 49;   CL 44, 45;
                DA 46, 54, 60;   DE 51, 64, 68;   DT 59, 64;
                HN 62;   NA 47;   LA 25, 34(2), 52, 60, 65;   MN 25,
                27, 34, 41, 42, 60, 63;   NP 25, 31, 35, 38, 42,
                43, 51, 54, 57;   NS 23;   PH 36, 49;   PT 43, 47,
                59, 68;   RC 46;   SL 23, 42, 43, 44, 45, 46, 48,
                49, 54, 56;   SF 61;   SE 46;   UT 67;   WA 46

23   Var for O Op 31   BN 61, 68(2);   CH 64, 67, 69;
                LA 65;   NP 50;   PH 29, 66;   SL 64

SCHOENFELD, HENRY   10   American Caprice   LA 24
   1857-1956   US   23   C Conc in g Op 80   CH 27
                     20   Impromptus for Str, Meditation and Valse Noble
                             CH 1899
                     30   Symph Pastoral Op 20   CH 1893

SCHOENHERR, Max   6   Perpetuum Mobile Op 29   WA 38
   1903-   Ger

SCHOLZ, Bernard   15   Suite, Wandering Op 74   CH 1894
   1835-1916   Ger   30   Symph B^b Op 60   NP 1885

SCHREIBER, Frederick   24   Conc Grosso for 4 Solo Instruments with O Op 53
   1895-   Aust/US   CH 54
                     13   Sinfonietta in G   DE 49;   PH 49;   SF 66

SCHREIBER, Louis   6   Conc for Cornet   NP 1854
              US   6   Fantasie Cappricioso, Cornet   NP 1860
                      6   Fantasie Stuck, Cornet   NP 1858

SCHREINER, Alexander   21   Conc for Org and O in b   UT 55
   1901   Ger/US

SCHREKER, Franz   25   Chamber Symph in 1 Mvt   NP 22
   or SCHRECKER   4   El's Lullaby from Der Schatzgräber Opera 1920
   1878-1934   Aust   CH 23, 28
                     22   Prelude to a Drama, Vorspiel zu einem Drama 1912
                             BN 21(2), 27;   CH 21, 33;   CT 24;   PH 26
                     11   Suite, Ein Tanzpiel   NS 23
                     21   Suite, The Birthday of the Infanta, Ballet 1923
                             CL 37;   DT 27, 34;   LA 31;   NP 33;   NS 24;
                             PH 28
                     10   Symphon Interlude from Act III of Der Schatzgräber
                             Opera 1920   CH 23

SCHROEDER, William   15   Pan, A Rhaps   PH 26
   1888-   US

SCHUBERT, Franz
1797-1828   Aust

[Orchestras rarely identify Schubert items on their title pages, and even the
program notes do not always give the specific sources or dates or opus
numbers. Since program notes were not available for these tabulations, many
small items such as songs in languages other than German, dances, marches,
minuets, etc., which are not listed in Groves' or other historical sources
cannot be properly identified.]

4	The Bee, arr Stock for O CH 08, 12
	Dances
15	Five German Dances NS 26; PH arr Stokowski 22, 25
10	Four Dances LA 45
10	For Str NP 38, 39
4	No 2 PH 49
4	No 6 in C PH 38, 61, 62
20	Six Dances arr Webern LA 68
30	Divertissiment a l'Hongroise Op 54, Andante-Allegretto CH 1892, 95
	-March CH 1892, 95
8	Fantasy on Praise of Tears NP 1856
17	Fantasia in f Op 103 BN 1885, 86, 95, 02; CH arr Mottl 1892, 95,
	02, 12; LA 33
20	Fantasie in C, The Wanderer for P and O Op 15 BA arr Liszt 66;
	BN 1884, 93, 02; CH 1897, 27; CT 1898; DE 62; DT 21, 56;
	MN 46; NP 1862, 64, 88, 97, 04, 09, 30, 54; NS 21; PT 63;
	SL 21; SF 49; SE 36; UT 50
18	Five Pieces for P CH 69
4	Impromptu Op 90 No 1 CH arr Scholz 02; RC arr for V and P 29
	Marches
5	Funeral March arr Liszt BN 1885, 87, 89, 95, 00; CH 1895(2), 96
2	March Militaire in D Op 41 No 1 BA arr Damrosch 26, 28, 50;
	BU 65; DT 54; HN 37; NP 54; NS arr Damrosch 1896, 12, 25;
	SF 60; UT 57; WA 32
4	Hungarian CH 1892, 95; NP 1912; PH 07, 10, 11
4	In b Op 40 No 3 BN 1883, 84, 94
4	In E^b Op 40 No 1 CH 01, 06, 16
4	Cavalry March arr Liszt CH 1892
4	Traummarsch NS 1882, 89, 93
10	Three Marches Op 40 arr Thomas CH 1893(2)
26	Mass No 6 in E^b (D950) DA 64; SE 64
25	Mass No 2 in G AT 57; BN 50; CL 60; NA 63; NR 60
3	Minuet DT 54
2	Moments Musical in f Op 14 CH 28; CT 45; DT 54
5	Offertorium No 1 Op 46 LA 53
25	Octet Op 166 in F for Str Quart CL 65; SE minuet only 27
	Overtures
7	Alphonso and Estrella, Opera Op 69 BN 1882, 84, 86, 99; CT 31;
	NP 37; SL 55, 61; SF 55
6	In B BN 1888
7	In e 1819 BN 1888, 02; CH 18
6	In Italian Style in C BA 62; CT 52; NA 61; KC 65
6	Romantic Op 34 BA 28; CH arr Kelley 32
9	Fierabras, Opera Op 76 NP 1858; WA 65

SCHUBERT, F. (Cont.)   Overtures (Cont.)
    7   to Des Teufels Lustschloss, Devil's Pleasure Palace Opera 1813
                 MN 28;   NP 66;   WA 65
    8   to Der hausliche Krieg, or Die Verschworenen Opera 1823   SF 64
    4   Psalm 23 for women's Chor Op 132   CH 02;   WA 38
   22   Quartet for Str in d No 14 1824   CH 35
    5   -Andante only   CL 28
    8   -Theme and Var on Death and the Maiden   CH 1891(2), 92, 97(2),
                 00, 06, 25;   NP 1889, 94, 96, 05;   SL 21
   44   Quintet for Str in C Op 163   CH 43;   NS 1881
             -Scherzo and Finale   CH 17, 35
   13   Grand Rondo for V and O in A Op 107 arr Weiner   CL 44;   NA 54;
              NP 34
          Rosamunde Op 26 Opera
   14   -Ballet Music   BA 50;   BN 1881, 82, 85, 88, 94, 99, 00, 30, 49,
                 67;   CL 34, 43;   DA 48;   DT 22, 32, 52, 59;   HN 36, 41;   KC 40
                 NP 12, 28, 29, 50;   NS 23;   PH 05, 13, 14, 18, 19, 21, 22, 23,
                 25, 29, 31, 48;   PT 38;   WA 32, 34, 41, 48
                -in G   CH 1899, 11, 39, 45;   SE 32
                -No 1 and No 2   CT 60
                -No 2   UT 61
    5   -Entr'acte   BN 1885, 89, 91, 94, 00, 08, 21, 49;   DT 18, 22,
                 32, 52, 59;   NP 1881, 12, 50;   NS 23;   PH 41;   WA 38, 41, 48
                -Entr'acte in b   CH 1898, 03, 04, 11, 21, 39;   NP 40;   RC 47, 53
                -Entr'acte in B^b CH 1898, 99, 01, 03, 11;   MN 28, 56;   RC 47, 53
    4   -The Magic Harp   RC 47, 53
   15   -Excerpts   KC 40;   RC 18(2)
                -Interlude and Dances   DT 28
   11   -Overt   BA 28(2), 43;   BN 1884, 87, 93, 96, 09, 52, 60;   BU 63;
                 CH 28, 45;   CT 10, 28, 37, 55, 60;   CL 61, 66;   DA 28, 48, 49;
                 DE 67;   DT 18, 19, 26, 28, 29, 55, 59, 63;   HN 31, 43, 50, 55,
                 69;   NA 57;   KC 55, 58, 64;   LA 61, 66;   MN 28, 46, 54, 56, 58;
                 NR 56, 64;   NP 11, 24, 28, 31;   NS 20, 23;   PH 52, 59;   PT 40,
                 42, 45, 63;   RC 28, 30, 35, 39, 53, 61, 66;   SL 10, 23, 26, 28,
                 32, 35, 39, 46, 47, 51, 58, 59, 61, 62, 67;   SF 44, 49, 60, 64,
                 67;   SE 56, 62, 67;   UT 59, 61;   WA 33, 43
   15   -Suite   MN 60
   20   Sonata for Arpeggione (Guitar-Cello) in a, also titled Conc, 1824
              arr Cassado   KC 38;   MN 38, 46;   NP 52;   SL 37
          Songs
    4   Im abentrot, for male Voices and O 1815   PH 13
    4   Die Allmacht Op 79 No 2   BN 42;   CH 03, 05, 06;   CT 03;
                 CL 22;   DT 21, 22, 23;   LA 28;   NS 1885, 96;   PH 06, 08, 09,
                 13;   SL 29
    4   Am Meer   NP 1888;   NS 1890
    4   An die leier Op 56 No 2   MN 47;   NP 1898;   NS 1888
    4   An die Musik Op 88 No 4   CT 31;   LA 28;   MN 28;   NP 1896;
                 SL 29
    4   An Eine quelle Op 109 No 3   SL 10
    4   An Schwager Kronos Op 19 No 1   CT 03;   NS 96
    4   An Sylvia, Who is Sylvia   BA 42;   CH 1895;   NP 1896;   SL 10
    4   Der Atlas   NP 1899;   SL 32
    4   Auf dem Wasser zu singen   MN 43;   NP 1896
    4   Aufenthalt   LA 28;   NP 1896;   SL 29

SCHUBERT, F. (Cont.) Songs (Cont.)
4   Ave Maria Op 52 No 6   BA 28(2);   CH 12;   CT 12;   HN 38, 43;
         NP 1853, 55;   PH 15;   SL 54;   SF 16
4   Der Doppelgänger 1828   CT 03, 07;   NP 1888;   NS 25;   SL 09
4   Du Bist die Ruh Op 59 No 3   BA 28;   CT 1895, 69;   DT 28;
         MN 31;   NP 1896, 13;   NS 25;   PH 13, 16;   SF 38
4   Der Erlkönig Op 1   BA 28, 43, 49;   CH 08, 26;   CT 1897, 19;
         CL 32;   DA 35;   DT 15, 21, 23, 25, 31, 54;   NA 38;   LA 20,
         28;   MN 49;   NP 1891, 11;   NS 1888, 95, 06(2), 20;   PH 10,
         13, 19;   SL 10, 11, 33;   SF 44
4   Die Forelle, The Trout Op 32   BA 28;   CL 22;   MN 49
4   Frühlingsglaube Op 20 No 2   CT 1895
4   Geheimes Op 14 No 2   PH arr Brahms 13
4   Gesang der Geister uber for male Voices and O   LA 57
4   Greisen gesang arr Brahms   PH 13
4   Grippe an der Tritains   NS 1887
4   Gretchen am Spinnrade Op 2   BA 28;   BU 45;   CH 1891, 93, 08;
         CT 1898, 32;   MN 49;   NP 1887;   NS 1888;   PH 06;   SL 33
4   Heiden roslein   NP 1878
4   Horch, Horch, die Lerch, Hark, Hark, the Lark   BA 42
4   Der Hirt auf dem Felsen, Huntsman, rest! Thy chase is done Op 192
         CH 12;   PH arr Brahms 13
4   Die jung Nonne Op 43 No 1   CH 06, 08;   NP 1888, 98;   NS 15;
         PH 06;   SL 44;   SF 44
4   Der Jüngling an der Quelle   SF 44
4   Der Kreuzzug   NP 1899
4   Kriegers Ahnung   NS 1890
4   Der leierman   CH 1895
4   Liebeslauchen or Liebesborschaft   MN 47, 49
4   Mein!   NP 1889
4   Morgenstandschen   NP 1855
4   Der Mussersohn   SL 11
4   Der Musensohn Op 92 No 1   SL 11
4   Litanei   NS 1896
4   Nachthelle   NP 1860
4   Nachtstuck   NP 1889
4   Neimwan   NS 1879
4   Die Post   NP 1851;   NS 1896;   PH 13
4   Rastlose liebe Op 5 No 1   CH 1895;   NP 12
4   Serenade   CH 1895(2), 25, 28;   WA 43
4   Song of the Harpist   NS 1884
4   Ständchen   NP 1887;   NS 1895;   PH 15;   SF 16, 44;   WA 38
4   Thine is   NP 1851
4   Der Tod und das Mädchen Op 7 No 8   CT 26;   CL 32;   DT 22;
         MN 43, 47, 49;   NP 12;   NS 06, 16;   PH 13
4   Soldier rest, Thy warfare o'er   CH 12
4   Ungeduld   NP 1887;   SL 10
4   Dem Unendlichen   CH 06, 26;   CT 26;   CL 28;   DT 26;   LA 28;
         MN 30;   NS 16;   PH 26;   SL 30
4   Waldenacht   NS 1896
4   Der Wanderer Op 4 No 1   CH 1891;   NP 1862, 87;   NS 1896
4   Warrior's Farewell   NS 1884
4   Wer sich der Einsamkeit ergibt   NS 1893
4   Wiegenleider   SL 09
4   Wohin   LA 28;   PH 16
4   Der Zweig   NP 1896

SCHUBERT, F. (Cont.) Songs (Cont.)
  20   Five Songs arr Webern   BU 66
   8   Songs   NS 1897

  37   Symph in E, sketch   CL 28
  26   Symph No 1   CL 66;   NA 60;   MN 64
  24   Symph No 2 in B^b 1815 (D 125)   BA 39, 59;   BN 44, 49, 59, 66;
           CH 60;   CT 42, 62;   CL 51;   DA 57, 63;   DT 65;   HN 55;
           NA 55, 58, 63;   KC 44, 64;   LA 28, 41, 46, 50;   MN 42, 55;
           NR 52, 55, 57, 60;   NP 36, 37, 39, 40, 49, 51, 53, 64;   PH 40;
           PT 50, 51, 53;   RC 59;   SL 52, 61;   SF 53, 67;   SE 53, 63
  23   Symph No 3 in D 1815 (D 200)   AT 67;   BN 56, 63;   CT 49, 50;
           CL 62, 64, 68;   DA 67;   DE 68;   DT 59;   KC 51, 69;   LA 56,
           63;   MN 60, 66;   NP 30, 33, 40, 61;   PH 37, 42, 49, 51, 65;
           PT 57, 59, 61, 68;   RC 61;   SF 56, 61;   SE 59
  25   Symph No 4 in c Tragic 1816   BA 37, 48;   BN 20, 28, 50, 60, 64;
           BU 64;   CH 61, 64;   CT 35;   CL 62, 69;   DE 67;   DT 62;
           LA 49, 52;   ML 68;   MN 60;   NR 62;   NP 34, 38, 39, 41, 60;
           PH 27, 61;   PT 55;   RC 28, 51;   SL 33, 40, 50;   SF 39, 41,
           57, 60;   SE 58, 66;   WA 40, 45
           -Andante   BN 1883, 84, 87;   DA 48
           -Scherzo   BA 28
  32   Symph No 5 in B^b 1816 (D 485)   AT 69;   BA 67;   BN 1882, 07, 24,
           28, 47, 52, 54, 58, 61, 65, 68;   BU 43, 50, 66;   CH 42, 46,
           54, 58, 59, 63, 68;   CT 33, 41, 47, 59, 68;   CL 49, 66, 69;
           DA 54, 56, 62;   DE 53, 64, 69;   HN 49, 53, 58;   NA 59;
           LA 38, 43, 51;   ML 64;   MN 35, 43, 50, 57, 61;   NP 37, 41, 47,
           56(2), 62, 65;   NS 27;   PH 05, 51;   PT 52, 59, 62, 65;
           RC 37, 49, 58, 66;   SL 45, 46, 54, 59, 60, 64;   SF 16, 46, 54,
           59, 62;   SE 28, 54, 68;   UT 56, 65;   WA 33, 60
   8   -Scherzo   WA 39
  25   Symph No 6 in C (D 589)   BN 1884, 85, 62, 66;   CH 56;   CT 64;
           CL 52, 67;   LA 57;   ML 68;   MN 45;   NP 66;   PT 56, 66;
           RC 45, 52;   SF 58, 66;   UT 67;   WA 56
  24   Symph No 8 in b Unfinished 1822 (D 759)   AT 49, 59, 67, 69;
           BA 28, 40, 43, 49, 55, 67;   BN 1881, 82, 83, 85, 86, 87, 88, 89,
           90, 91, 92, 94, 95, 96, 97, 99, 01, 03, 05, 06, 08, 11, 13, 16,
           18, 19, 23, 24, 28, 33, 35, 39, 42, 54, 57, 59, 62, 66;
           BU 49, 63, 69;   CH 1891, 93, 95, 96, 97, 98, 99, 00, 01, 02, 03,
           04, 05, 06, 07, 08, 09, 10, 11, 12, 14, 17, 18, 19, 21, 22, 27,
           28, 31, 35, 40, 42, 45, 52, 53, 54, 57, 59, 62, 64;
           CT 1895, 98, 99, 02, 07, 10, 12, 16, 20, 22, 25, 27, 28, 29, 34,
           36, 37, 39, 41, 43, 45, 46, 51, 58, 60, 65, 69;
           CL 18, 20, 21, 24, 25, 26, 27, 28, 30, 41, 43, 47, 50, 54, 58, 59,
           61, 65, 69;   DA 37, 46, 50, 52, 58;   DE 45, 47, 52, 58, 65, 68;
           DT 14, 17, 18, 22, 26, 33, 36, 38, 45, 48, 51, 53, 57, 61, 63;
           HN 32, 35, 38, 54, 58, 61;   NA 31, 40, 50, 64;
           KC 33, 36, 40, 43, 47, 50, 61;
           LA 19, 20, 21, 27, 39, 51, 55, 57, 64;
           MN 25, 27, 34, 43, 48, 53, 57, 59, 60;   NR 56, 58, 61, 63, 66;
           NP 1868, 70, 75, 80, 86, 90, 96, 99, 03, 08, 09, 10, 12, 15, 16,
           17, 18, 19, 22, 23, 25, 28, 30, 31, 41, 49, 54, 56, 59, 63, 67;
           NS 1878, 88, 03, 09, 10, 12(2), 15, 17, 18, 20, 21, 23, 25;
           PH 04, 06, 07, 08, 09, 10, 11(2), 12, 13(2), 15, 17, 18, 19, 20,
           21, 22, 23, 24, 25, 27, 28, 29, 31, 32, 33, 34, 36, 38, 41, 44,
           47, 50, 52, 53, 56, 57, 60, 63, 67, 69

SCHUBERT, F. (Cont.)   Symph No 8 (Cont.)
          PT 39, 41, 49, 52, 54, 65, 67;   RC 23, 24, 25, 36, 37, 39, 41,
          46, 50, 58, 63;   SL 09, 13, 16, 18, 19, 21, 23, 24, 25, 27,
          31, 34, 38, 42, 43, 55, 56, 58, 61, 66, 68;   SF 11, 12, 14, 17,
          27, 29, 30, 33, 38, 43, 50, 51, 63;   SE 37, 50, 61, 67;
          UT 41, 44, 46, 49, 52, 63;
          WA 31, 33, 35, 37, 39, 40, 44, 47, 51, 61, 67, 69
    8   -Allegro   NS 84
   12   -First and Second mvts   AT 65
    6   -First mvt   DA 28, 49;   MN 48
   50   Symph No 9 sometimes numbered 7 or 10 in C, the Great, 1828, (D944)
          AT 68;   BA 41, 49, 51, 60;
          BN 1881, 82, 84, 86, 88, 90, 91, 93, 94, 96, 98, 00, 02, 04, 05,
          06, 08, 10, 12, 14, 16, 19, 21, 28, 32, 34, 38, 39, 41, 42, 46,
          49, 53, 55, 58, 69;   BU 46, 51, 52, 54, 55, 57, 60, 62, 68;
          CH 1891, 94, 95, 96, 98, 00, 02, 04, 07, 10, 13, 15, 18, 19, 20,
          23, 26, 28, 30, 31, 34, 36, 38, 40, 41, 44, 46, 48, 50, 52, 53,
          54, 57, 60, 62, 65, 68;
          CT 1896, 06, 09, 13, 16, 21, 23, 25, 28, 32, 38, 40, 46, 48, 52,
          54, 58, 61, 63, 66;   CL 20, 29, 32, 35, 41, 43, 45, 46, 48, 50,
          52, 57, 59, 61, 64, 67, 69;   DA 46, 48, 50, 55, 57, 60, 63;
          DE 49, 56, 60, 63, 66;
          DT 19, 23, 27, 30, 33, 40, 41, 54, 60, 64, 67, 68;
          HN 36, 39, 42, 45, 48, 51, 52, 53, 59, 61, 64, 68;
          NA 34, 47, 57, 59, 62, 65;   KC 43, 45, 48, 52(2), 66;
          LA 27, 28, 33, 37, 41, 44, 46, 48, 51, 53, 55, 56, 58, 61, 62, 66;
          ML 61, 67;   MN 22, 28, 31, 32, 35, 38, 41, 44, 49, 51, 53, 55,
          58, 61, 63, 68;   NR 50, 54, 57, 64, 68;
          NP 1850, 52, 59, 61, 63, 67, 71, 77, 79, 81, 83, 89, 95, 06, 10,
          11, 12, 13, 14, 16, 21, 23, 24, 28, 30, 32, 35, 38, 39, 42, 45,
          50, 51, 56, 61, 63, 66;
          NS 1880, 84, 87, 91, 93, 96, 07, 09, 13, 15, 18, 19, 22, 23, 26;
          PH 02, 04, 06, 08, 10, 11, 12, 14, 17, 19, 20, 22, 24, 27, 28, 29,
          30, 33, 35, 36, 40, 41, 43, 45, 46, 47, 48, 51, 55, 57, 59, 63, 66;
          PT 45, 47, 49, 53, 58, 60, 62, 65, 69;
          RC 27, 33, 42, 46, 48, 50, 53, 55, 57, 62, 65, 68;
          SL 11, 14, 17, 22, 28, 35, 37, 39, 42, 47, 49, 51, 54, 55, 58,
          62, 67, 69;
          SF 15, 19, 22, 25, 26, 28, 31, 32, 37, 40, 44, 46, 48, 52, 55, 58,
          62, 63, 65, 67, 68;
          SE 33, 46, 57, 65;   UT 48, 57, 61;
          WA 38, 44, 50, 55, 58, 64, 69

SCHULLER, Gunther   12   American Tryptich, Three Studies in Texture 1964
    1925-   US   CT 65;   LA 67;   NR 64;   SF 66
                     12   Composition in Three Parts, 1962   MN 62;   PH 68
                     19   Concertina for Jazz Quart and O   CT 60;   MN 60
                     15   Conc for Horn and O 1944   CT 44
                     25   Conc for Double Bass and Chamber O   NP 67
                     20   P Conc 1962   CT 62
                     23   Contours   CT 59
                     12   Diptych for Brass Quint and O   BN 66;   CL 67
                      9   Dramatic Overt   CT 58;   LA 61;   NP 56
                     14   Five Bagatelles   BU 67;   RC 65;   SL 67
                     12   Gala Music 1965   CH 65

SCHULLER, G. (Cont.)   23   Seven Studies on Themes of Paul Klee 1959   AT 63,
                               67;   BN 63;   CH 64;   CT 67;   CL 60, 64;
                               DA 62;   DE 64;   DT 65;   MN 59, 64;   ML 69; LA 66;
                               NP 67;   NR 65;   PH 64;   PT 63, 67;   SL 66;
                               RC 63;   SF 67; SE 65;   UT 67;   WA 60, 63
                       12   Shapes and Designs   AT 69;   RC 69
                       23   Spectra   BN 69;   CL 65;   NP 59;   MN 69
                       30   Symph No 1 1964   DA 64
                       20   Symph   MN 65
                       18   Symph for Brass and Percussion BA 68;   CL 62;   NP 56

SCHUMAN, William   9   American Festival Overt 1939   BA 62;   BN 39, 48;
1910-   US   CH 39, 48;   DE 46;   DT 68;   NA 54;   LA 56;
                               MN 42, 54, 58;   NR 61;   NP 42, 47, 58;   PT 41,
                 62;   SL 41, 46;   SF 40, 48, 50;   WA 40, 41, 49, 63;   UT 69
        8   Circus Overt, Side Show for O 1944   CH 44;   CL 44, 49;   NA 45;
            LA 60;   MN 48;   PT 44, 60;   UT 47;   WA 52
       26   V Conc 1946   BN 49;   BU 65;   CT 61;   MN 59
       18   Credendum 1956   BN 56;   BU 61;   CH 63;   MN 57, 60;   NP 56, 64;
            PH 55, 57;   SF 57, 64, 69;   SL 69;   WA 61
       22   A Free Song, Cantata No 2 1942   BN 42;   LA 43;   MN 47;   WA 51, 55
       17   In Praise of Shahn, Canticle for O   NP 69
        4   Jubilee Var on a Theme by Goossens 1945   CT 45, 54
       50   Judith, Coreographic Poem 1949   BA 52; DA 54;   DT 52;   NP 55;   SE 69
       13   New England Triptych   BN 59;   CT 59, 66, 68;   CL 56;   DE 56;
            HN 62;   NA 59;   KC 58;   LA 56, 59;   MN 56, 67;   NR 57, 64;
            NP 52;   PH 65;   PT 58;   RC 56;   SF 56, 61;   UT 60;   WA 60, 65
        8   Newsreel in Five Shots 1941   MN 57
       15   Prayer in Time of War 1943   BN 44; DE 50;   NR 54;   NP 42;   PH 46;
            PT 42, 43
       20   A Song of Orpheus, Fantasy for C and O   BA 65;   BN 65;   CL 63;
            DE 61;   HN 63;   NA 61
       20   Symph No 2 One mvt 1937   BA 39;   BN 38
       30   Symph No 3 1941   BN 41, 47, 62;   BU 62;   CH 48, 62;   CT 52;   CL 51;
            DT 45;   HN 67;   MN 49;   NP 44, 60, 63;   PH 50;   SF 42, 47, 63
       24   Symph No 4 1941   BU 47;   CL 41;   PH 41
       17   Symph No 5 for Str 1943   BN 43;   CH 59;   CT 59, 68;   CL 61;
            DA 59;   HN 68;   MN 60;   NR 59;   NP 59, 66;   SL 52, 63
       24   Symph No 6 1948   DA 48;   NP 57;   PH 51, 53
       26   Symph No 7 1960   BN 60;   PH 67
       30   Symph No 8   NP 62;   SF 65
       23   Symph No 9   AT 69;   PH 68
       15   To the Old Cause, Evocation for Oboe, Brass, Trump and Str   NP 68
       25   Undertow, Ballet 1945   KC 61;   LA 45;   NP 46
        8   William Billings Overt 1943   BA 50;   CT 54;   NP 43

SCHUMANN, George   150   Amor and Psyche, for Chor and O Op 3
1866-1925   Ger   -Dance of Nymphs and Satyrs   CH 05, 10, 13, 17,
                               21, 28, 30, 34;   CL 34;   LA 20, 21;   PH 32,
                               58;   SF 26, 29;   WA 39
                       15   Liebesfrühling, The Dawn of Love Op 28   BN 02;
                         CH 1895(2), 06, 07, 08, 09, 10, 11, 13, 14, 16,
                         17, 20, 21, 22, 23, 25, 29, 31, 36, 40;   NS 06;
                         PH 03, 05;   SL 11, 22, 24;

SCHUMANN, G. (Cont.)   20   Humoreske in Var Op 74   CH 33
                        21   In Carnival Time Op 22 Overt   BN 03;   PH 05
                        15   Overt to a Drama Op 45   CH 10
                        15   Overt Lebensfreude, The Joy of Living   CH 11, 12
                        10   Ruth, Oratorio Op 50 Three Choruses   CH 09
                        25   Serenade Op 34   CH 06, 29
                              -Two Excerpts   CH 06
                        24   Var on Chorale, Wer den lieben Gott Op 24   BN 01,
                              16;   CH 00
                        16   Var and Double Fugue on a Merry Theme Op 30
                              BN 06;   CH 03, 05, 08;   CT 07;   NS 03(2), 08,
                              17;   PH 04;   SF 16
                        32   Var and Gigue on Handel Theme, Op 72   CH 26, 30

SCHUMANN, Robert   4   Abendlied Op 85 No 12 arr Stock   CH 24;   CT 1896;
1810-1856   Ger   NA 36;   NS arr Saint Saens 13
                        12   Andante and Var for Two P Op 46   NP 1848
      4   Arabesque C for P Op 18   NP 1874
      4   Bride of Messina Op 100 Overt   BN 1882;   CH 1898, 10;   MN 37
     25   Carnaval for P Op 9 arr for O Liadov, Glazounov, Rimsky-Korsakoff
           and Tcherepnine   BN 38;   CT 38, 44, 45;   HN 50
     31   P Conc in A Op 54
           AT 48, 51, 56, 58, 68;   BA 45, 49, 53, 57, 61, 69;
           BN 1882, 87, 89, 96, 00, 02, 04, 05, 11, 12, 13, 16, 20, 22, 24,
           27, 39, 47, 52, 58, 63;   BU 47, 51, 54, 59, 60;
           CH 1897, 02, 04, 10, 11, 12, 14, 15, 19, 20, 22, 23, 24, 26, 27,
           31(2), 34, 40, 42, 46, 51, 53, 57, 58, 62, 66, 68;
           CT 1897, 00, 11, 12, 14, 16, 19, 23, 26, 28, 30, 31, 32, 35, 37,
           41, 45, 48, 52, 54, 57, 59, 66, 69;   CL 19, 20, 22, 27, 30, 39,
           46, 47, 53, 59, 62, 63, 66;   DA 28, 34, 53, 57, 60, 66;
           DE 50, 53, 56, 59, 63, 66, 69;
           DT 22, 23, 26, 27, 29, 31, 34, 41, 45;
           HN 35, 39, 44, 47, 48, 50, 52, 56;
           NA 39, 47, 52, 56, 60, 62, 68;   KC 33, 34, 38, 47, 52, 57, 64;
           LA 21, 22, 23, 28, 30, 33, 39, 52, 54, 57, 60, 67;   ML 69;
           MN 22, 24, 28, 30, 31, 39, 42, 44, 45, 47, 54, 56, 59, 61;
           NR 56, 60, 63;
           NP 1858, 60, 67, 71, 74, 78, 80, 82, 85, 90, 08, 14, 17, 19, 20,
           22, 23, 24, 25, 27, 33, 40, 47, 48, 50, 51, 53, 55, 57, 58, 60,
           62, 63, 66, 69;   NS 1892, 03, 07, 12, 13, 19(2), 23, 24, 25(2),
           26, 27;   PH 02, 03, 04, 06, 07, 10, 13, 15, 20, 21, 24, 26, 33, 36,
           42, 44, 45, 47, 52, 54, 55, 62, 63, 64, 67;
           PT 38, 39, 41, 46, 55, 56, 59, 61, 66;
           RC 24, 28, 31, 34, 48, 55, 58, 63, 69;
           SL 12, 14, 17, 22, 23, 26, 27, 28, 31, 34, 35, 37, 41, 42, 44, 45,
           48, 51, 52, 55, 56, 57, 58, 65;
           SF 17, 21, 25, 30, 36, 42, 45, 49, 54, 59, 60, 62, 63, 66, 68;
           SE 30, 35, 36, 60;   UT 55, 59, 67;
           WA 37, 47, 50, 56, 65, 67, 69
      8   -First Mvt only   CT 64
     33   V Concerto in d Op Posth   BN 37, 60;   CL 48;   LA 38;   MN 39,   67;
           NP 37, 67;   PH 37;   SL 37
     22   C Conc in a Op 129   BA 44, 48, 67;
           BN 1887, 95, 10, 19, 30, 41, 43, 57, 66;   BU 60, 66;
           CH 10, 14, 24, 35, 38, 44, 55, 58, 61, 66, 68;   CT 19, 36, 62;

SCHUMANN, R. (Cont.)
      SONGS in GERMAN
4   Der Arme Peter Op 53 No 3   NP 1899
4   Brautgesange   CT 19;   LA 20
4   Dichter liebe Op 48   NP 1848, 49, 56, 1930;   NS 24, 25
4   Du bist wie eine Blume Op 25 No 24   NA 36;   SL 11
4   Er Ist's Op 79 No 23   CH 05
4   Fluten reicher Ebro Op 138 No 5   NS 1884
4   Fruhlings nacht Op 39 No 12   KC 40
4   Die beiden Grenadiere Op 49 No 1   CH 1891;   CT 21, 31;   DT 52;
      MN 49;   NS 1887
4   Der Hidalgo Op 30 No 3   NP 1898;   SL 11
4   Ich grolle nicht Op 48 No 7   CH 1893;   CT 03;   NS 1881
4   Ich Kann's nicht fassen Op 42 No 3   NP 46
4   In der Fremde Op 39 No 8   NS 1894
4   Die Lorerley Op 53 No 2   NS 1888
4   Die Lotusblume Op 25 No 7   CT 02;   SL 10
4   Mein Herz ist schwer Op 25 No 15   NP 00
4   Mit Myrthen und Rosen Op 24 No 9   CT 1895
4   Mond nacht Op 39 No 5   NP 46
4   Der Nussbaum Op 25 No 3   CH 05;   MN 27;   PH 08
4   Du Ring an meinem Finger Op 42 No 4   NS 1881
4   Der Sandmann Op 79 No 12   SL 10
4   Stille Tranen Op 35 No 10   SL 10(2)
4   Walddesgespricht Op 33 No 3   NS 1894
4   Widmung Op 25 No 7   AT 50;   CH 1893;   CT 04;   NP 20;   NS 1888

      SYMPHONIES
30   No 1 Spring in B^b Op 38
      BA 28, 62;   BN 1881, 84, 86, 88, 89, 90, 91, 92, 93, 95, 97, 99,
      01, 03, 05, 09, 11, 15, 17, 19, 21, 26(2), 28, 29, 30, 32, 35,
      37, 39, 42, 44, 47, 50, 56, 59, 66;   BU 54;   CH 1892, 95, 98,
      00, 02, 03, 05, 07, 10, 13, 16, 17, 18, 19, 22, 24, 27, 29, 36, 44,
      50, 51, 52, 53, 55, 61, 63, 66;   CT 1896, 03, 06, 12, 21, 25, 27,
      31, 32, 35, 40, 53, 58, 64;   CL 23, 28, 35, 38, 39, 42, 45, 48,
      51, 54, 56, 58, 62, 67;   DA 49, 60, 63, 68;   DE 50;   DT 18, 21,
      27, 29, 32, 54, 57, 68;   HN 31, 40, 46, 50, 53;   NA 33, 50, 52,
      58, 64;   KC 40, 45, 52, 58;   LA 22, 23, 31, 48, 52, 56, 62;
      ML 68;   MN 22, 32, 42, 43, 56, 61;   NR 58;   NP 1852, 59, 62,
      64, 67, 73, 79, 82, 86, 90, 95, 02, 11, 14, 18, 20, 23, 25, 31,
      32, 34, 38, 40, 45, 46, 49, 53, 54, 55;   NS 1885, 91, 96, 05,
      07, 08, 09, 10, 13, 16, 22;   PH 01, 03, 05, 07, 08, 10, 13, 15,
      17, 27, 28, 38, 41, 46, 57, 66;   PT 40, 44, 52, 57;   RC 26, 48,
      56, 59;   SL 12, 20, 23, 28;   SF 15, 20, 30, 38, 53, 55, 59, 65;
      SE 42, 48, 54, 63;   UT 54, 61;   WA 49, 50
30   -Mahler Version   PH 33
8   -Finale   MN 45
34   No 2 in C Op 61
      BA 56, 67;   BN 1881, 85, 87, 88, 90, 92, 94, 96, 98, 00, 02, 04,
      09, 11, 18, 20, 29, 36, 44, 45, 46, 52, 55, 58, 65, 67;   BU 63;
      CH 1891, 94, 96, 98, 00, 02, 04, 08, 11, 14, 33, 38, 49, 55, 57,
      60, 62, 66;   CT 1898, 10, 14, 16, 18, 23, 34, 37, 39, 42, 45, 62,
      69;   CL 32, 36, 37, 39, 48, 50, 52, 56, 60, 65, 68;   DA 46, 63;
      DE 48, 53, 62, 64, 65, 68;   DT 24, 29, 55, 58, 62, 66;   HN 33,
      47, 48, 51, 55, 69;   KC 53, 59;   LA 30, 47, 51, 54, 58, 67;
      ML 66;   MN 36, 37, 40, 47, 50, 54, 61, 63;   NR 62, 65, 69;

Time in
Minutes
SCHUMANN, R. (Cont.)   Symph No 2 in C (Cont.)
                        NP 1853, 56, 60, 63, 66, 69, 72, 76, 80, 83, 85,
                        89, 92, 98, 06, 10, 15, 32, 35, 38, 41, 46, 47,
                        49, 50, 54, 55, 56, 61, 62, 63, 66, 67, 68;
                        NS 1878;   PH 02, 05, 12, 13, 15, 19, 22, 24, 30,
                        31, 33, 36, 38, 44, 47, 48, 52, 56, 58, 62, 64,
                        68, 69;   PT 45, 49, 50, 55, 59, 64, 66, 68;
                        RC 33, 45, 46, 54, 57, 61, 69;   SL 10, 14, 19,
                        37, 40, 41, 45, 49, 53, 57, 62, 65;   SF 18, 39,
                        46, 49, 57, 61, 66;   SE 60;   WA 49, 57, 69
       8   -Adagio Expressione   CT 50
       8   -Second mvt   MN 47
     31   No 3 Rhenish in E^b Op 97
                        AT 50;   BA 59;   BN 1883, 84, 87, 89, 91, 92, 96,
                        98, 00, 04, 10, 16, 19, 22, 28, 31, 43, 51, 54,
                        64;   BU 65;   CH 1893, 97, 99, 01, 03, 06, 12,
                        36, 41, 48, 53, 54, 56, 57, 59, 63, 69;   CT 99,
                        14, 17, 20, 30, 33, 44, 49, 63;   CL 38, 43, 48,
                        52, 54, 57, 60, 62, 66;   DA 48, 54;   DE 69;
                        DT 22, 51, 56, 58, 67;   KC 55, 63;   LA 35, 40,
                        43, 51, 54, 68;   MN 35, 37, 41, 44, 46, 48, 53,
                        66;   NR 64;   NP 1860, 65, 70, 74, 78, 81, 84,
                        89, 93, 10, 12, 24, 30, 33, 35, 40, 49, 51, 53,
                        62, 68;   NS 1890, 95, 06, 09(2), 14;   PH 05, 11,
                        14, 16, 33, 47, 51, 56, 60, 63;   PT 41, 46, 51,
                        60;   RC 25, 37, 40, 52;   SL 11, 26, 30, 51, 59;
                        SF 14, 24, 40, 44, 48, 51, 55, 60, 68;   SE 57,
                        66;   UT 52
       8   -Third mvt   PT 53
     25   No 4 in d Op 120   AT 69;   BA 38, 55, 56, 58,
                        62;   BN 1882, 84, 86, 89, 90, 91, 93, 94, 96,
                        97, 99, 01, 03, 05, 08, 10, 12, 14, 18, 20, 23,
                        25, 27, 34, 36, 37, 38, 40, 47, 49, 50, 51, 54,
                        56, 60, 62;   BU 51, 53, 55, 58, 61, 68;
                        CH 1891, 94, 96, 97, 99, 01, 03, 04, 07, 08, 09,
                        12, 13, 15, 16, 17, 18, 21, 23, 25, 31, 33, 35,
                        43, 44, 45, 46, 54, 55, 59, 60, 65;   CT 1895,
                        96, 01, 04, 07, 11, 13, 15, 31, 36, 43, 45, 46,
                        47, 51, 57, 61, 67, 69;   DA 35, 58, 61, 64, 67;
                        DE 51, 56, 66;   DT 16, 17, 19, 23, 26, 29, 34,
                        36, 38, 41, 45, 48, 51, 53, 57, 60, 61, 64;
                        HN 44, 49, 52;   NA 38, 46, 54, 66;   KC 34, 44,
                        50, 54, 55, 69;   LA 30, 33, 45, 49, 50, 53, 59,
                        61, 63, 68;   MN 27, 33, 36, 39, 43, 46, 50, 62,
                        68;   NR 53, 56;   NP 1858, 61, 65, 68, 71, 75,
                        83, 87, 90, 96, 99, 05, 09, 23, 24, 30, 31, 37,
                        38, 42, 43, 44, 47, 49, 50, 56, 59, 60, 61, 64,
                        65, 66;   NS 1880, 82, 84, 86, 93, 95, 07, 11(2),
                        13, 15, 18, 24, 27;   PH 01, 04, 06, 12, 14, 16,
                        18, 21, 23, 27, 29, 35, 42, 52, 59, 60, 62, 63,
                        65;   PT 37, 42, 47, 49, 51, 54, 65;   RC 30, 38,
                        58, 67;   SL 09, 22, 56, 57, 60, 61;   SF 17, 23,
                        25, 31, 45, 47, 50, 52, 59, 63;   SE 49, 55, 64,
                        68;   UT 48, 64, 69;   WA 49, 52, 59, 62, 67
     30   -arr Mahler   CT 28;   CL 34, 41, 47, 48, 51, 54,
                        55, 56, 59, 61, 64, 69;   PH 32, 33, 34

SCHUMANN, R. (Cont.) Symph No 4 in d Op 120 (Cont.)
    30   -arr Stock   CH 21, 22, 23, 25, 30
    30   -Original Version   BN 1891;   CT 29;   NP 1891, 52, 55, 60
     4   Toccata in c arr L. Damrosch Op 7   NS 1894
    10   Three Pieces in Canon Form   BN 22
     4   Traumerei Op 15 No 7   CH 1893, 96, 02;   CT 1895;   HN 31; NA 33; NS 09

SCHUTT, Edward   30   P Conc in f No 2 Op 47   BN 1896, 99
1856- 1933   Aust

SCHUTZ, Heinrich   30   The Annunciation   Mezzo-Sopr, Tenor, Chor and O
1585-1672   Ger   CT 63
                   30   Christmas Story Sopr, Tenor, Bass, Chor and O
                        CT 63

SCHUYTEN, Ernest   35   Symph in f   NR 50
1881-   Belg/US

SCHYTTE, Ludwig   30   P Conc in c# Op 28   CH 09;   CT 06;   SL 10
1848-1909 Ger/Dan   6   Loch Lomond   CT 1896

SCLAVOS,
 see SKLAVOS

SCOTT, Cyril   24   P Conc in d Op 5   CH 20
1879-1959   Brit   25   P Conc in C 1915   DT 20;   PH 20
                   12   Festival Overt   SE 37
                    4   The Jasmine Door.Song   CT 43;   SL 41
                    4   Lotus Eaters Op 47 No 1   NP 55
                    4   Lullaby, Song Op 57 No 2   CT 37
                   10   Noel, Christmas Overt and Nativity Hymn for Chor
                        and O 1913   CT 32
                    7   Two Passacaglias on Irish Themes 1916   BN 20;
                        CH 20;   CT 33;   PH 20
                   16   Tropic Ballet   DT 34;   KC 33;   PH 20

SCRIABIN, Alexander 28   P Conc in f# Op 20   CT 07;   LA 25
1872-1915   Russ   38   The Poem Divine, Symph No 3 Op 43   BN 23, 25, 37,
                        39, 65;   CH 22, 23, 24, 25, 27, 28, 30, 35, 41;
                        CT 33; CL 33, 39;   DT 20(2), 21, 27, 34;
                        LA 30;   MN 34;   NP 34; NS 21, 27;   PH 15,
                        16, 27, 30, 39;   RC 26;   WA 37
                   24   The Poem of Ecstasy Op 54   AT 69;   BN 10, 17, 20,
                        24, 26, 28, 31, 33, 35, 38, 46, 60;   CH 20, 23,
                        33, 36;   CT 23, 32, 50;   CL 22, 24, 25, 30, 37,
                        66;   DA 62, 69;   DT 24, 66;   HN 58;   LA 24,
                        25, 26, 37, 47, 65;   ML 64;   MN 28, 29, 36, 49,
                        66;   NR 50;   NP 56, 64(2);   NS 20, 21, 23, 24;
                        PH 17(2), 18, 32, 63;   RC 23, 27, 63, 69;   SL 26,
                        32;   SF 37, 43, 47
                   25   Prometheus, Poem of Fire with P, Org, Chor and
                        Color Keyboard Op 60   BN 24, 41;   CH 14, 30, 37;
                        MN 69;   NP 52;   PH 21, 30, 31;   RC 30, 67
                    3   Reverie in E Op 24   CT 00;   RC 28
                   45   Symph No 1 in E with Soli, Chor and O Op 26   NP 07

SCRIABIN, A. (Cont.)
	50	Symph No 2 in c Op 29 BN 68; CH 69; DT 20; NP 68; WA 49
	4	Two Etudes arr Spier Op 2 No 1 in c# WA 40, 43, 46
	4	-Op 8 No 12 in d# WA 40, 46

SEARLE, Humphrey   20   Symph No 2 Op 33   LA 62;   SF 65
1915-   Eng

SEAY, Virginia   8   Theme, Var and Fugue for O   MN 45
             US

SEEBOECK, Wm. Chas.   20   P Conc No 2 in d   CH 1894
1859-1907   US

SEIBER, Matyas   8   Notturno for Horn and Str O 1944   MN 59
1905-1960 Hung/Brit

SEKLES, Bernhard   17   Gesichte, Phantastische Miniaturen for small O
1872-1934   Ger   Op 29   PH 24

SELMER, Johan Peter   10   Carnival of Flanders Op 32   CH 1894
1844-1910   Nor

SEMMLER, Alexander   6   Overt, Times Square   BA 41
             US   4   Serenade for Str   BA 40

SEREBRIER, Jose   8   Elegy for Str   MN 59
1938-   Hung/Urag   8   Fantasia for Str O   CL 69
                         28   Partita 1960   WA 60
                         20   Sinfonia No 1 for large O   HN 57

SERLY, Tibor   6   American Elegy   NP 51
1900-   Hung/US   11-12   Six Dance Designs   PH 35
                         18   Symph No 1 in three mvts   PH 36

SERVAIS, Adrian   20   Fantasia for C, Le Desir   CH 1891
1807-1866   Belg   5   Fantasia for C, Grand   NP 1858
                          5   Fantasia for C, O Cara Memoria   CH 1892

SESSIONS, Roger   35   V Conc in b 1935   BN 65;   MN 47;   NP 58;   SF 67
1896-   US   23   The Black Maskers,O Suite 1928   AT 67;   BN 54;
                               CH 63;   CT 30, 62;   CL 62;   DT 64;   LA 33;
                               MN 55;   PH 58, 59;   PT 61;   SF 41;   SE 63;
                               UT 64
                         10   Psalm 140 for Sopr and O   BN 65
                         18   Str Quart No 2 in e 1936   SF 65
                         22   Symph No 1 in e 1926   BN 26;   PH 35
                         25   Symph No 2 1946   CT 59;   NP 49;   SF 46, 66
                         32   Symph No 3 1957   BN 57;   CH 65
                         24   Symph No 4 1959   MN 59;   PT 65
                         30   Symph No 5   PH 63
                         25   Symph No 7   CH 67

SEVERN, Edmund   25   V Conc for V in d   NP 15
1862-1942 Brit/US

SEVERN, Thomas   4   Lullaby   DA 38
1801-1881   Brit

SEVITZKY, Fabian   5   To Old Glory   NA 42
1893-1969 Russ/US

SGAMBATI, Gioccomo   35   P Conc in g Op 15   BN 1890;   CH 08;   CL 23
1841-1914   It   40   Symph in D Op 16   BN 1894, 97, 12;   CH 18;
                                 CT 1897, 10;   PH 08
                          8   -Serenade   NS 11
                          10   Te Deum Laudamus   Str O and Org Op 28   BN 10;
                                 CH 1894

SHANNON, James R.   8   Week End Suite, Sunrise on Sabbath and Aftermath
1881-1946   US   on Monday Morning   HN 41

SHAPERO, Harold S.   11   Overt, The Travelers   HN 48
1920-   US   17   Partita in C for P and small O   DT 60;   SE 61
                          40   Symph in B^b for Classical O 1946   BN 47;   CL 48
                          8   -Adagietto   NP 49, 66

SHAPEY, Ralph   20   Rituals for Symph O 1965   NP 65
1921-   US

SHAPORIN, Yury A.   40   Symph in c for Chor and O Op 11   BN 36
1889-   Russ

SHAW, Arti   7   Fantasy on 3 American Songs arr Shaw   WA 50
1910-   US

SHAW, Martin   4   Gloria in Excelsis   MN 44
1875-1958   Brit

SHAW, Robert   8   Arr of Plain Song   AT 48
1916-   US

SHELLEY, Harry R.   15   Symphon Poem, Francesca de Rimini   CH 1891
1858-   US

SHEPHERD, Arthur   27   Choreographic Suite 1931   CL 31;   LA 32
1880-1958   US   18   Fantasy on a Garden Hymn P and O 1916   BN 20;
                                 CL 20;   NA Dance Episode 43
                          10   Fantasy on Down East Spirituals 1946   CL 47;
                                 NA 46;   MN 48
                          6   Festival of Youth, Overt 1915   SL 15
                          10   The Lone Prarie Suite two mvts   NA 37
                          12   Overt to a Drama 1919   CL 23, 24, 41, 49;   UT 48
                          20   Song of the Pilgrims, Cantata 1937   CL 37;   NA 38
                          41   Symph No 1 Horizons 1927   CL 27, 29, 30, 36, 53;
                                 DT 45;   NP 32;   UT 52
                          40   Symph No 2 in d 1938   BN 40;   CL 39
                          20   Theme and Var 1956   CL 56

SHERRIF, Noam   12   Festival Prelude   PT 58
              Is

SHIFRIN, Seymour   10   The Modern Temper   SF 67
1926-   US   17   3 Pieces for O 1951   MN 51

SHILKRET, Nathaniel 10   Creation for Narrator, Chor and O 1942   UT 46
1895-   US

SHOSTAKOVICH, Dmitri 20   Ballet Suite No 1 in Six mvts Op 84   NR 58
1906-   Russ 22   Conc for P, Str and Trump Op 35   CT 46;   DE 47,
                               62;   LA 35;   ML 62;   MN 44;   NP 35, 46;
                               PH 46;   PT 47;   SL 35;   SF 46;   WA 47
        22   P Conc No 2 for P and O Op 102   CL 36;   NP 57
        35   V Conc in a Op 99   BA 67;   BN 64;   CH 63, 66;   NA 68;   MN 64;
                  NP 55;   PH 61, 67, 69;   PT 61;   SF 60;   WA 61
        30   V Conc No 2 in c#   MN 68;   NP 67
        27   C Conc No 1 in E^b Op 107   DA 63;   HN 61, 63;   LA 59;   MN 65;
                  NP 63;   PH 59;   SE 63
        27   C Conc No 2 Op 126   CH 66;   CT 68;   CL 63;   PT 68;   SL 68
        16   Golden Age, Ballet Suite Op 22   CH 67;   CT 61;   CL 35;   KC 43;
                  NP 39;   RC 36;   SL 41, 68
         4   -Final Dance   SL 41
         4   -Polka   BA 44;   HN 44;   WA 41
         6   -Polka and Dance   PT 41, 42;   SL 43
         6   -Polka and Fugue   AT 48
        10   -Three mvts   LA 41
        14   Lady Macbeth of Minsk, Suite from Opera Op 29
         6   -Two Entr'actes   NP 34;   PH 35, 43
        14   -Revised version of the Opera entitled, Katerina Ismailova Op 29/114
         6   -Three Preludes   MN 67
        18   The Nose, Suite from Opera Op 15a   CT 38;   MN 36;   RC 36
         4   Overt Festivo Op 96   HN 50;   NP 55;   PT 69;   SL 67;   SE 58;
                  UT 55
         4   Prelude in e^b Op 34 No 14 arr Stokowski   CH 57, 62;   CT 56;
                  LA 39;   NP 47;   PH 35, 39;   SF 52
         8   Prelude and Scherzo for Str Op 11   CH 65;   PH 42
        12   Five Preludes arr Adomian   SL 47
         5   Satirical Polka   WA 45
        25   Symphony No 1 in f Op 10   AT 51, 56, 60;   BA 62, 68;   BN 35, 39,
                  43, 49, 57, 64;   BU 59;   CH 28, 30, 36, 42, 43, 44, 45, 55, 64,
                  69;   CT 35, 47, 55, 56;   CL 34, 36, 37, 40, 44, 52, 62;
                  DA 38, 65;   DE 53, 56, 66, 69;   DT 43, 53, 59, 64;   HN 43, 57,
                  60, 64;   NA 51, 57, 65;   KC 42, 44, 60, 65;   LA 29, 35, 38, 48,
                  61, 65;   ML 60;   MN 29, 43, 59, 61;   NR 54, 58, 62;   NP 30,
                  35, 36, 41, 42, 43, 46, 55, 59, 61;   PH 28, 31, 33, 37, 45, 50,
                  52, 59, 65;   PT 38, 41, 49, 63, 67;   RC 31, 50, 57;   SL 38, 42,
                  47, 54, 55, 61, 62, 69;   SF 61;   SE 46, 56, 65;   UT 45, 56, 63;
                  WA 36, 52, 53, 64
        28   Symph No 3, May Day Op 20   CH 32;   PH 32
        60   Symph No 4 Op 43   PH 62;   WA 63
        50   Symph No 5 Op 47   AT 55, 58;   BA 52, 55, 64, 66, 67;   BN 38, 40(2),
                  41, 42, 43, 44, 47, 52, 56, 61, 64, 66;   BU 41, 42, 58, 65;
                  CH 43, 45, 46, 57, 60, 63, 68;   CT 42, 46, 54, 57, 59;   CL 41,
                  42, 43, 45, 58, 68;   DA 49, 53, 60, 66;   DE 55, 63, 64, 65, 69;
                  DT 44, 60, 63;   HN 44, 47, 49, 51, 53, 60, 63, 66;   NA 43, 44,
                  48, 55, 60, 63;   KC 45, 47, 51, 62, 67;   LA 42, 44, 55, 60, 65, 68

SHOSTAKOVICH, D. (Cont.) Symphony No 5, Op 47 (Cont.)
        ML 62, 64, 68;   MN 40, 41, 44, 47, 50, 60, 63;   NR 53, 56,
        59(2), 62, 65, 1 mvt 69;   NP 41, 42, 45, 52, 58, 61, 66, 68;
        PH 38, 42, 44, 47, 48, 57, 59, 64, 65, 67;   PT 40, 43, 48, 59,
        65, 68;   RC 41, 42, 45, 51, 61, 66;   SL 40(2), 41, 42, 44, 45,
        46, 48, 49, 51, 53, 56, 59, 63;   SF 41, 42, 47, 57, 62, 63;
        SE 44, 45, 60, 67;   UT 57, 62, 64, 66;   WA 41, 51, 54, 57, 59,
        62, 67, 69

8   -Largo   UT 42
6   -Rouge et Noir ballet mvt   MN 39
33   Symph No 6 Op 53   BN 41(2), 42, 44;   CH 41, 58, 67;   CT 41, 69;
        CL 44, 51, 61;   DE 58;   NA 69;   LA 45;   NP 42, 46, 63, 67;
        PH 40, 43;   PT 42, 44;   RC 59;   SL 44;   SF 44;   SE 69;
        WA 49, 56, 66
72   Symph No 7 Leningrad Op 60   BN 42, 48;   BU 46;   CH 42;   CT 42,
        43;   CL 42;   LA 43;   MN 42;   NP 42(2), 62;   PH 42;   RC 46,
        62;   WA 42
64   Symph No 8, Op 65   BA 44, 1st mvt 45;   BN 43, 44;   CT 45;   NP 43,
        44
24   Symph No 9 Op 70   BA 69;   BN 46, 61;   BU 61;   CH 46;   CT 69;
        DA 46, 64, 69;   DT 46, 65;   HN 46, 52;   KC 46, 68;   LA 46;
        MN 46;   NR 66;   NP 46, 65;   PH 65, 67, 69;   PT 46;   SL 48,
        49, 68;   SF 46, 59, 64;   SE 64;   WA 46, 65
50   Symph No 10 in e Op 93   BN 62;   CH 61, 65;   CL 67;   DA 54;
        DT 68;   HN 55;   NA 62;   LA 67;   MN 66;   NR 54;   NP 54, 55;
        PH 67;   PT 55;   RC 55;   SF 68;   UT 55;   WA 55, 60
60   Symph No 11, Year 1905 Op 103   CH 60;   HN 57;   LA 66;   RC 58
40   Symph No 12, The Year 1917 Op 112   KC 69;   MN 69
30   Symph No 13   PH 69

SHULMAN, Alan   24   C Conc   NP 49
1915-   US   9   A Laurentian Overt 1951   AT 53;   BA 59;   DE 52;
                MN 51;   NP 51
            8   Nocturne for Str   AT 48
          11   Pastoral and Dance V and O   BA 47
            6   Piece for Str O 1941   BA 41
          14   Theme and Var for Vla and O   CH 43;   DE 48;   LA 46
            9   Waltzes   AT 50;   LA 46

SHURE, R. Deane   25   Circles of Washington Symphon Suite in four mvts
1885-   US   WA 35, 36

SIBELIUS, Jean   20   Aallottaret, The Oceanides, Tone Poem Op 73
1865-1957   Fin   BN 16;   CH 15;   CT 15;   NP 15;   PH 39, 55
            5   The Bard, Symphon Poem Op 64   DT 66
          16   Belshazzar's Feast, Incidental Music Op 51   NP 47
          15   The Captive Queen, Chor and O Op 48   BN 37
            8   Canzonetta for Str O Op 62a   KC 39;   NA 33
34   V Conc in d Op 47   AT 52, 69;   BA 49, 64;   BN 06, 11, 28, 29, 33,
        34, 55, 59, 65;   BU 43;   CH 06, 08, 31, 33, 41, 43, 48, 51, 63, 64;
        CT 07, 37, 46, 50, 59, 65, 67, 69;   CL 21, 31, 33, 36, 37, 42, 44,
        47, 55, 59, 65;   DA 53, 56, 61, 65;   DE 47, 50, 52, 54, 55, 60,
        62, 65;   DT 32, 36, 44, 55, 65, 67;   HN 49, 52, 60, 64, 69;
        NA 40, 43, 51, 64;   KC 41, 53, 55, 68;   LA 31, 41, 55, 64, 66;
        MN 41, 46, 49, 52, 55, 62, 65;   NR 52, 54, 61, 65;
        NP 06, 10, 21, 36, 37, 40, 48, 51, 54, 55, 62;
        PH 13, 18, 21, 32, 36, 40, 43, 50, 53, 55, 62, 68;

SIBELIUS, J. (Cont.) Pohjola's Daughter (Cont.)
           PH 37, 40, 50, 54;   SF 47
    12   Rakastava, The Lover, Suite for Str   Op 14   NA 52;   PH 55;   WA 55
    18   En Saga, Symphonic Poem Op 9   BA 39;   BN 09, 39;
           CH 03, 10, 37, 59, 63, 65;   CT 07, 31, 36, 58;   CL 31, 33, 53, 55,
           65;   DT 27, 28, 33, 40, 64;   HN 40, 43;   LA 32, 50, 55;
           NP 30, 32, 35;   PH 17, 35, 39, 55, 62;   PT 37, 65;   RC 24, 45;
           SL 13, 15, 18, 35;   SF 17, 52;   WA 33, 50
           SONGS
     4   Flicken Kom, The Tryst Op 37 No 5   DT 65
     4   Men men Fagel marks dock, My Bird is Long in Homing Op 36 No 2 NP 65
     4   Sav, Sav, Susa, Sigh, Sedges, Sigh Op 36 No 4   DT 65;   NP 65;
           SE 65
     4   Svarta Roser, Black Roses Op 36 No 1   DT 65;   MN 49;   NP 65; Se 65
     4   Varen flyktar hastigt, Spring Flies Fast Op 13 No 4   NP 65;   SE 65
     4   War dat en drom, Was it a Dream? Op 37 No 4   DT 65
    20   Five Songs Op 38   WA 65
     4   No 1 Autumn Eve   SE 65
    10   Varsang, Spring Song, Symphon Poem Op 16   BN 08
    20   Svanevhit, Swan White, Suite from Incidental Music Op 54   BN 35
    35   Symph No 1 in e Op 39   AT 53, 63;   BA 37, 65;
           BN 06, 12, 14, 16, 20, 23, 25, 27, 30, 32, 35, 37, 39, 41, 45, 46,
           52, 67;   CH 07, 18, 27, 32, 33, 35, 37, 63, 68;
           CT 09, 15, 36, 39, 43, 51;   CL 20, 21, 25, 30, 33, 36, 41, 63;
           DA 49, 59, 63, 69;   DE 47, 51, 56, 62;
           DT 27, 28, 31, 32, 33, 35, 37, 40, 44, 45, 47, 48, 54, 57, 62, 64,
           68;   HN 39, 40, 42, 45, 60, 63;   NA 44, 53, 46, 64;   KC 35, 40,
           65;   LA 24, 27, 28, 32(2), 33, 40, 43, 53, 63;
           MN 28, 31, 34, 36, 40, 47, 49;   NR 52, 55, 59, 69;
           NP 30, 33, 36, 37, 64, 66;   PH 08, 10, 15, 30, 32, 34, 35, 38, 40,
           41, 44, 46, 52, 55, 61;   PT 39, 42, 44, 51, 57, 65;
           RC 29, 38, 39, 40, 44, 58;   SL 09, 11, 15, 23, 27, 36, 40;
           SF 18, 37, 46, 67;   SE 28, 29, 30, 37, 38, 47, 53, 63;   UT 60
           WA 45, 48, 52, 54, 57, 64
           -Scherzo   MN 45
    35   Symph No 2 in D Op 43   AT 50, 55, 60, 68;   BA 37, 43, 47, 49, 53;
           BN 03, 09, 10, 15, 21, 23, 29, 31, 32, 33, 35, 37, 38, 40, 42, 44,
           47, 50, 53, 57, 62, 64, 68;   BU 40, 44, 49, 55, 61;
           CH 03, 10, 19, 26, 33, 36, 42, 43, 46, 55, 60, 62, 64;
           CT 11, 37, 38, 46, 52, 56, 64, 68;
           CL 27, 32, 34, 36, 40, 43, 44, 45, 51, 52, 54, 55, 57, 60, 63, 66;
           DA 50, 51, 58, 65;   DE 50, 54, 63, 67;
           DT 20, 28, 35, 36, 39, 40, 43, 45, 51, 55, 58, 62, 64;
           HN 41, 42, 44, 49, 52, 54, 55, 58, 62, 66;
           NA 39, 40, 42, 45, 48, 50, 54, 57, 66;   KC 37, 38, 39, 46, 49, 63,
           69;   LA 21(2), 28, 31, 33, 37, 42, 46, 51, 54, 68;   ML 65, 68;
           MN 32, 35, 36, 38, 41, 45, 46, 50, 55, 57, 62, 64;
           NR 51, 52, 54, 58, 64;
           NP 16, 34, 35, 36, 38, 39, 40, 52, 54, 55, 57, 60, 62, 65; NS 13
           PH 12, 32, 35, 36, 38, 41, 43, 45, 47, 48, 50, 52, 54, 56, 58, 62,
           64, 65;   PT 40, 47, 48, 53, 58, 64, 65;
           RC 32, 34, 36, 39, 54, 56, 61, 65;
           SL 10, 33, 35, 37, 39, 40, 44, 45, 48, 52, 55, 57, 62, 64, 66, 69;
           SF 39, 45, 48, 59, 68;   SE 31, 34, 40, 42, 51, 62, 68;
           UT 46, 50, 55, 65;   WA 35, 40, 43, 46, 50, 53, 55, 60, 65

SIBELIUS, J. (Cont.)
27   Symph No 3 in C Op 52   AT 58;   BN 28(2), 32, 38;   CH 39;   CT 33;
       CL 46, 69;   DT 62;   LA 57;   NP 33, 37, 46, 65;   PH 36;
       SF 41
35   Symph No 4 in a Op 63   BA 38;   BN 13, 14, 17, 31, 32, 39;   CH 31,
       34, 37, 39, 56;   CT 36;   CL 35, 53, 63, 65;   DT 25;   LA 36, 50;
       MN 38, 67;   NP 30, 34, 45, 49, 65, 69;   NS 12;   PH 31, 32, 35,
       37, 43, 54, 61, 68;   RC 29;   SL 35, 52;   SE 45, 66
27   Symph No 5 in E Op 82   BN 21, 22, 27, 32, 33, 34, 36, 38, 40, 41, 42,
       43, 45, 47, 50, 51, 61, 63, 66, 68;   BU 64;
       CH 40, 44, 45, 46, 48, 57, 64;   CT 32, 39, .47, 55, 66;
       CL 29, 38, 39, 41, 42, 44, 50, 59, 64, 68;   DA 50, 57;
       DE 51, 55, 65;   DT 35, 46, 48, 69;   HN 43, 48, 61, 64, 67;
       NA 48, 50, 56;   KC 47, 56, 67;   LA 35, 45, 51, 60, 69(2);
       ML 64;   MN 34, 39, 65;   NR 61, 67;   NP 21, 35, 41, 43, 46, 56,
       60, 65, 69;   PH 21, 25(2), 37, 40, 41, 42, 44, 45, 48, 51, 60, 63,
       68;   PT 45, 54, 62;   RC 33, 48, 51, 59, 68;
       SL 34, 38, 40, 50, 57;   SF 40;   SE 49, 65;   WA 49
27   Symph No 6 in C Op 104   BA 56;   BN 29(2), 32, 40, 45, 51;
       CH 47;   DT 41, 67;   HN 65;   KC 65;   MN 41;   NR 56;   NP 66;
       PH 25, 51, 55;   PT 56;   SF 51;   WA 56
20   Symph No 7 in C Op 105   BN 26, 30, 32, 34, 36, 38, 40, 45, 48, 55,
       57, 65;   BU 56, 62;   CT 38, 40, 42, 50, 57, 63;   CL 47, 49, 64;
       DT 51, 66;   HN 57;   NA 59;   LA 38, 48, 52, 65;   MN 40, 43, 68;
       NP 42, 50, 55, 59, 65;   NS 26;
       PH 25, 39, 40, 44, 45, 46, 49, 50, 52, 55, 59, 65, 67;
       PT 59, 63, 68;   RC 50, 55;   SL 37, 39, 41, 42, 53;   SF 40, 65;
       WA 50, 53, 55, 61
19   Tapiola, Symphonic Poem Op 112   BN 32, 35, 37, 39;   CT 46;
       CL 34, 55;   DA 57;   HN 49;   KC 65;   NP 34;   NS 26;
       PH 34, 38, 55;   RC 12, 60;   SF 54;   SE 65;   WA 65
20   The Tempest, Incidental Music Op 109   CT 54;   DT excerpts 45, 46;
       HN 65
 4   -Berceuse   HN 55;   PH 32
 4   -Overt   NP 26;   SE 30
 4   -The Storm   PH 32;   SF 30
 8   Tulen Syntry for Baritone, Chor and O   BN 53
 6   Valse Triste Op 44   BA 38;   BN 09;   CH 16;   DA 26, 28, 37, 38;
       DE 45, 65;   DT 14, 27;   HN 17, 37;   MN 46;   NS 16;
       PH 12(2), 17, 29, 31;   RC 30, 39;   SL 09, 17, 39;   SF 13, 37;
       UT 43;   WA 33, 39, 40

SIEBMANN   10   Two Intermezzi, Romanza and Scherzo   CH 1895
              US

SIEGAL, Alvin   14   Six Var on Volga Boatman 1943   SE 43
              US

SIEGMEISTER, Elie   20   Condura Symphon Suite from the film music   NA 59
1909-   US   16   Ozark Set   MN 44;   SL 47
                            15   Sunday in Brooklyn   KC 46;   LA 48
                             6   Wilderness Road 1945   MN 45;   UT 45

SIEMONN   6   Carnival Time, song with P   DT 26
              US   4   Ulysses, song with P   NA 36

	Time in Minutes	
SILVA, Romeo or Oscar da, 1872- Portugal	4	Corone, Song with O RC 40
SILVESTRI, Constantin 1913- Roum	8	Prelude and Fugue Op 17a No 2 PH 61
SIMONI It	15	Suite Sefardi SL 40

SINDING, Christian
1856-1941   Nor
	36
	15
	
	20
	
	8
	
	35
	
	35
		P Conc No 1 in D^b Op 6 CH 02
		V Conc in A Op 45 BN 05, 12; CH 00, 06;
		    DT 25; NP 1899, 16
		Episodes Chivalresque, Suite in F for O Op 35
		    BN Nos 1, 2, 4 04; CH 1899; PH 02
		Rondo Infinito Op 42 BN 09; CH 1895, 06, 07, 11,
		    18, 26, 32, 33
		Symph No 1 in d Op 21 BN 1897, 06, 12; CH 1893,
		    95; PH 17; NP 1893
		Symphon No 2 in D Op 85 NP 18

SINGER, Otto 1833-1894 US	10	Symphon Fantasie BN 1887

SINIGAGLIA, Leone
1868-1944   It
	5
	
	8
	
	16
	8
	13
		Concert Etude for Str Op 5 CH 06, 07, 10;
		    NS 16; SL 24
		Overt Le Baruffe Chizzotte Op 32 BN 10, 14, 16;
		    CH 08, 09, 16, 18, 22, 27, 32, 35, 38; CT 10,
		    17, 19, 28, 33; CL 29; DT 15, 16, 21, 32, 35;
		    NA 56, 65; LA 32; ML 60; MN 24, 42, 46;
		    NP 10, 27, 37; NS 11, 12, 20; PH 08, 09, 10,
		    11, 31; PT 47; RC 24; SL 12, 15, 18, 25,
		    38; SF 18
		Suite Piemontesi Op 36 with V Solo CH 14
		Two Character Pieces for Str NS 22
		Two Piedmontese Dances Op 31 CH 07; DA 27;
		    DT 16

SIQUEIRA, José 1907- Brazil	15	Senzala DT 45
SITT, Hans 1850-1922 Aust	30 20	V Conc in d Op 65 CH 1897 Concert Piece for Vla Op 46 CH 1894
SJOBERG, Svante 1873-1935 Swed	4	Tonerrsa, Song CT 49
SJOGREN, Emil 1853-1918 Swed	6	Two Songs NA 46
SKALKOTAS, Nikos 1904-1949 Gk	14	Greek Dances 1933 CT 49, 69; MN 38; NP 54, 55; PT 59; WA 66
SKILES, Marlin 1906- US	5	Ballade fr Cyrano de Bergerac CL 41

SKILTON, Chas.   35   Suite Primeval on Tribal Indian Melodies 1920
 Sanford   CH 26;   KC 33
 1868-1941   US   10   -Excerpts   BN 22;   NP 21
                         5   Two Short Pieces, No 1, Autumn Night   DT 30
                         5   No 2, Shawnee Indian Hunting Dance   DT 30
                        10   Two Indian Dances, Deer Dance and War Dance 1915
                               CH 17;   CT 17;   DA 25;   PH 18;   WA 31
                         6   No 2 War Dance   BA 28;   UT 57

SKLAVOS, George   8   The Eagle, Fantasia on Greek Themes 1922   MN 38
 1888-   Roum/Gk

SKROWACZEWSKI,   8   Conc for English Horn   MN 69
 Stanislaw   9   Symph for Str Op 25   MN 63;   CL 59
 1923-   Pol

SMETANA, Bedřich   7   The Bartered Bride, Opera 1866: Overt
 1824-1884   Czech   AT 47, 68;   BA 43, 44, 61;   BN 1887, 88, 94, 97,
                               99, 03, 06, 09, 11, 12, 14, 16, 19, 23, 24, 38,
                        42, 53;   CH 1893, 96, 99, 04, 06, 08, 09, 10, 11, 13, 14, 15, 17,
                        18, 20, 22, 24, 26, 32, 37, 39, 41, 44, 46, 49, 51, 52, 55, 60;
                        CT 99, 07, 10, 13, 17, 23, 25, 26, 27(2), 31(2), 32, 36, 40, 41,
                        44, 48, 52, 56, 58, 60, 62, 65;   CL 21, 29, 32, 33, 37, 44, 48,
                        50, 54, 57, 60, 64, 69;   DA 27, 49, 67, 69;   DE 47, 49, 50, 54,
                        55, 58, 62, 63, 69;   DT 18, 22, 25, 37, 52, 55, 61;
                        HN 32, 38, 55, 63, 68;   NA 39, 52, 53, 57, 63, 69;
                        KC 34, 39, 41, 53, 58;   LA 25, 30, 32, 35, 48;   ML 63;   MN 26,
                        37, 47, 56;   NR 52, 56, 63;   NP 09, 14, 17, 18, 22, 26, 27, 30,
                        33, 37, 39, 49, 54, 62, 64;   NS 1887, 92, 97, 08, 14, 15, 19,
                        23, 26;   PH 10, 11, 13, 14, 15, 17, 18, 19, 26, 29, 31, 32, 33,
                        38, 45;   PT 38, 41, 47, 49, 50, 56, 63, 65;   RC 23, 26, 33, 34,
                        47, 59;   SL 13, 16, 20, 21, 23, 26, 28, 32, 36, 40, 44, 47, 49,
                        50, 58, 61;   SF 11, 13, 16, 18, 32, 39, 46, 48, 54;   SE 33, 42,
                        53, 64;   UT 51, 66;   WA 41, 46, 61;   BU 45, 52, 57
                6   -Three Dances   BA 42;   CL 62;   DA 37, 38;   DE 52;   NA 55;
                      NP 2 dances 33;   SE 45
                4   -Entrance of Comedians   WA 37
                      Country Dances arr Byrnes fr P music 1877   CT 43
               15   Dance Suite arr Byrnes fr P music   CT 41;   CL 40;   NP 41;   PT 69
                4   Hubicka, The Kiss, Opera 1875: Overt   BN 04;   RC 48
                4   -Cradle Song   NP 10, 43
                9   Libusie, Opera 1869: Overt   BN 05;   CH 20
               50   Má Vlast, From My Life, Cycle of Symph Poems 1874-79   CH 52, 68;
                      NP 15;   SF 68
               30   -3 Excerpts   CL 49
               15   -1 Excerpt   WA 67
               10   No 1 Vysebrad, The High Castle   BA 59;   BN 1895, 98, 03, 06, 13,
                      15;   CH 1895, 00, 06, 10, 12, 19, 30, 34, 52;   CT 14, 47;
                      DT 65;   LA 63;   ML 60, 65;   NP 11;   SL 10;   CL 46
               16   No 2 Vltava, The Moldau   AT 58;   BN 1890, 93, 97, 98, 08, 10, 17,
                      22, 41, 42, 60, 66;   CH 1893(2), 94, 96, 97, 02, 06, 07, 08, 09,
                      10, 11, 12, 13, 14, 18, 19, 26, 33, 35, 52;   CT 1896, 01, 09, 32,
                      36, 39, 42, 44, 46, 47, 48, 50, 51, 56, 59, 61;   CL 38, 43, 47,
                      52, 59, 62;   DA 35, 46, 48, 52, 60;   DE 51, 53;   DT 15, 26, 35,
                      39, 43, 46, 47, 51, 62;   HN 41;   NA 35, 44, 49;   KC 33, 34, 42,
                      57;   LA 22, 26, 40, 60, 63;   ML 61;   MN 28, 33, 49, 54;

SMETANA, B. (Cont.) Má Vlast, No 2 Vltava, The Moldau (Cont.)
                NR 56, 65;   NP 08, 10, 11, 14, 19, 20, 29, 30, 35, 40, 44, 50;
                NS 06, 15, 24;   PH 00, 08, 09, 10, 11, 12, 14, 31, 44, 49, 57;
                PT 40, 43, 51, 52, 54;   RC 36, 38, 41, 49;   SL 17, 22, 27, 30;
                SF 15, 53, 56;   SE 26, 36, 65;   UT 43, 47, 48, 56, 60, 67, 68;
                WA 35, 36, 48, 49, 54
      9   No 3 Šárka, The Amazon Queen   BN 1894;   CH 1895, 98, 12, 52;
                CT 03, 05;   LA 63;   ML 61;   MN 29;   PH 06, 64
     12   No 4 Zčeských, from Bohemia's Fields and Groves   BA 55, 65;
                BN 00, 14, 44;   CH 50, 52;   CT 14, 33, 37, 63;   CL 48;   DT 48;
                LA 63;   NP 12, 50;   NS 09;   PH 35;   SL 14, 52;   NR 66
      8   No 5 Tabor   CH 52
     15   No 6 Blanik   CH 46, 52;   CL 41;   NP 41, 43
      9   Richard III, Symphon Poem 1858   BN 02, 15;   CH 1896
     25   Str Quart No 1 in e from My Life, arr Szell for O   BN 42;   BU 45,
                52, 57;   CH 48;   CL 44, 48;   MN 46;   NP 43;   PH 43;   SE 46;
                SF 52
      4   Dvě vdovy, Two Widows, Opera 1873: Aria of Carolina   DT 46
      8   Wallenstein's Camp, Symphon Poem 1858   BN 1896, 16, 21;   CH 1896;
                LA 21

SMIT, Leo   17   Capriccio for Str 1961   NP 61
1921-   US   15   P Conc   BU 68
                           7   Overt The Parcae in c# 1953   BN 53
                          30   Symph No 1 B^b 1956   BN 56;   SF 63;   WA 56
                          18   Symph No 2 six mvts   BU 64;   NP 65

SMITH, David S.   10   Credo, Poem for O Op 83   LA 41;   PT 41
1877-1940   US   15   Epic Poem Op 55   BN 34
                          11   Fete Galante, Fl and O Op 48   BN 22;   DT 23; NS 21
                          20   Impressions Suite Op 40   CH 19
                          10   Prince Hal   Overt Op 31   CH 14, 17;   CT 15;   CL 22;
                                 DT 23;   NS 15
                          15   A Satire 1929 Op 66 No 1   NP 33
                          40   Symph No 1 Op 28   CH 12
                          42   Symph No 2 in D Op 42   CH 18;   NP 18
                          30   Symph No 3 in c Op 60   CL 30
                          30   Symph No 4 Op 78   BN 38
                           5   Tomorrow Overt 1933   CL 34
                          10   Youth, Poem Op 47   BN 21

SMITH, Hale   9   Contours   CL 65;   CT 66
1925-   US

SMITH, John C.   10   Miniature Suite arr H. McDonald   DE 45, 50;   PH 39
1712-1795   Brit

SMITH, Lani   12   Prelude and Scherzo for Brass, Timpani, Str 1957
1934-   US   CT 57

SMITH, Leland C.   7   Overt to Santa Claus   SF 62
1925-   US

SMITH, Russell   12   Magnificat for Sopr and Chor   CL 68
1927   US

SMITH, William O.   12   Interplay   BU 64;   CT 66

SMYTH, Dame Ethel   9   The Wreckers 1906: Overt   NP 35
1858-1944   Brit   9   -Prelude, Act III   CH 21

SODERMAN, Johan   10   Overt The Maid of Orleans, Incidental Music   CH 21
1832-1876   Swed   4   Trollsjon   SF 39

SOLLBERGER, Harvey D. 15   Grand Quart for 4 Fl   SF 67
1938-   12   Stereocophony for O SL 68

SOMERS, Harry S.   18   Suite for Harp and Chamber O   DT 67
1925-   Can

SOMERVELL, Sir Arthur 5   Old Welsh Melody All Through the Night   CH 1893;
1863-1937   Brit   NS 1893

SONZOGNO, Guilio C.   14   Il Negro for C and O   NP 34
1906-   It   8   Tango for O   CL 35;   MN 35;   NP 34;   PH 36

SOR, Fernando   2   Alegretto for Guitar   DE 54
1778-1839   Sp   2   Allegro for Guitar alone   NR 67
                          6   Introd and Allegro   AT 58
                          4   Study, Guitar   AT 61
                          6   Study for Solo Guitar   NR 61
                         10   Var.Guitar   PT 60

SOUSA, John P.   5   El Capitan, March   CT 29
1854-1932   US   2   Semper Fidelis, March   NA 54
                          5   Stars and Stripes Forever   CL 41;   DA 46;   SF 50
                         27   -arr Kay, for Ballet 5 scenes   CT 61, 64;   WA 58
                          5   -Pas de Deux   NR 61

SOWERBY, Leo   5   Comes Autumn Time, Overt 1916   AT 50;   CH 20, 42;
1895-   US   DT 20;   NA 41, 48, 52;   KC 42;   LA 20, 21, 28;
                                MN 24;   NP 34;   NA 17;   PH 20;   SL 20, 31, 34;
                                UT 54;   WA 40
                         29   Conc in C for Org and O 1937   BN 37;   CH 38;
                                CT 39;   DT 64;   PH 63
                         30   P Conc No 1 in F 1919   CH 19, 24;   NS 20;   SL 20
                          5   Country Dance Tunes   HN 34
                          3   Fanfare for Airmen 1942   CT 42
                         20   From the Northland Suite 1923   CH 25, 29;   CT 24;
                                MN 25;   SL 25
                          2   Irish Washerwoman 1916   CH 23
                         17   King Estmere, Ballad for 2 P and O 1922   CT 25;
                                MN 23, 34
                         18   Mediaeval Poem for Org and O 1926   CH 26, 27, 31,
                                36;   NP 54;   WA 51
                          3   Money Musk 1924   LA 25
                         18   Passacaglia, Interlude and Fugue 1931   CH 33, 37,
                                55
                         16   Portrait, Fantasy in Triptych 1946   NA 53

SOWERBY, L. (Cont.)
17   Prairie, Symphon Poem 1929   BN 31;   CH 30, 34;
      CT 31;   MN 32;   PH 32
14   A Set of Four Suite: Ironies   CH 17, 18;   SF 22
30   Symph No 1 in e 1917   CH 21
25   Symph No 2 in b 1939   CH 28
40   Symph No 3 in f# 1941   CH 40
30   Symph No 4 1949   BN 48

SPAETH, Dr. J. Duncan 8   Shakespeare in Music   HN 36
US

SPATHY   4   Greek Folk Song: Lagarni   SE 56
Gk

SPELMAN, Timothy M. 12   Assisi, Tone Poem   BN 25
1891-   US   8   Christ and the Blind Man, Tone Poem 1918   CH 22

SPIER, LaSalle   10   Impressions of the Bowery 1934   WA 34
1889-   US   5   Jubiloso   WA 40
12   Suite Eulogistic 1951   WA 51
10   Symphon Visions 1939   WA 39

SPINELLI, Nicola   6   Prelude to Act III, A Basso Porto Opera 1894
1865-1906   It   CH 22

SPISAK, Michal   17   Conc Giacoso for Chamber O   MN 61
1914-   Pol   17   Conc Giacoso for Str O 4 pts   DA 59

SPOHR, Louis   30   Conc Clar and O No 2 in E^b Op 57   CH 00
1784-1859   Ger   15   Conc Str Quart and O Op 131   BA 63;   NP 1858;
      PH 63
18   V Conc No 1 in a Op 1   NP 1846;   NS 1881
20   V Conc No 7 in e Op 38   BN 1890;   NP 1898
18   V Conc No 8 in a Op 47   BN 1881, 85, 98, 01;
      CH 1896, 01, 16, 24, 27;   CT 1898;   CL 48, 59;
      MN 24, 28, 67;   NP 1857, 72, 88;   NS 1896, 16;
      SL 24
20   V Conc No 9 in d Op 55   BN 1887, 06;   CH 22, 41;
      MN 22;   NP 1873, 14, 40;   NS 1885
20   V Conc No 11 in G Op 70   BN 1885
10   Concertina No 14 for O Op 110   NP 1853, 57
4   Faust, Opera Op 60 1816: Aria and scene   NP 1888
5   -Overt   BN 1885;   NP 1853, 75, 15;   NS 84
4   Jessonda, Opera Op 63 1823: Aria   NP 1842, 52, 53,
      54, 58, 89
4   -Duet   NP 1847
6   -Overt   BN 1883, 84, 85, 95;   CH 1894, 00, 06,
      09, 19, 21;   NP 1844, 46, 49, 52, 67
10   Notturno for Wind Instruments and Turkish Band
      Op 34   BN 29
30   Symph No 1 in E^b Op 20   NP 1847
24   Symphon No 2 in d Op 49   NP 1843
30   Symph No 3 in c Op 78   BN 1891;   NP 1874
30   Symph No 4 Die Wiche der Tone Op 86   BN 1887, 99;
      DA 52;   NP 1846, 47, 49, 51, 53, 57, 59, 69, 75, 90

SPOHR, L. (Cont.)

	30	Symph No 7 for Double O Op 121 NP 1848
	30	Symph No 9 The Seasons Op 143 NP 1853
	30	Symph No 11 BN 1885
	4	Zemire und Azore, Opera 1819: Aria, Rose Softly Blooming CH 16; CT 43

SPONTINI, Gasparo L.   6   Olympia, Opera 1821, Overt   BN 1883;   NP 1854
1774-1851   It   4   La Vestale, Opera 1807: Aria, Tu che Invoco con
                          Orrore   RC 42
                      6   -Overt   BN 22;   NP 1850

SPRIGG   10   Maryland Portraits in Contrast 1953   BA 53
        US

STAHLBERG, Fred.   6   Mark Twain, a tale in tune   DT 33
1877-1937   US   20   Suite for O   NP 15
                        6   Symphon Scherzo   NP 12
                       20   Symph, A. Lincoln   NP 08

STAMITZ, Carl   10   Vla Conc in D   CH 45
1745-1801   Ger   18   Symphon Konzertante in F   NP 53

STAMITZ, Johann   9   Symph in E^b CH 44;   LA 48
1717-1757   Ger   12   Symph in G Op 3 No 3   BA 48, 49

STANFORD   13   Irish Rhaps No 1 in d Op 78   CH 05, 23, 33;
  Sir Charles V.   CL 29;   DT 30, 47;   PH 18;   RC 25, 30, 33
1852-1924   Brit   11   Irish Rhaps No 5 Op 147   CH 17(2)
                       15   Songs of the Sea for Baritone, Chor and O Op 91
                              HN 32
                       10   Serenade in G Op 18   NP 1883
                            Old Irish Melodies arr for O
                        4   My Love's an Arbutus   CH 1893
                        4   Patrick Sarsfield   CH 1893
                        4   Elmer's Farewell   CT 1895
                       36   Symph No 3, in f Op 28 Irish   BN 1889;   NP 10;
                              NS 1887, 07, 16;   PH 12, 23
                            Songs
                        4   Revenge   CT 11
                        4   Chiefton   NS 1892
                        4   March   NS 1892
                        4   Ye Dead   NS 1894
                        4   Zephyrs   NS 1893
                        4   Verdun, Tone Poem   NP 18

STRANGE, Max   4   Damon Song   CT 02;   NP 11
1856-1932   Ger

STRANGER, Russell   6   Buffoons A Merry Overt   SE 64
        US

STANLEY, Albert A.   15   Symphon Poem Attis   CH 20
1851-   US

STARER, Robert	20	Conc a Tre for Clar, Trump, Tromb and Str PT 65
1924- US	25	Conc for V, C and O PT 68; BN 69
	16	P Conc No 2 CT 60; DE 60
	26	Conc Vla, Str and Percussion NP 59
	11	Mutabili, Variants NA 68; PT 66
	12	Symph No 2 in 1 mvt RC 54
	25	Samson Agonistes Symphon Portrait 1961 CH 68; NP 67; PT 67

STAROKADOMSKY, Mikhail 1901- Russ — 17 — Conc for O Op 14 1937   BN 37;   CL 38

STEARNS, Theodore 1880-1935 US — 10 — Suite Caprese   NS 27

STEIN, Leon 1910- US — 13 — Three Hassidic Dances 1940   AT 53;   CT 53

STEINER, Geo 1900- Hung/US — 11 — Rhapsodic Poem for Vla and O   DA 50

STEINERT, Alexander L. 1900- US
- 14 — Conc Sinfonico P and O 1934   BN 34
- 15 — Leggenda Sinfonica 1931   BN 30
- 18 — Nightingale and Rose, Symphon Poem   PH 49
- 12 — Southern Night 1926   BN 26

STEINHAUSER US — 4 — Culver Polka   BA 28

STEINMAN, David Ward 1937- US — 18 — C Conc   SE 67 / Prelude and Toccata   NR 67

STENHAMMAR, Wilhelm 1871-1927 Swed — 13 — Midwinter, Tone Poem   PH 26

STEPHAN, Rudi 1878-1915 Ger — 19 — Music for O   CH 14, 16;   DT 31

STEVENS, Halsey 1908- US — 15 — Symphon Dances 1958   MN 58;   SF 58;   WA 59 / 16 — Symph No 1 1945   LA 49;   SF 45

STEWART, Robert 1825-1894 Ir — 8 — Prelude   AT 60

STIGELLI, George 1820-1868 US — 4 — Die Thrane, Song   NP 1859

STILL, William Grant 1895- US
- 6 — Combo y Congo from Danzes de Panama   DE 69
- 28 — Afro-American Symph 1931   CH 36;   DT 48;   KC 37; LA 3rd and 4th mvt 42;   NP 35;   UT 2nd and 3rd mvt 50 -Scherzo   DE 69
- 7 — Bells   SL 46
- 17 — Ebon Chronicle 1935   PH 36
- 3 — Fanfare for American Heroes 1942   CT 42

STILL, W.G. (Cont.)
	10	Festive Overt 1944 BU 45; CT 44, 52; DE 45; NA 64; NP 46
	6	In Memoriam, Negro Soldiers 1943 BN 44; CL 46, 64; LA 48; NP 43, 45
	15	Kaintuck, Poem for P and O 1935 CT 35; NA 42
	10	Peaceful Land DE 61
	15	Poem for O 1944 CH 50; CL 44
	8	Plain Chant for America, Baritone Org and O 1941 LA 42; NP 41; PH 42; PT 41
	30	Symph in g 1937 CL 39; PH 37
	27	Wood Notes CH 47

STOCK, Frederick
1872-1942   Ger/US
	35	C Conc CH 28, 38, 39; NP 31
	28	V Conc in d Op 22 CH 16, 20, 25, 29, 30, 42; NS 16; PH 16
	20	Elegy CH 23; PH 23
	5	Festival Fanfare 1940 CH 40(2)
	8	Festival March 1910 CH 10(2), 19, 24
	20	Festival Prologue 1915 CH 15
	15	Improvisations CH 07
	10	March and Hymn to Democracy CH 18(2), 19, 24, 42
	15	Musical Self Portrait CH 31, 45
	15	Overt, Life's Springtime Op 20 CH 13
	10	Overt To a Romantic Comedy 1918 CH 17
	25	A Psalmodic Rhaps for Solo Voice, Chor and O CH 29
	54	Symph No 1 in c Op 18 BN 15; CH 09(2), 15; PH 14
	24	Symphon Sketch, Summer Evening 1912 CH 12
	30	Symphon Poem, Eines Menschenleben's 1904 CH 04
	30	Symphon Var in b Op 7 CH 03, 05, 14, 22, 42; SL 21
	8	Symphon Waltzes Op 8 CH 07, 10, 11, 14, 30, 33, 35, 41; NS 10; SF 11

STOCKHAUSEN,
  Karlheinz
1928-   Ger
	15	Carre for 4 O and 4 Choirs, MN 69
	10	Mikrophonic I SF 66
	8	Momente BU 63; SF 66
	10	Punkte, Points SL 65
	30	Telemusick SF 66
	12	Zyklus SF 66

STOEHR, Richard
1874-   Aust/US
	15	Suite for Str O 3 parts Op 8 SL 10

STOELZEL, Gottfried
1690-1749   Ger
	15	Conc Grosso in D CT 66
	15	Conc Grosso a Quattro Chori NP 30

STOESSEL, Albert
1894-1943   US
	22	Conc Grosso for P and Str O 1936 CL 36; MN 38; SL 36
	13	Suite Antique, 2 V and Chamber O 1922 NS 23
	15	Suite from Opera Garrick 1936 CL 38; SL 37
	8	Symphon Paraphrase, Song of the Volga Boatmen 1925 BA 28; DA 28

STOJOWSKI, Sigismund 30   P Conc No 2 Op 32   BN 15
1869-1946   Pol/US   20   Suite in E^b Op 9   NP 14;   SL 11
                       6   -Theme and Var   BA 36
                      35   Symph in d Op 21   BN 19
                      10   Symphonic Rhaps P and O Op 23   NS 10
                       6   Two Ancient Liturgical Melodies   HN 57

STOKOWSKI, Leopold   5   Prelude on Ein Feste Burg   NP 41
1882-   US   11   Negro Rhaps for a Capella Chorus   RC 40

STORCH, M. Anton   4   Night Witchery, Chor for male Voices   CH 08
1813-1888   Aust

STRADELLA, Alessandro 4   Per Pieta, Signore,from Il Fioridoro   BU 44;
1642-1682   It   CT 33, 41;   DA 50;   DE 51;   DT 35;   NA 46;
                             LA 45;   NP 1861;   NS 25;   PH 15;   SL 44

STRAESSER, Ewald   40   Symph in G Op 22   CH 12
1902-   Ger

STRANG, Gerald   5   Intermezzo   LA 38
1908-   Can/US

STRANSKY, Josef   15   Three Melodies, Voice and O   NP 20
1872-1936   Czech/US 10   Three Symphon Songs   NP 19
                       8   Two Symphon Songs   NP 12, 15

STRAUSS, Edward   4   Babn Frei, Galop   PH 54, 55, 51
1835-1916   Aust

STRAUSS, Franz   6   Nocturne for Horn   CH 03
1822-1905   Ger

STRAUSS, Johann, Jr. 45   A Gala Program of Waltzes, Marches and Polkas
1825-1999   Aust   SF 64, 65, 66; or Viennese Favorites   LA 64
                       3   Annen Polka   CL 61;   DA 48, 53;   HA 38, 42
                       4   Artist's Life Waltz Kunsterlerleben Op 316
                             CH 53, 59;   DA 26;   HN 42, 45;   NA 36;   KC 41;
                             NP 40;   NS 06;   PT 38, 43;   WA 33, 35
          10   Blue Danube An der schönen blauen Donauu   OP 314   BA 26, 28, 37, 43;
                BN 32;   CH 1894, 99, 25;   CT 60(2);   CL 61;   DA 46;   DE 45,
                52, 56;   DT 36;   HN 36;   NA 33, 40;   KC 33;   MN Ballet 37, 38;
                NP 31, 50, 54, 55;   NS 15;   PH 25, 32, 38, 42, 58;   RC 63;
                SL 39, 65;   SF 25, 33, 37;   SE 29;   UT 52;   WA 32, 35, 41
           5   Champagne Polka Op 211   PT 42, 45
           7   Caglisstro in Wien, Operetta 1875: Waltzes Op 370   PH 54, 55, 61
           5   Elekrafer Polka   PH 48
          10   Emperor's Waltz,Kaiserwalzer Op 437   BU 49;   CH 93(2), 30, 31, 40,
                56, 59;   CT 99;   CL 43, 52, 60;   DA 46;   DT 43;   HN 41;
                KC 34, 41;   LA 57;   MN 44;   NP 39;   NS 13, 26;   PH 37, 39, 41,
                43, 45, 46, 47, 48, 51, 54, 55, 56, 57, 60;   PT 52, 59;   RC 37,
                66;   SL 59;   SF 41;   SE 44, 47;   UT 43, 48, 51;   WA 38
           5   Fast Track Polka   SE 51
          10   Four Famous Polkas   PH 52

STRAUSS, J. Jr. (Cont.)
```
 60    Fledermaus, Opera 1874: Act I and II    PT 60
 70      -Concert Version   PT 63, 69
 15      -Excerpts   SL 65
 15      -Fantasia for 2 P and O   DE 60;   PT 58
 20      -Suite arr Ormandy   AT 59;   HN 51;   KC 64;   PH 50, 51, 54
  9      -Overt   AT 49;   BA 37, 44;   BU 48, 54;   CH 53, 63;   CT 30;
         CL 33, 51, 67;   DA 28, 49;   DE 45, 48, 51, 52;   DT 24;   HN 36,
         39, 42, 53;   NA 66;   KC 41, 43;   LA 42, 66;   MN 32, 45, 49;
         NR 67;   NP 37, 54;   PH 37, 48;   PT 42, 45;   RC 63;   SL 59,
         60, 67;   UT 40, 44;   WA 35, 48
  4      -Czardos   NA 30;   KC 52;   SL 59
  4      -Laughing Song   CT 59;   SL 59
  4      -Look Me Over   PT 53
  5      -Oriental Ballet   DE 52
  5      -Waltz, Du und Du Op 367   CH 02;   NA 30
 48    Graduation Ball, arr as one act Ballet, Dorati   AT 55;   CT 52;
         DA 46
  4    Gypsy Baron, Operetta, 1885: Aria   SL 59
  7      -Overt   AT 51;   BA 36, 39;   CT 61;   DA 53;   HN 38;   NP 37,
         38, 39, 40;   PH 37, 42, 49, 54;   RC 63, 66;   SL 65;   UT 44
 15      -Paraphrase arr Byrnes   LA 42, 64
 10      -Suite   KC 66
         -Treasure Waltz   CH 53, 59;   MN 49;   PT 41, 45
       Indigo, Operetta 1871: Overt   NS 27
  5    In Krapfenwalde, Polka francaise Op 336   PH 54
  6    Night in Venice, Eine Nacht in Venedige Operetta 1883: Overt   CT 61;
         PH 51
       New Vienna, Neu Wien Op 342   BN 65
  5    Perpetual Motion, Musical scherzo Op 257   BA 36;   BN 1894, 32;
         CT 59, 60;   CL 33, 43, 48, 60;   DA 49;   DE 48;   DT 35;
         HN 38;   KC 43;   LA 42;   NR 56;   NS 18, 22, 27;   PH 37, 38,
         48;   PT 66;   SL 30, 65;   SF 56;   WA 38
  5    Pizzicata Polka (written with brother, Josef) Op 449   BA 36;   CT 58;
         CL 43, 60, 61;   DA 49(2);   DE 45, 48;   NR 56;   NP 54;   PH 37,
         38, 41, 53, 54, 56, 58, 59, 61;   RC 63;   SL 59, 65;   SF 56;
         WA 35, 48
       Queen's Lace Handkerchief, Das Spitzentuch der Königin Operetta 1880:
         Overt   MN 50;   PH 52
 10    Roses of the South Rosen aus dem Suden Op 388   BA 38;   CH 04, 59;
         CT 26, 61;   DT 32;   HN 40;   LA 42;   NP 37;   NS 14, 18, 21, 22;
         PH 55;   PT 42, 45, 54
       Ritten Pazman, Operetta 1892: Ballet   NS 27
       Seid umschlungen Millionen Op 443   CH 1892
  5    Thunder and Lightning Polka   CH 53;   PT 45, 54;   WA 35, 38
  5    Trisch-Tratsch Polka Op 214   CT 58;   CL 48, 61;   DA 59;   NP 54;
         PH 53, 59;   PT 66
 11    Tales of the Vienna Woods Geschichten aus dem Wienerwald Op 325
         AT 51, 59;   BA 36, 37, 42;   CH 1894, 54;   CL 32, 33, 42, 51;
         DE 45, 47, 48;   DT 35;   HN 38, 44;   NA 35;   KC 35, 40, 42;
         LA 29, 31, 32, 42;   MN 41, 47, 48;   NP 28, 37, 44, 54;   NS 22;
         PH 25(2), 37, 41, 43, 45, 49, 52, 55, 59, 61;   PT 47;   RC 63;
         SL 65;   SF 56;   SE 39, 45, 46;   UT 40;   WA 40, 42
  6    Thousand and One Nights, Tausend und eine Nacht Op 346   CH 1892;
         HN 37;   NA 31;   NS 10
       Tout Vienne   CH 1892
```

  Time in
Minutes
STRAUSS, J. Jr. (Cont.)
         Viener Blut,Vienna Blood Op 354   BA 38, 42, 49, 50;   CL 44;
            DA 29, 49, 53;   NA 34, 42;   NP 40, 41;   PH 59;   PT 40, 42;
            WA 35, 39
    6   Voices of Spring Frühlingsstimmen Op 410   BA 43;   BN 32;   DA 29;
            HN 43;   NA 44;   MN 34;   PH 40, 49, 56, 59;   WA 36, 37, 39, 48
         Vortanzer   BA 37
   10   Wine, Women and Song Wein, Weib und Gesung Op 333   BA 36;   CH 02,
            27;   CT 59;   HN 39, 44;   KC 43;   MN 50;   NS 19, 23, 27;
            PH 40, 51, 56, 61;   SE 28;   WA 34
         Waldmeister, Operetta 1895: Overt   PH 38, 41, 53, 61
         Where Citrons Bloom, Wo die Zitronen bluhn Op 354   MN 44;   WA 39

STRAUSS, Johann, Sr.   10   3 Polkas   PH 49
1804-1849   Aust   8   Radetsky March, Op 228 1848   DA 49;   PH 42, 52, 54

STRAUSS, Josef   4   Dynamiden Waltz Op 173   KC 66;   PH 48, 58, 60
1827-1870   Aust   7   Delirien Waltz Op 212   AT 64;   CT 61;   CL 51, 61
                       5   Feuerfest, Polka   PH 55
                       5   Frauenberg, Polka-Mazurka   PH 42;   WA 36, 38
                            Mailuft   PH 55
                            Polka-Mazurka, Dragon Fly, Die Libelle Op 204
                               NS 19, 22;   PH 54
                            Spharen Klange, Music of the Spheres, Op 235
                               CH 1891;   DA 49;   ML 63;   MN 56;   NP 30;
                               PH 38, 42, 44;   PH 54;
                            Waltz, Village Swallows, or Flappermaulchen Op 164,
                               or 245   CH 04;   ML 65;   NP 48;   PH 54, 55
                            Waltz, Schwert und Leyer   PH 54

STRAUSS, Richard   50   Alpine Symphony Op 64   BN 25(2), 29;   CH 16, 52;
1864-1949   Ger   CT 45;   LA 31;   NP 16, 30, 47, 55;   PH 15
                      47   Aus Italien Symphonic Fantasy Op 16   BA 61;
            BN 1888, 00, 05, 09, excerpts 14;   CT 06;   CL 49;   NS 11;
            PH 08;   SL 64
            -Neapolitan folklife   CH 11
            -Shores of Sorrento   CH 00, 02, 04, 09, 11, 16, 25, 35, 36, 38, 40
   35   Burger als Edelmann from Incidental music for Ariadne auf Noxos or
         Bourgeosie Gentilhomme, Suite Op 60   BA 59;   BN 20, 33, 63;
         BU 55, 59;   CH 26, 28, 32, 37, 55, 63;   CT 23, 28, 45, 50;
         CL 34, 51, 68;   DA 49;   DE 69;   HN 65;   KC 48, 66;   LA 29,
         36;   NP 30, 37, 64;   NS 23;   PH 21, 29, 63, 64, 68;   PT 45,
         46;   SL 53;   SF 41, 54, 64, 66
   20   -Excerpts   RC 54
    6   -Overt   CH 55
   17   Burlesque in d for P and O 1885   BA 45, 61;   BN 02, 16;   CH 25, 31,
         43, 45, 55, 56, 66;   CT 25, 31, 37, 53, 57, 63, 65;   CL 38, 48,
         53, 61;   DA 53, 66;   DE 59;   DT 21, 25, 59;   HN 60;   KC 37, 50,
         66;   LA 26, 55, 62, 65;   MN 26, 31, 43;   NR 56, 64;   NP 21, 26,
         32, 44, 50, 53, 57, 62;   NS 17;   PH 11, 21, 24, 38, 54;   PT 47,
         54, 57;   RC 26, 33, 48;   SL 25, 53, 62;   SF 24, 41, 56, 66;
         SE 57, 66;   UT 67;   WA 36, 52
   20   Concertina Duet for Clarinet, Bassoon, Str and Harp 1947   AT 59;
         CH 59;   DA 49
   23   Conc for Oboe and small O 1945-6   BN 65;   CH 64;   HN 65;   RC 57
   17   Conc for Horn in E^b No 1 Op 11   CH 1891, 07;   CL 61;   DT 64;
         LA 57;   MN 37, 64;   PH 45;   RC 24;   SL 67

STRAUSS, R. (Cont.)
   29   Conc in d Op 8   CH 06
   25   Dance Suite from Harpsi pieces by Couperin 1923   BA 36, 64;   Ch 43,
         63
   20   Eine Deutsche Motette for Soli, Chor and O Op 62   PH 33
   10   Divertimento for small O after Couperin Op 86   BN 52
   23   Death and Transfiguration, Tod und Verklärung Symphon Poem Op 24
         AT 61;   BA 33, 40, 45(2), 47, 50, 52, 56, 57, 63, 67;   BN 1896,
         98, 02, 05(2), 08, 10, 11, 13, 15(2), 20, 23, 25, 26, 28, 30, 32,
         35, 37, 40, 41, 43, 46, 48, 51, 53, 57, 59, 61, 62;   BU 41, 43,
         44, 47, 56, 62;   CH 1894, 00, 02, 03(2), 05, 06, 07, 08, 09, 12,
         13, 15, 16, 17, 20, 21, 22, 24, 25, 28, 30, 31, 33, 35, 37, 43,
         44, 46, 47(2), 48, 49, 51, 54, 56, 59, 60, 63, 66;
         CT 1899, 01, 04, 07, 09, 10, 13, 14, 16, 22, 24, 27, 29, 30, 36,
         38, 49, 60, 62, 64, 66;
         CL 20, 21, 23, 24, 27, 30, 32, 33, 35, 36, 40, 42, 44, 47, 49, 53,
         55, 56, 58, 61, 65;   DA 50, 52, 57, 60;
         DE 48, 51, 56, 64, 68;   DT 19, 25, 28, 31, 37, 40, 43, 44, 45, 47,
         48, 52, 54, 58, 60, 62, 65, 69;   HN 38, 45, 51, 58, 61, 63;
         NA 42, 49, 51, 54, 58, 62;   KC 33, 34, 35, 49, 52(2), 55, 56, 60,
         62, 68;   LA 21, 22, 24, 26, 30, 32, 35, 36, 40, 45, 52, 55, 57,
         62, 65;   ML 64;   MN 22, 26, 30, 32, 33, 36, 39, 40, 41, 43, 46,
         49, 52, 57, 58(2), 63;   NR 51, 57, 61, 63, 65;
         NP 1891, 01, 03, 07, 09, 10, 11, 12, 13, 14, 15, 16, 17, 20, 21,
         22, 26, 27, 29, 33, 35, 36, 40, 49, 53, 54, 56, 61, 64, 67;
         NS 03, 05, 14, 22, 25;   PH 03, 05, 08, 09, 11, 12, 13, 14, 15(2),
         16, 20, 21(2), 22, 23, 24, 25, 26, 27, 28, 29, 30, 31, 32, 33(2),
         34, 36, 37, 38, 39, 40, 41, 42, 43, 44, 45, 47, 48, 49, 51, 52,
         56, 59, 64;   PT 37, 40, 44, 46, 48, 49, 53, 56, 62, 66;
         RC 24, 31, 33, 37, 42, 46, 53, 58, 68;   SL 15, 20, 22, 24, 26, 27,
         28, 30, 31, 33, 34, 35, 38, 40, 41, 42, 43, 46, 50, 52, 54, 55, 63,
         67;   SF 16, 20, 21, 22, 23, 25, 28, 29, 31, 32, 33, 36, 38, 42, 44,
         46, 48, 50, 51, 61, 63, 65, 67, 68;
         SE 26, 27, 30, 39, 58;   UT 45, 48, 55, 64, 67;
         WA 34, 36, 39, 43, 51, 52, 54
   17   Don Juan, Symphon Poem Op 20   AT 53, 61;   BA 36, 37, 42, 43, 45,
         46, 47, 53, 57, 62;   BN 1891, 98, 02, 04, 06, 09, 14, 16, 21, 23,
         24, 25, 27, 29, 32, 33, 36, 39, 42, 45, 46, 47;   BU 42, 45, 49,
         53, 54, 55;   CH 1897(2), 01(2), 02, 03, 04, 05, 06, 07, 08, 10,
         11, 12, 14, 15, 16, 17, 20, 21, 22, 23, 24, 25, 26, 27, 28, 30, 31,
         32, 35, 38, 40, 42, 44, 45, 46(2), 49, 52, 54, 55, 57, 59, 64, 68;
         CT 04, 05, 10, 12, 14, 17, 22, 23, 24, 25, 26, 28, 30, 31, 33, 37,
         41, 47, 48, 52, 57, 59, 60, 61, 64, 69;
         CL 21, 22, 24, 26, 28, 31, 33, 42, 45, 46, 47, 49, 50, 52, 55, 58,
         60, 62, 64, 66;   DA 46, 48, 49, 50, 56, 57, 59, 62, 66;
         DE 47, 48, 50, 52, 53, 54, 55, 57, 61, 66, 68;   DT 20, 24, 27, 28,
         30, 32, 35, 36, 38, 41, 44, 45, 46, 47, 48, 51, 53, 56, 61, 63, 67;
         HN 37, 41, 46, 50, 51, 53, 62, 69;   NA 40, 46, 50, 55, 56, 63, 65;
         KC 34, 36, 37, 38, 39, 40, 46, 51, 61, 65;
         LA 22(2), 23, 24, 26, 28, 31, 35, 37, 43, 46, 47, 52, 57, 59, 61,
         64, 67;   ML 63, 65;
         MN 22, 27, 29, 31, 32, 36, 41, 45, 48, 49, 56, 58, 59, 62, 64, 67;
         NR 50, 52, 56, 59;   NP 05, 09, 12, 13, 14, 15, 17, 20, 21, 22,
         24, 25, 29, 30, 31, 32, 36, 37, 41, 42, 51, 55, 56(2), 59, 60, 61,
         63;   NS 09, 22, 23, 26, 27;   PH 07, 08, 09, 12, 13, 15, 16, 20,
         22, 23, 24, 25, 27, 28, 29, 30, 31, 32(2), 35, 40, 42, 43(2), 46,

STRAUSS, R. (Cont.)   Don Juan Op 20, PH (Cont.)
        48, 50, 54, 57, 59, 60, 61, 63;   PT 39, 40, 42, 44(2), 46, 49, 50,
        53, 55, 65, 66, 68, 69;
        RC 23, 29, 31, 33, 34, 36, 38, 41, 44, 47, 50, 54, 55, 56, 62, 68, 69;
        SL 10, 12, 16, 22, 23, 25, 26, 27, 28, 30, 31, 33, 35, 37, 39, 43,
        44, 48, 49, 52, 56, 57, 58, 61, 67;   SF 11, 15, 17, 20, 21, 22, 23,
        24, 26, 27, 29, 30, 31, 32, 38, 41, 43, 45, 48, 51, 53, 55, 60, 63,
        65, 67;   SE 27, 33, 37, 45, 48, 53, 60, 68;
        UT 47, 52, 61, 68;
        WA 32, 35, 38, 42, 44, 50, 53, 55, 63, 65
  40   Don Quixote, Fantastic Var for C, Vla and O Op 35   AT 69;   BA 60, 63;
        BN 03(2), 09, 10, 15, 21, 31, 32, 34, 39, 42, 44, 47, 49, 51, 58,
        63, 67;   BU 57, 63;
        CH 1898, 10, 16, 24, 27, 33, 35, 36, 43, 45, 49, 52, 55, 57, 58, 60,
        67, 68;   CT 24, 27, 36, 50, 52, 54, 60, 66;
        CL 31, 41, 48, 50, 52, 55, 57, 60, 67;   DA 53, 59, 63, 69;
        DT 31, 38, 41, 52, 58, 63;   HN 48;   NA 41, 48, 53;   KC 51;
        LA 29, 37, 41, 45, 48, 50, 54, 57;   MN 24, 27, 34, 35, 42, 49, 53,
        55, 62;   NR 59, 64;   NP 24, 26, 29, 30, 36, 38, 43, 45, 47, 50,
        57, 60, 63, 68;   NS 11, 16, 22, 23;   PH 25, 36, 39, 41, 44, 47,
        49, 52, 55, 60, 67, 68;   PT 41, 47, 49, 54, 59, 63, 66, 68;
        RC 27, 51, 59;   SL 28, 30, 45, 46, 63, 68;   SF 26, 28, 36, 42,
        46, 51, 59, 63, 67, 68;   SE 56, 66;   UT 58, 66;
        WA 49, 54, 63, 68
  12   Festival Prelude, Festliches Praeludium for Org and O Op 61   BN 13;
        CH 13;   NP 13, 53;   PH 64
  43   Ein Heldenleben, Tone Poem Op 40   AT 64;   BA 67;   BN 01, 08, 10,
        24, 27, 30, 62, 65;   BU 65;   CH 1899, 01, 06, 11, 21, 22, 24, 26,
        27, 29, 30, 32, 33, 35, 36, 37, 38, 42, 43, 44, 46, 47, 53, 56, 58,
        62, 64, 68;   CT 26, 29, 48, 64;   CL 27, 28, 34, 37, 39, 40, 51,
        60;   DA 53, 64;   DT 22(2), 24, 34, 39, 61, 63;   HN 67;   KC 57;
        LA 27, 30, 47, 58, 63, 66;   MN 22, 31, 34, 36, 48, 52, 63;   NR 50;
        NP 00(2), 05, 10, 13, 15, 21, 26, 27, 28, 29, 31, 32, 34, 44, 50,
        55, 58, 62, 67;   PH 13, 15, 16, 20, 21, 22, 27, 28, 30, 32, 37, 38,
        42, 46, 51, 56, 60, 63;   PT 47, 58, 65;   RC 10, 61, 69;   SL 54,
        68;   SF 26, 27, 45, 47, 49, 58, 65, 69;   SE 59;   UT 53, 56, 63;
        WA 47, 56, 60
  20   Joseph's Legend, Ballet Op 63: a Symphonic Fragment 1947   CT 49;
        PT excerpts 38
  18   Macbeth, Tone Poem Op 23   AT 62;   BN 10;   CH 01, 06, 15, 22, 29,
        34;   CT 33, 53, 63;   DA 64;   LA 59;   MN 60;   NP 16, 33;
        NS 1891; RC 42;   SE 64;   WA 51
  28   Metamorphoses for 23 Solo Str 1944-5   BN 46;   CH 48;   CL 69;
        DT 53;   KC 64;   NP 47;   PH 64;   SL 47
        OPERAS
   4   Arabella Op 79: Arabella's aria Act I and with Monologue Act III SL 38
   4   -Aria, Das War sehr gut   KC 63
   4   -Prelude to Act III   CT 36;   NP 53;   SL 38
  16   -Symphon Synthesis, Fantasia   DA 53
 100   Ariadne auf Noxos Op 60, see also Burger als Edelmann   BN 68
   5   -Zerbinetta's aria   BA 62;   BU 56;   CH 17, 21, 53;   CT 53, 60;
        CL 24;   DA 63, 68;   DT 22, 47, 57, 62;   KC 54;   LA 24; MN 57;
        NR 68;   PT 53;   SL 21;   SF 23;   SE 63;   WA 48, 63
   5   -Ariadne's Monologue   CH 36, 40, 55;   DA 49;   KC 63;   ML 63;
        MN 49;   NS 17;   PH 21, 56;   PT 44, 53

STRAUSS, R. (Cont.) Operas (Cont.)
```
  15    Capriccio Op 85: Closing Scene    CH 54;    DT 59;    NR 60;    NP 60;
        RC 55;    SE 61;    WA 59
        Daphne Op 82    BN 66;    DE 61
   7    -Aria of Apollo    MN 49;    NP 13, 37
  20    -4 Excerpts    PH 57, 64
        Die Frau ohne Schatten, The Woman without a Shadow Op 65: Aria  KC 63
  20    -Fantasie  KC 58;    MN 54;    NP 53;    PH 55, 56
  20    -Interludes    BN 60, 63;    CH arr Leinsdorf 60
   4    Egyptian Helen Op 75: Aria    BA 63
   4    -Awakening    BN 64
 105    Elektra Op 58 Complete    BA 58;    CH 47, 55;    DT 45;    KC 62;    PT 68
  90    -Concert Form    MN 54;    NP 49, 57, 64
  20    -Excerpts    BU 57;    KC 38;    NP 36;    SE 60
   4    -Monologue, Finale    CH 40;    RC 18, 32, 54;    WA 53
   4    -Lament    DA 56
  20    Feuersnot Op 50: Excerpts    NA 50;    SL 61
   8    -Love Scene    BN 01, 08, 11;    CH 01(2), 02, 04, 06, 08, 11, 23, 26,
        27, 28, 31, 37;    CT 03, 04, 06, 10;    NA 50;    KC 38;    LA 50;
        NP 01, 03, 11(2), 14, 20;    PH 12, 51;    PT 59;    SL 13, 22, 63;
        SF 16, 59
  10    Guntrum Op 25: Festival Music    NP 16
  12    -Final Scene    BN 64
   4    -Friedenerzahlung    CH 05;    NP 01;    PH 02
   4    -Prelude Act I    BN 1896;    CH 1895, 01, 05, 15, 26;    NP 12, 15;
   4    -Prelude Act II    BN 04;    CT 00;    NS 1895
   4    -Prelude Act III    BN 04
   4    Intermezzo Op 72: Dreaming    CH 59, 61;    NP 53
   8    -Interlude    BN 29, 64;    CH 4 interludes 49;    KC 4 interludes 58;
        NP 25, 53;    NS 27;    CT 29
  10    -Waltz Scene    CH 26;    NP 25;    PH 63
  14    Die Liebe der Danae Op 83: Excerpts    PH 64
  20    Der Rosenkavalier Op 59: Excerpts    CH 53;    LA 58;    WA 48
   8    -Finale    DA 46;    PT 38
   4    -Marschallin's Dialogue    SE 61
   4    -Overt    PT 38
   4    -Singer's Aria    CL 51;    SE 51
  27    -Suite    BA 37, 45(2), 46, 48, 50, 56, 57, 67;    BN 48, 52, 55, 67,
        68;    BU 41, 60;    CH 47, 48, 50;    CT 44, 48, 49, 52, 57, 64;
        CL 45;    DA 48, 50, 62, 63, 67;    DE 49, 50, 53, 55, 57, 61, 63,
        65, 67, 69;    DT 46, 54, 62;    HN 46, 52, 56, 62, 63, 66;    NA 48,
        53;    KC 51, 53, 55, 57, 61, 63;    LA 45, 49, 50, 53, 55;    MN 31,
        44, 46, 48, 50, 65, 67;    NR 50, 57, 61, 63;    NP 44;    PH 44(2),
        45, 46, 47, 48(2), 49, 51, 52, 53, 55, 57, 59, 60, 62, 63;    PT 37,
        41, 48, 50, 54, 57, 63, 66;    RC 49, 56, 58, 60, 63;    SL 46, 47,
        49, 50, 52, 57, 59;    SF 45, 47, 50, 57, 60, 64, 65, 67, 69;
        SE 58, 65;    UT 49, 69;    WA 49, 52, 54, 57, 62
  20    -Waltzes    AT 51, 58, 59;    BN 63;    BU 49;    CH 11, 32(2), 36,
        38, arr Reiner 56;    CT 62, 64;    CL 38, 40, 42;    DA 49;
        DE 45, 48, 54;    DT 16, 44, 45;    HN 60;    NA 42, 49, 50, 62;
        KC 34, 39, 44, 48;    LA 43, 65;    ML 60;    MN 34, 42;    NP 30,
        46, 54;    PH 11, 31, 37, 38, 39, 41, 43, 46, 56, 67;    PT 43, 69;
        RC 35, 37, 39, 40, 46, 54;    SL 33(2), 34, 37, 39, 40, 41, 42, 43,
        48, 57;    SE 44, 52, 61;    WA 33, 37, 39, 43, 47
```

STRAUSS, R. (Cont.) Operas (Cont.)
 90   Salome Op 54 Complete   LA 64;   WA 57
 60   -Concert Form   MN 51, 65
 12   -Dance of the Seven Veils   BA 37, 54, 65;   BN 11, 23, 24, 26,
            28, 30, 36, 45, 54, 64;   BU 55, 66;   CH 07, 08, 15, 16, 22, 31,
            32, 39, 43, 45, 50, 53, 57, 61;   CT 10, 11, 23, 31, 51, 67;
            CL 28, 35, 37, 41, 47;   DA 46, 49, 56, 64, 69;   DE 51, 56;
            DT 35, 37, 44, 55, 57, 68;   HN 47, 49, 53, 58;   NA 50, 55;
            KC 37, 38, 45, 57, 58;   LA 31, 44, 46, 51, 54;   MN 31, 49, 60,
            64;   NR 65, 67, 69;   NP 22, 26, 28, 29, 30, 34, 36, 52, 54, 55;
            NS 26, 27;   PH 12, 13, 21, 22, 23, 25, 27, 28, 35, 40, 43, 45,
            46, 53, 58, 62;   PT 45, 56, 62;   RC 28, 40, 50, 54, 56;   SL 26,
            29, 36, 48, 57;   SF 27, 37, 40, 52, 61;   SE 29, 54, 64, 68;
            UT 65;   WA 54, 55, 56, 62
 12   -Finale   BA 52, 57;   BU 55;   CH 15, 16, 39, 55, 61;   CT 16,
            38, 44, 53;   DA 49, 69;   DE 52, 55;   DT 43, 44, 55, 63, 69;
            KC 54;   LA 51, 56;   NR 56, 67;   NP 15, 37, 62;   PH 15, 54;
            PT 45;   RC 54, 62;   SL 15, 40, 51;   SE 54, 68;   WA 52, 55, 62
 10   -Solo Scene   CL 37
  5   -Third Scene   PT 45
 20   Die schweigsame Frau, The Silent Woman Op 80 Potpourri arr Strauss
          CT 36
  4   -Overt   KC 58;   PH 35

 10   Serenade for 13 Wind Instruments in E^b Op 7   AT 54;   CH 1899 04,
          06, 07, 21, 29, 31, 35, 39;   CT 06, 11, 15, 33;   CL 25, 51, 63;
          DA 34, 49;   DE 48, 60;   DT 29;   NA 39;   NR 53;   NP 11, 20,
          23;   NS 09;   PH 04, 11, 13, 29;   SL 16, 25;   SF 21
        -Andante   PH 04
        SONGS
  4   Allerseelen Op 10 No 8 All Soul's Day   BN 35, 54;   CH 39, 51;
          CT 51;   DA 34;   DT 36, 41;   NA 41;   LA 37;   ML 60;   MN 33;
          SL 38;   PT 38
  4   Amor Op 68 No 5   CH 57;   CT 59;   PT 60
  4   Befreit Op 39 No 4   MN 45;   NP 15
  4   Cacilie Op 27 No 2   CH 32, 39;   CT 04, 12, 22, 33;   CL 25, 27;
          DE 49;   DT 23;   LA 24, 35, 36, 38, 44;   MN 22, 30, 40, 45;
          NP 05;   NS 04, 26;   PH 03, 26, 30;   PT 38, 41;   RC 46;
          SL 09, 24, 32;   SF 28, 39
  4   Death the Releaser   DT 21
 29   Drei Hymnen for Sopr and O Op 71   CT 68
 22   Four Last Songs   AT 57, 61, 65;   BA 57, 68;   BU 42, 66;   CH 54,
          58, 65;   CT 51, 63;   CL 58;   DA 61;   DE 68;   DT 57, 66;
          HN 61, 66;   NA 62;   KC 57;   ML 63;   MN 58, 64;   NP 57, 67;
          PH 54;   PT 57, 69;   RC 59, 69;   SF 59, 69;   SE 55, 69
  6   No 2 Beim Schlafengehen   CL 51
  5   No 3 September   CL 51
  8   No 4 Im Abendrot   CL 51;   SL 51
  4   Freundliche Vision Op 48 No 1   CH 32, 56;   CT 29;   CL 36;
          DE 58;   DT 21;   HN 48;   LA 29;   NP 10;   SL 30
  4   Die heiligen drei konige Op 56 No 6   CH 16;   DT 67
  4   Heimkehr Op 15 No 5   CH 32;   CT 29;   DE 58
  4   Heimliche Aufforderung Op 27 No 3   BN 35;   CH 12, 51;   DT 41;
          NP 10, 15;   PH 04;   PT 38;   SF 36
  4   Hymnus Op 33 No 3   CH 03, 05;   NP 00, 03, 07, 09

STRAUSS, R. (Cont.) Songs (Cont.)

4	Ich trage meine Minne Op 32 No 1 CH 51
4	Kling! Op 48 No 3 HN 48
4	Das Lied des Steinklopfers Op 49 No 4 NP 03
4	Liebeshymnus Op 32 No 3 CH 03; CT 04, 06; NP 03; PH 03, 09
8	Two Lieder Frühlingsgedrange, and O wärst du mein Op 26 KC 49; SE 38
4	Meinem Kinde Op 37 No 3 BA 67; CH 03; DT 67; PH 03
6	Morgen Op 27 No 4 BA 67; BN 54; BU 44, 54; CH 12, 21, 32, 56; CT 04, 12, 22, 29, 33, 45, 51; CL 22, 25, 27, 36; DE 49; DT 21, 25, 31, 52, 67; KC 35; LA 23, 24, 29, 43, 44; ML 60; MN 22, 30, 31, 35, 45; NR 68; NP 15; NS 26; PH 03, 15, PT 41; SL 24, 30, 53; SF 16, 28, 29, 36, 39, 44;
4	Muttertändelei Op 43 No 2 BA 67; CH 03; DT 67; PH 03
4	Pilger's Morgenlied Op 33 No 4 CH 05; NP 00, 03, 10
4	Das Rosenband Op 36 No 1 CH 03; CT 04, 33; PH 03
6	Ruhe, meine seele Op 27 No 1 BA 47, 67; CT 34; DT 67; LA 31, 45; SL 31
8	Two Songs for Baritone and O Op 51 Das Tal and Der Einsame PH 02
4	Sausle, Liebe Myrte Op 86 No 3 CH 57; CT 59; PT 60
4	Sehnsucht Op 32 No 2 NP 03
4	Sehnechtes Wetter Op 69 No 5 CH 39
6	Standchen, Serenade No 2 Op 17 BN 54; BU 54; CH 21, 32, 57; CT 22, 30, 59; CL 22, 27, 36; DE 49; DT 21(2), 23, 25, 31, 41, 52; NA 41; LA 23, 29, 37, 44; ML 60; MN 22, 27, 31, 35; PH 15; PT 38, 60; RC 46; SL 30, 53; SF 28, 29
30	Die Tageszeiten, Song Cycle for men's Chor Op 76 BN 63; NA Tomorrow 41; NP 28
4	Traum durch die Daemmerung, Dream in the Twilight Op 29 No 1 CT 36, 51; DT 36; MN 33; NP 05; SF 29
4	Verfuhrung Op 33 No 1 MN 43; NP 10, 13, 37
4	Waldseligheit Op 49 No 1 BA 67; DT 67
6	Wiegenlied Lullaby Op 41 No 1 BA 67; BN 54; CH 03, 32, 57; CT 12, 22, 30, 33, 59; DT 21; LA 36; ML 60; MN 34, 40; PH 03; PT 38, 60; RC 46; SL 24
4	Zueignung, Dedication Op 10 No 1 BA 43; BN 35; CH 51, 56; DE 49; DT 34, 36, 41, 52; NA 36, 41; LA 24, 29, 35; MN 33, 35; NS 08; PT 38; RC 46; SL 32, 35, 38, 53; SF 36, 39; WA 33
4	Suite for Winds Op 4: Romanze CH 12
4	-Gavotte CH 12, 32
4	-Introduction and Fugue CH 12, 32
4	-Prelude CH 32
25	Suite, Schlagobers, Ballet Op 70 NP 32; CT 32
18	Sinfonia Domestica Op 53 BA 64; BN 06(2), 09, 11, 23(2), 27, 29, 30, 33, 35, 41, 45, 49, 58; CH 07, 29, 44, 56, 61; CT 12, 16, 28, 30, 55; CL 39, 50, 62, 63; DT 26, 27; LA 38, 53, 68; MN 40, 67; NP 23, 25, 27, 33, 40, 45, 49, 53, 56, 60; NS 07; PH 04, 10, 16, 37, 45, 52, 59, 64; PT 52; SF 40; SE 69
18	-Parergon zur Sinfonia Domestica for P, left hand and O Op 73 CT 34; NA 69; SF 46
45	Symph in f Op 12 BN 1893, 99; NP 1884; SL 14

STRAUSS, R. (Cont.)
  15   Til Eulenspiegl's Merry Pranks, Symphon Poem Op 28
         AT 50, 54, 64;   BA 36, 37, 50, 51, 53, 55, 57;
         BN 1895, 99, 05, 07, 09, 11, 12, 14, 16, 20, 22, 24, 26, 29, 31, 33,
         35, 37, 39, 40, 41, 43, 44, 46, 48, 51, 54, 56, 58, 59, 60, 62, 65,
         66, 69;   BU 46, 50, 54, 59, 62, 63, 69;
         CH 1895(3), 98, 00, 02, 03(2), 04(2), 05, 06, 07, 08, 09(2), 11, 13,
         16, 24, 25, 28, 30, 31, 32, 33, 35, 36, 37, 38, 39, 40, 42, 43, 46(2),
         47, 48, 51, 52, 53, 57, 61, 62, 63, 65, 66, 67;
         CT 05, 11, 13, 14, 22, 25, 26(2), 28, 29, 31, 33, 34, 37, 39, 42,
         44, 46, 48, 55, 58, 59, 61, 65, 68, 69;
         CL 23, 25, 29, 31, 33, 34, 36, 37, 38, 39, 40, 42, 43, 44, 45, 46,
         48, 49, 51, 54, 56, 59, 64, 69;   DA 46, 49, 50, 54, 57, 61, 65, 67,
         68;   DE 49(2), 50, 52, 57, 65, 68;   DT 19, 23, 25, 27, 28, 29, 31,
         35, 36, 40, 47, 48, 51, 52, 55, 58, 60, 61, 62, 63, 66;
         HN 46, 47, 49, 53, 55, 61;   NA 37, 42, 45, 47, 49, 53, 55, 59, 64,
         67;   KC 39, 40, 47, 50, 53, 59, 66;
         LA 23(2), 25, 29, 32, 35, 36, 38, 40, 41, 46, 49, 51, 53, 58, 64,
         69(2);   ML 68;   MN 22, 26, 28, 31, 33, 34, 35, 38, 40, 42, 44,
         47, 49, 51, 54, 61, 66;   NR 52, 55, 57, 62, 68;
         NP 02, 03, 05, 09, 10, 14, 15, 16, 20, 21, 22, 23, 26, 27, 28, 29,
         30, 32, 36, 37, 41, 43, 44, 45, 51, 52, 54, 55, 56, 57, 58, 62, 63,
         64, 67;   NS 06, 15, 21, 22, 23(2), 24, 25, 27;   PH 03, 04, 06,
         07, 08(2), 10, 11, 13, 14, 22, 23, 24, 27, 28, 29, 31(2), 35(2),
         37, 38, 40, 42, 44, 45(2), 49, 50, 51, 52(2), 54, 55, 57, 58, 60,
         63, 66, 68;
         PT 37, 39, 41, 44, 46, 47, 48, 49, 50, 51, 53, 55, 59, 60, 61, 64,
         65, 69;
         RC 24, 25, 28, 30, 32, 35, 38, 40, 43, 48, 55, 57, 65;
         SL 11, 12, 21, 23, 25, 27, 30, 32, 34, 35, 36, 38, 39, 40, 45, 46,
         47, 48, 50, 51, 56, 57, 59, 60, 61, 62, 66;
         SF 15, 21, 24, 27, 29, 35, 43, 46, 48, 50, 52, 53, 60, 62, 63, 64, 66;
         SE 45, 49, 54, 62, 67;   UT 46, 50;   WA 46, 49, 51, 53, 57, 60, 64
  35   Thus Spake Zarathustra, Symphon Poem Op 30   BN 1897, 99, 08, 09, 11,
         14, 15, 22, 28, 31, 32, 34, 36, 38, 40, 42, 46, 48, 60, 63, 67;
         BU 67;   CH 1896(2), 97, 98, 00, 03, 05, 13, 24, 28, 29, 30, 31,
         32, 33, 34, 35, 36, 38, 39, 40, 44, 45, 47, 53, 54, 59, 61, 65;
         CT 26, 30, 49, 69;   CL 34, 36, 51;   DA 48, 50, 55;   DT 23, 28;
         HN 68;   NA 47;   KC 54, 60, 63;   LA 32, 37, 50, 52, 60, 64, 67; ML 69
         MN 29, 35, 39, 47, 50, 65;   NR 69;   NP 08, 10, 21, 25, 41, 43,
         48, 52, 55, 57, 62, 64;   PH 26, 28, 31, 36, 54, 58, 62, 63, 68, 69;
         PT 38, 61, 67;   RC 26, 60;   SL 29, 37(2), 39, 63, 66, 69;
         SF 29, 40, 64;   SE 61;   UT 54;   WA 67

STRAVINSKY, Igor   22   Agon Ballet   BN 57, 64;   CH 59;   SF 58
  1882-1971   Russ   30   Apollon Musagète, Ballet Suite 1928   BN 28, 29, 33,
                             39;   CL 54;   HN 48;   LA 33, 34;   MN 48;
         NP 39;   PT 39;   SL excerpts 46, 66;   SF 47
   5   Babel, for Narrator, Chor and O in 7 Parts, Text from Genesis by
         various composers, Milhaud, Toch, Schoenberg, Stravinsky et al
         1944   UT 46
  50   Le Baiser de la fée The Fairy's Kiss Ballet   1928   BN 62, 67;
         CT 55;   CL 55;   DE 54, 67;   MN 50, 65;   NR 65, 69;   PH 46,
         59, 64;   SF 41;   WA 59
   8   -Dance Suisses   BU 63

STRAVINSKY, I. (Cont.)
   17   Canticum Sacrum for Tenor, Baritone and Mixed Chor   BN 57;   MN 62
  15-20   Capriccio for P and O 1929   BN 36, 39, 48, 55;   BU 58, 63;
          CH 53, 67;   CL 50;   DA 54;   KC 56;   LA 40;   NP 36, 61;
          PH 65;   SL 39, 65;   SF 43, 56, 64;   WA 67
   25   Chant du Rosignole, Song of the Nightingale, Symphon Poem 1917
          BA 68;   BN 25(2), 48, 60, 68;   BU 69;   CH 23, 24, 56, 60, 68;
          CT 26, 44;   CL 24, 64;   DA 64;   DE 57;   DT 51, 62, 68;   LA 56;
          MN 50;   NR 62, 68;   NP 23, 24, 39, 42, 56, 64, 69;   NS 23, 25;
          PH 23, 24, 48, 67;   PT 42, 50, 61;   SL 52, 62;   SF 48, 59;
          SE 64
    6   Circus Polka for Elephants 1942   BA 44, 52;   BN 43;   CL 46;
          LA 47, 59, 66;   MN 43;   NR 53;   NP 44;   PH 46;   RC 44;
          SL 45;   SF 47
   19   Conc for P and Wind O 1924   BN 24;   CH 35(2);   CL 48;   NP 24,
          44, 59;   RC 60
   22   V Conc Op 48   AT 69;   BN 31, 69;   CL 35, 66;   DA 65;   DT 38, 68;
          LA 64, 69(2);   NP 60;   PH 31, 41, 67;   PT 59;   SL 31, 64, 68;
          SF 48, 62, 64, 68;   SE 67
   12   Conc for Str in D, 3 mvt 1946   BN 48;   HN 48;   NP 47;   PT 47;
          SF 47, 59, 66;   SL 68
   19   Danses Concertantes for small O 1941   BN 53;   SF 67
   20   Divertimento 1934   AT 63;   BN 36, 40, 41, 51, 57;   CH 34, 53,
          57, 58, 59;   CT 48;   CL 64;   DA 53, 57, 63;   DE 63;   HN 48,
          55;   LA 36, 47, 58;   MN 40;   NR 53;   NP 52, 59;   PT 66;
          SF 47;   SE 63;   WA 48
   12   Dumbarton Oakes, Concerto in E^b for 16 Winds 1938   CT 44;   CL 63
    6   Fantasie   NR 65
  27-30   The Firebird, Ballet Suite 1910   AT 59, 67, 69;   BA 38, 43, 44(2),
          45, 48(2), 50, 52, 53, 58, 62;
          BN 14, 24, 26, 27, 29, 30, 34, 38, 43, 45, 52, 56, 57, 59, 63, 65,
          66, 68, 69;   BU 40, 41, 44, 46, 53, 58, 62;   CH 20, 24(2), 26,
          27, 28, 29, 31, 32, 33, 34(2), 36, 38, 40, 42, 46, 50, 53, 55,
          56, 61, 62, 65, 66, 67;   CT 24, 25, 29, 31, 32, 34, 38, 39, 42,
          43, 44, 48, 49, 54, 56, 59, 63, 68, 69;   CL 21, 24, 26, 27, 29,
          30, 31, 33, 36, 37, 39, 41, 44, 45, 47, 49, 51, 55, 56, 58, 60,
          62, 64, 66, 69;   DA 49, 50, 51, 52, 57, 58, 64;
          DT 24, 25, 26, 27, 33, 36, 37(2), 43, 44, 45, 46, 48, 53, 56, 59,
          61, 62, 66;   HN 47, 53, 54, 55, 56, 57, 65, 67;
          NA 45, 51, 55, 57, 62, 65,68;   KC 34, 36, 41, 51, 53, 61, 67;
          LA 27, 28, 29(2), 33, 34, 36, 37, 38, 39, 40, 44, 48, 50, 54, 58,
          60, 61, 63, 68;   ML 64;
          MN 27, 31, 33, 35, 36, 39, 40, 45, 48, 51, 53, 55, 57, 60, 67;
          NR 53, 55, 57, 60, 61, 65;
          NP 23, 24, 29, 30, 31, 32, 34, 36, 37, 38, 39, 41, 43, 45, 46, 53,
          54, 57, 58, 61;   NS 16, 20, 27;
          PH 17, 21, 23(2), 24(2), 25(2), 28, 29, 30, 31, 32, 33(2), 34, 35,
          38, 39, 40, 42, 43, 44, 45, 46, 47, 50, 52, 58, 61, 63, 64, 65, 68, 69;
          PT 39, 41, 43, 44, 45, 50, 51, 56, 61, 67;
          RC 24, 31, 35, 40, 44, 49, 57, 62, 68, 69;
          SL 22, 25, 26, 30, 31, 33, 36, 39, 41, 42, 43, 44, 45, 46, 47, 49,
          54, 57, 62, 69;   SF 21, 23, 24, 28, 29, 30, 32, 33, 36, 41, 50, 54,
          57, 63, 65, 66, 67;   SE 27, 29, 45, 47, 48, 49, 51, 55, 61;
          UT 47, 50, 52, 56, 60, 62, 64, 66;   WA 46, 58, 65
    5   -Berceuse   CL 25;   DE 46, 48, 50, 53;   DT 52;   MN 41, 47, 55;
          NP 52;   WA 39

STRAVINSKY, I. (Cont.)   The Firebird, Ballet Suite (Cont.)
```
12      -Excerpts   DE 51, 69;   HN 48;   NA 37, 39, 42;   WA 48
 7      -Finale   CH 35;   CL 25;   DE 46, 48, 50, 53;   MN 47, 55;
          NP 52;   SF 45;   WA 39
 5      -Firebird's Dance   DE 46, 48, 50, 53, 54
 5      -Introd   DE 46, 48, 50, 53, 54
 5      -King Kastchez Dance   DE 46, 48, 50, 53, 54;   MN 41, 47, 55;
          NP 23;   NS 21
 6      -Princesses Dance   DE 46, 48, 50, 53, 54
 5      Fireworks Op 4   BN 14, 34, 62;   CH 14, 40, 44;   CT 22, 27, 32,
          63, 65;   DT 56, 69;   MN 34, 65;   NP 14, 24, 29, 34, 36, 61;
          PH 20, 22, 24(2), 27, 34, 42, 44, 61, 67;   PT 45, 55;   RC 24,
          28;   SL 24;   SF 59
 9      Four Norwegian Moods 1942   BA 52;   BN 43;   BU 48;   LA 47;   MN 48;
          NR 53;   NP 44;   PH 45, 68;   RC 44;   SL 45;   SF 47, 69
 3      Greeting, Prelude, Happy Birthday   BN 69;   CT 69;   NP 61;   SF 69
15      Huit Pieces Enfantine, Little Suite 8 pieces   LA 33, 34;   NP Parts
          I and II 26,   69;   WA 36, 49, 51
20      L'Histoire d'un Soldat, Dramatic Piece 1918   NP 69;   SF 68, 69
19      The Card Party Ballet, Jeu de Cartes 1937   BA 52, 69;   BN 39, 43,
          49, 52, 56, 60, 65;   CH 39, 63, 67, 69;   CT 40, 68;   CL 63;
          DA 52;   LA 37, 40, 55, 67;   MN 40, 66;   NP 39, 52;   PH 37, 67;
          PT 39;   RC 66;   SF 39
25      Mavra, Opera Buffa in One Act 1922   CH 59
 7      Monumentum ad Carlo Geswalde   CL 63;   SF 60
10      Les Noces, Ballet with Chorus 1923   CH 52, 65
 8      Octet for Winds 1923   LA 67;   NP 68
10      Ode in 3 parts for O 1943   BN 43, 48, 67;   BU 66;   CL 52, 63;
          LA 62;   NP 44;   PH 59
55      Oedipus Rex, Opera-Oratorio 1927   BN 27, 39, 47, 51;   BU 66;
          CL 61;   LA 59, 66;   NP 69;   PH 30
 4      -Jocasta's Aria   CH 66
25      Orpheus, Ballet Suite 1947   BN 48, 54;   BU 59;   CL 62;   LA 49;
          MN 68;   SF three scenes 68
10      -Fragments   SF 50
48      Persephone, Narrator, Tenor, Chor and O 1934   BN 34;   BU 67;
          CT 62, 64;   LA 62;   MN 56;   NP 56;   PH 63;   SE 69
42      Petrouchka, Ballet Suite 1911   AT 54, 61, 65, 69;   BA 68;
          BN 20, 24, 25, 27, 31, 32, 39, 40, 42, 45, 52, 56, 57, 59, 63, 65,
          66, 68, 69;   BU 46, 58, 60, 61;
          CH 30, 33, 34, 37, 39, 40, 43, 49, 50, 53, 56, 60, 62, 65, 66;
          CT 24(2), 25, 30, 32, 47, 61;   CL 32, 34, 36, 42, 44, 46, 49, 55,
          61, 67;   DA 54, 61;   DE 67;   DT 35, 38, 51, 57, 63, 67;
          HN 52, 57, 69;   KC 44, 62;   LA 27, 31, 33, 34, 35, 36, 43, 58,
          63, 69;   MN 24, 32, 36, 39, 40, 42, 58, 62;   NR 52, 59;
          NP 23, 34, 35, 36, 39, 46, 50, 51, 56, 59, 64, 68;   NS 22, 25, 27;
          PH 24, 26, 27, 28, 31, 34, 36, 37, 40, 42, 46, 48, 49, 53, 66, 69;
          PT 38, 39, 45, 54, 63, 65, 66;   RC 25, 35, 36, 39, 43, 48, 56, 59;
          SL 28, 36, 50, 52, 56, 58, 61, 62, 64;
          SF 30, 35, 48, 50, 56, 61, 64, 67;   SE 31, 49, 60;
          UT 51, 57, 63, 67;   WA 49, 56, 58, 61, 67
30      -Excerpts   KC 48;   MN 68
 4      -Hocus Pocus   HN 50
15      -Part I and Part IV   NP 25, 33
 5      -Russian Dance   HN 50;   NR 65
```

STRAVINSKY, I. (Cont.)   Petrouchka (Cont.)
```
  10       -Scenes   CH four scenes 69;    DA 49;   RC 44
   5       -Shrovetide Fair   SF 45
   4     Pastorale, Wordless Song 1908    DT 43;    PH 38, 64
  22     Pulcinella Suite, Ballet after Pergolesi 1920   BA 52, 60;   BN 22,
           31, 43, 56, 64;    BU 46, 57, 64;   CH 34, 55;    CT 24, 29, 30,
           58, 67;    CL 37, 51, with song 52, 62, 66;    DT excerpts 54;
           HN 62;    KC 64;    LA 61;    NR 67;    NP 24, 35, 38, 52, 59;
           NS 25;    PH 34, 46, 56;    PT 45;    SL 30, 39, 53, 65;    SF 54;
           SE 65
   8       -Excerpts   SL 59
   8       -Scene   CL 46;    SL 59
  12     Quatre Études for O 1929    BN 68;    NP 52, 60, 68;    PH 31
  10     Ragtime for 11 Instruments 1918   NS 25
   6     The Rakes Progress, Opera 1951: Act I, Scene III    CH 53
   4       -Anna's Aria   CT 59;    PH 58
  15     Reynard the Fox from the Ballet for Chamber O and Vla 1922    PH 23
  13     Requiem Canticle   LA 69
  33     Sacre de Printemps, The Rite of Spring, Ballet 1913    AT 68;
           BN 23(2), 24, 26, 32, 33, 35, 38, 46, 50, 54, 56, 65;    BU 63, 69;
           CH 24, 25, 48, 50, 62, 64, 67, 69;    CT 35, 40, 50, 62, 65, 69;
           CL 34, 48, 56, 63, 65, 67;    DA 48, 49, 56, 61, 68;    DT 57, 63,
           65;    HN 56;    NA 67;    KC 65;    LA 30, 51, 54, 56, 59, 64, 67;
           ML 68;    MN 49, 53, 59, 63, 65;    NR 64;    NP 24, 30, 36, 39, 46,
           50, 57, 60, 68;    NS 25;    PH 21, 27, 29, 30, 32, 38, 54, 63, 67;
           PT 53;    RC 61;    SL 63, 65;    SF 38, 44, 65, 69;    SE 58, 66;
           UT 54, 62;    WA 65, 66
  16     Scherzo Fantastique Op 3 1908    CH 24, 69;    CT 24;    NP 27, 38;
           PH 24;    SF 57
   5     Scherzo a la Russe for Jazz Band 1944    CT 65;    CL 46;    HN 46;
           LA 47;    NR 53;    PH 46;    PT 55;    SF 45
  15     Scènes de Ballet 1944    AT 54;    BN 45;    CH 45;    CL 46;    HN 57;
           LA 47;    NR 53;    NP 45;    PH 46, 53;    PT 54;    SF 45, 50;
           SE 53;    WA 48, 49, 55, 60
   6     Star Spangled Banner arr for Chor and O 1941    UT 41;    WA 42
  10     Suite for small O No 1 1921    CT 28;    SF 53
  10     Suite for small O No 2 1926    CT 28;    NS 26
  30     Symph No 1 in E$^b$ 1905    CH 34
  40     Symph in C 1938    BA 50;    BN 40, 43, 68;    CH 40, 61, 67;    CT 40;
           CL 52;    DA 65;    LA 40, 65;    MN 60;    NP 63, 68;    PH 63, 65;
           RC 65;    SL 41;    SF 41, 66
  23     Symph des Psalmes for Chor and O 1930    AT 63, 67;    BN 30(2), 31,
           35, 39(2), 41, 46, 58, 62;    CH 32, 55, 63;    CL 53, 56, 66;    DA 61;
           DE 66;    HN 68;    LA 65;    MN 54, 66;    NR 63, 69;    NP 33, 34,
           60, 63;    PH 31, 43;    PT 62, 65;    RC 65;    SL 55, 62, 66;
           SF 36, 53, 65;    UT 67
  24     Symph in Three mvts 1945    BA 47, 49;    BN 45, 46, 47, 61, 66;
           CH 60, 67;    CT 55;    CL 46, 63, 66;    DA 61;    DE 62;    DT 66;
           HN 63;    LA 47, 52, 62, 67;    ML 65;    MN 64;    NR 66;    NP 45,
           63, 67;    PH 62;    PT 64;    RC 53, 54, 67;    SL 54, 61, 66;
           SF 45;    UT 62;    WA 48, 69
10-12    Symph d'instruments a Vent, Symph for Wind Instruments 1920    BN 55,
           68;    BU 65;    CH 67(2);    CT 65;    CL 50;    HN 67;    NP 65, 68;
           PH 23;    PT 69
  12     Three Songs from Shakespeare    AT 62
```

  Time in
  Minutes
STRAVINSKY, I. (Cont.)
  15   Three Lyrical Poems for Voice and O from the Japanese 1912   CT 23;
          PH 22
   6   Var for P and O 1964   BN 69;   CH 66;   SL 65;   SF 65
   5   Volga Boatmen, Song for Winds and Percussion arr Stravinsky 1917
          BN 23;   CH 24, 34(2);   CT 24;   NP 24;   PH 24
   7   Zvezdoliki, Cantata, female Chor and O   BN 61;   LA 65

STRIEGLER, Kurt Emil   9   Rondo Burlesque   NS 27
1886-1958   Ger

STRINGFIELD, Lamar   13   Dixie 1950   NA 50
1897-   US   20   Suite: From the Southern Mountains Op 38   WA 32

STRINGHAM, Edwin J.   13   Nocturne No 1 Symphon Poem 1932   CH 36;   CT 38;
1890-   US   SL 38;   SF 41
                    12   Nocturne No 2 1938   CH 38;   SL 43
                    20   Symphon Poem, The Ancient Mariner 1926   MN 28
                    30   Symph No 1 in b^b 1929   MN 29

STRONG, George T.   7   Chorale on a Theme of Leo Hassler, When Our Last
1856-1948   Ger/US   Hour is at Hand   PH 34;   RC 35;   WA 34
                    20   Symphon Poem, Une Vie d'Artiste, The Life of an
                            Artist   CL 25;   NP 26
                    30   Symph No 2, Sintram   NP 1892

STRUBE, Gustave   25   American Rhaps   CH 25
1867-1953   Ger/US   4   Black Bass   BA 26, 28
                    23   V Conc in f# 1924   BN 05, 06
                    23   V Conc in G   BN 1897
                    23   C Conc in e   BN 09
                    10   Fantastic Dance Vla and O   BN 07, 11, 17;   LA 26
                    10   Fantastic Overt   BN 03
                    15   Harz Mountain, Poem 1940   BA 42
                    15   Longing, Symphon Poem Vla and O   BN 04, 07
                     8   Die Lorelei   BN 12
                     6   Maid of Orleans, Overt   BN 1894
                     8   Narcissus and Echo   BN 12
                     4   Prelude No 2   BA 28, 64;   BN 20
                     8   Puck, A Comedy Overt   BN 09, 10;   CH 10, 17;
                            CT 11;   PH 12;   SL 10
                    15   Rhaps for O   BN 00
                    20   Sinfonietta   BA 40
                    10   Suite   WA 32
                    20   Symph Americana 1930   BA 36
                    35   Symph in b   BN 08, 11
                    30   Symph in c   BN 1895
                    12   Symphon Fantasy   BA 26
                    10   Var on Original Theme   BN 14;   NP 18;   PH 15;
                            CH 16

STURM, Louis   15   Prelude, Theme and Var in e Op 34   CT 14
        US

SUDERBERG, Robert   10   Orchestra Music I   SE 69
        US

SUESSE, Dana   20   Conc for 2 P in e   CT 43
1911-   US

SUK, Joseph   20   A Fairy Tale, Incidental Music Op 13   BN 02;
1874-1935   Czech   CL 49, 64;   SL 66
                       30   Fantasia V and O Op 24   CL 54, 65;   CH 36;
                             MN 46;   PH 24
                        8   Meditation on an Ancient Chorale Op 35a   CL 35, 57;
                             CH 50;   DT 37
                       31   Pohadka, A Summer Tale Symphon Poem Op 29: Ein
                             Marchen   CH 01(2), 04, Funeral Music only 51;
                             NR 52;   NP 01
                       14   Scherzo Fantastique Op 25   CH 06, 07;   LA 22;
                             NS 05, 14
                       25   Serenade for Str in E^b Op 6   CH 05;   PH 01
                       40   Symph No 1 in E Op 14   BN 04;   NP 00;   PH 02

SULEK, Stephen   12   Classical Conc for O No 1   NP 60
1914-   Yugo

SULLIVAN, Sir Arthur   5   Overt to the Devil   CL 49
1842-1900   Brit   5   The Templar's Soliloquy from Ivanhoe, Opera 1891

SUPPÉ, Franz von   7   Overt to Beautiful Galatea, 1865 CH 54; NP 40; PT 38
1819-1895   Aust   6   Overt to Light Cavalry 1866   HN 42;   SL 60

SURINACH, Carlos   16   Conc for O   PT 66
1915-   Sp/US   21   Dramas Melorhythmic   CT 68;   DT 67;   NR 67;   PT 67
                             SE 67;
                        6   Feria Magica   NA 57
                       20   Ritmo Jondo   ML 65;   RC 56
                       12   Sinfonietta Flamenco   HN 55;   UT 55
                       28   Symphony No 2   DA 53

SUTERMEISTER,   47   Missa da Requiem with Soli Chor and O 1953   DE 61
  Heinrich
1910-   Swiss

SVENDSEN, Johan   11   Carnival in Paris Op 9   BN 1891, 94, 02, 08, 19;
1840-1911   Nor   CH 1891, 04, 10;   DT 21;   NA 31;   NP 00, 10;
                             PH 02, 09, 10, 11, 14, 15, 17, 18;   RC 23;
                             SL 10, 27;   SF 12, 22;   SE 37;   UT 45
                        8   Carnival of Norwegian Artists for O Op 16   DA 30;
                             LA 20
                       20   C Conc in d Op 7   CH 03
                        7   Coronation March for Oscar II Op 13   CH 10;
                             HN 13, 15
                       10   Norwegian Rhaps No 1 Op 17   NS 1878;   RC 40
                       10   Norwegian Rhaps No 2 Op 19   BN 1889;   PH 17
                        6   Octet for Str in a Op 3   CH Scherzo and andante
                             only 09
                        8   Romeo and Juliet, A Phantasy Overt Op 18   NA 33;
                             NP 1880

SVENDSEN, J. (Cont.)
	30	Symph No 1 in D Op 4 CH 00, one mvt only 05, 07, 11
	30	Symph No 2 B♭ Op 15 BN 1883, 90, 03
	4	Violet, A Song CH 1892
	10	Zorahyde, Legend for O Op 11 BN 1892, 17; CH 04, 11; SF 24

SWANSON, Howard
1909-   US
	25	First Symphony DE 51
	12	Short Symphony CH 51; CL 51; DT 52; HN 51; NP 50; PH 51; SL 52

SWEELINCK, Jan Peter
1562-1621   Neth
	4	Born Today NS 16
	9	Chromatic Fantasy arr Kindler WA 48

SWEET, Reginald
1885-   US
	15	Overt Sketches NP 18
	5	Riders to the Sea NP 20

SWERT, Jules de
1843-1891   Belg
	16	C Conc in d Op 32 CH 08
	15	C Conc in c No 2 Op 38 AT 48; CH 15; PH 04

SWIERZYNSKI, Michal
1868-   Pol
	4	Wien, Wien KC 64

SYDEMAN, William
1928-   US
	8	The Lament of Electra SF 65
	8	In Memoriam John F. Kennedy BN 66
	12	Study for O No 2 BN 63
	10	Study for O No 3 BN 65

SZABELSKI, Boheslav
1896-   Pol
	6	Toccata CH 57; PT 64

SZALOWSKI, Antonin
1907-   Pol
	7	Overt PH 38; WA 39

SZELL, George
1897-1970   Hung/US
	16	Var on an Original Theme Op 4 SL 29

SZYMANOVKI, Karol
1883-1937   Pol
	23	V Conc No 1 Op 35 BN 54; CH 27, 29; CL 27; DT 69; LA 31; MN 30, 61, 67; PH 24;
	20	V Conc No 2 Op 61 BN 34; CH 43; CL 34; DT 63; MN 64; NP 45, 51; PH 47; PT 65; SL 62
	40	Harnasie, Ballet Op 51 Tenor, Chor and O CL 36; NP 36
	20	Stabat Mater for Soli, Chor and O Op 53 MN 61
	20	Symphonie Concertante for P and O Op 60 BN 39; LA 52; MN 44, 65; NP 43, 51; PH 42, 65; PT 52; SF 40
	30	Symphonie Concertante No 4 P and O CL 33, 41
	35	Symph No 2 Op 19 BN 21; NP 68 -Finale PT 66
	20	Symph No 3, Song of the Night for Tenor, Chor and O Op 27 CH 30; NP 26; PH 26
	8	Three Poems for V Op 30 No 1 La Fontaine d'arethuse SF 40

TAILLEFEERE, Germaine 1892- Fr/US	10 16 12 20	Jeux de Plein Air 1923 BN 25 Conc for Harp PT 55 P Conc in D BN 24; PH 24; NP 24 V Conc SF 37
TAKAHASHI, Yuji 1939- Japan	10	Orphika BU 69
TAKACS, Jeno 1902- Aust/US	17 11	Antiqua Hungarica Op 47 CT 69 Eisenstadt Divertimento CT 65

TAKEMITSU, Toru
1930-   Japan
	12
	
	6
	20
		Green, for O, November, Steps II CL 69; NP 67;
		    PH 68; SF 68
		The Dorian Horizon SF 66; BU 68
		Requiem for Str O MN 62; NP 64; PH 65;
		    PT 64; SF 67; DT 68

TALLIS, Thomas 1505-1585 Brit	4	O Nata Lux MN 42
TALMA, Louise 1906- US	21 12	Dialogues for P and O BU 65 Toccata 1944 BA 45

TANEYEV, Sergei
1856-1915   Russ
	5
	
	19
	
	32
		Entr'acte from Orestes, an Opera Trilogy 1895
		    DT 27; PH 28
		Overt to the Trilogy, Orestes Op 6 BN 00, 02;
		    CH 17
		Symph No 1 in c Op 12 BN 01, 35

TANGSTROM Swed	4	Tristan's Death NA 46

TANSMAN, Alexander
1897-   Pol/Fr
	4
	17
	16
	20
	24
	
	18
	12
	9
	
	6
	
	10
	10
	11
	15
	14
	17
	16
	10
	15
	
	8
		Aria and Alla Polacca SF 36
		Adagio for Str O 1936 SL 36, 42
		Concertina P and O 1931 SF 36
		Conc for O BN 56; CH 32; SL 36, 56
		P Conc No 2 1927 BN 27; CH 29; CL 32; LA 31;
		    PH 37; SL 32; SF 28
		Conc for Vla and O 1936 PH 39
		Deux Moments Symphoniques 1931 SL 32, 38
		Four Polish Dances 1931 CH 37, 43; CL 42;
		    NP 32; PH 35; SL 33, 40
		The Garden of Paradise 1923: La Sorciere's Dance
		    BN 26
		-Adam and Eve UT 46
		La Nuit Kurde Opera 1925, Symphon Suite NP 28
		Rhapsodie Polonaise 1940 CL 41; MN 42; SL 41
		Ricercare 1949 SL 49
		Serenade No 3 1942 LA 45; SL 45
		Sinfonia Piccolo DE 67; SL 54
		Sinfonietta 1924 BN 25
		Suite Baroque NP 60
		Suite in Spanish Fashion, Voyage of Magellan 1940
		    DE 65; DT 31; LA 53; SL 51, 52, 55, 57
		Symphon Overt 1926 PH 28

TANSMAN, A. (Cont.)

	28	Symph No 1 in a 1925 BN 26; CH 29
	22	Symph in d No 5 1942 MN 44; NP 43; SF 42
	25	Symph No 7 1944 SL 47
	8	Tocatta 1929 PH 31
	8	Transatlantique, Sonatine for O CL 39; DE 31; RC 32
	16	Triptyche for Str O 1930 CH 50; MN 31; NP 31; SL 31, 34, 43
	14	Var on a Theme of Frescobaldi 1938 DE 64; MN 49; SL 37, 46, 50, 52

TARTINI, Giuseppe
1692-1770   It

	12	C Conc in a PH 62
	12	Conc in F No 58 for 2 Oboes, 2 Horns and Str SL 48
	22	V Conc in d CH 43, 53; DT 38; NA 49; NP 44; WA 40, 65
	11	Pastorale for V and Str arr Respighi CH 27
	20	Sonate, Devil's Trill arr Zandoni CL 28; DE arr Levy 69; NP 00
	6	Var Symphoniques on a Corelli Theme NS 1883

TAURIELLA, Antonio
1931-   Arg

| | 15 | P Conc   NA 68 |

TAVARES, Henkel
1896-1970   Brazil

| | 8 | Capriccio Brasilienne for Str O   DE 60 |
| | 30 | Conc in Brazilian Forms for P and O Op 105 No 2 CH 41;   KC 40 |

TAVARES, Mario
              Brazil

| | 8 | Prelude and Dance   SL 53 |
| | 35 | Symph No 4 in f Op 36   SL 53 |

TAYLOR, Clifford
1923-   US

| | 12 | Theme and Var for O   PT 56;   WA 55 |

TAYLOR, Deems
1885-   US

	6	Ballet Music from Incidental Music Casanova Op 22 LA 37; WA 38
	10	Christmas Overt NP 43
	22	Circus Day a Fantasy Op 18 CH 34(2)
	14	Elegy for O Op 27 NA 46; LA 44
	3	Fanfare for Russia arr Turner CH 44
	18	Fantasy on Two Themes Op 17 DT 43 Jurgen, Symphon Poem Op 17 CH 27; NS 25; PH 29; SF 28
	14	Marco Polo Takes a Walk, Var Op 25 BA 42; NA 43; NP 42; RC 42(2), 44; SE 43
	8	Processional Op 24 BA 40
	15	Restoration Suite 1950 NA 50
	20	Siren Song, Symphon Poem Op 2 NP 22
	14	Suite from Opera Peter Ibbetson Op 20 BA 39; DT 41; NA 37
	28	Through the Looking Glass Suite Op 12 BA 28, 39, 41; CH 23, 26, 31, 33; CL 23, 34; DA 35; DT 24; HN 37; NA 40; KC 37; LA 28, 31, 36; MN 23, 29; NP 24; NS 22; PH 23, 31; SE 28
	4	-White Knight BA 47; NR 57
	4	-Jabberwocky BA 47

TCHAIKOVSKY, André   21   Ballet Suite No 2 Op 43   LA 58
              Russ

TCHAIKOVSKY, Peter I. 12   Allegro Brilliante c 1863   WA 60
1840-1893   Russ   8   Andante Cantabile from Str Quart No 1 in D Op 11
                          arr for C and O   BA 26, 42, 47;   CH 08, 50;
          CL 24, 42;   DA 29;   DT 25, 26, 31, 54, 55(3);   HN 35;   KC 39,
          40;   LA 31;   MN 45;   NP 20;   NS 1897;   RC 27, 29;   SL 52;
          UT 45;   WA 32
       16   Capriccio Italien Op 45   AT 46, 50, 56, 65;   BA 41;   BN 1897, 99,
          04, 39, 53;   BU 60;   CH 1892, 99(2), 18, 56;   CT 17, 48, 63,
          69;   CL 57;   DA 32, 52;   DE 46, 51, 57, 63;   DT 17, 23, 28,
          35, 39, 65;   HN 32, 39, 40;   NA 36, 39;   KC 36, 61;   LA 19,
          23;   MN 60, 63;   NR 65;   NP 08, 14, 19, 21, 23, 59;   NS 1886;
          PH 05, 08, 09, 10, 11, 23;   PT 41, 55;   RC 25, 45;   SL 09, 13,
          21, 23, 26;   SE 42, 49, 53;   UT 43, 46, 61, 67
        6   Chant sans Paroles arr for V and O from Op 2 No 3 in F   NS 03
        4   Cherubim Song, or Paternoster, or Our Father for Chor and O 1884
          CH 09;   NS 1896
       28   Concert-Fantasie in G for P and O Op 56   BN 54;   BU 63;   CH 1891;
          DA 55
       30   P Conc No 1 in B^b Op 23   AT 53, 55, 59, 62, 64;   BA 41, 42, 43, 46,
          47, 52, 61;   BN 1884, 90, 96, 97, 01, 02, 03, 06, 08, 09, 11, 15,
          24, 25, 30, 41, 43, 50;   BU 41, 49, 53, 56, 58, 65;   CH 1891, 96,
          00, 01, 02, 03, 05, 06, 07, 08, 09, 12, 15, 16, 18, 19, 20, 22, 23,
          26, 28, 33, 36, 39, 40, 41, 44, 45, 47, 50, 53, 55, 57, 59, 61, 66;
          CT 1895, 99, 01, 09, 11, 12, 15, 23, 33, 35, 40, 41, 42, 44, 45,
          48, 52, 58, 62, 64, 66, 69;
          CL 20, 21, 29, 36, 38, 40, 42, 48, 54, 61, 62, 68;   DA 46, 48, 49,
          51, 60, 62, 65, 69;   DE 46, 49, 51, 55, 58, 61, 63, 67;
          DT 15, 17, 18, 24, 29, 30, 40, 44, 55, 59, 62, 63;
          HN 40, 45, 49, 51, 54, 63, 64, 68;
          NA 37, 39, 44, 46, 49, 54, 57, 63, 67;
          KC 35, 41, 43, 47, 48, 51, 53, 55, 58;
          LA 19, 20, 23, 27(2), 29, 30, 33, 45, 48, 50, 60, 61, 64, 66, 69(2);
          MN 25, 29, 41, 43, 45, 46, 49, 53, 64, 65;   NR 50, 56, 59, 62, 66,
          69;   NP 1879, 87, 94, 00, 05, 06, 07, 13, 17, 18, 19, 21, 22, 23,
          27, 39, 40, 44, 45, 50, 51, 54, 63, 67;   NS 05, 15, 17, 18, 20;
          PH 00, 02, 05, 06, 14, 15, 16, 20, 22, 25, 31, 37, 38, 40, 44, 47,
          51, 54, 56, 59, 60, 66, 67;
          PT 40, 42, 44, 48, 51, 54, 61, 62, 66;   RC 23, 27, 42, 45, 51, 65;
          SL 12, 13, 14, 15, 16, 18, 20, 21, 25, 26, 28, 32, 33, 35, 38, 39,
          42, 44, 45, 47, 48, 49, 52, 54, 55, 56, 57, 58, 61, 64, 66;
          SF 12, 14, 23, 31, 35, 41, 46, 47, 51, 55, 61, 66;
          SE 44, 48, 51, 63, 67;   UT 43, 50, 62, 65, 68;
          WA 32, 38, 42, 48, 49, 50, 51, 53, 56, 57, 61, 64, 66
       30   P Conc No 2 in G Op 44   BN 1897, 12;   CH 10;   CT 48, 67;   CL 67;
          DT 20, 68;   ML 67;   MN 67;   NP 1881, 03, 23;   NS 1897, 06, 07;
          PH 12, 23, 48, 67;   RC 49;   UT 68
       35   V Conc in D Op 35   AT 47, 49, 60, 62, 66;   BA 26, 43, 44, 49, 52,
          53, 63, 67;   BN 1893, 99, 00, 04, 06, 08, 09, 10, 13, 21, 23, 33,
          45, 46, 51, 52, 57, 58, 67;   BU 40, 42, 45, 59, 61, 67;
          CH 1899, 00, 06, 08, 11, 12, 13, 16, 17, 18, 20, 22, 23, 28, 35,
          39, 41, 42, 43, 45, 61, 62, 63, 69;

TCHAIKOVSKY, P.I. (Cont.)   V Conc in D Op 35 (Cont.)
        CT 1899, 00, 10, 13, 14, 18, 23, 30, 35, 36, 42, 44, 47, 49, 52,
        57, 60, 63, 65, 68;   CL 24, 27, 32, 33, 37, 38, 40, 41, 42, 43,
        45, 46, 48, 51, 53, 54, 55, 58, 59, 63, 65, 69;
        DA 32, 34, 49, 55, 63, 67;   DE 45, 47, 51, 54, 57, 59, 62;
        DT 16, 17, 19, 20, 24, 27, 29, 37, 44, 45, 48, 51, 53, 55, 58, 61,
        64, 69;   HN 39, 44, 48, 50, 55, 60, 63, 67;
        NA 38, 44, 59, 65, 69;   KC 34, 39, 42, 43, 49, 56, 63, 69;
        LA 20, 24, 29, 30, 36, 37, 39, 45, 47, 52, 55, 59, 63, 67; ML 64, 69;
        MN 23, 26, 29, 34, 37, 43, 45, 47, 49, 50, 53, 55, 57, 60, 61, 65;
        NR 50, 52, 54, 55, 58, 60, 62, 63;
        NP 1899, 04, 10, 12, 13, 16, 18, 23, 25, 27, 28, 31, 38, 39, 43(2),
        44, 45, 47, 48, 50, 51, 53, 54, 55, 57, 62, 64, 66;
        NS 1888, 92, 08, 12, 14, 19, 20, 21, 24;
        PH 04, 06, 08, 09, 11, 13, 15, 17, 20, 24, 27, 36, 43, 44, 45, 46,
        48(2), 50, 51, 53, 54, 55, 57, 58, 59, 60, 61, 63, 64, 67, 68, 69;
        PT 37, 39, 42, 44, 46, 48, 51, 53, 55, 58, 62, 64, 66, 67;
        RC 23, 32, 44, 51, 55;   SL 14, 17, 18, 19, 20, 21, 29, 35, 37,
        42, 43, 44, 49, 58, 60, 63, 65, 69;
        SF 12, 25, 28, 29, 30, 35, 37, 40, 44, 45, 50, 55, 65, 68;
        SE 30, 49, 54, 62;   UT 47, 48, 56, 60;
        WA 32, 35, 37, 40, 42, 43, 47, 55, 62, 67

8	-First mvt CH 10, 15
4	Coronation Cantata Moscow, Sopr, Baritone, Chor and O Prayer 1883 MN 41
	Coronation March 1883 CT 35
15	Danish National Hymn, Festival Overt Op 15 CH 1898, 19; RC 37
4	Eugene Onegin, Opera Op 24: Aria SL 23
6	-Aria of Prince Gremin KC 45; NS 11; PT 45
4	-Aria of Lemski NS 1896; RC 24, 27
60	-Concert form NS 07
12	-Letter Scene BA 63; BN 36, 47; CH 20; CT 33; CL 21, 65; DA 49; DE 67; DT 20, 43, 67; NA 39, 67; LA 33; NP 16; NS 08, 11, 18; PH 20, 49; PT 49; WA 47
6	-Polonaise CH 11; CT 34, 35, 37, 55; CL 33; DA 28; LA 29; ML 60; MN 48; PT 43; RC 27, 29; SE 37; WA 32, 36, 47
6	-Waltz MN 47; NS 11; WA 31, 35, 49
6	Medley for P and O arr Borge NR 67
6	Nocturne in c op 19 No 4 CL 25
18	Nutcracker Ballet Suite Op 71 AT 46, 54, 57; BA 40, 43; BN 08; CH 1892, 98, 04(2), 08, 23, 52, 55; CT 50; CL 23, 26, 29, 39; DA 25, 29, 37, 38, 58; DE 59, 61, 62, 63, 64; NA 31, 33, 46; MN 23, 43(2), 46; NR 69; NP 45, 55, 59; NS 03, 06, 08, 24; PT 42, 63; RC 26, 54, 55; SF 56; SE 27, 37, 47; UT 41, 45, 46, 49, 53; WA 66, 67
12	-Suite No 1 Op 71a CT 47; DT 15, 26, 27, 40, 46, 47, 48, 60; HN 38, 42; PH 11, 14, 16, 17, 20, 22, 23, 25, 48, 50, 53, 56, 58, 63, 66; SL 24; WA 33, 34, 37, 40, 57
10	-Suite No 2 Op 71b CT 47
6	-Dances BA three 28, 38; NA four 33
4	-Dance Arabe DE 45, 46, 52; HN 31; WA 41, 42, 48
2	-Chinese Dance DE 45, 46, 52; WA 48
2	-Dance de Mihrtons, Toy Flutes BA 43; DE 45, 46, 52; WA 42
2	-Dance Russe, Trepak BA 42; DE 45, 46, 52; HN 31; SL 65; WA 41, 42, 48
2	-Dance of the Sugar Plum Fairy BA 42; DE 45, 46, 52, 59; HN 31; WA 42

TCHAIKOVSKY, P.I. (Cont.)   Nutcracker Ballet Suite (Cont.)
```
 5      -Finale    DE 59
 4      -Marche    DE 52
 3      -Overt    DE 45, 46;    HN 31;    SL 65
 4      -Pas de Deux    CT 64;    DE 59;    MN 43;    NR 57, 58, 62
20      -Selections    CH 59;    SF 61
 4      -Tarantelle    DE 59
 7      -Waltz of the Flowers    AT 63;    DE 45, 46;    HN 13, 31, 45;
         SL 65;    WA 40
 4      -Coda    DE 59
 4      Oprichnik, The Guardsman Opera Op 69 Overt    PH 49, 51
15      Overt for the Year 1812 Op 49    AT 51;    BA 43;    BN 1893, 95, 97,
         01, 02, 09, 29, 41, 61;    CH 1893(2), 95(2), 96, 97, 98, 01, 02,
         03, 05, 09, 10, 12, 21, 24, 55;    CT 03, 10, 18, 21, 58, 63;
         CL 21, 23, 27, 29, 41;    DA 53, 63;    DT 15(2), 22, 66;    HN 31;
         KC 40, 41, 42;    LA 21;    MN 29, 42, 49, 68;    NP 11, 17, 19, 20,
         22, 24;    NS 08;    PH 08, 09, 10, 11(2), 12, 14, 16, 17, 20, 22(2),
         25(2), 29;    PT 41;    RC 23, 25, 30, 38, 39, 41, 45, 51;
         SL 11, 22, 24, 26, 63;    SF 14, 61;    SE 63;    UT 41, 65;    WA 42
 8      Pezzo Capriccio for C Op 62    NA 39
 8      Quartet No 3 in E$^b$ Op 30: Andante funèbre arr Glazounov    CT 30, 42
 4      Queen of Spades, Pique Dame.Opera Op 68: Aria    DT 21;    LA 29
 8      -Overt    BN 64
15      -Selections    SF 56
        -Suite    BU 53;    NR 57;    NP 53, 55;    RC 55
18      Romeo and Juliet, Fantasy Overt 1869    AT 59, 66, 67;
         BA 38, 39, 43, 44, 46, 68;
         BN 1889, 90, 92, 95, 98, 02, 05, 06, 10, 11, 14, 20, 23, 24, 28,
         32, 37, 40, 42, 53, 54, 55, 60;    BU 46, 52, 58, 63;
         CH 1892, 95, 97, 02, 04, 05, 07, 09, 12, 15, 18, 22, 38, 40, 42,
         43(2), 44, 46, 47, 53, 61, 62, 63;
         CT 1897, 02, 12, 14, 17, 18, 30, 33, 37, 39, 41, 43, 45, 46, 47,
         49, 51, 53, 55, 64, 69;    CL 19, 21, 23, 24, 26, 28, 30, 32, 34,
         40, 42, 43, 46, 51, 58, 64;    DA 46, 48, 49, 51, 52, 57, 60;
         DE 45, 46, 49, 51, 53, 55, 56, 57, 60, 61, 65, 69;
         DT 16, 17, 18, 21, 22, 24, 28, 29, 31, 36, 40, 41, 43, 45, 46, 47,
         48, 52, 54, 57, 62, 68;    HN 35, 36, 43, 46, 50, 51, 55, 57, 60;
         NA 35, 36, 39, 43, 49, 51, 53, 55, 57, 58, 63, 67, 69;
         KC 34, 36, 37, 39, 43, 44, 51, 56, 60, 61, 63;
         LA 20, 21, 29, 41, 46, 54, 63;    MN 23, 27, 31, 35, 38, 43, 46, 49,
         51, 56, 58, 66, 67;    NR 54, 58, 60;
         NP 1875, 98, 04, 07, 09, 12, 14, 17, 18, 20, 22, 23, 29, 31, 35,
         39, 43(2), 45, 49, 50, 51, 53, 55, 67;
         NS 1893, 95, 06, 07, 08, 21, 22, 23;
         PH 03, 07, 12, 15, 17, 19(2), 22, 24(2), 25, 26, 28, 29(2), 31,
         32, 33, 36, 37, 39, 41(2), 43(2), 45, 47, 48, 50, 53, 58, 60, 63,
         68;    PT 40, 42, 44, 46, 48, 50, 60, 67, 68;
         RC 23, 25, 29, 32, 33, 37, 41, 42, 44, 51, 57;
         SL 11, 14, 16, 17, 19, 20, 21, 23, 25, 27, 30, 32, 35, 36, 41, 45,
         52, 53, 58, 61, 63;    SF 14, 18, 19, 21, 25, 29, 32, 38, 41, 47,
         52, 56, 59, 60, 63, 66;    SE 28, 32, 36, 39, 40, 43, 46, 50, 51,
         57, 60, 66;    UT 40, 44, 46, 48, 67;    WA 32, 36, 42, 46, 49, 50, 67
        -Excerpts    DA 28, 50
20      -Serenade, Sonatine, Waltz, Adagio    SE 41
```

TCHAIKOVSKY, P. I. (Cont.)
```
 23    Francesca da Rimini, Fantasy Op 32    AT 53;    BA 53, 56, 63, 68;
          BN 1895, 97, 01, 05, 09, 37, 43, 45, 47, 55;    BU 45, 59, 63, 67;
          CH 1896, 02, 05, 07, 09, 16, 18, 20, 21, 28, 29, 34, 41, 47, 53,
          61;    CT 16, 32, 38, 40, 44, 62;    CL 25, 30, 35, 45, 51, 64;
          DA 49, 52, 68;    DE 59;    DT 18, 21(2), 24, 26, 41, 44, 55;
          HN 49, 58, 65, 69;    NA 42;    KC 35, 40, 54;    LA 53;    ML 63;
          MN 33, 42, 48;    NR 60;    NP 1878, 00, 06, 10, 19, 20, 24, 37,
          47, 49, 53, 65;    NS 21, 22;    PH 16, 21, 24, 30, 31, 33, 37, 42,
          46, 54, 58;    PT 40, 45;    RC 24, 27, 32, 34, 41, 65;
          SL 10, 14, 22, 29, 41, 42, 43, 45, 47, 49, 52, 66, 69;
          SF 24, 25, 28, 39, 44, 67;    SE 31, 33, 35, 41, 42, 53, 62, 67;
          UT 53;    WA 33, 34, 39, 42, 47, 54, 64, 69
 18    Hamlet, Fantasy Overt Op 67    BN 1891, 99, 15, 54, 67;    CH 1891,
          95, 99, 14, 16;    CT 62, 66;    DA 46;    HN 58;    MN 25, 45;
          NP 1889, 01;    NS 1891, 94, 03;    PH 05;    RC 45, 52;    SL 15,
          20;    SF 31, 40;    SE 69
  6    Jeanne d'Arc, Opera 1878: Adieu, Forêts  AT 56, 58;  BA 46; BN 44; BU 44
          CH 01, with Recitative 17;    CT 1897, 27;    CL 22, 29;    DA 46; DE 64;
          DT 22, 43;    NA 42;    LA 45;    ML 62;    MN 30, 44;    NP 18;
          NS 10, 13, 15, 26(2);    PH 17, 22;    RC 26;    SL 12, 32, 44, 62;
          SF 14;    WA 35
  8    -Ballet music    NS 10
  8    -Finale, Act I    NS 10
  6    Legende Op 54 No 5 Christ in His garden arr Fuerst    NP 38;    NS 1896
  6    March Solennelle for the Law Students, Chor and O Moscow 1885
          CT 40;    DT 15;    SF 61
  7    March Slave Op 31    AT 49, 62;    BA 26, 38, 42, 43, 47;    BN 1882;
          CH 1892, 93, 95, 97, 01, 02, 06, 07, 11, 12, 19, 20, 29, 30, 31;
          CT 04, 11, 38, 44;    CL 18, 21, 23, 25, 27, 31, 51;
          DA 28, 32, 38(2), 54;    DT 14, 17, 21, 29;    HN 33, 37, 41;
          KC 51;    LA 29;    MN 48;    NP 08, 13, 18, 19, 20, 21, 22, 23;
          PH 08, 09, 10, 11, 12, 14, 16, 17, 18, 20, 21, 24, 29;    RC 25,
          27, 28, 57;    SL 20, 24;    SF 14;    SE 36, 40;    UT 57;    WA 43;
          NS 1896, 03, 26
  5    Mazeppa Opera 1881: Battle of Poltavo    RC 24, 27
  4    -Cradle Song    CT 28
  6    -Danse Cosaque    CH 1894;    CT 1898
 30    Serenade in C for Str O Op 48    AT 49, 52, 54, 65;    BA 41;
          BN 1888, 93, 17, 56;    CH 1893, 95, 00, 04, 17, 30, 56;    CT 45,
          55;    DA 46, 62;    DE 55;    DT 25, 40, 48;    HN 61;    NA 43, 64;
          KC excerpts 34;    LA 49;    MN 44, 67;    NP 05, 26;    NS 1884, 86,
          08, 18;    PH 00, 39, 42, 45, 47, 48, 52, 56, 59;    PT 53, 54;
          RC 41;    SL 58, 64;    SF 61;    SE 42;    WA 54, 58, 66
          -2nd mvt    CT 1895
          -3rd mvt    CT 1895, 99
          -Elegy    CT 1895, 99;    MN 25;    NP 08;    SL 22, 24;    UT 53
          -Elegy and Waltz    CH 06
          -Sonatine, Waltz, Adagio    SE with Ballet Russe 41
          -Waltz    CT 1895;    DE 49;    UT 46
          -Waltz and Finale    PT 50
  9    Serenade Melancolique in B♭ for V and O Op 26    HN 14;    MN 60;
          NS 03, 08;    RC 24;    SL 60;    SF 13
```

TCHAIKOVSKY, P.I. (Cont.)
5   Sleeping Beauty, Ballet Op 66a: Aurora's Wedding   MN 37
4   -Blue Bird   MN 43
9   -Introd and Waltz   NP 55
4   -Pas de deux Classique   BU 63;   CT 64;   MN 43;   NR 57, 62
4   -Princess Aurora   AT 55;   DT 44;   MN 42, 43
10   -Suite   CH 00;   NP overture 55;   PH 52;   RC 29;   SF 56
7   -Waltz   CH 1894, 02, 05;   CL 26, 28, 31;   DA 28;   NA 35
     Solitude Op 73 No 6 arr Stokowski   PH 36
     Songs
4   Berceuse, Cradle Song Op 16 No 1   NS 05
4   The Cuckoo Op 34 No 8   NP 1899
4   Don Juan's Serenade Op 38 No 1   NS 1897, 08;   SE 38
4   Im Mitten des Balles In the midst of the Ball Op 38 No 3   DT 23
4   Invocation to Sleep Op 27 No 1   NS 08
4   None but the Lonely Heart, Longing Op 6 No 6   CT 1896, 03, 38, 41;
         CL 29;   DT 34;   HN 41;   NS 1886, 08, 21;   SL 40;   WA 38, 43
4   Pilgrim's Song Op 47 No 5   HN 19
4   Romanze   NS 1896
     Souvenir of Florence Sextet for Str Op 70   CH 1892;   NP 1892
     The Sorceress, Enchantress, Opera 1885: Ariosa of Kama   CL 65
     The Storm, L'Orage Overt Op 76   CH 1899;   PH 08
     Strains from Olympus   DA 32
     Suite No 1 in d, Childhood Dreams Op 43   BN 1898, 09, 16;   CH 1894,
         95, 02, 03;   NP 10, 23, 53, 54;   NS 1879
       -Intermezzo and Divertimento   PH 02, 16
       -Introd and Fugue   CH 15, 26, 27, 39, 41, 45;   MN 25, 29;   SE 31
       -Marche Miniature   CT 1896, 04
     Suite No 2 in C Op 53: Danse Baroque   CH 1895
       -Rêves d'Enfant   CH 1895, 03
     Suite No 3 in G Op 55   BN 1891, 02, 10, 63;   CH 1893, 97;   CT 1898,
         07, 17, 39;   NP 1894, 97;   NS 1892, 06, 09;   PH 06, 47;   PT 41;
         SF 17, 25;   SE 65;   SL 16
8   -Elegie   CH 13;   MN 25
       -Excerpts   BN 04
       -Finale   SL 18
       -Polonaise   CT 35, 40, 45;   RC 30
       -Polonaise and Finale   CH 1894, 02, 05, 09, 17
8   -Scherzo   CH 13;   NS 14, 23
8   -Theme and Var   AT 54;   CH 1893, 94, 02, 05, 09, 17;   CT 1899,
         00, 13, 31, 52;   CL 24, 27, 28, 32, 34;   DT 17, 24, 30, 38;
         NA 47;   KC 36;   LA 31;   MN 28;   NP 02;   PH 32;   RC 27, 29,
         33, 47, 51;   SL 27;   SE 27, 36, 40
25   Suite No 4, Mozartiana Op 61   BN 1898;   CH 1891, 95, 05, 14;
         CT 62;   DT 16, 19, 66;   MN 28, 45;   NP 44;   NS 08, 10, 12,
         15;   PH 46;   RC 29;   SF 20
12   -Var   BN 54;   CT 62;   SE 37
60   Swan Lake, Ballet Op 20   AT 56, Act II 60
22   -Suite Op 20a   CH 57;   CT 30;   MN 37, 39, 43, 56;   NP 55;
         RC 30, 41;   SF 56;   UT 58, 65
       -Excerpts   DT 39;   HN 56;   NA 35;   ML 69;   WA 50
44   Symphony No 1 in g Winter Dreams Op 13   BN 33, 69;   CT 29;
         CL 30;   DT 18, 31;   KC 46;   NA 45(2);   NP 1895, 69;   NS two
         mvts 08;   PH 69;   PT 51;   WA 69

Time in
Minutes
TCHAIKOVSKY, P.I. (Cont.)

33   Symph No 2 in c Little Russian Op 17   AT 50;   BA 45;   BN 1896, 40,
            45, 47, 61;   CH 01, 15, 16, 19, 20, 22, 38, 39, 57, 65;   CT 29,
            40, 53;   CL 25, 42, 50;   DA 54, 68;   DT 26, 59;   HN 47, 56, 67;
            NA 68;   ML 68;   MN 29, 45, 64;   NR 52, 53;   NP 10, 44;
            NS 1883, 88, 94, 08, 16;   PH 67;   RC 26, 44, 62;   SL 41, 68;
            SF 39, 54, 59, 62;   SE 53;   WA 63

40   Symph No 3 in D Polish Op 29   BN 1899;   CT 42;   DE 52;   KC 58;
            NP 1878, 36, 69;   PH 44;   PT 50;   WA 41

48   Symphony after Byron's Manfred Op 58   BA 61, 69;   BN 00, 01, 04,
            10, 20, 38;   CH 1898(2), 99(2), 02, 05, 09, 13, 15, 17, 19, 21,
            22, 24, 26, 31, 34, 39, 41, 54, 62, 68;
            CT 03, 05, 31, 44, 62;   CL 48, 51;   DA 63;   DT 29;   NA 41, 45;
            LA 28, 44;   MN 25;   NP 1886, 00, 05, 08, 13, 19, 32, 66, 69;
            NS 14, 15, 22;   PH 02, 09, 10, 11, 58, 61, 63;   PT 62;   RC 30;
            SL 12(2), 13, 15, 19, 22;   SF 14, 29;   SE 63

43   Symph No 4 in f Op 36   AT 48, 52, 55, 59, 62, 65, 67;
            BA 42, 43, 44, 45, 46, 48, 52, 54, 56, 58, 62;
            BN 1896, 03, 05, 09, 11, 13, 15, 17, 21, 25, 27, 30, 33, 35, 38,
            42, 46, 48, 52, 55, 57, 59, 61, 64;   BU 42, 47, 56, 64;
            CH 1899, 04, 07, 10, 14, 17, 18, 19, 21, 23, 24, 30, 32, 36, 39,
            47, 51, 52, 53, 55, 57, 61, 64, 69;
            CT 1897, 10, 12, 17, 28, 30, 33, 37, 39, 40, 41, 45, 46, 48, 52,
            55, 57, 59, 60, 63, 65, 67, 69;
            CL 21, 22, 26, 29, 32, 33, 35, 37, 40, 43, 46, 48, 50, 51, 52, 53,
            54, 56, 57, 58, 59, 60, 62, 63, 65, 67;
            DA 37, 38, 48(2), 49, 50, 51, 56, 59, 63, 69;
            DE 45, 47, 49, 50, 51, 54, 56, 57, 61, 65, 67, 69;
            DT 16, 17, 22, 25, 32, 39, 41, 44, 48, 54, 58, 60, 62, 65;
            HN 36, 39, 41, 44, 47, 50, 52, 54, 55, 58, 63;
            NA 37, 43, 49, 52, 55, 61, 64, 67;
            KC 33, 34, 35, 37, 40, 42, 44, 45, 49, 60, 62;   LA 19, 21, 23, 25,
            27, 28, 31(2), 32, 35, 41, 50, 51, 55, 57, 61, 66;   ML 60, 64;
            MN 23, 26, 29, 31, 37, 39, 45, 48, 51, 56, 62, 65;
            NR 51, 54, 56, 58, 60, 61, 66;   NP 1892, 02, 04, 07, 11, 13, 15,
            16, 18, 19, 23, 28, 38, 40, 41, 43, 45, 47, 48, 50, 51, 54, 55,
            57, 62, 64, 66, 68;
            NS 1889, 92, 03, 08 12, 14, 17, 18, 21, 22, 24, 26(2), 27;
            PH 05, 07, 08, 09, 10, 11, 13, 14, 15, 17, 18, 19, 20, 21, 22, 23,
            24, 25, 26, 27, 28, 29, 30, 32, 33, 37, 39, 40, 41, 42, 43, 44, 45,
            47, 49, 50, 53, 54, 55, 60, 63, 67;
            PT 37, 40, 45, 46(2), 48, 49, 52, 56, 58, 62, 65, 66;
            RC 23, 24, 25, 28, 35, 39, 41, 43, 50, 54, 56, 59, 66;
            SL 10, 11, 13, 15, 17, 19, 22, 24, 26, 32, 36, 40, 47, 50, 55, 62,
            65, 67;   SF 12, 17, 19, 21, 22, 23, 25, 30, 33, 36, 39, 42, 51,
            58, 60, 61, 67, 69;   SE 27, 36, 34, 41, 43, 46, 47, 51, 61;
            UT 40, 43, 45, 46, 50, 57, 64, 67;   WA 37, 38, 41, 44, 47, 51,
            63, 68

 8   -Pizzicato Ostinato   SL 29
 8   -Scherzo   BA 42;   RC 29
20   -2nd and 3rd mvts   MN 46
15   -Excerpts   BN 1890

49   Symph No 5 in f Op 64   AT 49, 53, 56, 60, 63, 68;   BA 26, 28, 41,
            42, 43, 46, 47, 49, 53, 55, 59;   BN 1892, 97, 98, 00, 02, 07, 08,
            10, 24, 26, 28, 31, 32, 33, 37, 39, 41, 43, 44, 51, 52, 56, 68;
            BU 40, 43, 48, 51, 58, 66;   CH 1891, 92, 94, 96, 00, 03, 04, 07,

TCHAIKOVSKY, P.I. (Cont.) Symphony No 5 in f (Cont.)
>08, 10, 11, 13, 14, 16, 17, 18, 20, 21, 25, 27, 29, 37, 40, 42, 43,
>45, 46, 47(2), 48, 52, 55, 60, 63, 65, 67;   CT 1896, 98, 00, 03,
>04, 06, 09, 11, 13, 15, 17, 20, 24, 27, 32, 36, 38, 39, 42, 43, 46,
>47, 48, 49, 51, 53, 56, 58, 61, 66;   CL 19, 21, 23, 24, 25, 26,
>27, 28, 30, 32, 33, 34, 35, 38, 39, 41, 42, 43, 44, 46, 50, 52, 54,
>56, 57(2), 63, 67;   DA 29, 49, 52, 54, 57, 58, 68;   DE 45, 46,
>47, 49, 50, 51, 53, 55, 57, 61, 62, 65, 67;   DT 17, 19, 21(2), 23,
>25, 28, 31, 33, 40, 43, 45, 47, 48, 52, 54, 57, 61, 64, 67;
>HN 34, 39, 40, 42, 46, 49, 51, 53, 55, 56, 59, 60, 62, 64, 66, 68;
>NA 30, 34, 36, 38, 42, 48, 51, 54, 57, 60, 63, 64, 67;
>KC 33, 34, 36, 38, 40, 41, 48, 52, 55, 57, 58, 64;
>LA 20, 26, 27, 30, 32, 36, 39, 40, 42, 45, 48, 51, 57, 61, 67; ML 61;
>MN 23, 25, 27, 30, 32, 34, 38, 40, 41, 44, 46, 48, 51, 55, 57, 64;
>NR 50, 53, 55, 59, 62, 63, 67;   NP 1889, 90, 93, 99, 02, 03, 04,
>06, 08, 12, 14, 15, 16, 17, 22, 24, 25, 26, 29, 32, 35, 38, 41, 42,
>44, 46, 47, 49, 51, 53, 58, 59, 65;
>NS 1891, 05, 07, 08, 09, 11, 13, 18, 20, 21, 22(2), 25;
>PH 06, 08, 12, 13, 14, 17, 18, 19, 21, 22(2), 23, 24, 28, 29, 30,
>32, 33, 34, 35, 37, 39, 40, 42, 43, 45, 46, 47, 48, 49, 50, 52, 53,
>57, 66;   PT 39, 42, 47, 48, 50, 54, 57, 59, 61, 64, 68;
>RC 23, 25, 31, 38, 44, 46, 49, 51, 54, 57, 61, 68;
>SL 10, 12, 14, 16, 18, 20, 21, 22, 24, 26, 29, 34, 38, 40, 42, 43,
>45, 46, 48, 52, 54, 56, 59, 63, 66;   SF 13, 18, 20, 22, 24, 28,
>30(2), 32, 38, 50, 53, 55, 60, 64, 65, 67(2);
>SE 26, 29, 31, 33, 37, 38, 40, 45, 56, 62, 66, 68;
>UT 40, 42, 46, 49, 59, 66;
>WA 32, 38, 39, 42, 43, 49, 51, 53, 55, 58, 60, 65

12   -Andante   HN 35
14   -Andante Cantabile and Valse   CH 1896
12   -Second mvt   WA 32
12   -Third mvt   MN 44
47   Symphon 6 in b Pathetique Op 74   AT 47, 51, 54, 58, 61, 64, 69;
>BA 38, 40, 42, 43, 45, 46, 57, 63, 67;   BN 1894(2), 95, 96, 97,
>98, 01, 04, 06, 08, 10, 23, 25, 27, 29, 34, 36, 38, 39, 41, 44,
>45, 47, 49, 51, 52, 53, 54, 56, 58, 61, 63, 65, 69;
>BU 42, 43, 46, 51, 52, 58, 67;
>CH 1893, 95, 97, 98, 99, 01, 03, 04, 06, 07, 08, 09, 11, 12, 14,
>18, 22, 39, 41, 42, 44, 51, 56, 63, 68;
>CT 1899, 02, 04(2), 09, 10, 12, 13, 14, 18, 19, 22, 23, 26, 28,
>32, 35, 39, 44, 47, 49, 54, 59, 61, 64, 68;
>CL 20, 22, 23, 24, 25, 26, 28, 29, 31, 34, 36, 40, 41, 42, 43, 44,
>45, 47, 49, 52, 53, 55, 56, 57, 61, 68;
>DA 27, 46, 48, 55, 57, 59, 64;   DE 46, 48, 52, 54, 57, 64, 68;
>DT 15, 17, 18, 21, 22, 24, 27, 34, 35, 38, 40, 43, 44, 45, 46, 51,
>52, 56, 60, 63, 66;   HN 37, 41, 45, 48, 50, 52, 53, 54, 57, 61,
>62, 65;   NA 39, 40, 44, 46, 50, 53, 55, 58, 62, 65, 68;
>KC 33, 38, 42, 43, 47, 50, 53, 54, 62, 66;
>LA 19, 20, 22, 24, 29, 39, 42, 43, 45, 49, 56, 58, 65, 69;   ML 65;
>MN 24, 26, 28, 30, 33, 36, 39, 42, 47, 54, 61, 66;   NR 56, 62, 64;
>NP 1896, 98, 01, 03, 04, 05, 06, 07, 08, 09, 12, 14, 15, 16, 18, 21,
>24, 25, 26, 33, 42, 43, 44, 46, 47, 48, 50, 56, 61, 63, 67;
>NS 1893, 94, 96, 04, 08, 10, 14, 17, 19(2), 23, 25, 26, 27;
>PH 01, 03, 04, 05, 06, 07(2), 08(2), 09(2), 10(2), 11, 12, 13, 14,
>16, 17, 18(2), 20, 21, 22, 23, 24, 25, 31, 32, 33, 36, 38, 39, 40,

TCHAIKOVSKY, P.I. (Cont.)   Symphony No 6 in b (Cont.)
        41, 42, 43, 44, 46, 47, 49, 51, 52, 56, 57, 59, 60, 61(2), 64, 66,
        67;   PT 37, 38, 42, 44, 48, 51, 53, 56, 59, 63, 67, 69;   RC 23(2),
        26, 33, 36, 37, 38, 40, 42, 45, 48, 53, 55, 57, 63, 69;
        SL 11, 13, 14, 16, 17, 18, 19, 20, 21, 23, 25, 27, 28, 31, 33, 37,
        39, 41, 42, 43, 44, 45, 48, 50, 51, 52, 55, 56, 57, 58, 61, 62, 64,
        67;   SF 11(2), 16, 20, 21, 23, 26, 29, 30, 32, 40, 44, 46, 49, 50,
        53, 56, 65, 69;   SE 26, 28, 29, 32, 35, 39, 46, 48, 52, 58, 64;
        UT 41, 47, 52, 56, 61, 65, 69;
        WA 33, 35, 38, 39, 46, 50, 52, 55, 59, 62, 67, 69

10	-Adagio lamentoso CH 1896, 00; PT 44	
9	-Allegro molto vivace CH 00	
8	-Second Mvt WA 33, 36	
20	-Second and Third Mvt DA 48	
12	-Third Mvt MN 49; UT 43	
37	Symph No 7 DE 68; PH 61, 67	
23	The Tempest Fantasy Op 18 CH 1894; CL 34; HN 45; NP 32, 60;	
	NS 04, 08, 10, 20(2); PH 43; PT 39; SF 23; WA 52	
10	Trio for P, V and C in a Op 50 CH arr Stock 36, 38, 40, 49; CT 38	
	-Theme and Variations arr Rapee CL 40	
17	Var on a Rococo Theme for C and O Op 33 BA 68; BN 08, 18;	
	CH 04, 13, 24, 33, 39, 64; CT 01, 25, 66; CL 24, 42, 53, 55;	
	DA 53, 66; DE 61; DT 18, 34, 44, 65; HN 63; NA 37, 45,	
	48, 59; KC 34, 44, 46; LA 35, 67; ML 62, 64; MN 39, 66;	
	NP 00, 14, 18, 26, 47, 51; NS 07, 22; PH 03, 08, 10, 27, 50,	
	68; PT 42, 48, 62, 66; RC 54, 60, 63; SL 13, 35; SF 57;	
	SE 55, 59; UT 54, 64; WA 56, 66	
12	Var on a Mozart Theme SE 37	
10	Le Voyvode, Dream on the Volga, Symphon Ballad Op 78 BN 02;	
	CH 1897; CL 26; DE 54; NP 16; NS 1897; PH 45, 69;	
	SF 19; SE 59; WA 67	

TCHEREPNIN,	20	Conc for Harmonica and O Op 86 DE 61
Alexander	15	P Conc in a Op 22 BN 50; CH 51
1899- Fr	18	P Conc in c# Op 30 BN 22; NS 19
	15	P Conc No 5 Op 96 KC 68
	10	Dances Russes Op 50 RC 40
	20	Divertimento Op 90 CH 57; PT 68
	8	Evocation LA 49
	8	Magna Mater Op 41 BN 32
	16	Rhaps Georgienne for C and O Op 92 CH 61; MN 44
	8	Romantic Overt Op 67 NA 52; KC 51; SL 52
	5	Symphon March Op 80 PT 56; SL 55
	9	Symphon Prayer Op 93 BN 60; KC 65; MN 64;
		PT 64; DE 68
	20	Symph No 1 Op 42 DA 50
	25	Symph No 2 in E^b Op 77 CH 51; KC 53
	28	Symph No 3 Op 83 NA 54
	25	Symph No 4 Op 91 BN 58; CH 64; DE 60
	18	Suite for O Op 87 CH 54

TCHEREPNIN, Nikolay	18	P Conc Op 30 in c# BN 22; NS 19
1873-1945 Russ/Fr	15	8 Miniatures BN 31
	10	Prelude in Memory of Rimsky-Korsakoff BN 31
	25	Sonatine Op 61 NA 38
	12	Three Pieces for O after Poc BN 33
	8	-The Enchanted Kingdom BN 31

TEDESCO, Ignatz	20	V Conc Italiano DT 33
1817-1882 Czech	10	Le Passe for P Op 47 NP 1860

TELEMANN, George   10   Conc for Fl and V   BN 67
1681-1767   Ger   16   Conc for 2 Horns, Str and Cembalo in E^b MN 56, 57
8   Fantasia for 2 P and O   MN 47
20   Overt in C   BN 63;   SL arr Saar 36
15   Passacaglia in e arr Collins   LA 47
21   Suite in a Fl and Str   CH 52;   DE 48;   HN 51;
     NA 44;   PH 39, 51, 62;   RC 60;   SF 42;   SE 69
19   Suite in f Oboe and Str arr Dorati   DE 68;
     MN 53, 65
28   Suite, Tafelmusik, Table Music in B^b arr Steiffert
     DT 34;   PT 60;   RC 54
12   -Excerpts   NP 31

TEMPLETON, Alec   18   Concertino Lirico   WA 47
1909-   Brit/US   15   Mozart Matriculates for P and O   MN 48

TEN HAVE, Jean   15   Arcadia Tone Poem   CT 43
1878-1952   US   10   Symphon Prelude 1938   CT 38

THARICHEN, Werner   20   Conc for Timpani and O Op 34   HN 66;   PT 63
1921-   Ger   24   Conc for Voice and O Op 38   SL 59

THATCHER,   20   Symphon Fantasy   BA 26
 Sir Reginald
1888-   Brit

THEODORAKIS,   15   Suite No 2 for O   MN 61
1925-   Gk

THIERIOT, Ferdinand   10   Sinfonietta in E   BN 1892
1838-   Ger

THIRIET, Maurice   8   Poéme, for small O   SL 36
1906-   Fr

THOMAS, Ambroise   4   Le Caid, Opera Comique 1849: Air de Tambour-Major
1811-1896   Fr   CH 07
4   La Folie, Opera Comique: Scene   CT 1895, 00, 01,
     19, 55
4   Hamlet, Opera 1868: Drinking Scene   NA 36
8   -Grand Scene d'Ophelia   NP 1894;   NS 1889;
     SL 10
7   -Mad Scene   AT 62;   CH 1894;   CT 1895, 00, 01,
     19, 55, 39;   NA 63;   MN 23, 26;   PH 00;
     PT 54;   SL 12, 19
4   Mignon, Opera Comique 1866: Connais-tu le pays
     AT 56;   CH 19;   DT 19;   HN 36;   ML 65;   WA 46
4   -Elle ne Croyait pas   DT 26;   NA 49
4   -Je suis Titania   CT 04;   DE 50, 57;   DT 37;
     ML 64;   SL 10
8   -Overt   BA 42, 43;   CH 05;   DA 26;   HN 36, 39;
     NA 34;   MN 42;   NS 19;   SE 47

THOMAS, A. (Cont.)   Mignon, Opera (Cont.)
                       4   -Polonaise   BA 26;   CH 1897
                       4   -Romanza   PH 07
                       7   Raymond, Opera Comique 1851, Overt   PT 42

THOMAS, Arthur   4   Ma Voisine, Song   CH 1891
1850-1892   Brit   4   My Heart is Weary from the Opera Nadeschda 1885
                                PH 15
                       4   Time's Garden   CT 1895

THOMAS, John   5   Fantasia for Harp   NP 1853
1826-1913   Brit   4   Home Sweet Home for Harp   NP 1854

THOMASI, Henri   12   Ballade for Sax and O   BN 57
1901-   It

THOME, Francis   4   Légende for Harp and O Op 122   CH 15
1850-1909   Fr

THOMPSON, Randall   32   Americana for Chor, P and O 1932   PT 40
1899-   US   26   Fantasy for O, Voyage to Nahant   BN 56;   PH 54(2)
                      28   Symph No 2 1931   BN 33, 39, 54;   CH 58;   CT 40;
                                CL 43, 45, 49;   NA 64;   LA 41, 45;   NP 33, 40,
                                68;   PH 39;   PT 39;   SE 34, 39;   UT 48, 63
                       7   -Largo   UT 47, 55
                      32   Symph No 3 in a   BN 49;   CT 51;   CL 49;   RC 49
                      25   Testament of Freedom, men's Chor, P and O 1943
                                BN 44;   NA 64;   RC 55

THOMSON, Virgil   15   Acadian Airs and Dances, Suite No 2 of Louisiana
1896-   US   Story 1948   DT 52;   NA 61;   KC 59;   LA 55;
                                NR 50, 58;   PH 51;   PT 51
                      22   C Conc 1949   CH 53;   PH 49
                      15   Conc Fl, Str, Harp and Percussion   DT 56;   NP 55;
                                PH 55;   PT 55;   SF 57
                       3   Fanfare for France 1942   CT 42;   SL 42
                      15   Fantasy, Homage to England   PT 56
                       8   Feast of Love, Baritone and O   PH 68
                      15   Filling Station, Ballet Suite 1937   PH 41
                      16   Five Songs from Blake, Bar and O   PH 52
                      50   Four Saints in Three Acts Opera 1928 Acts II and IV
                                NP 59
                       5   The Harvest According, Ballet   CT 52
                      17   Louisiana Story, Suite 1937   BN 49;   BU 48, 56;
                                CT 49;   CL 49;   DT 56;   HN 49;   NA 50;   KC 50;
                                MN 53;   PH 48, 57;   PT 50;   RC 53;   SL 49;
                                SF 49, 56;   SE 50;   WA 50
                      10   Mother of us all, Suite from the Opera 1947:
                                Interlude and aria   RC 47
                      15   The Plough that Broke the Plains, Suite 1936   AT 69;
                                DA 49;   DE 49;   DT 43;   NA 44;   KC 46;   MN 47;
                                PH 42;   PT 44;   SL 44;   SF 44;   SE 48
                       5   Sea Piece with Birds   BU 66
                      10   The Seine at Night 1947   DE 48;   DT 48;   KC 47;
                                LA 49;   NP 47, 61;   RC 48;   UT 48

THOMSON, V.(Cont.)
                  8   Shipwreck and Love Scene from Byron's Don Juan   NP 67
                  8   Solemn Music 1949   NP 61
                12   Solemn Music and Joyful Fugue   PH 62, 64
                12   Suite, 5 Portraits 1929   PH 44(2);   PT 46
                16   Symph No 2 in c   1931   BU 62;   CT 42;   NP 50;
                        PH 41;   SL 42;   SE 41
                21   Symph on a Hymn Tune 1928   NR 56;   NP 44;   PH 47,
                        59;   PT 55;   SF 57
                6   Wheat Field at Noon 1948   NA 52;   NP 48;   SL 52
                19   Three Pictures for O   CT 53;   DT 56;   MN 53;
                        PH 53;   WA 50

THORNE, Francis   Burlesque Overt   MN 67
  1912-   US   13   Elegy for O   DE 66;   NA 65;   PH 64

THRANE, Waldemar   4   Norwegian Echo Song, Kom Kjyra   CT 49;   WA 51
  1790-1828   Nor

THUILLE, Ludwig   4   Komme Doch, Song   CH 32;   MN 27;   SL 31
  1861-1907   Ger   9   Romantic Overt Op 16   CH 00
                6   Rosenlied Op 29 for women's Chor and O   NS 11
                6   Symphon Festival March Op 38   CH 07, 10

TILY, Herbert J.   10   Christmas Morning   PH 38
            US

TINEL, Edgar   Suite for O Op 21 1906 from Incidental Music to
  1854-1912   Belg 6   Polyeucte 1878: Fête dans le Temple de Jupiter
                      No 3   CH 1892
                6   -Overt No 1   CH 07
                8   -Three Symph Pictures   BN 06

TIPPETT, Sir Michael   25   P Conc   HN 68
  1905-   Brit   22   Conc for Double Str O 1939   BA 50(2), 54;   CH 69;
                      DT 69;   PT 68;   RC 69
                32   Conc for O   SL 67;   SF 67
                18   Fantasia Concertante on Theme of Corelli for Str O
                      1953   SF 65
                23   Ritual Dances from The Midsummer Marriage Opera
                      1952   HN 56

TIPTON, Albert   12   Serenade for Fl   DT 64
  1917-   US

TIRINGDELLI, Pietro   15   V Conc in g   CT 00
  1858-1937   It   10   L'Intruse, Poem Op 56   CT 06, 18, 21
                10   Legende Celeste, Poem   CT 03
                4   Oh to Love, Song   CT 1898

TOCH, Ernst   20   Big Ben Var, a Phantasy 1934   BN 34;   CT 42;
  1887-1964   Aust/US   LA 40, 62;   NP 42;   PT 53, 62;   RC 51;   SL 53
                18   Bunte Suite 1929   BN 31
                5   Circus Overt   NP 54;   SL 54;   SF 56;   UT 62
                15   Comedy for O Op 42   LA 62

TOCH, E. (Cont.)

22	P Conc Op 38 BN 28, 31	
4	The Covenant UT 46	
20	Fantastic Night Music Op 27 NS 22	
12	Hyperion, Dramatic Prelude Op 71 CL 47; RC 49	
27	The Idle Stroller, Suite 1938 LA 38	
16	Little Theatre Suite Op 54 BN 31; NP 31	
18	Music for O and Baritone Op 60 LA 46; PH 50	
11	Nocturne Op 77 NA 62	
5	Overt to The Fan, Der Fächer, Opera Op 51 LA 49; PH 31; PT 42	
15	Peter Pan Op 76, A Fairy Tale for O HN 55; NA 56; PT 57; SE 55	
7	Pinocchio A Merry Overt 1936 AT 47; BN 39, 44; CH 37, 38; CT 39; CL 42, 62; LA 36; ML 60; MN 42; NR 51; PT 40; RC 62	
40	Symph No 1 Op 72 PT 52	
31	Symph No 2 Op 73 BN 52, 54; LA 52; MN 54	
29	Symph No 3 Op 75 PT 55, 56, 66	
24	Symph No 4 MN 57	
21	Symph No 5 A Rhapsodic Poem, Jephtha in 1 mvt BN 63; NA 66	

TOMMASINI, Vincenzo
1880-1950   It

13	Il Beata Regna, Symphon Poem 1920 NS 22
12	Carnevale of Venice, Var after Paganini 1929 CH 30; CT 36; DT 29; RC 29; WA 29
14	Chiara de Luna: Serenade and Moonlight 1914 CH 18; NP 30; NS 19; SL 27
14	Paesaggi toscani, Symphon Poem 1922 NP 25; NS 22
14	Prelude, Fanfare and Fugue 1927 CH 29; NP 28
12	Suite for Ballet fr Scarlatti's Good Humored Ladies 1916 CL 39; PH 46

TONI, Alceo
1884-   It

15   Theme Var and Fugue   DT 37

TOPLIFF
          Brit

4   Consider the Lilies, Sacred Song   NP 1858

TORELLI, Giuseppe
1658-1709   It

4	Aria, Tu Lo sai DE 55
9	Sinfonia con due Trombi for 2 Trombones arr Berger MN 56

TOURNIER, Marcel
1879-1951   Fr

10   Féerie for Harp and Str   BN 29;   CH 23

TRAPP, Max
1895-   Ger

30	Conc for O Op 32 CH 36
20	P Conc Op 26 CH 34
24	Symph No 4 Op 24 CH 31

TRAVIS, Roy Elihu
1922-   US

12   Symphon Allegro   KC 56;   NP 51

TRIGGS, Harold
1900-

The Bright Land   SL 42

TRIMBLE, Lester   10   Closing Piece   PT 57
1923-   US   10   Five Episodes for O   DT 67;   PT 68
                       16   Symph in 2 mvts   WA 64

TRUBITT   6   Overt in D   HN 63
                US

TRYTHALL, Harry G.   30   Symph No 1   SF 58
19 30-   US

TURCHI, Guido   20   Five Comments on Bacchae of Euripides   PT 60
1916-   It   14   Piccolo Conc Notturno   CH 57;   SF 62

TSCHESNOKOFF   4   Salvation is Created   MN 44, 48
                Russ

TUBIN, Edward   20   Symph No 5   WA 66
1905-   Swed

TUREMAN   8   English Suite in D 4 parts   DE 50, 53
                US   6   The Valley of the Wild Deer   DE 46

TURINA, Joaquin   40   Canto a Sevilla, Song Cycle from Seville Op 37
1882-1949   Sp   DE 54, 63;   DT 52;   SF 62;   SE 66
                        8   La Oracion del Torera, The Toreador's Prayer
                                Op 34   LA 43;   SL 43;   SF 58;   NR 50
                       18   Danzas Fantasticas Op 22   BN 22;   CH 31, 38;
                                CT 31, 43;   RC 37, Orgia only 39, 40
                       15   -For Guitar arr Segovia   SL 54
                        9   Procession del Rocio Op 9   AT 66;   BN 28;   CH 23,
                                28;   CT 35, 41, 50;   CL 27;   KC 65;   NR 64;
                                NS 19;   PH 20;   RC 35, 36, 42;   SL 28;   SF 27,
                                43, 52;   SE 30;   WA 54
                       22   Sinfonia Sevillano 1920   BN 56;   CT 37;   CL 37
                        5   -Andante and Allegro   RC 40
                        5   -Fiesta a San Juan   CT 42
                        5   -Por el Guadalquivir   CT 42
                        5   -Sacro-Monte arr Cailliet   PH 35, 36

TURNER, Charles   8   Encounter   CT 58;   CL 55; DT 55;   NP 57
1921-   US   13   The Marriage of Orpheus   NP 65

TURNER, Godfrey   10   Trinity Conc, Larghetto   SF 47
1913-   US

TUTHILL, Burnet C.   7   Bethlehem, Pastorale Op 8   CT 34;   CL 36;   DA 34;
1888-   US   SL 36
                        6   Come Seven, Rhapsody Op 11   SL 43

TYLER, Abram R.   4   Voice, Spring Has Come from Hiawatha   PH 00
1868-   US

UGARTE, Floro M.   15   Suite No 2 De mi Tierra   RC 38
1884-   Arg

UHLIG, Theodore   4   My Country   SL 42
1822-1853   Ger

URACK, Otto   25   Symph No 1   BN 13
1884-   Ger

URSPRUCH, Anton   5   Overt to Der Sturm   CH 02
1850-1907   Ger

USIGLI   10   Don Quixote   SF 29
1899-   It/US   18   Passacaglia and Fugue   SF 49
                         5   Song of the ruin in Night of War   SF 31

USSACHEVSKY, Vladimir   9   Concerted piece for Tape Recorder and O in colla-
1911-   Russ/US   boration with Luening   MN 60;   SL 60
                        17   Rhapsodic Var for Tape Recorder and O with Luening
                                 SF 55

VALENTINI, Giuseppe   10   Conc Grosso for Str O arr Tinayre   SL 39
c 1681   It   12   Suite for C and O   DT 27

VALLS, Josep   18   Conc for Str Quart and O   NA 42
1904-   Sp

VAN DER STUCKEN,   Festival March, Shir Zion Op 12   CH 09;   CT 00
  Frank V.   8   Festival Suite Op 12   CT 04
1858-1929   US   -March   CH 09
                        10   Idylle for O Op 20   CT 02, 04, 06
                         5   Louisiana Festival March Op 32   CH 08, 18;   CT 05
                         5   Night of Spring, Pagina d'amour for O Op 10
                                 CT 1898, 03
                        10   Pax triumphans, a Symphon Prologue Op 26   BN 04;
                                 CT 02;   CH 11
                        10   Wm. Ratcliffe, Symphon Prologue Op 6   BN 00;
                                 CH 07;   CT 1899, 07;   NP 1899
                        15   Souvenir Op 39   CH 11
                        20   The Tempest Incidental Music 1882: Suite Op 8   CH 15
                         6   -Caliban's Pursuit   CT 1898, 06
                         6   Valasda, Opera Op 9; Introd to Act II   CT 00, 04
                               Songs
                         4   Fallih Fallah   CH 1894;   CT 1895, 96
                         4   Jugenliebe   CT 1896
                         4   O come with me   CT 1895, 01

VAN DER VOORT, Paul   15   Sinfonietta   SL 40
1903-   US

VAN GELDEN, Lex   18   Conc for Harp and O 1955   WA 55
              Neth

VAN GELDER, Martinus   20   Symph No 2 in A   PH 03
              US

VAN GILSE, Jan   5   Prelude Eine Lebansmesse   LA 23
1881-1944   Neth

VANNAH, Kate   4   My Bairnie Song   CT 03
  ? -1933   US

VACTOR, David Van   10   Comedy Overt No 1 1935   NA 40;   SL 38
  1906-   US   6   Comedy Overt No 2 1941   AT 49;   NA 52;   KC 44;
                                PH 42;   SL 43;   WA 43
                      20   Conc Vla and O 1940   CH 40
                      15   Conc Grosso for 3 Fl, Harp and O 1935   CH 34
                      30   Credo, Contral, Chor and O 1941   NA 41
                       4   Fanfare for O, Salute to Russia 1943   NA 42
                      25   Music for the Marines 1943   NA 42
                      10   Passacaglia and Fugue in d 1933   AT 48;   WA 37, 48
                      32   Symph in D 1937   CH 38;   CL 39;   NP 38
                      26   Symph No 2 in c 1958   AT 63;   PT 58
                       4   Theme harmonized and Orchestrated by 12 Americans:
                                Van Vactor, Oldberg, Sowerby, Carpenter, Ganz etc.
                                CH 40

VARDELL,   30   Symph No 1 in g Carolinian 1938   PH 39
  Charles G. Jr.
  1893-   US

VARÈSE, Edgard   20   Ameriques   PH 25;   UT 65
  1883-1965   Fr/US   18   Arcana   CH 64;   MN 68;   NP 58;   PH 26
                      24   Deserts   BN 68;   BU 64;   NP 63;   PT 65;   SE 68
                       6   Hyperprisms   PH 24;   SL 66
                      20   Integrales   CT 69;   LA 63;   NP 66, 68;   SF 60;
                                SL 68
                      10   Offandres   SF 65;   SL 69

VARMAN, Norodom S.   8   Cambodian Suite 3 parts arr Kostelanetz   AT 54
             Cambodia

VASQUEZ, Jose   12   Suite for Str, Romantic Style   NA 48
  1895-   Mex   10   Triptych Symph   NA 48

VASSILENKO, Sergey N. 15   Epic Poem Op 4   BN 20
  1872-1956   Russ

VAUCLAIN, Constant   15   Symph in One mvt   PH 46
  1908-   US

VAUGHAN-WILLIAMS,   16   V Conc Accademico in d 1925   CH 28;   CT 62;
  Ralph   PH 43
  1872-1958   Brit   17   Conc for Oboe 1944   LA 63
                      18   Conc for Bass, Tuba and O   LA 66;   SF 64
       16   Conc for 2 P in C   AT 60;   BN 49;   CT 49;   HN 60;   NA 62;
                NP 51;   PT 68;   RC 50, 65
       34   Dona Nobis Pacem, Cantata Soli, Chor and O 1936   MN 49;   UT 65
        4   Fantasia on Greensleeves 1929   DT 58;   UT 64, 66
       14   Fantasia on Christmas Carols   AT 54;   BA 48;   CH 45;   CT 49, 52;
                CL 43;   NP 38;   PH 33, 45
                -arr for O alone   CT 43
       14   Fantasia on a Theme of Thomas Tallis   AT 57, 62, 64;   BA 53, 57;
                BN 22, 23, 32, 38, 41, 42, 52, 56;   BU 40, 41, 43, 49, 54, 57;
                CH 23, 30, 37, 51, 57, 60;   CT 32, 37, 64, 68;   CL 23, 27, 32,

Time in
Minutes
VAUGHAN-WILLIAMS, R. (Cont.)   Fantasia on a Theme of Thomas Tallis (Cont.)
           49, 62, 68;   DA 50;   DE 50, 53, 56, 58, 64, 69;   DT 33, 40,
           44, 45, 54;   HN 51, 52, 60, 62, 64, 69;   NA 45;   KC 56, 62, 65;
           LA 30, 35, 44, 50, 54, 61;   MN 29, 42, 44, 49, 62;   NR 53, 57,
           59, 69;   NP 28, 29, 38, 40, 42, 45, 47, 53, 61;   NS 21(2), 24,
           26;   PH 26, 27, 33, 46, 63;   PT 41, 52, 64;   RC 50, 51, 57, 62;
           SL 33, 36, 38, 42, 43, 53, 56;   SF 38, 47, 51, 62, 63;
           SE 45, 49, 51, 60, 68;   WA 49, 50, 65

11-12   Fantasia on the Old 104th Psalm Tune for P, Mixed Chor and O 1949
           BN 51, 63;   CT 50
        Four Hymns for Tenor, Vla and O 1914   DT 64
22   Five Tudor Portraits for Soli, Chor and O 1936   PT 52
10   Five Variants on Dives and Lazarus 1935   CT 41;   LA 41;   NP 41;
           RC 42
15   Flos Campi, Suite for Vla, Chor and O 1925   BU 66;   CT 55;
           SF 56;   UT 65
40-45   Job, A Masque for Dancing 1931   AT 58;   BN 45, 48;   CT 5 scenes
           only 48, 49, 51, complete 53;   NR 61;   NP 36;   PH 54;   RC 52
13   The Lark Ascending, Romance for V and O 1914   CL 64;   UT 68
18   Magnificat for Contralto, women's Chor and O 1932   CH 40;   PH 69
30   Mass in g for Solo and Double Chor 1922   CH 38
10   Three Norfolk Rhaps 1904: No 1 in e   BN 26, 33;   CT 28;   DE 57;
           DT 28, 30;   MN 30;   NP 35;   PH 28, 30;   SL 28
24   On Wenlock Edge, Song Cycle for Tenor and O 1909   BA 45;   CH 20
20   Partita for Double Str O 1948   WA 62
22   Sancta Civitas for Chor and O 1926   BU 54
13   Serenade to Music for Speaker, Sopr, Children's Chor and O 1940
           BA 50;   SF 59
3   Seventeen Come Sunday   WA 45
10   Suite on Folksongs arr for O by Jacob   BA 45, 47
23   Suite for Vla and small O   SF 68
40-45   Symph No 2, A London Symphony 1914   AT 54;   BN 20(2), 22, 33, 40, 44;
           CH 21, 22, 23, 24, 27, 28, 32, 34, 36, 40, 63;   CT 33, 40;
           CL 23, 24, 40;   DE 54;   DT 24;   HN 55;   NA 53;   KC 39;
           LA 39;   MN 23, 27, 44;   NP 28, 34, 35, 39;   NS 20, 22, 24(2);
           RC 47, 54;   SL 24, 25, 50, 69;   SF 40;   SE 29, 37
35   Symph No 3 A Pastoral Symphony 1922   BN 32;   CH 30, 38, 56;
           CL 28;   CT 25, 42;   MN 29;   NP 22, 33, 38, 42;   PH 24;
           RC 43;   SL 27
32   Symph No 4 in f 1935   CH 60;   CT 57;   CL 37, 58, 64;   DA 49;
           DE 53;   DT 59;   HN 68;   NA 67;   LA 47;   MN 40;   NP 35, 42,
           49, 52, 54, 55, 65;   RC 43;   SL 64;   SE 54, 59;   UT 69;
           WA 59
35   Symph No 5 in D 1943   BN 46;   CH 44;   CL 46;   DA 55;   ML 67;
           NP 44, 46;   RC 43, 60;   SF 54, 57, 60;   WA 52, 54, 64
34   Symph No 6 in e 1947   BA 48, 49;   BN 48, 64;   CL 50;   HN 63;
           NA 49;   LA 57;   MN 48;   NR 64;   NP 48;   PH 49;   SL 53;
           SE 64;   UT 65, 66;   WA 50
40   Symph No 7 Sinfonia Antarctica 1951   CH 52;   CL 54;   HN 67;
           MN 54
26   Symph No 8 in d   AT 59;   BN 57;   CH 59;   CL 56;   DA 56, 64;
           DT 65;   HN 57, 59;   NA 63;   KC 59;   LA 58;   MN 67;   NR 59;
           NP 58;   PH 56;   PT 69;   SL 59;   SF 58;   WA 57, 61
29   Symph No 9 in e   CT 56, 58;   DT 67;   HN 58;   PH 58;   PT 59;
           WA 58

VAUGHAN-WILLIAMS, R. (Cont.)
    13   Toward The Unknown Region 1905, rev 1918   KC 51
     8   The Wasps, Overt to Aristophanes, Play 1909   BA 43;   BU 47;
          CH 68;   CT 31, 51, 52;   DE 55;   DT 41, 47, 63, 68;   HN 55, 65;
          NA suite 58;   PH 54;   RC 30;   SE 40

VEIT, Wenzel   4   Song: King in Thule   NP 1867
1806-1864   Czech

VENTH, Carl   8   Pan in America, Lyric Dance Drama   DA 26
1860-   Ger/US   8   Symphon Suite for O, Dionysius   DA 30
                             10   Symph, Romantic   DA 28
                              6   Two Numbers fr Str O   DA 29

VERDI, Guiseppe   Attila, Opera 1846: Aria D'aghi immortali   NP 1855,
1813-1901   It   59
                                      -In entre gionfiarsi   NR 69
                                      -Te sol quest anima   NR 69
                            120   Aida, Opera 1872 Concert Form   BU 56;   DE 48
                             40   -Act IV, complete   RC 53
                              4   -Aria   BA 51;   PH 02, 46
                              4   -Ballet Music   HN 42;   KC 62
                              4   -Celeste Aida for Tenor   BA 43;   CT 1899, 10, 15,
                                      17, 18, 21;   DT 20;   NA 55;   MN 30;   SL 15, 41
                              8   -Finale, Act II Scene II   SL 63
                              4   -Judgment Scene   NA 55
                              4   -Prelude   HN Act I 41, Act III 42
                              4   -Ritorna Vincitor, Soli, and Chor   CT 42;   DE 46,
                                      59;   DT 66;   HN 41;   ML 66;   MN 23, 27, 40, 46;
                                      NR 69;   NS 06;   PT 37;   SE 69;   SF 69;   UT 65
                              4   -O Skies of Blue, O cieli azzuri, O patria mia
                                      DE 46;   MN 22, 27, 40, 46
                              4   -Triumphal March   BA 42;   DA 52;   KC 62;   MN 48
                                   La Battaglia di Legnano, Opera 1849: Overt   DA 55
                              4   Don Carlo Opera 1849: Aria unidentified   DA 34, 52;
                                      DE 55, 57;   NR 53
                              4   -O Carlo ascolta Act IV   AT 52;   BA 67;   CT 52;
                                      NA 69
                              4   -O Don fatale Act IV   CH 16;   CT 99, 53;   DE 45,
                                      58;   DT 39, 43, 63;   HN 44;   NA 49, 55;   KC 46,
                                      63;   LA 19, 22, 38;   MN 37, 41, 59;   NS 13, 16;
                                      PH 13, 40;   SL 62;   SE 56
                              4   -Dormir sol nel Marto   AT 53;   MN 44
                              4   -Ella giammai m'amo Act IV   AT 53;   BA 28;
                                      CT 45, 49;   HN 49;   NA 41;   MN 40; NR 68;   PT 57;
                                      RC 41;   SL 19;   SE 40;   UT 40
                              4   -Per me giunto e di supremo Act IV   AT 52;   BA 46,
                                      67;   CT 52;   SL 40;   WA 46
                              4   -Tuche le vanita   LA 60
                              4   Ernani, Opera 1844: Aria unidentified   MN 64;
                                      NS 13, 20, 25
                              4   -Ernani involami Act I   BU 60;   CT 46;   DT 65;
                                      PT 51;   SF 37
                              4   -Infelice che un brando   KC 39;   NR 68
                              4   -Oh de'vend anni mie   AT 53;   BA 28;   HN 49;
                                      NA 41;   MN 40;   PT 57;   SL 19;   SE 40;   UT 40

VERDI, G. (Cont.) Ernani, Opera (Cont.)
 5   -Scene and Aria   NP 1847
 4   Falstaff Opera 1893 Aria   DA 58
 4   -Ford's Monologue   MN 58
 4   -Quand'ero paggio   NA 61
 4   La forza del destino Opera 1862: Aria unidentified   BU 43;   DA 30;
        DE 54, 59;   NP 14, 47;   RC of don Alvaro 53;   SL 45
 4   -Duet   RC 53;   SE 51
 4   -Excerpts   RC 53
 4   -Finale, Act V   RC 53
 4   -Madre, Pietoso Vergine   DT 18
 7   -Overt   BN 60;   BU 53, 57, 61;   CT 47, 57, 61, 64;   CL 52, 55,
        62, 67;   DA 50;   DT 38, 59, 64, 69;   HN 53, 62, 65;   NA 55;
        KC 62;   LA 50, 54, 60;   ML 64;   MN 56, 58, 59, 64;   NP 54, 61,
        69;   PT 54, 56, 64;   RC 53, 56;   SL 57;   SF 68, 69;   SE 51,
        59, 65;   WA 69
 4   -Pace, Pace   AT 54;   BA 51;   CL 26, 47;   DA 69;   DE 53;
        DT 51, 66;   HN 36, 42, 51;   NA 40;   LA 31, 36, 45;   MN 25,
        27, 29, 45, 46;   RC 53, 56;   SL 18, 26, 30;   SF 45;   SE 38,
        46, 54;   UT 45, 65;   WA 37, 61
 4   -Scene of the Monks   RC 53
 4   -Tuche in seno   UT 51
        Giovanno d'Arco, Opera 1845: Overt   NR 69
 6   Louisa Miller Opera 1849: Overt   MN 53;   NP 41
        I Lombardi alla prima crociata Opera 1843: Non fu sogno   NP 1845
         -Quando le sere al placido   NR 69
 4   Macbeth, Opera 1847: Aria   HN 51
 4   -La luce langue   DA 69;   NR 69
 4   -Scene and Cavatina   MN 33
 4   -Sleepwalking Scene, Una macchia e qui tuttora   AT 62;   NA 63;
        SL 50
 4   Un ballo in maschera, The Masked Ball Opera 1859: Aria unidentified
        BA 67;   RC 26, 29;   PH 14, 37, 40;   SE 38, 58
 4   -Aria of Ulrica   RC 53
 4   -Eri tu che macchiavi Act III   CT 13, 34, 36, 39, 47, 56;   CL 24;
        DT 25;   HN 36, 41;   KC 36, 38;   NA 36, 37, 40, 56;   LA 34;
        MN 33;   NS 26;   PT 51;   SL 30, 38;   WA 32, 52
 4   -Forze la sogli alta Act III   CT 56;   KC 67;   MN 60;   ML 68
 4   -Invocation   SE 59
 4   -Ma se me forza perditi   CT 67;   HN 55;   LA 54
 4   -Saper Vorreste   DT 23;   NS 22
 4   -Scene   NA 68
 8   Nabucco Opera 1842: David's Air   PH 40
         -Overt   LA 58;   MN 47, 59;   NP 48, 53;   SL 28
        Otello Opera 1887: Four Acts with Narrator, Chor and O   SE 56
 4   -Ave Maria, Act IV   AT 54;   BA 59, 67;   BU 52, 60;   CH 16;
        CT 38, 46;   DT 51;   NA 63;   ML 63;   WA 66
 4   -Ballet Music   DA 50;   RC 48, 52, 53, 54
 4   -Canzone del salce, Act IV   CT 46
 4   -Credo, Iago's Creed, Act II   AT 51;   CT 31, 36, 47, 48;   CL 26,
        29;   DA 52;   DE 50, 53, 59;   DT 27, 37;   HN 36, 46;   KC 36, 39,
        60;   NA 56, 69;   LA 31, 34, 54;   ML 60;   MN 29, 36, 58;   NR 69;
        NS 24;   PH 40;   RC 29, 43, 57;   SL 47;   SE 31, 35, 55;
        WA 33, 49
 4   -Death Scene   NA 46
 4   -Dio, me petevi scagliar   AT 64

VERDI, G. (Cont.) Otello, Opera (Cont.)
    4   -Duet from Act I   AT 64;   BA 59
           -Finale, Act I   WA 35, 44
           -Recitative and Aria   DE 60;   PH 36
           -Salce Salce, Ave Maria   AT 62;   DT 51, 67;   NA 63;   ML 63
           -Three Dances   NS 26
        Rigoletto Opera 1861: Complete   AT 66;   NA 66
    4   -Aria   BA 50;   RC 25
    4   -Caro Nome   BA 42, 66;   CT 54, 62;   DA 28;   DT 24, 37;   HN 39;
           KC 52, 54, 65;   ML 64;   MN 66;   NS 24;   PT 52;   SL 13
    4   -Cortigiani vil razza   CT 40, 48;   HN 44;   MN 39
    4   -Donna e mobile   BA 43;   KC 44;   MN 31;   PT 37
    4   -Ella mi fu rapita   NP 1875
    4   -Parmi   MN 60, 64;   SF 38
    4   -Prelude   HN 42;   RC 25
    4   -Quartet   DT 25
    4   -Questa o Quella   PT 59
    4   -Vengeance Chorus   HN 42
    4   Sicilian Vespers Opera 1855: Aria unidentified   DA 35
    4   -Bolero   CT 34;   DT 35;   PT 44
    4   -Merce diletti Amiche   MN 33
    4   Simon Bocanagra Opera 1857: Aria Il lacerato spirito   DE 49, 57, 60;
           KC 47, 53;   MN 40, 44;   PT 51;   RC 41;   UT 40
           -Prologue   CT 43
    9   -Overt   BA 59;   BN 67;   CT 54, 63, 69;   CL 39, 50, 55;   DA 52;
           DT 35, 38, 66;   HN 31, 48;   KC 61, 62, 68;   LA 33, 34;   MN 47,
           55, 63;   NR 59;   NP 34, 47, 49, 55;   PH 35, 48;   PT 50, 55;
           RC 54, 56, 68;   SL 63;   SF 69;   SE 37;   UT 66
    4   La Traviata Opera 1853: Aria   NR 69;   NP 66;   SL 22, 48;   SE 51; UT 51
           -Addio del passato   NP 67
           -Ah fors e lui Act I   BA 26, 42;   CT 16, 36, 37, 48, 49, 66;
           DT 17;   HN 42;   NA 69;   KC 45, 62, 65;   ML 64;   MN 30, 36;   PH 35
           -Dance   DE 52
           -Dei miei bollenti spiriti   NA 55;   PT 59
           -Di Provenza Act II   AT 51, 52;   KC 37;   ML 60;   MN 28;   NA 69
    4   -Overt   BU 54;   DA 35;   HN 39;   ML 66;   UT 41, 65
           -Parigi, O Cara, duet from Act IV   AT 53
           -Pura siccome un angelo   SL 48
           -Prelude and Aria   DA 28, 52;   DE 52, 58, 59;   **NP** 67
           -Prelude, Act III   DT 37;   MN 40;   UT 41
           -Recitative and Aria   AT 53
           -Scenes from Act III   DE 60
           -Sempre libera   CT 16, 36, 37, 48, 49;   DT 46;   NA 69;   KC 52, 56
    4   Il Trovatore Opera 1853: Anvil Chor   NR 69
    4   -Cavatina   NP 1855
    4   -Condotta ell' era in ceppi   CT 47
    4   -D'amor sull ali rose   NP 67
    4   -Tacca La Notte   ML 65;   UT 65
    4   Willow Song   AT 54
    4   Gio nello notti   KC 64
        Sacred Works
   90   Requiem Mass for Manzoni 1874   AT 53, 68;   BA 52, 55, 63, 67;
           BN 54;   BU 46, 64, 67;   CT 59, 65;   CL 36, 52, 56, 63, 67;
           DA 46, 50, 56, 60, 66;   DT 57, 65;   HN 50, 54, 62, 67;   NA 42;
           KC 59;   LA 45, 54, 62;   MN 49, 56, 59;   NR 54, 67;   NP 54, 65, 68;

VERDI, G. (Cont.)   Sacred Works, Requiem Mass (Cont.)
     PH 41, 51, 56;   PT 39, 49, 55, 61;   RC 60, 63;   SL 63; 35, 69;
     SF 59;   SE 53, 58, 66, 68;   UT 49, 53, 66;   WA 49, 58, 62
     -Excerpts   KC 49
     -Inquineseo   MN 60
  15 Stabat Mater for Chor and O 1898   BN 61;   BU 57;   PH 59
   8 Te Deum for double Chor and O 1898   AT 63;   BN 18, 61;   BU 51, 64;
     CL 59, 66;   HN 66;   NA 52;   NP 30, 55;   PH 59;   PT 55;
     SE 55;   WA 54
     Laudi alla Vergine Maria for 4 part Chor and O 1898   BN 61;
     BU 56;   NS 11
   8 Four Sacred Pieces   BU 57;   CL 69;   KC 56;   NP 68;   LA 69
     Sacred Pieces   MN 62
  23 String Quartet in e   NP 35, 64;   PT 63;   SE 69

VERESS, Sandor   30 Minneapolis Symph 1953   MN 53
 1907- Hung/Swiss

VERHEY, Theodore 15 Fl Conc Op 43   CT 32
 1848-1929 Neth

VERLEY   6 Chanson Tourangelle   SL 45
 1867-   Fr 4 Cloches dans la vallée   SL 35
         4 Pastel Sonore   SL 38, 42

VERRALL, John   17 Concert Piece for Str and Horns   NP 40
 1908-   US 12 Portrait of St. Christopher, Tone Poem   SE 56
        10 Prelude and Allegro for Str   SE 48
        20 Symph Suite, Portrait of a Man 1941   MN 40
        18 Symph No 1 in E 1940   MN 39
        10 A Winter's Tale   SE 49

VERETTI, Antonio 18 Sinfonia Sacra   MN 50
 1900-   It

VICTORIA, Tomas   5 Motet   NP 46
 1540-1613 Sp 4 O Magnum Mysterium for Chor and O   WA 48

VIDAL, Paul   10 Danses Tanagreennes   NS 18
 1863-1931 Fr 5 Song, arietta   NS 05

VIERNE, Louis   5 Improvisation on a Given Theme   CH 26
 1870-1937 Fr 9 Symphon Piece for Org and O   CH 26

VIEUXTEMPS, Henri 15 Adagio and Rondo, V and O   NP 1848, 55;   NS 1884
 1820-1881 Fr 10 Ballade and Polonaise, V and O Op 38   NP 1865, 75;
           NS 04;   PH 41
        35 V Conc No 1 in E Op 10   CH 1893, 21;   CT 21;
           NS 21
        10 -Rondo and Allegro   CH 07
        14 V Conc No 2 in f# Op 19   NP 1860;   PH 00
        25 V Conc No 4 in d Op 31   BA 63;   BN 1884, 92, 95;
           CH 1895, 98, 07, 16, 38, 52;   CT 02, 45;   CL 18;
           DT 39, 43, 56;   HN 57;   LA 53;   MN 39, 43;
           NR 56;   NP 22, 38, 50, 53;   PH 01, 16, 44, 56;
           PT 54;   UT 68;   WA 45

VIEUXTEMPS, H. (Cont.)
        18   V Conc No 5 in a Op 37   BA 51;   BN 1884, 89, 98,
                 01;   BU 67;   CH 14;   CL 50;   DA 55;   DT 47;
                 MN 68;   NP 1866;   PH 02;   PT 40;   SL 15;   SE 62
        16   Fantasia Appassionata V and O Op 37   CH 14
        15   Fantasie-Caprice, V and O Op 11   NP 1843, 53, 62, 64
        15   Fantasia on Slavonic Melodies for V and O   BN 82

VIGO,   5   Currito de la Cruz   DE 58
        Sp

VILLA-LOBOS, Hector   10   Alma Brasilenia   WA 43
    1887-1959   Brazil   8   Alvorado Na Florensta,Tropical Overture, Dawn in a
                            Tropical Forest   CL 56;   HN 57;   PH 52
    17   Bachianas Brasileiros No 1 for 8 C and O 1930   DA 53;   DE 51, 53;
             KC 55;   NP 56;   PH 2 mvts 52
     4   -Prelude   PT 51;   SF 51
    20   Bachianas Brasileiros No 2 1930   CT 43;   CL 44, 67;   DT 41, 65;
             NP 44;   PT 43;   KC 57
     5   -Toccata, The Little Train   BN 44;   CH 42;   CT 48;   DE 53;
             KC 44, 51;   MN 49;   NP 44, 55;   UT 48
     4   -Fugue   BN 44;   KC 51
     3   -Dance, Memories of the Prairie   CH 42
    20   Bachianas Brasileiros No 4 1936   HN 65;   ML 64;   WA 67
    11   Bachianas Brasileiros No 5 1938   BA 47, 65;   DE 50;   DT 62;
             KC 45;   LA 65;   MN 49, 55;   CT 42;   NR 55, 67;   NP 44;
             SL aria only 53
     5   -Cantilena   CL 63;   NA 49;   PT 60
     6   -Prelude   NR 52;   PH 45, 50
    30   Bachianas Brasileiros No 7 1942   BN 44;   CL 56;   SE 54, 58, 67;
             HN Toccata and Fugue only 51;   NR 66, 67
    20   Bachianas Brasileiros No 8 1944   DA 57;   PH 54
    12   Choros No 1 for Guitar 1920   WA 51
    20   Choros No 6 for O 1926   AT 56;   BU 51;   CL 56;   HN 55;   NR 55;
             NP 56;   PH 54;   PT 52;   SL 55;   SE 54;   WA 51
     8   Choros No 7 for Str and Winds 1924   SF 66
    20 ' Choros No 8, 2 P and O 1925   NP 44;   PH 28
    30   Choros No 9 for O 1929   NP 44
    20   Choros No 10 for Chor and O   BN 40, 41;   BU 63;   CL 39;   KC 39;
             NR 60;   PH 59;   RC 62;   SL 61, 63, 67;   SE 62;   WA 52, 55, 59
    40   Choros No 12 for O 1929   BN 44
    25   P Conc No 1 1945   CH 50;   DA 46;   WA 53
    20   P Conc in a No 2   NP 54
    20   P Conc No 4   PT 52
    12   P Conc No 5   AT 56;   CL 56
     5   Conc Guitar and O   HN 55
    30   Conc for Harp and O   PH 54
    14   Danses Africanes 1914   BA 48;   HN 42, 57;   NR 55;   PH 28
          Descobrimento Do Brasil
    15   Suite No 1 1937   BU 51;   CH 42;   CT 41;   LA 42;   NP 40, 42;
             PH 41;   SF 42
    15   Suite No 2, C and Sopr 1937   LA 43
    15   Emperor Jones   DT 61
    20   Erosao, The Origin of the Amazon, Symphon Poem   SL 55;   SF 62;
             WA 51, 54, 58

VILLA-LOBOS, H. (Cont.)
```
13    Fantasia C and O 1945    BU 66;    PT 51
15    Fantasia de Movimentos Mixtos V and O three mvts 1922    BN 48
24    Madona, Symphon Poem    BN 47;    CH 47;    CL 53;    HN 59
20    Mandu Carara Cantata Profana    NP 56
15    Magic Window Suite    NA 43
25    Momo Precose, Carnival of Brazilian Children, P and O 1929    CT 60;
          NA 50;    SL 63;    SF 42
 8    Overt to Olympiad    SF 55
24    Pobra Peregrino Modinnas e Cancoes    HN 59
32    Poem de Italia, or Itabira    DT 54
40    Rudepoema    BN 44
25    Symph No 1, O Imprevisto 1916    NR 55
55    Symph No 2, The Ascension 1917    HN 55
20    Symph No 6    BU 51
35    Symph No 7, Peace Odyssey    DA 49
20    Symph No 8    PH 54
20    Symph No 11    BN 55
 2    Study for Guitar    DE 54
18    Uirapuru, Symphon Poem The Enchanted Bird, Ballet 1917    CH 64;
          CT 53;    HN 48;    NP 49;    SE 60;    WA 49
18    Six Songs on Folk Themes    DT 41;    KC 5 only 40
```

VINCENT, John   18   Festival Symph in D in one mvt   AT 62;   DE 58;
1902-   US   LA 56;   PH 56;   SE 58;   WA 57
                        4   Merry June, Chor and O   BA 26
                        8   Rondo Rhaps   WA 65
                       15   Symphon Poem after Descartes   AT 63;   LA 61;   PH 58
                       15   Three Jacks, Ballet in three mvts, Suite   LA 54

VIOLA, Anselmo   23   Conc for Bassoon and O   BN 65
1738-1798   Sp

VIOTTI, Giovanni B.   27   V Conc in a No 22   BN 1895, 13;   CH 12;   CT 12,
1753-1824   It   39;   CL 64;   MN 64;   NP 32, 42, 53;   NS 12;
                                 PH 39, 60;   SL 12;   SF 29;   WA 61
                                 -Andante   CH 09

VISÉE, Robert de   15   Suite in D for Guitar   AT 61;   PT 60;   NR 61
c 1650-1725   Fr

VISKI, Janos   26   C Conc   NP 65
1906-   Hung

VITALI, Tommaso   10   Chaconne   DE 64;   DT 37;   NA arr Gibilaro 41;
1665-   It   KC 61;   NR arr Akon 58;   SL arr Levy 47, 48, 49,
                              53, 54, 56

VIVALDI, Antonio   Few orchestras record both number and key signature
1675-1741   It   for Vivaldi's concertos on their title pages, and they
                        are often omitted also in the program notes available to
     the author. Timings for the concertos vary from 8 to 15 minutes and those
     which could be found in publishers' catalogues were recorded. Arrangers
     are also recorded where available.

VIVALDI, A. (Cont.)
        CONCERTO GROSSI
  11   Op 3 No 1 in d   BA 52;   DE 50, 57, 66;   HN 50, 52, 57;   LA arr
        Franko 35;   MN 29, 49;   NR 67
  15   Op 3 No 8 in a   CT 61;   DT 16, 23, 26, 35;   LA 45;   ML 65;   RC 62
  12   Op 3 No 10 in b for 4 V and O   AT 69;   BA 64;   BN 65;   CT 54;
        CL 54;   DE 64;   NA 30;   LA 42;   MN 29, 49, 63;   PH 29;   PT 56;
        SL 36, 37, 66;   WA 51
  12   Op 3 No 11 in d   BA 54(2), arr Siloti 56;   BN 52, 54, 60, 63;
        BU 57;   CH arr Siloti 27, 32, 47, 48;   CT arr Siloti 30, 53, 57;
        arr Giannini 47, 49, 51;   CL arr Siloti 38, 45;   DE 68;   DT 37,
        40, 68;   NA arr Siloti 47;   LA arr Siloti 32, 50;   MN 64;
        NP 43, 45, 49, arr Stokowski 48;   PH 22, 31, 32, 34, 52, 53, 55;
        PT 48, 60, 66;   SL 50, 59;   RC 48, 60, 67;   SE 58, 67;   UT 45;
        WA 63
   3   -Largo   BN 56
        Op 4 in d   DA 59;   SL 24, 30, 32, 38, 45, 47, 49;   WA arr Bach
        transcribed Kindler   32, 36, 42, 43
        No 1 in g   DT arr Torrefranco 57;   KC 43;   NR arr Molinari 51;
        NP 69;   PH 49;   WA 58
        No 2 arr Molinari   BN 27
  10   In A Op 11 No 4 Str and Cembalo   NR arr Molinari 53, 67;   NP 53;
        PT 50
        In a with Harpsi   MN 31;   PH arr Cailliet 38, 41
  14   In C   BA 61;   SF arr Casello 54;   WA 62
        In D   NR 53, 67
  11   In d Op 9 No 13   DA 62;   RC 29
        In E   NR 3 parts 58

        CONC for STRINGS
  14   In a   BN 26;   CL 21;   NP 27, 29, 31;   NS 11, 13, 22;   PH 13, 14,
        21, arr Molinari 35, 45;   SL 13;   SF 24
        In b, Al santo sepulcro, arr Fanna   CH 52
        In e arr Mistovski   BN 25;   LA 43, 51;   NP 36;   RC 29
        In G   MN 49, 56
        In g arr Mistovski   NP 37

        CONC for SOLO INSTRUMENTS arranged alphabetically according to
          Instrument and Key
  10   Conc for Bassoon   PT 63;   WA 65
        Conc for Cello in B^b DA 58
        Conc for Cello in D   CH 30
        Conc for Cello and Str, Sonata No 3 arr Dallapiccola   CT 55
  10   Conc for Cello and O in e   CL 60
        Conc for Flute, Str and Harpsichord in c   NP 58
        Conc for Flute in D   BA 59;   NA 40
  12   Conc for Flute in F Op 10 No 5   MN 38
  12   Conc for Flute in G Op 10 No 4   MN 38
   8   Conc for Flute and Bassoon in g   WA 63
        Conc for Guitar in C   NA 68
  11   Conc for Guitar in D   CH 65
        Conc for 2 Guitars   DE 62
  10   Conc for 4 Guitars arr from Op 3 No 1 for 4 V   ML 67;   SL 66
        Conc for Harpsichord, Flute and Strings in C   NP 58
        Conc for Harpsichord, Piccolo and Strings in C   HN 66;   SF 66;
        UT 64

VIVALDI, A. (Cont.)   Conc for Solo Instruments (Cont.)
       Conc for Harpsichord and Str Op 11 No 4   NP 53
       Conc for Harpsichord and 2 Horns arr Malipiero   LA 60
9   Conc for 2 Mandolins   BU 65;   NP arr Casella 56, 58
       Conc for Oboe in C   DE 65;   WA 63
15   Conc for 2 Oboes, Bassoon and String in g   SL 64
       Conc for Organ in a   CT 22, 31
       Conc for Organ in b arr d'Antalffy   NP 25, 39, 54, 58;   PH 42;
         SF 56
       Conc for Organ in d arr Siloti   BN 24, 29, 35, 38, 41, 43, 48;
         NP 27;   NS 15
       Conc for 4 Pianos in a arr J.S. Bach   NP 32;   SF 33
10   Conc for Piccolo and O in a   BU 67;   CL 55;   PH arr Malipiero 54;
         RC 66
       Conc for 4 Trumpets and Strings in c   RC 57
10   Conc for 2 Trumpets in C   ML 62;   MN arr Malipiero 52;   RC 57
       Conc for Viola d'Amore in d   NA 68
       Conc for Viola and O arr Dallapiccola   AT 56
       Conc for Violin in a arr Nachez   BN 41;   CH 23, 29;   MN 30;   NP 27
       Conc for Violin in C   CH 13
       Conc for Violin in D   NP 07
       Conc for Violin in g Op 12 No 1   PH 68
14   Conc for Violin in g No 8   BN 12;   CH 13;   CL 63;   DE 62;   DT 23,
         59;   SL 16
       Conc for 2 Violins in A arr Molinari   PH 56
       Conc for 2 Violins in a arr Molinari   SF 33
       Conc for 2 Violins and Strings in c   CL 56
15   Conc for 2 Violins in d   SE 64
10   Conc for 3 Violins and O   SF 47
12   Conc for 4 Violins and O   AT 69;   MN 29, 49
       The four Seasons Op 8 for Violin and Strings   CH 55, 61;   DE arr
         Molinari 60;   SL 27, 52;   SF 60
10   Spring in E No 14   BN arr Molinari 36;   CL 61;   DT 28;   LA 59,
         67;   ML 68;   NP 27, 54, 62;   NR 66;   PH 31, 54, 59;   RC 31
10   Summer in g No 15   LA 67;   NP 63;   PH 59
10   Autumn in F No 16   DT 30;   LA 67;   NP 54, 63;   PH 59, 60
10   Winter   BA 60;   DT 29, 36;   LA 67;   MN 65;   NP 35, 63;   NR 66;
         PH 31, 54, 57, 59;   RC 31;
       Conc for Woodwinds and Strings arr Siloti   NS 21

31   Gloria Mass   AT 58;   BU 61;   CH 64;   CT 51;   WA 52

VIVES, Amadeo   5   Bolero from Dona Francisquita Opera 1923   CT 43, 44;
1871-1932   Sp   RC 42, 43, 44

VLADIGEROFF, Pantcho 8   Bulgarian Rhaps, Vardar Op 16 1934   SL 30
1899-   Bulgaria 20   Bulgarian Suite in four mvts Op 21   MN 32;
               PH three mvts 33
           31   Conc for P Op 6   CH 31
           35   Conc for V Op 11   CH 27

VLIJMEN, Jan   10   Serenata II Fl and O   CH 69
1935-   Neth

VOGEL, Vladimir   Two Orchestral Etudes 1931
  1896-   Russ/Swiss 13   Ritvica Funebre   BN 31;   PT 69;   PH 31
                          7   Ritvica Scherzo   BN 31;   PT 69;   PH 31

VOGRICH, Max   25   P Conc in e   BN 1888
  1852-1916 Aust/US   30   V Conc E pur si muovi   CH 15;   NS 16;   PH 16

VON KOCH, Erland   Conc Piccola for 2 Saxophones and O   RC 65
  1910-

VOLBACH, Fritz   12   Alt Heidelberg, du feine, Ein Fruhliugagedicht
  1861-1941   Ger   Op 29 Symphon Poem   CH 07
                        6   Serenade in d for C and Str   CT 1895
                       15   Symphon Poem, Es Waren Zwei Königskeinder Op 21
                                       CT 03;   CH 02
                       17   Symphon Poem, Easter Op 16   CH 05
                       25   Symph in b Op 33   BN 14;   PH 09, 10

VOLKMANN, Robert   20   C Conc in a Op 33   BN 1883, 85, 86, 91, 04, 06,
  1815-1883   Ger/Hung   15;   CH 1892, 99, 07;   LA 21;   NP 1884, 08,
                                       15;   PH 61;   PT 47;   SL 12, 14
                        8   Festival Overt Op 50   BN 1889, 95
                        6   Fantasie, Night for Alto and O Op 45   NS 1879
                       10   Overt Richard III Op 68   BN 1884, 85, 90, 93, 96,
                                       01, 06;   NP 1884;   PH 07;   SF 19
                       15   Serenade No 2 in F Op 63 for Str   BN 1882, 88, 91,
                                       08, 15;   CH 1892;   NS 13;   WA 32
                       15   Serenade No 3 in d Op 69   BN 1884, 89, 93, 03, 12;
                                       CH 1896, 02, 12, 17;   NP 1877;   NS 1878, 82,
                                       90, 17;   PH 05;   SL 09;   SF 14
                       25   Symph No 1 in d Op 44   BN 1884(2), 90, 94, 98, 03;
                                       NA 36;   NP 1866;   NS 1883;   PH 06
                       20   Symph No 2 in B^b Op 53   BN 1883, 89, 92

VOŘÍŠEK, Jan Hugo   15   Sinfonia in D   MN 66
  1791-1825   Czech

VREULS, Victor   19   Jour de Fete, Poem   CT 20
  1876-1944   Belg

VRIONIDES, Christos   6   Three American Indian Melodies   UT 42
  1894-   US

VUILLEMIN, Jean B.   4   Bourrée   DA 26
  1798-1875   Fr   4   Pavane   DA 26

WAGENAAR, Bernard   35   Conc, Triple.for Fl, Harp, C and O 1935   PH 37
  1894-   Neth/US   7   Concert Overt Op 25   DT 54;   SL 54
                       20   Divertimento 1927   CT 31;   DT 29;   MN 36;   WA 36
                        3   Fanfare for Airmen 1942   CT 42
                       14   Five Tableaux for C and O   NP 55
                       14   Overt, Cyrano de Bergerac   CH 15, 26
                        6   Song of Mourning for the Dutch Patriots 1944
                                       CL 51;   SL 47;   WA 44
                       12   Sinfonietta for small O 1929   NP 29
                       25   Symph No 2 1930   NP 32

Time in
Minutes
WAGENAAR, B. (Cont.)
     24   Symph No 4 1946   BU 49

WAGNER, Richard   6   Albumblatt for P in C 1861 for Princess Metternich
  1813-1883   Ger   arr Reichelt for O   CT 02, 06, 07;   DE 59;
                                NP 02;   SL 09
      4   Adagio for Clar and Str   HN 66
      4   An Weber's Grabe 1844 for unaccompanied men's Chor 1844 arr for O
           Stock   CH 05;   NP 1894
      5   Centennial March in 'G 1876   BN 1894, 04;   CH 1899;   NP 16
     10   Christopher Columbus Overt 1835   CT 14;   NS 07;   PH 07(2)
     12   A Faust Overt 1840   BA 61;   BN 1882, 85, 88, 90, 91, 93, 95, 98,
           02, 04, 06, 07, 09, 11, 12, 14, 16, 20, 29, 31, 36, 46, 53;
           CH 1891, 92, 95, 98, 99, 00, 03, 05, 06, 09, 10, 12, 14, 16, 21,
           26, 27, 32, 40, 44, 53, 57, 67(2);   CT 1895, 02, 07, 10, 14, 19,
           20, 31, 35, 39, 68;   CL 22, 49, 54, 65;   DA 30, 49;   DE 52;
           DT 16, 22, 31;   HN 49;   NA 33;   KC 49, 59;   LA 22, 44, 55, 61;
           ML 66;   MN 22, 25, 27, 45, 47;   NR 56;   NP 1856, 59, 62, 65,
           68, 73, 77, 80, 82, 87, 91, 95, 98, 00, 03, 06, 09, 10, 12, 13,
           14, 16, 17, 19, 28, 29, 32, 40, 46, 52, 54, 61;   NS 1879, 05, 08,
           13, 20, 23;   PH 00, 01, 03, 04, 05, 06, 09, 12, 14, 21, 24, 38,
           48, 55, 56, 60;   PT 44, 60, 62;   RC 41;   SL 10, 13, 15, 22, 23,
           29;   SF 15, 17, 20, 24, 49, 54;   SE 29;   WA 66
     20   Fragments from Der Ring des Nibelungen   SF 56, 61
     13   Huldingungsmarch March of Homage 1864   BN 1882, 87, 89, 91, 93, 95,
           00, 05, 09;   CH 1891, 95, 96, 97, 98, 99, 02, 03, 04, 05, 07, 09,
           11, 22, 26, 27, 28, 31;   CT 1898, 00, 04, 35, 39, 44;   DT 27;
           NP 01;   PH 09, 11, 12, 15, 16, 23;   SL 09, 12, 25
      9   Kaisermarsch 1871   BN 1881, 83, 85, 92, 94, 97, 98, 02, 03, 07;
           CH 1891, 93, 94, 95, 96, 97, 98, 99, 00, 02, 03, 04, 07, 12;
           CT 1896, 99, 00, 02, 03, 04, 05, 06, 07;   NP 1888, 09, 11;
           NS 1878, 91, 95, 06;   PH 01, 12, 14, 24;   PT 62;   SL 13;   SF 13
      6   Das Liebesverbot Opera from Shakespeare's Measure for Measure 1835
           Overt   SF 58
     10   Polonia Overt 1836   CH 07, 35, 40;   LA 23;   PH 08
      3   Rule Brittannia Overt 1836   CL 41
           Songs
      4   Erwartung   NP 1895
      6   The Two Grenadiers 1839   CH 1895;   CT 1899
      4   Wiegenlied 1840   NS 06, 13
     16   Wesendonck Songs five songs 1857   BA 58;   BU 67;   CT 28;   DA three
           63;   DE 58, 64(2);   DT 59, 67;   HN 50;   KC 54, 60;   ML 66;
           NP 51;   RC 54, 68;   SF 61
      2   No 1 Der Engel   CH 04, 14, 50;   CT 04, 25;   NS 12;   PH 53
      4   No 2 Stehe Still   CH 04, 50;   CT 25, 32;   NP 10, 11;   NS 06,
             12, 13;   PH 14, 53
      4   No 3 In Treibhaus   BN 35, 42;   CH 15, 50;   CT 56;   CL 21;
             DT 17, 21, 35;   LA 34;   NP 02, 10;   NS 12, 13, 27;   PH 17,
             21, 36, 53
      2   No 4 Schmerzen   BN 35, 42;   BU 42;   CH 04, 14, 15, 50;   CT 25,
             32, 43, 45, 50, 56;   CL 21;   DT 17, 21, 22, 35, 48;   LA 34;
             MN 22, 35;   NR 55;   NP 1895, 02, 10, 11;   NS 1895, 12, 17,
             27;   PH 14, 17, 21, 36, 53;   PT 40;   RC 38;   SL 09, 21, 52;
             UT 53;   WA 37

WAGNER, R. (Cont.) Wesendonck Songs (Cont.)
  3   No 5 Traume   AT 49;   BN 35, 42;   BU 42;   CH 04, 14, 15, 50;
           CT 1897, 02, 03, 07, 13, 25, 32, 38, 43, 50, 56;   CL 19, 21;
           DT 17, 21, 22, 34, 35, 36, 48;   HN 32;   NA 31;   KC 35;
           LA 20, 34;   MN 22, 35, 45;   NS 1890, 95, 06(2), 12, 25, 27;
           PH 06, 14, 17, 21, 36, 53;   RC 36;   SL 09, 21, 38, 52;
           SF 16;   UT 53, 62;   WA 32, 35, 37
  5   -arr by Thomas   CH 04, 06, 07(2), 08, 09, 11, 12, 14, 16, 17,
           25;   CT 04;   CL 19;   NP 1888, 95, 02, 10, 11, 13, 19
  5   -arr for V Solo   NS 11, 23, 25;   WA 35, 40, 42, 45
  21   Siegfried Idyl 1870   AT 53, 59;   BA 39, 43, 59;   BN 1882, 84, 85,
           87, 92, 93, 95, 96, 99, 02, 06, 07, 08, 10, 11, 12, 13, 19, 31,
           34, 36, 42, 44, 47, 48, 49, 60, 63, 65, 68;   BU 40, 65;
           CH 1891, 92, 93(2), 95, 96, 97, 98, 99, 00, 05, 08, 10, 12, 15,
           16, 24, 29, 36, 47, 60, 62, 65;
           CT 1896, 06, 09, 12, 17, 19, 20, 23, 27, 29, 32, 38, 44, 53, 57,
           61, 63, 67;   CL 20, 26, 34, 39, 43, 47, 50, 53, 57, 60, 69;
           DA 48, 58;   DE 45, 48, 50, 52, 54, 56, 61, 65, 68;
           DT 14, 20, 27, 30, 38, 46, 52, 55, 60, 66;   HN 32, 35, 50, 51, 63;
           NA 34, 44, 58, 62;   KC 35, 48, 58, 65;
           LA 19, 22, 23, 26, 30, 40, 41, 51, 56, 57, 61, 62, 68;
           ML 61, 66;   MN 22, 26, 27, 36, 42, 47, 63;   NR 52, 59;
           NP 1884, 87, 93, 98, 04, 09, 10, 11, 13, 14, 15, 17, 19, 20, 21,
           23, 31, 39, 51, 60;
           NS 1888, 92, 04, 05, 07, 08(2), 13, 21(2), 23, 24, 26;
           PH 07, 08, 09, 10(2), 16, 19, 22, 24, 25, 31, 34, 38, 40, 45, 46,
           47, 49, 51, 54, 57, 59;   PT 44, 52, 62, 67;   RC 43, 51, 52, 57;
           SL 09, 13, 16, 19, 20, 21, 24, 27, 31, 33, 37, 39, 43, 47, 48,
           51, 53, 59, 63, 67;   SF 12, 13, 15, 27, 31, 35, 38, 40, 43, 47,
           50, 52, 55, 56, 57, 66, 67;   SE 32, 34, 36, 46;
           WA 33, 50, 55, 63
  26   Symph in C 1832   BN 1887;   CH 10;   CT 53, 56;   DE 60;   NS 10
  6   -Scherzo only   NS 24
         DRAMATIC WORKS
  4   Die Feen, The Fairies Opera in Three Acts 1834: Aria, Weh Mir   CH 15
  12   -Overt   CH 15;   CT 22;   MN 32, 46;   NP 1856;   PH 32
  4   Der Fliegende Holländer, The Flying Dutchman 1841: Aria   NP 1881,
           14;   NS 80;   SL 25
  6   -Die frist ist um, Recitative and Aria   CT 12, 67;   DT 24, 61;
           MN 23;   PH 10;   PT 38;   RC 52
  25   -Excerpts   LA 43
  8   -Jo-ho-hoe, Senta's Ballad for Sopr and Chor   BN 54;   CH 1892,
           56;   CT 16, 29, 37;   CL 21;   DA 26;   DT 16, 27;   HN 69;
           NA 38;   KC 36;   LA 30;   MN 28;   NR 55;   NS 06, 10, 20;
           PH 39;   RC 46;   SL 15, 21
  4   -Leave the Watch   CL 31
  4   -Love Duet, Like a vision   CH 1892, 96, 07, 56;   NP 1896
  11   -Overt   AT 50, 53, 62, 65;   BN 1889, 90, 92, 94, 95, 97, 99, 01,
           04, 08, 09, 10, 11, 13, 15, 19, 21, 25, 30, 37, 40, 56, 67;
           BU 48, 56, 58, 59;   CH 1891, 92, 93, 96, 97, 00, 02, 06, 07, 09,
           10, 11, 12, 13, 14, 15, 16, 21, 25, 27, 31, 35, 39, 42, 44, 52,
           54, 63;   CL 20, 23, 26, 30, 43, 48, 55, 59, 63;   CT 1896, 97,
           98, 00, 01, 04, 05, 06, 09, 13, 19, 20, 23, 29, 31, 38, 44, 45, 50,
           59, 64, 67;   DA 25, 26, 30, 34, 60;   DE 48, 50, 52, 61;

WAGNER, R. (Cont.) Dramatic works, Der Fliegende Holländer, Overt (Cont.)
        DT 15, 16, 19, 22, 31, 45, 48, 53, 54, 58, 60, 64, 67; HN 31,
        37, 40, 52, 63;   NA 36, 39, 50, 61, 66;   KC 35, 38, 40, 47, 54;
        LA 19, 36, 49;   ML 60;   MN 23, 25, 28, 32, 33, 40, 43, 60, 67;
        NP 1863, 74, 90, 99, 04, 09, 10, 11, 12, 13, 14, 15, 16, 17, 19,
        20, 25, 28, 30, 31, 32, 33, 36, 48, 53, 61;   NS 1880, 87, 91, 06,
        10, 26;   PH 02, 05, 06, 07, 08(2), 09, 10, 11, 12, 13, 14, 15,
        16, 17, 18, 19, 21, 23, 24, 25, 30, 39, 51, 52, 57;   PT 37, 47,
        49, 55, 58, 61, 62, 69;   RC 52, 56, 43;   SL 10, 11, 12, 13, 16,
        18, 21, 23, 25, 26, 27, 30, 32, 60, 63;   SF 14, 15, 19, 35, 45,
        48, 50, 53, 60, 63, 66;   SE 26, 33, 43, 57, 69;   UT 40, 48, 57,
        64;   WA 34, 35, 37, 40, 42, 45

4   -Spinning Song, Ballad for Chor   BN 05;   BU 58;   CH 1896;
        CL 29;   NP 20;   NS 10
         -arr for V   NS 23
4   -Steurmannsleid, Steersman's Song   CH 1891, 92, 11, 16, 58;
        CT 49
4   -Wie oft in Meeres, Aria for Baritone   CL 29
        Götterdämmerung, The Twilight of the Gods part 4, Ring des Nibelungen
        1869-74
6   -Act I Interlude   BN 64, 68;   RC 53, 54
6   -Act II Prelude   BN 64;   RC 53, 54
45   -Act III, Complete   NP 55;   NS 26
4   -Blitzend Gewolk von Wind getragen   CT 30
20   -Brunnhilde's Immolation, Finale   AT 53;   BA 43, 45, 49, 51;
        BN 1890, 92, 93, 99, 04, 11, 19, 53, 54, 57, 67, 68;   BU 67;
        CH 1891, 92, 93(2), 94, 00, 01, 03, 05, 06, 09, 13, 14, 15, 19,
        20, 21, 22, 24, 25, 26, 27, 28, 30, 32, 33, 35, 37, 38, 39, 41,
        44, 50, 54, 57, 61, 67;   CT 27, 29, 31, 36, 38, 42, 43, 48, 53,
        56, 61;   CL 20, 23, 25, 26, 28, 33, 43, 51, 56, 68;   DA 53, 63;
        DE arr Caston 47, 52, 56;   DT 16, 20, 25, 28, 37, 41, 44, 48, 53,
        57, 64;   HN 43, 47, 50, 57, 63, 69;   NA 40, 43;   KC 42, 50;
        LA 28, 30, 50, 51, 66;   ML 66, 69;   MN 24, 26, 27, 38, 40, 43,
        45, 48, 51;   NR 53, 57, 67;   NP 45;   NS 16, 20, 21, 24;
        PH 07, 12, 13, 14, 15, 16, 19, 20(2), 23, 24, 25, 27, 28, 30, 31(2),
        32, 34, 35, 36, 37, 38, 39, 40, 41, 42, 44, 46, 48, 50, 53, 55;
        PT 40;   RC 53, 54, 57;   SL 11, 14, 19, 22, 24, 26, 40, 59, 69;
        SE 43, with soloist 52;   UT 50, 62, 64;   WA 35, 39, 40, 47,
        55, 61
5   -Dawn   BN 64, 68;   CH 1891, 94;   CT 69;   CL 68;   DA 63;
        LA 51;   NR 57;   NP 1884, 85, 19, 20, 21, 22, 29, 32, 35;
        PT 40, 51;   RC 47, 53, 54, 57
14   -Dawn and Siegfried's Rhine Journey, Prologue   BN 31, 38, 49,
        51;   CT 05, 06, 17, 21, 22, 31, 33, 47, 48, 53, 61, 63, 69;
        NA 40;   NP 1897, 02
10   -Duet, March and Closing Scene   BN 1887, 00, 01, 05;   NS Duet
        only 22, 26
20   -Excerpts   BN 1887, 88, 90, 92, 94, 98, 03, 27, 60;   CL 52;
        KC 52;   NP 69;   PH 63;   PT fr Act III 47;   RC 53, 54;   SL 12;
        SF 58;   UT 50
7   -Gibichungchor arr Goossens   CT 28, 32, 33, 37, 42, 44, 45;
        DT 21, 29;   PT 37;   WA 38
8   -Prologue, Scene 2 arr Stock   CH 27, 33, 34
8   Siegfried's Apostrophe to Brunnhilde   CH 26, 27, 28;   NP 1876

WAGNER, R. (Cont.) Dramatic Works, Götterdämmerung (Cont.)
    7   -Siegfried's Death Music   BA 43, 49;   BN 1882, 88, 90, 93, 08,
           10, 11, 15, 19, 21, 24(2), 26, 35, 45, 48, 64;   BU 46, 56, 66;
           CH 1891, 92, 93(2), 94, 95, 96, 97, 98, 99, 00, 01, 03, 05, 06,
           07, 09, 10, 11(2), 12, 14, 15, 19, 20, 24, 25, 26, 27, 28, 32,
           35, 37, 41, 43, 44, 46, 47, 50, 58, 61, 65;
           CT 1897, 00, 02, 12, 13, 20, 21, 27, 32, 58, 61, 63, 67, 69;
           CL 21, 23, 25, 31, 33, 37, 39, 50, 56, 68;   DA 30, 37, 53, 57, 63;
           DE 47, 52;   DT 16, 17, 21, 24, 27, 31, 36, 39, 44, 47, 48, 60;
           HN 37, 40, 49, 57, 63, 69;   NA 31; 40;   KC 33, 38, 50, 65;
           LA 20, 22, 23(2), 28, 29, 30, 50, 53, 61, 63, 66;
           MN 22, 24, 31, 34, 35, 38, 40, 43, 48, 49, 51;   NR 53, 57, 67;
           NP 1876, 79, 82, 84, 85, 09, 12, 16, 19, 20, 25, 27, 29, 35, 36,
           37, 39, 41, 45, 49, 50, 59;   NS 1882, 09(2), 22, 25;   PH 04, 08,
           09, 16(3), 19, 20(2), 22(3), 24, 25, 26, 27, 28, 30(2), 31(2), 32,
           34, 35, 37, 39, 40, 41, 42, 44, 46, 48, 50, 53, 55, 56, 60, 67, 68;
           PT 40, 48, 49, 52, 54;   RC 43, 53, 54, 68;
           SL 13, 15, 17, 22, 24, 26, 31, 35;   SF 38;   SE 52;   UT 50, 62;
           WA 34, 61
   20   -Siegfried's Death and Brunnhilde's Immolation   NR 67;
           NP 1893, 95, 07, with voices 11, 16, 19, 20, 36, 37, 39, 45, 48,
           50, 51
   11   -Siegfried's Rhine Journey   BA 39, 43, 49, 53, 59;   BN 31, 38,
           56, 64, 68;   BU 40, 47, 49, 56, 64;   CH 1891, 92, 93, 94(2),
           96, 97, 98, 99, 04, 05, 06, 07, 09, 12, 15, 17, 21, 26, 27, 30,
           31, 33, 34, 39, 40, 43, 44, 45, 46, 47, 49, 50, 54, 57, 58, 61,
           63, 65, 67;   CL 20, 21, 24, 26, 28, 29, 32, 33, 35, 43, 45, 56,
           68;   DA 30, 35, 53, 57, 63;   DE 46, 47, 50, 52;   DT 25, 27,
           31, 37, 38, 44, 47, 48;   HN 40, 52, 57, 63, 69;   NA 38, 39, 40,
           52, 58;   KC 34, 37, 41, 42;
           LA 22, 28, 29, 30, 32, 42, 44, 46, 51, 53, 55, 56, 61, 66;   ML 67;
           MN 22, 24, 31, 36, 39, 40, 43, 48, 49, 50, 51;   NR 51, 53, 57, 67;
           NP 1884, 85, 12, 13, 14, 16, 19, 20, 21, 22, 29, 32, 35, 36, 37,
           39, 41, 47, 48, 49, 52, 59, 66(2);   NS 1891, 97, 03, 09(2), 11,
           13, 19, 21, 25, 26, 27;
           PH ʋ9, 12, 14, 15, 16, 19, 20, 21, 22, 23, 24, 25, 28, 29, 30,
           31(2), 35, 37, 39, 40, 42, 44, 48, 50, 53, 55, 60, 67, 68;
           PT 40, 51, 52, 63;   RC 39, 42, 47, 53, 54, 57;
           SL 10, 14, 24, 26, 27, 29, 35, 44, 59;   SF 31, 50, 54, 65;
           SE 29, 34, 38, 47, 52, 66, 68;   UT 50, 62;
           WA 35, 47, 50, 52, 61
   10   -Song of the Rhine Daughters   BN 1883;   MN 26;   NP 38;   NS 91,
           13, 21;   SL 09, 13, 32;   WA 35, 37, 45, 47
   12   -Symphon Study arr Hendl   DA 47
   15   -Symphon Synthesis   DT 43;   HN 53;   KC 39
    8   -Waltraute Scene, narrative   CH 09, 15;   CT 10, 15;   MN 35;
           NP 1851;   NS 1890, 14, 26;   PH 06, 12, 40;   SL 10, 15;   SF 28
 150   Lohengrin 1846-48 Complete   NA 51
    8   -Act II, Scene 2   PT 38
    5   -Bridal Scene   HN 69;   KC Concert form 58;   MN 48;   SL 16
    4   -Elsa's Dream, Einsam in truben Tagen   AT 53;   BA 43, 53;
           BU 42, 45;   CH 09, 25, 37, 44;   CT 14, 32, 48, 59;
           CL 24, 29, 31, 44;   DA 32;   DE 49;   DT 27, 39, 53;   HN 43;
           NA 41;   KC 44;   LA 20, 35;   MN 27;   NR 53, 55;   NP 1894;
           NS 20, 27;   PH 11, 50, 57;   PT 40, 43;   RC 43, 46;   SL 32;
           SF 42;   SE 60;   UT 50

WAGNER, R. (Cont.)   Dramatic Works, Lohengrin (Cont.)

```
  5       -Ensemble and Chorus Act I    NP 27
  4       -Entr'acte Act III    NA 49(2)
 12       -Excerpts    DA 25, 63;    SF 58
  4       -Feierlichen Zug    PH 13, 15
  4       -Lohengrin's Farewell    CH 1899, 06;    CT 31, 49;    DA 48;    NA 38,
            45;    MN 31;    SL 63;    SF 36;    WA 44
  5       -Lohengrin's Narrative, In fernem Land, or Gral Song    BU 45;
            CH 27;    CT 1899, 06, 07, 26, 31;    CL 22;    DA 30, 48;    DT 25,
            28, 35, 53;    KC 65;    LA 21;    MN 29, 31, 37, 38, 42;    NS 27;
            PH 36;    PT 38, 43;    SL 11, 26, 27, 31, 37, 63;    SF 27;    SE 37,
            40;    WA 44
  7       -Prelude to Act I    BA 26, 39, 56;    BN 1883, 90, 95, 96, 08, 10,
            11, 19, 24, 26, 45, 46, 64;    BU 69;    CH 1891, 93(2), 94, 95, 96,
            97(2), 98(2), 99(2), 00, 01(2), 02, 03, 04(2), 05, 06, 07(3), 08,
            09, 10, 11, 12(2), 13, 14, 16, 17, 19, 20, 21, 23, 26, 44, 46, 47,
            54, 59, 62;    CT 1896, 97, 99, 01, 03, 06, 12, 13, 14, 16, 19, 23,
            25, 27, 45, 46, 56, 59, 65, 69;    CL 20, 22, 25, 28, 32, 33, 36, 41,
            42, 43, 44, 47, 52, 59, 62, 63, 65;    DA 26, 34, 37, 38;
            DE 46, 49, 53, 55, 58, 60, 64, 67;
            DT 15, 22, 23, 25, 26, 35, 37, 40, 43, 44, 52, 58, 61, 63, 68;
            HN 32, 33, 35, 39, 41, 43, 44, 50, 56, 69;    NA 30, 31, 39, 41, 55;
            KC 36, 43, 56;    LA 19, 23, 30(2), 33, 34, 37, 45, 61;
            MN 22, 25, 27, 29, 34, 38, 43, 47, 50;    NR 55, 59, 69;
            NP 1859, 63, 66, 67, 81, 92, 94, 99, 03, 08, 09, 10, 12, 14, 15,
            16, 17, 19, 21, 26, 35, 46, 48, 49, 51, 61, 62;
            NS 06, 07, 08, 09(2), 11, 12, 19(2), 20, 22, 25(2), 27;
            PH 01, 06, 07, 08(2), 09, 10, 12, 13, 14, 15, 16, 19, 20, 22, 24(2),
            25, 27, 28, 29, 30, 32, 33, 34, 35, 37, 40, 45, 50, 54, 67;
            PT 39, 41, 43, 46, 49, 51, 55, 60, 62;    RC 42, 48, 53, 57;
            SL 09, 12, 21, 22, 25, 32, 33, 34, 36, 38, 39, 42, 43, 46, 47,
            49, 50, 52, 55, 56, 68;    SF 11, 12, 13, 16, 19, 27, 38, 42, 44,
            46, 48, 54, 63, 65;    SE 35, 42, 48, 52;    UT 41, 60;
            WA 33, 35, 36, 65
  4       -Prelude to Act II    DT 52
  3       -Prelude to Act III    AT 46, 51, 53, 62, 65;    BA 26(2), 43, 50;
            BN 1894, 95, 96, 97;    BU 69;    CH 1894, 13, 25, 49, 62;
            CT 31(2), 34, 36, 37, 43, 46, 56, 59;    CL 21, 22, 26, 28, 34,
            43, 60;    DA 26, 32, 34, 37, 38, 49;    DE 53, 55, 58;
            DT 14, 39, 60, 63;    HN 33, 36, 41, 49;    NA 49, 55;    KC 42, 56;
            LA 19;    MN 22, 25, 27, 29, 30, 48(2), 56, 59, 60;    NR 53, 56,
            59, 69;    NP 13, 14, 15, 16, 17, 19, 49;    NS 11, 19, 22;    PH 06,
            25, 35, 51, 59;    PT 38, 43, 46, 48;    RC 42, 57;    SL 09, 13, 16,
            22, 48;    SE 26, 28, 34, 38, 66;    UT 41, 50;    WA 35, 36, 37, 38
```

Die Meistersinger von Nürnberg 1862-67

```
  4       -Am Stillen Herd In Snowbound Hall    CH 01, 10;    CT 1895;
            MN 36;    PT 38;    SL 33
  4       -Aria    DE 52;    SL 12, 17, 22, 26, 27, 41
  8       -Two Arias    PH 45
  8       -Dance of the Apprentices    BA 48, 55, 63, 65;    CH 1892, 95, 96,
            97, 00, 04, 05, 06, 08, 11, 21, 25, 26, 27, 28, 47, 53, 54, 57,
            58, 65;    CT 01, 24(2), 32, 38, 43, 44, 45, 48, 50, 63, 69;
            CL 26, 27, 28, 29, 32, 33;    DA 26, 53;    DE 49, 53, 64;
            DT 33, 59;    HN 37, 41, 53, 60;    NA 45;    KC 62;    LA 23, 69;
            ML 60, 69;    MN 31, 33, 39, 44, 45, 47, 49;    NR 50, 53, 55, 57;
            NP 26, 52, 63;    NS 03, 07, 17, 18, 19, 21, 22;    PH 26, 31, 37,
            38, 47, 48, 52, 58, 59, 64;    PT 37, 40, 41, 43, 51;    RC 50;
```

WAGNER, R. (Cont.) Dramatic Works, Die Meistersinger von Nürnberg: Dance (Cont.)
         SL 11, 48, 52, 55;   SF 13, 31;   SE 41, 43, 44;   UT 41, 53,
         62;   WA 35, 36, 44, 45, 48, 51, 57, 62

4   -Ehrt lure deutchen Meister   RC 52

4   -Entrance of the Meistersingers   BA 48, 63;   CH 1892, 95, 96,
         97, 00, 04, 05, 06, 11, 13, 21, 25, 27, 28, 58;   CT 01, 38, 43,
         44, 45, 47, 48, 50, 63, 69;   DE 49, 53, 58, 62, 68;   HN 37, 41,
         53, 60;   KC 62;   ML 60;   MN 31, 33, 39, 44, 45, 47, 49;
         NR 53, 55, 57;   NP 26, 52, 63;   PH 37, 38, 52, 58, 59, 64;
         PT 37, 41, 43, 51;   RC 50, 52;   SL 52, 55;   UT 53, 62;
         WA 35, 36, 45, 51, 62

12   -Excerpts   BN 1881, 90, 92, 94, 99;   BU 41, 42, 45;   CH arr
         Thomas 03;   NR 63;   NP 43;   PH 40, 49;   RC 50, 52;   SL 48;
         SF 54, 57, 61, 64;   SE 63

9   -Excerpts from Act III   BA 38;   BN 52, 59, 67;   CL 43, 44, 50;
         NA 46, 48, 55;   KC 51, 62

8   -Finale BA 48, 55;   CH 1892, 96, 97, 00, 04, 05, 06, 08, 10, 11,
         13, 21, 23, 25, 26, 27, 28, 47, 54, 57, 65;   CT 24(2), 29;
         DT 59;   LA 29;   MN 46;   NR 50;   NP 26;   PH 26, 31, 37, 38,
         47, 48, 52, 58, 59, 64;   WA 41, 48, 49, 57

6   -Fliedermonologue, Wie duftet doch der flieder, Act II   CT 1899,
         51;   MN 23;   WA 47

8   -Hans Sachs Monologue, Wahn, Wahn   CH 1891, 10, 11, 12, 16, 22,
         50, 56;   CT 37, 38, 51;   CL 24, 29, 30;   DT 24;   MN 23, 33,
         39;   NP 00, 10;   NS 03, 11, 24, 25;   PH 10;   RC 47;   SL 15,
         24, 31, 36, 38;   WA 37, 47

5   -Homage to Hans Sachs   WA 35, 36, 45

8   -Magic of St. John's Eve arr Damrosch   NS 08;   PH 37

4   -Pogner's Address, Das Schöne Fest, Act I   CH 1893, 99;   CT 67;
         NP 42

4   -Preislied, Morgenlich leuchtend Morning was Glowing, Prize
         Song, Act III   BU 58;   CH 1892, 07(2), 11, 18, 25, 26, 27, 28;
         CH 1897, 06, 07, 20, 26, 44, 45;   CL 19, 22, 29;   DA 35;
         DT 27, 53;   NA 38, 45, 46;   KC 65;   LA 27;   MN 26, 28, 36, 64;
         NP 1896, 06, 09, 12, 17, 20;   NS 1883, 03, 07, 09(2), 11, 12, 16,
         22, 27;   PH 02;   RC 42;   SL 63;   SF 25, 27;   SE 40;   WA 33,
         44

9   -Prelude   AT 50, 56, 58, 66, 67;   BA 26, 28, 37, 42, 44, 47, 48,
         51, 55, 63, 65;   BN 1881, 82, 83, 84, 86(2), 88, 89(2), 92, 93,
         95, 97, 98, 99, 01, 03, 04, 06, 07, 08, 09, 10, 11, 12, 13, 14,
         16, 19, 22(2), 24, 26, 27, 28, 30(2), 32, 34, 35, 40, 42, 45, 46,
         48, 49, 54, 57, 59;   BU 40, 44, 46, 49, 51, 58, 59, 65;
         CH 1891, 92, 93(2), 94, 95, 96, 97, 98, 99, 00, 01(3), 02(2),
         03(2), 04, 05, 06, 07, 08, 09, 10, 11, 12, 13, 14, 15, 16, 17,
         19, 21, 22, 23, 25, 31, 32, 34, 38, 49, 50, 55, 58, 60, 61, 63,
         66, 68;   CT 1895, 97, 98, 99, 01, 02, 04, 05, 07, 10, 12, 13, 14,
         16, 19, 21, 22, 25, 26, 27, 28, 30, 33, 34, 36, 39, 47, 49, 51,
         53, 55, 58, 60, 62, 68;   CL 19, 20, 22, 24, 26, 28, 31, 33, 35,
         37, 40, 43, 44, 48, 49, 51, 54, 55, 56, 58, 59, 61, 62, 64, 67;
         DA 25, 27, 32, 37, 46, 48, 49, 51, 53, 58;   DE 45, 46, 48, 49,
         50, 51, 52, 53, 54, 57, 58, 59, 60, 62, 63;   DT 14, 15, 18, 20,
         21, 22, 24, 26, 29, 35, 36, 37, 39, 51, 52, 55, 60, 61, 62, 63, 68;
         HN 31, 35, 38, 39, 42, 46, 49, 53, 55, 58, 59, 60, 62, 65, 69;
         NA 34, 35, 36, 40, 42, 44, 50, 54, 57;   KC 35, 39, 42, 46, 50, 60;
         LA 20, 21, 22, 23, 24(2), 25, 26, 27(2), 32, 34, 36, 42, 47, 54,
         55, 56, 57, 63, 69;   ML 63;   MN 22, 23, 25, 28, 30, 31, 34, 36,

WAGNER, R. (Cont.) Dramatic Works, Die Meistersinger von Nürnberg: Prelude (Cont.)
                    38, 40, 42, 46, 48, 50, 52, 53, 58, 64, 67(2);   NR 54, 55, 57,
                    58, 62, 68;   NP 1871, 77, 79, 83, 87, 89, 92, 94, 97, 00, 02,
                    03, 04, 07, 09, 10, 11, 12, 13, 14, 15(2), 16, 17, 18, 19, 20,
                    21, 22, 24, 25, 26, 27, 29, 31, 32, 36, 37, 38, 44, 49, 50, 51,
                    53, 54, 55, 57, 59, 62, 63;   NS 1878, 82, 83, 87, 93, 03, 06, 07,
                    08, 09, 11, 12, 14, 16, 17, 19, 20, 21, 22, 23(2), 24, 25, 26(2),
                    27(2);   PH 04, 05, 07(2), 08(2), 09(2), 10(2), 11(2), 12(2), 13,
                    15(2), 16, 17, 18, 19, 20, 21, 22, 23, 24, 25, 26, 27, 28(2), 29(3),
                    30, 35, 38, 39, 40, 42, 43, 50, 51, 54, 55, 58, 60, 62, 64, 67, 68;
                    PT 38, 39, 40, 42, 44(2), 46(2), 48, 49, 50, 53, 56, 57, 60, 66;
                    RC 42, 44, 47, 50, 54, 57, 59, 64, 68;   SL 11, 13, 15, 16, 17, 18,
                    20, 21, 22, 23, 24, 25, 26, 27(2), 28, 29(2), 30, 32, 34, 35, 37,
                    38, 41, 43(2), 47, 50, 53, 54, 55, 57, 58, 63, 66;   SF 11(2), 12,
                    13, 14, 15, 16, 17, 19, 21, 24, 25, 26, 27, 30, 31, 32, 36, 50, 52,
                    56, 64, 65, 66, 67;   SE 27, 29, 32, 36, 38, 39, 40, 41, 43, 49,
                    51, 64;   UT 40, 45, 51, 55, 59, 65;   WA 32, 33, 35, 38, 39, 40,
                    41, 42, 44, 46, 60, 67, 69
        7   -Prelude to Act III   BN 1885, 24, 37, 45, 48;
                    CH 1891, 92, 96, 97(2), 99, 00, 04, 05, 06, 08, 11, 13, 16, 21,
                    22, 23, 25, 26, 27, 28, 32, 47, 53, 54, 57, 58, 65;
                    CT 29, 32, 43, 44, 45, 47, 48, 50, 63, 69;   CL 21, 26, 29, 32, 33;
                    DE 62, 64;   DT 25(2), 37, 39;   HN 37, 41;   NA 31, 38, 45, 63;
                    KC 62;   LA 23, 29, 69;   ML 60;   MN 28, 31, 33, 39, 49;
                    NP 1880, 06, 10, 16, 17, 19, 20, 22, 29, 52, 63;
                    NS 1883, 03, 07, 09(2), 11, 16, 17, 19;   PH 09, 10, 12, 14, 15,
                    16, 21, 23, 24, 28, 29, 31, 37, 38, 52, 58, 59;
                    PT 37, 40, 41, 43, 50, 51;   RC 60;
                    SL 10, 12, 14, 16, 26, 31, 33, 36, 40, 52, 55, 56, 59;   SF 16, 31;
                    UT 47, 53, 62;   WA 32, 35, 36, 41, 45, 48, 49, 50, 51, 52, 57, 62
        4   -Probelied, Trial Song, Fanget an, Act I   CH 01, 10, 19;
                    CL 22;   MN 36;   SL 33;   SF 27
        4   -Procession of the Guilds   CH 1892, 95, 96, 00, 04, 05, 06, 08,
                    10, 11, 13, 21, 23, 25, 26, 27, 28;   NA 45;   SF 12, 13;   SE 41
        4   -Quintet, Act III Scene 4, Selig, wie die Sonne   CH 1892, 96, 07,
                    25, 26, 27, 28;   CT 07;   LA 29;   NS 03
        4   -Verachtet mirdie Meister nicht Act III, Scene 5, Aria for Bass
                    RC 52
        6   -Wach' auf, Chorale, Awake Act III Scene 5   AT 48;   BU 51;
                    CH 08, 13, 21, 26, 28, 53;   CT 01, 31;   CL 29;   NP 1869;
                    NS 1878, 86;   RC 52
                  Parsifal 1877-82
      120   -Concert Form   MN 52;   NS 1894;   PH 32;   SE with Soloists
                    and Chor 57
      250   -Complete   CH 52
      200   -Acts I and III   WA 67, 69
        5   -Act II, Scene 3   PT 43
       35   -Act III   BN 65;   SL 65
        4   -Amfortas' Lament   NS 03, 25
       12   -Excerpts, unidentified   BN 62;   MN 67;   RC from Act I 47;
                    SF in Concert form 44
        8   -Excerpts from Act I   NS 1889
        8   -Excerpts from Act III   BN 69;   CL 40, 53;   NP arr Stokowski
                    61;   PH 14, 24, 26, 34, 35, 36, 39;   SL 54
       15   -Finale, Act I   DT 37;   HN 45;   NS 82
       12   -Finale, Act III   HN 57, 58;   NA 47;   MN 25;   NP 46, 47;
                    WA 45, 50

WAGNER, R. (Cont.) Dramatic Works, Parsifal (Cont.)
6   -Glorification   CH 1893, 94, 96, 97, 99, 01, 02, 03, 05, 06, 08,
        09, 11, 12, 13, 14, 15, 19, 20, 21(2), 22, 23, 24, 25, 27, 28, 29,
        36, 37, 39, 40, 41;   NP with Prelude 1892, 97, 99, 01, 07, 11,
        37, 41;   SF 42
9   -Good Friday Spell, Usually with Prelude to Act III, and often
        arr by conductor   AT 49, 66;   BA 37, 40, 65;
        BN 1883, 91, 98, 01, 05, 08, 10, 21, 25, 32, 45, 53, 60, 63;
        BU 41, 54;   CH 1891, 92, 95, 96, 97, 98(2), 01, 02, 03, 05, 06, 07,
        08, 09, 11, 12, 13, 14, 15, 17, 19, 20, 21, 22, 23, 26, 27, 28, 29,
        30, 31, 33, 36, 37, 38, 39, 40, 41, 42, 43, 46, 49(2), 53, 55, 57,
        59, 62;   CT 1897, 00, 10, 21, 25, 27, 33, 37, 38, 39, 47, 45, 54,
        58;   CL 20, 22, 25, 30, 38, 45, 47, 49, 50, 55, 57, 60, 67;
        DA 46, 51;   DT 20, 39, 43, 45, 53, 63;   HN 31, 33, 34, 40, 49, 57, 58;
        NA 32(2), 38, 54;   KC 33, 35, 42;   LA 22, 23, 29, 49, 51, 54, 55,
        57, 58, 68;   ML 64;   MN 22, 25, 27, 31, 35, 39, 40, 43, 47, 55,
        58;   NR 51, 64;   NP 08, 11, 12, 13, 14, 15, 16, 17, 19, 20, 27,
        28, '29, 32, 44, 46, 49, 50, 55, 63, 67;   NS 1882, 96, 03, 07,
        09(2), 13, 17, 18, 19, 21, 22(2), 24;   PH 03, 04, 06, 09, 10, 11,
        13, 17, 20, 22, 23, 24, 26, 27(2), 29, 30, 31, 35, 37, 41, 43, 46,
        47, 50, 54, 56, 57, 59, 69;   PT 40, 43, 44, 48, 56, 61, 68;
        RC 42, 50, 54;   SL 11, 13, 18, 22, 24, 29, 44, 61;   SF 13, 16,
        38, 47, 51, 65;   SE 51;   UT 47, 61, 67;   WA 35, 36
4   -Act III Interlude   RC 51
13   -Klingsor's Magic Garden and Flower Girls Act II   CH 1898, 08;
        MN 25, 46;   NP 44;   PH 03, 11, 37, 43, 54;   PT 53
4   -Kundry's Monologue, Ich Sah das Kind, Act II   AT 66;   CH 1895;
        NS 14, 16;   SL 09, 59
6   -Paraphrase for V and O on Parsifal Themes arr Wilhelm   CH 1893;
        NS 1897
25   -Parsifal Symph arr Foss, 3 mvts   BU 68
12   -Prelude Act I   BA 37, 40, 65;   BN 1882(2), 83, 88, 91, 96, 99,
        08, 10, 12, 15, 17, 19, 20, 22, 30, 32, 38, 40, 42, 51;
        CH 1891, 92, 93, 94, 95, 96, 97, 98, 99, 05, 06, 11, 14, 15, 25,
        32, 36, 42, 53, 59, 69;   CT 1895, 13, 19, 20, 29, 32, 36, 51, 58,
        64;   CL 27, 31, 37, 39, 41, 48, 53, 54, 69;   DA 35;   DE 50;
        DT 15, 20, 31, 36, 45, 47, 54;   HN 33, 40, 49, 52, 57;   NA 40,
        47, 54;   KC 33;   LA 31, 32, 44, 51;   MN 23, 25, 27, 35, 43, 47,
        64;   NP 1882, 13, 28, 29, 30, 32, 37, 40, 48, 50, 51, 53, 63;
        NS 1885, 89, 96, 03, 07, 19, 21, 22, 25;   PH 02, 07, 09, 10, 11,
        13, 14, 20, 22, 23, 24, 25, 26, 27, 29, 35(2), 37, 38, 40, 42,
        43, 45, 47, 48, 51, 54, 56, 60, 65, 66;   PT 53;   RC 51, 55;
        SL 09, 14, 20, 25, 27, 36;   SF 15, 22, 24, 26, 32, 36, 42, 46,
        49, 50, 57, 65;   WA 52, 67
6   -Prelude Act II   NA 47;   RC 51
3   -Prelude Act III   NA 47;   RC 51;   WA 67
8   -Procession of the Knights of the Holy Grail, Grail Scene
        BA 36;   CH 07, 08, 09, 14, 20, 21, 29, 31, 32, 33, 36, 37, 38,
        39, 40, 41;   CT 29, 33, 39, 41;   CL 31;   DA 27;   HN 45;
        MN 25, 43;   NP 17, 20;   NS 03, 06, 07, 15, 17, 24, 25;   PH 14;
        SL 14, 24;   SF 37
12   -Temple Scene Complete   NS 25
6   -Titurel's Funeral Procession   BN 63;   CH 1892, 95, 96, 97, 01

WAGNER, R. (Cont.)   Dramatic Works, Parsifal (Cont.)
20   -Transformation Scene, often with finale   AT 66;   BA 40;
            CH 1891, 98, 99, 02, 03, 05, 06, 08, 09, 11, 12, 13, 15, 19,
            20, 21, 22, 23, 24, 25, 27, 28, 29, 36, 39, 40, 41;   CT 33(2),
            38, 39;   CL 22, 30, 38, 47, 49, 52, 57, 60, 67;   DT 21;   HN 45;
            NP 44;   PH 03, 08(2), 09, 10(2), 11(2), 13, 14, 31, 37, 43, 54;
            SF 37;   WA 45, 50
          Das Rheingold, Part I of Der Ring des Nibelungen 1853-54
8   -Act I Scene 1, Awakening   NP 40;   NS 03, 12, 13, 21
15   -Act I Scene 3   CT 31
4   -Alberich's Curse   NS 03;   PH 15, 16, 20, 22, 24, 30, 31, 37, 68;
            SL 53
9   -Finale Entrance of the Gods into Valhalla   BN 1894;   CH 1894,
            96, 00, 04, 06, 07, 08, 09, 10, 11, 12, 13, 15, 16, 19, 20, 22,
            23, 24, 32, 39, 45, 47;   CT 1896, 99, 02, 03, 05, 07, 11, 17,
            20, 22, 25, 30, 31, 32, 38, 44;   CL 27, 33;   DA 37, 50, 53, 68;
            DE 45;   DT 17, 25, 30, 39, 45, 46, 63;   HN 43;   NA 40, 54;
            KC 33, 34, 36, 40;   LA 19, 21, 22, 24, 53;   ML 67;   MN 22, 24,
            27, 28, 31, 39, 46, 51;   NR 55;   NP 14, 15, 16, 17, 19, 20, 40,
            45;   NS 1878, 83, 85, 03, 13, 20, 21, 25, 26;   PH 00, 01, 09,
            10, 12, 13, 14, 15, 16, 19, 20(2), 21, 22(2), 23, 24, 25, 29, 30,
            31, 35, 37, 40, 54, 60, 68;   PT 50;   SL 15, 21, 25, 53;
            SF 23, 27;   SE 26, 29, 35;   WA 32, 36, 45, 50
4   -Erda's Warning, Weihe Wotan Weiche   CH 09;   CT 10, 26;   MN 31;
            NS 14, 25, 26;   SL 10, 16;   SF 12;   PH 06, 12, 23
8   -Excerpts   CH arr Thomas 01(2), 02, 03;   HN 36;   PH arr
            Stokowski 32, 33, 36
4   -Prelude   BN 1892;   CH 1894;   CT 31;   NA 40;   NP 40;
            NS 03, 12, 13, 21
4   -Loge's Tidings   NP 40
4   -Rainbow Scene   CH 12, 23
4   -Song of Rhinemaidens   CH 1894; 12, 23;   NA 40;   NS 03, 21, 25
8   -Wotan's Greetings to Valhalla   DT 22
          Rienzi 1838-40
4   -Andriano's Air, Gerechter Gott, from Act III   CH 1893, 01, 05,
            09, 12, 15, 23, 29, 40;   CT 1896, 03, 06;   DT 21, 23;   LA 21,
            22, 54;   MN 28;   NP 05, 10   NS 07, 10;   PH 01, 05, 06, 07,
            14, 16;   PT 38, 65;   SF 13, 28
4   -Aria   SL 09, 10, 16, 22
13   -Bacchanale   MN 30
4   -Battle hymn   NS 25
4   -Duet   NS 25
12   -Overt   AT 48, 53, 56, 61;   BA 41, 43, 50, 58;
            BN 1882, 92, 94, 95, 96, 97, 00, 03, 05, 09, 12, 22, 24, 67;
            BU 49, 60;   CH 1891, 93, 97, 99, 01, 06, 08, 09, 10, 12, 16,
            17, 19, 20, 24, 26, 30, 31, 57, 66;   CT 1897, 03, 06, 12, 21,
            38, 43, 66;   CL 25, 49, 54, 57, 65;   DA 26, 29, 53, 56;
            DE 47, 57;   DT 15, 16, 17(2), 22, 30, 34, 41, 43, 55, 59;
            HN 34, 40, 45, 47, 49, 59;   NA 31, 39;   LA 19, 28, 58;
            ML 66, 69;   MN 22, 23, 26, 28, 30, 41;   NR 60;   NP 1861, 63,
            07, 12, 13, 14, 16, 20, 39, 51, 52, 53, 54, 55;   NS 07, 12, 19,
            23, 24, 25;   PH 07, 08(2), 12, 14, 15, 16, 17, 19, 20, 23, 24,
            27, 29, 30, 35;   PT 37, 38, 39, 45, 49, 51, 55, 68;   RC 38, 42;
            SL 09, 14, 16, 22, 23, 27, 69;   SF 28, 59, 62;   SE 59, 68;
            UT 44, 62;   WA 31, 45, 47, 49, 65

WAGNER, R. (Cont.)   Dramatic Works, Rienzi (Cont.)
   4   -Peace Chorus   NS 25
   4   -Rienzi's Gebet Prayer, Allmacht 'ger Vater, From Act V   CT 44;
           CL 23;   MN 43;   NP 13;   NS 1885, 25;   WA 45
   6   -Recitative and Chor   NP 17
      Siegfried, Part 3 Der Ring des Nibelungen 1869-74
   4   -Act II Prelude   DT 29
   5   -Act II, Scene 3 Interlude arr Goossens   CT 31, 34, 37, 45
   4   -Act III Prelude   BN 63;   CT 31, 34, 37, 45;   NA 40
  25   -Act III   BN 34;   NS 1879, 22
  12   -Act III Final Scene, Scene 3   BU 64;   CH 10;   CT arr Reiner
           26, 27;   HN 65;   MN 48;   NP 65;   NS 1891, 17;   RC 48
   4   -Aria   NR 55
   5   -Brunnhilde's Awakening   BN 63;   NS 1891, 17, 03;   PH 32
          -Brunnhilde's Entreaty Ewig war ich, ewig bin ich   CT 30;
           MN 45;   NS 03
  20   -Excerpts   BN 1887, 88, 90, 92, 94, 98, 03, 21;   CH from Act II
           01, 10, 11, 14, 22, 26, 32;   PH 37;   SL 12
   9   -Forest Murmurs, Waldweben   BA 49;   BN 1890, 92, 94, 95, 96, 99,
           03, 08, 09, 19, 21, 26, 32, 36, 45, 63;   BU 45;
           CH 1892, 93, 94(2), 95(3), 96, 97, 98, 99, 00, 02, 03, 05, 06,
           07(2), 09, 12, 13, 14, 16, 21, 25, 29, 39, 40, 43, 45, 46, 47, 65;
           CT concert version 13, 20, 22, 23, 25, 29, 31, 63;   CL 21, 25, 31,
           33, 35, 37, 68;   DA 35, 50;   DE 51;
           DT 16, 17, 24, 25, 35, 36, 37, 39, 44, 53, 54, 58, 63, 66;
           NA 40, 54;   KC 34, 37, 42, 50;   LA 22, 25, 28, 40, 53, 61;
           ML 62, 67;   MN 24, 29, 31, 32, 45, 49;   NR 55, 67;   NP 1899,
           00, 12, 14, 15, 16, 18, 20, 29, 50, 55;   NS 1881, 86, 94, 03,
           05, 06, 13, 16(2), 17, 19;   PH 04, 08, 09(2), 10, 11, 13, 12,
           14, 15, 16, 19, 20, 21, 22, 23, 24, 26, 27, 28, 30, 31, 32, 35,
           37, 39, 40, 45, 51, 58, 59;   PT 37, 39, 46, 56;   RC 42;   SL 15,
           21, 22, 26, 29, 32, 34, 36, 40, 54, 56, 69;   SF 11, 12, 13, 14,
           45;   SE 29;   WA 47
   4   -Meeting with Fafner   NA 40
   4   -Nothung, Nothung! Forge Song, Schmelzlied   CT 26, 44;   SL 34
  25   -Overt   BN 54;   CH with Forge scene arr Stock 26;   NA 40
  20   -Siegfried's Ascent to Brunnhilde through the flames   BN 63;
           CH 1894; with Finale 13, 22, 23, 24, 25, 26, 27, 28, 29, 30, 31,
           32, 33, 34, 35, 38, 40;   NP 1897, 19, 20, 21;   NS 1891, 03,
           08;   PH 22, 23, 24, 30, 31, 32, 37
   5   -Siegfried and the Dragon arr Damrosch   NS 08, 09(2), 16
   4   -Wotan's reply to Mime   DT 22
   4   -Wotan's ride   NP 19, 20, 21
          -Hammer Song Schmiedelied, Ho, ho, Schmeide mein Hammer   CH 1896;
           CT 26, 44;   DT 53;   MN 37;   NP 1880, 13, 26;   PH 09, 32
      Tannhäuser 1843-44
   4   -Aria   BA 50, 53;   DA 26, 32, 53;   NR 53;   SL 11
   8   -Arias   SE 36, 37
   4   -Aria, Blick ich umber, Wolfram's Eulogy   CH 10, 12, 16;
           CT 13, 30, 38;   MN 39;   PH 38;   SL 13, 38;   WA 37
  12   -Bacchanale or Venusberg Music   BA 39, 49, 50, 57;   BN 05, 08,
           16, 21, 24, 33, 38, 56, 63;   BU 63;   CH 1891, 92(2), 93 94, 95,
           96(2), 97, 98, 99, 03, 04, 06, 07(2), 08, 09(2), 10, 11, 12, 14, 15,
           16, 17, 19, 20, 21, 23, 25, 49, 68;   CT 02, 15, 21, 29, 33, 69;
           CL 20, 21, 23, 24, 27, 30, 32, 33;   DA 46, 50, 63;   DT 36, 37, 41, 48,

  Time in
  Minutes
WAGNER, R. (Cont.) Dramatic Works, Tannhäuser: Bacchanale (Cont.)
              53, 58, 69;   HN 58;   KC 36, 37, 38, 61, 63;   LA 23, 34, 35,
              36, 39, 40;   MN 22, 23, 25, 28, 30, 41, 43;   NR 54, 59;
              NP 1899, 04, 14, 15, 17, 19, 20, 23, 29, 36, 39;   NS 1892, 95,
              09(2), 10, 12, 15, 16, 18, 19, 22, 23, 24, 26, 27;   PH 09, 10,
              11, 52, 59, 62;   PT 39, 40, 45, 46, 48, 53, 60, 62, 68;   RC 59;
              SL 09, 10, 32, 33, 37, 41, 44, 46, 53, 61, 62;   SF 16, 28, 68;
              SE 30, 36;   UT 41;   WA 40, 57, 63
     18   -Overt and Bacchanale   BN 05, 08, 16, 21, 24;   CT 28, 37, 40, 48;
              CL 43, 46, 51;   DE 51, 54, 64;   ML 61;   NR 69;   NP 1891, 10,
              51;   PH 13(2), 15, 16, 19, 20, 21, 22, 23, 24, 25, 26, 28, 29,
              30, 35, 36, 38, 40, 42, 45, 49;   RC 46, 52;   SL 12, 13, 15, 16,
              20, 24;   SF 31, 45;   SE 33;   WA 51
     15   -Bacchanale with Finale from Overt   CH 13, 26, 27, 29, 31, 32,
              34, 35, 37, 38, 42;   SF 14
      4   -Departing Pilgrims   CL 31
      6   -Elizabeth's Greeting, Dich theure Halle   AT 53;   BN 54;
              CH 1891, 92(2), 96, 10, 56;   CT 1898, 00, 05, 11, 29, 32, 37, 59;
              CL 26, 56;   DE 47, 63;   DT 22, 32, 35, 36, 39, 53, 66;
              HN 32, 36, 45;   KC 40, 60;   LA 27, 38;   ML 66;   MN 27, 30, 32,
              35, 41, 44, 46;   NP 1877;   NS 11, 14, 20, 21, 27;   PH 02, 05,
              07, 11, 57;   PT 37, 38, 40(2);   SL 12, 15, 23, 26, 27, 29, 40,
              62;   SF 15;   SE 40, 54, 60;   WA 32, 37
      6   -Elizabeth's Prayer, Allmacht'ge Jungfrau hor mein flehen   BA 53;
              CH 1893; 09, 14;   DE 55;   LA 19;   MN 27, 32, 35;   NP 1860;
              NS 08;   PH 05, 55;   SL 12, 38
      6   -Entrance of the Guests, Fest march   BN 63;   HN 43;   RC 42, 52
     10   -Fragments from Tannhäuser, orch Thomas   CH 00(2), 01, 02, 03
      6   -O Furstin, Duo of Tannhäuser and Elizabeth Act II   WA 37
     13   -Overt   AT 52, 56;   BA 28, 43, 45, 49, 50, 59, 62, 64;   BN 1882,
              84, 86, 89, 92, 94, 95, 97, 00, 03, 04, 07, 10, 11, 20, 23, 24, 27,
              31, 32, 36, 40, 48, 51, 54, 56, 59, 66;   BU 46, 50;   CH 1891(2),
              92(2), 93(2), 94, 95, 96(3), 97, 98(2), 99, 00, 01, 02(2), 03,
              04(2), 06(2), 07, 08, 10, 11, 12, 14, 19, 21, 23, 36, 51, 56, 59,
              60, 62, 64, 65;   CT 1895, 97, 98, 00, 01, 03, 06, 07, 11, 12,
              14, 15, 17, 22, 25, 26, 32, 45, 50, 60, 63;   CL 18, 20, 22, 23,
              24, 25, 31, 32, 35, 42, 48, 49, 52, 55, 56, 59, 61, 66;   DA 26,
              28, 32, 34, 46, 55, 63;   DE 45, 47, 50, 53, 55, 59, 61;
              DT 14, 15, 17, 18, 20, 21, 22, 24, 27, 32, 33, 35, 36, 38, 43,
              51, 52, 56, 62, 63, 65;   HN 31, 35, 36, 39, 42, 44, 48, 50, 56,
              58, 63;   NA 35, 38, 41, 44, 49;   KC 33, 34, 35, 36, 37, 42, 43,
              45, 48, 50, 56, 60, 61, 63, 65;   LA 19, 20, 21, 23, 24, 25, 28,
              37, 56;   MN 22, 23, 25, 26, 28, 30, 31, 32, 41, 43, 47, 49, 54,
              65;   NR 50, 54, 55, 56, 57, 59, 61;   NP 1854, 55, 57, 60, 62,
              66, 70, 72, 87, 88, 96, 98, 03, 06, 08, 09, 11, 13, 14, 15, 16,
              18, 19, 20, 21, 23, 25, 29, 38, 39, 50, 51, 52, 54, 57, 58, 60;
              NS 1878, 80, 93, 06, 07, 09, 10, 20, 21, 22, 24, 27;   PH 02, 03,
              04, 06, 07(2), 08(3), 09, 12, 17, 18, 19, 20, 22, 27, 28, 47, 52,
              56, 59, 62(2);   PT 37, 44, 45, 48, 51, 54, 56;   RC 43, 49, 57,
              59, 64;   SL 09, 10, 11, 14, 17, 20, 21, 23, 25, 27, 28, 29, 31,
              32, 34, 36, 40, 43, 44, 45, 46, 48, 52, 55, 56, 61, 62, 69;
              SF 12(2), 13, 15, 21, 22, 23, 24, 27, 32, 53, 56, 60, 62, 63,
              64, 66;   SE 26, 32, 38, 43, 52, 60;   UT 41, 46, 49, 56(2), 60,
              63;   WA 33, 35, 36, 37, 39, 44, 48, 57, 63, 65

WAGNER, R. (Cont.) Dramatic Works, Tannhauser (Cont.)
6   -Pilgrims Chorus or March   AT 49;   BA 42;   BN 1883;
CH 1894, 95(2), 96, 99, 02;   CT 01, 14;   CL 29, 31;   DA 27;
DT 21;   NA 31;   KC 34;   MN 46, 48;   NS 21;   SF 55;   WA 36, 42
4   -Prelude to Act II   MN 27
11   -Prelude to Act III   BN 1894;   CH 1892, 93, 95, 97, 05, 13, 14,
37;   CT 38, 45;   MN 27;   NS 08, 21;   PH 22, 24, 35, 39;
PT 62;   SF 59
4   -Romanza, To the Evening Star   CH 1892, 93;   CT 01, 13, 37;
CL 30;   DT 22;   HN 36;   KC 36;   LA 21, 53;   MN 33;   NP 1879,
89;   NS 26;   PH 38;   RC 52;   SL 13;   SF 31;   UT 56;   WA 37,
47
6   -Rome Narrative, Inbrunst im Herzen   CT 44;   PH 09, 13;
PT 57;   WA 45
5   -Scene   NP 1878
4   -Septet Finale Act I   CT 07;   KC 36, 37
     -Shepherd's Song   SL 16
     -Tournament of Songs   HN 69
     Tristan und Isolde 1857-59
209   -Act I, Act II and Act III   DT 34;   KC 61
64   -Act II   NP 38;   PT 57
12   -Act II, Scene 2 Liebesnacht   CT 34;   CL 27;   HN 57;   NA with
Introduction 47;   NS 1892, 94, 06, 07, 12, 16, 17, 19, 25, 27;
PH 33(2), 34, 35, 36, 37, 50, 51, 52;   RC 50;   SL 26
8   -Act III, Scene 1   CT 45
4   -Aria   PH 42(2), 48
     -Brangane's Aria, Erfuhrst du meine Schmach Act I, Scene 3   CT 49
     -Brangane's Warning, Einsam wachend   CT 46;   NS 06, 07, 25;   SL 12
8   -Act III, Scene 3   CT 30
60   -Concert Version   CT 52, 57;   MN 49;   WA 66
4   -Entr'acte, Act III   NA 49
20   -Excerpts   DA 46;   KC 40;   LA 26;   SF 58, 62
20   -Excerpts from Act II and III   PH 11, 31
16   -Excerpts from Act III arr Stock   CH 10, 11, 12, 13, 14, 20, 23,
24, 25, 27, 30, 31, 32, 34, 37
12   -Excerpts from Act I arr Reiner   CH 53
11   -Introd and Tristan's Vision, Act III arr Stock   CH 28
16   -Introd and Finale   NP 1879, 10, 11, 12, 23, 24, 25, 26, 29,
Finale only 36;   MN 31
6   -Isolde's Farewell   PT 41
8   -Isolde's Narrative, Act I, Scene 3   CH 06, 11, 24, 27, 30, 50;
CT 30, 34;   CL 26;   DE 49;   DT 25, 35;   HN 47, 52;   KC 50;
MN 51;   PT 41;   RC 50;   SL 45, 53
8   -King Mark's Narrative   CL 30
7   -Liebestod Love-Death   AT 69;   BA 39, 45, 51, 68;   BU 64;
CH 41;   CT 04, 19, 29, 30, 34, 47, 49, 69;   CL 23;   DA 28, 32,
37, 46, 48, 50, 54, 57, 60;   DE 45, 46, 47, 52, 53, 55, 57, 58,
64, 68;   DT 16, 17, 19, 22, 24, 25, 27, 28, 30, 31, 32, 33, 35, 36,
37, 39, 40, 43, 46, 47, 51, 53, 54, 58, 61, 63;   HN 39, 45, 47,
49;   KC 56;   LA 24;   MN 22, 23, 25, 27, 28, 29, 32, 36, 43,
46, 48(2), 49, 51, 58, 61, 67, 68;   NR 51, 54, 57, 60, 61;
NS 1879, 81, 84, 91, 92, 93, 97, 04, 06, 07, 08, 09(2), 14, 18(2),
19, 21, 22, 23(2), 25(2), 26(2), 27;   PH 53, 57;   PT 37, 38, 39,
40, 41, 63, 69;   PT 68;   RC 50, 56, 61, 64;   SL 69;   SE 43;
WA 39

WAGNER, R. (Cont.) Dramatic Works, Tristan und Isolde (Cont.)
```
 16      -Love scene Act II arr Stock    CH 09(2), 10, 11, 12, 13, 14, 17,
         23, 24, 25, 27, 28;    NS 1892, 94, 06, 07, 12, 16, 17, 19, 25, 27
  9      -Prelude Act I    BN 1882, 89, 12, 13, 15, 67;    BU 46, 63;
         CH 13, 14, 23, 24, 27, 30, 50;    CT 1898, 19, 34, 38, 43, 47, 49;
         CL 23, 50;    DA 28(2), 32, 37, 46, 48, 50, 54, 57, 60;    DE 45,
         46, 47, 52, 53, 55, 57, 58, 64;    DT 14, 15, 16, 17, 19, 22, 24,
         25, 27, 28, 30, 31, 32, 33, 35, 36, 37, 39, 40, 43, 46, 47, 51,
         53, 54, 58, 61, 63;    HN 39, 45, 47, 49;    MN 22, 23, 25, 27,
         28, 29, 32, 36, 43, 46, 48(2), 49, 51, 58, 61, 67;    NR 51, 53,
         54, 57, 60, 61;    NP 1865, 74, 22, 23;    NS 1879, 81, 84, 91, 93,
         97, 04, 08, 09(2), 14, 18, 19(2), 22(2), 27, 23(2), 25(2), 26(2);
         RC 50, 56, 61;    SF 27, 29;    PH 04, 07(2), 08(2), 09, 10, 11,
         12, 13, 15, 16, 17, 18, 19, 20, 21, 22, 23, 24, 25, 26, 27, 28,
         29, 31(2), 32, 34(2), 38, 39(2), 40, 41, 42, 44, 45, 46, 47, 48,
         49, 50, 51, 52(2), 53(2), 55, 58, 59, 60(2), 62, 64
  8      -Prelude Act III    BA 26, 28, 38;    BN 23;    CH 50, 66;
         CT 26, 34, 38, 44, 46, 49;    CL 24, 25, 27, 31;    DT 20, 35, 37,
         55, 60;    HN 31, 67;    NA 38, 47, 54;    MN 23, 26, 51;    NP 16,
         17, 18, 22, 37;    PH 13, 22, 23, 24, 42, 48, 53;    PT 52, 63;
         RC 50;    SL 33, 45, 46;    SF 28;    WA 32, 36, 38, 43, 47
 16      -Prelude Act III and Love-Death Liebstod    AT 53;    BA 42, 43,
         48(2), 49, 55, 61;    BN 1884, 85, 86, 92, 95, 97, 98, 02, 08, 09,
         11, 20, 22, 25, 26, 27, 32, 34, 39, 48, 52, 53;    BU 41, 42, 52,
         56, 60, 62;
         CH 1891, 92, 93, 94(2), 95, 96, 97, 98, 99, 00(2), 01, 02, 03, 04,
         05, 06, 07(2), 08, 11, 12, 15, 17, 18, 20, 21, 22, 33, 36, 38, 43,
         45, 47(2), 49, 55, 57, 61, 62, 63, 67;
         CT 1895, 02, 03, 04, 06, 10, 12, 14, 15, 17, 22, 27, 31, 37, 46,
         53, 65;    CL 20, 22, 24(2), 27, 28, 30, 32, 34(2), 35, 36, 37,
         42, 43, 44, 47, 49, 51, 54, 56, 58, 61;    HN 31, 35(2), 53, 55, 63;
         NA 37, 41, 45, 47, 49, 53, 58, 61;    KC 33, 34, 35, 36, 37, 38, 41,
         47, 50, 60, 65;    LA 19(2), 20(2), 23, 24, 27, 30, 34, 35, 37,
         39(2), 40, 45, 46, 52, 63;    ML 62;    MN 40, 41;    NP 1892, 97, 99,
         02, 03, 04, 09, 13, 14, 15, 16, 17, 18, 19, 20, 21, 22, 38, 41, 46,
         47, 49, 50, 56, 64;    PH 04, 07(2), 08(2), 09, 10, 11, 12, 13, 15,
         16, 17, 18, 19, 20, 21, 22, 23, 24, 25, 26, 27, 28, 29, 31(2), 32,
         34(2), 38, 39(2), 40, 41, 42, 44, 45, 46, 47, 49, 50, 51, 52(2),
         53(2), 55, 58, 59, 60(2), 62, 64, 67;
         PT 37, 38, 39, 40, 41, 45, 46(2), 48, 49, 51, 54, 61, 62, 63;
         RC 50, 56, 61, 64;    SL 10, 12, 13, 14, 15, 16, 17, 18, 19, 20,
         21(2), 23, 24, 25, 26, 27, 28, 29, 30, 31, 32, 34, 38, 39, 40, 45,
         47, 48, 52, 55, 57, 59;    SF 12, 13, 14, 15, 16, 19, 20, 21, 22,
         23, 24, 25, 28, 30, 32, 36, 41, 48, 51, 52, 53, 55, 63, 64, 65, 67;
         SE 29, 31, 32, 38, 40, 48, 52, 58, 65, 68;    UT 45, 46, 53, 55,
         62, 64;    WA 32, 36, 41, 43, 44, 47, 48, 52, 54, 59
 17      -Prelude Liebstod with voice    BN 1887, 93, 00, 16, 57
  4      -Shepherd's Tune    NS 26
 30      -Symphon Synthesis    DA 56
  4      -Thater du es wirklich    PH 38
  4      -Tristan's Death    CT 26, 34;    NS 26, 27;    RC 50
  4      -Tristan's Vision    SF 15, 28, 30, 32, 36, 41;    WA 43
```

WAGNER, R. (Cont.)
       Die Walküre Part II of Der Ring Des Nibelungen 1854-56

60   -Act I   BN 33, 61;   BU concert form 58;   CH 45;   CL 53;
         HN 54, 65;   KC Concert form 58;   MN 24, 37, 58;   NP 35;
         NS concert form 26;   PT 39, 47, 67;   RC concert form 68;
         UT 68
40   -Act I Scene 1 and 2   SE 40
6   -Act I Scene 3 Finale   BA 59;   CL 22, 24, 29, 32, 39;   NP 37,
         54;   NS 11;   PT 38;   SL 24;   WA 37
50   -Act III   NP 45
8   -Act III Prelude and Scene 3   CT 37
4   -Aria   NR 55;   PH 55
4   -Brunnhilde's Battle Cry Hoyo to Ho   DA 53;   DE 47;   LA 30;
         MN 35;   NR 55;   NS 25
6   -Brunnhilde's Plea; War es so schmalich, Act III   CH 1893;
         CT 50;   KC 44;   PH 37, 43, 45;   WA 44
120   -Concert Version with Soloists and Chor   WA 68
6   -Duet, Act I   PH 07, 11, 32;   WA 36
6   -Ein Schwert Verhiess mir der Vater, Siegmund's address to the
         sword   KC 65;   MN 49;   WA 45
25   -Excerpts   SL 29 arr Stokowski   PH 33, 35
15   -3 Scenes   LA 47
4   -Fort denn Eile   HN 45
6   -Magic Fire Scene   BA 26, 37;   BN 56, 63;   CT 67;   CL 25, 27,
         33, 68;   DA 26, 32;   DE 50, 53;   DT 29, 31, 34, 40, 44, 47,
         52, 55, 59, 61;   MN 48;   NS 1896, 20, 21;   PH 38;   RC 43, 57;
         SF 40;   UT 64
6   -Prelude to Act I   CH 1892;   CT 31, 34, 36, 38;   RC 48, 68
8   -Prelude to Act II and Ride of the Walkure   CH 26, 27, 28, 29,
         37, 39, 40
5   -Ride of the Walkure, Walküren ritt   AT 49, 52;   BA 39, 42, 43;
         BN 1890, 96, 97, 08, 23, 24, 26, 27, 63;   BU 40;
         CH 1891, 92, 93(2), 94(2), 97, 98, 99, 00, 01, 02, 03, 04, 05,
         06, 07, 08, 09, 10, 11, 12(2), 13, 14, 15, 16, 19, 20, 21, 22,
         23, 24, 28, 44, 47, 49, 56, 58, 65;
         CT 1897, 09, 14, 21, 22, 25, 29, 32, 40, 44, 56, 63;
         CL 21, 30, 33, 37, 39, 43, 68;   DA 25, 28, 32, 37, 38, 50, 53;
         DE 56, 60;   DT 17, 20, 22, 24, 30, 31, 33, 34, 36, 38, 39, 51,
         61, 63, 66;   HN 39, 43;   NA 36, 39, 40, 56;   KC 38, 39, 44;
         LA 21(2), 22, 23, 24, 32, 37;   MN 22, 24, 26, 36, 38, 46, 48,
         49, 67;   NP 1879, 88, 00, 06, 12, 13, 14, 16, 17, 19, 20, 22,
         29, 30, 39, 49, 54, 56;   NS 1886, 89, 90, 03, 06, 09, 11, 12,
         13, 17, 19, 20, 25;   PH 07, 10(2), 11(3), 12, 13, 14, 15, 16,
         19, 20(2), 22, 23, 24, 25, 27, 29, 30, 31, 32, 37, 45, 51, 52, 60;
         PT 37, 39, 45, 46, 48, 49, 51, 56, 61;   RC 43, 54;
         SL 11, 13, 21, 24, 31, 33, 35, 59, 63;   SF 11, 14, 52;   SE 27,
         34;   UT 53;   WA 33, 35, 38, 42, 43, 44
4   -Sieglinde's Narrative Du bist die Lenz, Thou art Spring, Act I
         BA 43;   CH 44;   CT 47, 48;   CL 28, 44;   DE 47, 55;   NA 40,
         43, 50;   KC 44;   LA 37;   MN 32;   NP 36;   PH 50;   PT 40,
         RC 42, 43, 46;   SL 15;   UT 50;   WA 37, 40
6   -Siegmund's Love Song Wintersturme, wichen dem Wonnemond, Winter
         Storms have waned, Liebeslied   CH 1892, 06;   CT 1895, 06, 26;
         DT 53;   HN 46;   NA 38;   MN 28, 49;   NP 06;   NS 12;   PH 15,
         36;   PT 38;   SL 14, 31, 34, 63;   WA 34, 36, 44

WAGNER, R. (Cont.) Dramatic Works, Die Walküre (Cont.)
    5   -Wotan's Farewell   BN 1882, 88, 91, 96, 97, 02, 12, 37;
           CH 1895(2), 10, 32, 39;   CT 67;   DA 26, 32, 37;   DE 53;
           DT 22, 25, 27, 31, 34, 40, 47, 52, 55, 59, 61;   KC 37;   LA 23;
           MN 37;   NS 21;   RC 47;   SF 31, 33;   UT 64
   18   -Wotan's Farewell and Magic Fire Scene   BA 26, 37, 65;   BN 37;
           BU 56;   CH 1891, 92, 93, 94, 96, 97, 99, 00, 02, 06, 10, 11, 12,
           16, 22, 30, 50, 56, 58;   CT 1898, 03, 11, 12, 20, 21, 25, 27,
           30, 31, 36;   HN 40, 44, 59, 65;   NA 39, 40;   KC 36;   LA 34;
           MN 23, 29, 31, 33, 36, 45;   NP 1878, 82, 88, 93, 95, 97, 98, 00,
           02, 16, 17, 19, 28, 47;   PH 01, 08(2), 09(2), 10(3), 11(2), 12,
           13, 14, 15, 16, 19, 20, 21, 22(2), 23(2), 24, 25, 27, 29(2), 30,
           31, 32, 36, 37, 45, 60;   PT 38, 50, 57;   RC 52;   SL 09, 12,
           15, 17, 22, 23, 25, 31, 35, 46, 47;   SE 33, 52;   WA 34, 40, 47,
           50

WAGNER, Siegfried   10   Barenhauter, Opera 1899: Overt   BN 1899;   CH 1899;
1869-1930   Ger   PH 07
             6   -Prelude, Act II   CT 03
           15   Symphon Poem, Sehnsucht 1895   NP 1897

WALD, Max   12   The Dancer Dead, Pagan Epitaph 1931   CH 43;   CT 34
1889-1954   US   14   In Praise of Pageantry 1945   CH 46
           10   Retrospectives 1925   CH 25

WALDROP, Gid   11   Prelude and Fugue   ML 63
1919-   US

WALDTEUFEL, Emile   6   Les Patineurs, Skaters' Waltz   WA 38
1837-1915   Fr

WALKER   6   Passacaglia from Address for O   DE 69

WALLACE, W. V.   15   Fantasy for 2 P on Halevy's L'Eclair   NP 1853
1812-1865   Brit   4   The Happy Birdling, Song   NP 1850
            4   The Restless Wind, Song   NP 1850
            5   Maritane, Opera: Overt   NP 1854
            4   -Aria: The Harp in the Air   NP 1858

WALLACE, William 25   Symphon Poem No 6, Villon 1909   BN 11, 17;
1860-1940   Brit   CH 15;   NS 10;   SL 14

WALTON, Sir William 38   Belshazzar's Feast, Baritone and O 1929   AT 62;
1902-   Brit   BN 32, 60;   BU 58;   CH 51;   CL 61;   DA 49;
                  DT 56, 69;   HN 60;   NA 44, 56;   MN 52;   NP 67;
        PH 33, 60;   RC 35, 61;   SL 36, 61;   SE 54, 67;   PT 67
   26   C Conc   BN 56;   NA 51, 54, 56;   SE 61
       P Conc   BN 27
   23   Conc for Vla 1928   AT 50;   BA 65;   BN 56;   CH 44;   CT 51;
        DT 45;   LA 42, 50;   HN 68;   MN 38, 51, 64;   PH 43, 58;   PT 55;
        SF 66;   UT 63
   30   V Conc 1939   CH 57, 64;   CT 40, 53, 58;   CL 39, 58, 67;   DA 66;
        HN 61;   NA 49, 52, 57;   LA 63;   MN 44;   NR 61;   PH 68;
        PT 58;   RC 55;   SL 40;   SF 66;   SE 63;   UT 66
    9   Crown Imperial Coronation March 1937   BA 42, 47;   WA 53

WALTON, Sir W. (Cont.)
- 19   Facade, for speaking Voice and six Instruments, on 21 Sitwell poems, 1922, revised 1942   BA 42;   CT 36;   CL 36;   DE 49, 50, 54;   KC 43;   PH 43;   SF 41, 49
- 10   -Suite No 1   CT 59;   DT 59;   NA 35, 36, 37;   HN 68
- 9   -Suite No 2   RC 38
- 3   Fanfare, Memorial for Wood 1944   NA 54
- 10   Improvisation on an Impromptu of Britten   SF 69
- 7   Johannesburg Festival Overt   BA 57;   BN 56;   BU 61;   HN 59, 60, 68;   NA 62;   SF 61
- 15   Partita for O   CL 57, 58, 59, 67;   CH 68;   DA 59;   HN 60;   NA 59;   PH 59;   RC 58;   SF 58;   SE 57, 58
- 6   Portsmouth Point Overt 1925   BA 65, 68;   BN 26, 29, 41;   CH 29, 30, 31, 32, 35, 38, 41, 60;   CL 45;   DA 49;   NA 39;   MN 45;   RC 48;   DE 69;   KC 69
- 12   Richard III Suite   WA 67
- 8   Scapino, Comedy Overt 1940   AT 69;   BN 45;   CH 40(2), 62;   CL 41;   NA 42, 63;   PH 62;   SF 63;   WA 63
- 19   Sinfonia Concertante, P and O 1927   BN 21;   CT 31
- 8   Spitfire, Prelude and Fugue 1942   NA 48
- 43   Symph No 1 in b^b 1935   BN 49;   BU 62;   CH 35;   DT 63;   HN 53, 56;   NA 63;   LA 67;   PH 36, 54;   PT 66;   SF 63;   RC 35;   WA 69
- 27   Symph No 2   CH 61;   CL 60;   DT 68;   HN 68;   NA 64;   PT 62;   SF 64
- 23   Var on a Theme of Hindemith   CL 62, 63, 64, 66, 69;   DT 67;   MN 68;   NP 69
- 20   Wise Virgins, Suite from the Ballet 1940   HN 67

WARD, Robert E.
1917-   US
- 12   Adagio and Allegro 1946   BA 50
- 5   America the Beautiful   DA 49
- 10   Euphony for O   CL 62;   DE 61
- 10   Festive Ode 1939   ML 66
- 8   Jubilation Overt 1946   BA 49;   DA 46;   DE 56;   LA 46;   ML 64
- 15   Symph No 1 1941   WA 44
- 24   Symph No 2   LA 49;   WA 48;   DE 57;   PH 49
- 23   Symph No 3   CT 53;   RC 57

WARD-STEINMAN
see STEINMAN

WARGO, George
        US
- 30   Symph No 1   WA 41

WARFIELD, Gerald
1940-   US
- 35   Three Movements for O   DA 65

WARLOCK, Peter
(pseudonym
Heseltine, Philip)
1894-1930   Brit
- 10   Capriol, Suite for Str 1926   BA 42, 47;   CH 44;   DT 41;   SE 33, 35, 36
- 10   Three Carols, Chor and O 1932   NP 38

WARNER, H. Waldo
1874-1945   Brit
- 22   Hampton Wick, Tone Picture Op 38   CT 34

WARNER, Philip   12   The Green Mansions: Symphon Poem, 6 parts, based on
1901-   US   novel by Hudson   AT 47
                          12   Perelandra, Symphon Poem   AT 49

WARNKE, F.M.   12   A New Symph in Olden Style   SF 27
               US   8   Suite, Impressions of a Mountain   RC 25

WARREN, Elinor Remick   8   Crystal Lake, Tone Poem   LA 45;   NA 58;   SL 61
1905-   US   6   Passing of King Arthur, Symphon Poem for Baritone,
                                   Tenor, Chor and O   LA 39;   NA 42
                          17   Suite for O 4 parts   AT 55;   LA 54

WASHBURN, Robert   6   Festive Overt   NA 68
1928-   US   20   Symph No 1   NA 61

WASILENKO, Serge   15   Hzrcus Nocturnus, Symphon Poem Flug der Hexen
1872-   Russ
(Vasilenko)

WAXMAN, Franz   6   Athaneal, the Trumpeter, Comedy Overt 1944
1906-   Ger/US   AT 49;   CT 48
                          15   Carmen, Fantasy for V   SL 46, 61

WEAVER, Powell   8   Fugue for Str   DE 48;   KC 41
1890-1951   US   17   The Sand Dune Cranes, Symphon Poem 1937   KC 50, 51
                          14   The Vagabond, Symphon Poem 1930   KC 34, 45, 52;
                                   MN 30

WEBBER, Amherst   20   Symph in c 1904   BN 05
1867-1946   Brit

WEBER, Ben   25   P Conc Op 52   HN 62;   NP 60
1916-   US   11   Prelude and Passacaglia Op 42   NP 55

WEBER, Carl Maria   18   Conc for Bassoon and O in f Op 75   DT 48;   PH 19
1786-1826   Ger   6   -Adagio and Rondo   NP 1853
                          21   C Conc No 1 in D Op 20   NA 37
    19   Conc for Clarinet in f No 1 Op 73   AT 51;   CH 1892;   DA 51;   SE 51
    12   Conc for Clarinet in E^b No 2 Op 26   BA 65;   BN 1883;   BU 52;
              CT 63;   DA 46, 50;   HN 52, 66;   NP 1844, 51;   SF 67;   SE 50, 60
    12   Conc for Horn in e Op 45   NP 1855
     4   Folksong   NP 12
     8   Grande Polonaise in E^b Op 21 arr Liszt   CT 20
     8   Introd and Polonaise   NP 1871
     6   Invitation to the Dance.Aufforderung zum Tanz Op 65   CL 22;   HN 31,
              35, 37;   NA 36, 38, 53;   NR 57;   PH 00, 07, 14, 16;   RC 38, 54,
              56;   SF 37;   SE 35, 36;   UT 50
     6   -arr Berlioz   BN 1882, 84, 86, 95, 97, 04, 66;   CH 1891, 96, 03,
              56;   CT 47, 51;   DA 25, 49;   DE 48, 50, 56, 59;   DT 14, 18, 31,
              58;   NP 31, 53;   SL 57
     6   -arr Weingartner   BN 21;   CH 1896(2), 97, 98, 99(2), 00, 01(2),
              04, 06, 09(2), 12, 14, 37;   CT 27;   KC 34, 40;   LA 19, 26, 31;
              NP 15, 25;   PH 00, 04, 20, 23, 25, 27, 31;   WA 32, 41
     6   -arr Ormandy   PH 40, 57

WEBER, C.M. (Cont.)

9	Jubilee Overt in E Op 59	CH 1895, 00, 15; CT 21, 53; DT 26; KC 58; LA 50; MN 28, 45; NP 1842, 43, 46, 48, 51, 60, 69, 1944; PT 41; SF 40, 48; UT 64
12	Konzertstück, P and O in f Op 79	BA 50, 53; BN 1885, 93, 95, 14; BU 58; CH 1891, 10, 13, 15, 16, 41, 45; CT 42, 66; CL 51, 60, 64; DA 25; DT 18, 22, 29, 59; HN 44; KC 40, 50, 55; LA 43, 55; MN 29, 39, 52; NP 1848, 52, 54, 67, 72, 86, 09, 36, 55; NS 1884, 09, 16; PH 01, 09, 14, 18; PT 44, 56; RC 60, 61; SL 17, 37, 67; SF 15, 38, 50, 56; SE 53; UT 52
5	Perpetuum Mobile arr Szell	MN 43; NP 53
8	Polacco, Polonaise, Brilliante for P and O in E, L'Hilaite arr Liszt Op 72	BN 1882; CH 1891, 96; NP 1864
12	Quintet for Clarinet and Str Op 34	NS 12
4	Romanza in F Op 3 No 2	NP 1863
8	Rondo brillante, La Gaiété in E^b Op 62	NP 1856
6	Rondo in C for 2 P	MN 47
6	Sonatine for C and P	MN 47
22	Symph No 1 in C Op 19	NA 40; NP 31, 51, 55
21	Symph No 2 in C 1804	NP 34; PT 34
5	Vienna-1814	DT 41

DRAMATIC WORKS

6	Abu Hassan, Opera 1811: Overt	BA 59, 64; BN 1895; CH 13, 14, 22, 23, 24, 26, 27, 28, 32, 35, 36, 37, 38, 39; CT 16, 56, 62; NA 52; LA 63; ML 66; SF 54; SE 55; WA 38
4	-Aria	NS 1892
4	Euryanthe, Opera 1823: Aria	NS 1880, 85; PH 02
4	-Glocklein im Thale	SL 38
6	-Overt	AT 50; BA 26, 43, 53, 55, 65; BN 1882, 84, 86, 88, 89, 90, 91, 93, 96, 97, 98, 00, 03, 05, 06, 08, 10, 12, 14, 16, 19, 20, 22, 25, 29, 35, 49, 56; BU 44, 49, 52, 54, 59; CH 1894, 96, 99, 00, 02, 04, 06, 07, 08, 09, 10, 11, 12, 14, 16, 18, 20, 23, 26, 33, 35, 39, 40, 48, 53, 54, 58, 62, 64, 67; CT 1895, 99, 00, 02, 09, 11, 12, 14, 18, 20, 26, 27, 31, 38, 41, 49, 54, 57; CL 23, 28, 31, 33, 34, 38, 41, 44, 47, 51, 57, 62, 63, 67; DA 25, 46, 50, 56, 63, 65; DE 45, 48, 51, 53, 55, 59, 62, 64; DT 17, 25, 30, 37, 40, 53, 55, 56, 63; HN 33, 39, 44, 55, 58; NA 35, 37, 39, 45, 60, 66; KC 35, 39, 44, 48, 56; LA 21, 26, 32, 35, 40, 46, 67; ML 60; MN 22, 23, 25, 29, 31, 32, 36, 39, 43, 46, 48, 51, 53, 57, 58, 60, 66; NR 51, 53, 58, 67; NP 1843, 45, 47, 49, 52, 55, 58, 63, 65, 69, 71, 74, 85, 93, 97, 01, 04, 08, 11, 15, 17, 19, 22, 24, 25, 31, 35, 37, 38, 39, 42, 49, 50, 54, 55, 62, 63; NS 1878, 08, 18, 23; PH 05, 07, 08, 09, 10, 12, 13, 16, 17, 20, 24(2), 25, 27, 30, 31, 32, 36, 39, 43, 46, 50, 52, 61, 65; PT 37, 39, 40, 46, 48, 49, 55, 63; RC 39, 44, 48, 56, 58, 62, 68; SL 09, 14, 20, 23, 26, 27, 33, 37, 45, 48, 50, 54, 56, 67; SF 12, 14, 16, 25, 39, 41, 44, 57, 67; SE 27, 36, 37, 39, 52, 53, 58, 66; UT 52; WA 33, 49, 52, 54
8	-Recitative and Aria	NP 1889
4	-Romanza	NP 1863
5	-Scene and Aria, I Fain Would Hide	CH 00
4	-Unter Cluhenden	NP 1865, 81
4	-Wo berg ich nich	CT 1899; NP 1880, 83, 87, 97

WEBER, C.M. (Cont.)   Dramatic Works (Cont.)
4   Der Freischütz, The Free Shooter 1821 Air   NS 22, 26;   SL 10, 13,
       33, 47;   SE 46
4   -Act I Aria for Tenor, Durch die Walder Through the Forest   CT 06;
       NP 1851
4   -Act I Max's Aria, Jetzt ist Wohl ihr Fenster offer   BA 45
4   -Hunter's Chorus, Jagerchor Was gleicht wohl auf Erden   HN 42
4   -Act II Leise, leise fromme Weise, Agatha's Prayer Softly, softly
       BA 52;   BN 41;   CT 1898, 01, 11, 14, 38, 45;   CL 29;   DE 46;
       DT 27, 40, 60;   HN 34;   NA 47;   KC 45;   LA 40, 44;   MN 34,
       35, 40(2), 42, 43, 46;   NP 1857;   SL 50;   SF 40;   WA 40
4   -Wie nahte mir der Schlummer, Agatha's Aria   CH 1892, 06, 08,
         11, 56;   DA 25, 49;   KC 35, 39;   NP 1854, 70, 73, 98;
         NS 1882;   PH 02, 06, 07, 09, 39, 49
5   -Scene   NP 1845, 63, 69, 77
6   -Overt   AT 48, 50;   BA 39, 42, 47, 52, 53, 55, 57, 67;
       BN 1882, 84, 86, 87, 89, 90, 92, 94, 96, 97, 01, 03, 05, 06, 08,
       10, 11, 12, 14, 18, 25, 26, 47, 51, 62;   BU 45, 49, 56, 62;
       CH 1892, 93, 95, 97, 99, 01, 03, 05, 06, 08, 09, 11, 12, 13, 14,
       19, 21, 30, 36, 39, 42, 48, 50, 51, 55, 56, 60, 62, 64;
       CT 07, 09, 12, 14, 15, 17, 26, 29, 30, 32, 36, 39, 40, 49, 59, 63;
       CL 22, 25, 26, 29, 32, 33, 39, 41, 42, 44, 49, 55, 59, 65;
       DA 32, 48, 65;   DE 46, 47, 50, 63;
       DT 16, 17, 19, 21, 22, 25, 26, 30, 33, 36(2), 38, 45;
       HN 31, 36, 41, 42, 43, 48, 55, 60, 62, 65;   NA 30, 33, 38, 46, 67;
       KC 34, 41, 47, 53, 57, 60, 62;
       LA 20, 22, 24, 27, 35, 53, 55, 56;   ML 63, 67;
       MN 22, 24, 28, 32, 35, 41, 46, 48, 52, 59, 62;   NR 57, 61, 62;
       NP 1842, 45, 46, 48, 67, 99, 03, 10, 11, 13, 14, 16, 21, 22, 23,
       25, 26, 30, 34, 35, 37, 38, 39, 46, 49, 51, 54, 55, 56, 58, 66;
       NS 1883, 87, 95, 10, 17, 19, 22, 23, 24(2), 25;
       PH 02, 03, 07, 12, 13, 14, 16, 18, 19(2), 20, 23, 24, 26, 28(2),
       29, 30, 35, 36, 38, 41, 42, 44, 47, 59, 61, 64, 66;
       PT 39, 45, 47, 49, 53, 58;   RC 42, 47, 57;   SL 11, 13, 16, 19,
       20, 21, 22, 23, 25, 29, 30, 31, 33, 35, 36, 38, 40, 47, 48, 49, 52;
       SF 18, 32, 47, 52;   SE 26, 32, 34, 35, 37, 47, 54, 63;
       UT 45, 49, 67;   WA 33, 37, 40, 63
     Oberon, The Elf King's Oath 1826
6   -Overt   AT 51, 57, 63, 69;   BA 26, 42, 52, 58, 62;
       BN 1881, 84, 85, 89, 90, 91, 92, 93, 95, 96, 99, 02, 04, 06, 08,
       10, 11, 12, 14, 21, 24, 26, 29, 32, 36, 46, 49, 58, 64;
       BU 40, 42, 43, 50, 58;   CH 1891, 95, 98, 01, 02, 05, 07, 09, 10,
       11, 14, 15, 16, 17, 20, 23, 24, 27, 28, 31, 34, 42, 49, 53, 54, 56,
       58, 60, 66;   CT 1895, 96, 02, 06, 10, 17, 21, 23, 25, 27, 31, 38,
       42, 45, 46, 49, 55, 59, 60, 65, 68;
       CL 26, 30, 32, 33, 35, 36, 39, 43, 46, 48, 54, 56, 60, 62, 63, 64;
       DA 27, 37, 46, 49, 52, 53, 58, 60, 67;
       DE 45, 47, 49, 51, 52, 56, 59, 63, 65;
       DT 16, 17, 19, 21, 22, 25, 29, 31, 35, 43, 53, 59, 61, 64;
       HN 32, 34, 36, 40, 47, 49, 55, 63;   NA 31, 43, 50, 56, 58;
       KC 33, 36, 38, 39, 40, 42, 43, 52, 56, 64;
       LA 19, 20, 22, 24, 27, 28(2), 36, 37, 40, 44, 54, 55, 58, 61, 62,
       66(2);   ML 61, 67;   MN 22, 25, 26, 28, 30, 31, 36, 45, 48, 49,
       55, 56, 67;   NR 51, 56, 60, 64;
       NP 1842, 44, 46, 48, 51, 59, 64, 68, 72, 76, 00, 04, 06, 20, 21, 26,
       27, 30, 33, 35, 37, 39, 42, 44(2), 45, 50, 51, 55, 60, 62, 64;

WEBER, C.M. (Cont.) Dramatic Works, Oberon, Overt (Cont.)
        NS 1886, 88, 07, 08, 14(2), 20, 23, 24, 27;
        PH 06, 07, 08, 09, 10, 12, 13, 14, 15, 19(2), 20(2), 22, 24, 26,
        29, 33, 35, 42, 46, 53, 55, 56, 59, 67, 69;
        PT 37, 40, 43, 46(2), 48, 49, 50, 52, 57, 59, 61, 64, 68;
        RC 42, 45, 49, 53, 57, 62(2), 63, 66, 69;   SL 12, 13, 15, 18, 22,
        27, 29, 32, 34, 35, 38, 41, 43, 44, 45, 46, 48, 49, 69;   SF 11,
        16, 30, 31, 39, 49, 51, 52, 53, 61, 64;   SE 27, 28, 32, 37, 49,
        61;   UT 41, 42, 47, 54, 56, 61, 65;   WA 49, 51, 53, 61, 65

6   -Act II Ozean, du Ungerheuer Ocean, Thou Monster   BA 47, 51, 58;
        CH 1891, 05, 25, 28, 65;   CT 09, 21, 24, 39, 51;   CL 25;   DE 53;
        DT 24, 28, 34;   HN 51;   KC 36, 60;   LA 22, 27, 35;   MN 28, 33,
        36, 42;   NP 1851, 56, 59, 67, 79, 84, 11, 20;   NS 1890, 96, 20,
        21, 22, 24, 25;   PH 05, 27;   RC 57;   SL 24, 30;   SF 15;
        SE 30, 36;   UT 65;   WA 32, 39, 42, 45, 53, 61

5   -Scene   NP 1842
6   Peter Schmall und sein Nachbarn, Opera 1803: Overt   LA 63
6   Preciosa, Incidental Music 1821: Overt   BN 1885;   CH 1896, 01;
      NP 1854, 12, 33
      Ruebezahl, or Derbeherrscher der Geister, Ruler of the Spirits 1805
6   -Overt   BN 00;   CT 09;   DT 21;   LA 45;   MN 37, 47;   NP 1843,
      58, 61, 74, 29, 36, 40;   PH 05;   RC 30
6   Specter de la Rose (used as ballet)   DT 39;   MN 37, 38
3   The Three Pintos, Opera,Die drei Pintos 1821 Entr'acte   BN 24
8   Turandot, after Schiller's translation of Gozzi, Incidental Music
      Op 37 1809 Overt and March   CL 36;   LA 63;   NP 36

WEBERN, Anton   6   Das Augenlicht Op 26   MN 65;   SL 64
1883-1945   Aust 13 Cantata No 2 Op 31   SL 65
               6   In Summer Wind   LA 69;   WA 66
               6   Five Pieces for O Op 19   AT 69;   BN 26, 58(2), 69;
                   BU 64, 66;   CH 63;   LA 68;   MN 65;   NP 65;
                   SL 63;   SE 66
             11 Five mvts for Str O Op 5   NP 58
             11 Passacaglia Op 1 1908   BN 63;   BU 62;   CH 43,
                   62, 68;   CT 68;   CL 49, 61;   DE 69;   LA 59,
                   68, 69(2);   MN 48, 61;   NP 59, 61;   PH 26, 61;
                   PT 69;   SF 62, 63;   SL 69;   SE 58, 69;
                   UT 63
             12 Six Pieces for O Op 6   AT 67, 69;   BA 69;   BN 61,
                   66, 69;   CH 57, 61, 66, 68;   CT 60;   CL 58, 68;
                   DA 62;   DT 64;   LA 60, 69;   MN 59, 61;   NP 57,
                   60, 64, 68;   PH 3 pieces only 66, 68, 69;
                   NR 65;   PT 57, 61;   RC 64, 68;   SL 62, 65;
                   WA 66
              3   Two Songs, for Voice and Chamber Ensemble Op 13
                   BU 66
             10 Symph Op 21   CT 66;   MN 69
              6   Var Op 30   BN 67;   RC 60;   PT 67

WEED, Maurice   20 Symph No 1   WA 55
1912-   US

WEHLI, James M.   12 Fantasy on Gounod's Faust   NP 1865
        US

	Time in Minutes	
WEIDIG, Adolf	22	Capriccio Op 13 CH 1899, 01
1867-1931 US	25	Concert Overt Op 65 CH 18
	25	Symphon Fantasie, Semiramis Op 33 CH 05, 17
	30	Symphon Suite CH 14, 15, 27
	17	Three Episodes Op 38 CH 07, 20
WEILL, Kurt	40	Das Berliner Requiem CT 69
1900-1950 US	33	V Conc for O of Wind Instruments Op 12 CH 64; CT 29
	25	Lindbergh's Flight, Cantata for Solo and Chor PH 30
	4	Lost in the Stars CT 57
	16	Suite from Dreigroschenoper arr Schonherr BN 68; CT 69
	10	Three Night Scenes NP 34
WEINBERGER, Jaromir	6	Bohemian Grenadiers, March BA 38
1896- Czech/US	20	Christmas Night for Org and O CH 30; NA 51
	9	Czech Rhaps WA 42, 43, 46
	24	Legend of Sleepy Hollow, Suite in four mvts DT 40
	45	A Lincoln Symph CT 41; NP 41; RC 41
	30	Passacaglia, Org and O 1931 NP 31
	8	Polka and Fugue from Schwanda The Bagpiper, Opera 1927 AT 48, 52, 55, 63; BA 42, 65; BN 32; CH 31, 32, 33, 34, 35, 36, 38; CT 30(2), 32, 38, 41, 45, 46, 50, 52; CL 32; DA 37; DE 48, 52, 53, 64; DT 32, 33, 45, 63, 65; HN 39, 40; NA 38, 40, 45, 50, 60, 63; ML 61; MN 31, 32, 39, 46; LA 30; NP 30, 36, 39, 42, 48; PH 31, 32, 37, 41, 43, 50; PT 38, 43; RC 38, 43, 48; SL 34, 35, 36, 37, 39, 42, 43, 47, 49, 52, 54; SE 44; UT 40, 49; WA 38, 40, 44
	5	Prelude and Fugue on Dixie BU 40; HN 42
	38	Preludes, Religious and Profane SL 55
	12	Under the Spreading Chestnut Tree, Var and Fugue on English Tune BA 39, 44, 47; CH 40; CT 40, 43; CL 39, 54; DT 39; NA 39, 67; MN 39; NP 39; RC 62; SL 40, 41; SF 39; SE 40
	20	Suite from Schwanda, Opera 1927 HN 56; KC 34, 35
WEINER, Leo	19	Concertina in e P and O Op 15 1928 PH 57; RC 36, 47
1885-1961 Hung	9	Carnival, Fasching Op 5 for small O CT 22, 26, 27; PT 44
	24	Csongor e Tunde, Prince Csongor and the Goblins, Incidental Music Op 10 CT 25
	9	-Introd and Scherzo CH 37, 38; NP 22
	9	Divertimento No 1 Op 20 After Old Hungarian Dances PT 43, 44; RC 33
	13	Divertimento No 2 Op 24 After Old Hungarian Folk Melodies NP 39; PH 39, 43
	15	Hungarian Folk Dances Suite Op 18 PT 40; SE 63
	7-8	Pastorale, Fantasy and Fugue for Str O Op 23 PT 45
	24	Suite Op 18 PT 40; RC 32
	20	Serenade in f Op 3 CH 07, 08, 16

WEINER, Stanley 1925- Hung/US	22	V Conc NA 67

WEINGARTNER, Felix
1863-1942   Aust
	15
	20
	10
	
	20
	30
	30
	4
	4
	4
		Elysian Fields, Symphon Poem Op 21 BN 02; NP 03
		King Lear, Symphon Poem Op 20 CH 1897; NP 03
		Lustige Overt, Festive Op 53 BN 13; CH 12;
		    NP 12, 13
		Symph No 1 in G Op 23 BN 00; CT 00
		Symph No 2 in E^b, Op 29 CH 01; NP 02, 04
		Symph No 3 in E Op 49 BN 11; NP 11
		Songs: Liebesfeier CH 21
		    -Erdriese NP 09; PH 09
		    -Letzter Tanz NP 09; PH 09

WEISGALL, Hugo 1912- US	10 17 25	Overt in F BA 67 Dances from Outpost Op 7a WA 49 Soldier Songs, Cycle for Baritone BA 65
WEISS, Adolph 1891- US	13	Theme and Var 1931 SF 35
WEISSENBORN, Julius 1837-1888 Ger	4	Turkish March for Bassoon and O CT 48, 49
WELD, Arthur Cyril 1844-1914 US	8	Italia BN 1889
WEPRICK, Alex 1899- Russ	15	Dances and Songs of the Ghetto Op 12 NP 32; PH 32
WERNER, Eric 1901- Aust/US	20 30	Suite Abraxas LA 51 Symph Requiem CT 43
WESSEL, Mark 1894- US	26	Symph Concertante for Horn, P and O 1929 CH 30

WETZLER, Hermann
1870-1943   US
	20
	17
	
	17
	
	18
	
	35
		Adagio and Double Fugue for Str O CH 41
		As You Like It, Incidental Music 1928: Overt CT 23;
		    DT 22; PT 40; SF 21
		The Basque Venus, Opera Op 14 1928: Dance in Basque
		    Style BN 29, 35; CH 28, 31, 41; CT 29;
		    DT 24; LA 31; NP 29; PH 29
		Legend, Assissi Op 13 CH 25, 33; CT 40;
		    SF 27; SE 41(2), 42; RC 41
		Visions, Six Symphon mvts Op 12 CH 24; DT 24;
		    NP 25

WEYSE, Christoph 1774-1842 Ger/Dan	4	O Day Full of Grace MN 43
WHITCOMB, Robert 1921- US	8	Suite for O: No 3 From the Ohio River CT 52
WHITE, Clarence 1880- US	4	Elegie WA 54

WHITE, Paul	8	Five Miniatures, 1933 CH 36; DA 38; DT 36;
1895- US		PH 35; RC 35, 43; WA 37
	10	Negro Chant PH 36
	4	A Pagan Festival Overt 1927 CH 30
	8	Lake Spray 1938 RC 39(2)
	18	Sea Chanty, Quintet for Harp and Str 1942 RC 41
	18	Sinfonietta for Str O 1936 RC 46
WHITHORNE, Emerson		The Aeroplane 1920 CL 25, 26
1884- US	32	V Conc 1931 CH 31
	16	The Dream Peddler, Symphon Poem Op 50 CT 31;
		LA 30; NP 40; PH 35
	8	Fandango 1931 SF 37
	20	Fata Morgana, Symphon Poem Op 44 NP 28
	25	Court of Pomegranates, Symphon Poem NP 21
	16	Moon Trail Suite Op 53 BN 33
	20	New York Days and Nights, Suite Op 40 CT 39;
		CL 28; NS 27; RC 29
	20	Poem for P and O Op 43 CH 26
	6	Sierra Morena, Symphon Poem Op 49 NA 38
	28	Symph No 1 in c Op 39 CT 33; CL 34
	33	Symph No 2 in f Op 56 CT 36
WHITING, Arthur B.	20	Fantasy for P and O in b^b Op 11 BN 1896, 00;
1861-1936 US		CH 03
	8	Conc Overt Op 3 BN 1885
	25	P Conc in d BN 1888
	20	Suite for Str and 4 Horns in g BN 1890
WHITMER, T. Carl	8	Two Dances from Syrian Night PT 49
1873- US		
WHITNEY, Robert	14	Conc Grosso 1933 CH 33
1904- Brit/US		
WHITTAKER, Howard	8	Two Murals for O CL 59
US		
WIDOR, Charles	13	Chorale and Var for Harp and O Op 74 BN 02;
1844-1937 Fr		CH 02, 04, 17, 20, 24, 37; NS 13; SL 26
	5	Marche Americans NS 23
	5	Overt Espagnole SL 23
	5	Romance for Fl and O NS 17
	15	Salvum Fac Populum Tuum for O, 3 Trumpets, 3 Trombones
		and Timpani Op 84 CH 17
	5	Scherzo for Fl and O NS 11, 17
	28	Sinfonia Sacra Org and O Op 81 CH 10
		Songs
	4	Le Plongeur CH 05
	4	Lie e sorte NS 1883
	29	Symph No 3 for Org and O Op 13 NA 16
	25	Symph No 6 Op 42 for Org and O CT 36; CL 27;
		DT 24; MN 25
	8	-Allegro and Moderato NA 54
	5	Toccata SL 54

WIECHOWICZ, Steven   10   Chmiel, Hopwine, Symphon Scherzo 1926   CL 39
1893-   Pol

WIENER, Jean   19   P Conc, Franco-American Op 27   SL 18
1896-   Fr

WIENIAWSKI, Henri   8   Air Varie for V and O Op 15   CH 1891
1835-1880   Pol   20   V Conc No 1 in f# Op 14   DE 51; LA 53; MN 68;
                              NP 51
                      18   V Conc No 2 in d Op 22   BN 1889, 90, 04;   BU 58;
                              CH 1897, 08;   CT 42, 49;   CL 26, 57, 58;
                              DA 50, 58;   DE 45, 58;   DT 62;   NA 46, 60, 66;
                              KC 47;   LA 44;   MN 41, 49, 62;   NP 58;   NS 27;
                              PT 45;   PH 03, 04, 06, 17, 20, 56;   RC 26, 59;
                              SL 18, 47;   SE 60, 68;   WA 63, 69
                      12   Fantasie on Faust, V and O Op 20   BN 02;   CH 01;
                              CT 1895;   HN 14;   NS 27;   PH 01
                       9   Legende for V and O Op 17   NS 1884
                       6   Scherzo-Tarentella for V and O in d   MN 49

WILCKENS, Friedrich   5   Bacchanale   KC 33
1899-   Aust   5   Country Dance KC 33
                       5   Jester's Dance   KC 33

WILDER, Alec   15   Pieces for O in 3 mvts   RC 47
1907-   US

WILHELMJ, August   10   Fantasiestuck for V and O   NS 1878
1845-1908   Ger

WILKES, Robert   7   Tolentine Overt 1944   WA 44
1883-   US   7   Twilight Dreams 1941   WA 41

WILLAN, Healey   23   The Trumpet Call   KC 41
1880-   Can

WILLEBYE, Charles   4   Song, Stolen Wings   CT 03

WILLIAMS,   15   Symphon Cycle, Pot-Pourri   NS 21
  John Gerrard
1888-1947   Brit

WILLIAMS, John T.   5   Essay for Str   HN 65;   PT 66
1932-   US   8   Legend   HN 49
                      20   Symph No 4   HN 68

WILLIS, Richard   9   Prelude and Dance   AT 58
1929-   US

WILLSON, Meredith   14   The Jervis Bay, 1941   SF 41
1907-   US   21   The Missions of Southern California, Symph No 2
                              LA 39
                       8   -Mvt II   BA 40

WILM, Nikolai   14   Concertstuck for Harp and O in c Op 122   CH 07
1834-1911   Russ/Ger

WILSON, Mortimer   4   America is Calling   HN 42
1876-1932   US   12   Suite, From My Youth   NP 18

WINKLER, Alexander   15   Conc for Fl in e   CH 09
1865-1935   Russ

WINKLER, Karl   40   Symph No 2, Spring, in D Op 47   BU 60
1899-   Aust

WIREN, Dag Ivan   18   Symph No 4   DE 57
1905-   Swed

WIRTEL, Thomas   15   Concertina for O   DA 66
1937-   US

WISSMER, Pierre   25   The Child and the Rose, Theme, Var and Finale for O
1915-   Swiss/Fr   1959   DA 59

WITKOWSKI, G. M.   25   Symph in d   BN 02
1867-1943   Fr

WOLF, Hugo   20   Christmas Night Cantata, Chor and O 1886   CT 49
1860-1903   Aust   120   Die Corregidor, Opera 1895
                         6   -Prelude and Entr'acte   CH 14, 37
                        20   der Feuerreiter, Chor and O 1892   BN 26, 42;   NS 11
                        12   Italian Prints, Ballet   AT 65
                         7   Italian Serenade 1892   BN 04, 08, 17;   CH 04, 05(2),
                                 08, 09, 14, 15, 22, 25, 34, 37, 55;   CT 22, 26,
                                 28, 31;   CL 28;   DE 62;   DT 51;   KC 55, 67;
                                 LA 46;   NS 05, 07, 12, 15, 16;   PH 05, 14, 37;
                                 PT 39, 57;   SL 26;   SE 30
                        21   Penthesilia, Symphon Poem 1883   BN 04, 07;   CH 03,
                                 37;   CT 14;   PH 09
                         6   Prometheus, Baritone and O 1890   BN 33;   PH 09
                              SONGS and CHORAL PIECES
                         4   Abgescheiden heit, Seclusion   DT 21
                         4   An die turen will ich schleichen   NA 64
                         4   Auf ein altes Bild 1889   CH 05, 25;   CL 25
                         4   Anakreon's Grab 1893   BA 49;   CH 37, 56;   NA 09,
                                 35;   PT 38;   SF 44
                         4   Dank'es o Seele 1888   CT 52
                         4   Er ists 1890   CH 09, 11, 12, 25, 33, 35, 56;
                                 CL 25;   DE 49;   DT 27;   NA 09, 11, 13, 16,
                                 35, 36;   KC 48;   LA 31;   PH 09, 12;   PT 38;
                                 NR 57;   SL 24;   SF 44
                         4   Elfin Lied, Chor and O 1889   CH 56;   NS 11
                         4   Der Freund   CH 11;   CT 25;   DT 21;   NA 05, 11,
                                 12, 16, 35;   PH 12;   SL 24
                         4   Frühling Ubers   CT 25
                         4   Der Gartner 1888   MN 34
                         4   Gebet 1890   CH 35;   CT 52;   NA 36
                         4   Heimiveh   CT 11, 27;   WA 52
                         4   Harfenspieler   CL 41
                         4   In der Frohe   CH 25, 33, 56;   DT 21, 27
                         4   In dem Schatten Meiner Locken   CH 12;   NA 13;
                                 MN 45;   NS 12

WOLF, H. (Cont.) Songs and Choral Pieces (Cont.)
                4   Karvoche 1889   CH 25
                4   Mignon's Song, Kenst du der lande 1893   CH 33,
                        37;   DT 44;   NA 61;   MN 34;   LA 31;   PH 49
                4   Morgenstimmung 1896   CH 37
                4   Nieu Leibe 1890   CH 25, 35;   DT 27;   MN 45
                4   Der Rattenfänger 1890   CH 30;   NA 09;   PH 09,
                        27
                4   Schlafindes Jesuskind 1890   CH 25, 33, 56;
                        CT 25;   DT 27;   KC 48
                4   Tretet ein, hoher Krieger   NA 13
                4   Verborgenheit 1888   CH 11, 12;   DE 49;   NA 05,
                        11, 13, 16, 36;   NS 12;   PH 12;   PT 38;
                        SL 24
                4   Wernie sein Brot   NA 64
                4   Wer sich der Einsamfeit   NA 64
                4   Wo find'ich Trost 1890   CH 05, 25;   DT 27
                4   Weyla's Song, Gesang Weylas 1888   CH 33, 37;
                      CT 25;   DT 44;   NS 08;   PT 38

WOLF, Kenneth   25   Conc No 1   UT 51
        US

WOLFE, Stanley   28   Symph No 3 Op 14   BU 62
  1916-   Brit   25   Symph No 4   HN 67

WOLF-FERRARI, Ermano   3   The Four Rustics, I quattro rusteghi, Opera 1906:
  1876-1948   It   Intermezzo   DT 38;   SL 28
                6   Jewels of the Madonna, I gioielli della Madonna,
                    Opera 1911: Intermezzo No 1 and No 2   HN 32;
                    KC 37, 40, 41;   ML 63, No 2 only 60, 65;   MN 46;
                    NP 45;   NS 11;   WA 35, 36
                4   -Meeting of the Camorrests   DA 29;   ML 63
                6   -Prelude Act II   PH 11(2)
              10   -Prelude Act III   AT 57;   DA 29;   HN 41;
                    PH 11
                5   -Serenade, Neapolitan Dance   WA 66
                    Secrets of Suzanne, Il segreto di susanna, Opera
              30   1909: Act I, complete   DT 34
                3   -Overt   AT 51;   BA 43;   CH 14, 15, 16, 17, 19,
                    21, 22, 23, 24, 27, 28, 31, 34, 57;   CT 32, 35,
                    38, 51;   CL 27, 28, 30;   DA 32, 49, 61;   DT 28,
                    30, 32, 35, 48;   KC 36, 39, 41;   HN 32;   MN 28,
                    30, 31, 42, 45;   NP 30, 51;   NS 11;   PH 27, 35;
                    PT 39, 51;   RC 30, 57;   SL 12, 17, 28;   SF 56;
                    UT 46;   WA 33, 44
                3   Vita Nuova Op 9, Cantata after Dante 1903: Dance
                    of Angels   CH 11, 35, 36, 37, 38, 40, 41;   CL 27;
                    DA 32

WOLPE, Stefan   40   Ballet Suite, Man from Midian, 1942   NP 51
  1902-1972 Ger/US   12   Piece for Two Instrumental Units   SF 67
               30   Symph No 1   NP 63

WOLTMANN, Frederick   8   Rhaps for French Horn and O   MN 38
1908-   US   6   Symphon Poem for Fl and O, The Colisieum at Night
                             MN 39;   SL 48

WOOD, Carl Paige   12   Three Dances for Str O   SE 35
               US

WOLDRIDGE, John D.   8   The Elizabethans, Concert Overt   HN 60
1911-1958   Brit   8   A Solemn Hymn for Victory   NP 44

WOOLLEN, Russell   15   Toccata for O Op 26   WA 56
1923-   US

WORK, Julian   16   Myriorama by Night, Suite in 4 mvts   LA 45
1910-   US

WYKES, Robert   10   Letter to an Alto-Man   SL 66
1927-   US   17   The Shape of Time 1965 for Percussion and Double-
                             Bass groups   SL 64, 67

XENAKIS, Yannis   10   Akrata for 16 Winds   MN 69
1922-   Gk   10   Eonta   NP 68;   SF 69
                            Many Wonders   WA 65
                      10   Pithoprakta   NP 63;   SF 65;   UT 68
                      10   Polla Ta Rhina   BA 65
                      12   Strategie for 2 O   SL 64

YARDUMIAN, Richard   17   Armenian Suite   CT 64;   NA 59;   PH 53
1917-   US   15   Cantus Animae et Cordis, Song of the Soul and Heart
                             for Str   PH 55
                      18   P Conc   PH 57
                      17   V Conc in 2 mvts   PH 50, 60
                       9   Chorale Prelude, Veni Sancte Spiritus   HN 59;
                             NA 61;   KC 59;   PH 58, 63
                   20-22   Desolate City in 2 mvts   NP 44
                      18   Passacaglia, Recitative and Fugue for P and O
                             DE 61
                      10   Psalm 130 for Tenor and O   PH 54
                      23   Symph No 1 in 3 mvts   PH 61
                      30   Symph No 2, Psalms, Voice and O   KC 66, 67;
                             NA 68;   PH 64;   SL 67

YON, Pietro   20   Conc Gregoriano, Org and O in 4 mvts   NS 20
1886-1943   US   3   Gesu Bambino, Song   SL 54

YOUNG, Victor   5   Arizona   PH 36
1900-1956   US   10   Symphon Synthesis from For Whom the Bell Tolls,
                             film score   LA 44

YSAYE, Eugene   12   Chant d'Hiver, Poem for V and O   CT 18
1858-1931   Belg   8   Exile Poem for Str O   CT 18, 21;   DT 19;   PH 18

YSAYE, Theophile   10   Les Abeilles, Poem for O Op 17   CT 21
1865-1918   Belg   20   P Conc in E^b Op 9   CT 21
                       4   Divertimento, Extase for V and O   PT 21

YSAYE, T. (Cont.)	7	Fantasy on Walloon Folk-Songs for P and O Op 13 CH 44; CT 17, 20; DT 21; MN 23; SL 14, 16
	6	Meditation, Poéme No 5 for C and O CT 19
	25	Symph No 1 in F Op 14 BN 21; CT 18, 20
YUN, Isang	30	Symphonic Scene LA 69
ZABEL, Albert 1830-1910 Ger	14	Conc for Harp in c Op 35 CH 09; KC 41
ZADOR, Eugen(Jeno) 1895- Hung/US	14	Aria and Allegro for Str and Bass LA 66; UT 68
	20	Biblical Triptych in 3 mvts 1943 CH 43; PH 43; SF 45
	8	Christmas Overt NA 62
	5	Caprice for O and Tarogoto 1935 MN 34
	16-18	Five Contrasts for O PH 64
	24	Dance Symph CT 39
	12	Divertimento for Str PH 56
	12	Elegy and Dance DE 52; PH 53
	8	Elegie PH 60
	10	Festival Overt DE 66; NA 66; LA 64; PH 67
	15	Fugue, Fantasia NA 59; PH 59
	20	Machine Man, Ballet Suite 1934 MN 35; PH 39
	10	Pastorale and Tarantelle CH 41; PH 41
	15	Rondo 1933 KC 37
	12	Rhaps for O 1930 LA 61; PH 62
	10	Tarentelle LA 32
	18	Var on a Merry Theme NA 64
	15	Var on Hungarian Folk Song 1928 LA 32; MN 26; PH 32; SF 29
ZAFRED, Mario 1922- It	30	Symph No 4 In Honor of the Resistance 1950 NP 58
ZANDONAI, Riccardo 1883-1944 It	28	Quadri Di Segantini, Symphon Poem NA 51
		Romeo and Juliet, Opera 1921 Excerpts SL 28, 29
	14	-Torch Dance and Calvacata DA 52; DT 30; NA 54
		-Symphon Episode DT 39; LA 31; NP 29, 56
	40	Terre Nativa, Symphon Impressions Suite No 1, Primavera in Val di Sole NS 16
	12	Serenade Medieval for C, 2 Horns, Harp and Str SL 27
ZECH, Frederick 1858- US	12	Lamia, Symphon Poem SF 17
ZECKWER, Richard C. 1850-1922 US	20	P Conc in e Op 8 PH 03, 13
	10	Jade Butterflies BN 23; CH 22; PH 22
	10	Sohrab and Rustum, Symphon Poem PH 15
ZEISL, Eric 1905- Aust/US	13	Passacaglia DT 46

ZEMACHSON, Arnold
1892-   Russ/US
	9	Chorale and Fugue in d Op 4 CH 31; CL 31;
		    DA 38; DE 48; DT 33; LA 32; MN 34;
		    PH 30, 34, 35

	20	Conc Grosso Op 8 CH 34

ZEMLINSKY, Alexander   25   Sinfonetta for O Op 23   BA 60
1872-   Aust/US 15   Songs from Dixieland   BA 64

ZIEHRER, C.M.   4   Wiener Madl'n Op 388   NA 36
                Ger

ZILCHER, Hermann   15   Rameau Suite Op 76   NP 35
1881-1948   Ger

ZIMBALIST, Efrem   11   American Rhapsodie   CH 35;   PH 42;   WA 47
1889-   Russ/US 23-24 P Conc in E^b 1958   NR 58
                       16   V Conc   PH 47
                       12   Concert Fantasy on Coq' d'Or   PH 43;   WA 44
                        5   Creole Songs   NS 16
                       20   Daphnis and Chloe, Symphon Suite   PH 31
                       16   Portrait of an Artist 1945   PH 45
                       10   Two Slavic Dances   CH 18;   PH 14

ZIMMERMAN, Bernd-Alois   Musique pour les soupers du Roi Ubu   CT 69
1908-   Gk

ZIMMERMANN,   4   Song of the Navy   UT 42
                US

ZOLLNER, Heinrich   8   Fantasia, Midnight at Sedan, Suite   BN 1895;
1854-1941   Ger   CH 1896;   CT 02
                        5   Interlude fr Bei Sedan, Opera   CT 02
                        5   Der Versunkene Glocke, Opera 1899 Prelude to act V
                              CT 01
                       12   Waldphantasie Op 83   CH 04